THE NARROW HOME PLAN™ COLLECTION

Since 1983, we at Design Basics have been bringing people home with many of America's most popular home plans. Our company began as a custom home plan design firm for the professional builders of our local community, Omaha, Nebraska. As the popularity of our designs increased, we expanded our focus from designing for the local market only, to designing plans that would be adaptable anywhere. Since then, builder as well as consumer interest in our plans has grown tremendously in all 50 states and countries around the world. Today, we are the nation's largest home plan design service, offering a variety of home plans as well as products and services which include, color renderings, material lists, custom changes and more.

Whether it's one of our home plans, a product or service, we take pride in serving you with our very best. It's all a part of our culminating efforts to lead people to their dreams of home.

Design Basics . . . *Bringing People Home*

THE NARROW HOME PLAN™ COLLECTION

IT'S A FACT OF HOME BUILDING that the size of a lot often dictates the kind of home that can be built on it. And over the years, there's been a growing need for designs that are suitable to lots that are narrow. That's why at Design Basics, we've created ***The Narrow Home Plan™ Collection,*** *a compilation of 150* ***Gold Seal™*** *and 67* ***Heartland Home Plans™*** *and 16* ***Nostalgia*** *home plans - all of which have a width of no more than 50 feet. Ranging from 962 - 2,586 square feet, each plan features the same thoughtful design qualities found in our other* ***Gold Seal™*** *and* ***Heartland Home Plans™*** *collections. And as an added benefit, many of these homes are what we have termed "plexable," meaning they can be formed into duplex plans in a variety of combinations. (For more information on our "plexable" plans, see our ad on page 294-295)* ***The Narrow Home Plan™ Collection*** *also features a special section of 25 duplex designs as an example of what we can provide for you using our "plexable" system. Whether multi-family or simply narrow, we believe each of these designs provide a solution to the challenge of building a suitable place to call home.*

THE NARROW HOME PLAN™ COLLECTION
is published by:
Design Basics Inc. • 11112 John Galt Blvd. • Omaha, NE 68137-2384

Library of Congress Catalog Card Number: 98-70601
ISBN: 892150-02-6

Table of Contents

GOLD SEAL™ HOME PLANS

With careful attention to detail and well-thought-out floor plans, this group of designs was meant to impress.

HEARTLAND HOME PLANS™

These home plans are more economical to build with simplified rooflines, foundations and floor plans, while maintaining their charm.

NOSTALGIA HOME PLANS COLLECTION™

An established, old-world feel marks this home plan collection featuring vintage elevations with today's modern floor plans and features.

DUPLEX DESIGNS

A collection of 25 multi-family designs features all the same efficient traffic patterns and amenities buyers have come to expect in Design Basics' home plans.

Welcome to

Gold Seal™ Home Plans

Designs that provide the best of two worlds: thoughtful features and alluring elevations.

You could say the homes from the Gold Seal™ Home Plans collection were meant to be shown off. These homes feature elevations with immediately striking street appeal and well thought-out floor plans. The Gold Seal™ designs on the following pages reflect this philosophy within a narrow lot situation. As a whole, all the plans in this collection provide the best of two worlds: thoughtful features and alluring elevations, making owning one of them nothing but pleasurable.

As an additional benefit, you can take advantage of our Gold Seal Plus™ offering a variety of special options. Just look for the Gold Seal Plus™ logo on any of the home plans on the following pages to receive options such as: right-reading reverse plans • immediately available Roof Construction Package™ (specific for each plan) to aid in framing the roof • custom changes from the Select Plan Change Directory in five days or half off the price of the custom change.

GOLD SEAL™ HOME PLANS

Plan Index & Guide to Symbols

CUSTOM CHANGES AVAILABLE

Changes can be made to any Design Basics plan. See page 293 in the back of the book for details.

PARADE HOME PACKAGE

Available for any Gold Seal™ plan. Includes *Materials and Estimator's Workbook, Color Rendering, Customized Promotional Handout Artwork* and acrylic literature holder. Only $149. See page 297 in the back of the book for details on each product.

ROOF CONSTRUCTION PACKAGE

Detailed roof framing plans available for all Design Basics plans. See page 297 in the back of the book for details.

PLEXABLE OPTIONS AVAILABLE

Plexable™ plans can be configured into a variety of duple designs. See page 294-295 in the back of the book for fur ther details.

GOLD SEAL™ HOME PLANS

BASE PLAN INFORMATION

Page No.	Width	Plan No.	Plan Name	Sq. Ft.
4	32'-0"	2568	Avery	962
11	38'-0"	1184	Lorain	975
22	44'-0"	1129	Calumet	1125
13	40'-0"	2376	Dover	1205
14	40'-8"	2825	Laurell	1261
29	50'-0"	1551	Logan	1271
30	50'-0"	969	Benton	1305
5	32'-0"	3907	Reynolds	1316
31	50'-0"	3102	Aspen	1339
23	47'-4"	2761	Mayberry	1341
17	42'-0"	1963	Kaplin	1347
31	50'-0"	3010	Quimby	1422
24	48'-0"	1379	Pendleton	1429
32	50'-0"	2173	Fraser	1451
17	42'-0"	3260	Kirby	1478
24	48'-0"	3019	Kelsey	1479
18	42'-0"	2550	Vinton	1486
25	48'-0"	2300	Adair	1496
19	42'-0"	2553	Gifford	1499
27	48'-8"	3555	Laramy	1518
33	50'-0"	3127	Haley	1554
34	50'-0"	1770	Bayley	1556
35	50'-0"	2196	Granite	1561
8	36'-0"	3899	Bradshaw	1577
26	48'-0"	2537	Tahoe	1580
36	50'-0"	2291	Bradley	1599
28	48'-8"	1767	Rosebury	1604
20	42'-0"	2377	Leighton	1636
9	36'-0"	3915	Ithaca	1643
21	42'-0"	2907	Ashley	1658
6	32'-0"	3889	Montclare	1684
10	36'-0"	3919	Dunbar	1699
7	32'-0"	3887	Winfield	1821
10	36'-0"	3894	Webber	1864
15	41'-4"	3891	Stockville	1883
12	39'-4"	3879	Thomasville	1885
16	41'-4"	3892	Tecumseh	2035

ONE STORY HOMES

9F-2568 Avery price code: 9

- High quality, erasable, reproducible vellums
- Shipped via 2nd day air within the continental U.S.

- comfortable and economical, this plan is perfect for narrow home sites
- simple efficiency is key to this thoughtful design
- expansive great room with sloped ceiling is warmed by fireplace
- adjacent to volume dining area, well-planned kitchen offers handy snack bar
- master bedroom includes walk-in closet
- optional finished basement plan offers inexpensive living areas including 2 bedrooms, bath, spacious family room and 2 storage areas

Rear Elevation

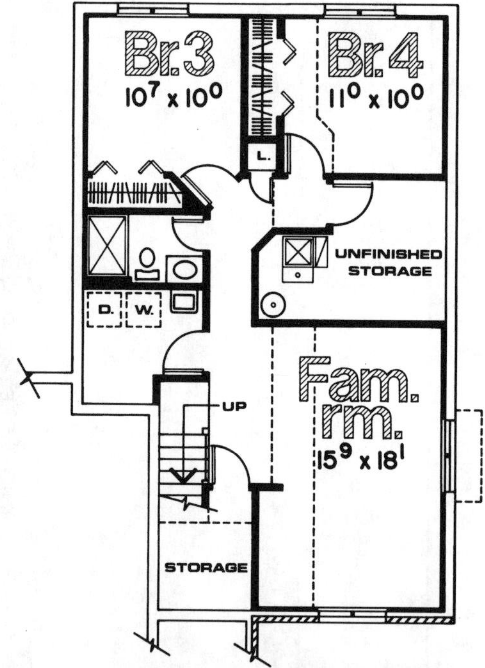

Optional Finished Basement Plan Included – Adds 668 Square Feet

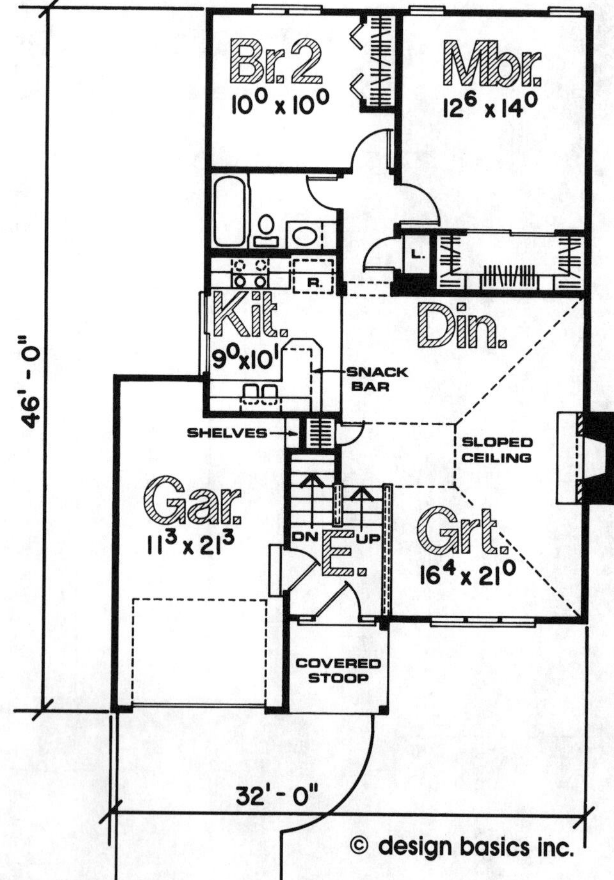

© design basics inc.

ORDER DIRECT
7:00-6:00 Mon.-Fri. CST
800-947-7526

962 Finished Sq. Ft.

9F-3907 Reynolds price code: 13

- High quality, erasable, reproducible vellums
- Shipped via 2nd day air within the continental U.S.

- brick half-wall with palladian arch detailing adds interest to the entrance of this one-story home
- entry centers on a view of the volume great room's fireplace
- kitchen is planned for convenience with a snack bar serving the breakfast area and immediate access to garage
- laundry room also serves as a mud entrance from the garage
- bedrooms are located to the rear of the home for added privacy
- French doors open to the master bath featuring his and her vanities, walk-in closet and compartmented stool

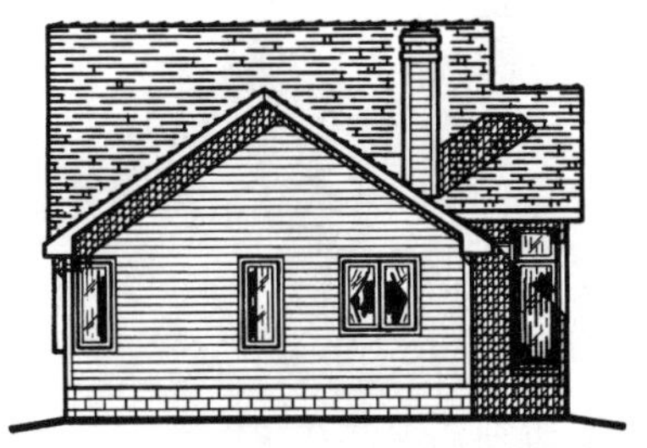

Rear Elevation

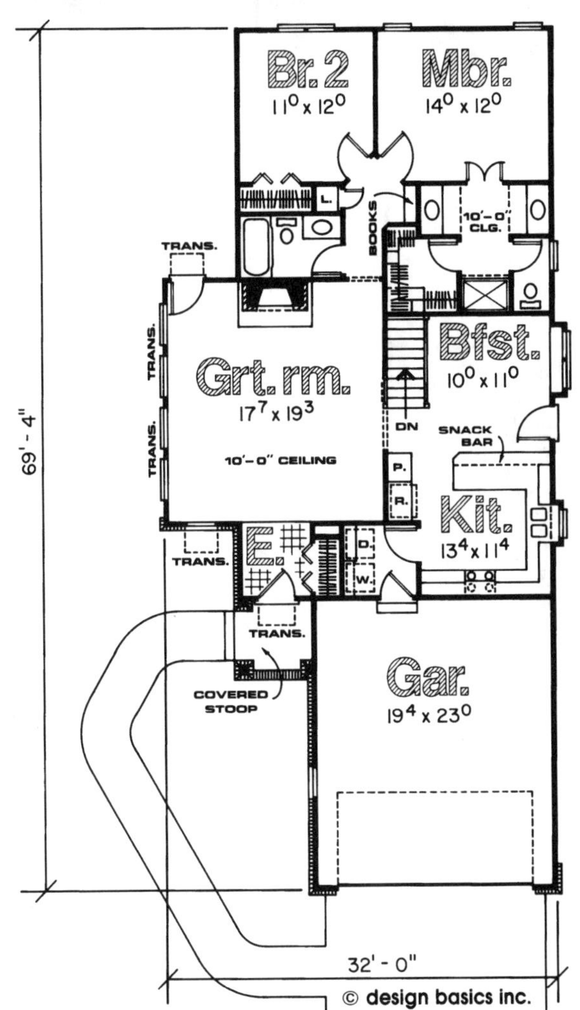

1316 Finished Sq. Ft.

9F-3889 Montclare price code: 16

- ▸ High quality, erasable, reproducible vellums
- ▸ Shipped via 2nd day air within the continental U.S.

Gold Seal™ PLUS

- arched brick detailing and columns at the covered stoop provide a refined air to the elevation
- hard-surfaced entry area gains definition from attractive cased opening
- living room is warmed by raised-hearth fireplace
- gourmet island kitchen adjoins spacious breakfast area with direct access to outdoors
- formal dining room opts as a secondary bedroom
- luxury master suite includes volume sloped ceiling, skylit dressing area with double vanity, whirlpool tub and walk-in closet

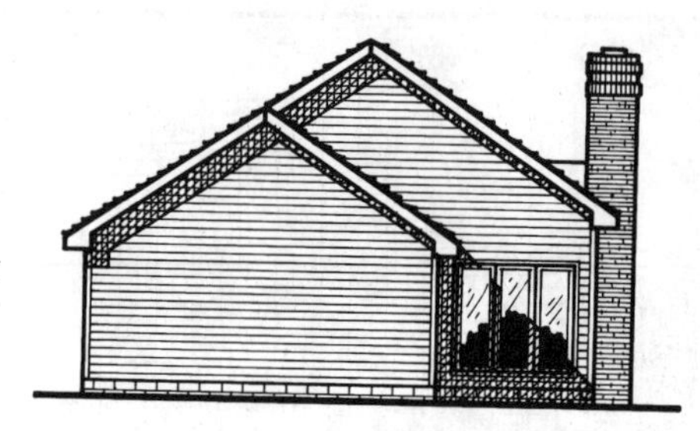

Rear Elevation

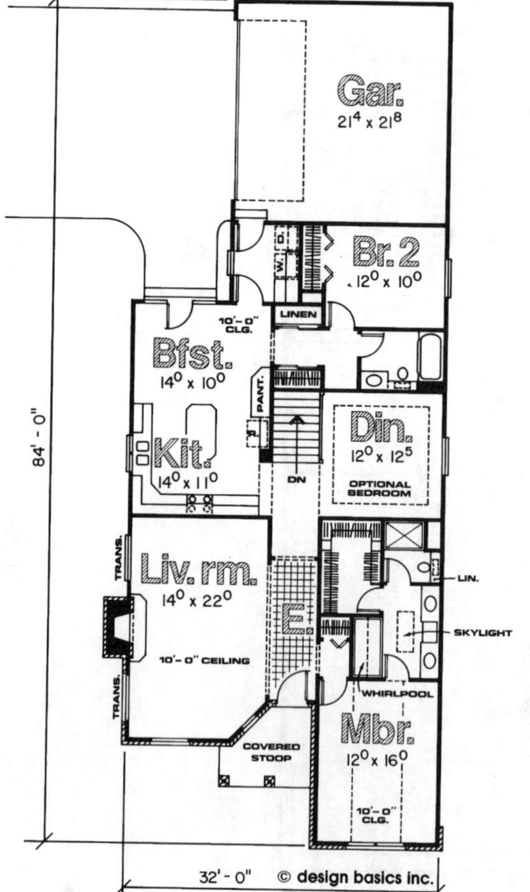

1684 Finished Sq. Ft.

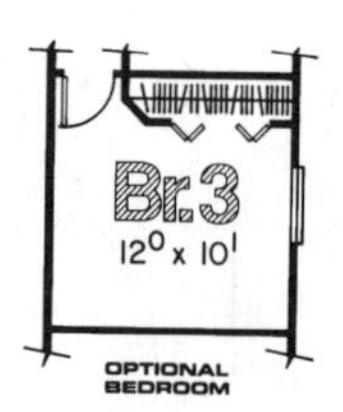

9F-3887 Winfield price code: 18

- High quality, erasable, reproducible vellums
- Shipped via 2nd day air within the continental U.S.

- special detailing allows a welcoming, yet sophisticated feel to the elevation
- volume great room is beautified by a palladian arch window and raised-hearth fireplace
- interesting angles and decorative column help define border between great room and formal dining room
- hard-surface breakfast area is open to kitchen with generous counter space, pantry, snack bar and plenty of natural light
- secondary bedrooms are accessed through angled doors and share a centrally located bath
- deluxe master suite features built-in bookcase, his and her vanities, whirlpool tub and walk-in closet

Rear Elevation

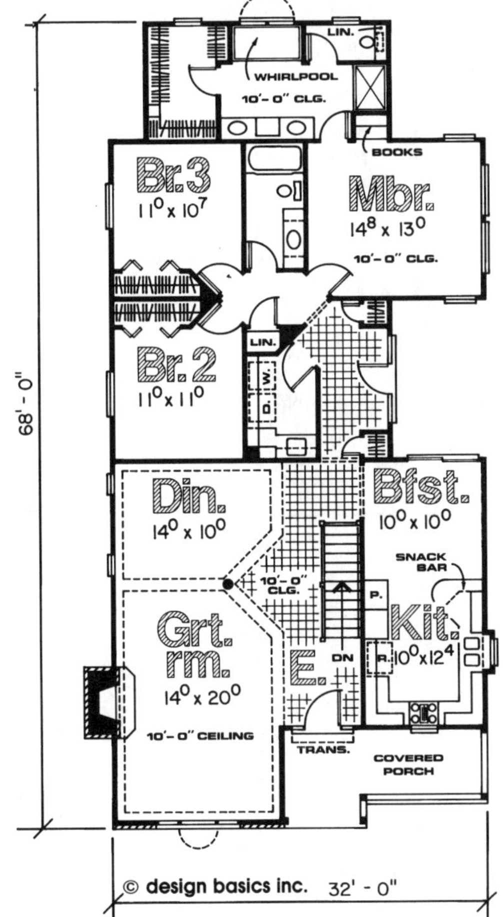

1821 Finished Sq. Ft.

9F-3899 Bradshaw price code: 15

Gold Seal PLUS™

- High quality, erasable, reproducible vellums
- Shipped via 2nd day air within the continental U.S.

- angled entry with covered porch adds interest to this exciting one-story design
- double doors reveal coat closet at entry
- raised-hearth fireplace centered under cathedral ceiling in expansive great room
- well-equipped kitchen with snack bar easily accesses bayed dinette and formal dining room
- private, covered rear patio accessed from dinette
- generous master bedroom offers 9-foot high boxed ceiling, walk-in closet and plenty of natural light
- window over whirlpool in master bath with dual lavs
- den easily optioned as secondary bedroom

Rear Elevation

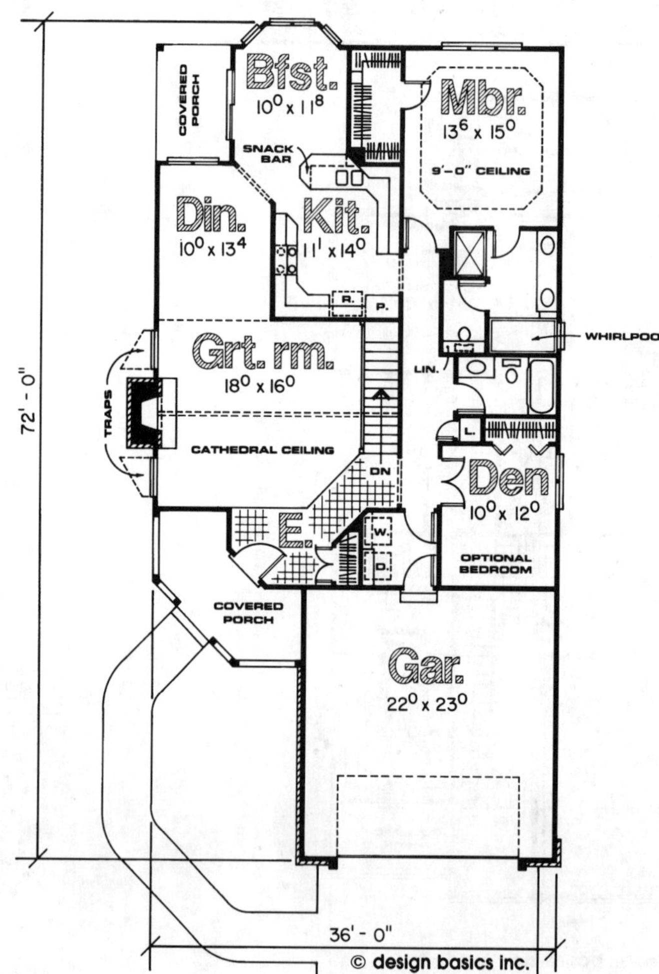

1577 Finished Sq. Ft.

9F-3915 Ithaca price code: 16

Gold Seal PLUS™

- ▶ High quality, erasable, reproducible vellums
- ▶ Shipped via 2nd day air within the continental U.S.

- covered porch provides a pleasant focal point on this home's front elevation
- great room and dining room are both connected and enhanced by openings that flank a see-thru fireplace and mantle
- kitchen with 2 lazy Susans, pantry, snack bar and abundant counter space, opens to spacious breakfast area with access to covered side porch
- comfortable master suite includes walk-in closet, double vanities, and luxurious corner whirlpool tub
- laundry room is located near bedrooms and hall bath for practicality and convenience

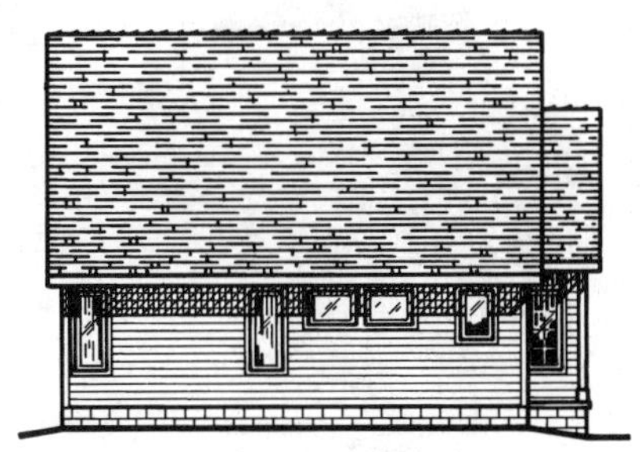

Rear Elevation

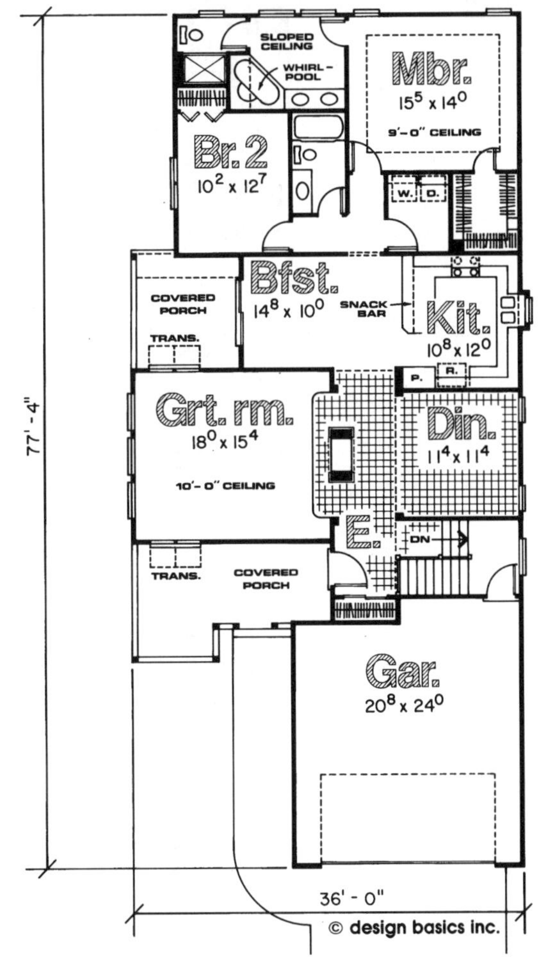

1643 Finished Sq. Ft.

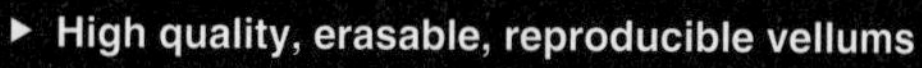
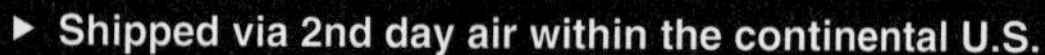

- High quality, erasable, reproducible vellums
- Shipped via 2nd day air within the continental U.S.

9F-3919 Dunbar price code: 16

- covered front porch shelters side entry and adds charming appeal
- entry provides an expansive view across great room, which freely connects to formal dining room
- kitchen with snack bar, pantry and window sink, adjoins spacious breakfast area with access to outdoors
- roomy master suite includes dressing area with double vanity, corner windows and a walk-in closet

1699 Finished Sq. Ft.

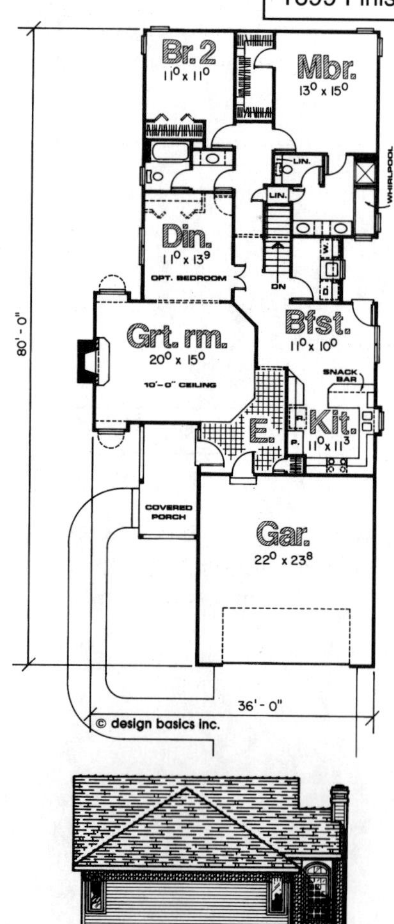

Rear Elevation

9F-3894 Webber price code: 18

- entry framed by sidelights and detailed trim adds character to this exciting one-story home
- inside, entry views elegant dining room and spacious great room, both of which enjoy tall, formal ceilings
- french doors access dining room from kitchen which features planning desk, pantry and corner sink with two windows
- dinette offers access to side yard
- laundry, with space for soaking sink, located near bedrooms

1864 Finished Sq. Ft.

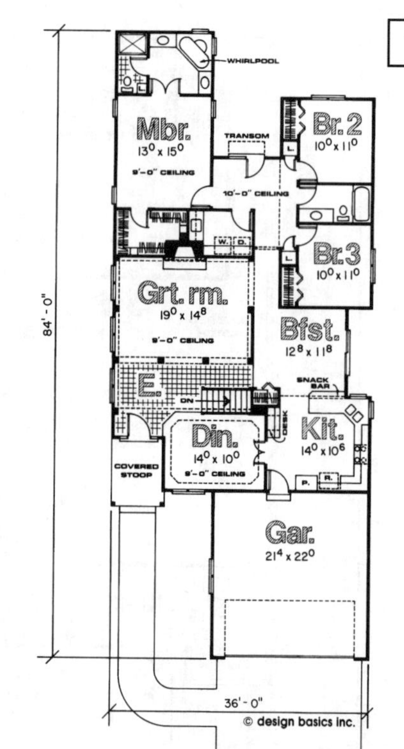

Rear Elevation

9F-1184 Lorain price code: 9

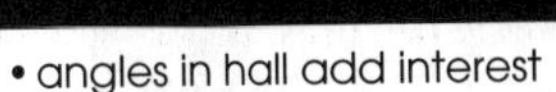

- High quality, erasable, reproducible vellums
- Shipped via 2nd day air within the continental U.S.

- convenient split-entry ranch design
- 2-car drive-under garage
- volume ceilings give home spacious feeling
- living and dining rooms open for expanded entertaining
- spacious basement area featuring bright windows to the front, is well suited for finishing
- kitchen includes snack bar, plant window at sink and lazy Susan
- angles in hall add interest
- large master bedroom with vaulted ceiling and mirrored bi-pass doors
- private access from master bedroom to full bathroom

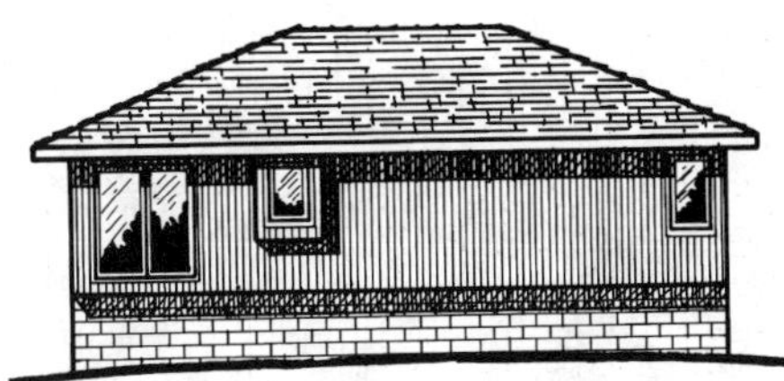

Rear Elevation

Alternate Elevation At No Extra Cost

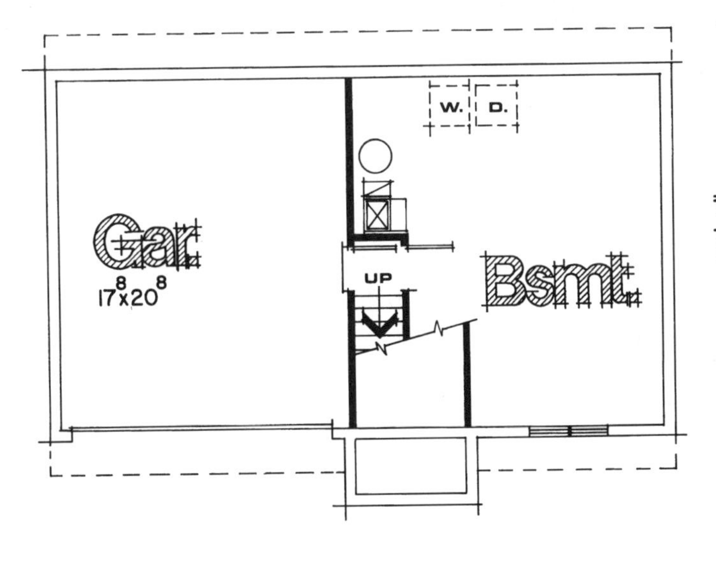

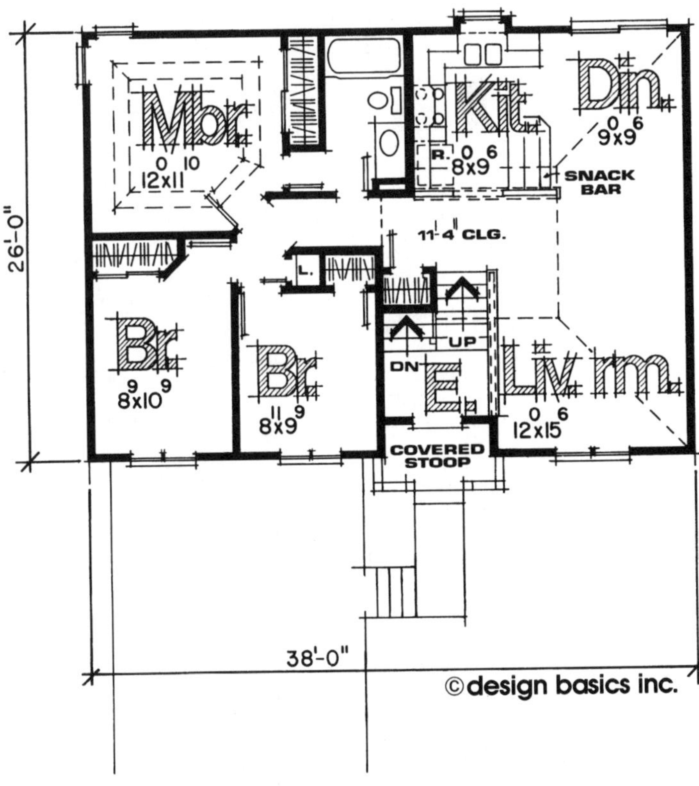

975 Finished Sq. Ft.

9F-3879 Thomasville price code: 18

Gold Seal PLUS

- High quality, erasable, reproducible vellums
- Shipped via 2nd day air within the continental U.S.

- successive tiers layer the front elevation, providing visual intrigue
- a covered entry opens to the formal dining room with special ceiling details and a see-thru fireplace
- great room features a flush-hearth fireplace, expansive views to the rear and open access to the dinette
- kitchen offers plenty of counter space, snack bar and pantry
- hall bath is centrally-located to secondary bedrooms, one of which features a walk-in closet
- master bath includes walk-in closet, whirlpool and double vanity under a sloped ceiling

Rear Elevation

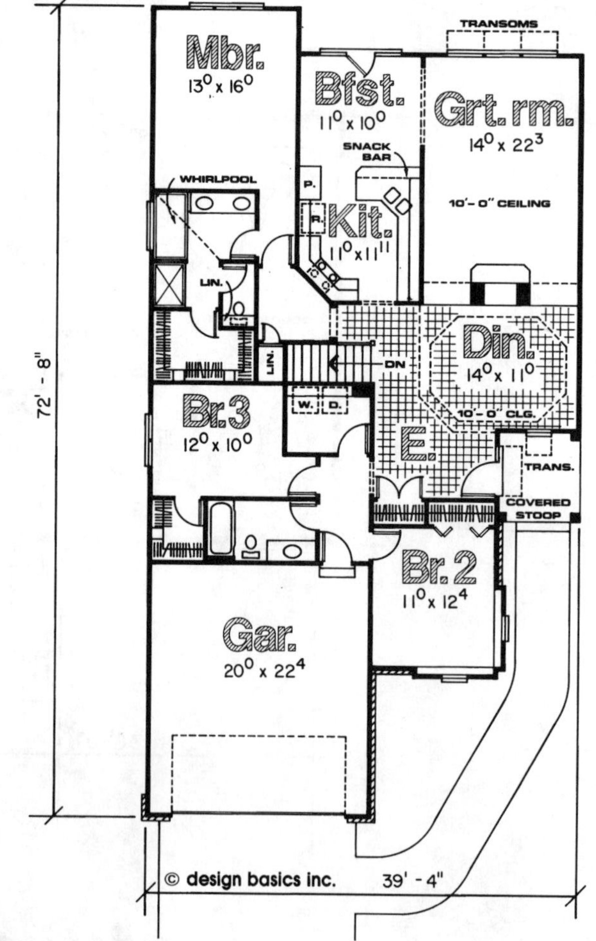

1885 Finished Sq. Ft.

9F-2376 Dover price code: 12

- High quality, erasable, reproducible vellums
- Shipped via 2nd day air within the continental U.S.

- elevation strikes cozy appeal
- lovely angled entry sports two plant shelves and roomy closet
- great room enjoys 10-foot ceiling, window-flanked fireplace, bookcase and easy access to kitchen/dinette
- sunny kitchen/dinette area offers convenient snack bar, wrapping counter and pantry
- cozy secondary bedroom offers privacy to guests or becomes a handy den
- master bedroom highlighted by lovely window and boxed ceiling
- luxurious master bath/dressing area includes whirlpool, roomy walk-in closet and dual lavs

Rear Elevation

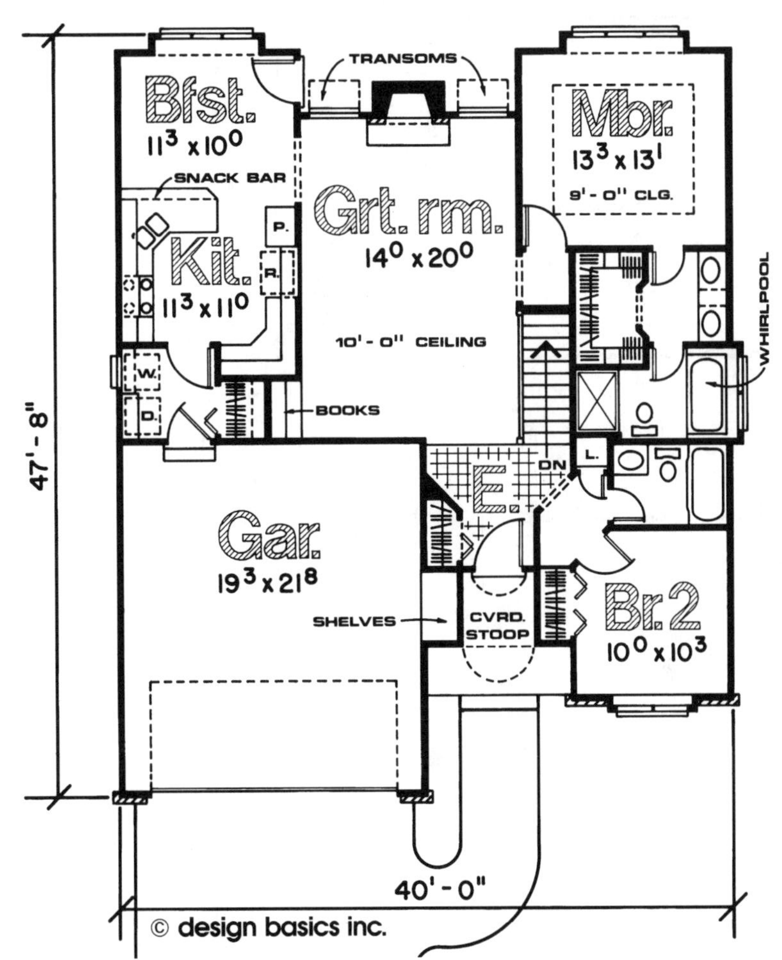

1205 Finished Sq. Ft.

9F-2825 Laurell price code: 12

- crisp, clean lines provide warm, homey allure to this front elevation
- entry provides immediate access to spacious great room or wood-railed staircase to lower level
- cooking is a breeze in well-designed kitchen, with handsome patio doors leading to covered porch from dinette
- plan offers option to choose formal dining room or create third bedroom
- shaded arbor provides added enjoyment to home
- vaulted ceiling and French doors into bath provide style in master bedroom
- dual lavs, spacious walk-in closet and glass block over whirlpool in master bath

Rear Elevation

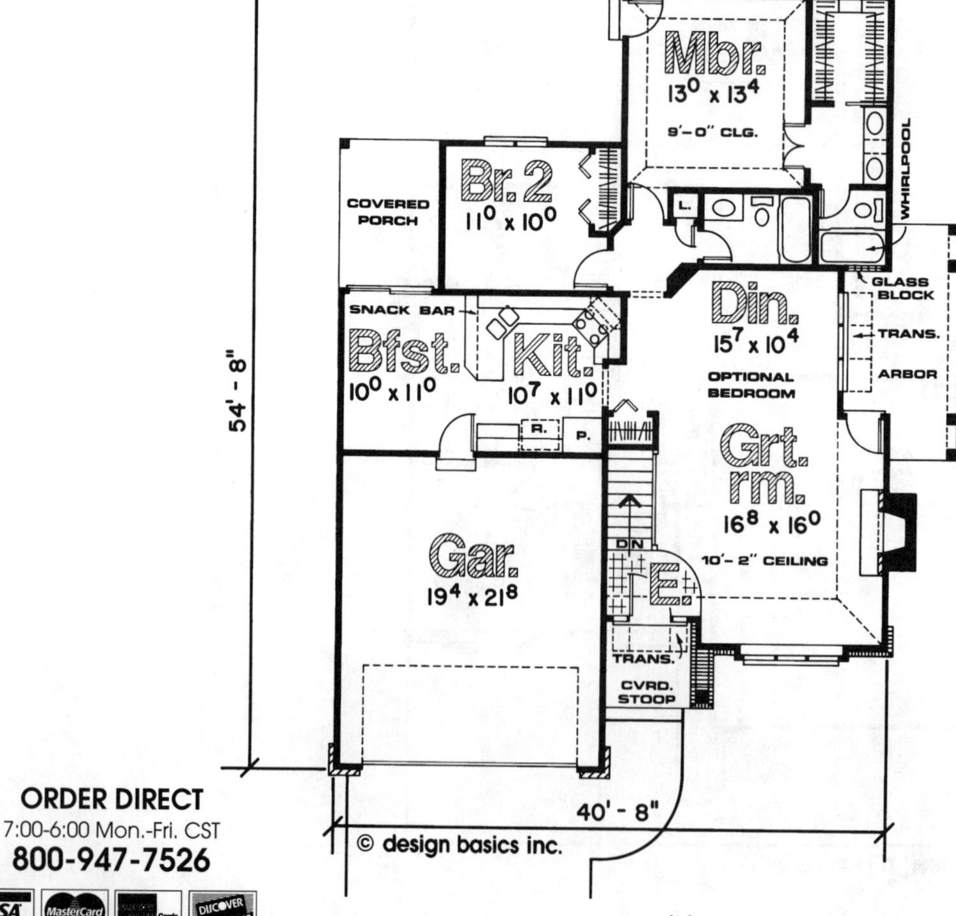

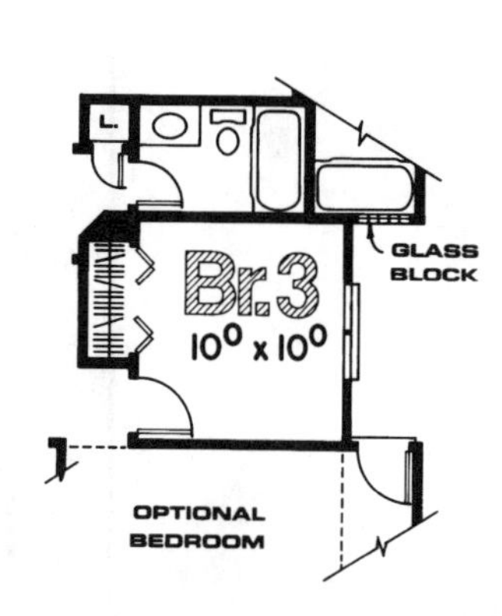

1261 Finished Sq. Ft.

9F-3891 Stockville price code: 18

Gold Seal PLUS

- High quality, erasable, reproducible vellums
- Shipped via 2nd day air within the continental U.S.

- entrance is granted privacy with spacious front courtyard
- impactful entry offers expansive views, extending through open, formal dining room, to sizeable great room with raised-hearth fireplace
- kitchen with pantry and snack bar adjoins breakfast area with direct access to covered porch
- powder bath and laundry room are convenient to both kitchen and garage
- secondary bedroom with sloped ceiling is brightened by attractive arched transom window
- roomy master suite with views to the rear offers skylit dressing area with double vanity, whirlpool tub and walk-in closet

Rear Elevation

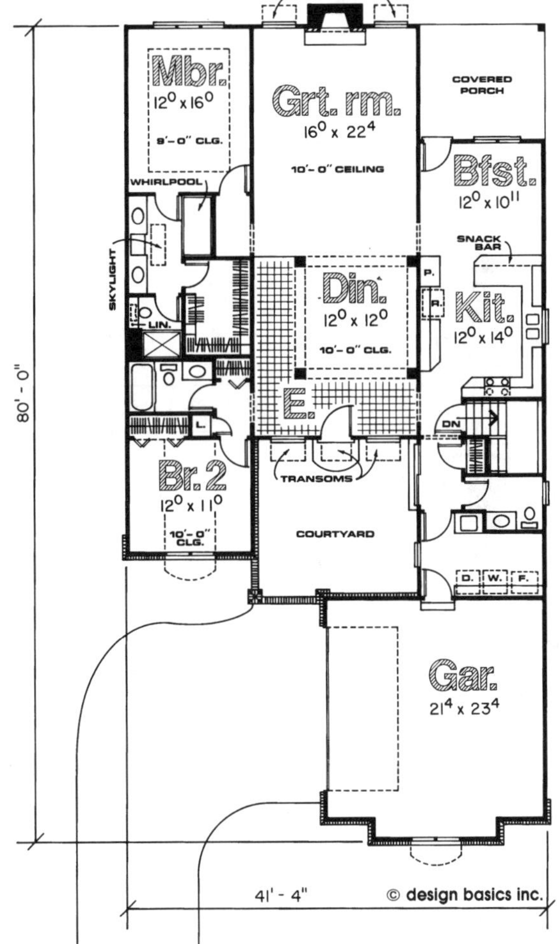

1883 Finished Sq. Ft.

9F-3892 Tecumseh price code: 20

- ▸ High quality, erasable, reproducible vellums
- ▸ Shipped via 2nd day air within the continental U.S.

- decorative brick wing walls grace the elevation and enhance the privacy of this home's romantic front courtyard
- spacious first impressions abound as the entry opens to dramatic views of dining room and great room beyond
- kitchen with snack bar, pantry and plenty of counter space adjoins breakfast area with direct access to covered rear porch
- natural light floods hallway leading to powder bath, laundry room and garage
- master bedroom with walk-in closet, opens to bath area with corner whirlpool and separate vanities
- master suite enjoys direct access to back yard

Rear Elevation

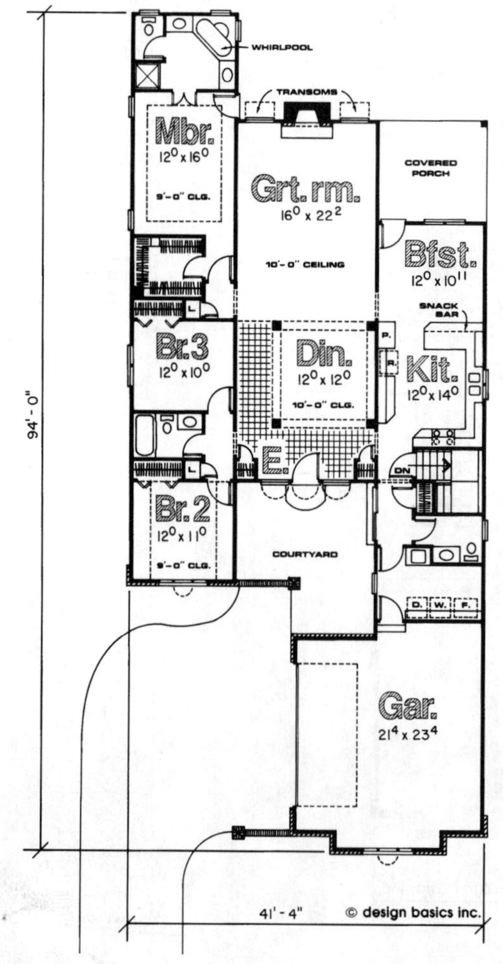

2035 Finished Sq. Ft.

9F-1963 Kaplin price code: 13

- 10-foot-high ceiling in entry and great room
- open staircase for versatile future finished basement
- picture windows with transoms above flank handsome fireplace in great room
- bedroom #3 easily becomes den with French doors off entry
- boxed window, built-in bookcase and tiered ceiling for master bedroom
- skylit dressing/bath area features double vanity and whirlpool on angle under window

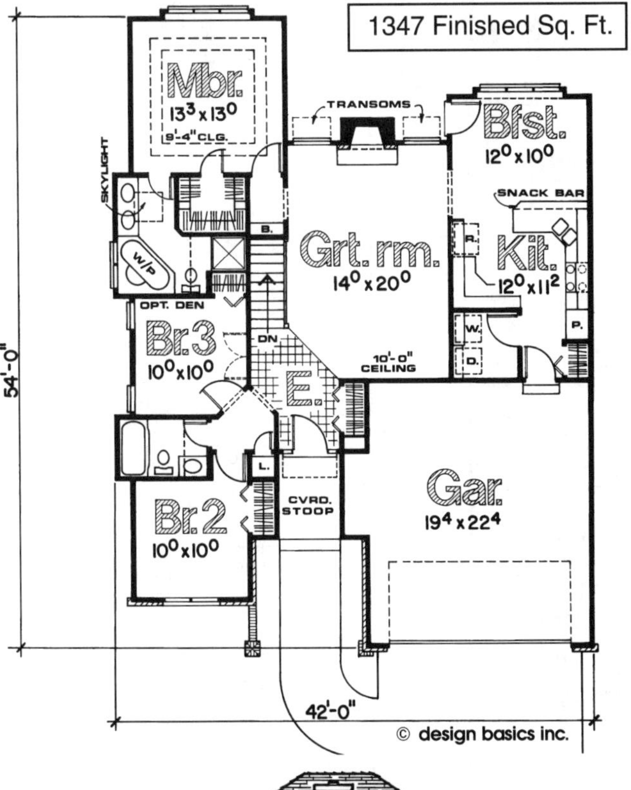

Rear Elevation

9F-3260 Kirby price code: 14

- ornate brick accents and transom windows compliment this quaint ranch style home
- gallery wall in entry has artistic appeal
- breakfast area provides access to rear covered porch
- spacious great room has brick fireplace and 11′-5″ ceiling
- master suite features access to covered porch, walk-in closet and corner whirlpool
- private den easily converts to optional bedroom

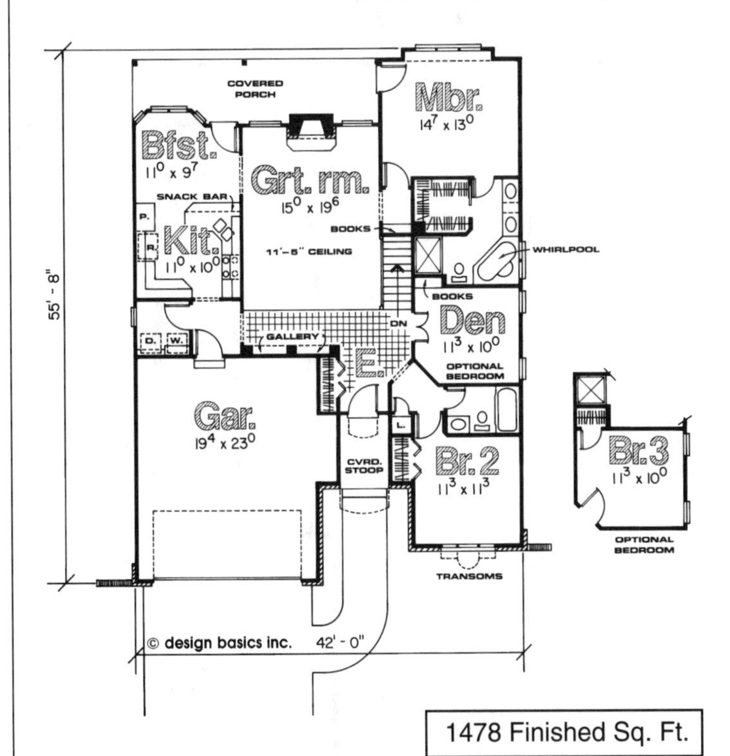

1478 Finished Sq. Ft.

Rear Elevation

9F-2550 Vinton price code: 14

- High quality, erasable, reproducible vellums
- Shipped via 2nd day air within the continental U.S.

- plan features optional bedroom or private den accessed by French doors
- staircase to lower level conveniently located off kitchen
- handy closet in laundry area which also serves as mud entry from garage
- great room features fireplace graced by tall windows
- dinette surrounds you with natural light with its bayed windows and patio door
- volume dining room complements entertaining with added hutch space
- sunny master bedroom boasts 9-foot ceiling and built-in bookcase
- master bath has dual vanities, large walk-in closet and oversized whirlpool

Rear Elevation

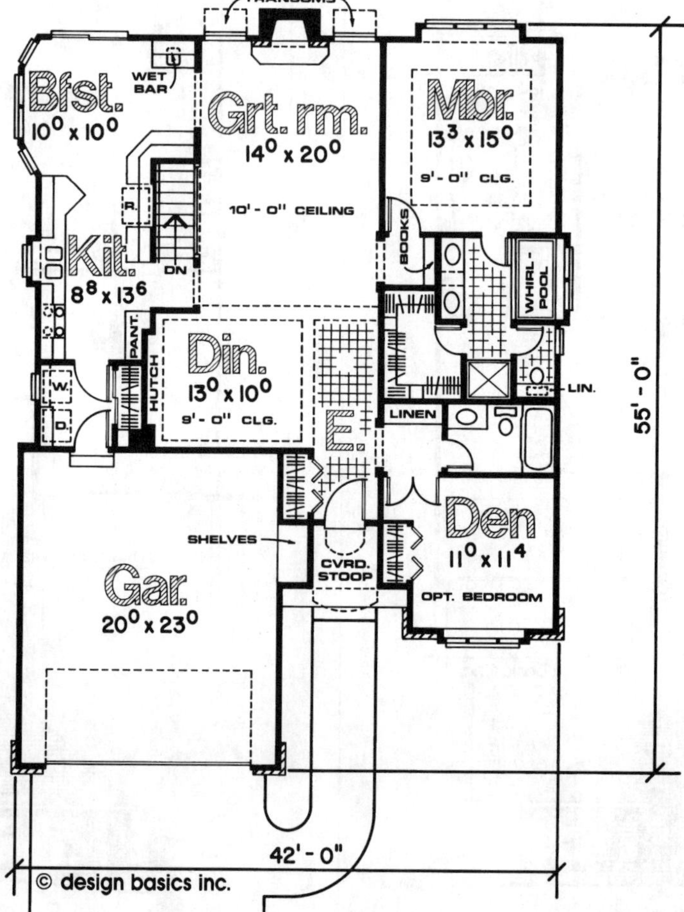

1486 Finished Sq. Ft.

ORDER DIRECT
7:00-6:00 Mon.-Fri. CST
800-947-7526

9F-2553 Gifford price code: 14

- High quality, erasable, reproducible vellums
- Shipped via 2nd day air within the continental U.S.

Gold Seal™ PLUS

- pleasant mix of materials, shapes, and textures create notable elevation
- practical use of space is demonstrated by placement of 2 closets in entry
- optional den/bedroom provides design flexibility
- lofty great room features fireplace flanked by large windows
- double doors from great room offer privacy from kitchen
- dinette, featuring desk and snack bar also provides convenient access to outdoors
- garage features built-in workbench
- roomy laundry area is accessed from garage and kitchen
- master suite features deluxe bath with sloped ceiling and plant shelves above an open shower

Rear Elevation

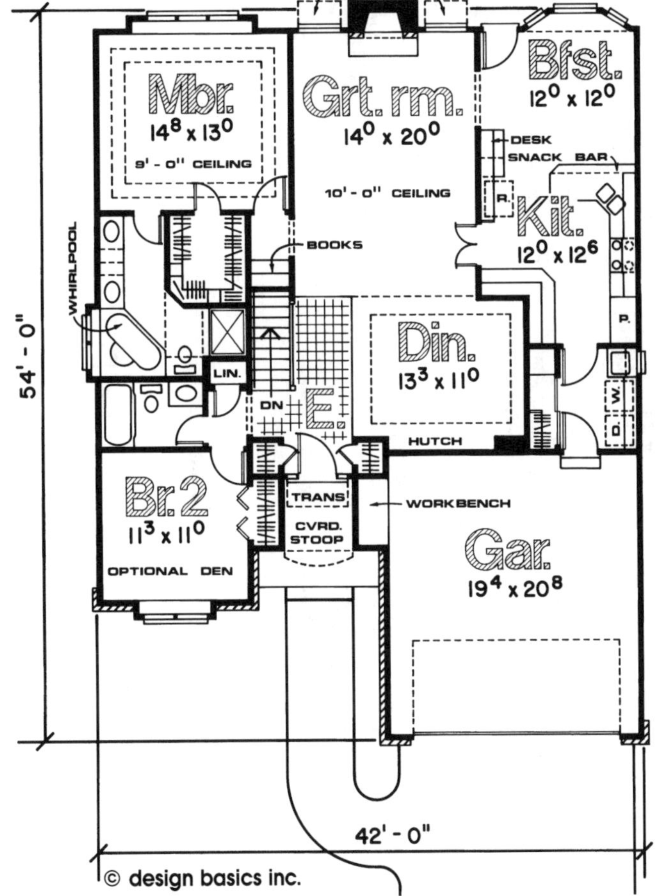

1499 Finished Sq. Ft.

9F-2377 Leighton price code: 16

- High quality, erasable, reproducible vellums
- Shipped via 2nd day air within the continental U.S.

Gold Seal™ HOME PLANS

- barrel vaulted porch highlights elevation of this comfortable ranch
- great room features cozy fireplace flanked by bright windows
- formal dining room features hutch space and easy access to kitchen area
- gourmet kitchen and bayed dinette includes snack bar for additional eating space, wrapping counters, planning desk and access to outdoors
- secondary bedrooms share bath; bedroom #3 designed as optional den
- master bedroom features tiered ceiling, bright window design and an ample walk-in closet
- master dressing/bath area includes skylight, his and her vanities and corner whirlpool

Rear Elevation

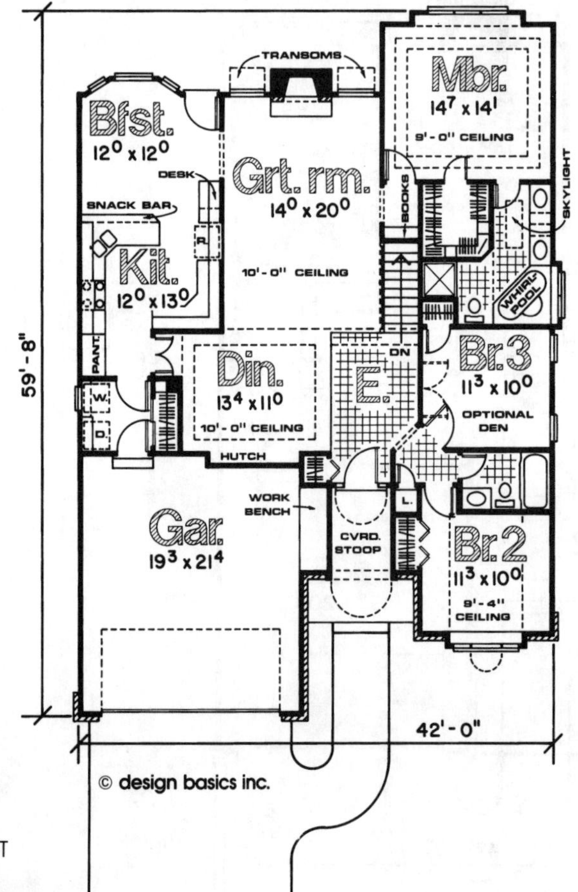

1636 Finished Sq. Ft.

9F-2907 Ashley price code: 16

- High quality, erasable, reproducible vellums
- Shipped via 2nd day air within the continental U.S.

- prominent entry commands captivating elevation
- entry captures fantastic views from great room to sun room with arched windows
- peninsula kitchen featuring corner sink and snack bar is open to breakfast area
- sun room offers access to breakfast area, great room and master suite or can option as a lovely dining room
- spacious master suite includes whirlpool bath with dual lavs and walk-in closet
- den off entry has bedroom option

Rear Elevation

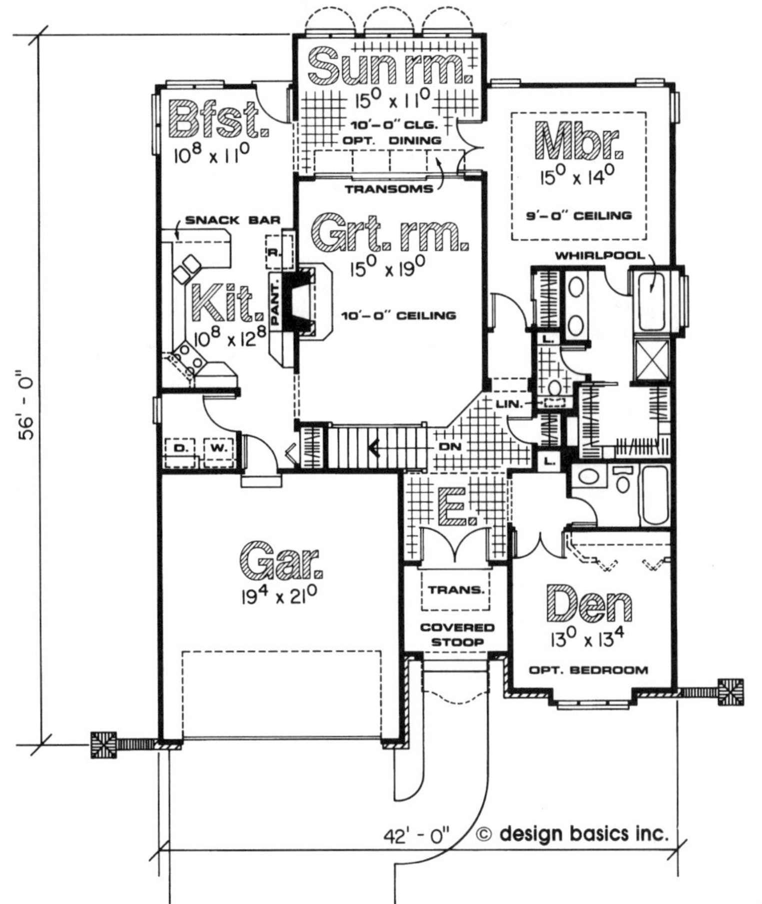

1658 Finished Sq. Ft.

9F-1129 Calumet price code: 11

Gold Seal™ HOME PLANS

- High quality, erasable, reproducible vellums
- Shipped via 2nd day air within the continental U.S.

- convenient split-entry ranch design
- 2-car garage
- large entry with coat closet on entry level
- volume ceiling for visual expansion
- efficient kitchen with snack bar, lazy Susan and window over sink
- basement area accessed from entry and garage, allowing for a variety of finishing options
- hallway segregates all bedrooms from primary living areas for privacy
- double doors open to large master bedroom with vaulted ceiling
- walk-in closet and private 3/4 bath complete the master suite
- secondary bedrooms share convenient hall bath

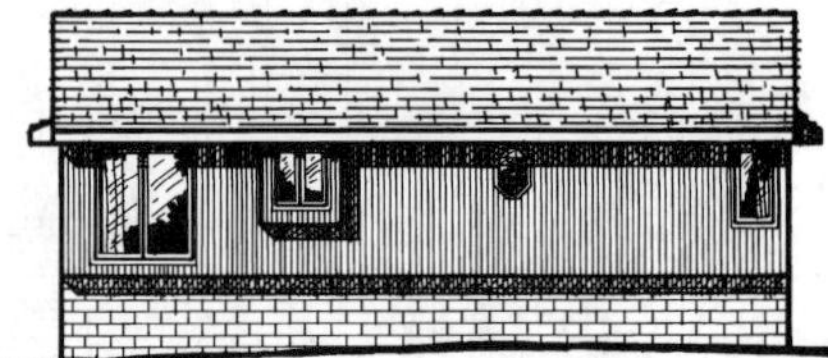

Rear Elevation

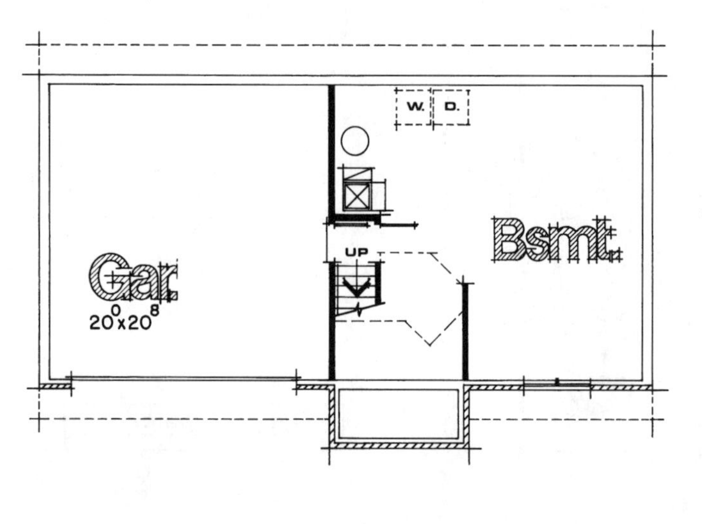

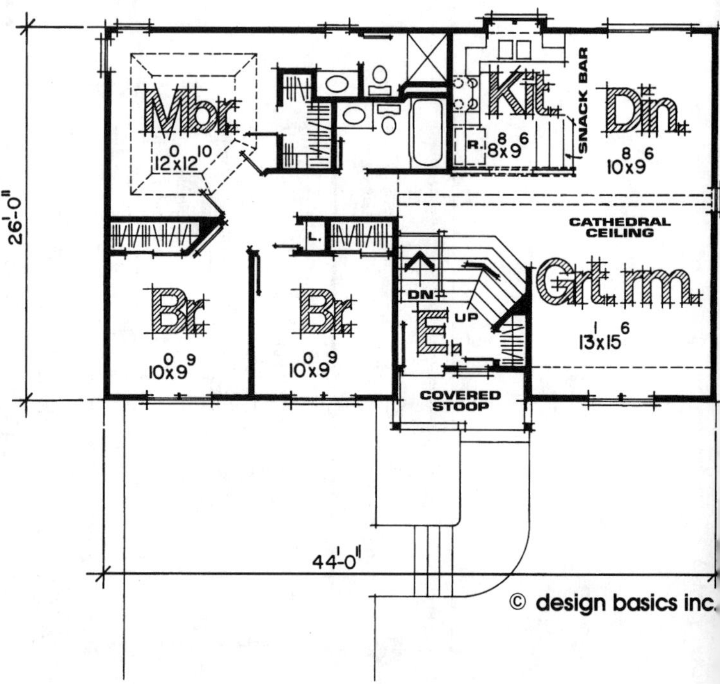

1125 Finished Sq. Ft.

ORDER DIRECT
7:00-6:00 Mon.-Fri. CST
800-947-7526

9F-2761 Mayberry price code: 13

- High quality, erasable, reproducible vellums
- Shipped via 2nd day air within the continental U.S.

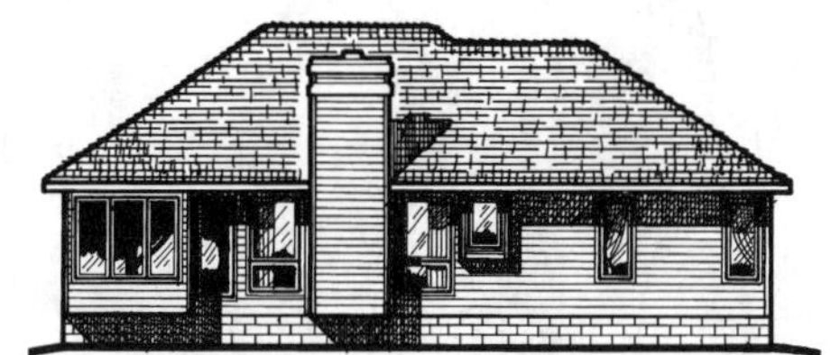

- offering basement or alternate slab foundation, this home is the epitome of economy and efficiency
- practical design with no wasted space offers amenities typically offered only in larger plans
- sloped ceiling, and fireplace flanked by large windows expands the great room
- kitchen is exceptionally well planned featuring large pantry, 2 lazy Susans and snack bar serving the dinette
- strategically located TV cabinet/entertainment center with lazy Susan affords viewing from great room, dinette or kitchen
- master suite features large walk-in closet and deluxe bath area with dual lavs and glass panel separating shower and whirlpool

Rear Elevation

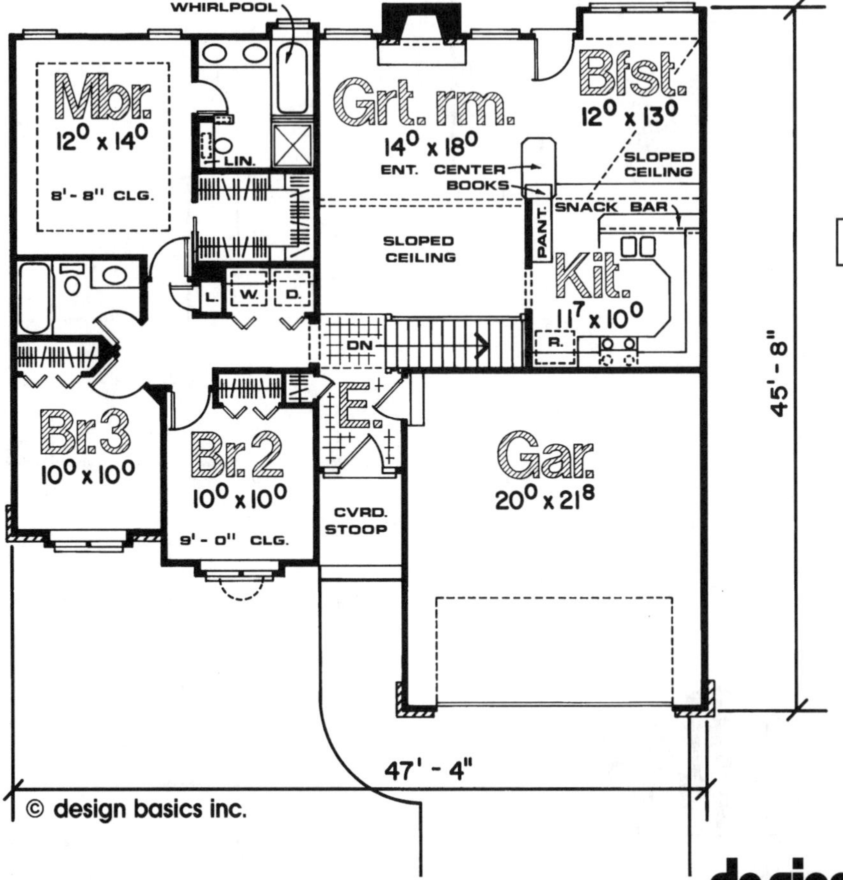

1341 Finished Sq. Ft.

- High quality, erasable, reproducible vellums
- Shipped via 2nd day air within the continental U.S.

9F-1379 Pendleton price code:14

Alternate Elevation At No Extra Cost

- optional elevation included with this plan at no addtional cost
- formal dining room open to large entry with coat closet and wide stairs
- great room with vaulted ceiling and fireplace as focal point
- double L-shaped kitchen includes boxed window at sink, pantry, space saver microwave and buffet counter
- core hallway opens to large master bedroom with walk-in closet and private bath

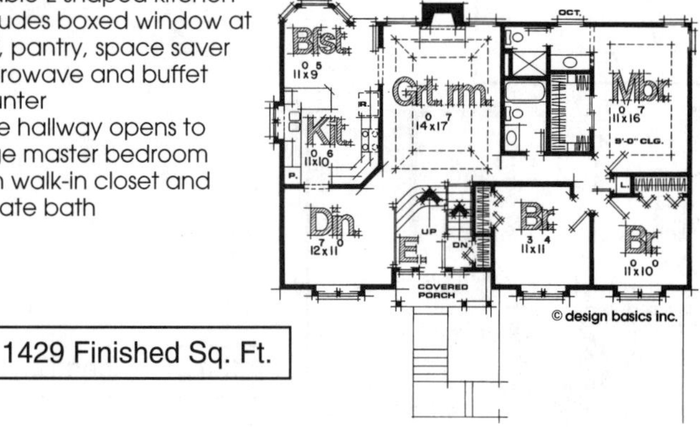

1429 Finished Sq. Ft.

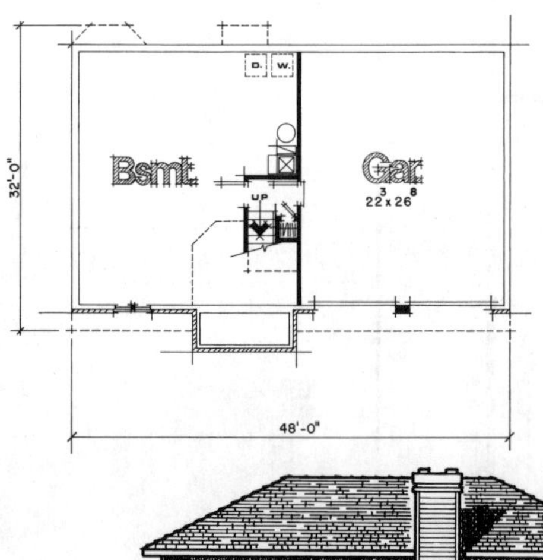

Rear Elevation

9F-3019 Kelsey price code:14

- covered porch adds charm to this ranch home
- sunny great room with 11-foot ceiling open to entry
- bowed breakfast area open to kitchen including island snack bar, corner sink and access to back yard
- secondary bedrooms share hall bath
- den with 10-foot-high ceiling and French doors options as a third bedroom
- volume master suite features whirlpool bath, dual lavs and mirrored doors to walk-in closet

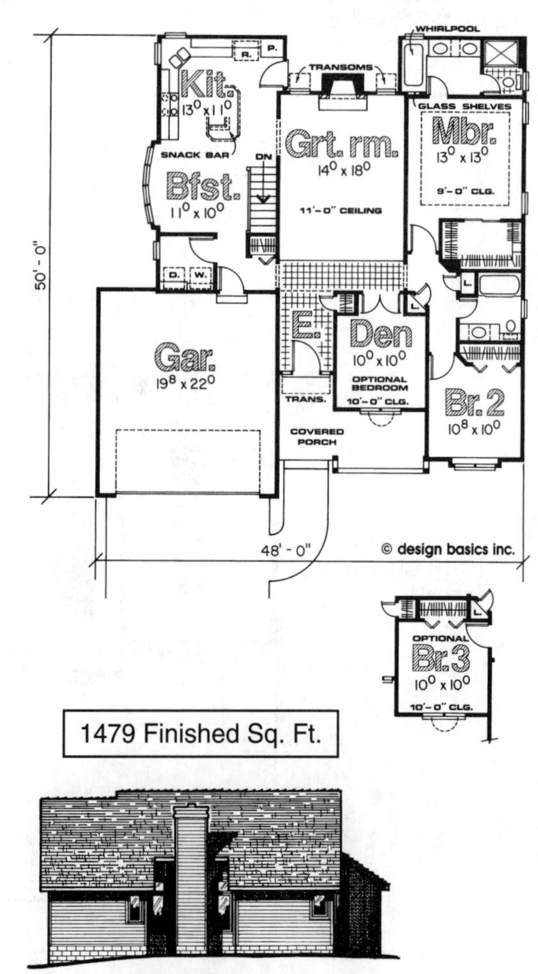

1479 Finished Sq. Ft.

Rear Elevation

9F-2300 Adair price code: 14

Gold Seal™ HOME PLANS

- ▶ High quality, erasable, reproducible vellums
- ▶ Shipped via 2nd day air within the continental U.S.

- sleek lines of this ideally compact ranch allude to sophistication within
- tiled entry views spacious great room with window-framed fireplace
- dining area strategic to great room enhances formal or family gatherings
- kitchen/breakfast area designed for enjoyment has utility room nearby
- convenient wet bar/servery serves both kitchen and dining area
- bedroom #3 designed for optional conversion to a den or home office
- comfortable secondary bedrooms share nearby bath and hall linen closet
- luxurious master suite enjoys sunlit whirlpool, dual lav dressing area and roomy walk-in closet

Rear Elevation

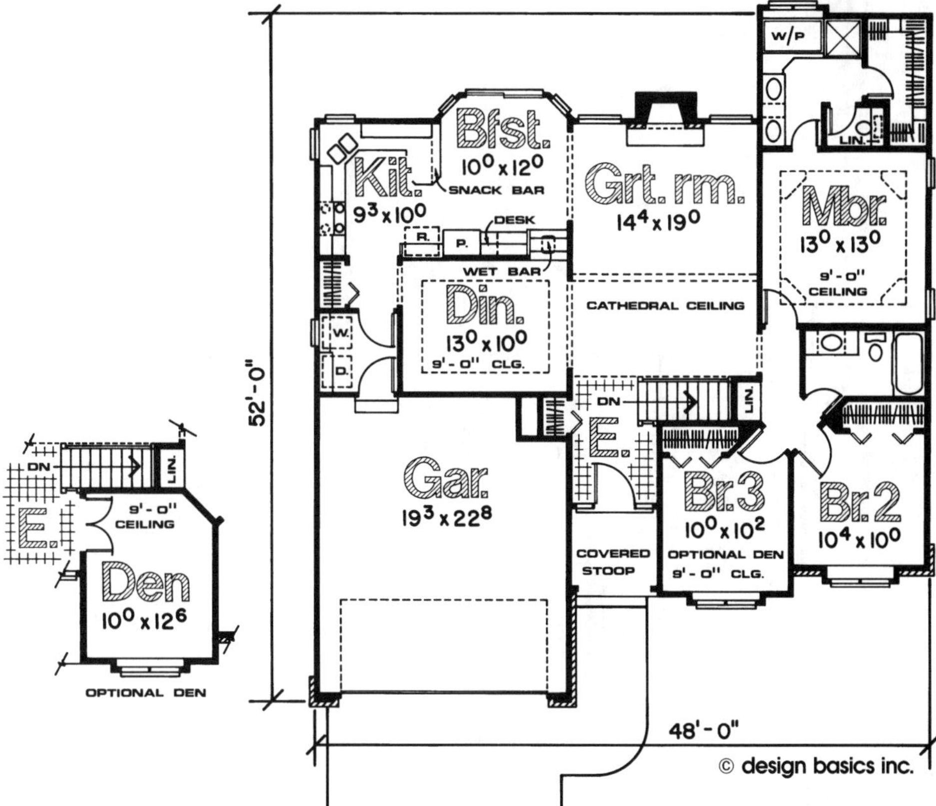

1496 Finished Sq. Ft.

9F-2537 Tahoe price code: 15

Gold Seal HOME PLANS™

- High quality, erasable, reproducible vellums
- Shipped via 2nd day air within the continental U.S.

- brick wing walls provide visually expansive front elevation
- from entry, traffic flows into bright great room with impressive 2-sided fireplace
- dining room opens to great room, offering view of fireplace
- French doors off entry open into kitchen
- kitchen features large pantry, planning desk and snack bar
- dinette accesses large, comfortable screen porch
- laundry room is strategically located off kitchen and provides for direct access from garage
- built-in shelves in garage
- French doors access master suite with formal ceiling and pampering bath

Rear Elevation

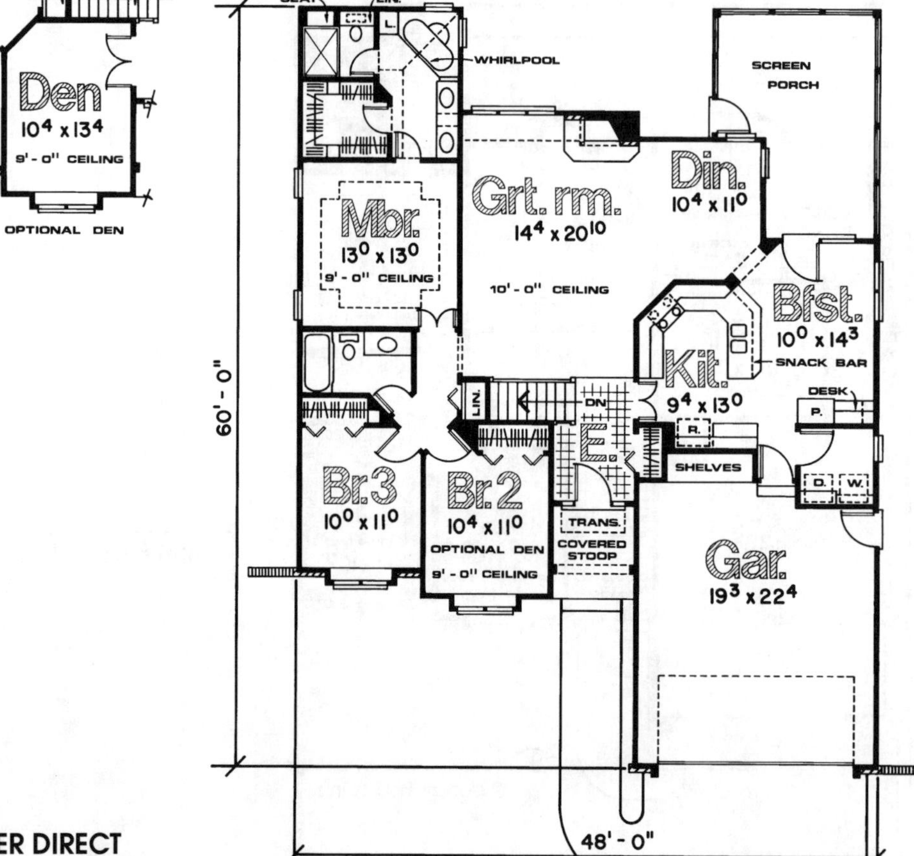

1580 Finished Sq. Ft.

9F-3555 Laramy price code: 15

- High quality, erasable, reproducible vellums
- Shipped via 2nd day air within the continental U.S.

Gold Seal™ HOME PLANS

- windows and brick detailing perfect this warm elevation
- volume entry adorned with arched transom above door
- kitchen enjoys view to family room through arched opening above sink
- breakfast area has planning desk and boxed window
- covered porch off breakfast area welcomes relaxation
- cathedral ceiling adds drama to family room with fireplace framed by windows
- master bedroom has 9'-0" ceiling and view to back
- spacious walk-in closet, whirlpool under glass and dual sink vanity serve master bath
- bedroom #2 has volume ceiling and shares full bath with bedroom #3

Rear Elevation

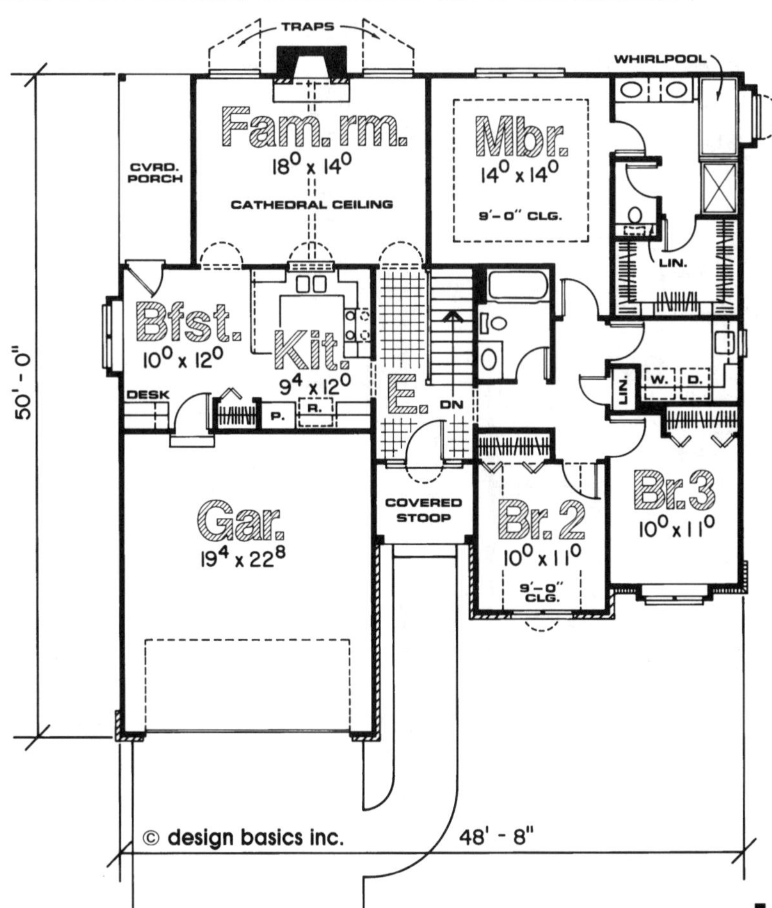

1518 Finished Sq. Ft.

design basics inc.® HOME PLAN DESIGN SERVICE

9F-1767 Rosebury price code: 16

Gold Seal HOME PLANS™

- ▶ High quality, erasable, reproducible vellums
- ▶ Shipped via 2nd day air within the continental U.S.

- spacious 10-foot entry
- large volume great room with fireplace flanked by windows to the back seen from entry
- see-thru wet bar between dinette and dining room with formal ceiling
- fully-equipped kitchen with desk, pantry and special window box above sink
- angles in hallway for secondary bedrooms create interesting effect
- secondary bedrooms share convenient hall bath
- roomy master suite with volume ceiling equipped with special amenities including skylit dressing/bath area with plant shelf, large walk-in closet, double vanity and whirlpool tub
- extra deep garage

Rear Elevation

Alternate Elevation At No Extra Cost

1604 Finished Sq. Ft.

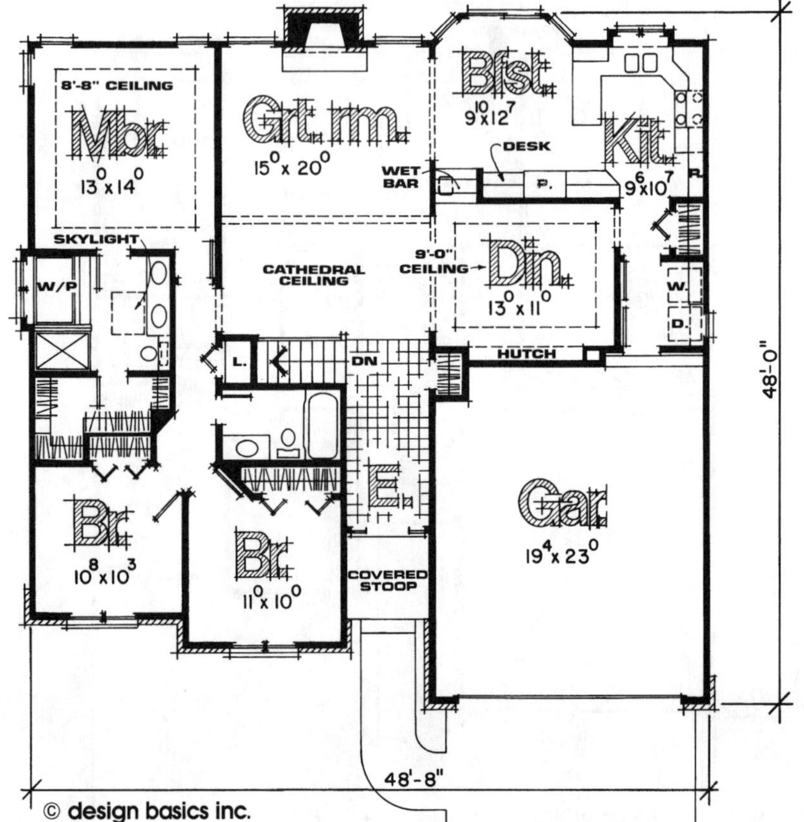

ORDER DIRECT
7:00-6:00 Mon.-Fri. CST
800-947-7526

9F-1551 Logan price code: 12

- High quality, erasable, reproducible vellums
- Shipped via 2nd day air within the continental U.S.

- fireplace centered in great room under cathedral ceiling and surrounded by windows
- efficient kitchen with window box, planning desk, lazy Susan and snack bar counter
- dinette with many windows has access to outdoors
- roomy secondary bedrooms
- accessible hall linen closet
- laundry room conveniently located near bedrooms
- master bedroom with corner windows and intriguing ceiling treatment
- master dressing area with large vanity, walk-in closet and compartmented stool and shower

Rear Elevation

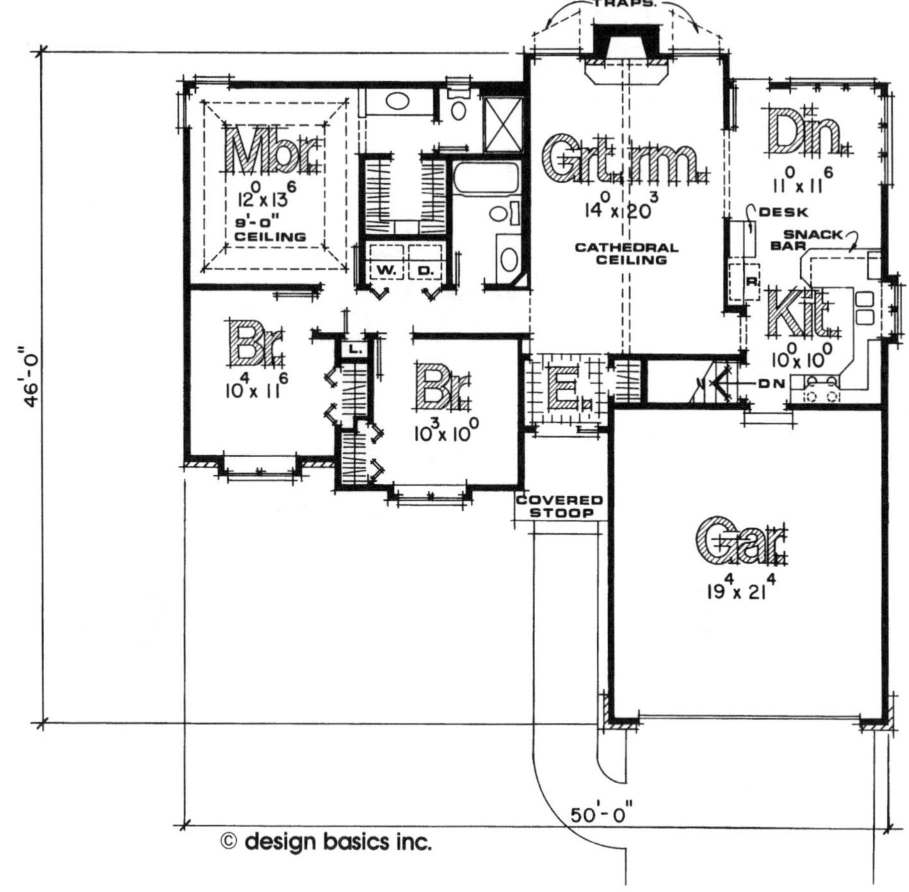

1271 Finished Sq. Ft.

9F-969 Benton price code: 13

- High quality, erasable, reproducible vellums
- Shipped via 2nd day air within the continental U.S.

- garage at entry level
- volume entry with coat closet, plant ledge and angled staircase
- great room features cathedral ceiling and fireplace framed by windows with elegant quarter-round transoms
- bayed window in dining area
- efficient kitchen with corner sink and access to outside
- central hallway angled for maximum privacy
- convenient split-entry ranch design
- double doors open into master bedroom with vaulted ceiling, his and her closets, and dressing area with vanity
- skylight provides the perfect accent for shared hall bath

Rear Elevation

1305 Finished Sq. Ft.

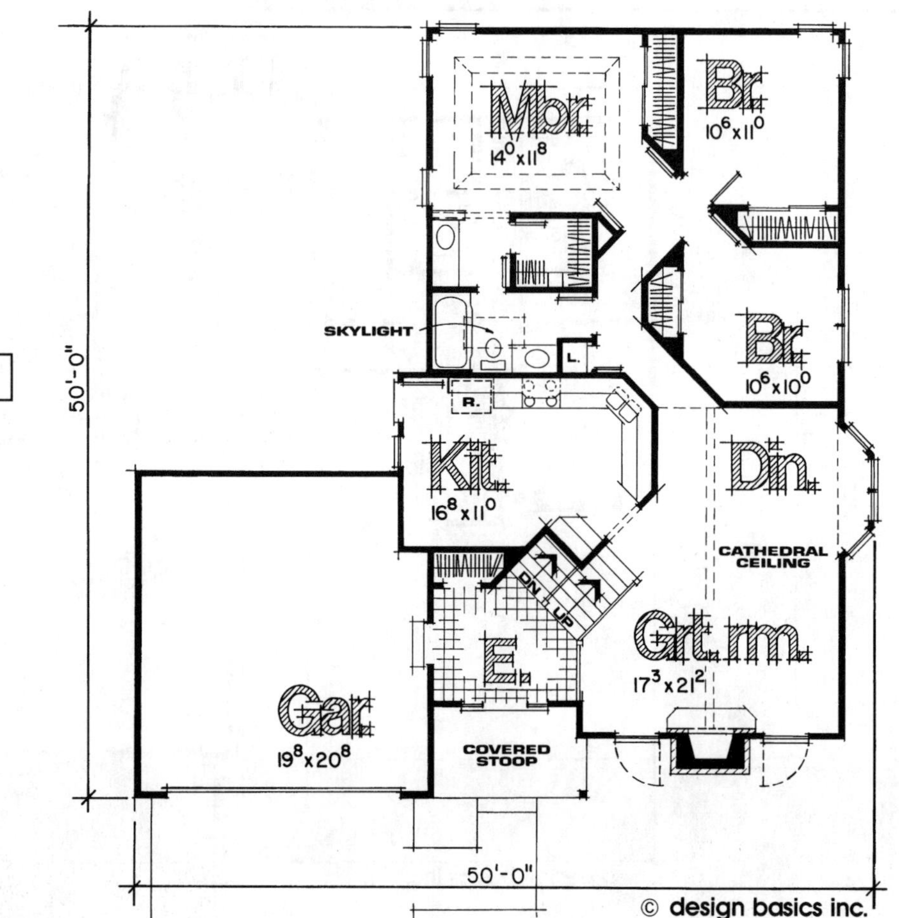

- ▶ High quality, erasable, reproducible vellums
- ▶ Shipped via 2nd day air within the continental U.S.

9F-3102 Aspen price code: 13

- arched entry highlights brick and siding elevation
- great room with arched windows creates beautiful view from entry
- kitchen features large snack bar and convenient access to spacious utility room
- window at sink overloooks versatile covered area outside
- master suite contains generous walk-in and whirlpool bath with compartmented stool and shower

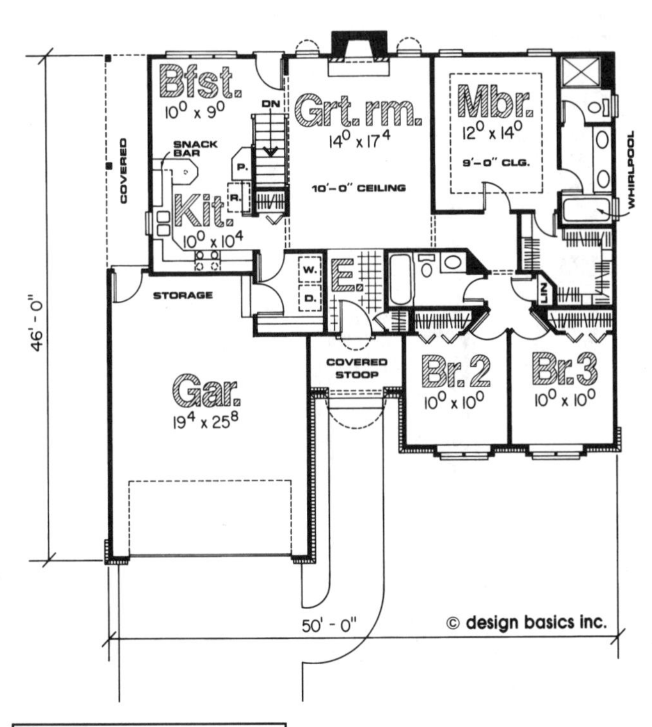

1339 Finished Sq. Ft.

Rear Elevation

9F-3010 Quimby price code: 14

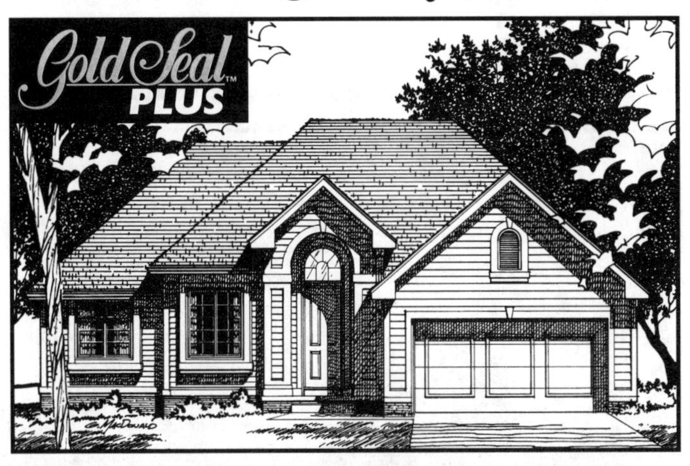

- 12-foot-tall ceiling integrates great room, semi-formal dining room and kitchen
- spacious covered porch accessed from dining room
- arched openings to kitchen with built-in bookcases provide dramatic backdrop for dining area
- hall bath serves secondary bedrooms, with bedroom #3 easily optioned to a den
- master suite features a boxed 9-foot-high ceiling, whirlpool bath and walk-in close

1422 Finished Sq. Ft.

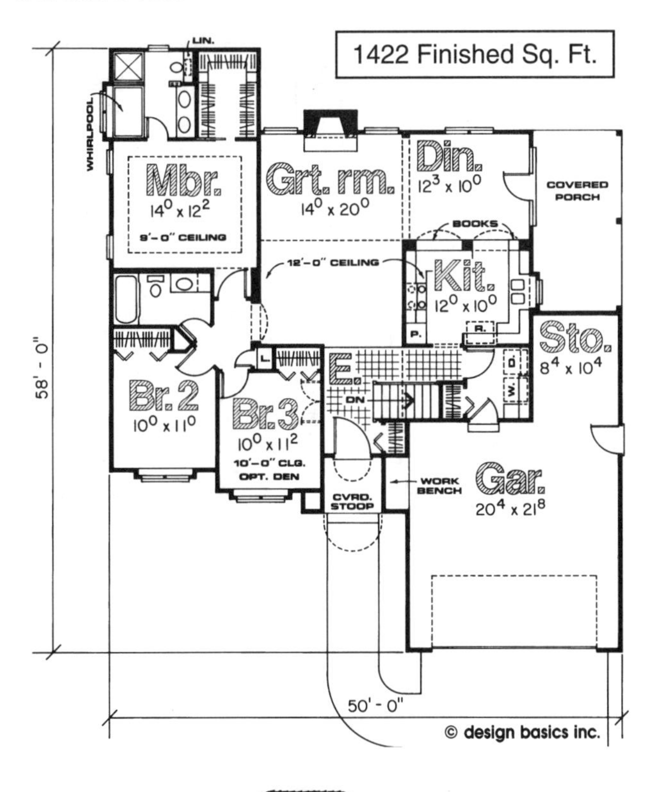

Rear Elevation

9F-2173 Fraser price code: 14

Gold Seal™ HOME PLANS

- ▶ High quality, erasable, reproducible vellums
- ▶ Shipped via 2nd day air within the continental U.S.

- bright volume entry open to volume great room
- handsome fireplace flanked by tall windows in great room
- versatility with living room/bedroom option
- snack bar and generous pantry in kitchen adjacent to pleasant dinette
- hanging space and cabinet in convenient laundry room access from garage entry
- angles throughout enhance architectural interest
- boxed window in private secondary bedroom
- spacious master bedroom with boxed ceiling and walk-in closet
- master bath features his and her lavs and whirlpool tub under skylight

Rear Elevation

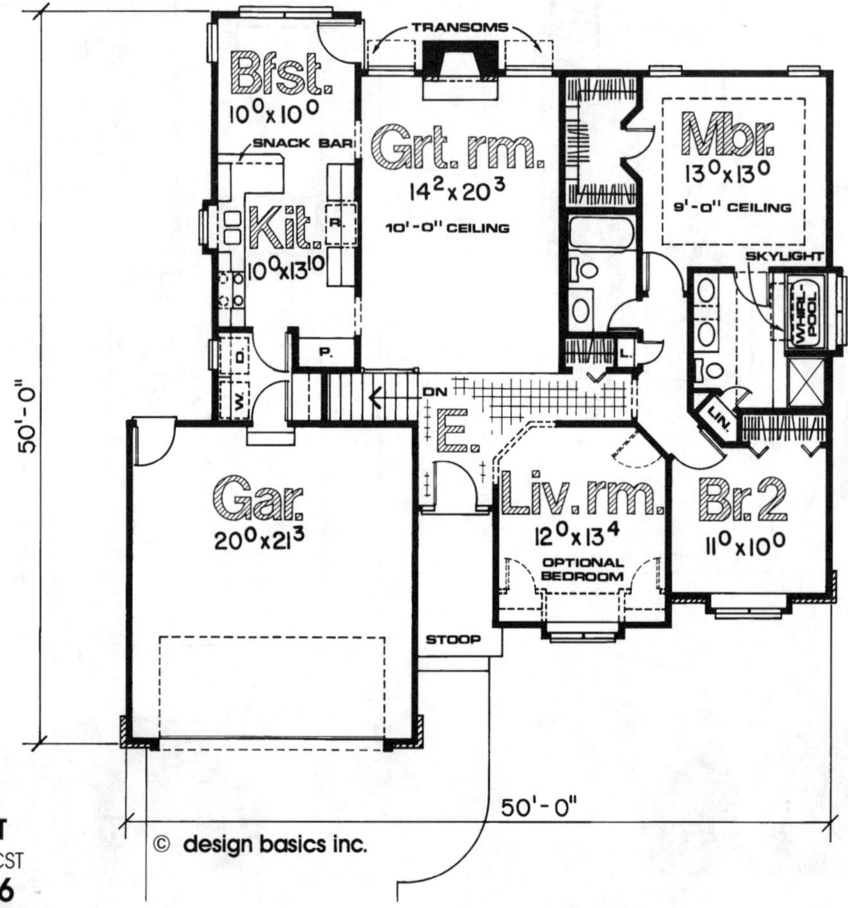

1451 Finished Sq. Ft.

9F-3127 Haley price code: 15

- High quality, erasable, reproducible vellums
- Shipped via 2nd day air within the continental U.S.

- corner wrapping porch provides focal point for cozy ranch
- entry open to great room with cathedral ceiling and formal dining room with 10-foot-high ceiling
- spacious kitchen features corner sink, built-in bookcase and shares snack bar with breakfast area
- bedroom wing has convenient laundry access
- plan offers versatility with optional third bedroom
- French doors open to master suite with volume ceiling, mirrored doors to walk-in closet and sunny whirlpool bath

Rear Elevation

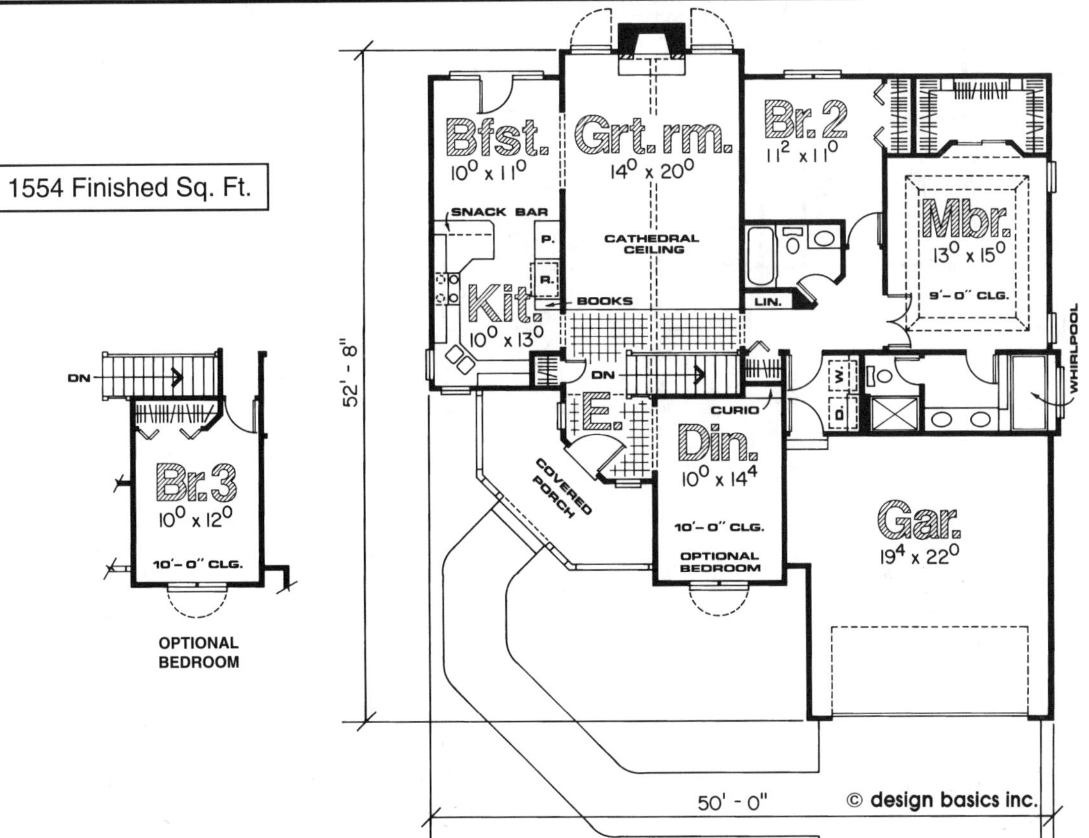

design basics inc.®
HOME PLAN DESIGN SERVICE

9F-1770 Bayley price code: 15

- High quality, erasable, reproducible vellums
- Shipped via 2nd day air within the continental U.S.

- large entry with interesting angled staircase to living areas
- attached garage at entry level
- large great room with cathedral ceiling features fireplace framed by beautiful windows
- bayed dining area open to great room for expanded entertaining
- efficient kitchen with pantry, desk and sunny dinette leading to covered patio
- convenient split-entry ranch design
- corridor hallway accesses bedroom wing
- large master suite with vaulted ceiling and French doors from hallway includes his and her closets, whirlpool, 2 lavs with make-up counter and private access to covered patio

Rear Elevation

1556 Finished Sq. Ft.

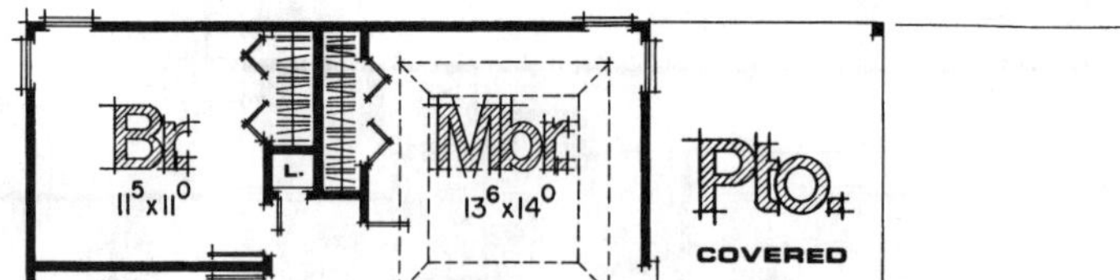

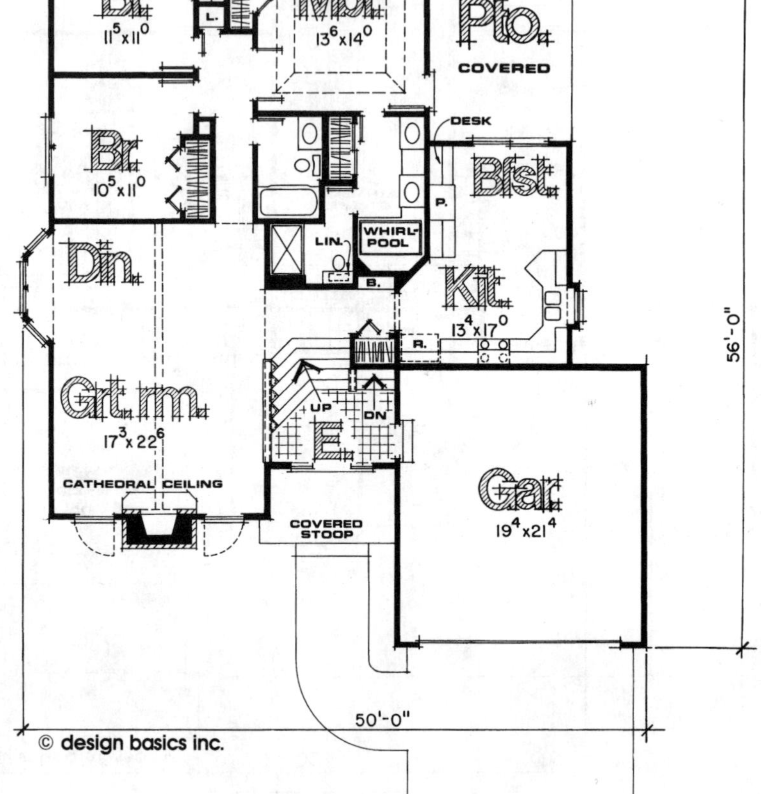

© design basics inc.

9F-2196 Granite price code: 15

- High quality, erasable, reproducible vellums
- Shipped via 2nd day air within the continental U.S.

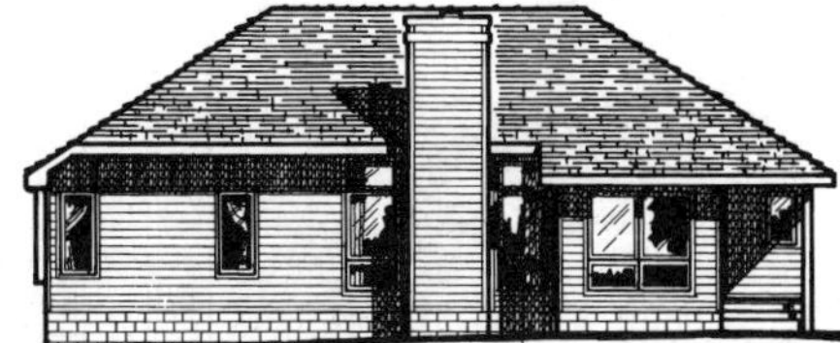

- volume entry with transoms above door offers view of great room fireplace
- flexible dining area and great room share 10-foot ceiling
- formal living room converts to optional third bedroom
- kitchen features pantry, lazy Susan and corner sink with windows
- breakfast area has built-in desk and access to covered deck or great room
- laundry room with closet serves as mud entry from garage
- master bedroom features clever indented walk-in closet
- master bath includes whirlpool tub separated from shower by glass panel, double vanity and skylight

Rear Elevation

1561 Finished Sq. Ft.

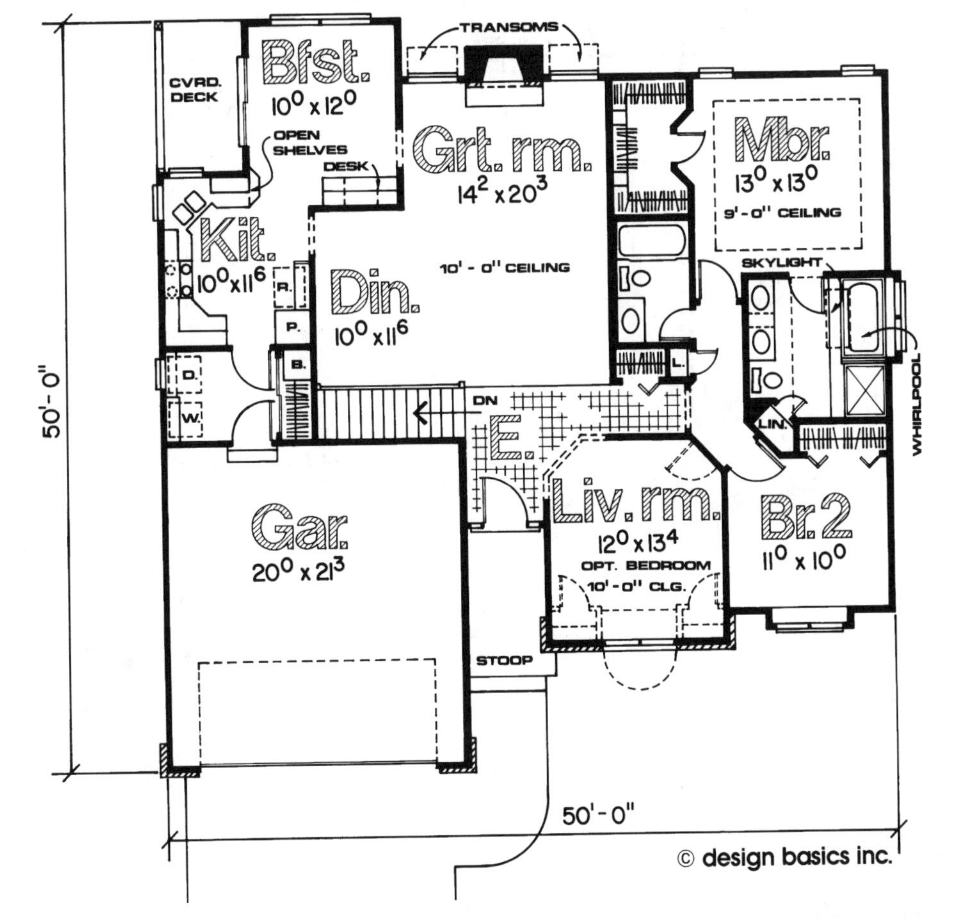

9F-2291 Bradley price code: 15

Gold Seal™ HOME PLANS

- High quality, erasable, reproducible vellums
- Shipped via 2nd day air within the continental U.S.

- clean lines on elevation add volume to this compact raised ranch
- appealing entry opens to living room with cozy bayed window with a built-in seat
- family room opens to kitchen and has cozy fireplace and cathedral ceiling
- premium eight-sided dining room features two corner windows and two arched openings to hall
- well-designed kitchen/breakfast area with wrapping counters and snack bar extends aspects of comfortable living
- roomy secondary bedrooms separate from master suite include window seats
- natural light from a bayed window floods the charming master suite featuring a tiered ceiling, walk-in closet, whirlpool and dual vanities

Rear Elevation

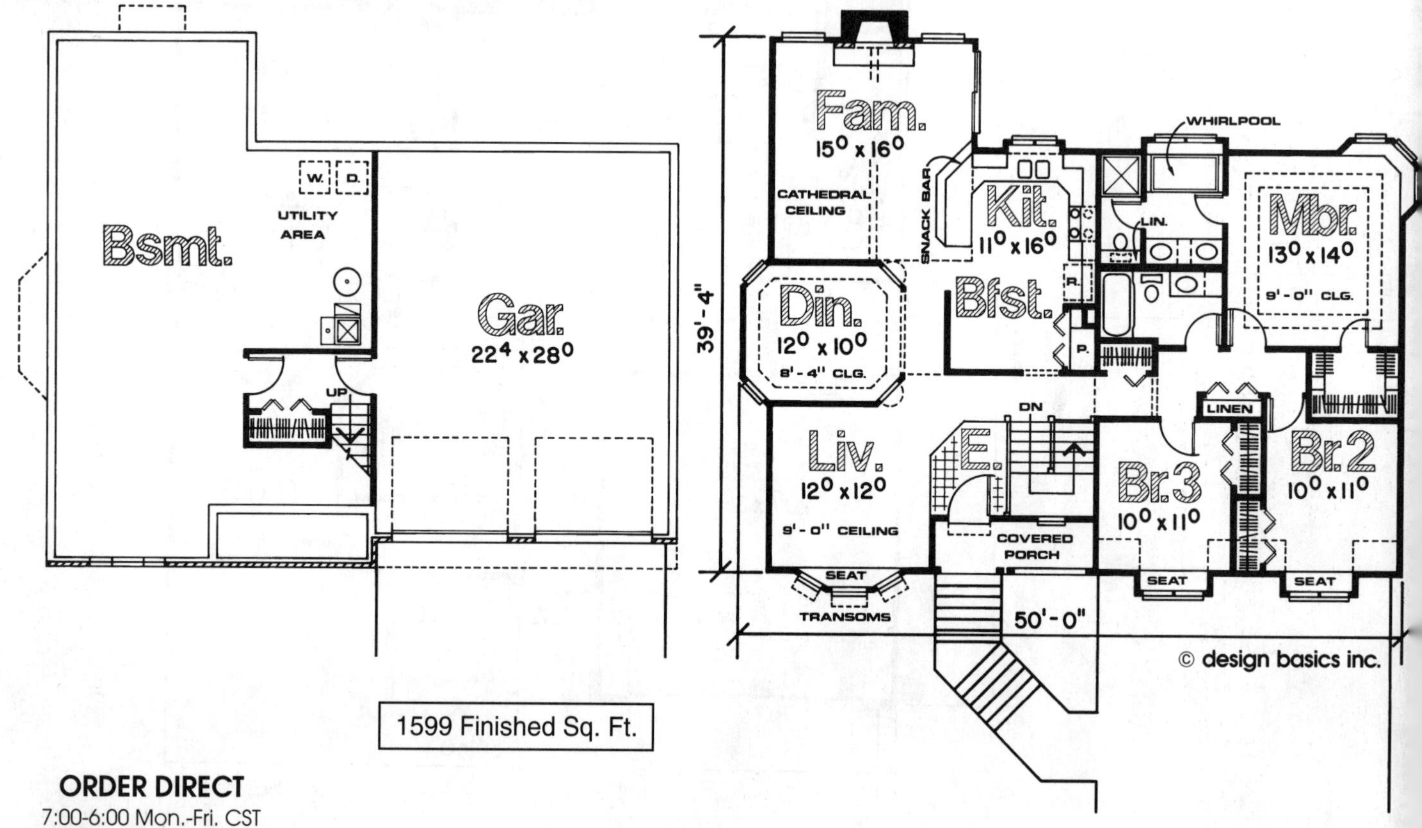

1599 Finished Sq. Ft.

ORDER DIRECT
7:00-6:00 Mon.-Fri. CST
800-947-7526

VISA MasterCard Discover NOVUS

GOLD SEAL™ HOME PLANS

BASE PLAN INFORMATION

Page No.	Width	Plan No.	Plan Name	Sq. Ft.
62	50'-0"	3464	Jenkins	1546
63	50'-0"	3123	Bethany	1596
56	46'-0"	3121	Bellamy	1660
47	40'-8"	2578	Kaiser	1675
64	50'-0"	1734	Crescent	1731
49	42'-0"	2330	Pomeroy	1751
50	42'-0"	2486	Fowler	1772
60	48'-0"	3090	Jarret	1783
65	50'-0"	3385	Brittany	1788
38	29'-4"	3931	Medora	1801
51	42'-0"	3065	Foster	1841
48	40'-8"	2569	Ohern	1845
66	50'-0"	1867	Langley	1901
67	50'-0"	1727	Spencer	1905
52	42'-0"	2551	Girard	1927
43	38'-0"	3908	Chapman	1929
68	50'-0"	2292	Inglewood	1943
53	42'-0"	2554	Lansing	1948
39	30'-0"	3925	Elmwood	1980
61	48'-0"	3382	Higgins	1991
54	42'-0"	3075	Grant	2019
44	38'-0"	3892	Tecumseh	2033
59	46'-8"	2951	Newlin	2109
69	50'-0"	2220	Gentry	2139
57	46'-0"	1417	Sanborn	2142
46	40'-0"	3909	Ashland	2162
55	44'-0"	2328	Birchley	2170
70	50'-0"	3375	Gilchrist	2201
45	39'-4"	3874	Lawton	2252
41	34'-0"	3878	Marysville	2290
42	36'-0"	3900	Harris	2292
58	46'-0"	2927	Morgan	2403
40	30'-0"	3921	Bakersfield	2419

1½ STORY HOMES

9F-3931 Medora price code: 18

- High quality, erasable, reproducible vellums
- Shipped via 2nd day air within the continental U.S.

Gold Seal PLUS

- well balanced elevation with covered porch offers warm, friendly welcome
- entry provides immediate access to great room
- expansive great room features ceiling that slopes to 2-stories high
- complete island kitchen includes snack bar, lazy Susan, pantry and plenty of counter space
- a sloping ceiling in dining area provides a comfortable space for both formal and informal eating
- first-floor luxury master suite offers 9-foot high boxed ceiling
- large laundry accessible from kitchen and garage
- loft easily converted to a 4th bedroom

Rear Elevation

Main	1228 Sq. Ft.
Second	573 Sq. Ft.
Total	1801 Sq. Ft.

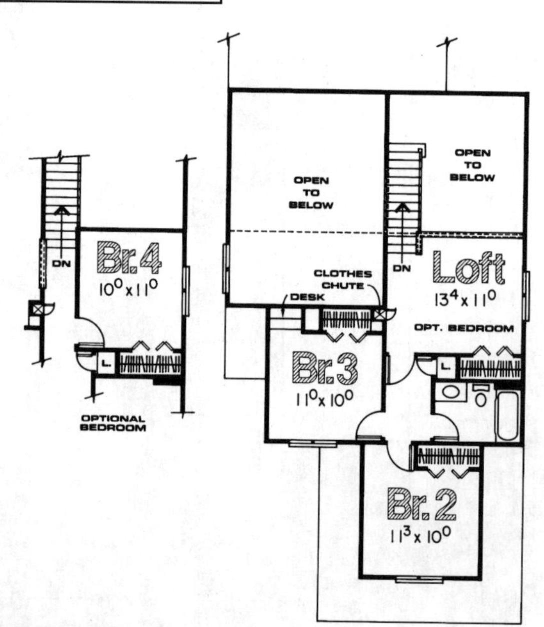

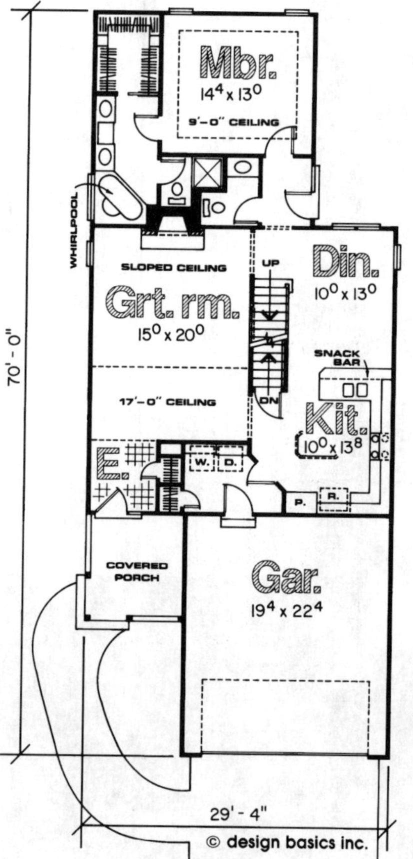

ORDER DIRECT
7:00-6:00 Mon.-Fri. CST
800-947-7526

9F-3925 Elmwood price code: 19

- High quality, erasable, reproducible vellums
- Shipped via 2nd day air within the continental U.S.

- stylish arches and gables impart a refined character to the elevation
- raised-hearth fireplace provides a handsome focal point for the great room
- unloading groceries is made easy with convenient access from garage to kitchen
- comfortable breakfast area allows access to outdoors
- sizeable master suite includes corner windows, walk-in closet and double vanity under arched transom window
- upper-level secondary bedrooms share centralized bath with separate vanities and compartmented stool and tub

Rear Elevation

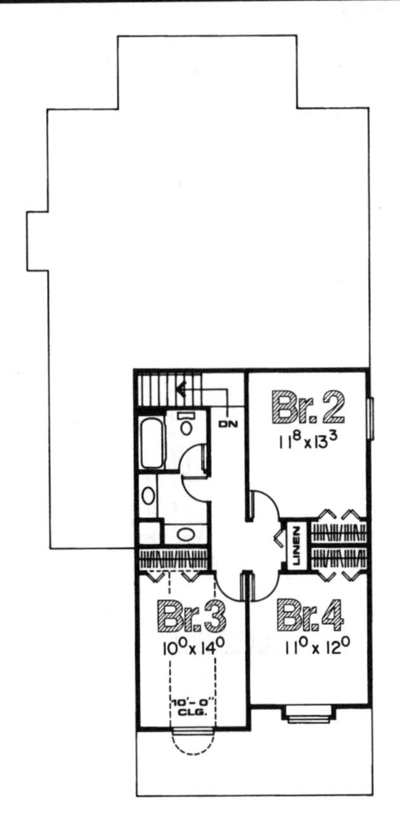

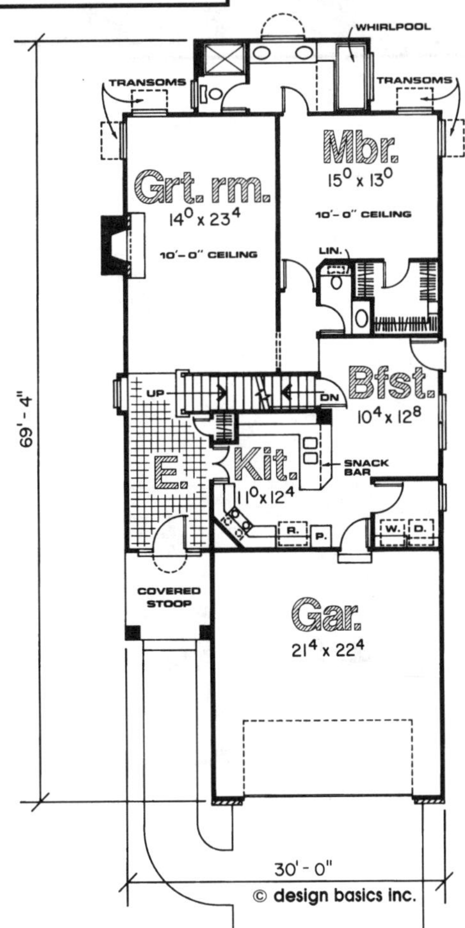

Main	1311 Sq. Ft.
Second	669 Sq. Ft.
Total	1980 Sq. Ft.

9F-3921 Bakersfield price code: 24

Gold Seal PLUS

- High quality, erasable, reproducible vellums
- Shipped via 2nd day air within the continental U.S.

- wood and brick details highlight elegant elevation
- view from entry reveals gracious dining room and volume great room with 10-foot high ceiling
- great room is enhanced by raised-hearth fireplace flanked between large windows
- sunny kitchen/dinette area offers convenient island, snack bar, lazy Susan, pantry and easy access to side yard
- laundry room convenient to garage entrance into home
- master suite includes generous walk-in closet, whirlpool, compartmented stool and shower

Rear Elevation

Main	1727 Sq. Ft.
Second	692 Sq. Ft.
Total	2419 Sq. Ft.

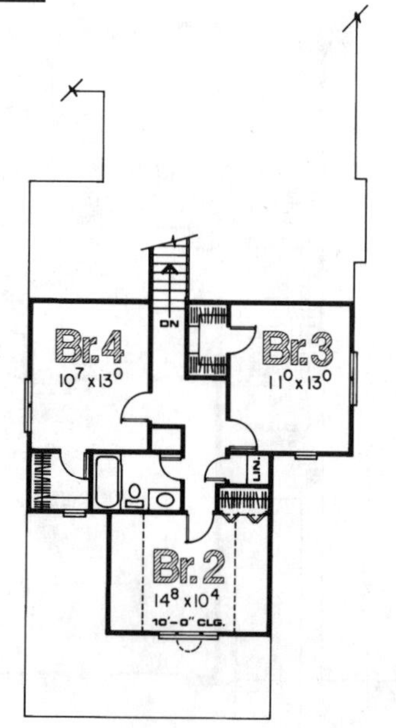

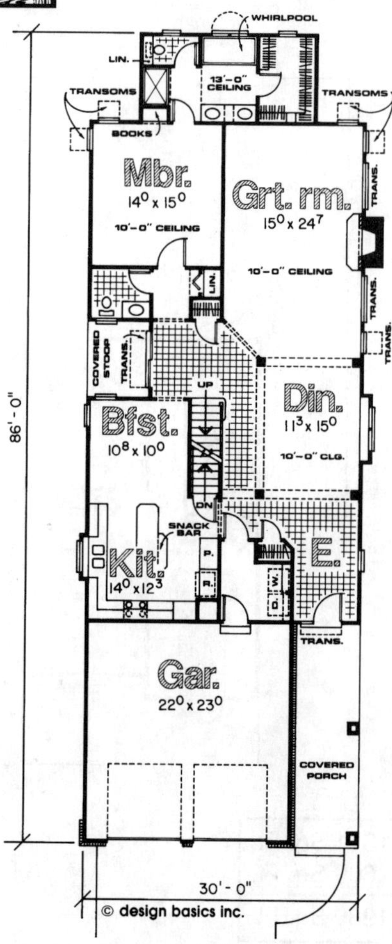

9F-3878 Marysville price code: 22

- dormers and traditional trim detailing charm this perfectly balanced elevation
- sunken great room is immediately viewed from 2-story entry
- French doors in dining room open to conveniently located kitchen
- rear stairway provides private access to upstairs secondary bedrooms
- luxury master suite features double vanity, walk-in closet and whirlpool tub beneath boxed window
- secondary bedrooms share centrally located hall bath
- upstairs, unfinished area opts as a hobby room, study, or fifth bedroom

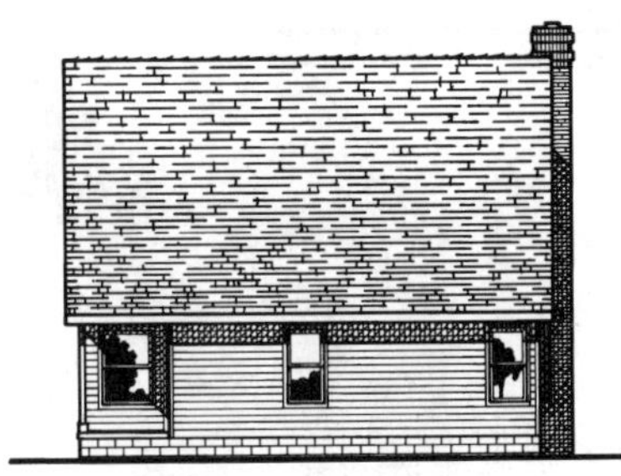

Rear Elevation

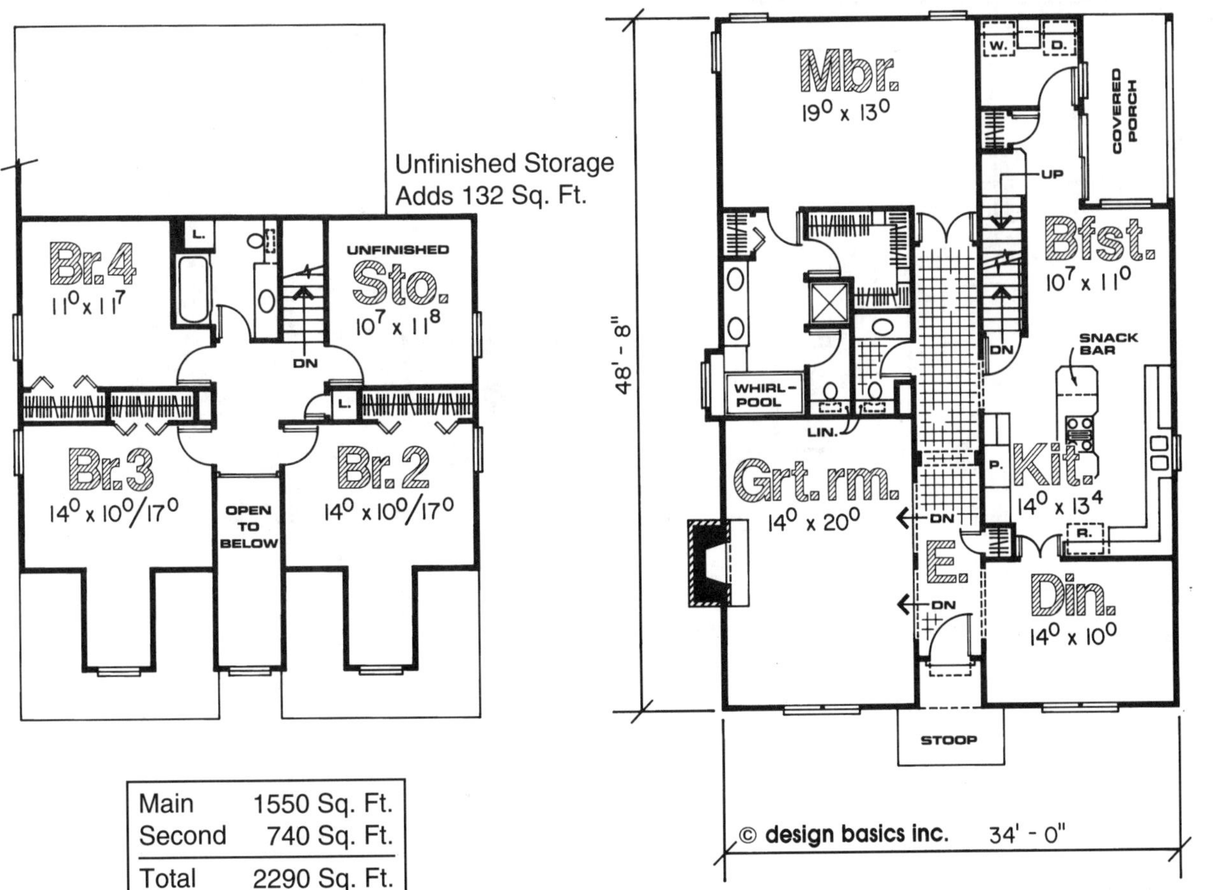

Main	1550 Sq. Ft.
Second	740 Sq. Ft.
Total	2290 Sq. Ft.

9F-3900 Harris price code: 22

- High quality, erasable, reproducible vellums
- Shipped via 2nd day air within the continental U.S.

- arched entry highlights brick and lap siding on elevation
- great room enjoys 10-foot ceiling, corner windows with transoms and raised-hearth fireplace
- well-designed kitchen/dining area with patio door leading to side yard from dinette
- kitchen features pantry, 2 lazy Susans, snack bar and generous counter space
- large master suite includes 9-foot high ceiling, whirlpool, 2 lavs with make-up counter and walk-in closet
- study area upstairs, connects bedrooms

Rear Elevation

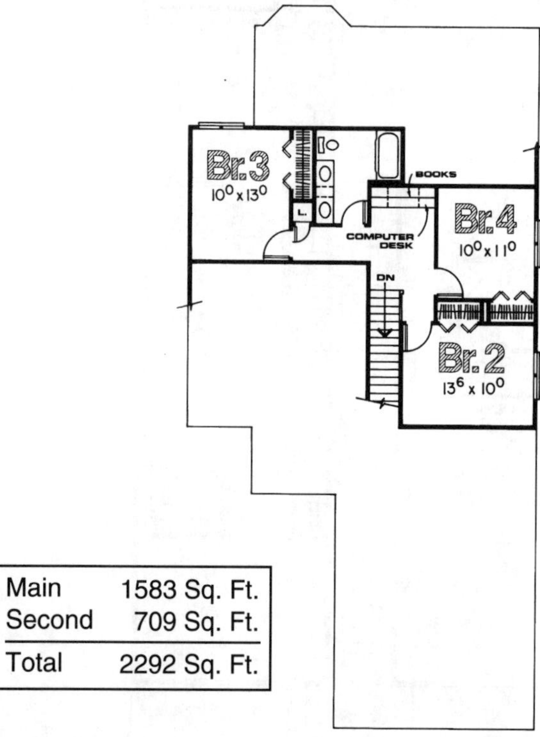

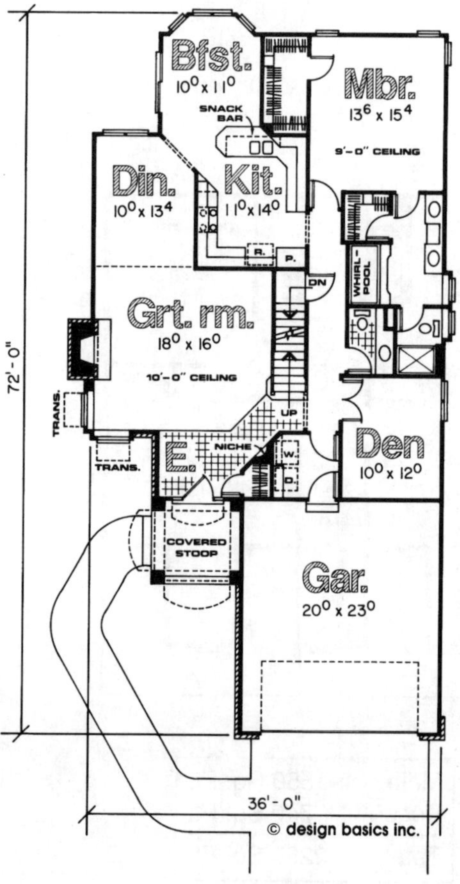

Main	1583 Sq. Ft.
Second	709 Sq. Ft.
Total	2292 Sq. Ft.

9F-3908 Chapman price code: 19

- High quality, erasable, reproducible vellums
- Shipped via 2nd day air within the continental U.S.

- well-balanced elevation uses brick, gable rooflines and keystones to set it apart
- entry offers impressive long views through great room
- great room features ceiling that slopes to 2-stories high, plus tall windows surround fireplace
- excellent working triangle in spacious kitchen, with window over sink and snack bar
- dinette offers easy access to private, covered rear porch
- first-floor master suite crafted with distinctive ceiling treatment, sizable bath/dressing area, and angled walk-in closet

Rear Elevation

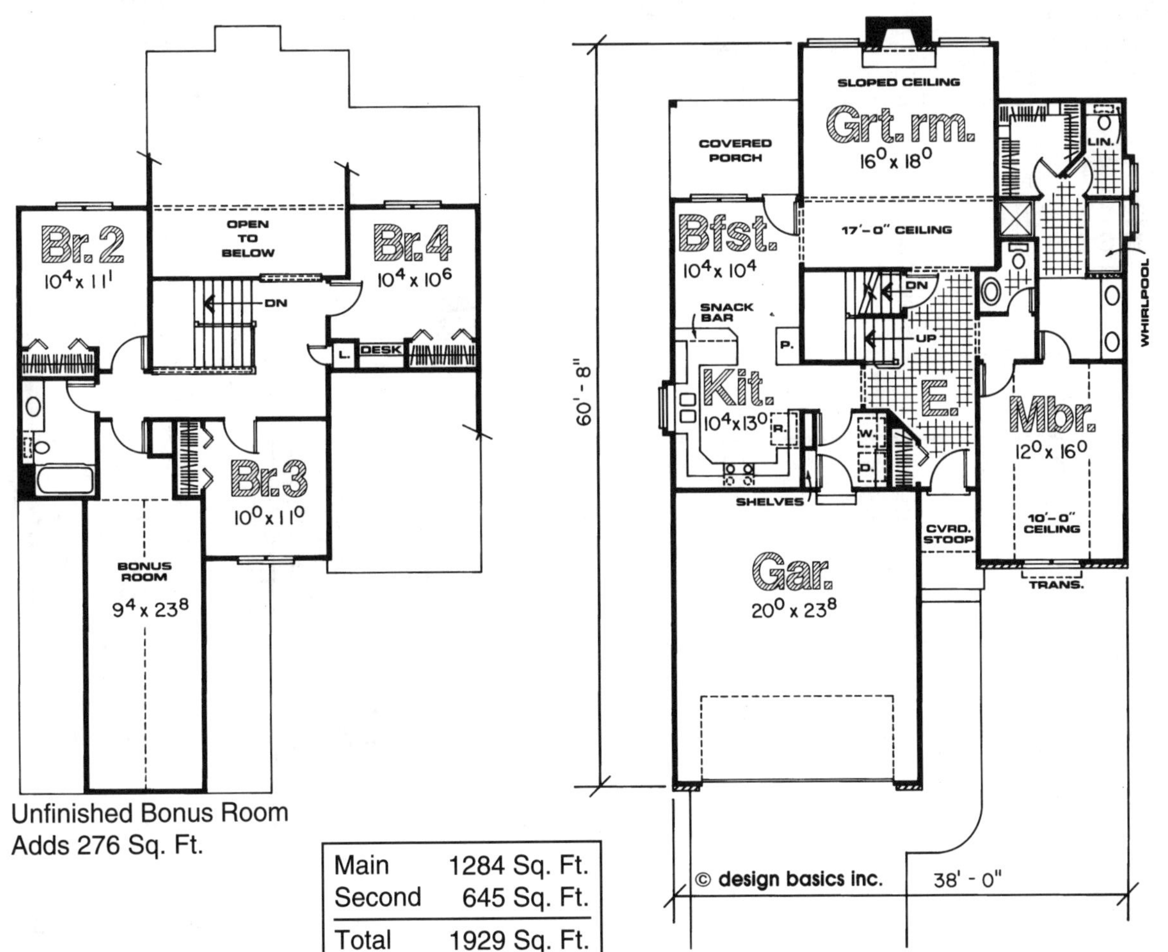

Unfinished Bonus Room
Adds 276 Sq. Ft.

Main	1284 Sq. Ft.
Second	645 Sq. Ft.
Total	1929 Sq. Ft.

9F-3920 Fairbury price code: 20

▸ High quality, erasable, reproducible vellums
▸ Shipped via 2nd day air within the continental U.S.

Gold Seal PLUS

- attractive elevation offers a pleasing balance of brick and lap siding, enhanced by gables and a covered front porch
- entry views U-shaped staircase and formal dining room which opts as a den
- family room situated for privacy allows views to the rear, through large windows flanking a raised-hearth fireplace
- kitchen with snack bar and pantry adjoins breakfast area with direct access to covered rear porch
- main floor master suite includes double vanity, whirlpool tub and spacious walk-in closet
- upper-level secondary bedrooms share a centrally located bath with double vanity and compartmented tub and stool

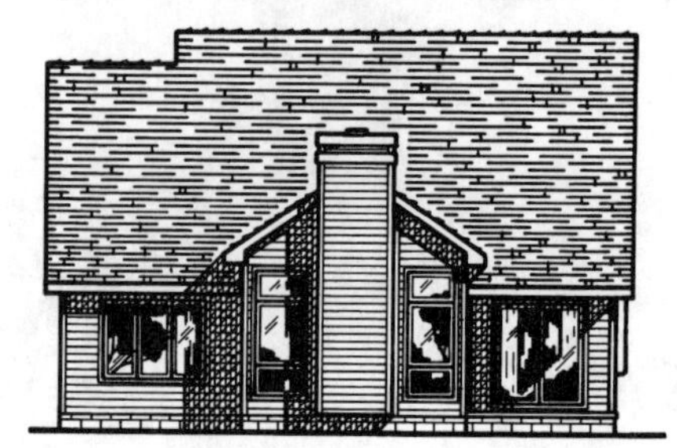

Rear Elevation

Main	1397 Sq. Ft.
Second	636 Sq. Ft.
Total	2033 Sq. Ft.

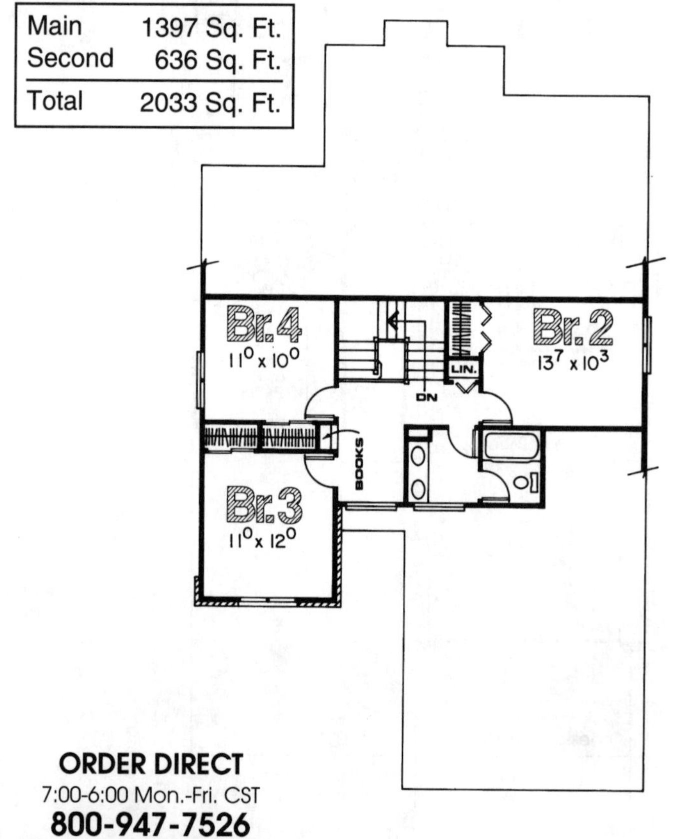

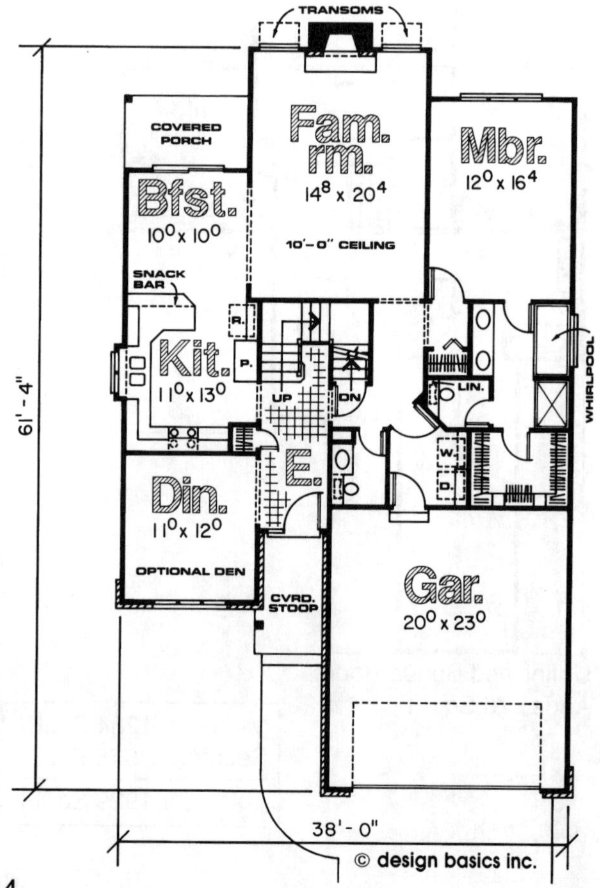

© design basics inc.

9F-3874 Lawton price code: 22

▶ High quality, erasable, reproducible vellums
▶ Shipped via 2nd day air within the continental U.S.

- a pair of covered porches add unique balance to this home's appearance
- entry opens directly into volume great room with raised-hearth fireplace and access to rear covered stoop
- dining room is situated at the back of the home for privacy
- kitchen with two lazy Susans, pantry and snack bar, is open to bayed breakfast area with access to outdoors
- French doors in master bedroom open to private covered porch on front of the home
- elegant master bath includes dual vanities, corner whirlpool, compartmented stool and large walk-in closet

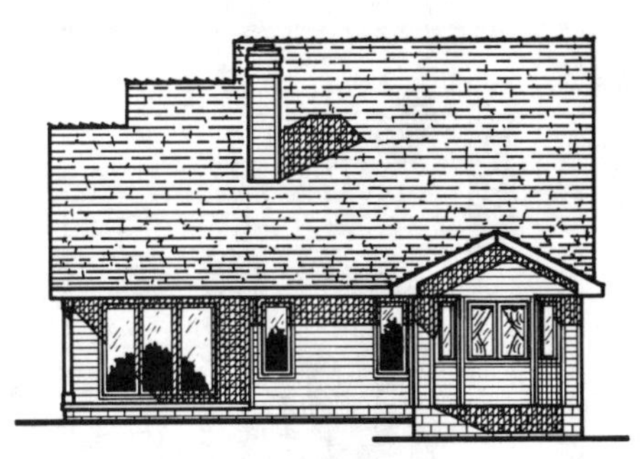

Rear Elevation

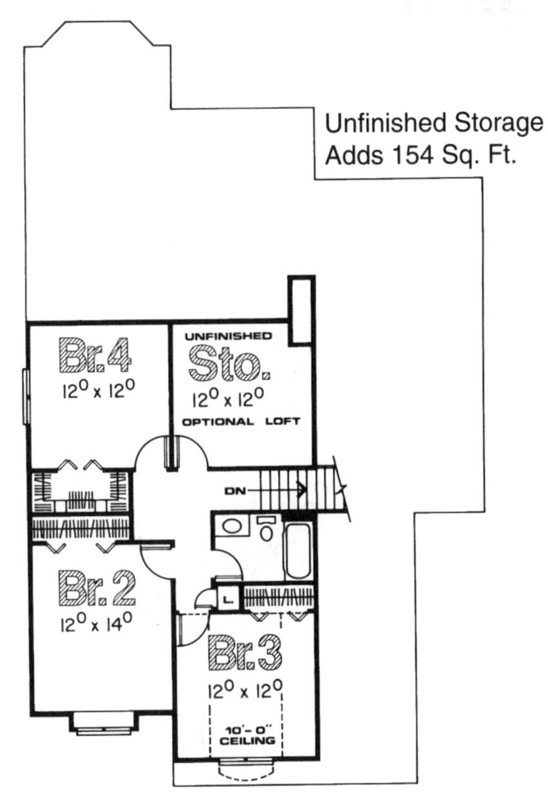

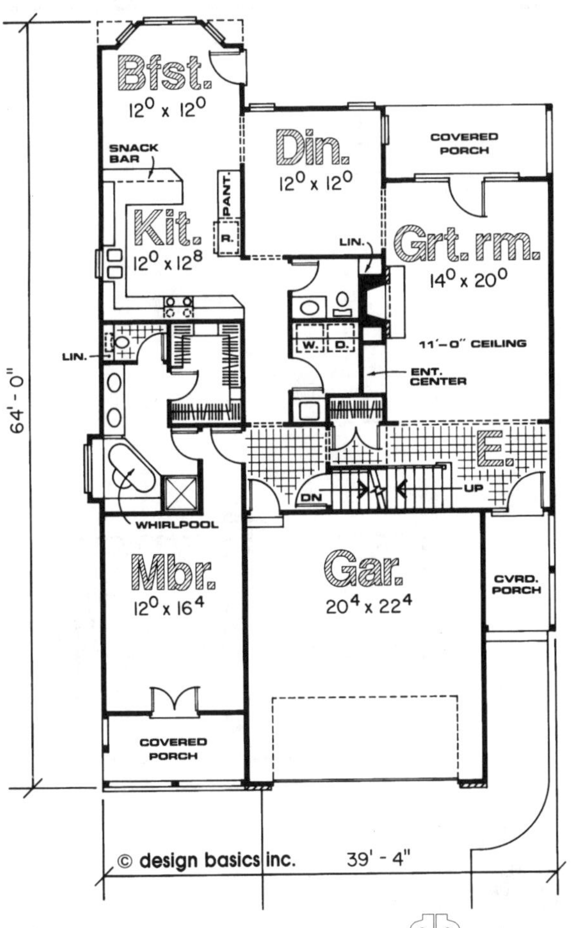

9F-3909 Ashland price code: 21

- traditional colonial design elements create a warm, yet stately elevation
- expansive great room with raised-hearth fireplace, opens to entry for a dramatic welcome
- formal dining room is serviced by adjacent kitchen with snack bar, pantry and plenty of counter space
- breakfast area with sloped ceiling is brightened by attractive arched transom window and sliding patio door
- double doors lead to elegant master suite with double vanity, whirlpool and direct access to private covered porch
- two of the three upstairs secondary bedrooms include spacious walk-in closets

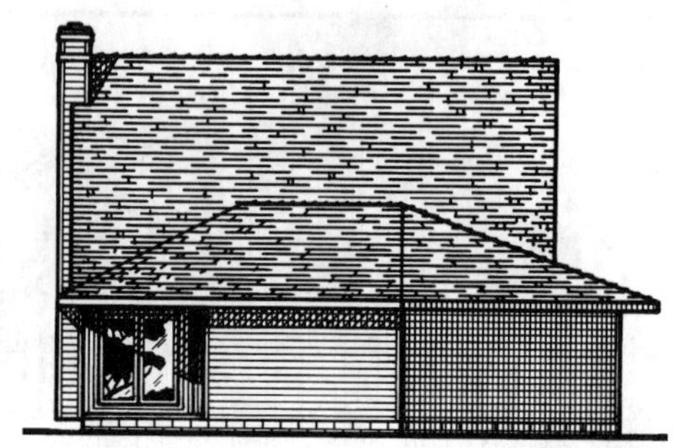

Rear Elevation

Main	1456 Sq. Ft.
Second	706 Sq. Ft.
Total	2162 Sq. Ft.

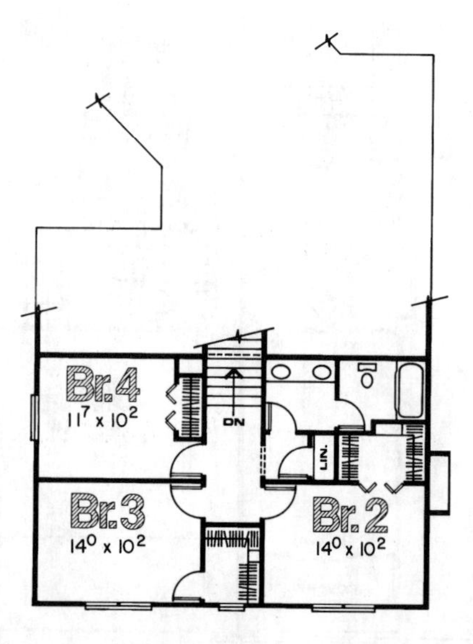

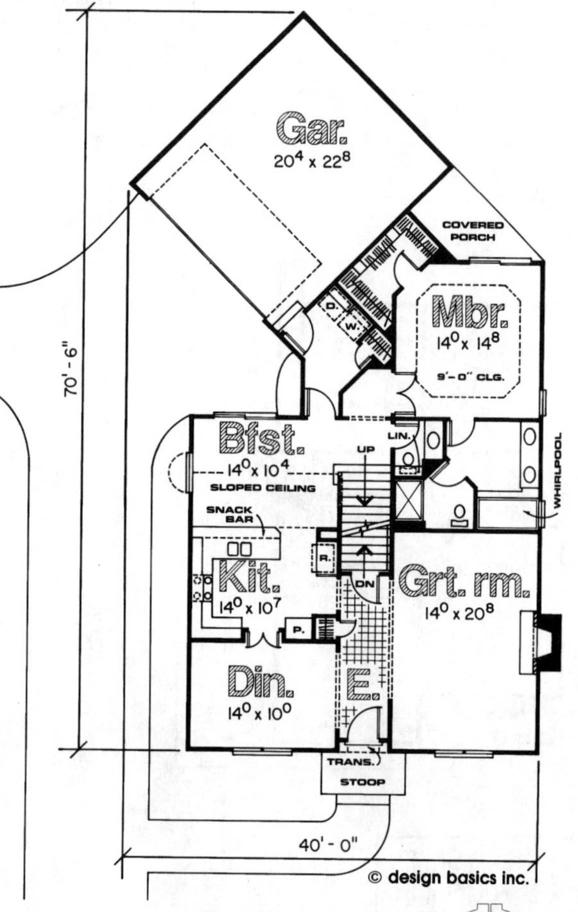

9F-2578 Kaiser price code: 16

- ▶ High quality, erasable, reproducible vellums
- ▶ Shipped via 2nd day air within the continental U.S.

- suited for narrow lots, this home demonstrates design efficiency
- paladian arch supported by stylish columns shelters entry stoop
- off entry, wide-cased opening leads to bright formal dining room
- volume entry is accented by glass blocks that spotlight decorator plant shelf above guest coat closet
- great room with its 10'-8" ceiling, full wall of windows and brick fireplace create inviting atmosphere
- dinette achieves light, open sensation with its 10-foot ceiling and large windows
- master bedroom, with its 9-foot boxed ceiling and expansive window area, affords maximum privacy

Rear Elevation

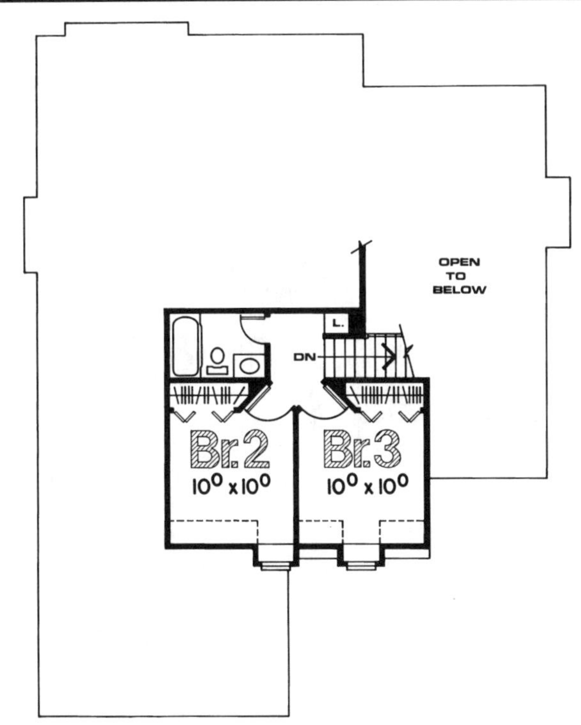

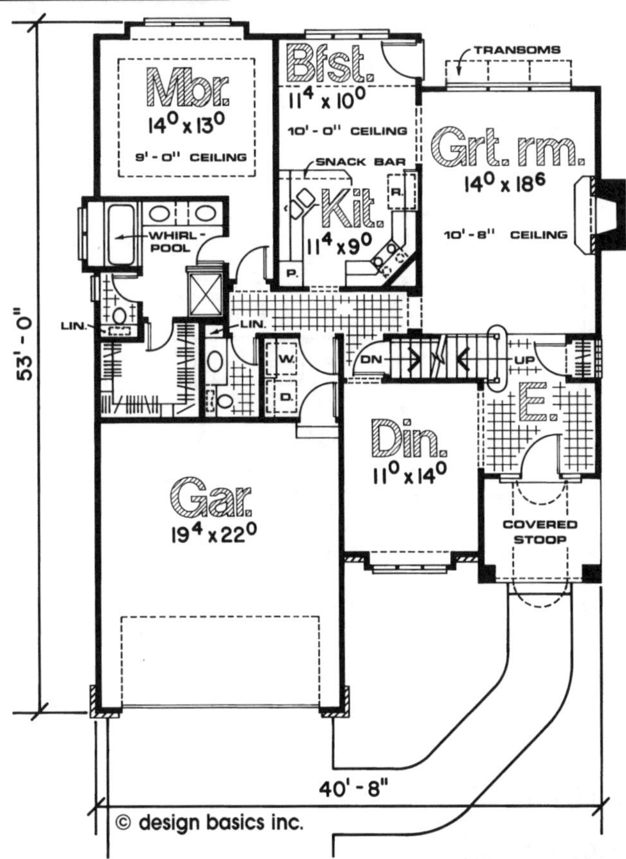

Main	1327 Sq. Ft.
Second	348 Sq. Ft.
Total	1675 Sq. Ft.

design basics inc.®
HOME PLAN DESIGN SERVICE

9F-2569 Ohern price code: 18

- High quality, erasable, reproducible vellums
- Shipped via 2nd day air within the continental U.S.

- eye-catching design is highlighted with brick accents and a large covered stoop distinguished by handsome wood columns
- spacious entry offers view of the great room with its grand 10'-8" ceiling and dramatic use of windows
- 10-foot-high ceilings give a distinctive personality to the thoughtfully planned kitchen and spacious dinette
- laundry area serves as mud entry from garage
- secluded from the traffic flow, the master suite offers privacy
- luxurious master bath features dual lavs, whirlpool, compartmented stool and walk-in closet

Rear Elevation

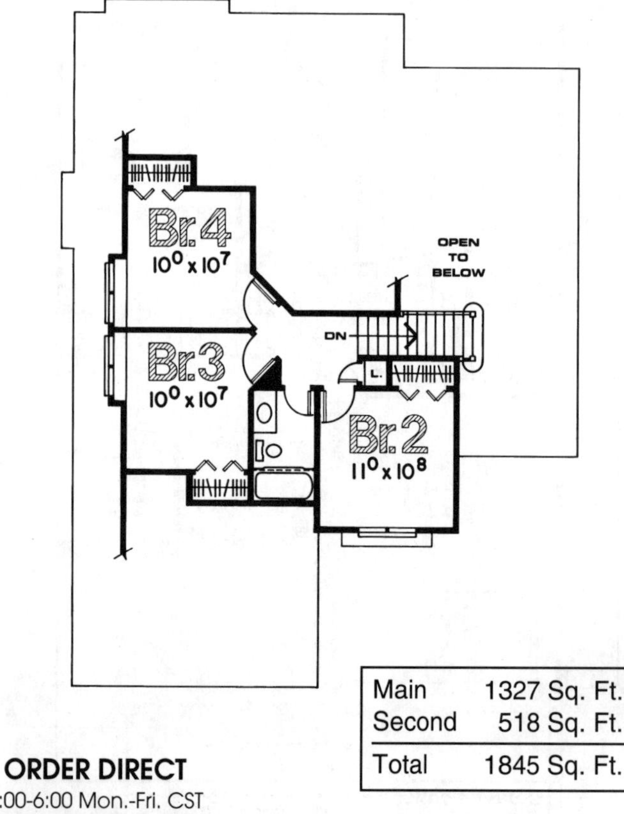

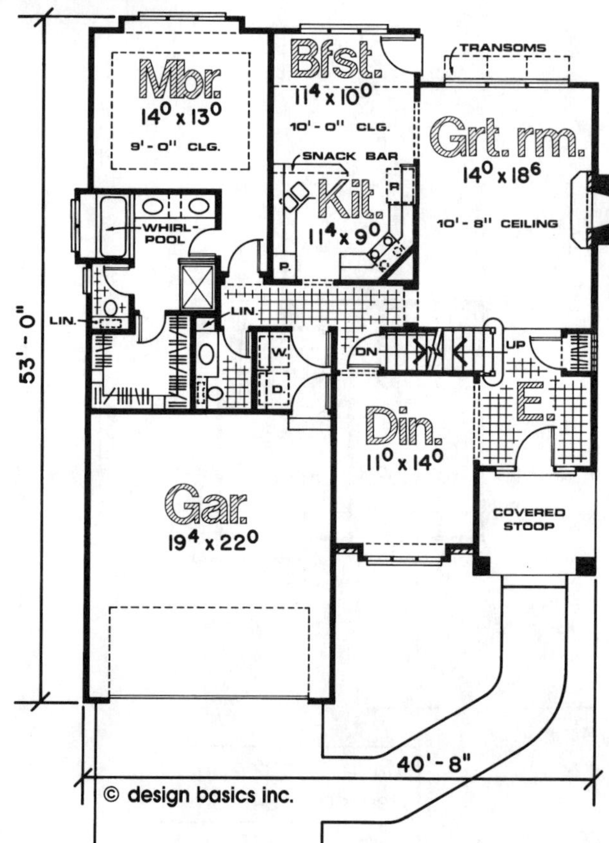

Main	1327 Sq. Ft.
Second	518 Sq. Ft.
Total	1845 Sq. Ft.

9F-2330 Pomeroy price code: 17

Gold Seal PLUS

- ▶ High quality, erasable, reproducible vellums
- ▶ Shipped via 2nd day air within the continental U.S.

- attractive brick and wood siding and covered porch makes elevation suitable for narrower lots
- entry surveys dining room with hutch space
- bright and airy great room with volume ceiling and windows framing fireplace
- kitchen with French door entry, ample counters, planning desk and roomy pantry
- bayed window dinette features opening to great room and door for outdoor entertaining
- private bedroom #3 with ample bath
- pampering main level master suite with roomy walk-in closet, corner whirlpool and dual lavs
- bedroom #2 can become an optional den

Rear Elevation

Main	1517 Sq. Ft.
Second	234 Sq. Ft.
Total	1751 Sq. Ft.

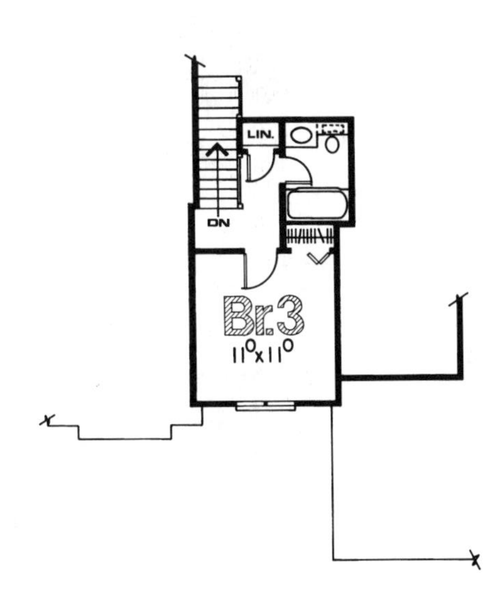

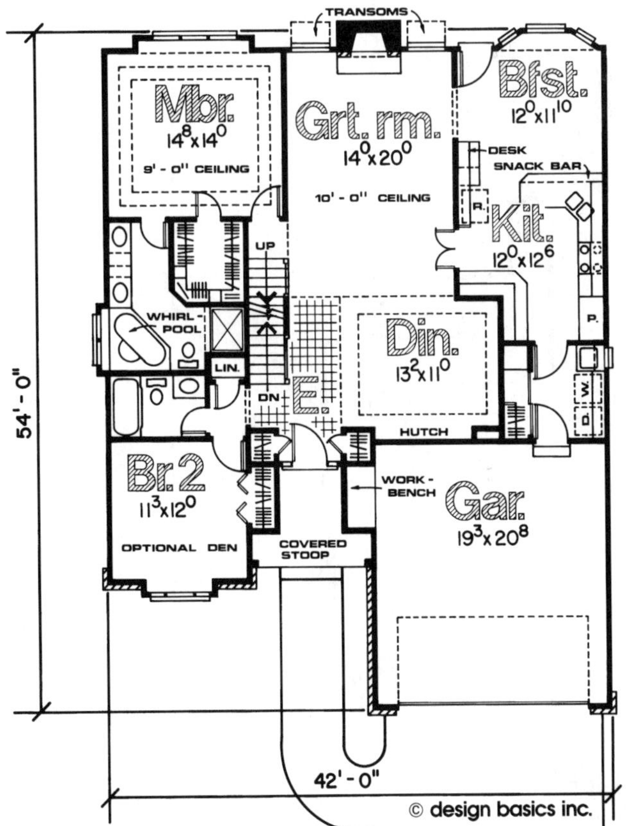

9F-2486 Fowler price code: 17

- High quality, erasable, reproducible vellums
- Shipped via 2nd day air within the continental U.S.

- entry introduces spacious formal dining room designed to accommodate hutch or buffet
- handsome kitchen delights with pantry, plant window over sink, and space-saver microwave
- staircase to second floor is conveniently located at back of house
- dinette features bayed windows, 10-foot ceiling, wet bar, and wide patio doors
- luxurious great room features fireplace and lofty 10-foot ceiling
- master retreat offers bright windows, bookcase and volume ceiling
- master bathroom provides dual vanities, separate whirlpool and shower areas, and large closet

Rear Elevation

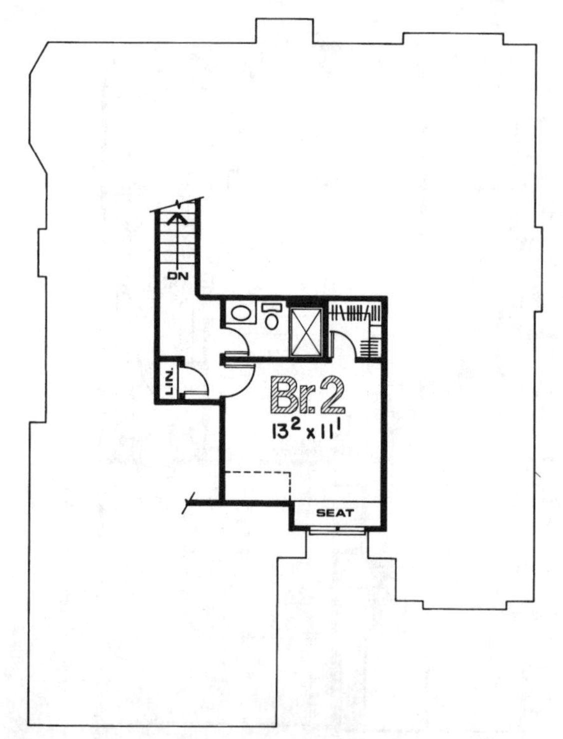

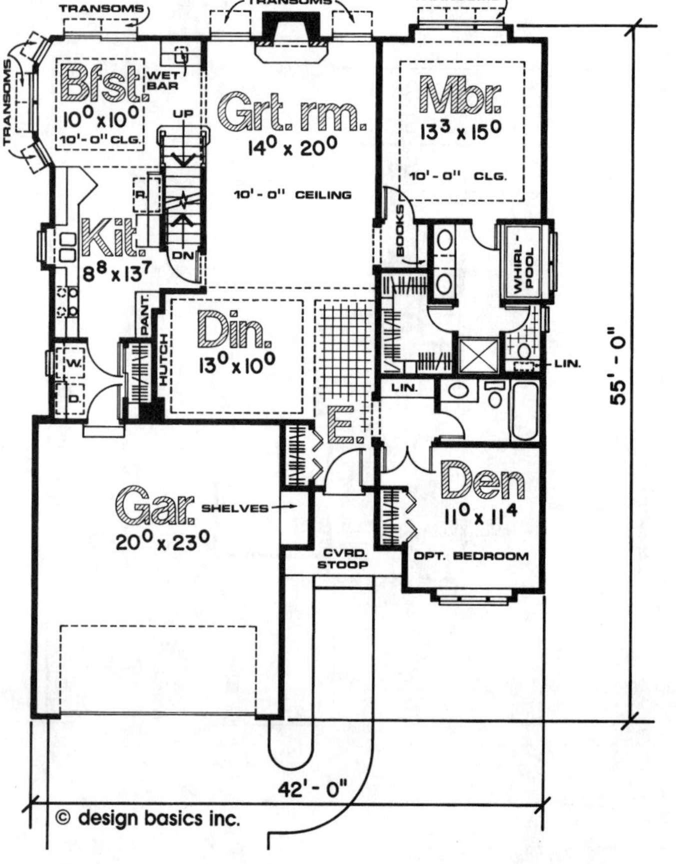

Main	1486 Sq. Ft.
Second	286 Sq. Ft.
Total	1772 Sq. Ft.

PLEXABLE

9F-3065 Foster price code: 18

- ▶ High quality, erasable, reproducible vellums
- ▶ Shipped via 2nd day air within the continental U.S.

- attractive $1^1/_2$ story well suited for narrower lots
- U-stairs enhance entry with views of volume dining room and great room
- French doors to peninsula kitchen with 2 pantries and corner sink add drama
- breakfast area highlighted by boxed 10-foot-high ceiling, direct access to back yard and great room
- cathedral ceiling, arched windows and brick fireplace create a beautiful great room
- private master suite features 10-foot-high ceiling, whirlpool bath with open shower and generous walk-in closet
- upstairs secondary bedrooms, each with built-in desk, share large bath

Rear Elevation

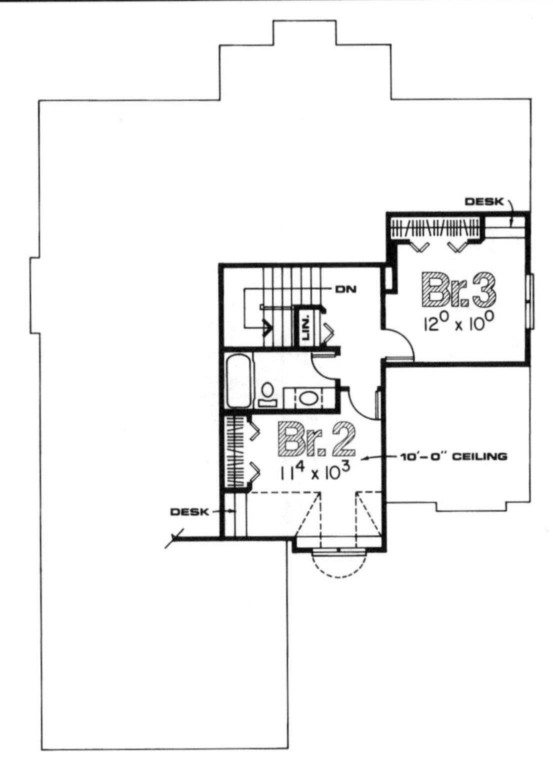

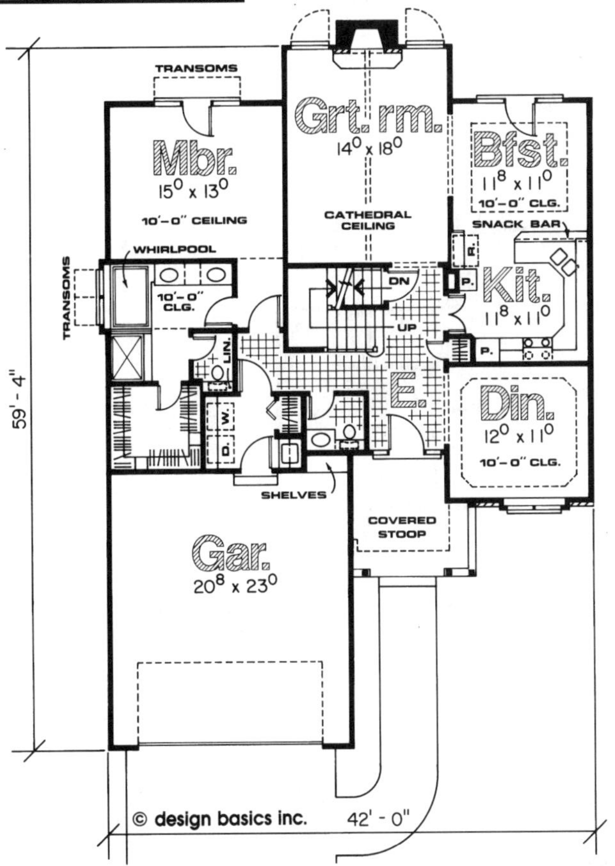

Main	1402 Sq. Ft.
Second	439 Sq. Ft.
Total	1841 Sq. Ft.

9F-2551 Girard price code: 19

- High quality, erasable, reproducible vellums
- Shipped via 2nd day air within the continental U.S.

- convenient for a private home office, French doors off entry reveal an optional den
- staircase to second level is conveniently located at back of house, off of kitchen
- lofty, open great room features raised hearth fireplace flanked by 2 large windows
- wet bar placed for easy access from great room and dinette
- extensive windows and volume ceiling make dinette bright
- seclusion is optimized in well-appointed master suite
- second level front bedroom has delightful window seat and ample walk-in closet

Rear Elevation

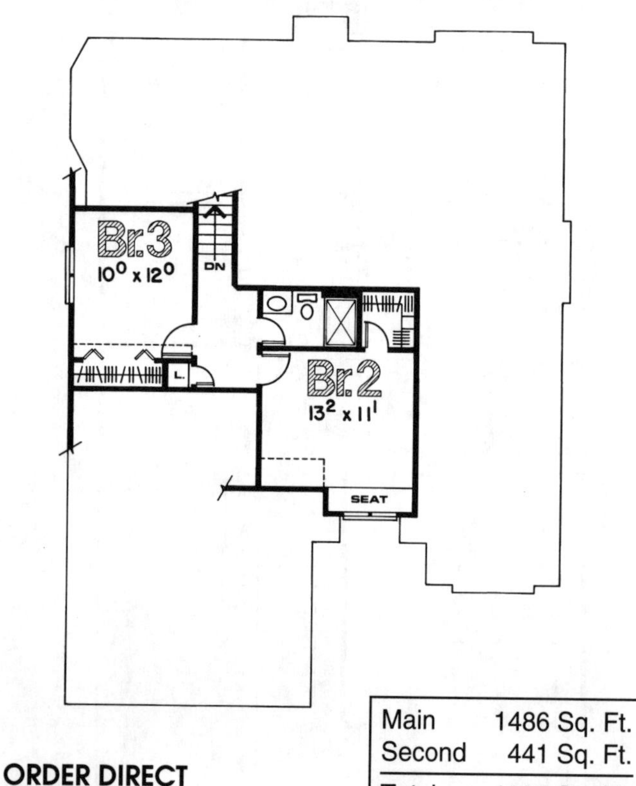

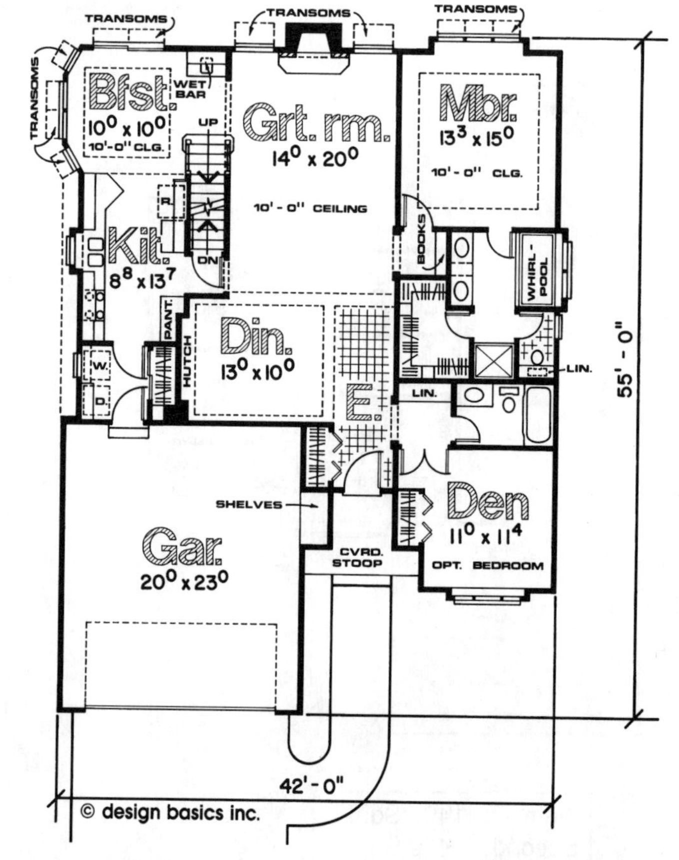

Main	1486 Sq. Ft.
Second	441 Sq. Ft.
Total	1927 Sq. Ft.

9F-2554 Lansing price code: 19

- ▶ High quality, erasable, reproducible vellums
- ▶ Shipped via 2nd day air within the continental U.S.

- rhythmic use of arches creates a notable elevation
- practical use of space is demonstrated by the placement of 2 closets in the entry
- optional den is accentuated by dramatic windows and a dramatic ceiling
- lofty open great room features a fireplace flanked by large windows
- dinette featuring a desk and snack bar also provides convenient access to the outdoors
- garage features built-in workbench
- master suite features a deluxe bath with whirlpool and dual lavs and large walk-in closet
- second level front bedroom achieves a feeling of spaciousness with a 10-foot ceiling and arch-top window

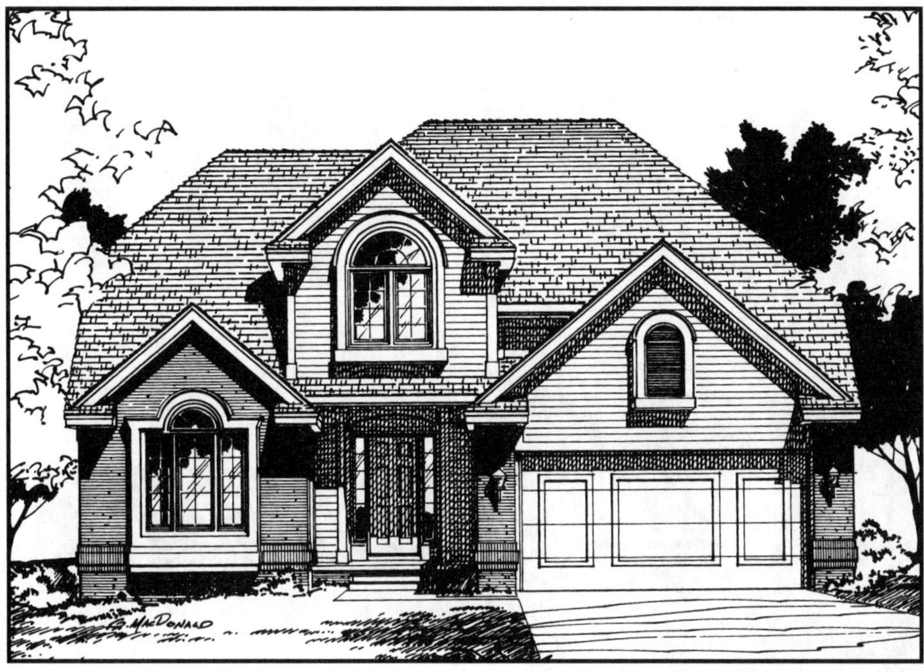

Rear Elevation

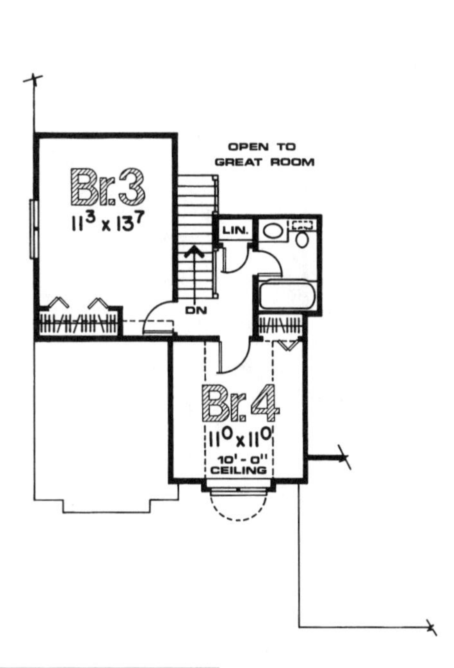

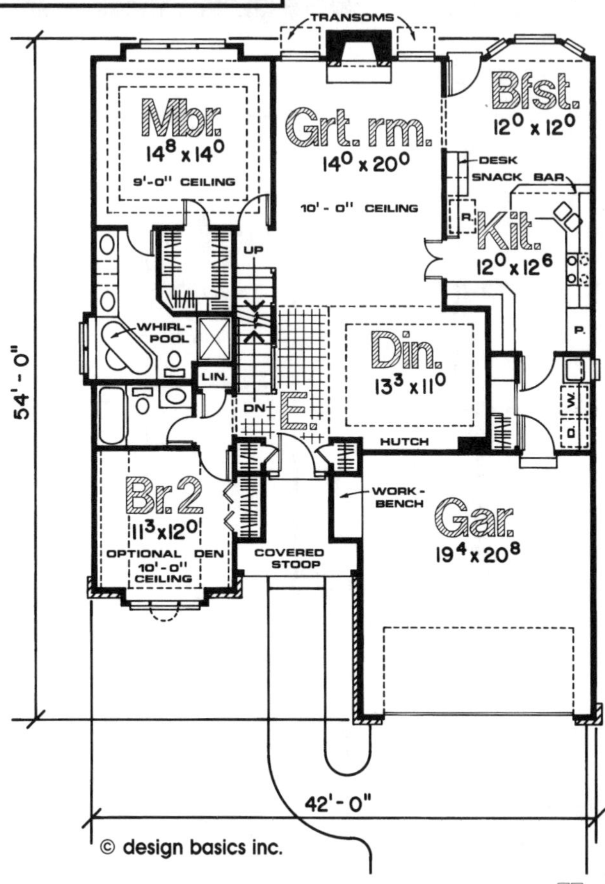

Main	1517 Sq. Ft.
Second	431 Sq. Ft.
Total	1948 Sq. Ft.

9F-3075 Grant price code: 20

- High quality, erasable, reproducible vellums
- Shipped via 2nd day air within the continental U.S.

Gold Seal™ PLUS

- gabled roof and limited brick use add affordability to this great elevation
- elegant U-stairs, French doors to kitchen and views to formal dining and great rooms create wonderful entry
- great room has cathedral ceiling, brick fireplace between large windows and direct access to breakfast area
- efficient kitchen offers corner sink, 2 pantries, lazy Susan and snack bar
- large laundry with sink and closet
- master suite has atrium door to rear yard, great whirlpool bath with open shower and generous walk-in closet
- upstairs, 3 secondary bedrooms share compartmented bath

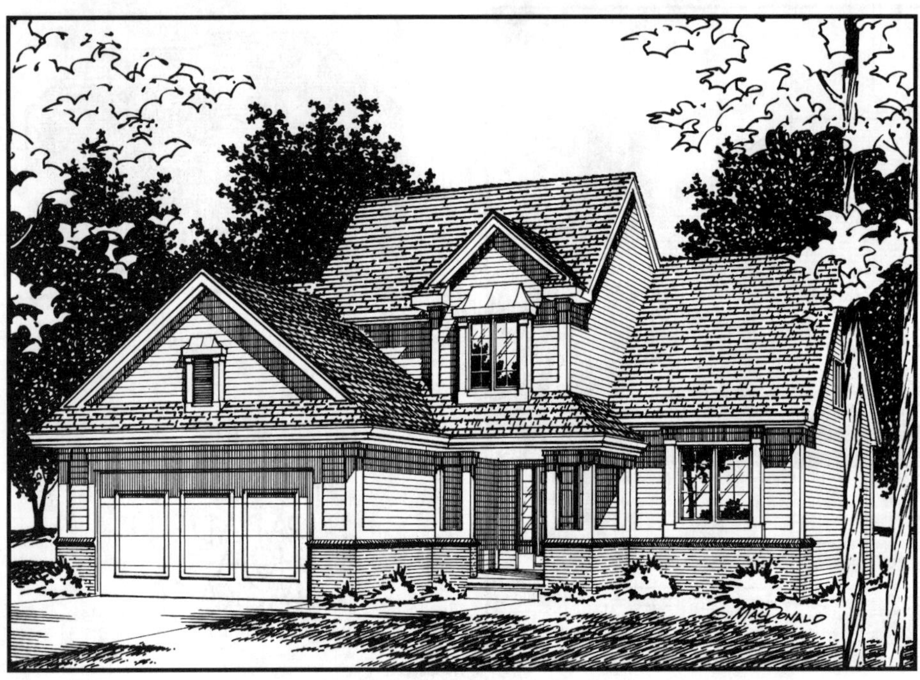

Rear Elevation

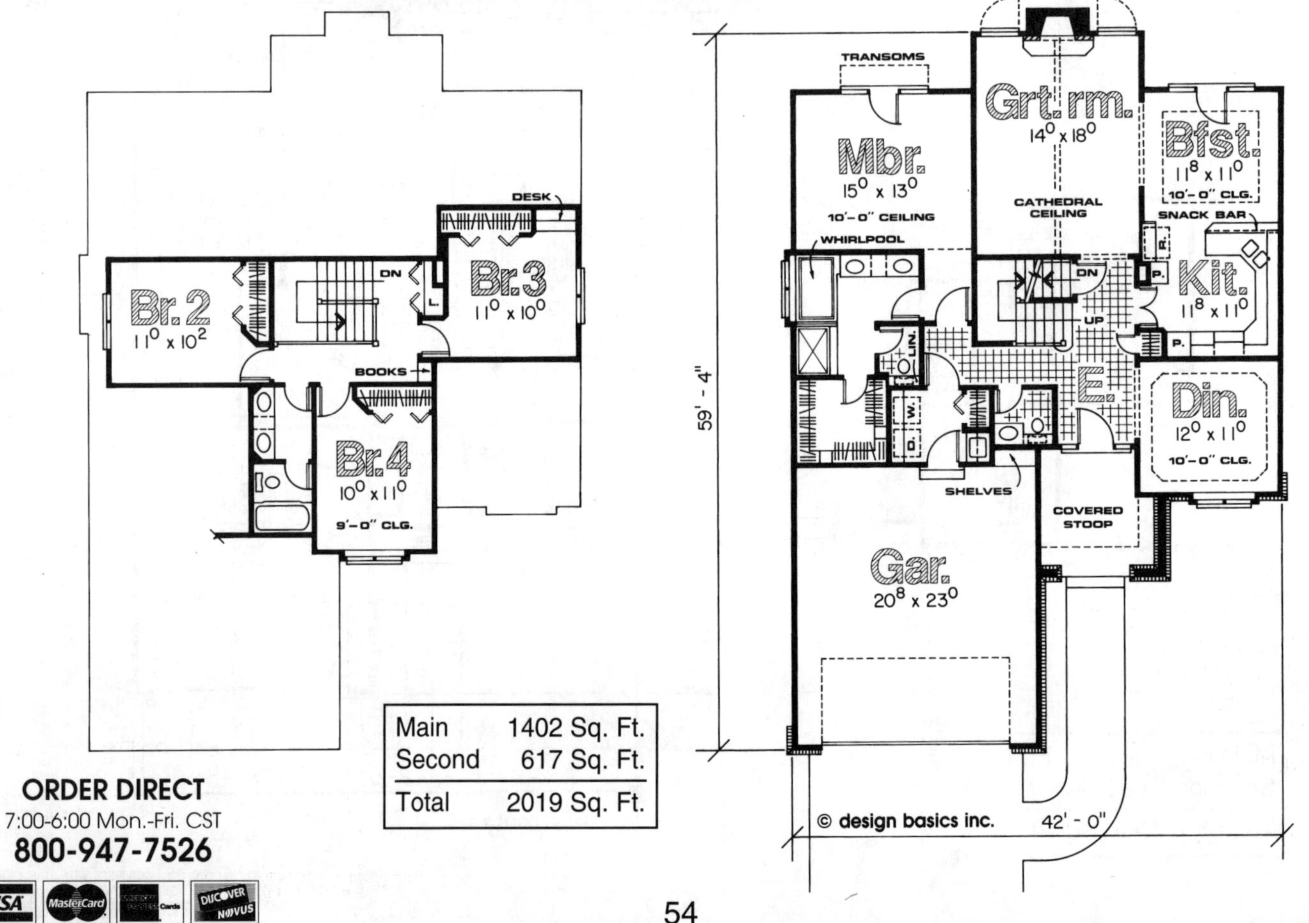

Main	1402 Sq. Ft.
Second	617 Sq. Ft.
Total	2019 Sq. Ft.

9F-2328 Birchley price code: 21

- ▸ High quality, erasable, reproducible vellums
- ▸ Shipped via 2nd day air within the continental U.S.

- alluring brick elevation
- entry includes roomy closet
- openness of dining room enhanced by elegant columns
- great room with bright windows includes raised hearth fireplace
- kitchen and bayed breakfast area support leisure or entertaining activities
- second floor features optional den/loft with built-in desk and bookshelves
- bath with dual lavs serves secondary bedrooms
- elegant main floor master bedroom enjoys privacy, special window and tiered ceiling
- pampering bath/dressing area features whirlpool, his and her vanities and large walk-in closet

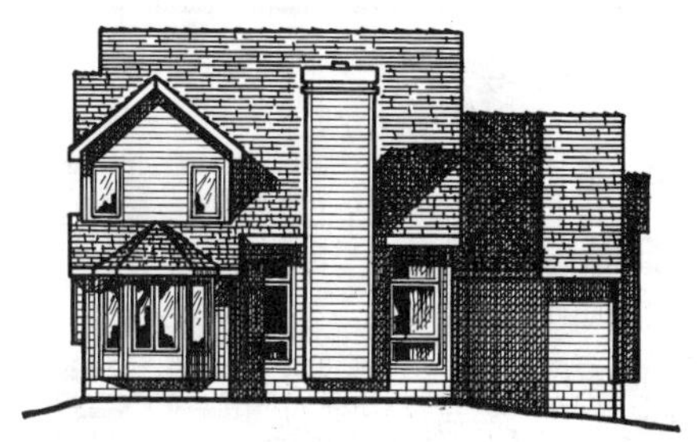

Rear Elevation

Main	1509 Sq. Ft.
Second	661 Sq. Ft.
Total	2170 Sq. Ft.

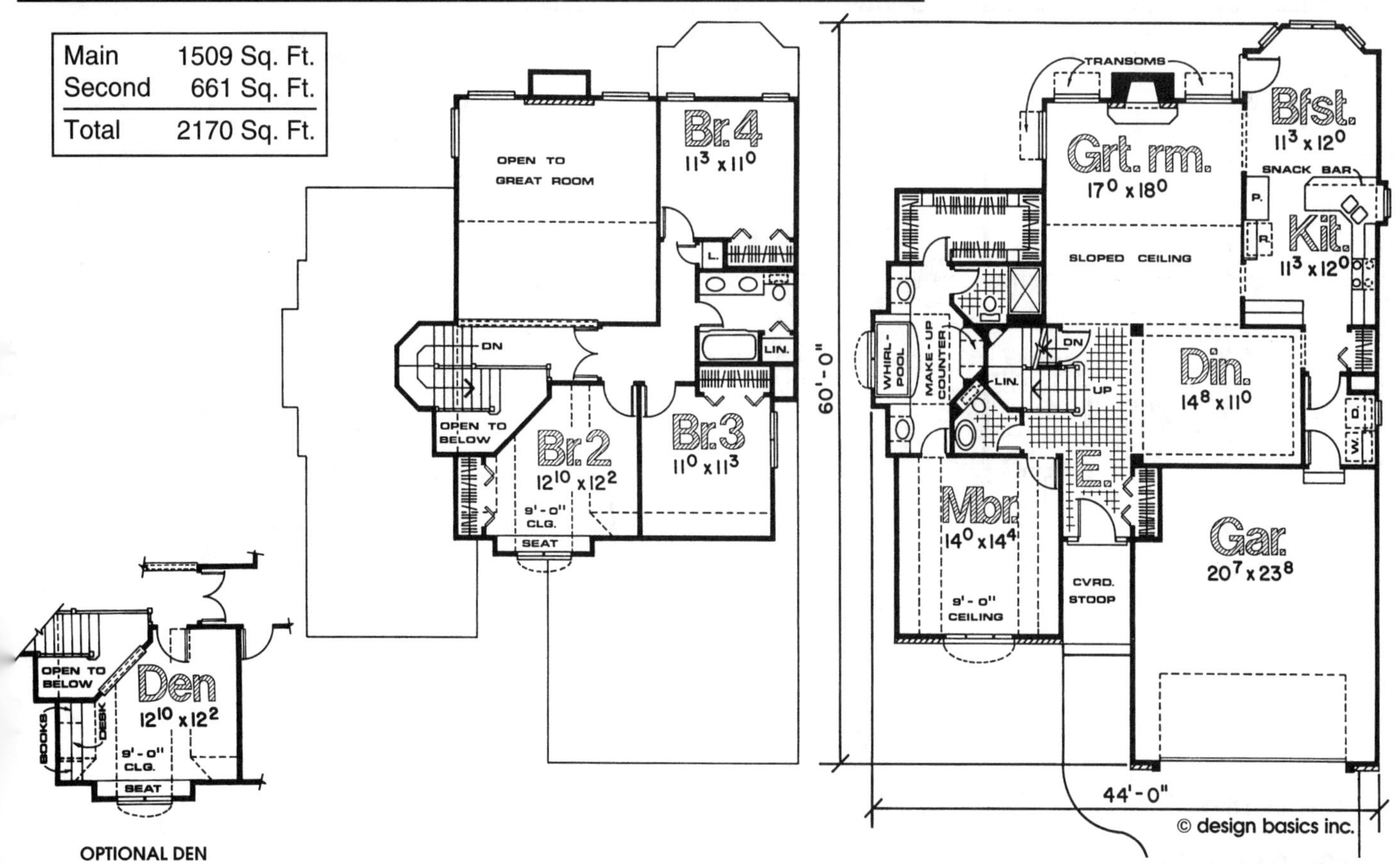

OPTIONAL DEN

9F-3121 Bellamy price code: 16

- ▶ High quality, erasable, reproducible vellums
- ▶ Shipped via 2nd day air within the continental U.S.

- welcoming elevation achieved with subtle window treatment, front porch and repreating gables
- formal dining room off entry has parlor option
- French doors at base of stairs open to kitchen and breakfast area
- sun-filled great room, with raised hearth fireplace, features 13-foot ceiling
- secluded master suite has volume ceiling, well-designed whirlpool bath and walk-in closet
- upstairs secondary bedrooms accessed off hallway with built-in bookcase

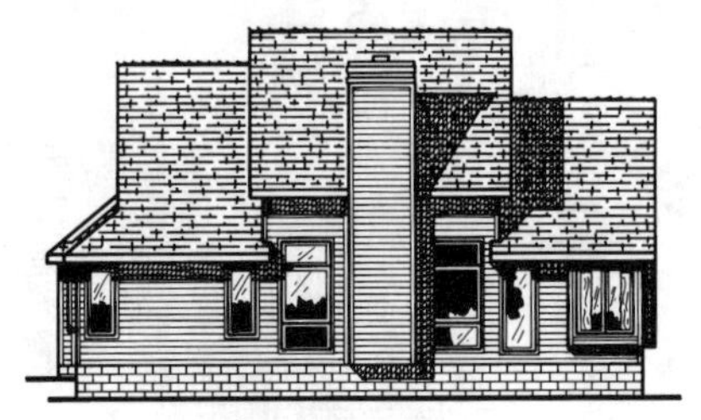

Rear Elevation

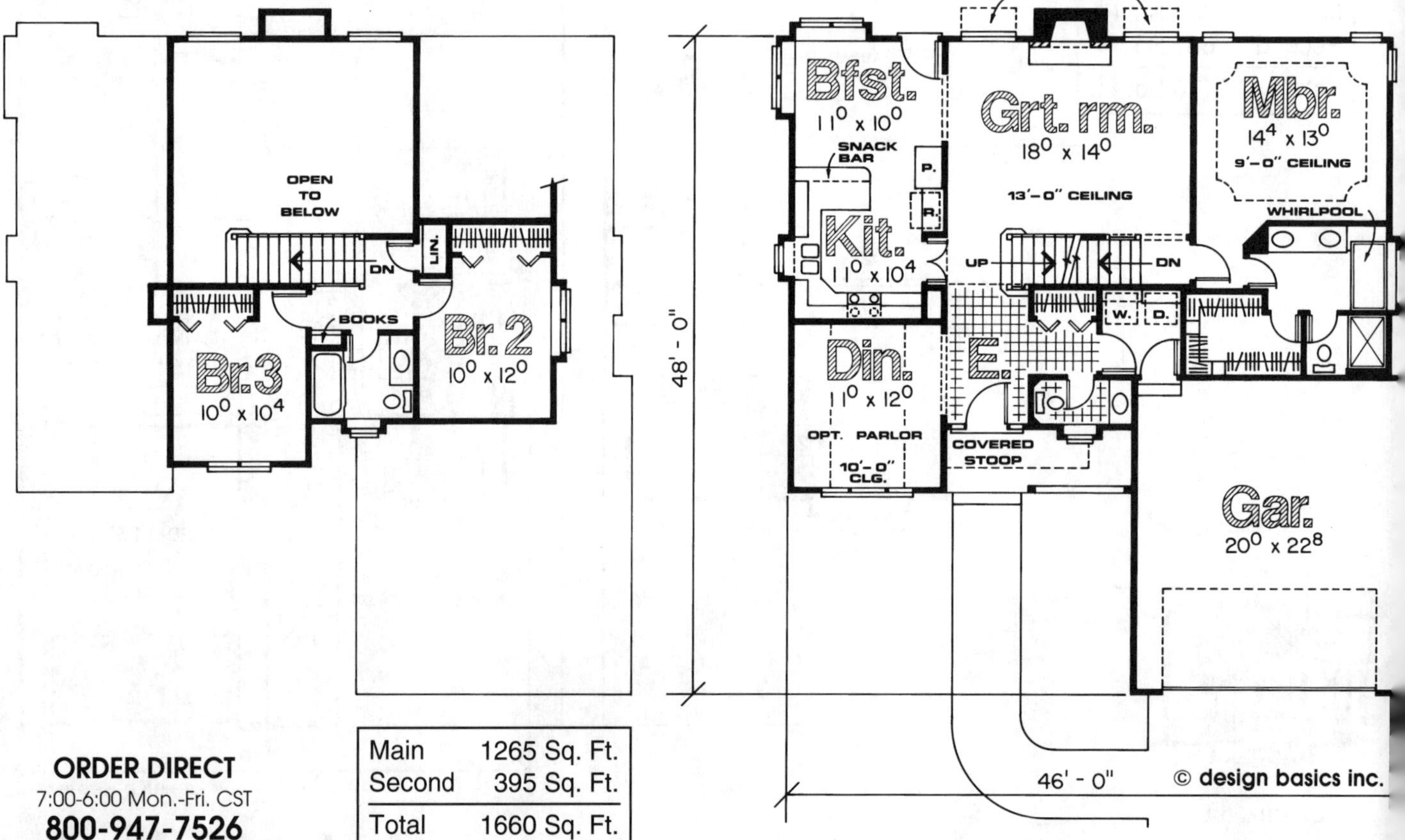

Main	1265 Sq. Ft.
Second	395 Sq. Ft.
Total	1660 Sq. Ft.

9F-1417 Sanborn price code: 21

- High quality, erasable, reproducible vellums
- Shipped via 2nd day air within the continental U.S.

- diagonal views through house from entry
- 10-foot ceilings at entry and in living and dining areas
- volume living room with sunny bayed window and handsome fireplace
- formal dining room with hutch space
- service entry from garage through laundry/mud room with coat closet
- French doors into deluxe master bedroom
- skylit master bath/dressing area with whirlpool and large walk-in closet
- upstairs corridor hall connects secondary bedrooms
- large linen closet in compartmented bath with double lavs

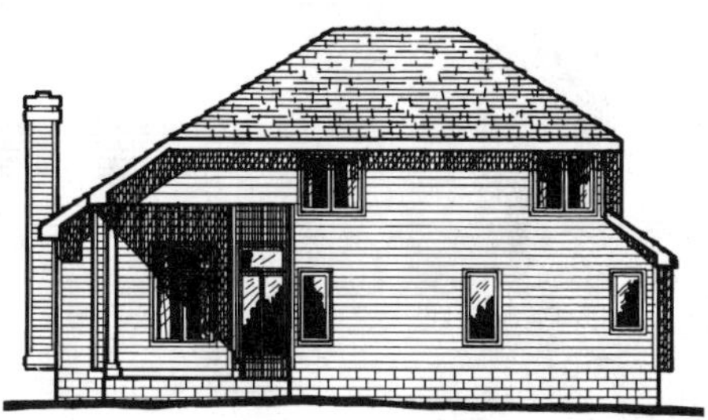

Rear Elevation

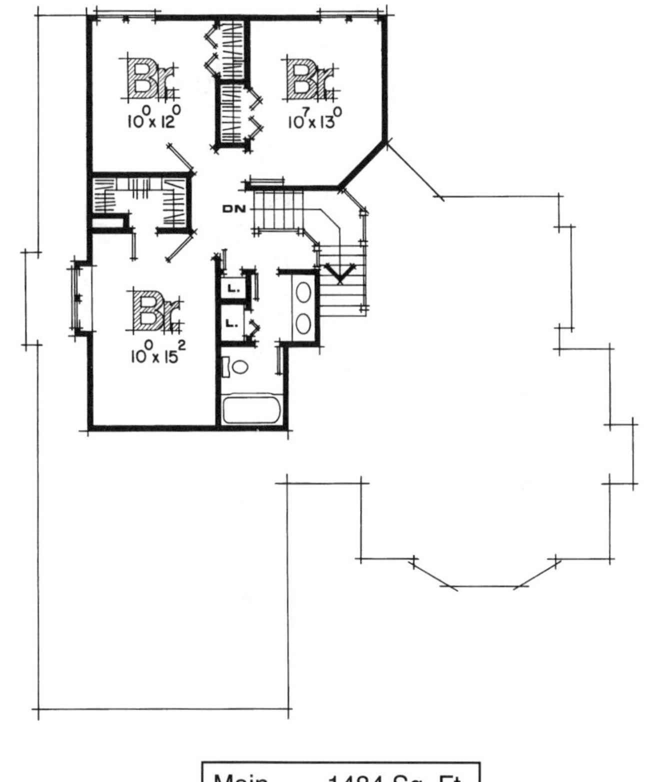

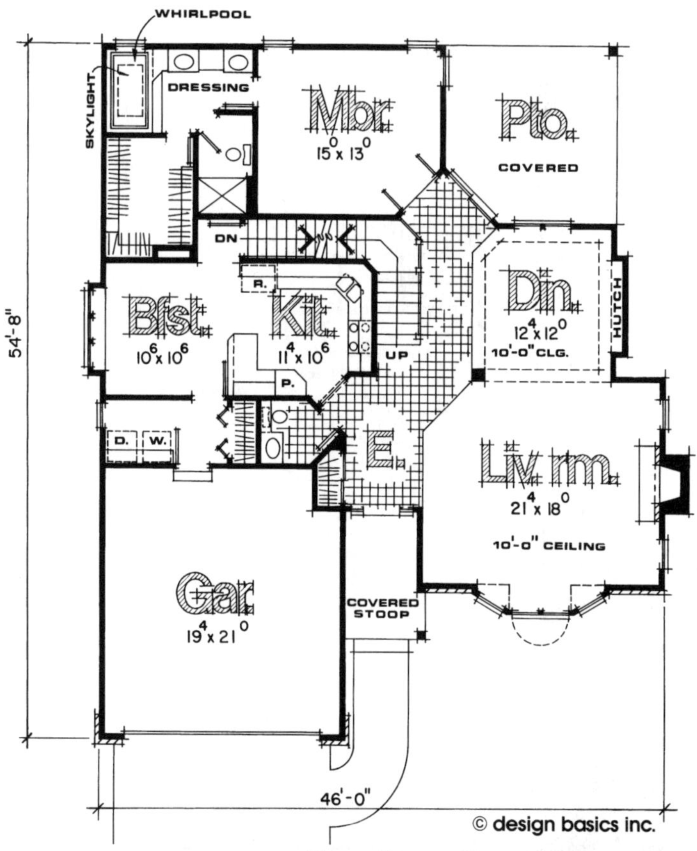

Main	1484 Sq. Ft.
Second	658 Sq. Ft.
Total	2142 Sq. Ft.

9F-2927 Morgan price code: 24

- High quality, erasable, reproducible vellums
- Shipped via 2nd day air within the continental U.S.

- powerful entry and brick accents enhance beautiful elevation
- volume living room and U-shaped stairs create elegant views from entry
- French doors, brick fireplace and cathedral ceiling in gathering room
- well-organized kitchen, open to breakfast and gathering room, offers angled sink, large pantry and wrap-around snack bar
- large laundry is easily accessible from garage or convenient side-yard door
- master suite features whirlpool tub, dual lavs, open shower and extensive walk-in closet
- secondary bedrooms share large compartmented bath with dual lavs
- special unfinished bonus room above garage has private access off stair landing

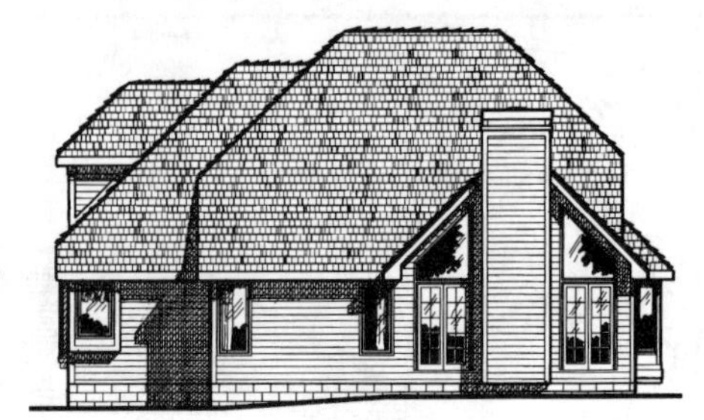

Rear Elevation

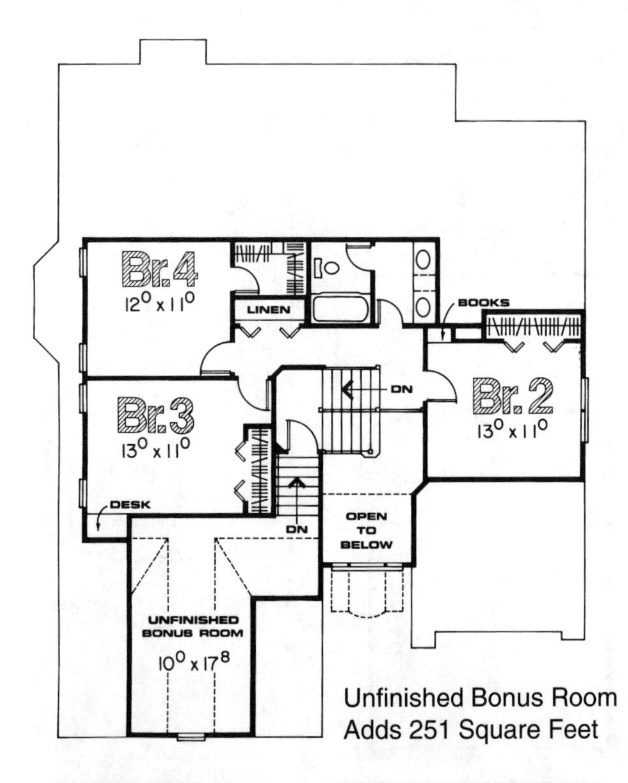

Unfinished Bonus Room
Adds 251 Square Feet

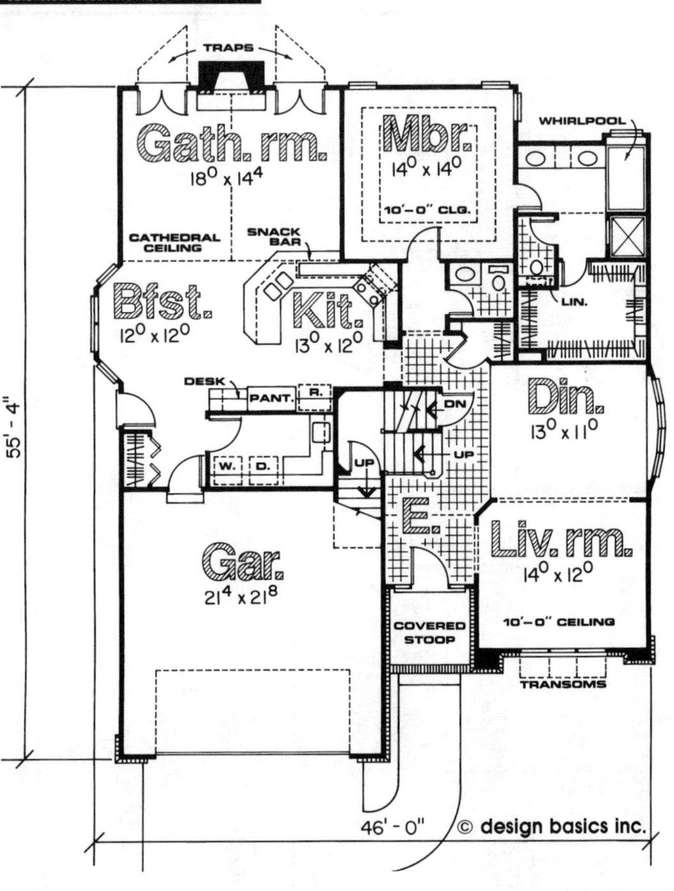

Main	1688 Sq. Ft.
Second	715 Sq. Ft.
Total	2403 Sq. Ft.

9F-2951 Newlin price code: 21

- High quality, erasable, reproducible vellums
- Shipped via 2nd day air within the continental U.S.

- brick wing walls anchor magnificent elevation
- formal dining room is enriched by 2-story entry
- great room enhanced by 10-foot-high ceiling and brick fireplace
- exciting kitchen provides corner sink, large pantry and snack bar
- spacious dinette with large windows has access to back yard
- master suite features whirlpool bath, open shower and ceiling detail
- second level bridge overlooks entry and staircase
- secondary bedrooms share large bath and deep linen closet

Rear Elevation

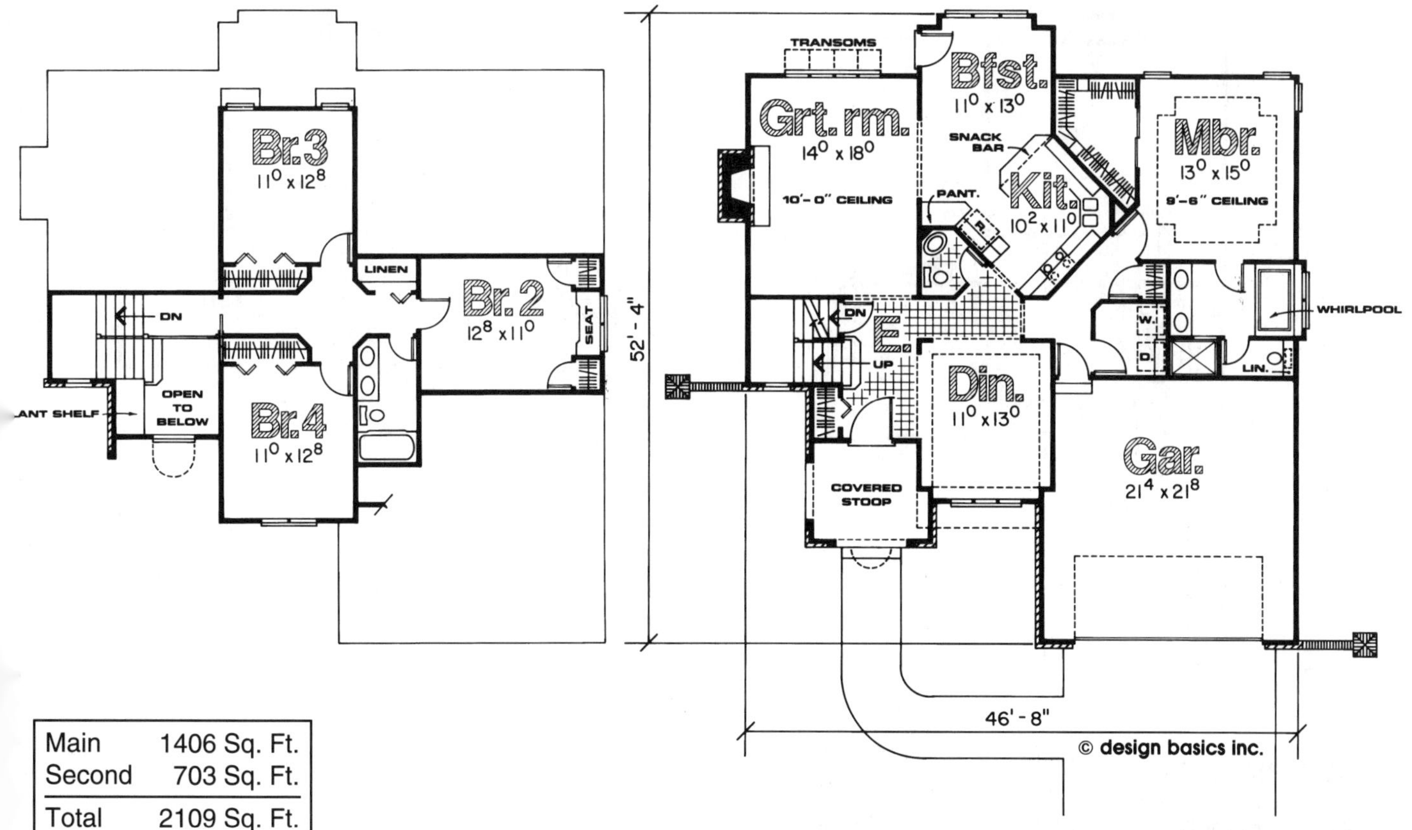

Main	1406 Sq. Ft.
Second	703 Sq. Ft.
Total	2109 Sq. Ft.

design basics inc.®
HOME PLAN DESIGN SERVICE

9F-3090 Jarret price code: 17

Gold Seal HOME PLANS™

- High quality, erasable, reproducible vellums
- Shipped via 2nd day air within the continental U.S.

- versatile dining room off entry has 10-foot volume ceiling and parlor option
- French doors at base of stairs create an elegant passage to peninsula kitchen with snack bar
- corner boxed windows create sunny and inviting breakfast area
- volume ceiling allows staircase to overlook great room
- secluded master suite features dual lavs, whirlpool bath and generous walk-in closet
- upstairs, 3 secondary bedrooms share hall bath with seat at tub

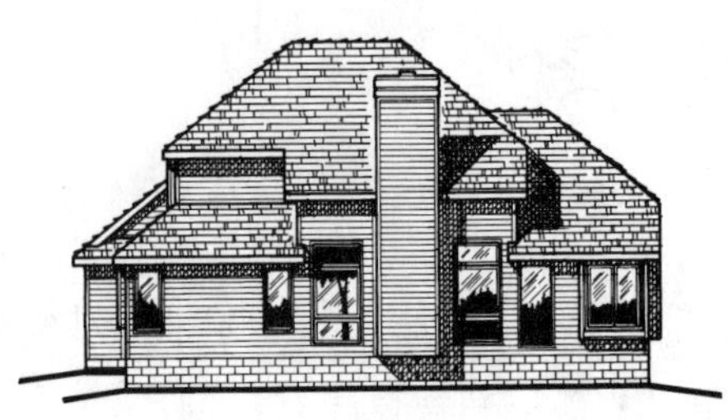

Rear Elevation

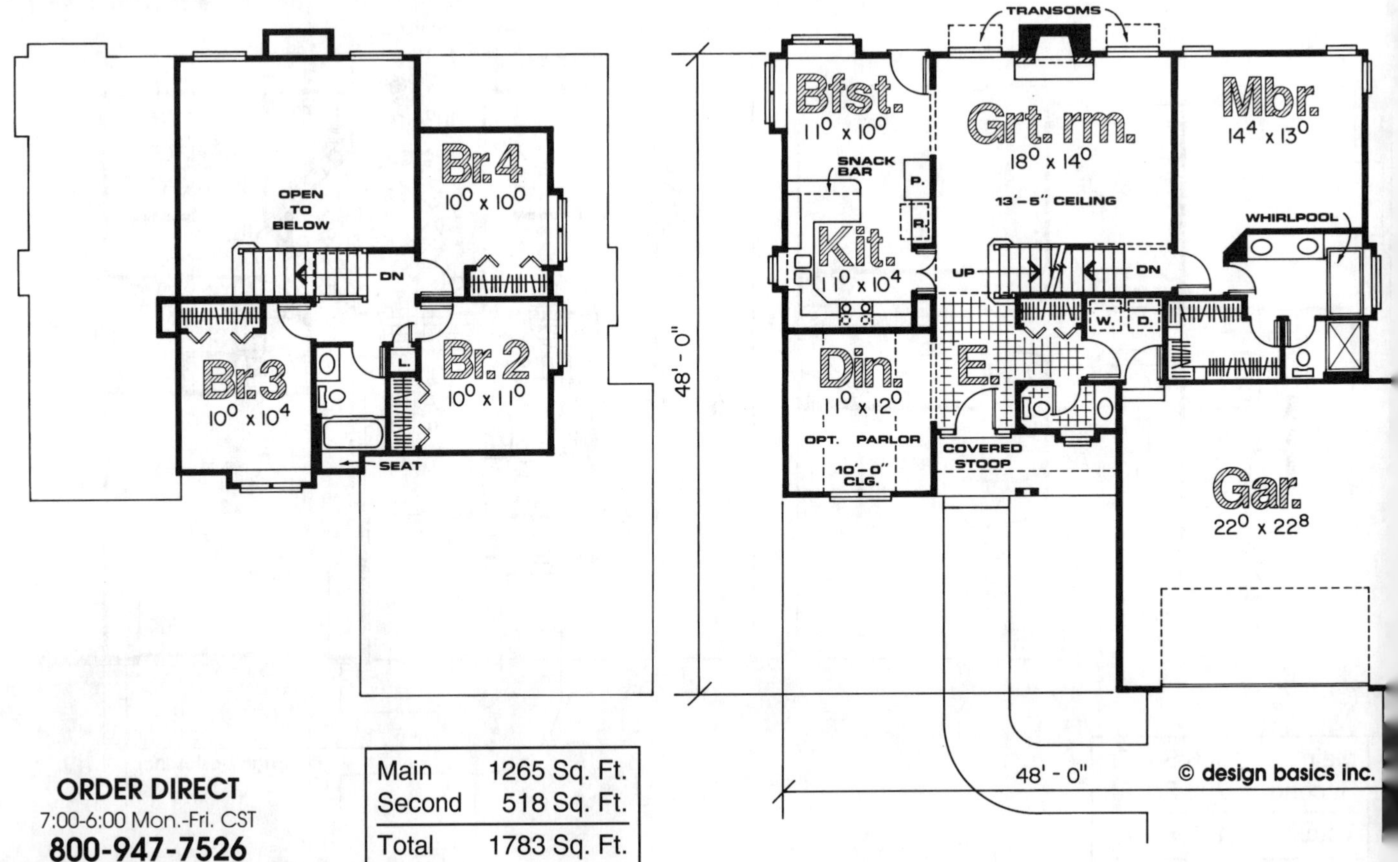

ORDER DIRECT

7:00-6:00 Mon.-Fri. CST

800-947-7526

Main	1265 Sq. Ft.
Second	518 Sq. Ft.
Total	1783 Sq. Ft.

9F-3382 Higgins price code: 19

- High quality, erasable, reproducible vellums
- Shipped via 2nd day air within the continental U.S.

- notable exterior features captivate attention
- bayed windows and vaulted ceiling displayed in dining room
- snack bar and boxed window above sink accommodate kitchen
- breakfast area enhanced by two corner boxed windows
- great room unfolds tall windows framing fireplace
- secluded master suite reveals roomy walk-in closet and sunny whirlpool
- bedroom #3 has 10'-0" ceiling and bayed window with arched transom
- all three secondary bedrooms are served by full bath

Rear Elevation

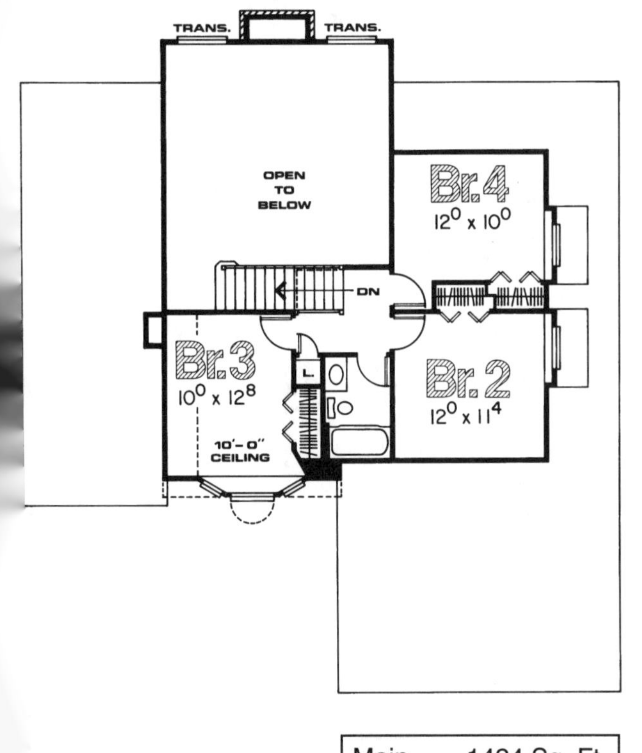

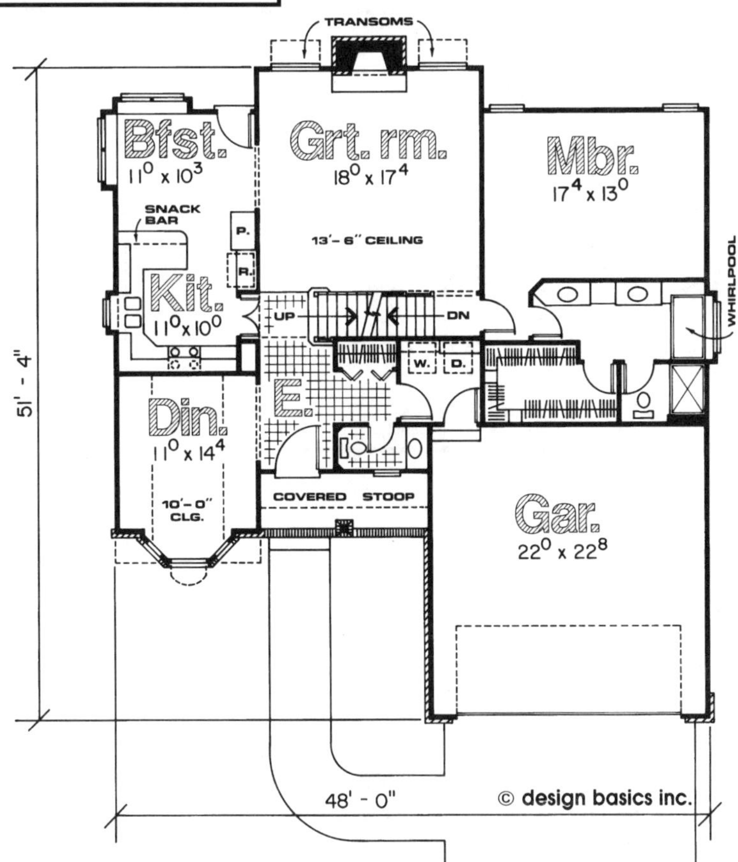

Main	1424 Sq. Ft.
Second	567 Sq. Ft.
Total	1991 Sq. Ft.

PLEXABLE™

9F-3464 Jenkins price code: 15

Gold Seal PLUS™

- High quality, erasable, reproducible vellums
- Shipped via 2nd day air within the continental U.S.

- well designed, economical home has appeal of a summer cottage
- oak entry and parlor make stunning impression upon entry
- parlor is easily adaptable as dining room
- two lazy Susans and wrapping counters in kitchen
- bayed breakfast area offers access to deck
- family room boasts cathedral ceiling and raised hearth fireplace
- master suite features twin vanities and large walk-in closet
- second floor reveals two bedrooms that share full bath
- mud entry off garage allows a quick path to kitchen for grocery unloading

Rear Elevation

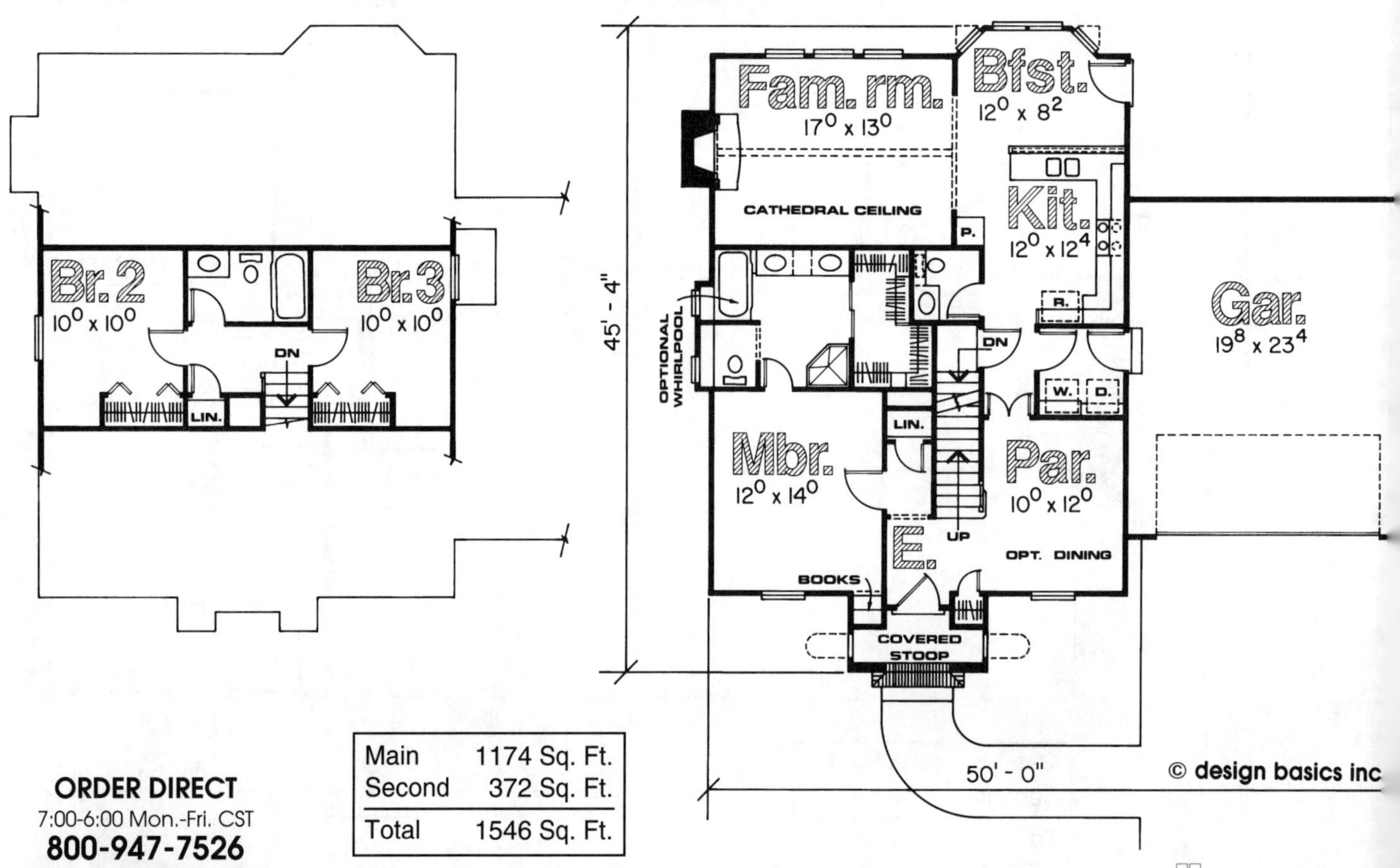

Main	1174 Sq. Ft.
Second	372 Sq. Ft.
Total	1546 Sq. Ft.

9F-3123 Bethany price code: 15

- High quality, erasable, reproducible vellums
- Shipped via 2nd day air within the continental U.S.

- charming country style elevation has wrapping porch and oval accents
- spacious great room, directly accessible from 2-story entry and breakfast area with bowed window
- angled wall adds drama to peninsula kitchen and creates private entry to master suite
- master suite contains boxed 9-foot ceiling, compartmented whirlpool bath and spacious walk-in closet
- second level balcony overlooks U-stairs and entry
- twin linen closets just outside upstairs bedrooms serve compartmented bath with natural light

Rear Elevation

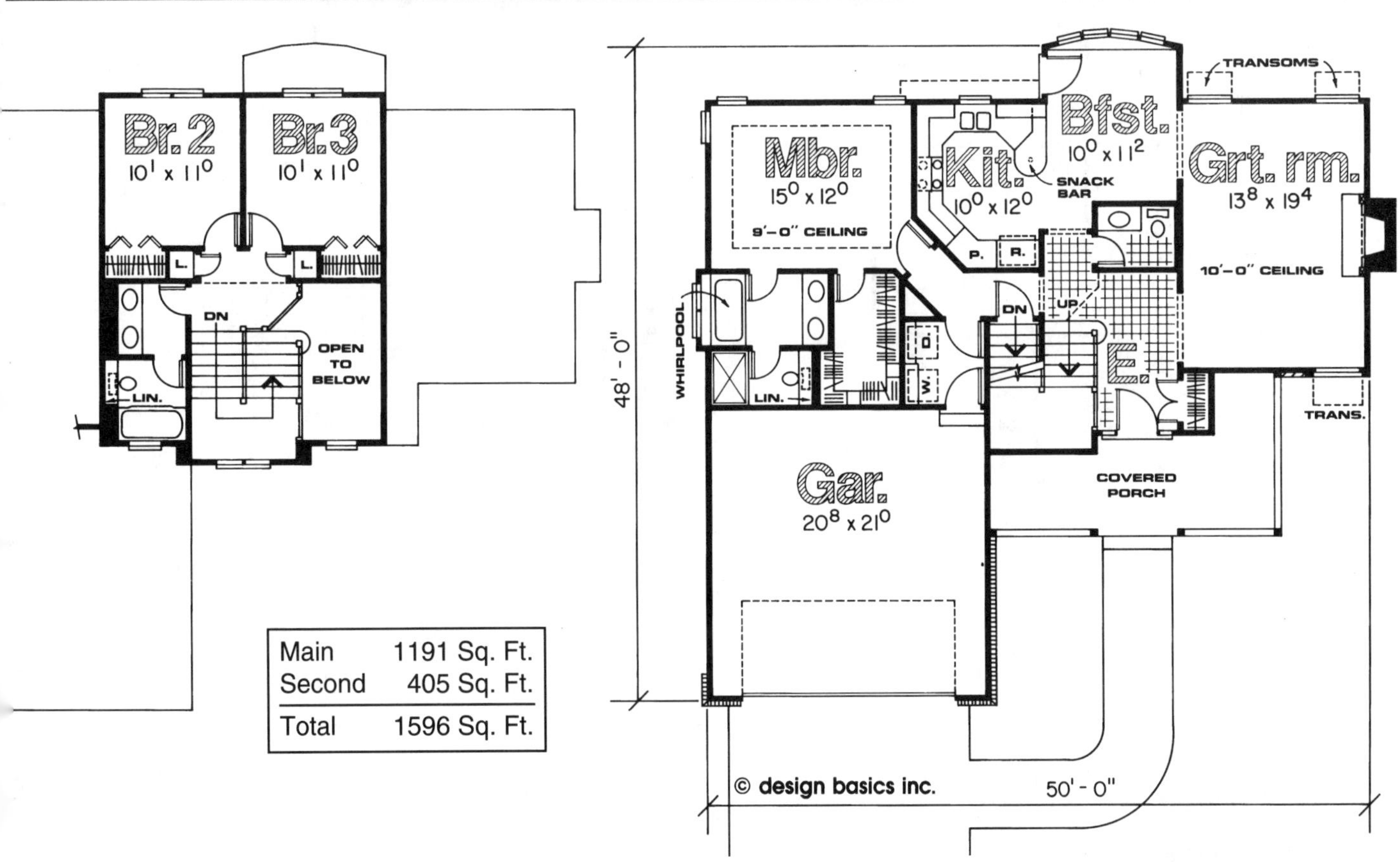

Main	1191 Sq. Ft.
Second	405 Sq. Ft.
Total	1596 Sq. Ft.

design basics inc.®
HOME PLAN DESIGN SERVICE

9F-1734 Crescent price code: 17

Gold Seal™ HOME PLANS

- ▶ High quality, erasable, reproducible vellums
- ▶ Shipped via 2nd day air within the continental U.S.

- covered front porch
- well-planned kitchen includes island cooking center, wrapping counters and windows over sink
- covered patio accesses home through breakfast area
- excellent traffic patterns thoughout
- sunny dining room opens up to volume great room with fireplace framed by picturesque windows
- large master bedroom with volume ceiling and bayed window
- deluxe master bath with his and her closets and two lavs
- interesting staircase leads to bridge overlooking great room and entry below
- secondary bedrooms share centrally located hall bath

Rear Elevation

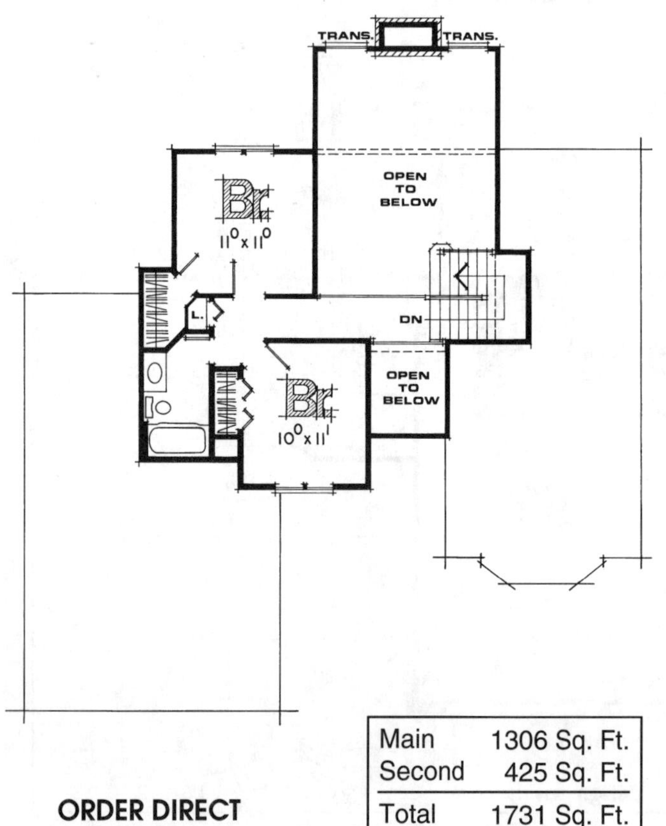

TRANSOMS
Grt.rm. 14⁸x19⁰
Pto. COVERED
Din. 11⁰x11⁰
UP
DN
10'-0" CLG.
WHIRLPOOL
Bfst. 10⁰x10⁸
R.
Kit. 11⁴x12⁸
D.
W.
E.
Mbr. 15⁴x13⁶ 9'-0" CEILING
COVERED PORCH
Gar. 20⁰x21⁰
52'-0"
50'-0"
© design basics inc.

Main	1306 Sq. Ft.
Second	425 Sq. Ft.
Total	1731 Sq. Ft.

9F-3385 Brittany price code: 17

- High quality, erasable, reproducible vellums
- Shipped via 2nd day air within the continental U.S.

- exciting curb appeal enhanced by long front porch and gingerbread accents
- transom windows and 11'-0" ceiling adorn great room
- interesting angles and unique snack bar highlight unforgettable kitchen
- bowed breakfast area links great room and kitchen
- master bedroom has 9'-0" boxed ceiling, large walk-in closet and pampering bath
- centrally located main floor powder room
- U-shaped staircase leads to second floor where balcony views entry below
- three secondary bedrooms served by full bath and two hall linen closets

Rear Elevation

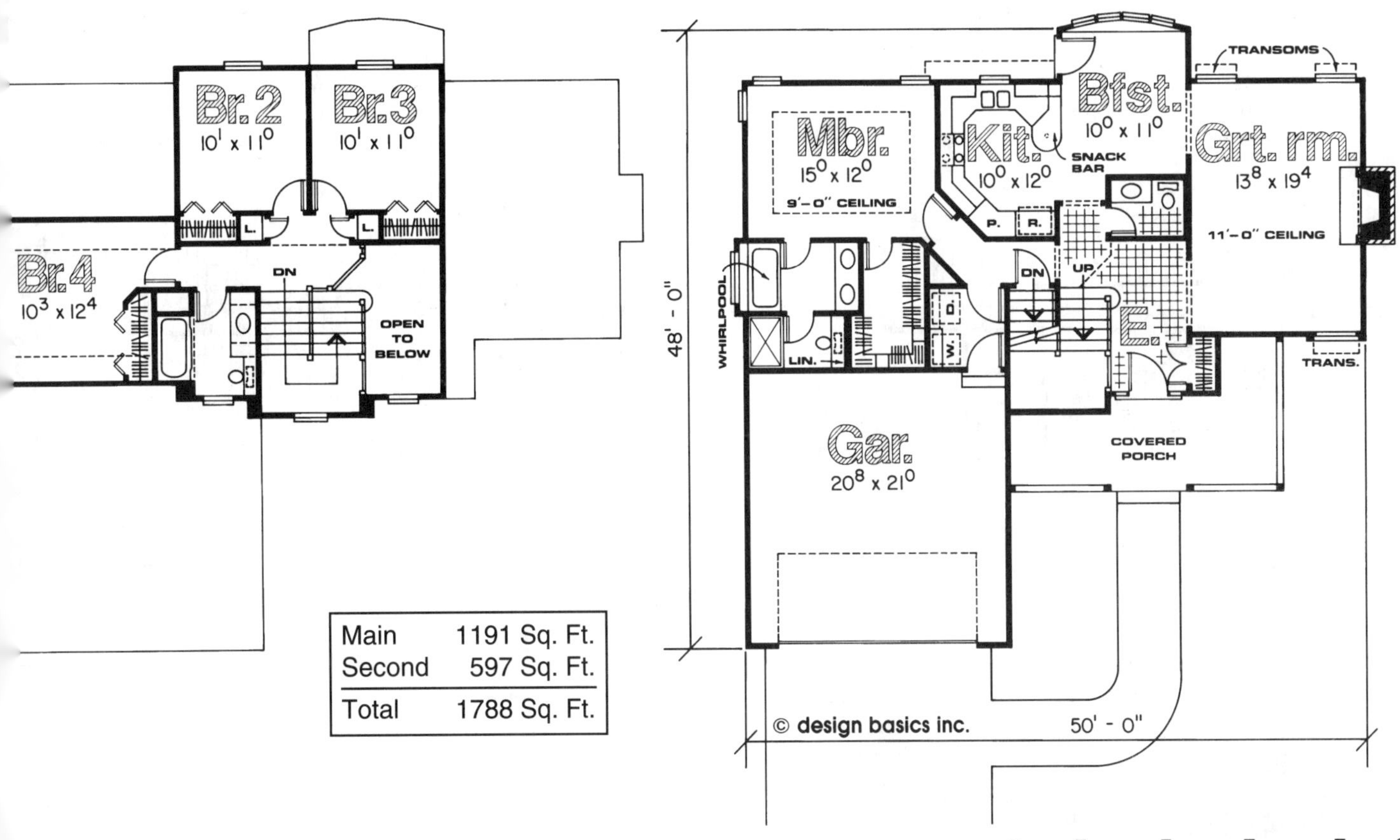

Main	1191 Sq. Ft.
Second	597 Sq. Ft.
Total	1788 Sq. Ft.

design basics inc.®
HOME PLAN DESIGN SERVICE

9F-1867 Langley price code: 19

- High quality, erasable, reproducible vellums
- Shipped via 2nd day air within the continental U.S.

Gold Seal HOME PLANS™

- sleek lines coupled with impressive detailing enhance elevation
- entry opens into volume great room with fireplace flanked by cheerful windows
- dining room off great room offers entertaining options
- kitchen and breakfast area has cooktop in island and access to covered patio
- bridge overlook on second level
- secondary bedrooms share compartmented bath with dual lavs
- master bedroom secluded on first level includes decorative ceiling and bright boxed window
- luxurious master bath has two closets, separate wet and dry areas, dual lavs and whirlpool tub

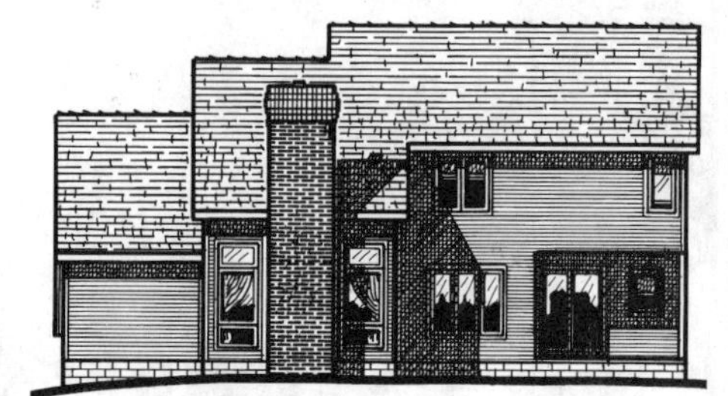

Rear Elevation

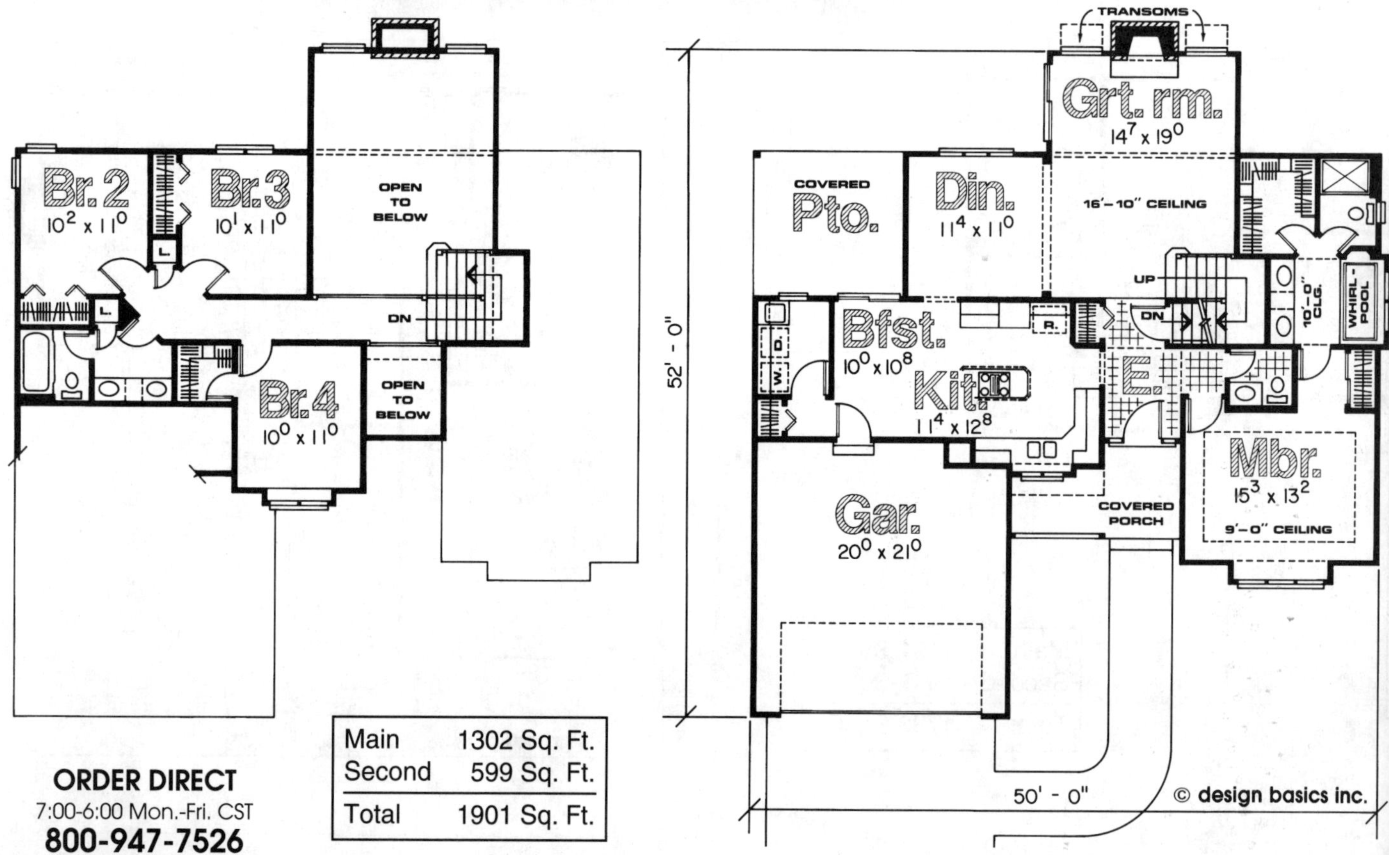

Main	1302 Sq. Ft.
Second	599 Sq. Ft.
Total	1901 Sq. Ft.

9F-1727 Spencer price code: 19

- ▸ High quality, erasable, reproducible vellums
- ▸ Shipped via 2nd day air within the continental U.S.

Gold Seal™ HOME PLANS

- volume hard-surfaced entry with coat closet
- volume ceiling in great room with fireplace flanked by windows
- dining room open to great room for expanded entertaining
- island kitchen adjoins breakfast area with access to covered patio
- laundry room with sink, closet and window to the back
- upstairs landing overlooks entry and great room below
- master bedroom with volume ceiling and arched bayed window adjoins luxury skylit dressing/bath area with whirlpool, walk-in closet and plant shelf
- secondary bedrooms share generous compartmented bath

Rear Elevation

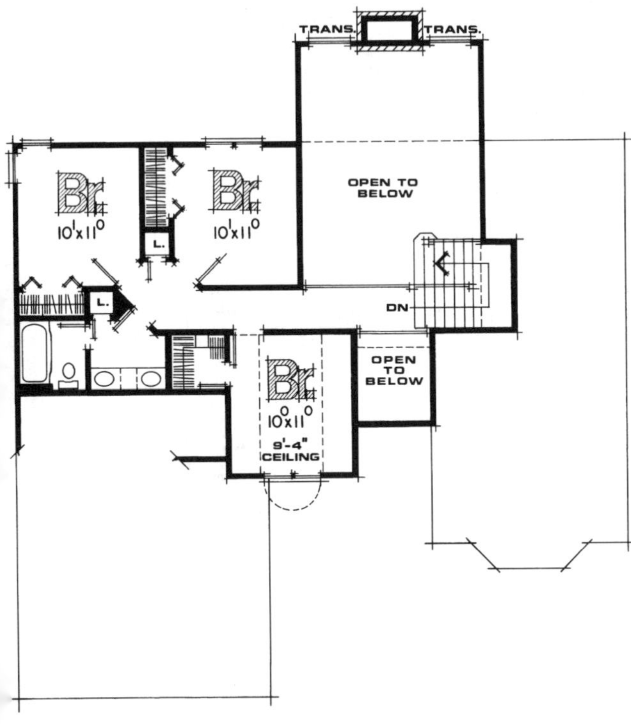

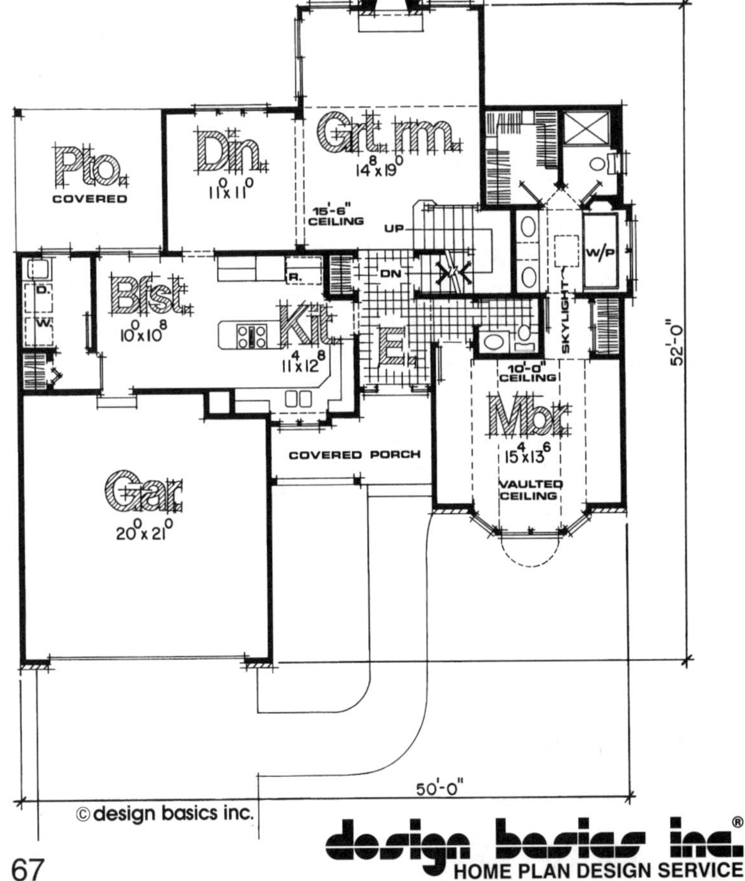

Main	1306 Sq. Ft.
Second	599 Sq. Ft.
Total	1905 Sq. Ft.

design basics inc.®
HOME PLAN DESIGN SERVICE

9F-2292 Inglewood price code: 19

- stone accents and inviting porch enrich front elevation
- entry views volume great room with captivating window-framed fireplace
- formal dining area allows entertaining ease
- gourmet island kitchen has snack bar, handy desk and walk-in pantry
- dinette has access to large covered patio ideal for leisure activities
- two secondary bedrooms share a roomy bath with its own linen closet
- handy unfinished storage on second level
- French doors open to pampering main level master suite with boxed ceiling
- master dressing area with two closets, dual lavs with knee space between and window-brightened whirlpool

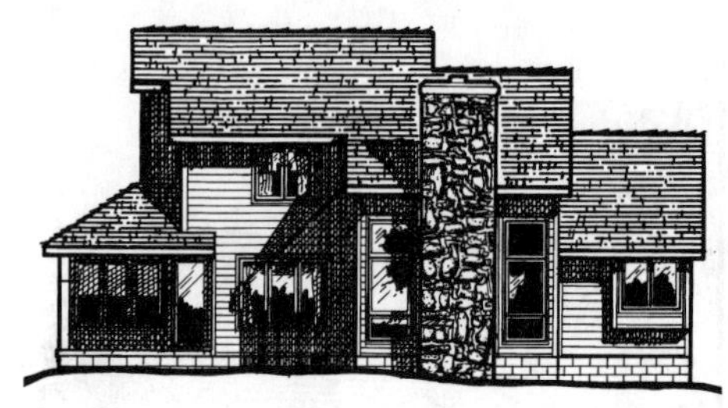

Rear Elevation

Main	1507 Sq. Ft.
Second	436 Sq. Ft.
Total	1943 Sq. Ft.

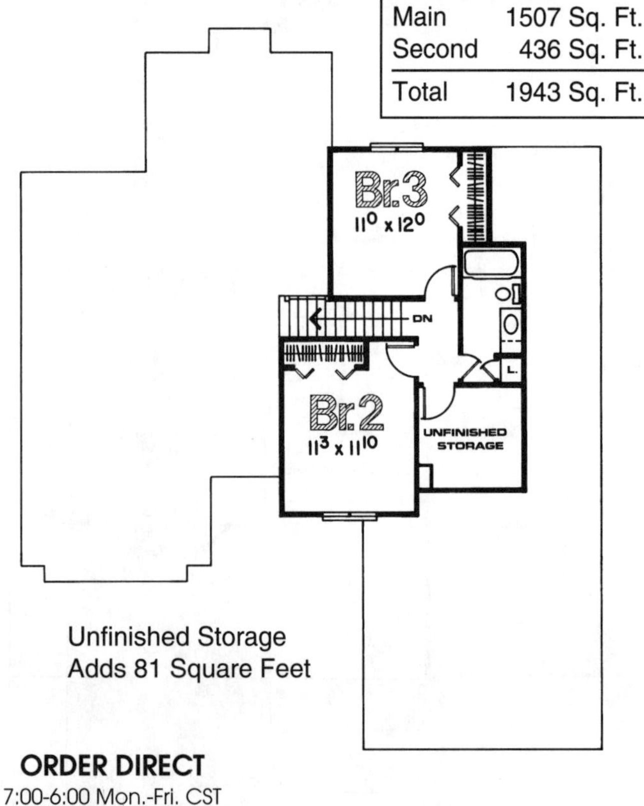

Unfinished Storage Adds 81 Square Feet

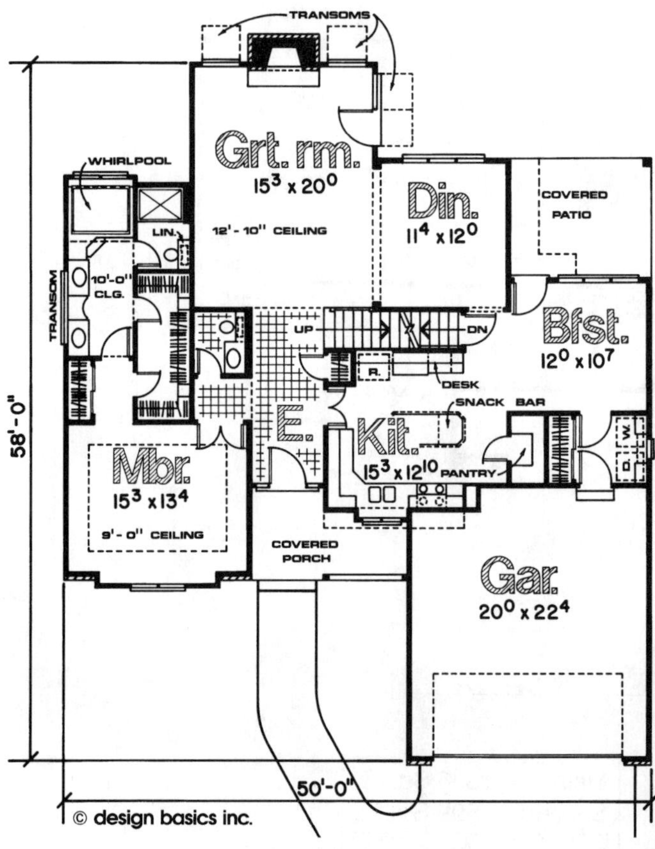

9F-2220 Gentry price code: 21

- High quality, erasable, reproducible vellums
- Shipped via 2nd day air within the continental U.S.

- arched window is seen in volume entry
- volume great room with handsome fireplace and windows out the back
- service doors to close off kitchen
- dining room and dinette both feature large windows out the back
- gourmet kitchen includes snack bar on island counter, desk and walk-in pantry
- convenient family entrance through laundry with closet
- beautiful arched window, double doors and sloped ceiling in master suite
- master dressing area includes 2-person whirlpool, his and her vanities and decorator plant ledge
- compartmented hall bath serves secondary bedrooms

Rear Elevation

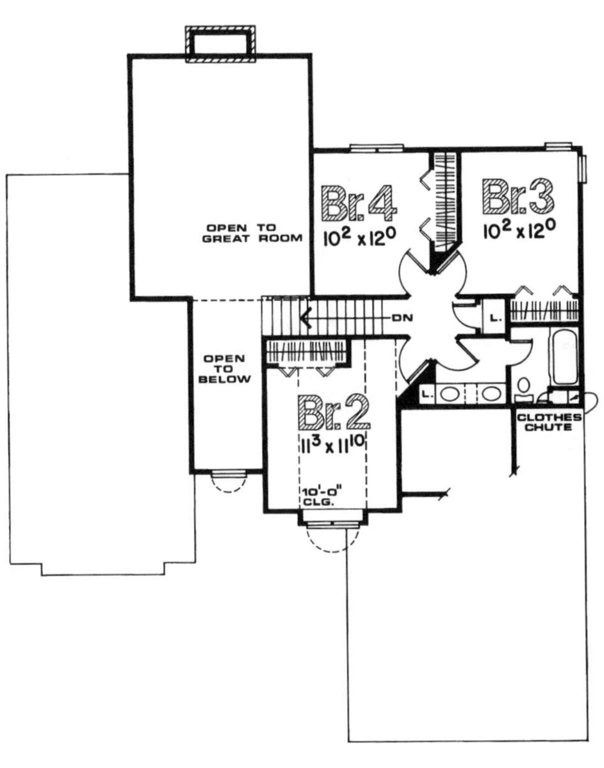

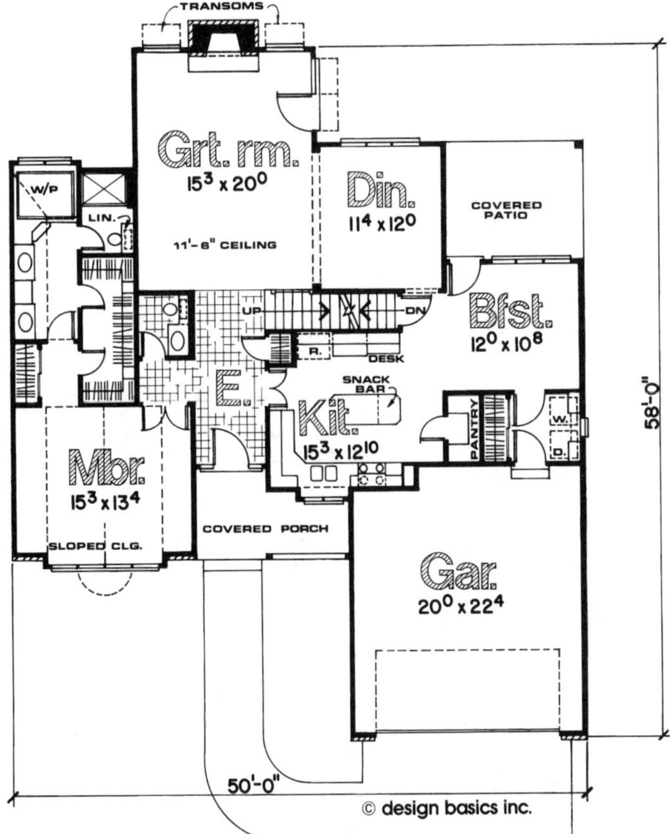

Main	1506 Sq. Ft.
Second	633 Sq. Ft.
Total	2139 Sq. Ft.

9F-3375 Gilchrist price code: 22

- ▶ High quality, erasable, reproducible vellums
- ▶ Shipped via 2nd day air within the continental U.S.

- intricately detailed elevation is reminiscent of days past
- dining room offers wonderful atmosphere for formal meals
- large great room is enhanced by fireplace and 10'-8" high ceiling
- snack bar and wrapping counters in unique kitchen
- private master suite boasts 10'-8" high ceiling, walk-in closet and luxurious whirlpool tub
- second floor landing overlooks entry below
- secondary bedrooms share convenient hall bath
- unfinished bonus room offers storage or expansion options
- 9'-0" main level walls

Rear Elevation

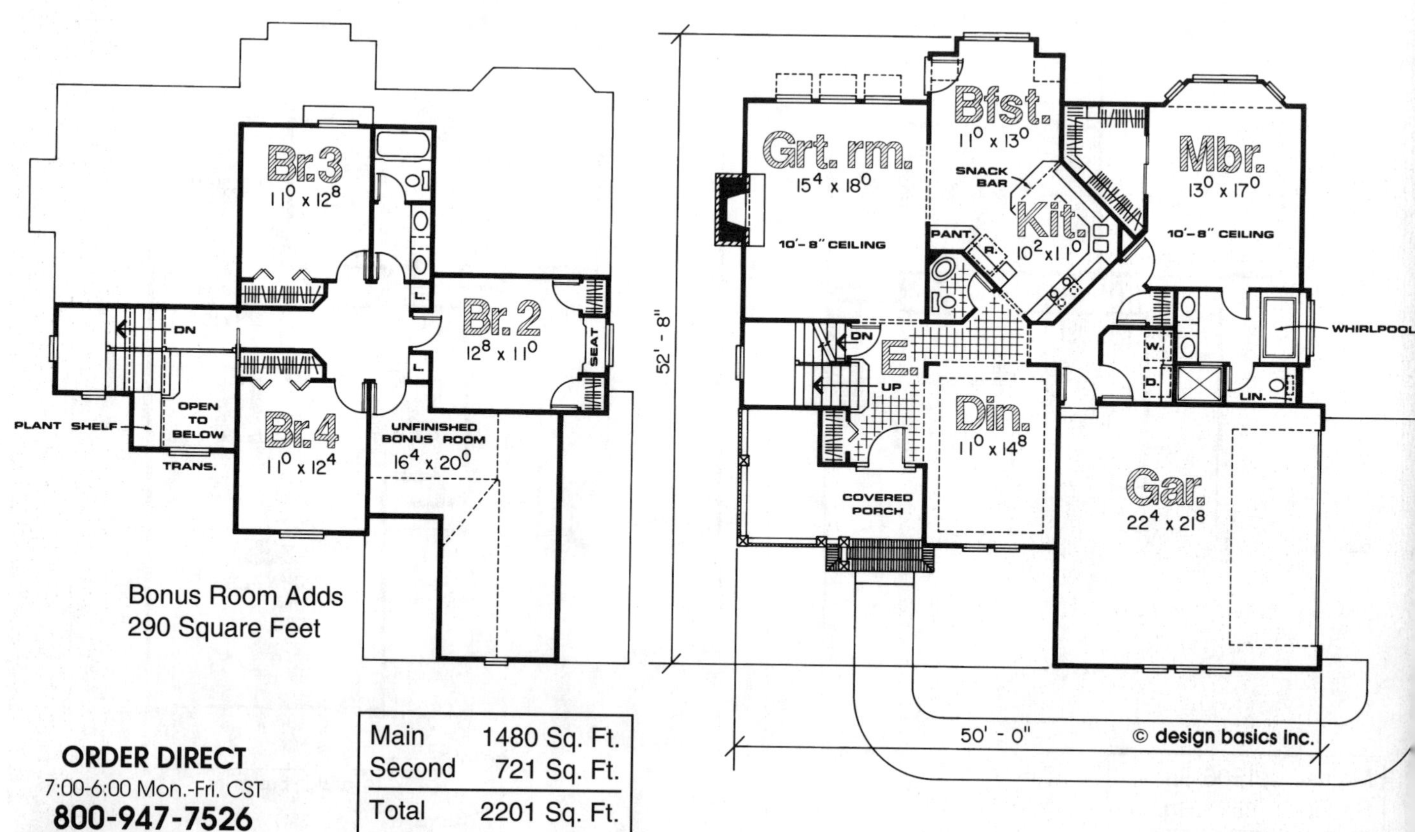

Main	1480 Sq. Ft.
Second	721 Sq. Ft.
Total	2201 Sq. Ft.

GOLD SEAL™ HOME PLANS

BASE PLAN INFORMATION

Page No.	Width	Plan No.	Plan Name	Sq. Ft.
122	48'-0"	3459	Jamestown	1561
73	28'-0"	3842	Salem	1561
79	38'-0"	2579	Bartels	1594
86	40'-0"	2526	Arbor	1605
96	42'-0"	3098	Duncan	1621
99	44'-0"	2248	Laverton	1650
84	39'-4"	3582	Webster	1651
87	40'-0"	2559	Archer	1699
107	46'-0"	3103	Ashworth	1700
123	48'-0"	3554	Cheyenne	1710
88	40'-0"	2545	Deming	1728
89	40'-0"	2700	Creston	1739
83	38'-8"	2890	Jefferson	1732
105	44'-8"	3097	Lincoln	1745
97	42'-0"	971	Optima	1748
80	38'-0"	2594	Jaymes	1764
95	40'-8"	3096	Torrey	1768
85	39'-4"	3581	Paige	1771
108	46'-0"	2308	Juniper	1775
100	44'-0"	2246	Augusta	1776
109	46'-0"	3576	Walton	1791
101	44'-0"	3383	Hackett	1792
106	45'-4"	2952	Francis	1799
75	32'-0"	3888	Quentin	1816
81	38'-0"	2699	Benson	1824
90	40'-0"	2547	Jasper	1841
110	46'-0"	1868	Somerset	1842
124	48'-0"	2100	Fenton	1845
102	44'-0"	1752	Lancaster	1846
111	46'-0"	2950	Herald	1849
125	48'-0"	3567	Yorktown	1858
112	46'-0"	746	Monroe	1875
120	47'-4"	2948	Peyton	1879
113	46'-0"	2305	Austin	1897
103	44'-0"	1572	Burton	1912
126	48'-0"	3386	Mansell	1915
76	36'-0"	3841	Springfield	1919
77	36'-0"	3840	Petersburg	1933
137	48'-8"	3568	Melrose	1947
139	50'-0"	2648	Cyprus	1951
138	49-4"	3384	Frederick	1992
127	48'-0"	2154	Galvin	1995
140	50'-0"	3552	Ballobin	2028
114	46'-0"	1769	Hampton	2031
115	46'-0"	846	Ardmore	2062
121	47'-4"	3028	Ferguson	2063
116	46'-0"	1870	Bristol	2078
104	44'-0"	2217	Yorke	2085
78	36'-0"	3893	Holdredge	2087
128	48'-0"	1179	Sawyer	2090
129	48'-0"	1552	Landon	2091
130	48'-0"	2156	Graham	2093
131	48'-0"	3209	Foresman	2099
141	50'-0"	2638	Linden	2103
132	48'-0"	2216	Collier	2174
72	26'-0"	3869	Matson	2177
133	48'-0"	669	Kinston	2191
117	46'-0"	1536	Livingston	2193
142	50'-0"	3588	Stratman	2198
143	50'-0"	790	Cormorant	2208
91	40'-0"	2327	Brighton	2218
74	30'-0"	3868	Norfolk	2223
92	40'-0"	2612	Clifton	2229
134	48'-0"	1865	Arlington	2233
144	50'-0"	1857	Cambridge	2251
93	40'-0"	3867	Riverdale	2255
118	46'-0"	2408	Crawford	2270
94	40'-0"	2351	Hastings	2292
135	48'-0"	2157	Lauderdale	2305
136	48'-0"	1754	Sydney	2345
98	42'-0"	2949	Hartley	2404
145	50'-0"	1033	Santee	2430
119	46'-0"	2792	Primrose	2475
146	50'-0"	3274	Whitmore	2517
82	38'-0"	3871	Brookdale	2586

TWO STORY HOMES

TWO STORY HOMES

9F-3869 Matson price code: 21

- ▶ High quality, erasable, reproducible vellums
- ▶ Shipped via 2nd day air within the continental U.S.

- several large casement windows give this home's elevation an open feel
- an expansive view of the family room's fireplace is enjoyed immediately upon entering
- flanking the entry, the open living and dining rooms expand the home's sense of space
- kitchen is well-planned for convenience with direct access to the dining room and utility area
- a second-level catwalk leads to the secondary bedrooms and overlooks the volume dinette
- French doors open to the master suite with his and her vanities, compartmented stool and walk-in closet

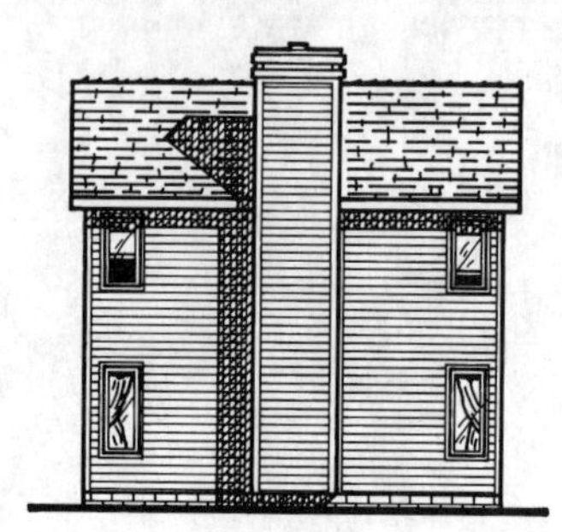

Rear Elevation

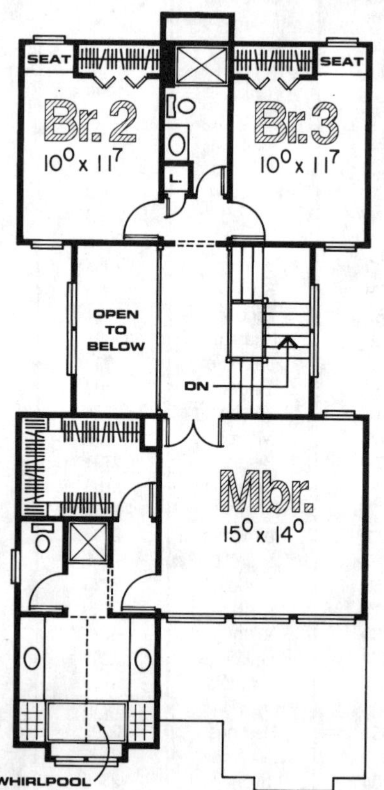

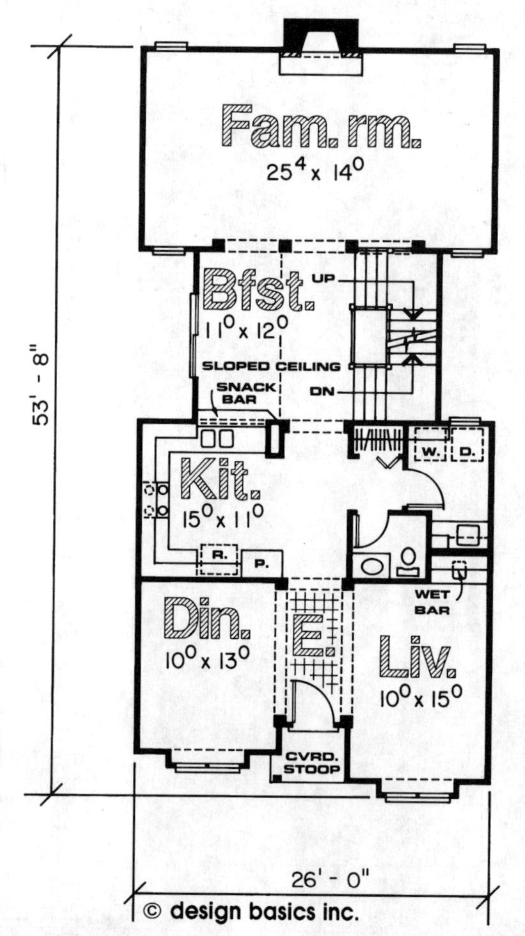

Main	1245 Sq. Ft.
Second	932 Sq. Ft.
Total	2177 Sq. Ft.

9F-3842 Salem price code: 15

- High quality, erasable, reproducible vellums
- Shipped via 2nd day air within the continental U.S.

- sunburst pediments and lighted, brick stoop columns provide a sophisticated charm to this home's elevation
- entertaining options are enhanced by an attractive cased opening which connects the formal dining room and family room
- well-planned kitchen features lazy Susan, pantry and convenient snack bar adjoining the breakfast area
- hall bath serves secondary bedrooms with views to the rear
- large master suite features French doors that open to dressing area with his and her vanities, compartmented stool and walk-in closet

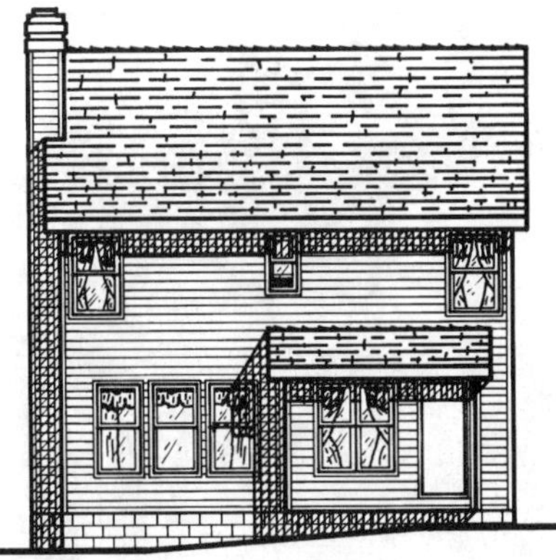

Rear Elevation

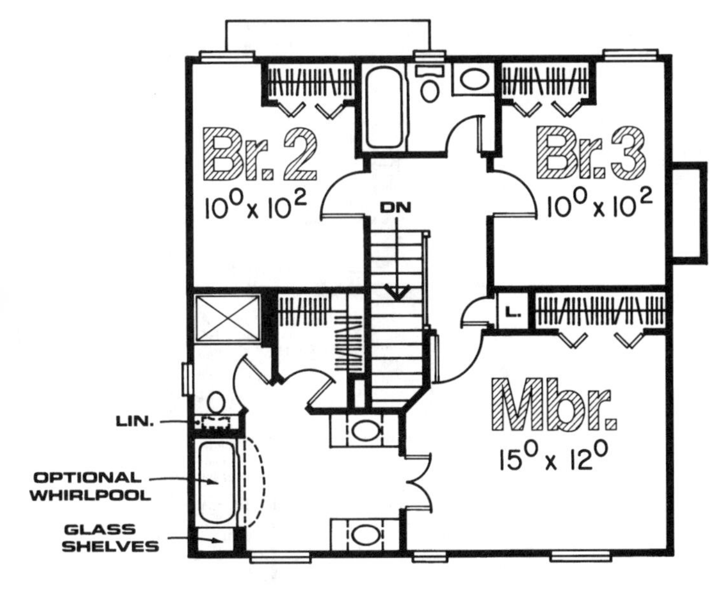

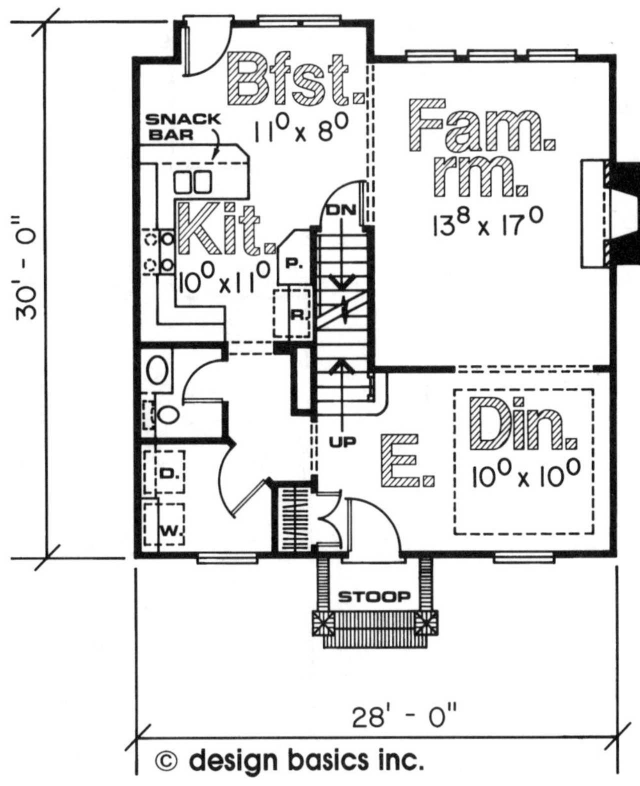

Main	807 Sq. Ft.
Second	754 Sq. Ft.
Total	1561 Sq. Ft.

9F-3868 Norfolk price code: 22

- ▸ High quality, erasable, reproducible vellums
- ▸ Shipped via 2nd day air within the continental U.S.

Gold Seal™ PLUS

- staggered gables, an arched transom window and a quaint covered stoop add visual interest to the elevation
- angled 2-story entry with balcony above, opens to formal dining room with built-in hutch space
- great room is situated for privacy and is highlighted by a raised-hearth fireplace and views to the rear.
- kitchen with snack bar and pantry adjoins bayed breakfast area
- optional den/bedroom on second level provides functional flexibility to the design
- master suite boasts his and her walk-in closets, a built-in dresser, his and her vanities and a step-up corner whirlpool tub

Rear Elevation

Main	1033 Sq. Ft.
Second	1190 Sq. Ft.
Total	2223 Sq. Ft.

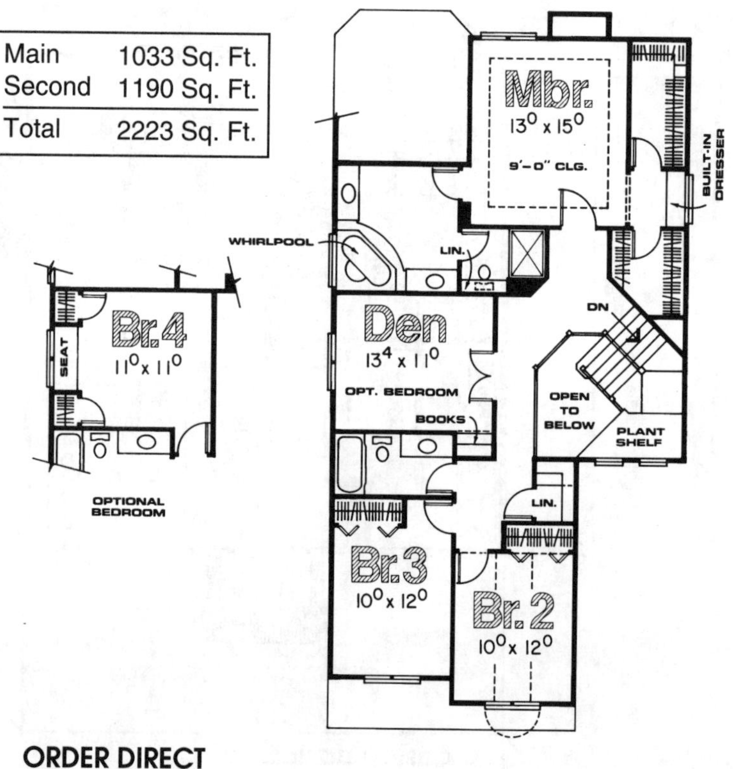

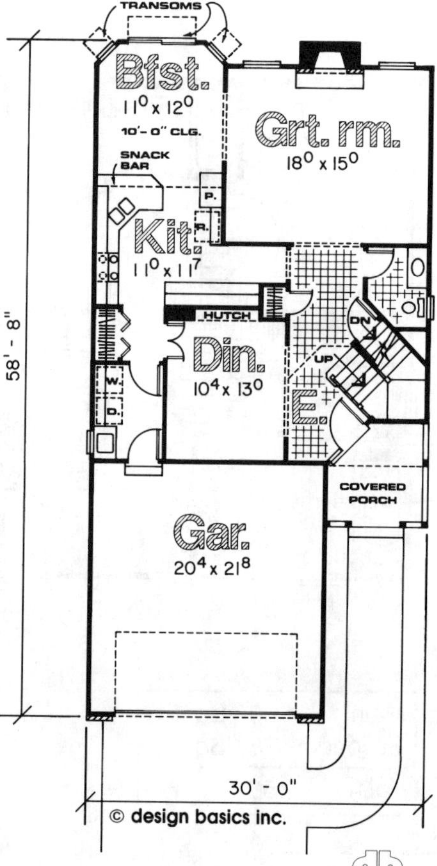

ORDER DIRECT

7:00-6:00 Mon.-Fri. CST

9F-3888 Quentin price code: 18

- High quality, erasable, reproducible vellums
- Shipped via 2nd day air within the continental U.S.

Gold Seal PLUS

- double-hung windows, brick accents and a quaint covered porch contribute to this homes inviting appeal
- 2-story entry offers immediate access upstairs
- great room with views to the rear, is warmed by the glow of a raised-hearth, see-thru fireplace
- roomy kitchen with snack bar and pantry shares the comfort of the breakfast area's fireplace
- impressive upstairs master suite showcases special ceiling details and includes a whirlpool, walk-in closet and double vanity
- angled doorways add special interest to secondary bedrooms

Rear Elevation

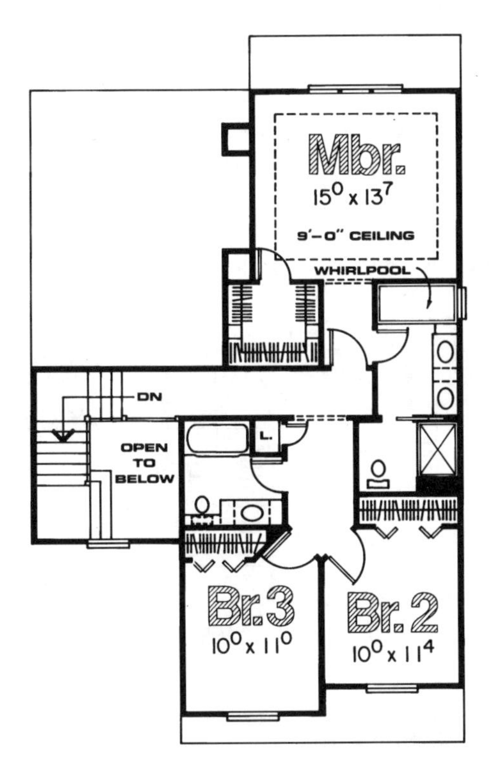

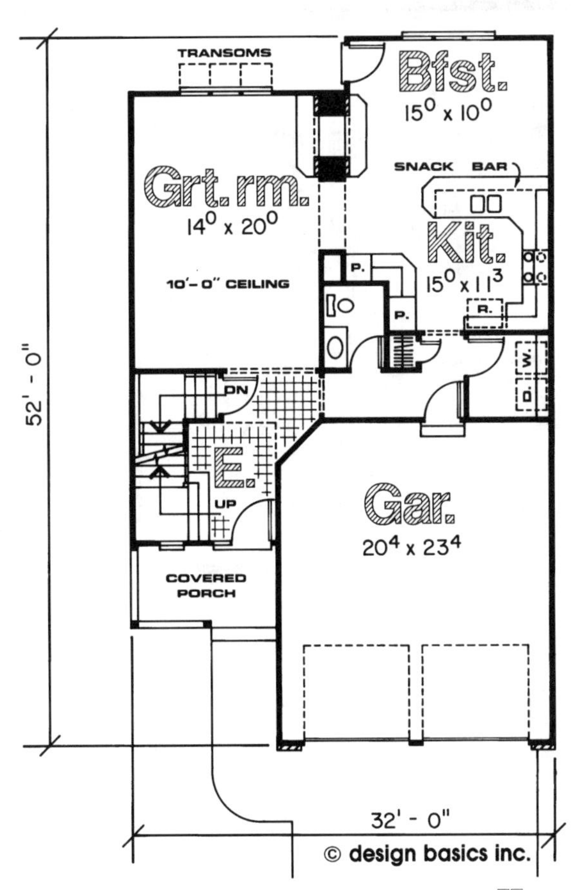

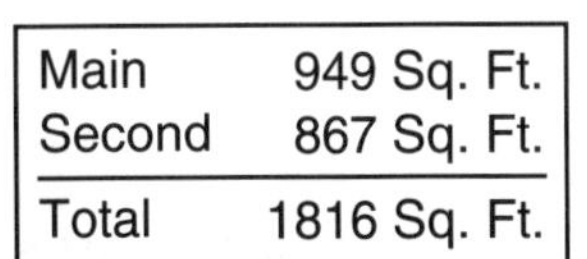

Main	949 Sq. Ft.
Second	867 Sq. Ft.
Total	1816 Sq. Ft.

9F-3841 Springfield price code: 19

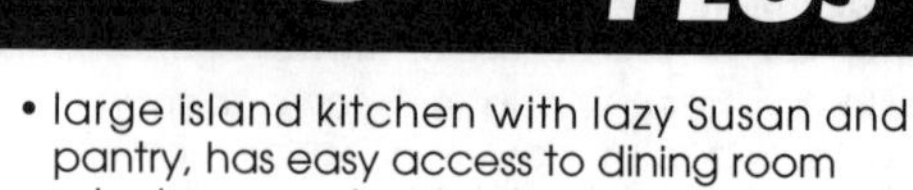

- High quality, erasable, reproducible vellums
- Shipped via 2nd day air within the continental U.S.

- inviting elevation with covered stoop has colonial charm
- dining room with built-in curio cabinet is open to 2-story entry
- expansive great room with raised-hearth fireplace offers view to the rear covered porch
- attractive cased opening connects great room to bayed breakfast area
- large island kitchen with lazy Susan and pantry, has easy access to dining room
- private secondary bedrooms flank conveniently located hall bath
- master suite features double vanities, dressing area, whirlpool and walk-in closet

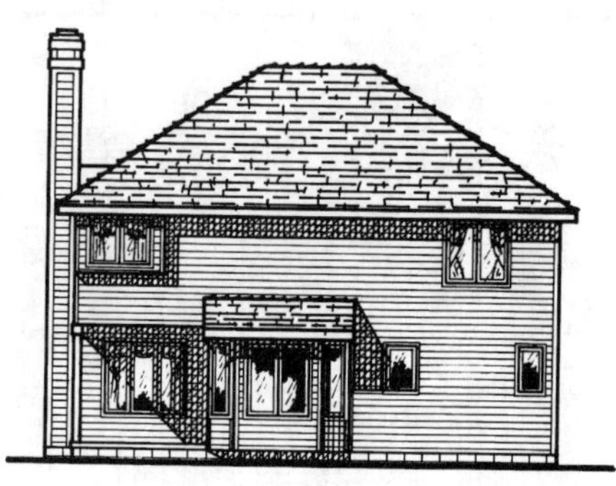

Rear Elevation

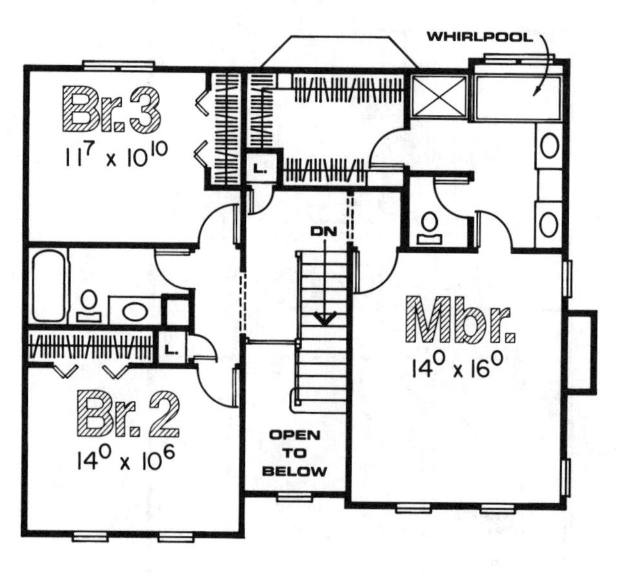

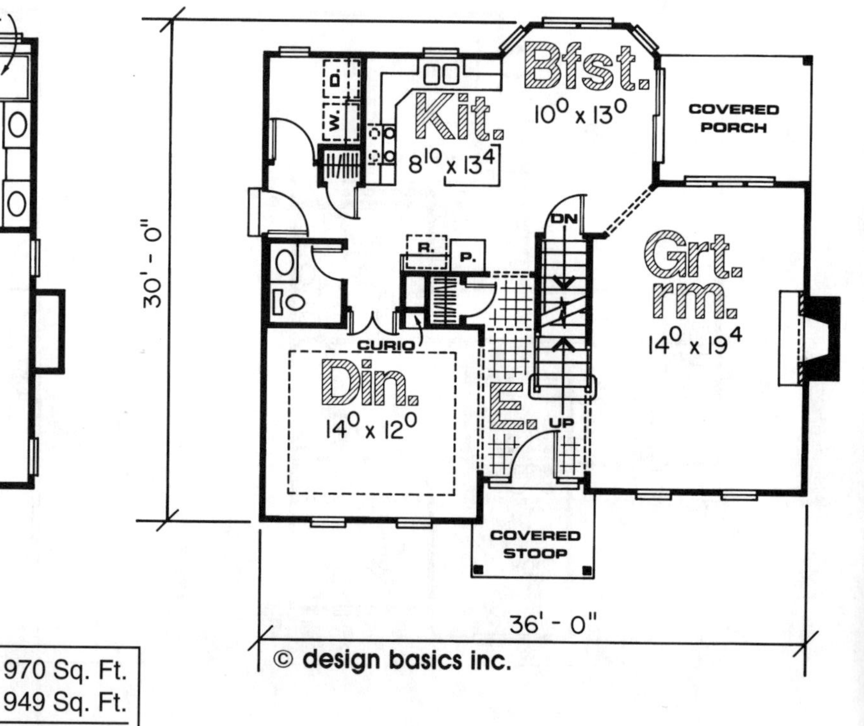

Main	970 Sq. Ft.
Second	949 Sq. Ft.
Total	1919 Sq. Ft.

9F-3840 Petersburg price code: 19

- ▶ High quality, erasable, reproducible vellums
- ▶ Shipped via 2nd day air within the continental U.S.

Gold Seal™ PLUS

- shake siding and six-over-nine, double-hung windows enhance the historical overtones of this grand elevation
- balcony provides impressive overviews of 2-story entry
- great room is open to entry and enjoys the warmth of a raised-hearth fireplace
- French doors connect spacious dining room to kitchen area and convenient servery
- large, sunlit breakfast area accesses covered porch
- second-level bath with dual lavs services secondary bedrooms
- impressive master suite features a nine-foot ceiling, walk-in closet, whirlpool bath and dressing area

Rear Elevation

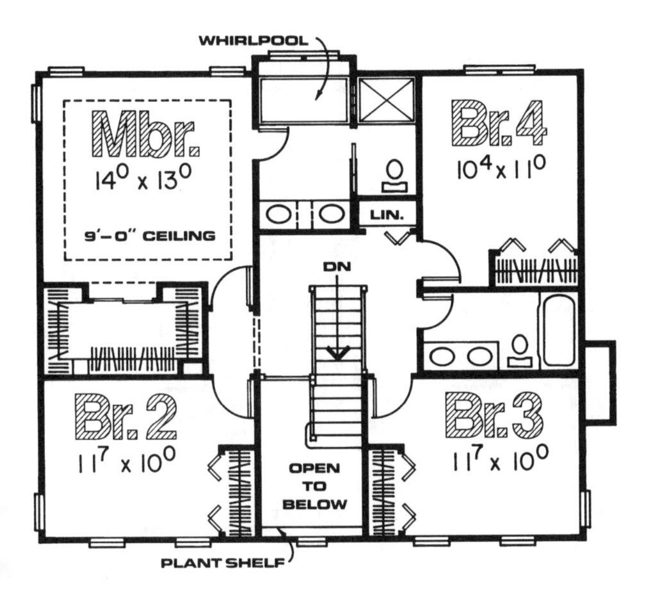

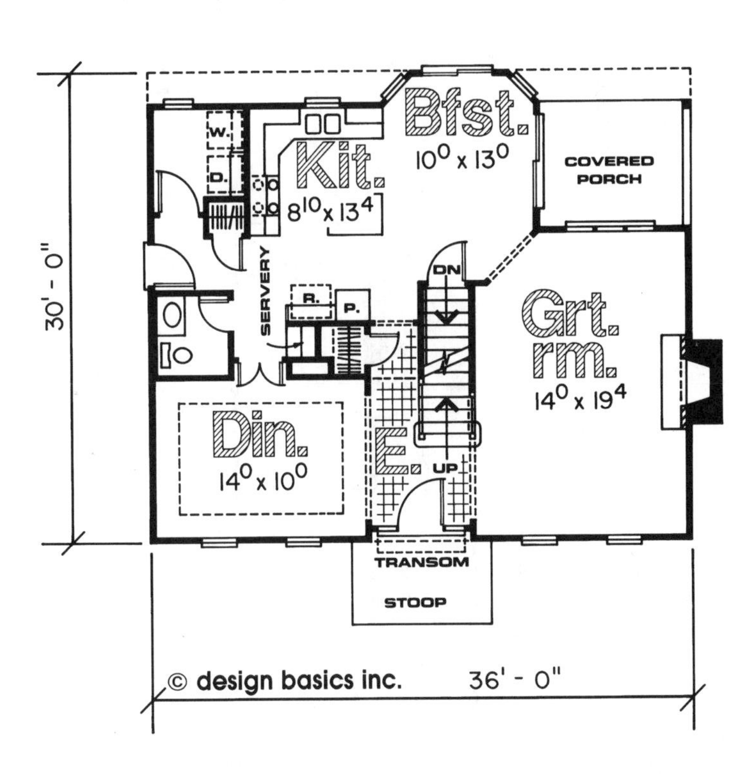

Main	941 Sq. Ft.
Second	992 Sq. Ft.
Total	1933 Sq. Ft.

9F-3893 Holdredge price code: 20

Gold Seal PLUS

- High quality, erasable, reproducible vellums
- Shipped via 2nd day air within the continental U.S.

- stylish elevation uses repeating details, twin gables centered over bright windows and impactful front porch to command attention
- deep garage offers storage options
- volume entry with plant shelf open to formal dining room
- kitchen offers pantry, dual lazy Susans, window over sink and built-in snack bar
- volume dinette visually connects with the outside through windows and atrium door
- large, sunken family room has fireplace framed by windows
- master bedroom has twin walk-in closets
- loft, overlooking tall windows in dinette, is ideal space for relaxing or can be optioned as fourth bedroom

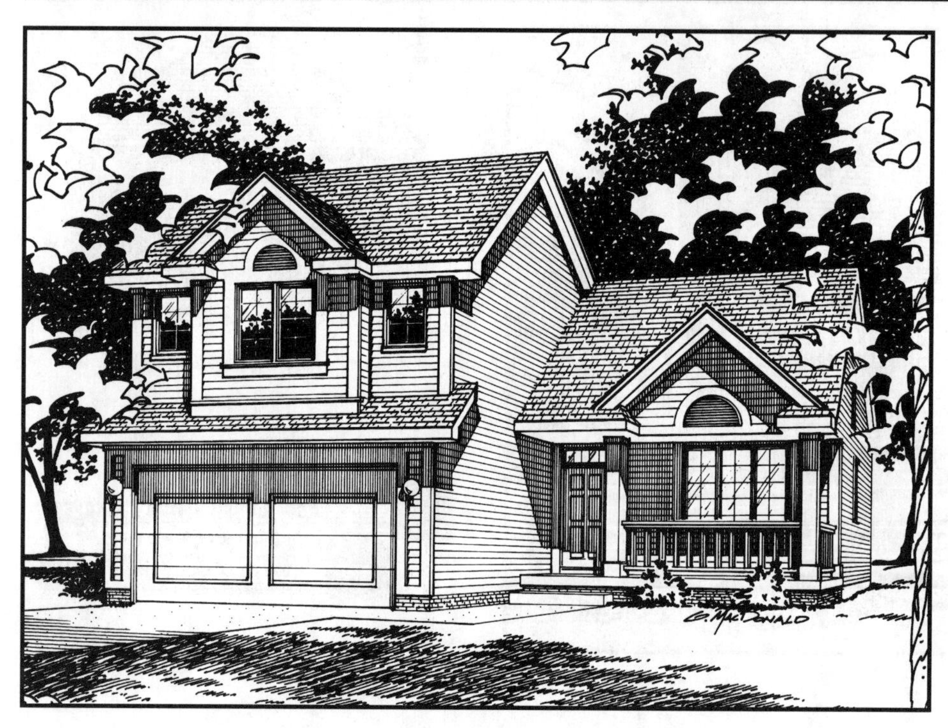

Rear Elevation

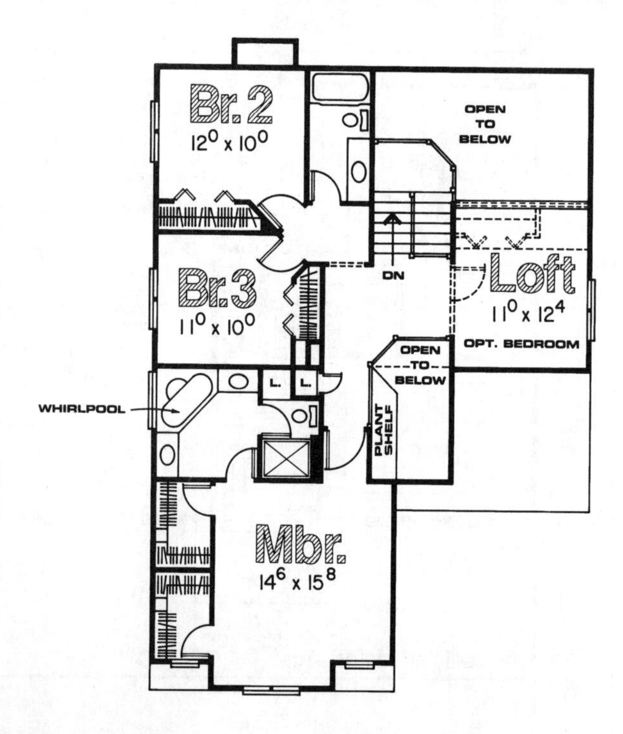

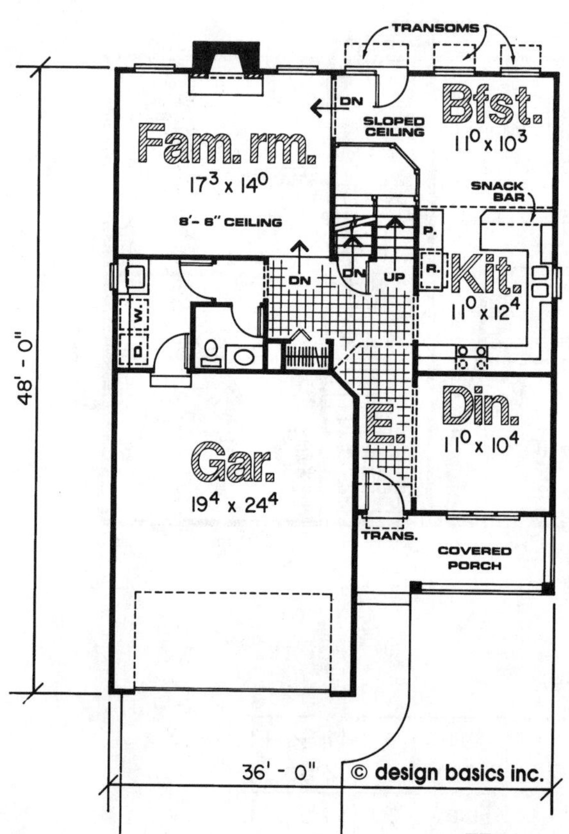

ORDER DIRECT
7:00-6:00 Mon.-Fri. CST
800-947-7526

Main	1016 Sq. Ft.
Second	1071 Sq. Ft.
Total	2087 Sq. Ft.

PLEXABLE

9F-2579 Bartels price code: 15

Gold Seal HOME PLANS™

- High quality, erasable, reproducible vellums
- Shipped via 2nd day air within the continental U.S.

- columned front porch adds visual appeal to this livable design
- from the entry, step down into living room distinguished by raised hearth fireplace centered under cathedral ceiling
- French doors seclude formal dining room from kitchen
- ample kitchen and dinette provide amenities available in larger plans such as large pantry and center island with snack bar
- private den strategically located off dinette
- grand master bath features dual lavs and whirlpool
- spacious walk-in closet highlights master bedroom

Rear Elevation

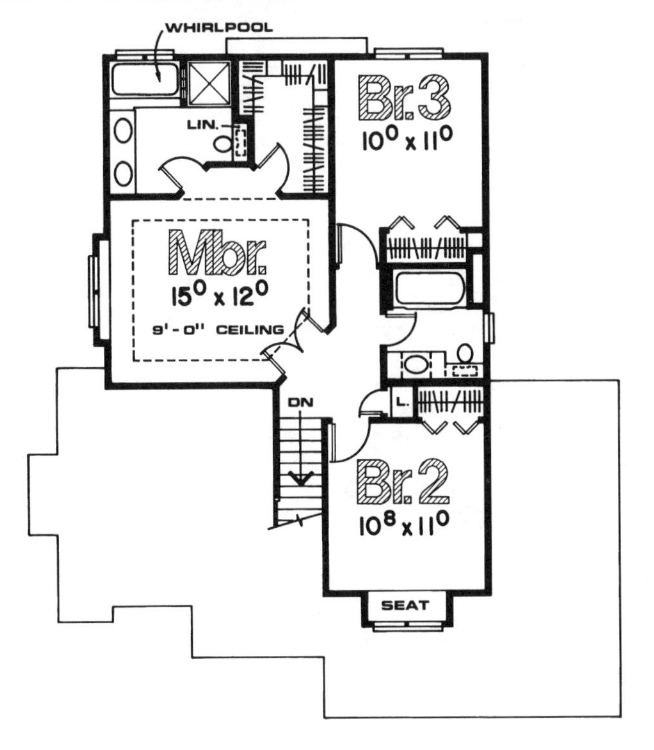

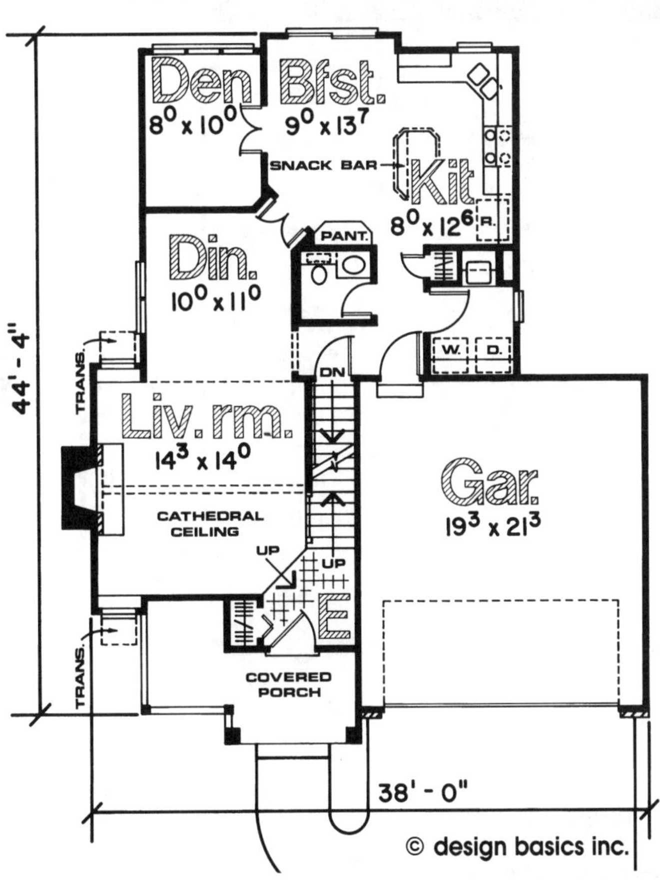

Main	869 Sq. Ft.
Second	725 Sq. Ft.
Total	1594 Sq. Ft.

design basics inc.®
HOME PLAN DESIGN SERVICE

9F-2594 Jaymes price code: 17

- ▶ High quality, erasable, reproducible vellums
- ▶ Shipped via 2nd day air within the continental U.S.

Gold Seal HOME PLANS™

- this simple but charming design presents a well-balanced elevation for narrow lots
- from entry, step down into volume living room open to formal dining area for expanded entertaining flexibility
- double doors access formal dining room from kitchen
- open kitchen/dinette features large pantry, center island with snack bar and corner sink
- private den may be converted to sunroom
- laundry room conveniently located off dinette
- master suite includes volume ceilings, walk-in closet, dual lavs and whirlpool tub

Rear Elevation

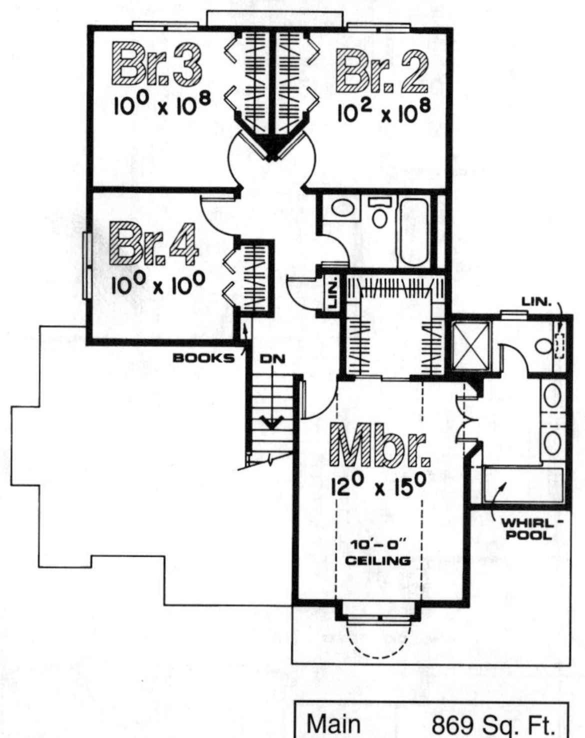

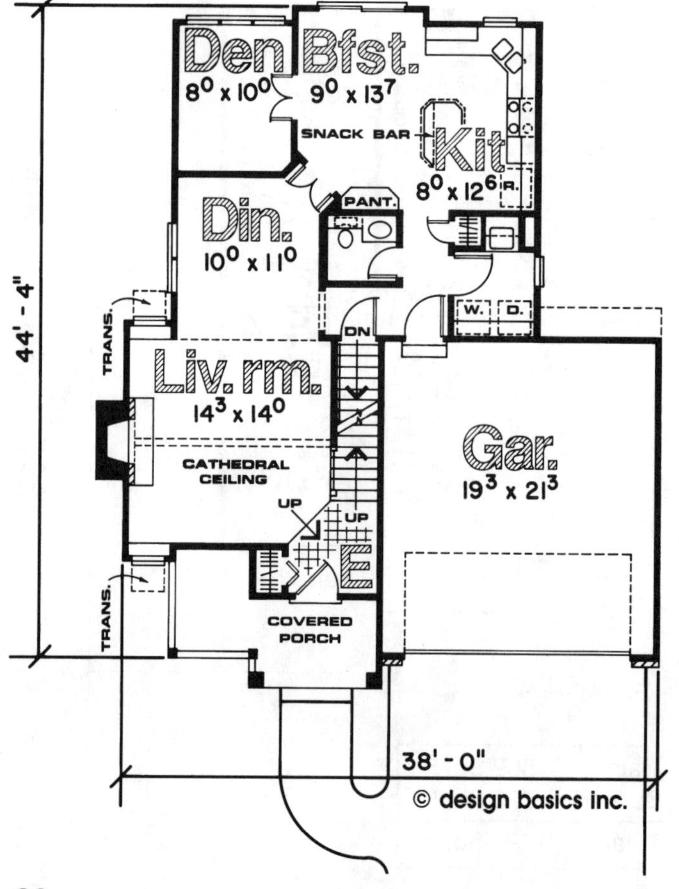

Main	869 Sq. Ft.
Second	895 Sq. Ft.
Total	1764 Sq. Ft.

9F-2699 Benson price code: 18

- High quality, erasable, reproducible vellums
- Shipped via 2nd day air within the continental U.S.

- brick and glass block accents, plus wood-railed porch create front elevation that's contemporary, yet nostalgic
- dining room offers ample space for formal dinner occasions
- family room with raised hearth fireplace provides open feeling and endless decorating options
- kitchen features 2 lazy Susans, centrally-placed range and handy snack bar
- master bath is conveniently laid out with separate vanities
- master bedroom boasts 9-foot-high ceiling and spacious dressing area
- well-appointed master bath includes step-up whirlpool and plant shelf

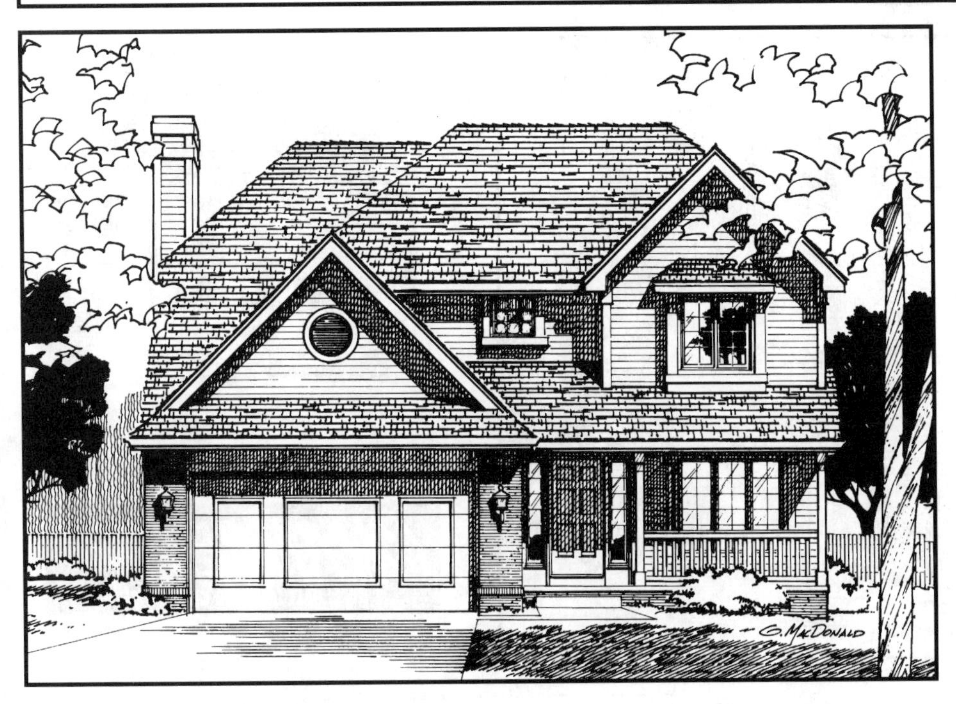

Rear Elevation

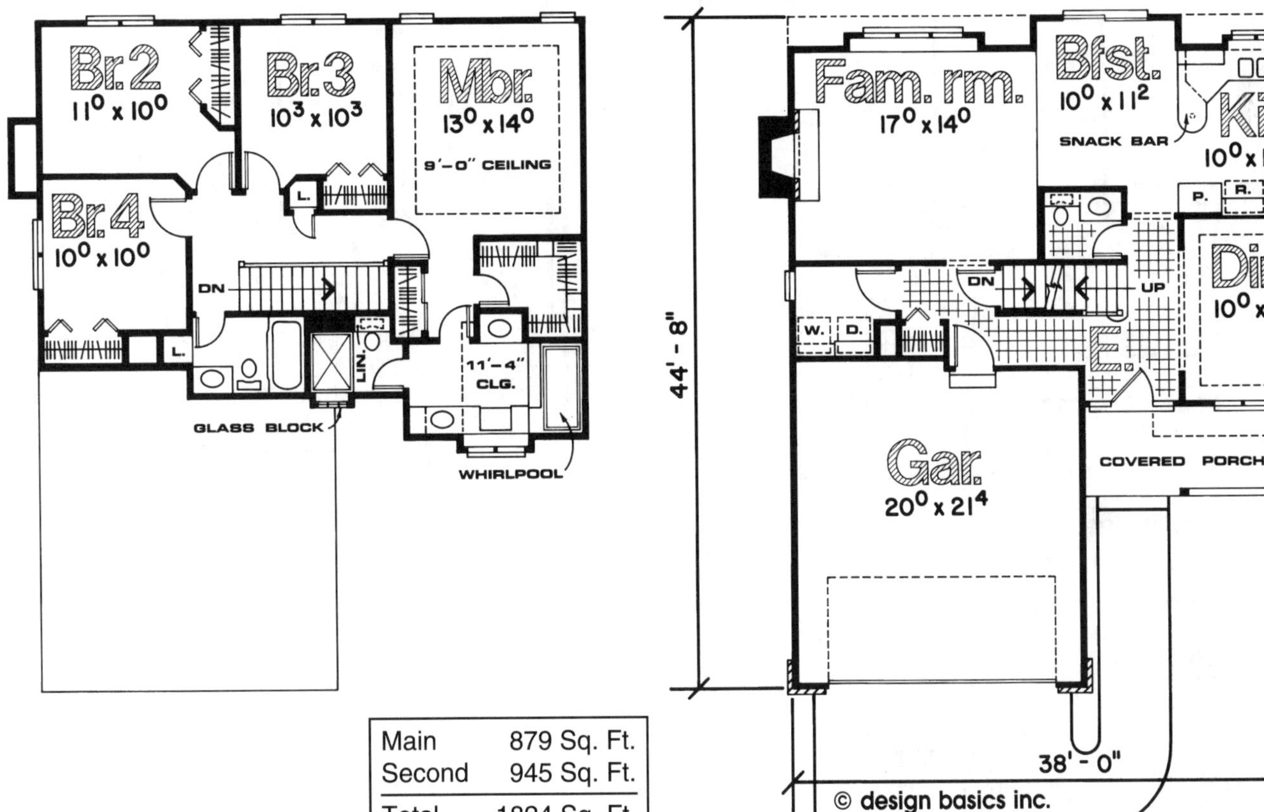

Main	879 Sq. Ft.
Second	945 Sq. Ft.
Total	1824 Sq. Ft.

design basics inc.®
HOME PLAN DESIGN SERVICE

9F-3871 Brookdale price code: 25

- High quality, erasable, reproducible vellums
- Shipped via 2nd day air within the continental U.S.

Gold Seal™ PLUS

- a tasteful blend of brick and siding enhances curb appeal
- nine-foot main level walls throughout
- dining room is open to reading room with built-in bookshelf and raised-hearth fireplace
- great room enjoys see-thru fireplace and open views to the rear
- kitchen offers snack bar, pantry and plenty of counter space
- sunny breakfast area opens to great room and has direct access to the outdoors
- secondary bedrooms are served by centralized hall bath with dual vanities
- luxury master suite features his and her vanities, oval whirlpool, compartmented stool and large walk-in closet

Rear Elevation

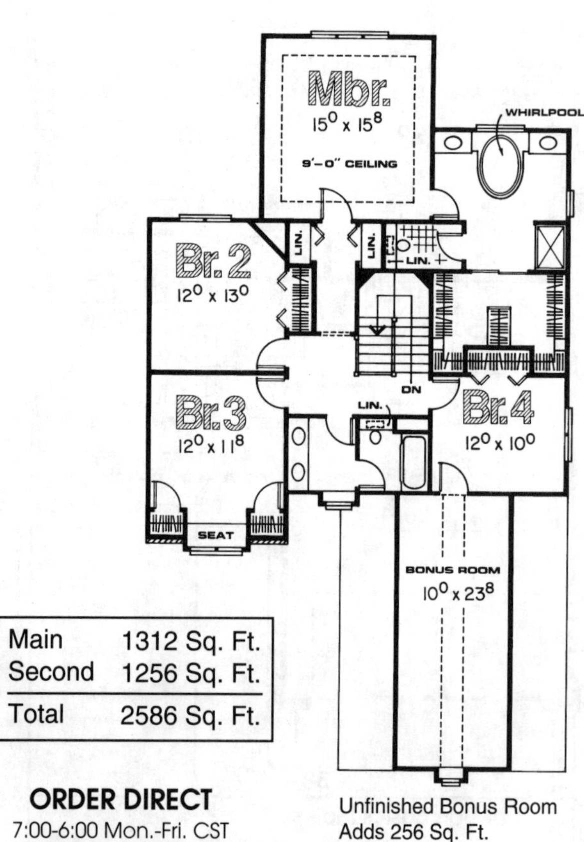

Unfinished Bonus Room Adds 256 Sq. Ft.

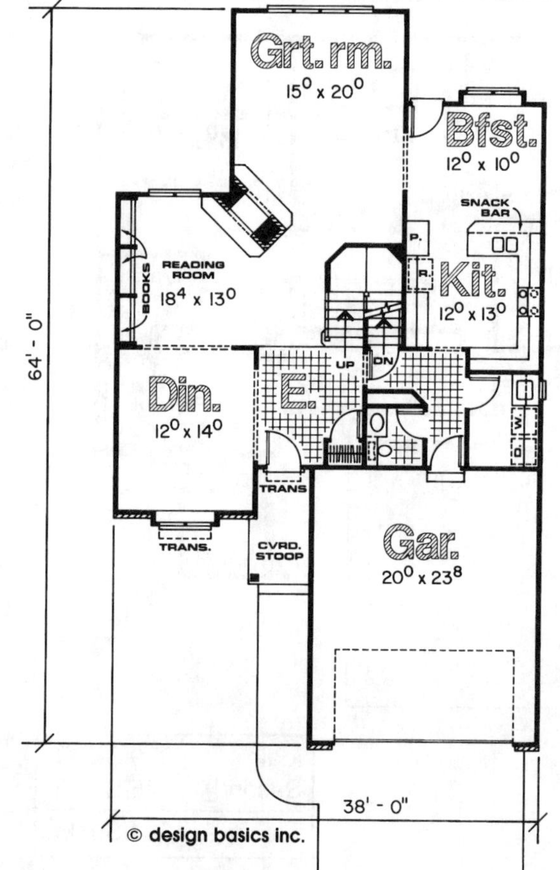

© design basics inc.

Main	1312 Sq. Ft.
Second	1256 Sq. Ft.
Total	2586 Sq. Ft.

ORDER DIRECT
7:00-6:00 Mon.-Fri. CST
800-947-7526

PLEXABLE™

9F-2890 Jefferson price code: 17

- High quality, erasable, reproducible vellums
- Shipped via 2nd day air within the continental U.S.

- angled U-stairs are focus for 2-story entry
- formal living room off entry features fireplace between built-in bookcases and view to dining room with hutch space
- bayed dinette adds to oversized island kitchen with large pantry, snack bar and convenient access to laundry room
- bedroom #2 contains beautiful arched window and volume ceiling
- secondary bedrooms share compartmented bath with dual lavs
- great master suite has whirlpool bath with dual lavs, make-up counter and generous walk-in closet

Rear Elevation

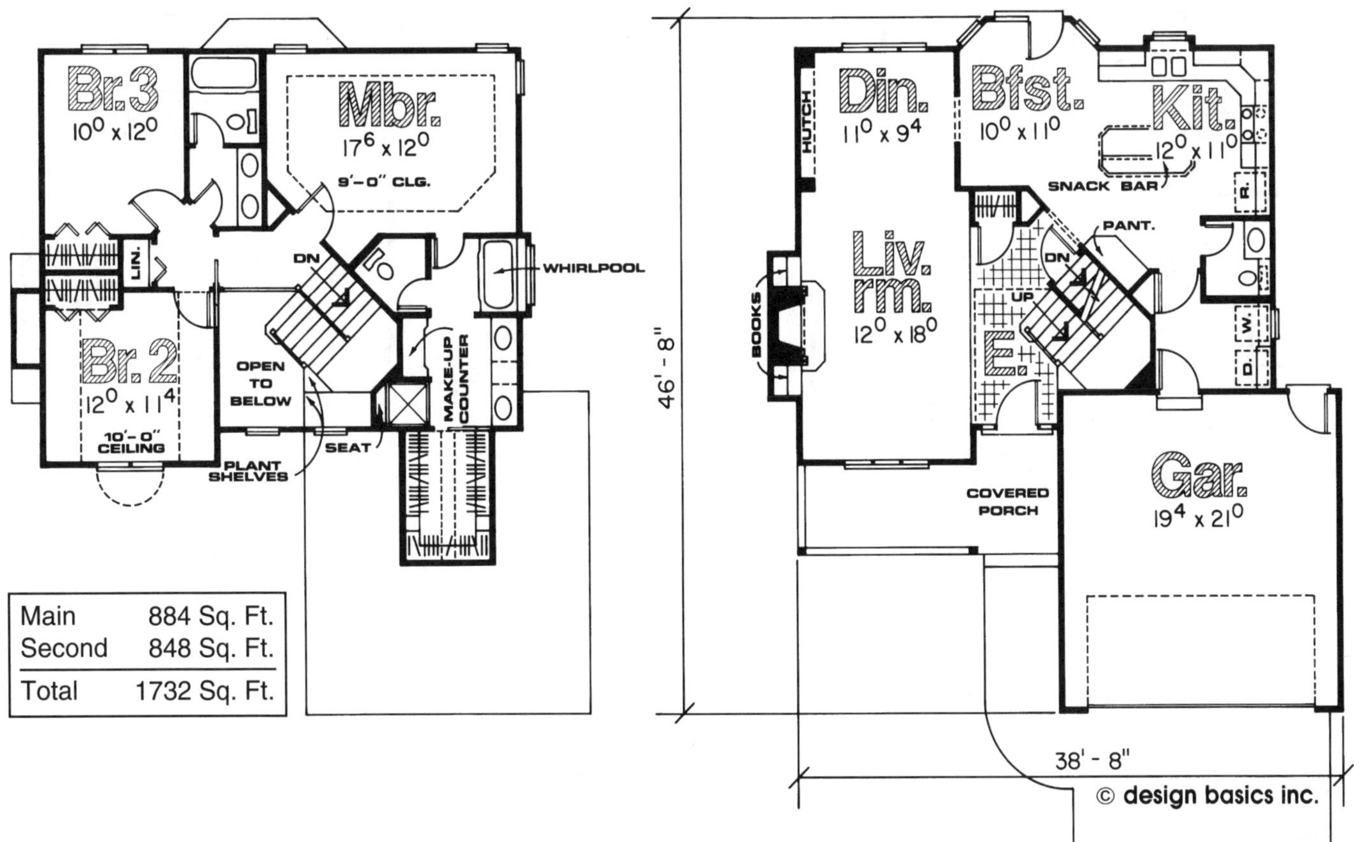

Main	884 Sq. Ft.
Second	848 Sq. Ft.
Total	1732 Sq. Ft.

9F-3582 Webster price code: 16

Gold Seal PLUS

- High quality, erasable, reproducible vellums
- Shipped via 2nd day air within the continental U.S.

- mixture of charm and elegance creates curb appeal
- formal dining with 10'-0" ceiling is flexible as parlor
- kitchen with snack bar opens to sunny breakfast area
- centrally located main floor powder room
- wall of windows and fireplace highlight family room
- laundry room equipped with shelves and rod for hanging clothes
- designated storage space in garage
- master suite presents sunlit whirlpool and walk-in closet
- bedroom #2 has window seat
- hall bath serves secondary bedrooms

Rear Elevation

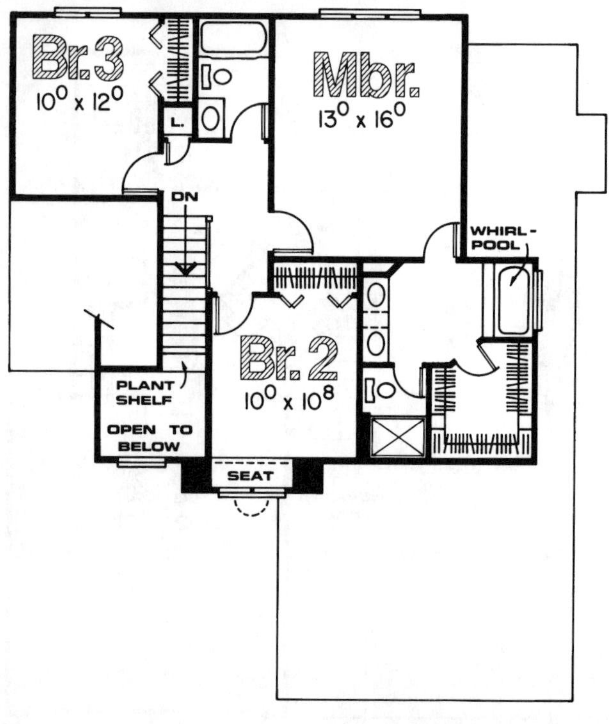

Main	866 Sq. Ft.
Second	785 Sq. Ft.
Total	1651 Sq. Ft.

9F-3581 Paige price code: 17

- ▶ High quality, erasable, reproducible vellums
- ▶ Shipped via 2nd day air within the continental U.S.

Gold Seal™ PLUS

- quaint, cozy exterior
- covered porch leads to entry with double-door coat closet
- formal dining room is flexible as parlor
- sunny kitchen has wrapping counters
- patio doors leads to back from breakfast area
- spacious family room boasts fireplace and three lovely windows
- extra deep garage offers storage options
- second floor master suite hosts roomy walk-in closet and whirlpool tub
- three secondary bedrooms share central hall bath
- open area above entry easily converts to optional toy closet

Rear Elevation

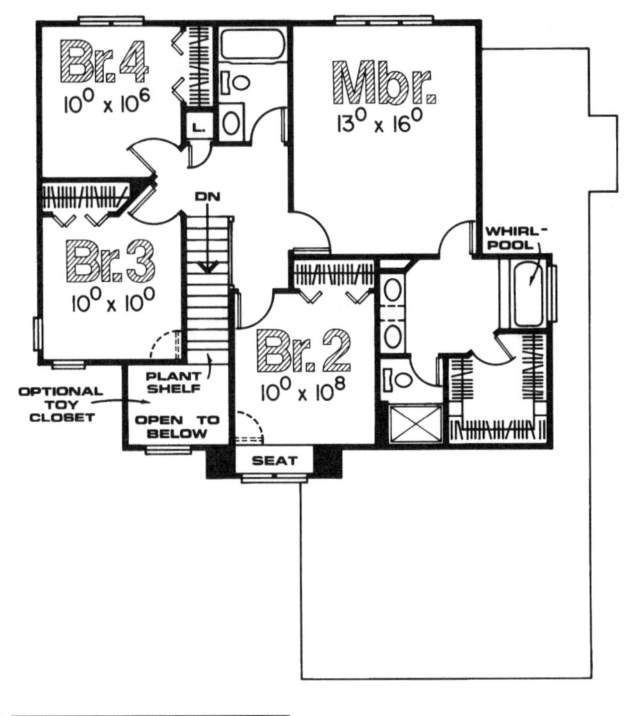

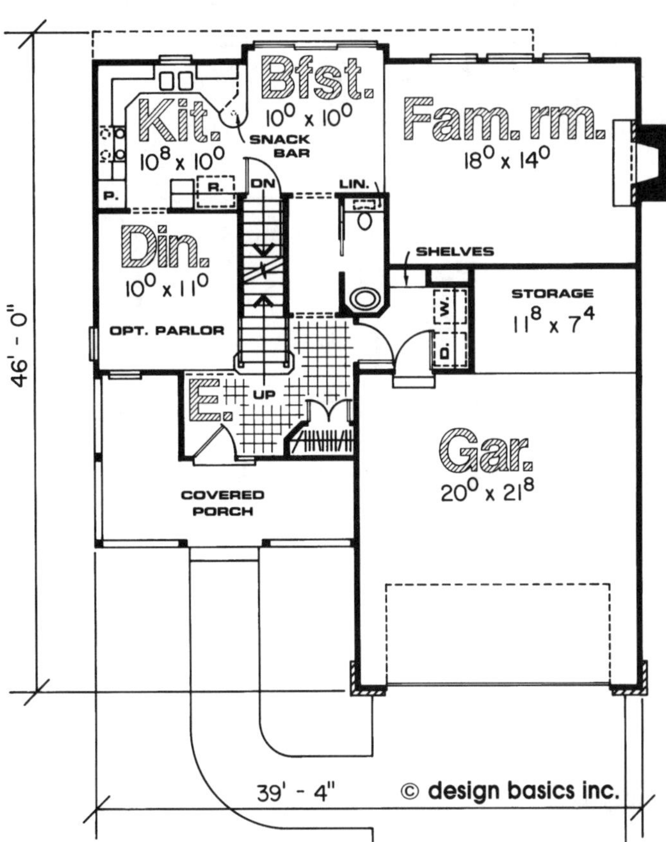

Main	866 Sq. Ft.
Second	905 Sq. Ft.
Total	1771 Sq. Ft.

9F-2526 Arbor price code: 16

- High quality, erasable, reproducible vellums
- Shipped via 2nd day air within the continental U.S.

- gabled roof, brick accents and covered front porch combine to present striking elevation
- ceiling slopes from 9 foot to 16'-10", plus raised hearth fireplace of great room makes dramatic presentation
- formal dining room features built-in hutch
- efficient kitchen with snack bar serves dinette, which has planning desk and large pantry
- laundry area has window, broom closet and hanging rod
- French doors access master suite with 10-foot-high ceiling, and second set of French doors lead to private dressing area with dual lavs
- natural light floods master bath above whirlpool tub

Rear Elevation

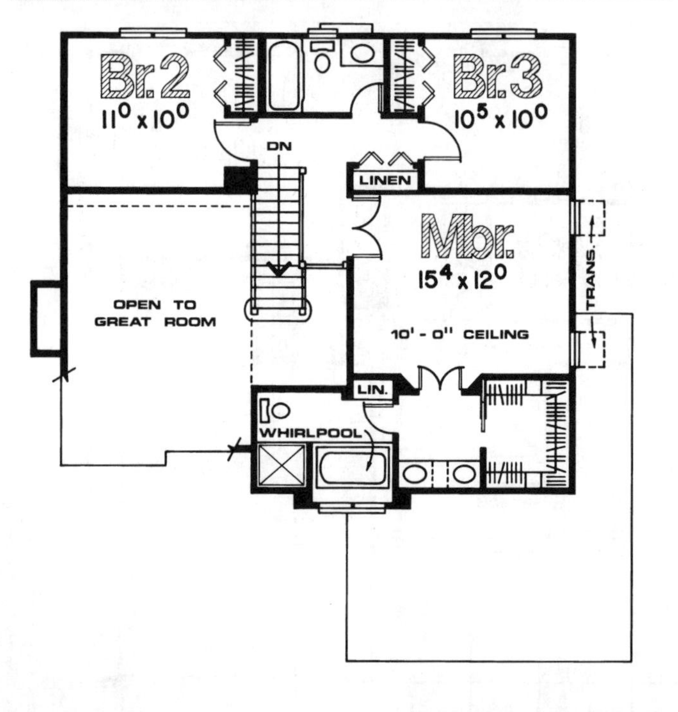

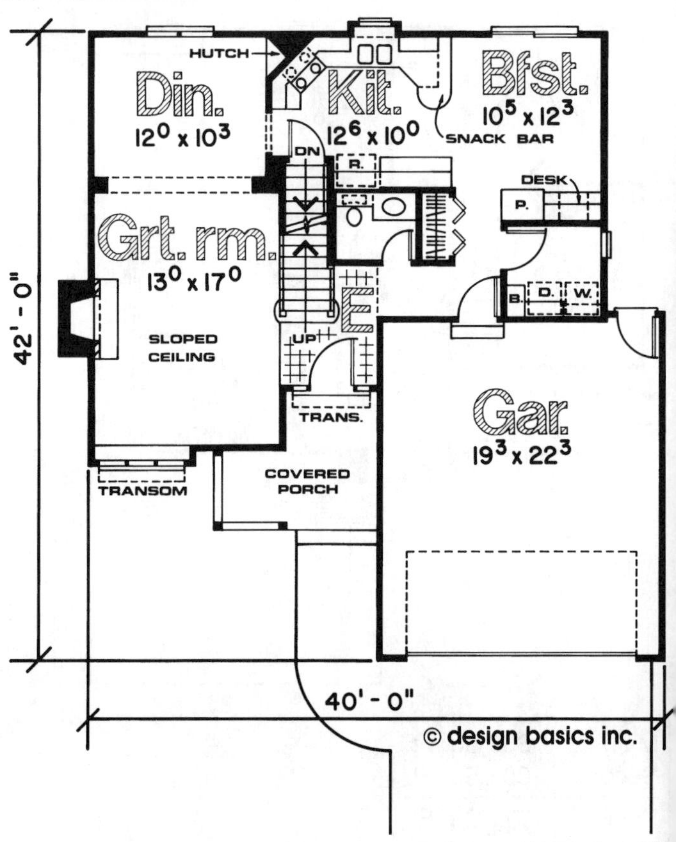

Main	845 Sq. Ft.
Second	760 Sq. Ft.
Total	1605 Sq. Ft.

9F-2559 Archer price code: 16

- High quality, erasable, reproducible vellums
- Shipped via 2nd day air within the continental U.S.

- covered stoop offers warm, friendly welcome
- delightfully large living room, with 10-foot ceiling and tall windows, provides distinctive character and presents many entertaining options
- wood floors integrate family room, dinette and kitchen into unified living space
- large laundry room is practically located off family room and garage
- impressive double doors lead to gorgeous master bedroom distinguished by his and her walk-in closets
- French doors open to the luxurious master bath with dual lavs and whirlpool

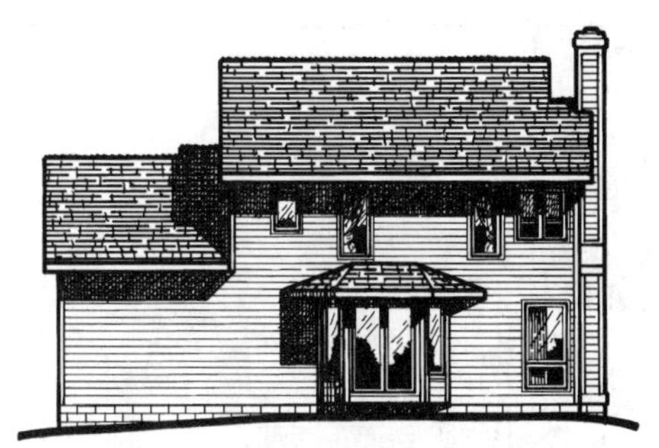

Rear Elevation

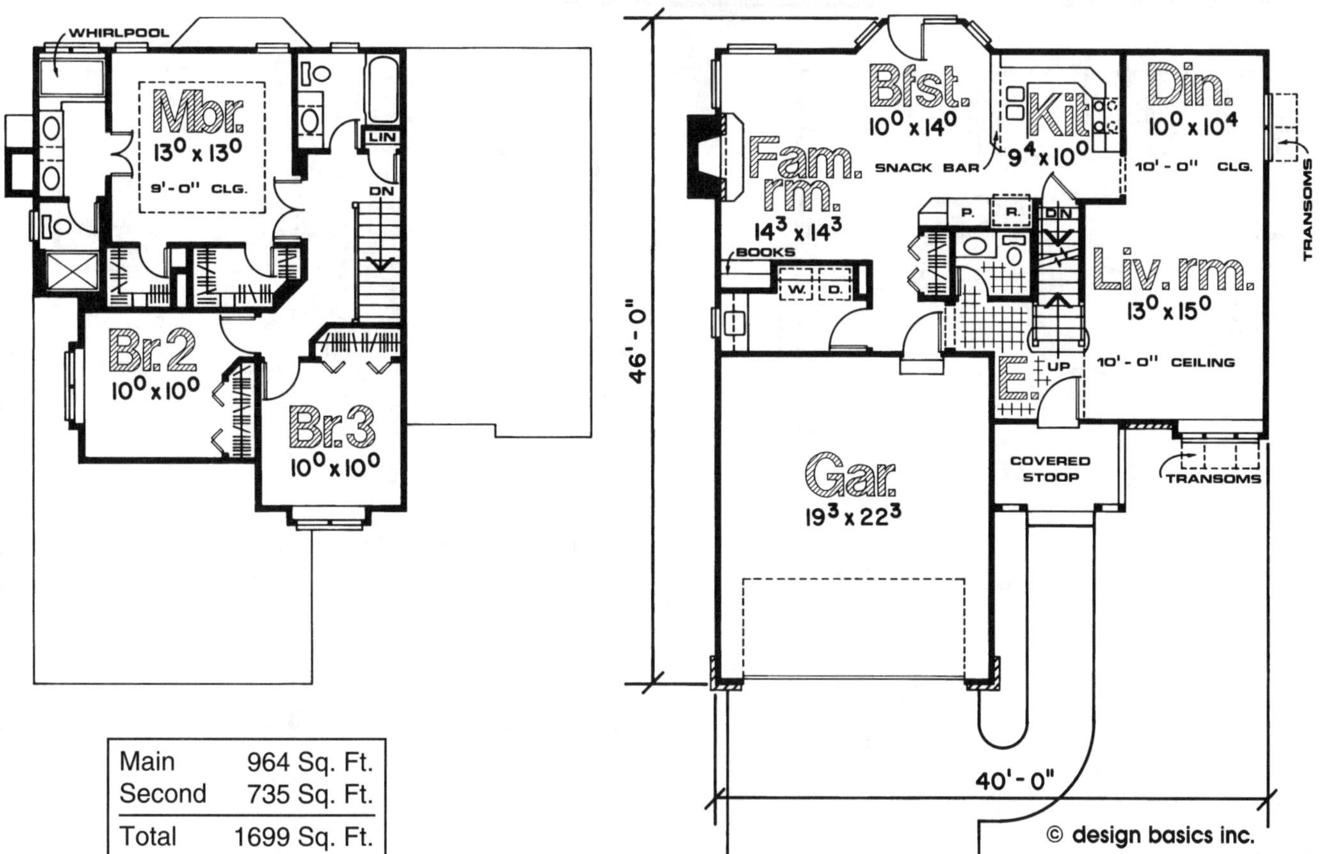

Main	964 Sq. Ft.
Second	735 Sq. Ft.
Total	1699 Sq. Ft.

9F-2545 Deming price code: 17

- High quality, erasable, reproducible vellums
- Shipped via 2nd day air within the continental U.S.

- quaint covered porch suggests comfortable living in this two-story design
- great room features raised hearth fireplace, sloped ceiling and transom windows that allow more natural light
- wrap-around kitchen with peninsula snack bar is located between formal dining room and family dinette
- staircase with nostalgic wood railing offers dramatic view of great room
- double doors invite you into master bedroom with high 10-foot ceiling
- master bath with dual lavs, whirlpool and shower adjoins large closet
- large linen closet services upstairs bath areas

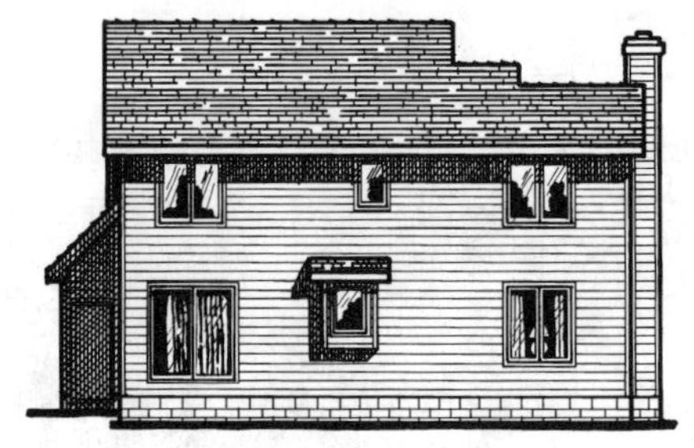

Rear Elevation

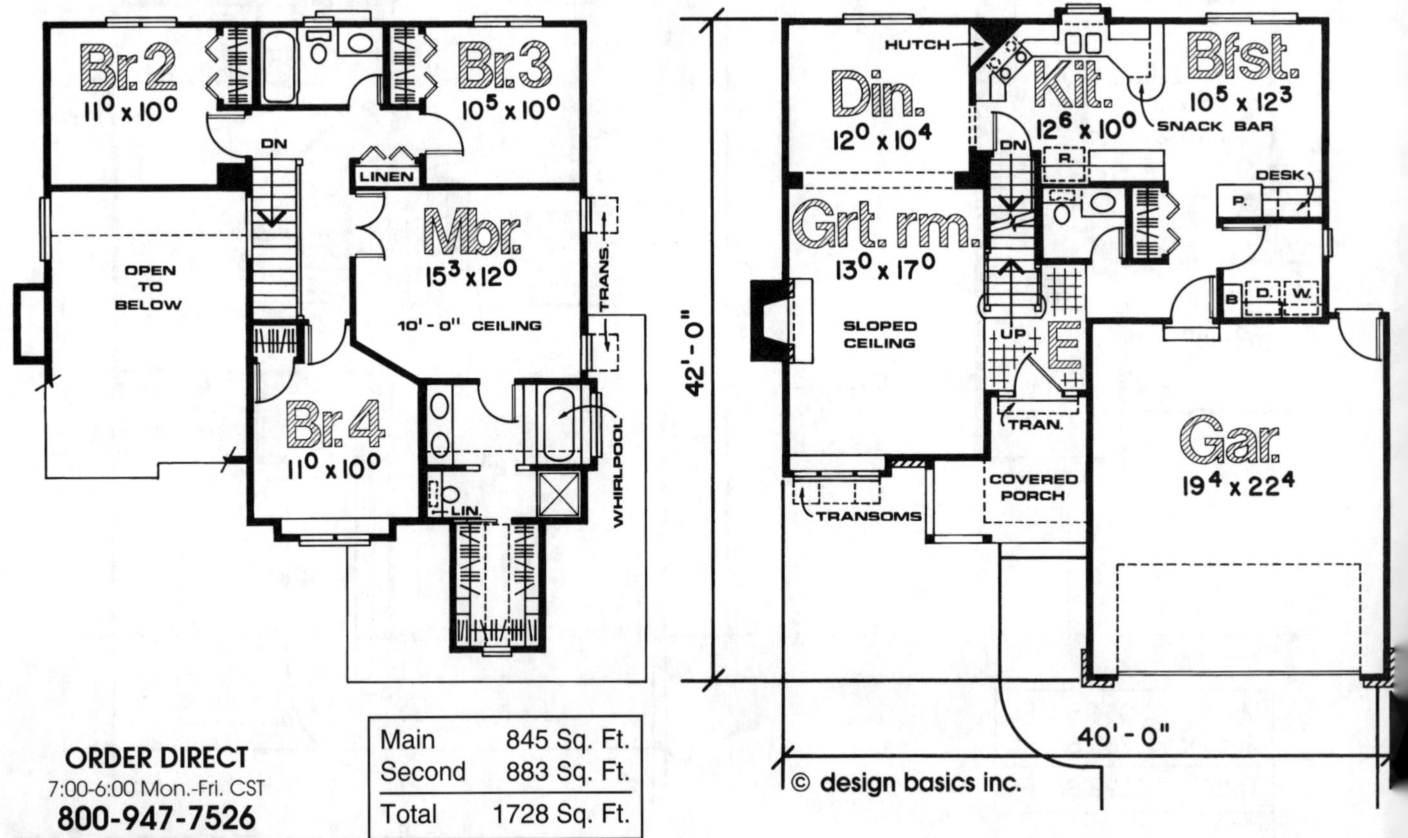

Main	845 Sq. Ft.
Second	883 Sq. Ft.
Total	1728 Sq. Ft.

9F-2700 Creston price code: 17

- High quality, erasable, reproducible vellums
- Shipped via 2nd day air within the continental U.S.

- quaint front porch provides nostalgic theme to this front elevation
- comfort and style blend together in spacious family room with fireplace and bayed windows
- convenient T-shaped staircase
- natural light floods sizeable dining room
- kitchen is designed for convenience, and maximizes counter space
- master suite is complemented by 2 sets of mirrored by-pass doors accessing spacious closets
- compartmented master bath features dual lavs, whirlpool and shower with glass block accents
- angled openings of secondary bedrooms create interest

Rear Elevation

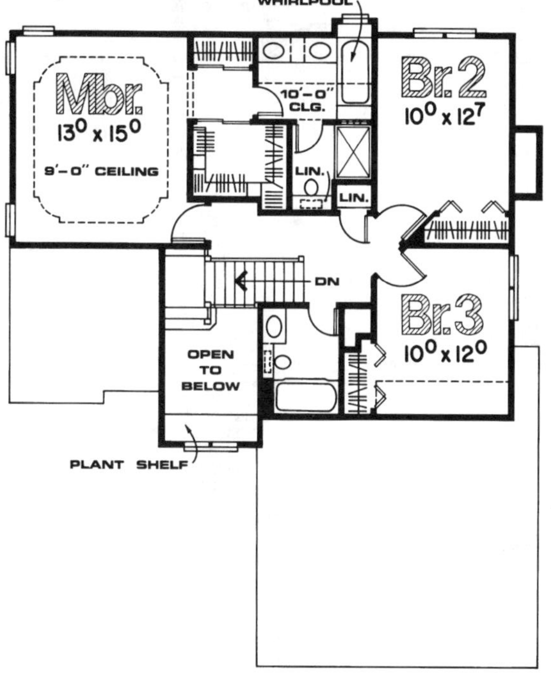

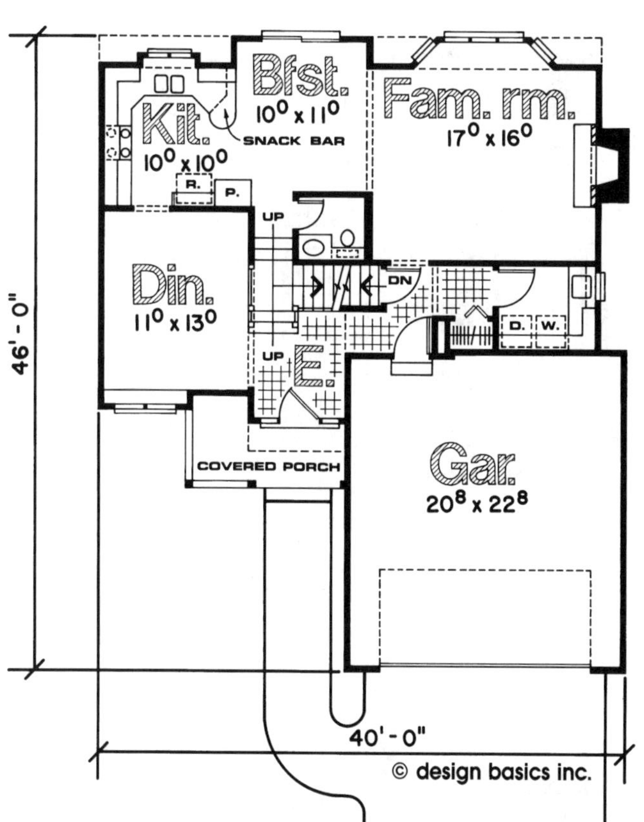

Main	912 Sq. Ft.
Second	827 Sq. Ft.
Total	1739 Sq. Ft.

9F-2547 Jasper price code: 18

Gold Seal HOME PLANS™

- High quality, erasable, reproducible vellums
- Shipped via 2nd day air within the continental U.S.

- attractive 2-story home with brick accenting front elevation
- handsome wood floor joins the family room, dinette and kitchen
- family room is highlighted by a fireplace and useful built-in bookcase
- dinette is a bright point featuring delightful bayed windows
- formal entertaining options multiply as dining room opens to volume living room
- impressive double doors lead to a distinctive master bedroom distinguished by his and her walk-in closets
- French doors open to luxurious master bath featuring dual vanities, large whirlpool and separate shower area

Rear Elevation

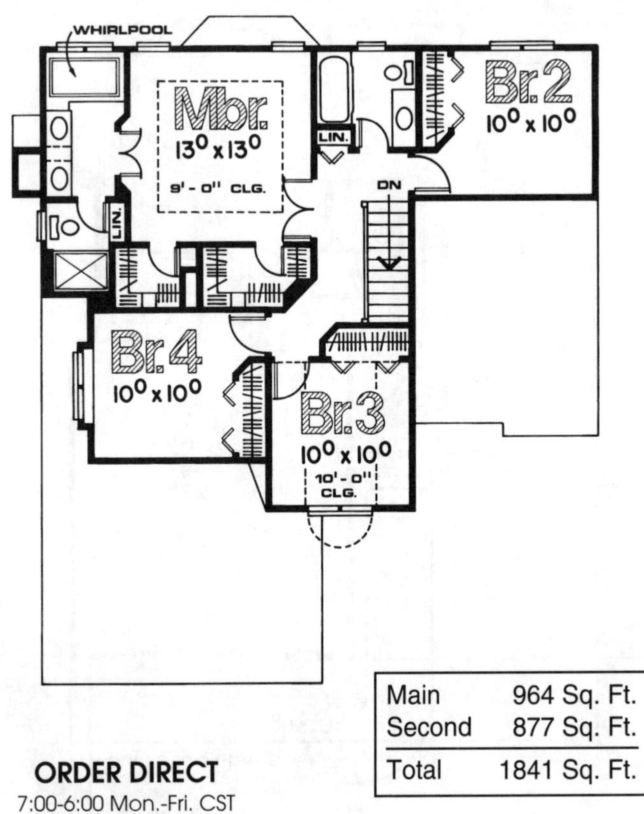

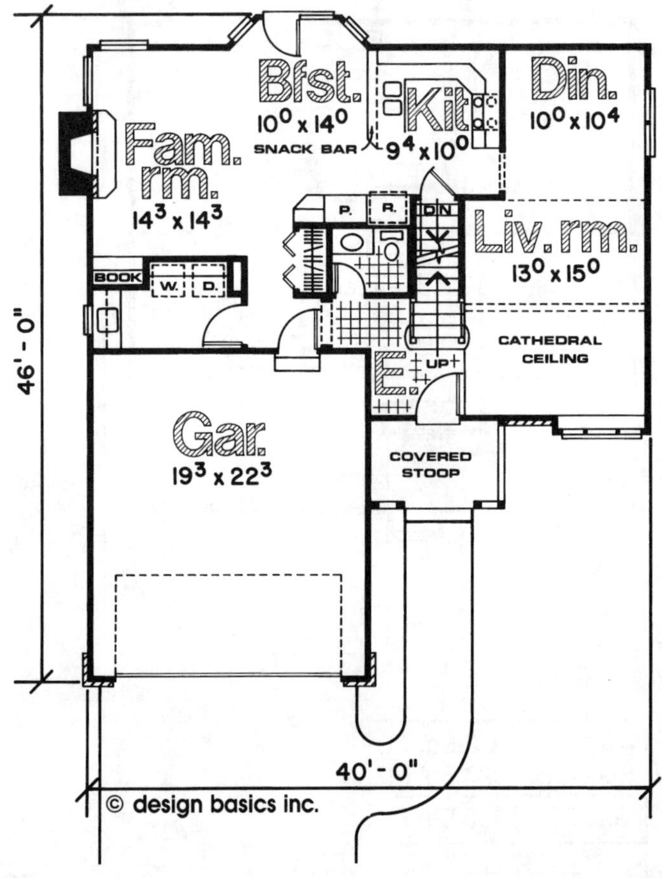

Main	964 Sq. Ft.
Second	877 Sq. Ft.
Total	1841 Sq. Ft.

ORDER DIRECT

7:00-6:00 Mon.-Fri. CST

800-947-7526

9F-2327 Brighton price code: 22

- High quality, erasable, reproducible vellums
- Shipped via 2nd day air within the continental U.S.

- charming front elevation invites attention from the street
- elegant tiled entry views living, dining and great rooms
- living room sports cathedral ceiling and impressive arched transoms
- sunny kitchen features bayed breakfast area with quick access to outside
- secondary bedrooms share bath and nearby linen closet, bedroom #2 can be used as optional loft
- luxury master bedroom enriched by elegant ceiling details
- pampering master bath/dressing area includes separate vanities, whirlpool and superb walk-in closet

Rear Elevation

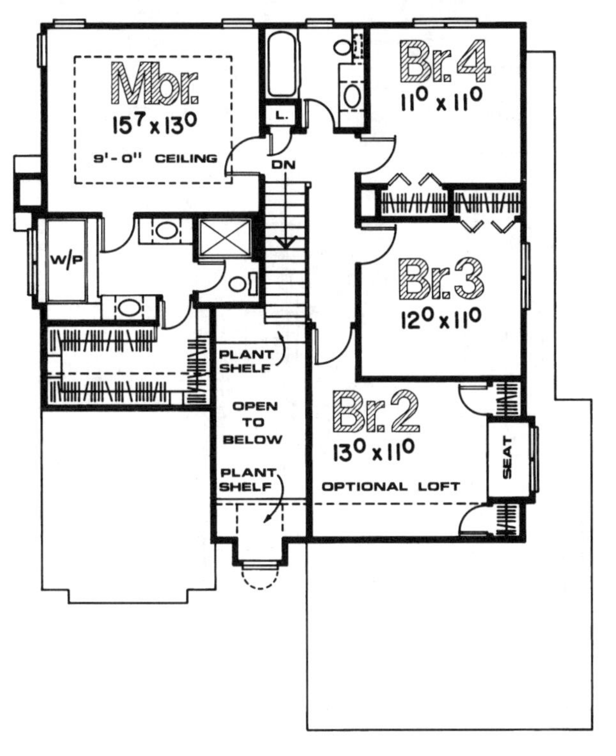

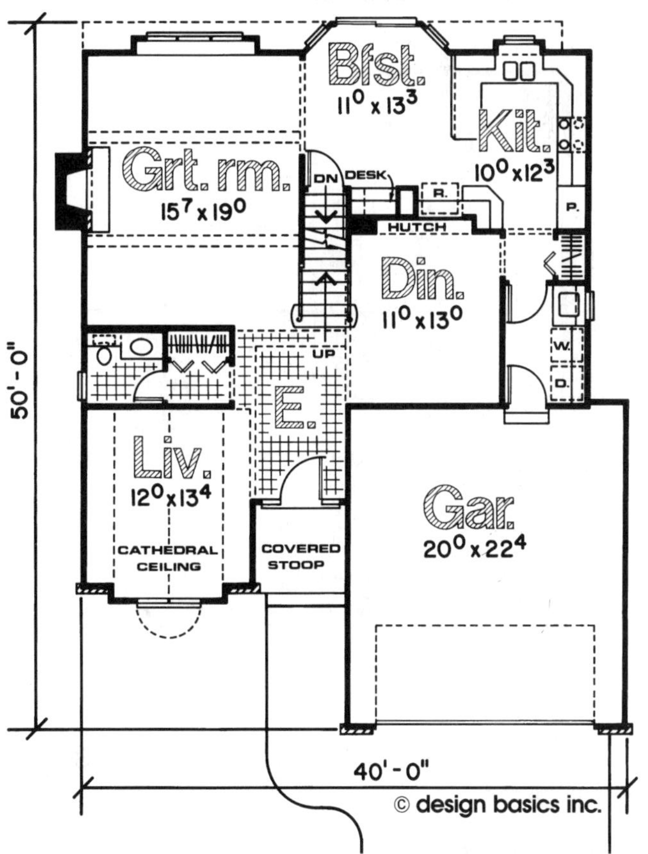

Main	1180 Sq. Ft.
Second	1038 Sq. Ft.
Total	2218 Sq. Ft.

9F-2612 Clifton price code: 22

Gold Seal HOME PLANS™

- ▶ High quality, erasable, reproducible vellums
- ▶ Shipped via 2nd day air within the continental U.S.

- majestic front elevation features arched wood-railed porch and quaint window treatment
- versatile den is styled with spider-beamed ceiling and built-in bookcase
- great room showcased by sloped ceiling and fireplace framed by twin media centers
- formal dining room uniquely set in back of home facilitating more privacy
- well planned wrap-around kitchen offers spacious pantry and quick access to centrally located laundry
- plush master suite features unique angled entrance with double doors, plus built-in dresser and entertainment center

Rear Elevation

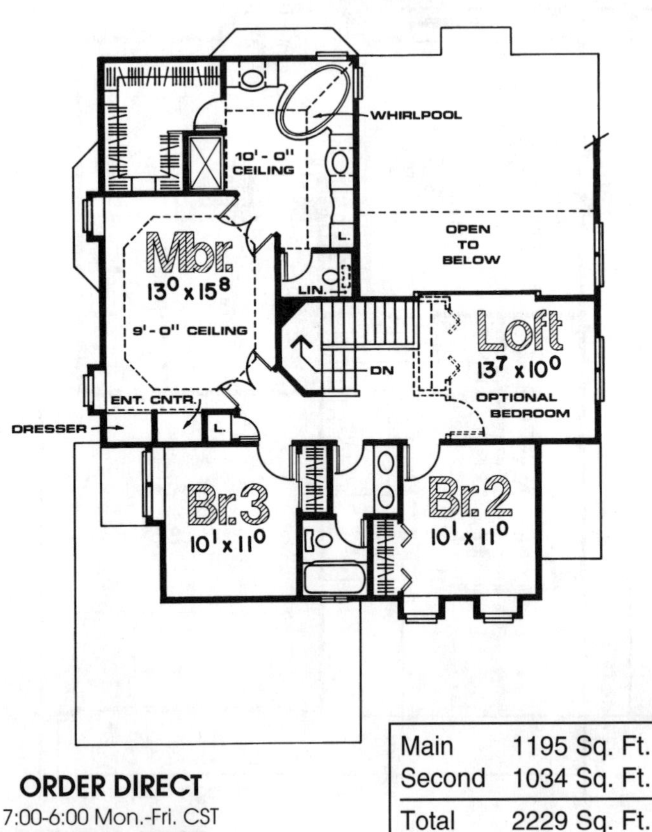

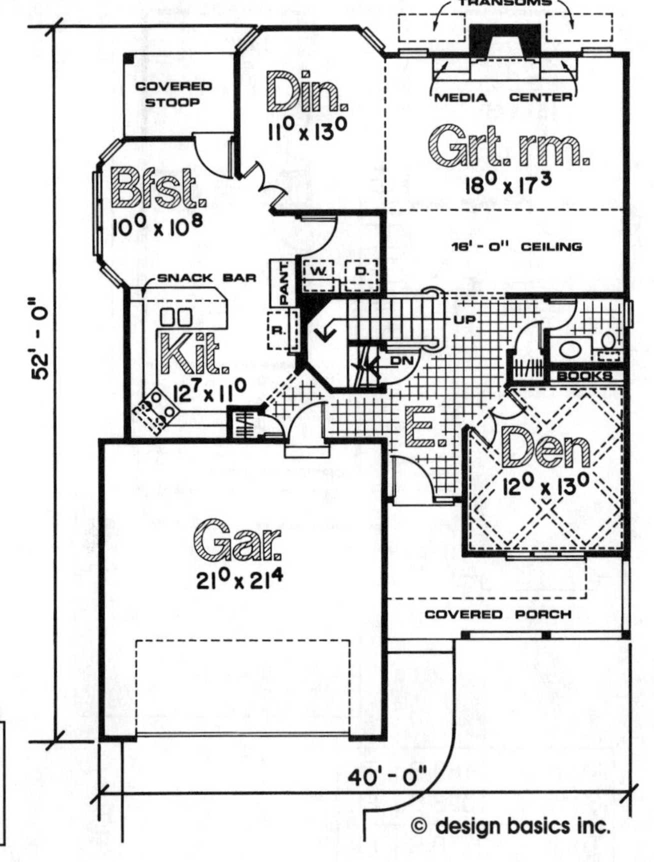

Main	1195 Sq. Ft.
Second	1034 Sq. Ft.
Total	2229 Sq. Ft.

9F-3867 Riverdale price code: 22

Gold Seal™ PLUS

- ▶ High quality, erasable, reproducible vellums
- ▶ Shipped via 2nd day air within the continental U.S.

- welcoming elevation is charmed by a covered porch with railing
- angled garage helps accommodate narrow building sites
- entry offers immediate view of formal dining room
- great room with raised-hearth fireplace accesses covered rear stoop
- kitchen with snack bar and pantry is conveniently located to both utility area and garage
- secondary bedrooms are serviced by two linen closets and a centrally-located hall bath
- spacious master suite enjoys two walk-in closets, dual vanities and a compartmented stool

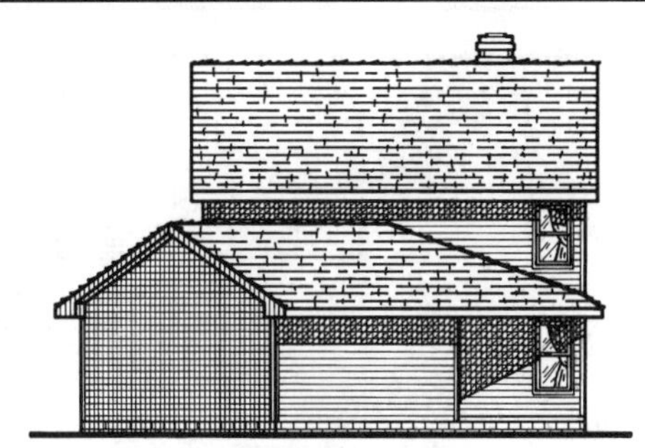

Rear Elevation

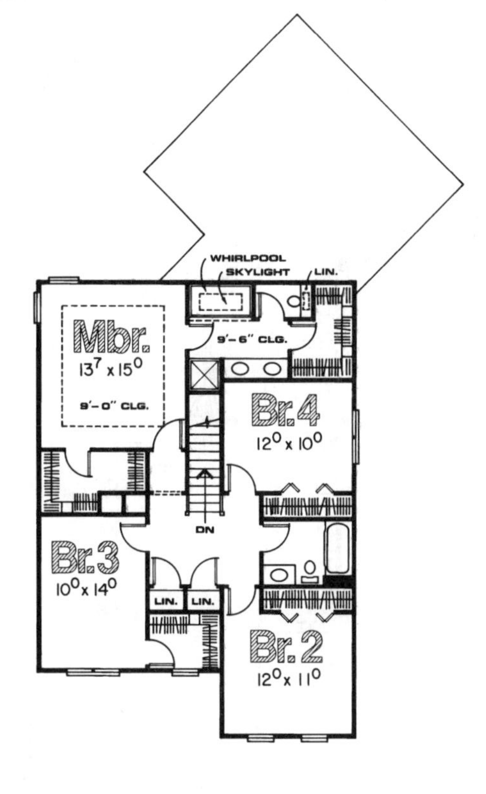

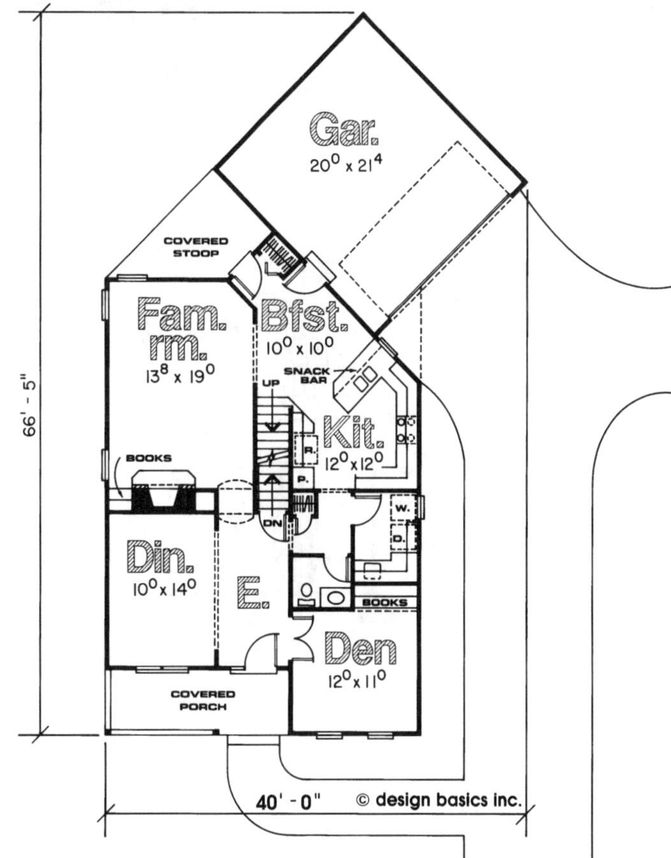

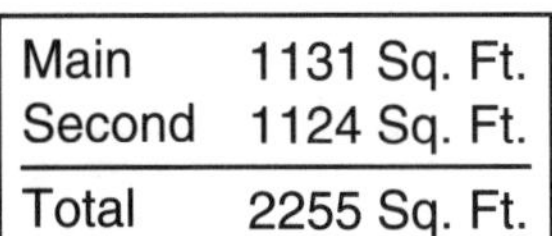

Main	1131 Sq. Ft.
Second	1124 Sq. Ft.
Total	2255 Sq. Ft.

9F-2351 Hastings price code: 22

- High quality, erasable, reproducible vellums
- Shipped via 2nd day air within the continental U.S.

- elegantly detailed elevation enhances first impressions of this home
- spectacular entry includes window above
- living room open to dining room highlighted by bowed windows
- island kitchen/dinette contain wrapping counters, pantry and convenient desk
- family room enjoys toasty fireplace, bayed windows and French door to den/optional bedroom
- comfortable secondary bedrooms
- master bedroom has cathedral ceiling, walk-in closet and French door to private balcony overlooking entry below
- luxurious bath/dressing area includes walk-in closet, whirlpool, and his and her vanities with knee space

Rear Elevation

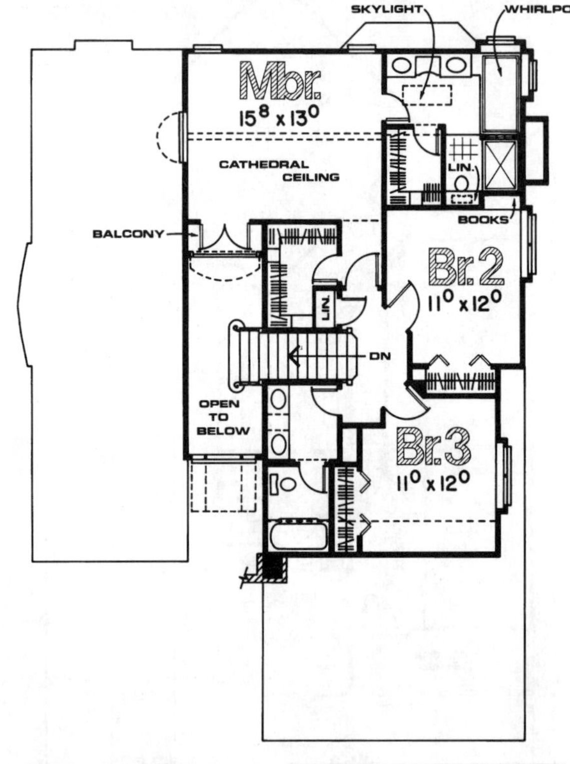

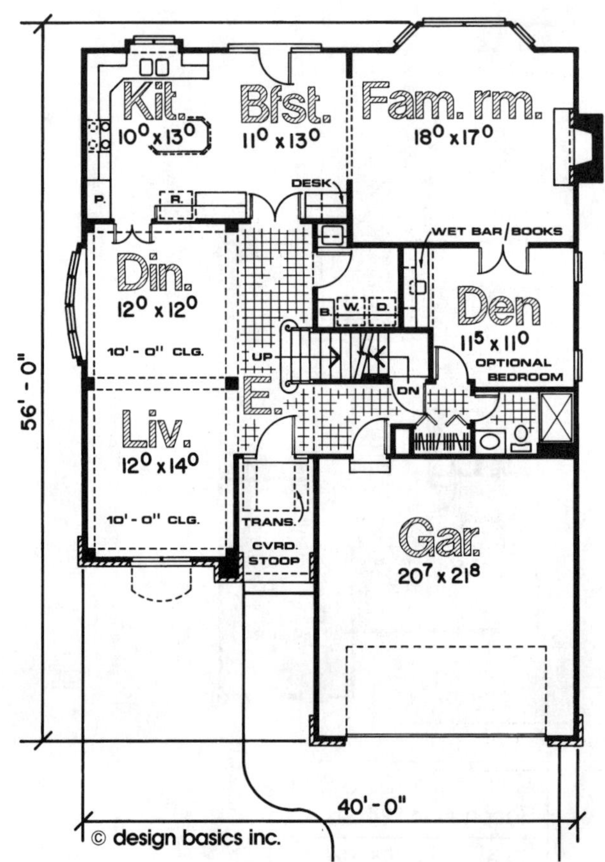

Main	1401 Sq. Ft.
Second	891 Sq. Ft.
Total	2292 Sq. Ft.

9F-3096 Torrey price code: 17

- High quality, erasable, reproducible vellums
- Shipped via 2nd day air within the continental U.S.

- covered porch and Victorian accents create this classical elevation
- double doors to entry open to spacious great room and elegant dining room
- gourmet kitchen features island/snack bar and large pantry
- French doors lead to breakfast area with access to covered porch and kitchen
- cathedral ceilings in master bedroom and dressing area add an exquiste touch
- his and her walk-in closets, large dressing area with dual lavs and whirlpool complement master bedroom
- vaulted ceiling in bedroom #2 accents window seat and arched transom window

Rear Elevation

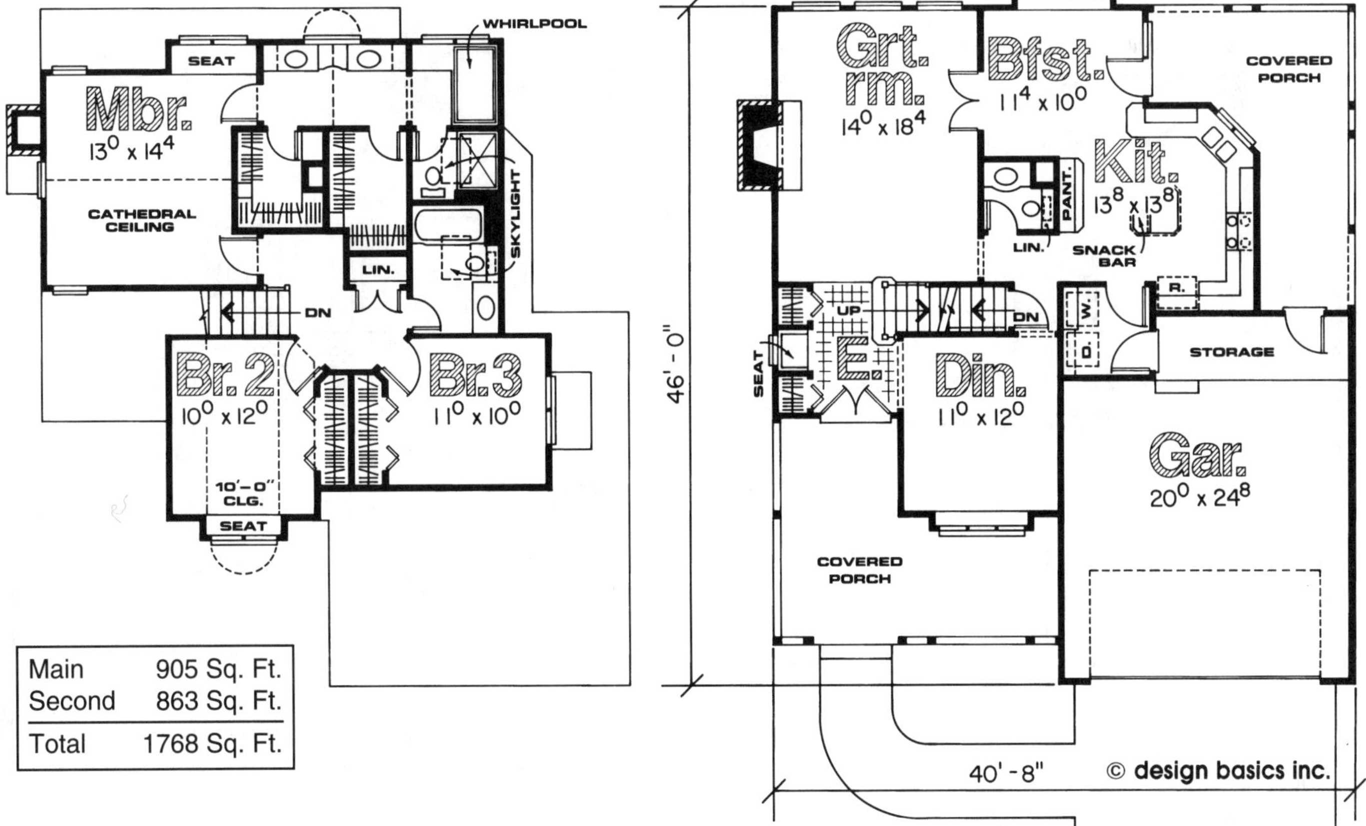

Main	905 Sq. Ft.
Second	863 Sq. Ft.
Total	1768 Sq. Ft.

9F-3098 Duncan price code: 16

- High quality, erasable, reproducible vellums
- Shipped via 2nd day air within the continental U.S.

- 2-story entry with plant shelf, open to great room
- formal dining and great room are well arranged for entertaining
- breakfast area features large patio door and useful built-in bookcase
- upstairs, secondary bedrooms have ample closet space and hall bath
- kitchen has 2 lazy Susans and snack bar
- bedroom #2 offers a built-in desk
- terrific master suite offers his and her closets and compartmented whirlpool bath

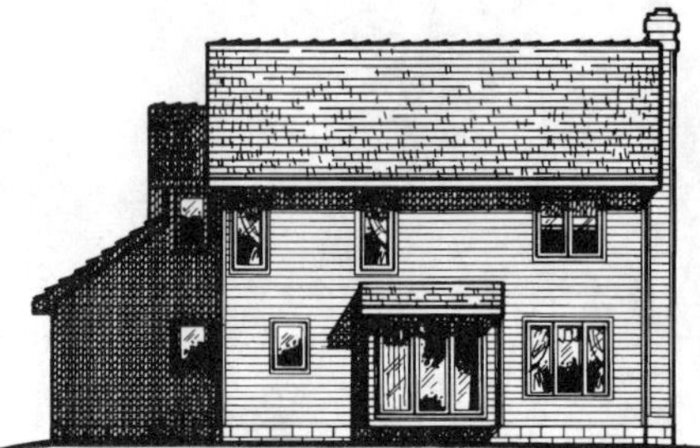

Rear Elevation

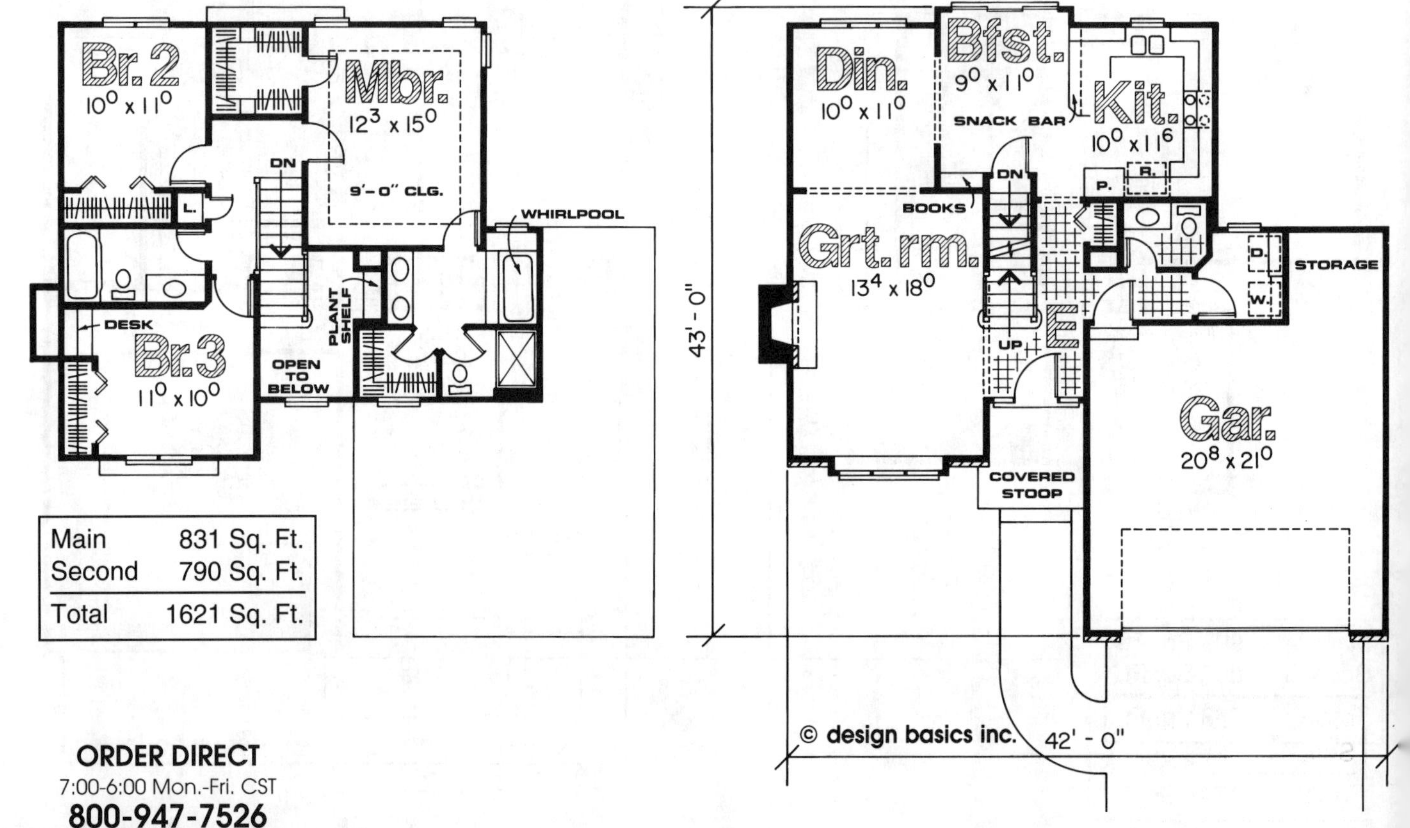

Main	831 Sq. Ft.
Second	790 Sq. Ft.
Total	1621 Sq. Ft.

ORDER DIRECT
7:00-6:00 Mon.-Fri. CST
800-947-7526

9F-971 Optima price code: 17

- hard-surfaced entry area with coat closet
- great room with sloped ceiling, bookcase and fireplace framed by windows
- laundry room with utility sink and iron-a-way
- island kitchen with lazy Susan and breakfast area accessing back yard
- stairway leads up to attractive curved balcony overlooking great room
- master bedroom with vaulted ceiling segregated from secondary bedrooms
- master dressing/bath area features skylight, walk-in closet, and compartmented stool and shower
- front bedroom has volume ceiling and beautiful arched window
- hall bath shared by secondary bedrooms

Rear Elevation

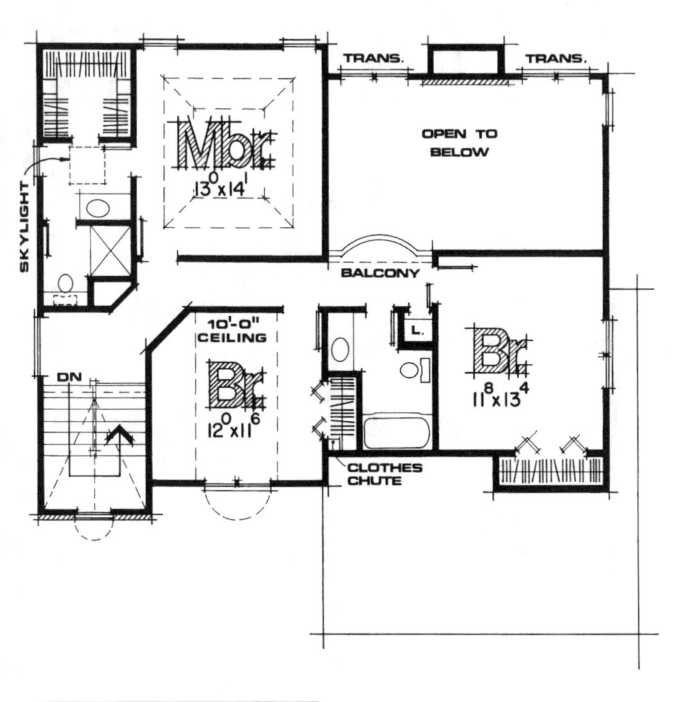

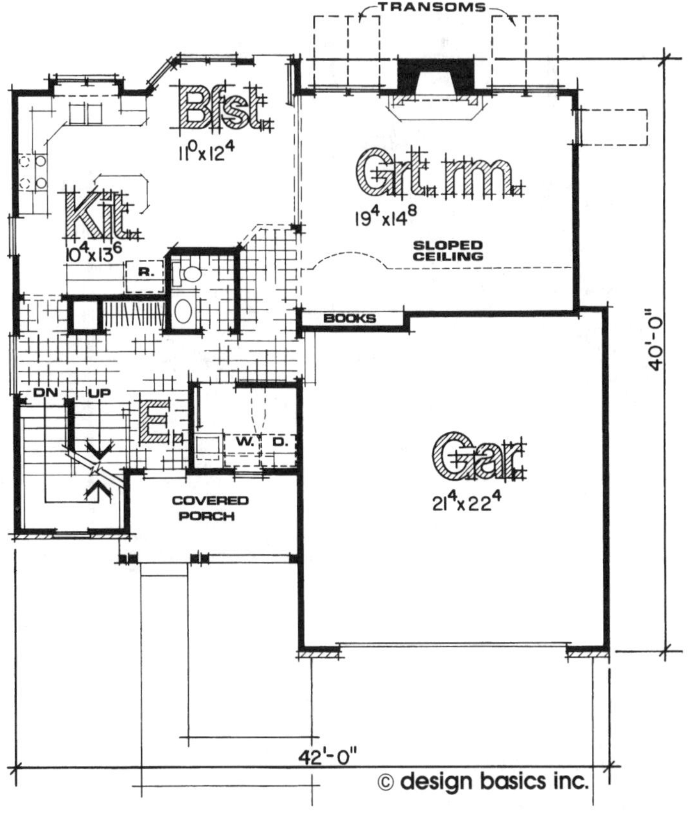

Main	890 Sq. Ft.
Second	858 Sq. Ft.
Total	1748 Sq. Ft.

9F-2949 Hartley price code: 24

Gold Seal™ HOME PLANS

- ▶ High quality, erasable, reproducible vellums
- ▶ Shipped via 2nd day air within the continental U.S.

- gabled roof and simple foundation provides affordability to this wonderful 2-story
- generous stairway landing overlooks 2-story great room highlighted by built-in cabinets surrounding a tile fireplace
- formal dining room features built-in wet bar/buffet
- well-integrated kitchen and breakfast area offers island sink with snack bar
- upstairs 3 secondary bedrooms share compartmented bath with two lavs
- cathedral ceiling with arched transom at 11-foot-high brings sophistication to master bedroom
- angled whirlpool tub, his and her vanities, walk-in closet and private shower highlight master bath

Rear Elevation

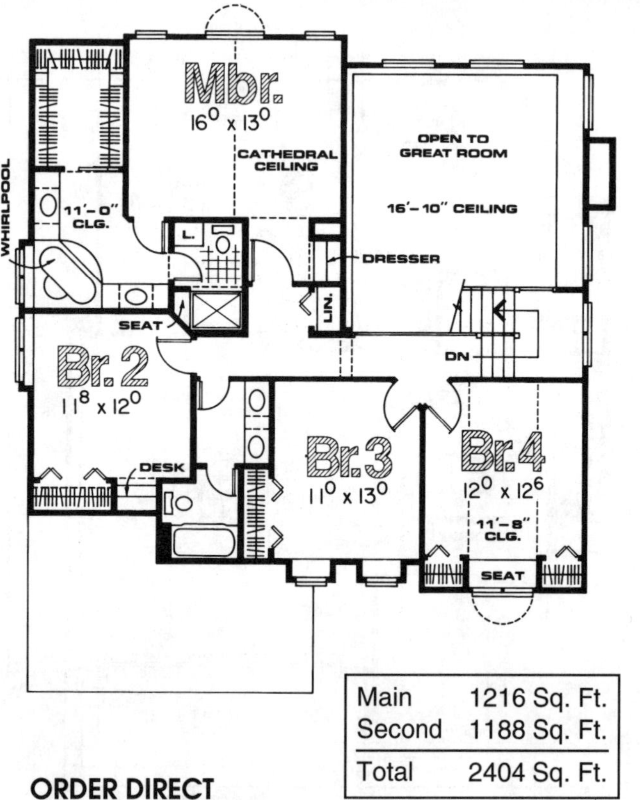

Main	1216 Sq. Ft.
Second	1188 Sq. Ft.
Total	2404 Sq. Ft.

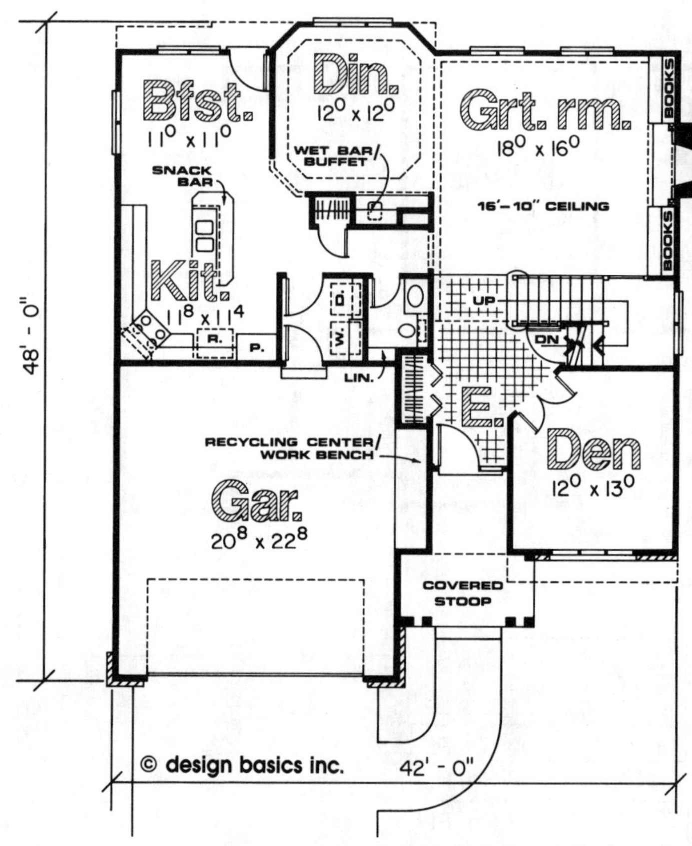

9F-2248 Laverton price code: 16

- High quality, erasable, reproducible vellums
- Shipped via 2nd day air within the continental U.S.

- quaint covered porch
- volume entry with decorator plant ledge above closet
- formal dining room with boxed window seen from entry
- large great room with fireplace and boxed window out the back
- open dinette with built-in desk
- pantry and window above sink in kitchen
- window and closet in laundry room
- upstairs landing overlooks entry below
- bedroom #3 with beautiful arched window under volume ceiling
- master bedroom with walk-in closet and pampering dressing area with double vanity and whirlpool under window

Rear Elevation

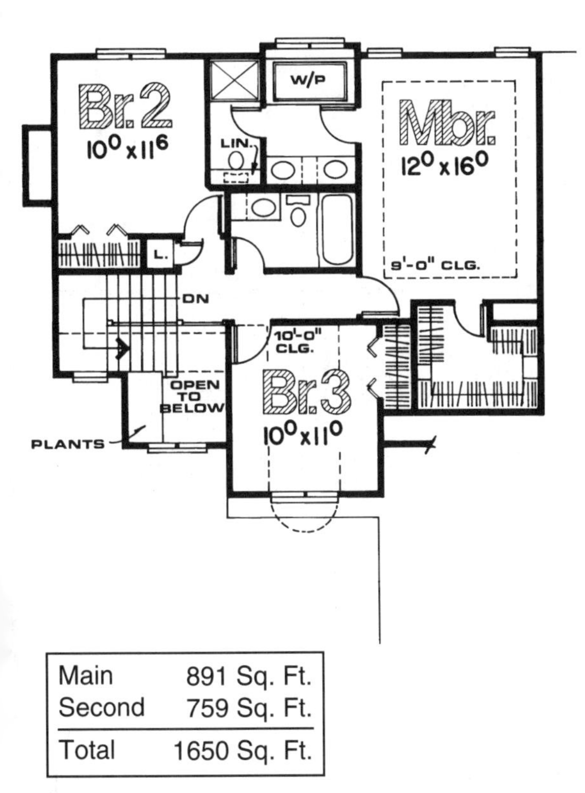

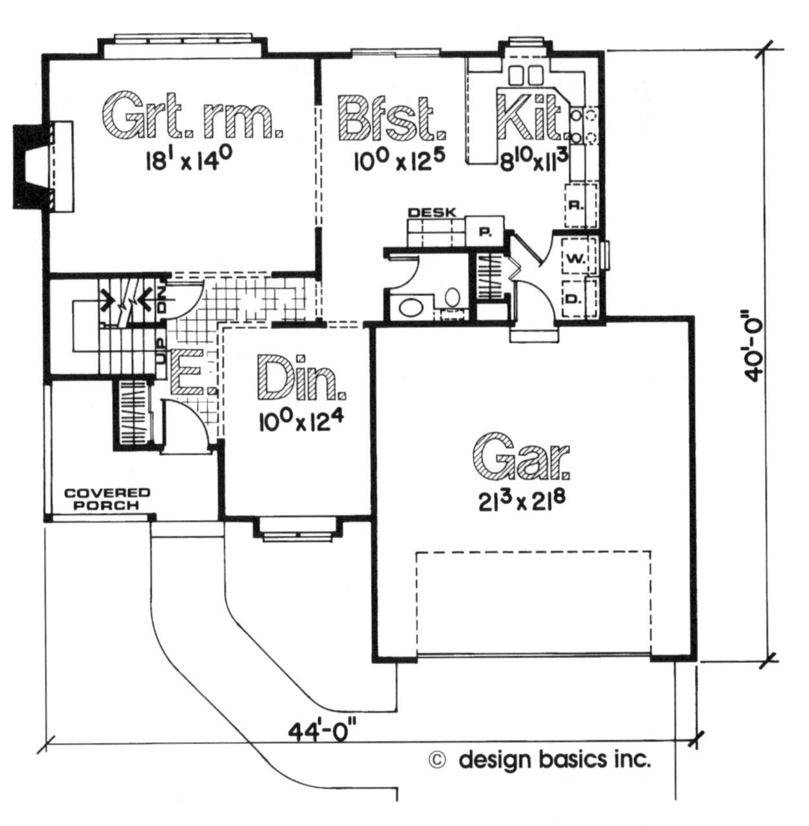

Main	891 Sq. Ft.
Second	759 Sq. Ft.
Total	1650 Sq. Ft.

9F-2246 Augusta price code: 17

- High quality, erasable, reproducible vellums
- Shipped via 2nd day air within the continental U.S.

- inviting wrap-around front porch
- entry open to formal dining room with boxed window and interesting staircase
- large great room with windows out the back and raised hearth fireplace
- open dinette with built-in desk
- windows over sink plus pantry in kitchen with handy access to laundry room
- convenient entrance with closet from garage
- upstairs landing views decorator plant ledge and entry below
- beautiful arched window and volume ceiling in bedroom #4
- boxed ceiling in master bedroom with generous closets and corner windows
- master bath area with double vanity, whirlpool and private stool and shower

Rear Elevation

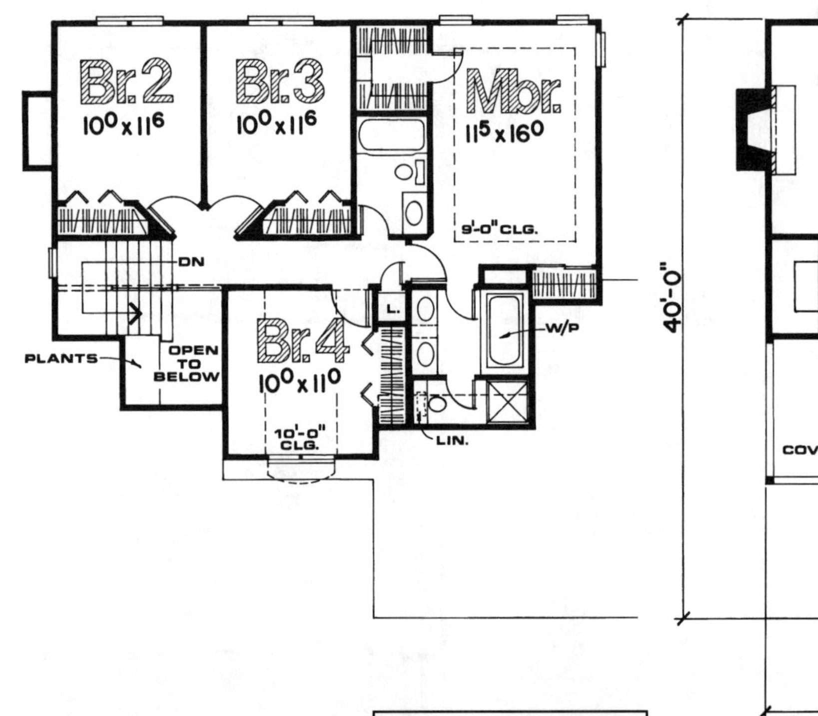

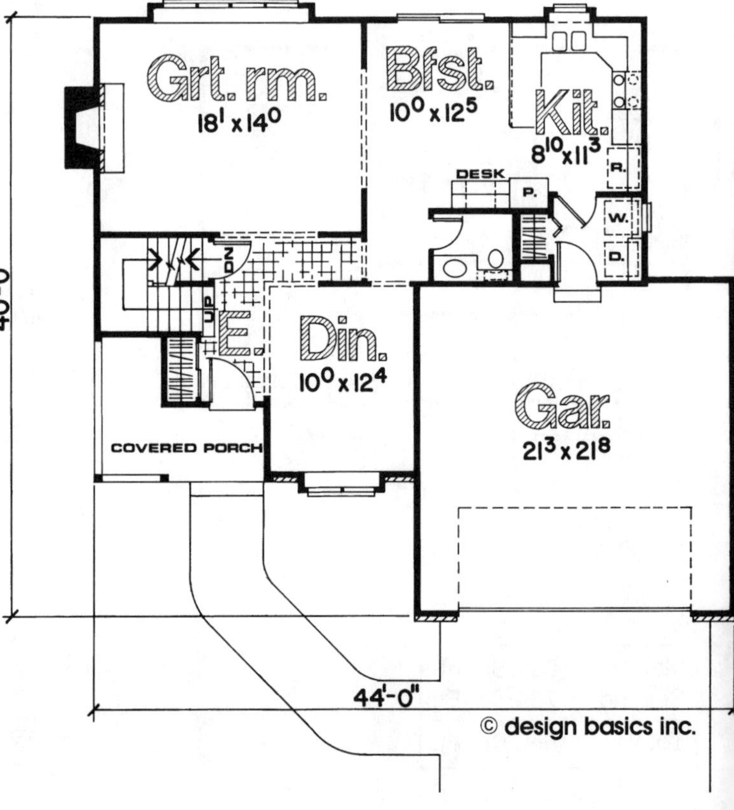

Main	891 Sq. Ft.
Second	885 Sq. Ft.
Total	1776 Sq. Ft.

9F-3383 Hackett price code: 17

- High quality, erasable, reproducible vellums
- Shipped via 2nd day air within the continental U.S.

- exciting curb appeal enhanced by long front porch and gingerbread accents
- transom windows and 11'-0" ceiling adorn great room
- interesting angles and unique snack bar highlight unforgettable kitchen
- bowed breakfast area links great room and kitchen
- master bedroom has 9'-0" boxed ceiling, large walk-in closet and pampering bath
- centrally located main floor powder room
- U-shaped staircase leads to second floor where balcony views entry below
- three secondary bedrooms served by full bath and two hall linen closets

Rear Elevation

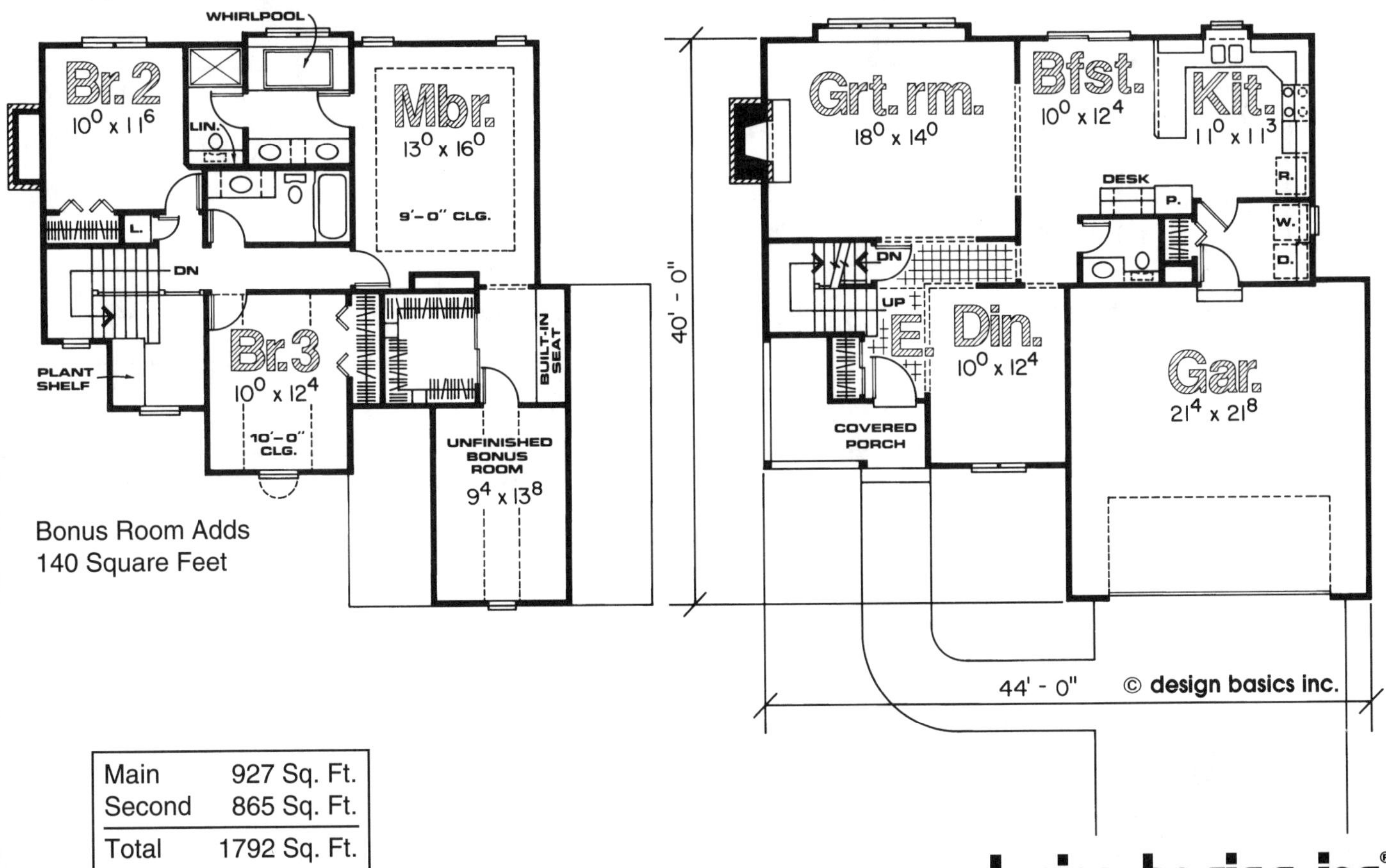

Bonus Room Adds
140 Square Feet

Main	927 Sq. Ft.
Second	865 Sq. Ft.
Total	1792 Sq. Ft.

design basics inc.®
HOME PLAN DESIGN SERVICE

9F-1752 Lancaster price code: 18

- High quality, erasable, reproducible vellums
- Shipped via 2nd day air within the continental U.S.

- 2-story entry with large coat closet and plant shelf above
- strategically located staircase
- great room with many windows
- island kitchen with boxed window over sink
- large bayed dinette
- convenient powder bath location
- main floor laundry
- volume ceiling and arched window in front bedroom
- pleasant secondary bedrooms with interesting angles
- large master suite with his and her walk-in closets, corner windows and bath area featuring double vanity and whirlpool bath

Rear Elevation

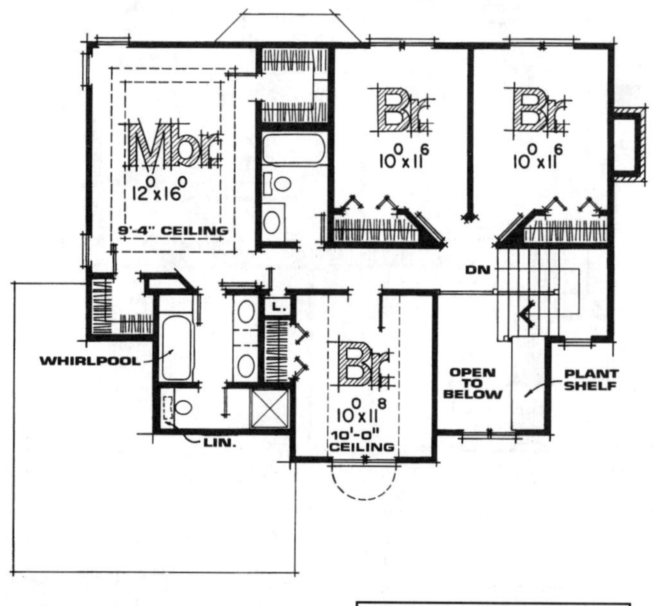

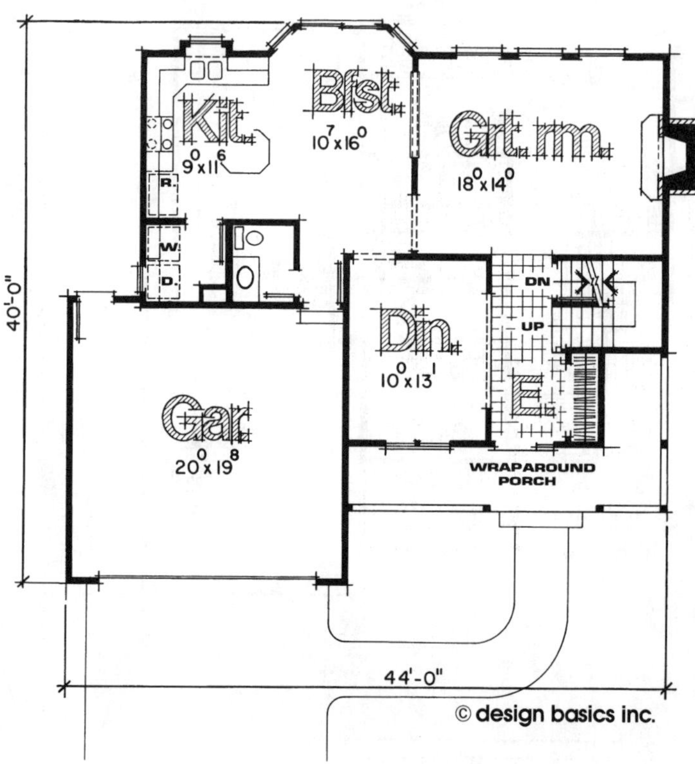

Main	919 Sq. Ft.
Second	927 Sq. Ft.
Total	1846 Sq. Ft.

ORDER DIRECT
7:00-6:00 Mon.-Fri. CST
800-947-7526

9F-1572 Burton price code: 19

- High quality, erasable, reproducible vellums
- Shipped via 2nd day air within the continental U.S.

- tasteful balace of brick and siding
- view from entry to see-thru fireplace and wall of windows in great room
- thoughtful traffic patterns
- strategic powder bath location
- bayed breakfast area into island kitchen with fireplace and built-in pantry
- staircase open to entry
- plant ledge above entry closet
- clothes chute and double lavs in hall bath
- French doors into master bedroom with vaulted ceiling and walk-in closet
- double lavs and whirlpool tub in master bath
- generous secondary bedrooms

Rear Elevation

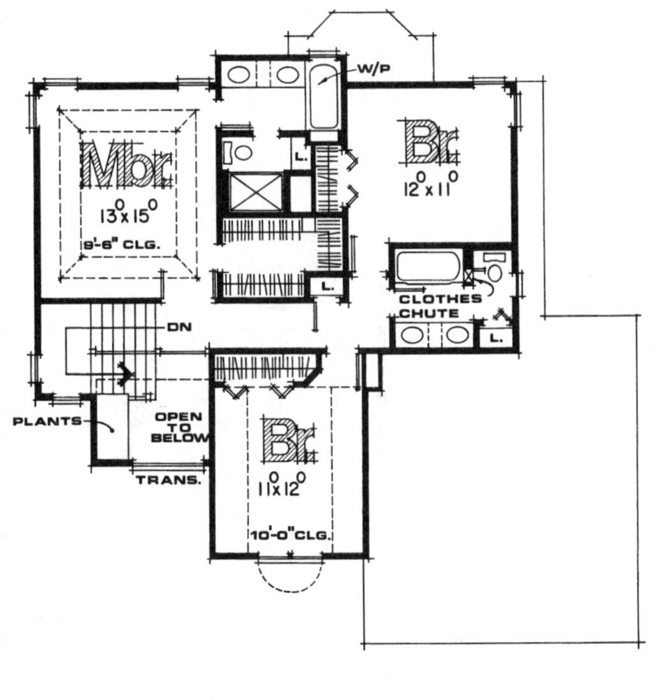

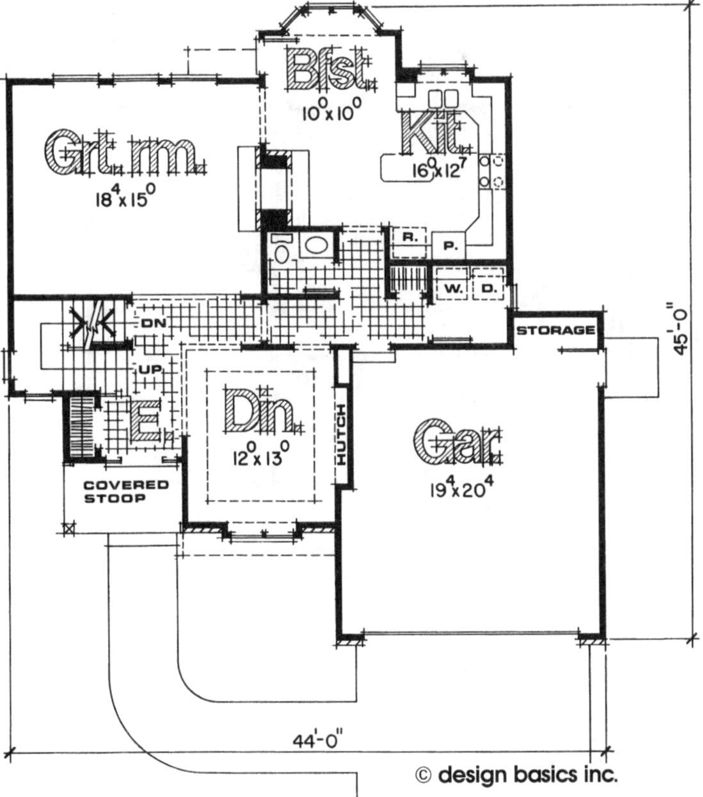

Main	1012 Sq. Ft.
Second	900 Sq. Ft.
Total	1912 Sq. Ft.

9F-2217 Yorke price code: 20

- 2-story entry open to interesting staircase and formal dining room with boxed window and hutch space
- great room with large windows, entertainment center and see-thru fireplace
- hearth room takes advantage of see-thru fireplace
- island counter, desk and pantry in kitchen open to bayed dinette
- closet for garage entrance
- window in laundry room
- vaulted ceiling and unique angle into walk-in closet and dressing area make this a special master suite
- irresistible oval whirlpool under arched window and his and her vanities in master bath/dressing area

Rear Elevation

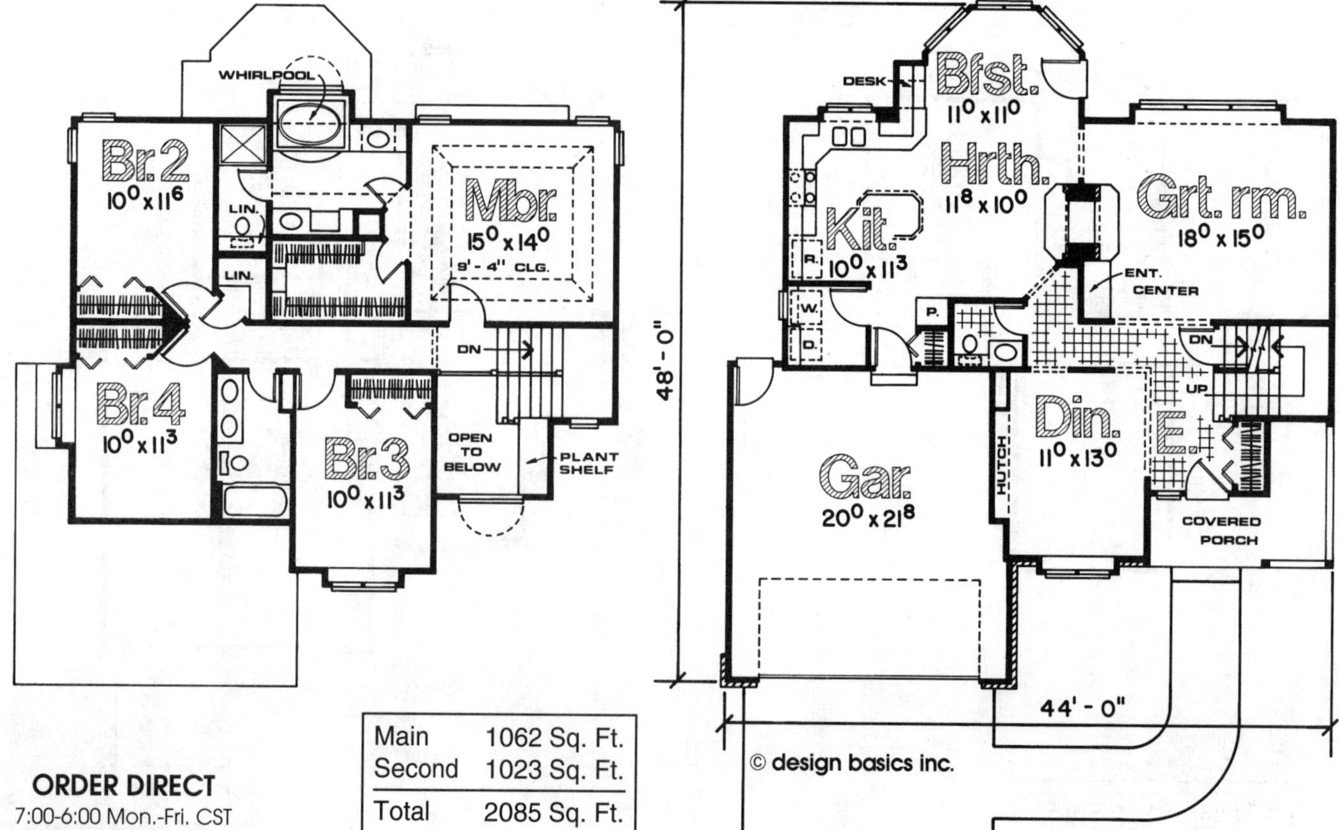

Main	1062 Sq. Ft.
Second	1023 Sq. Ft.
Total	2085 Sq. Ft.

9F-3097 Lincoln price code: 17

- ▶ High quality, erasable, reproducible vellums
- ▶ Shipped via 2nd day air within the continental U.S.

Gold Seal HOME PLANS™

- traditional elevation combines aesthetics and economy
- symmetrical coat closets and cased openings frame view to great room and entry
- versatile dining room has parlor option
- bayed dinette with back yard access and staircase to second level
- deluxe laundry room and built-in bookcase provide ample amenities to fantastic upper level
- luxurious master suite contains built-in dresser between his and her walk-in closets
- roomy compartmented dressing area with whirlpool
- extra storage in deep garage

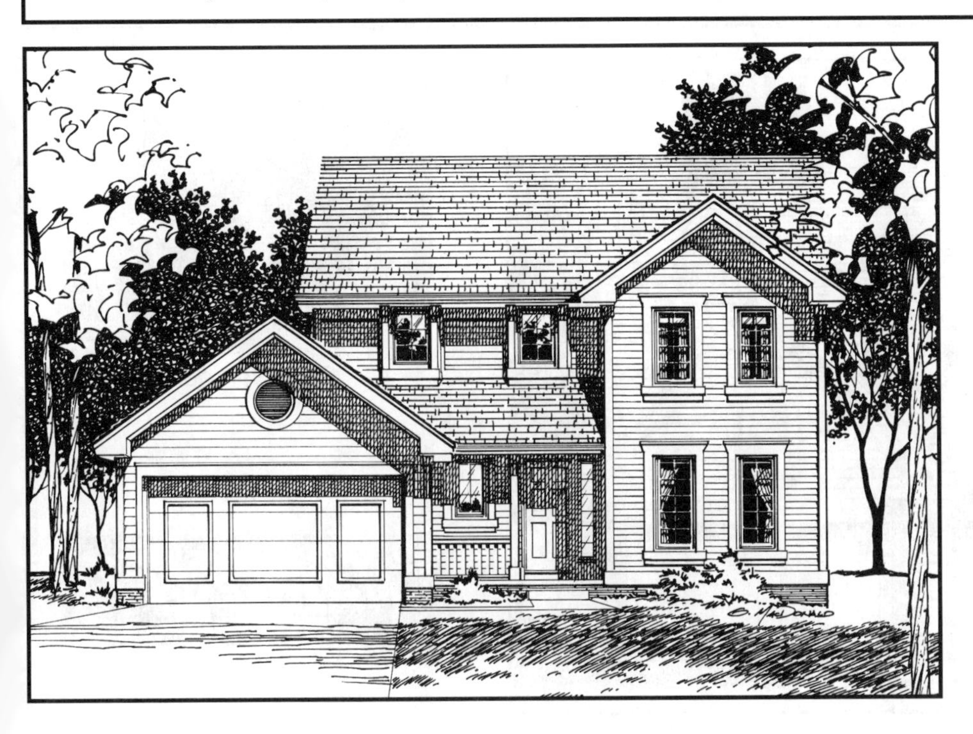

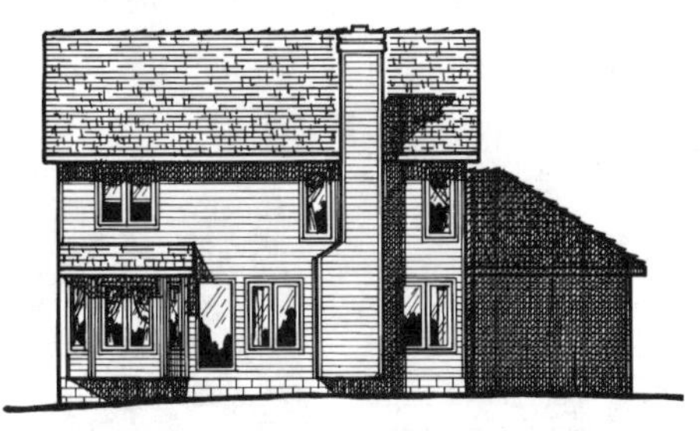

Rear Elevation

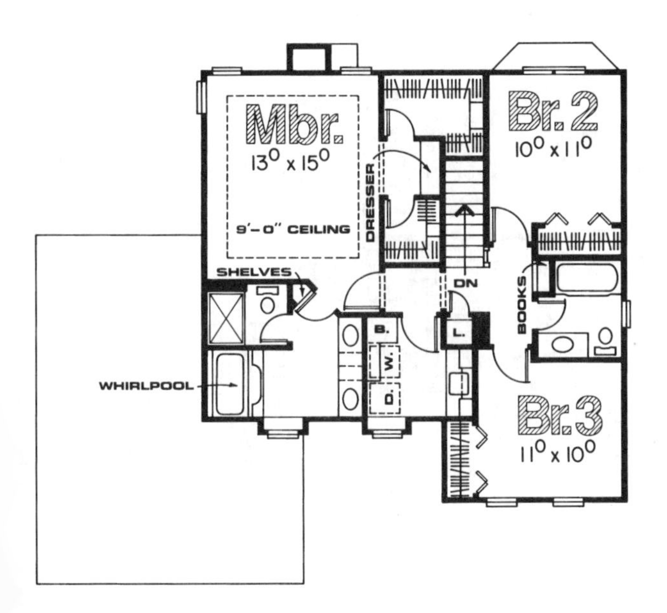

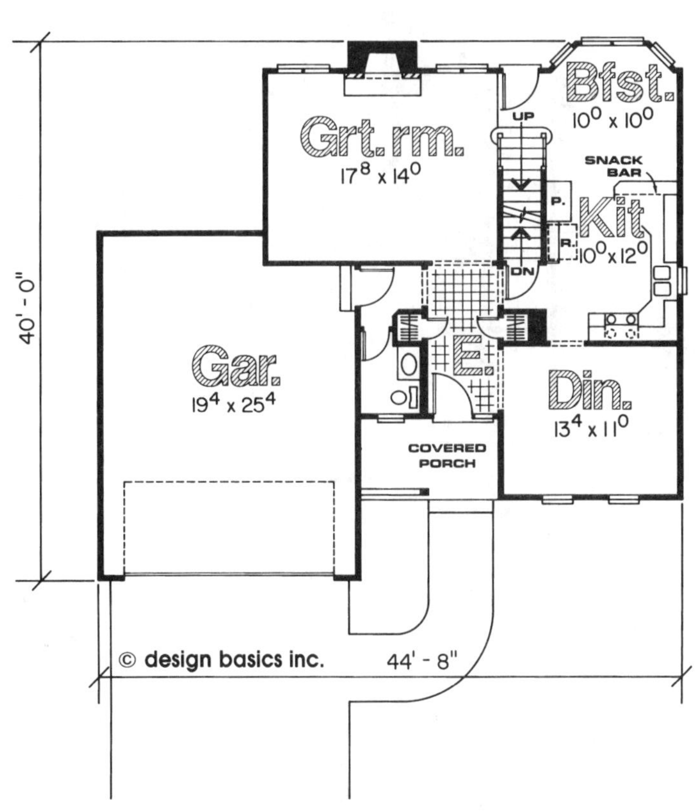

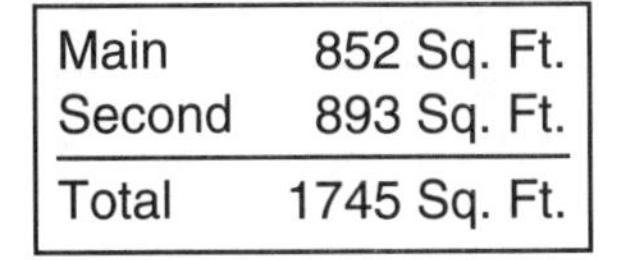

Main	852 Sq. Ft.
Second	893 Sq. Ft.
Total	1745 Sq. Ft.

9F-2952 Francis price code: 17

- ▸ High quality, erasable, reproducible vellums
- ▸ Shipped via 2nd day air within the continental U.S.

- gabled roof, arched window and covered porch add to this country style home
- formal parlor offers 10-foot ceiling and dining room option
- French doors in entry open to breakfast area with patio door to covered deck
- island kitchen features wrapping pantry and convenient access to large family room
- upstairs, secondary bedrooms each have a desk
- large bonus room accessible from main hall is perfect for kids' use
- whirlpool bath with arched opening and French doors highlight sun-filled master suite

Rear Elevation

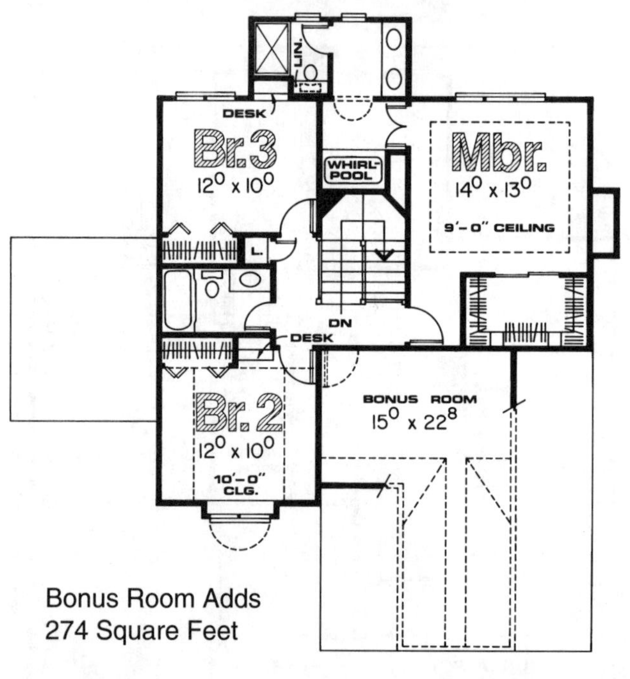

Bonus Room Adds 274 Square Feet

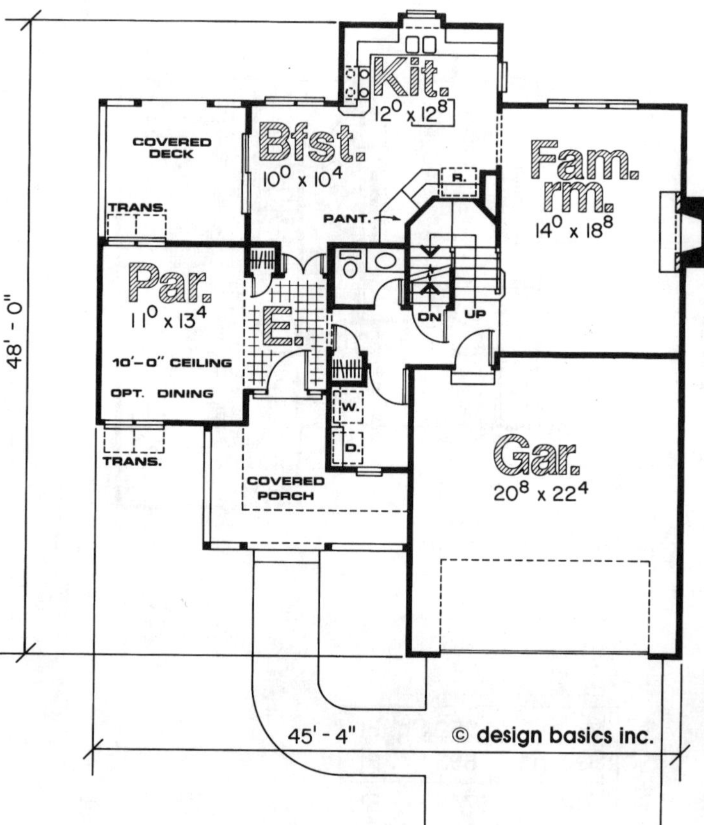

Main	976 Sq. Ft.
Second	823 Sq. Ft.
Total	1799 Sq. Ft.

9F-3103 Ashworth price code: 17

- High quality, erasable, reproducible vellums
- Shipped via 2nd day air within the continental U.S.

- traditional elevation with covered porch provides mass appeal
- U-stairs and French doors highlight entry
- large cased openings define formal dining room and great room without restricting space
- bayed kitchen and breakfast area have functional access to utility area and side yard
- secondary bedrooms share generous compartmented bath with dual lavs
- his and her walk-in closets, 9-foot-high boxed ceiling and whirlpool bath create stately master suite
- workbench and extra storage space in garage

Rear Elevation

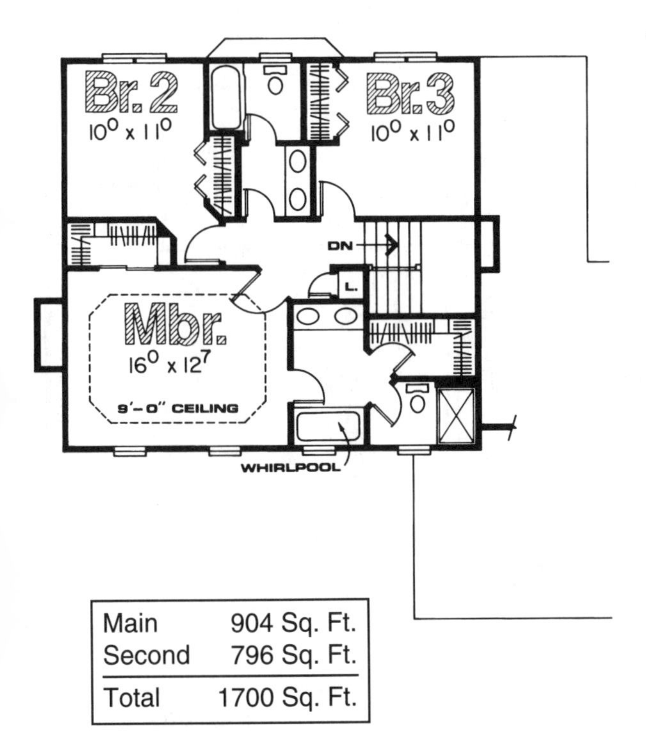

Main	904 Sq. Ft.
Second	796 Sq. Ft.
Total	1700 Sq. Ft.

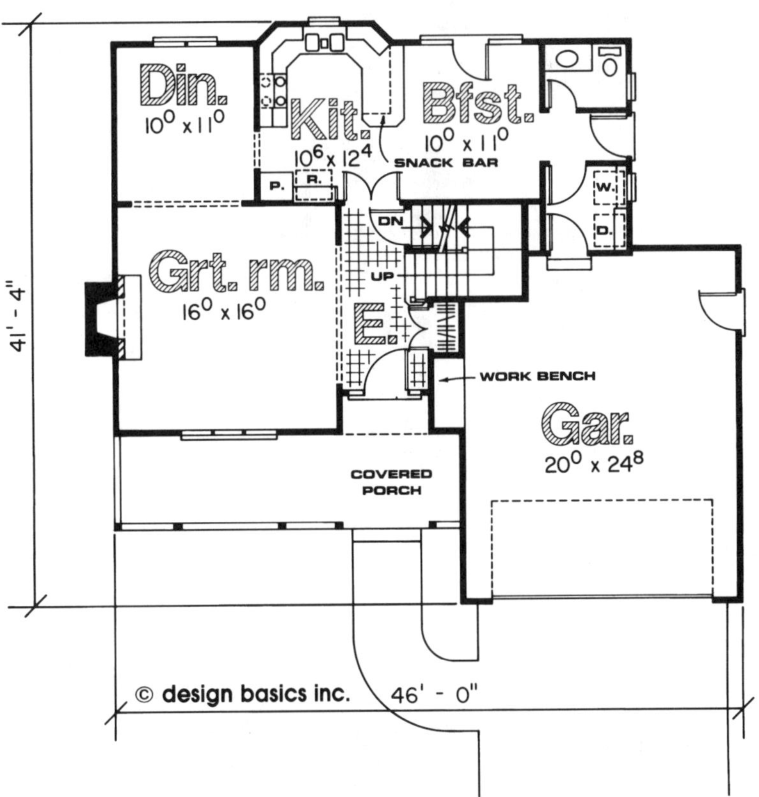

9F-2308 Juniper price code: 17

- sleek lines, covered porch and window details enhance elevation
- volume entry views bright living room with adjoining dining room
- kitchen enjoys gourmet features and bayed dinette
- family room enhanced by window-brightened wall and raised-hearth fireplace
- garage includes extra storage space
- bedroom #2 includes huge walk-in closet
- secondary bedrooms convenient to bath
- hall design affords seclusion to luxurious master suite with boxed ceiling
- pampering master bath/dressing area includes two closets, whirlpool with plant sill and double lavs

Rear Elevation

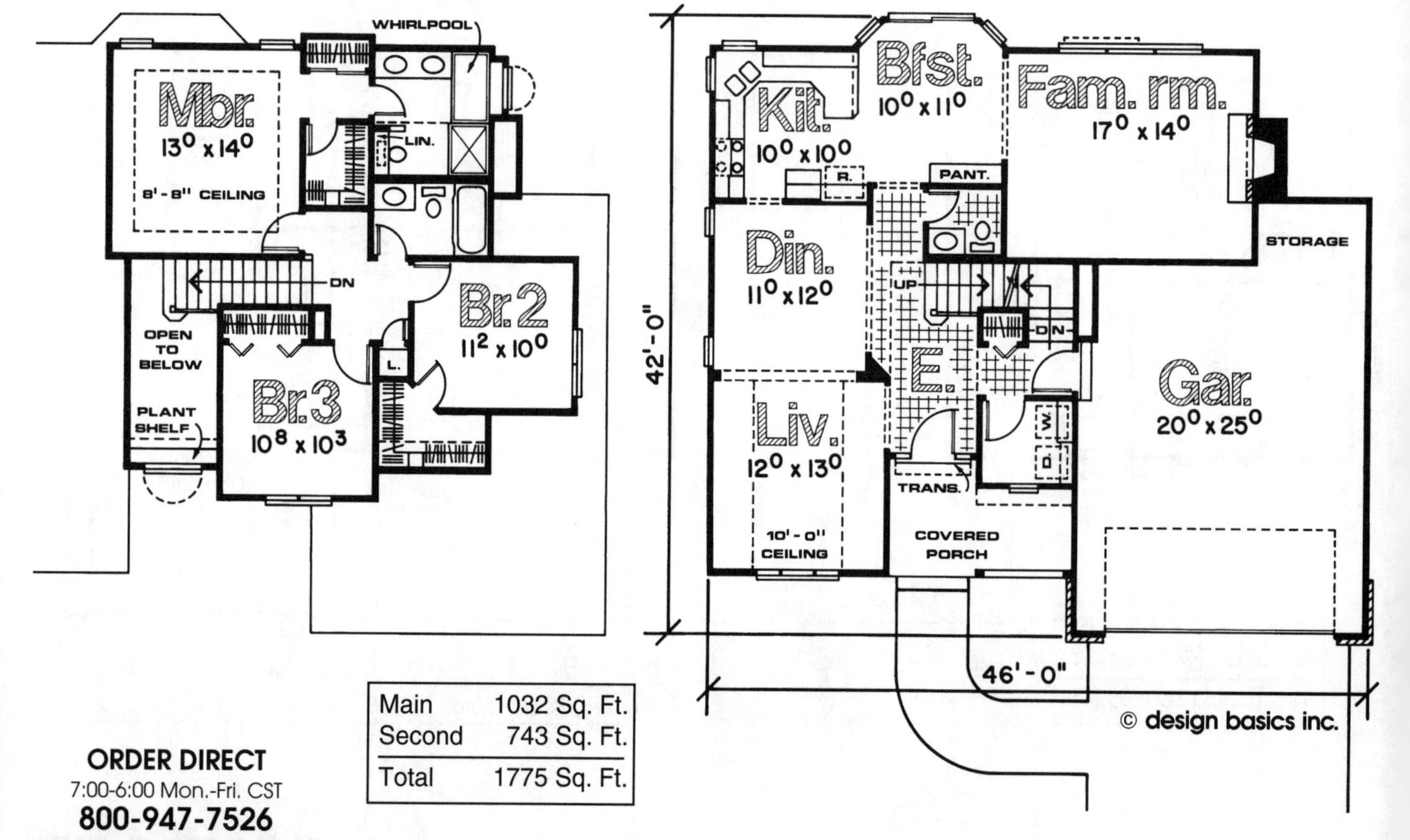

Main	1032 Sq. Ft.
Second	743 Sq. Ft.
Total	1775 Sq. Ft.

9F-3576 Walton price code: 17

Gold Seal PLUS

- High quality, erasable, reproducible vellums
- Shipped via 2nd day air within the continental U.S.

- wrapping porch brings out farmhouse charm
- oak entry views formal parlor with French doors connecting it to kitchen
- family room displays fireplace and view to backyard
- flexible dining area showcases boxed window and accesses covered side-yard porch
- two lazy Susans and snack bar equip kitchen
- second floor landing overlooks volume entry
- walk-in closet and whirlpool complement master suite
- two secondary bedrooms are served by full bath
- laundry room boasts soaking sink and sunny window

Rear Elevation

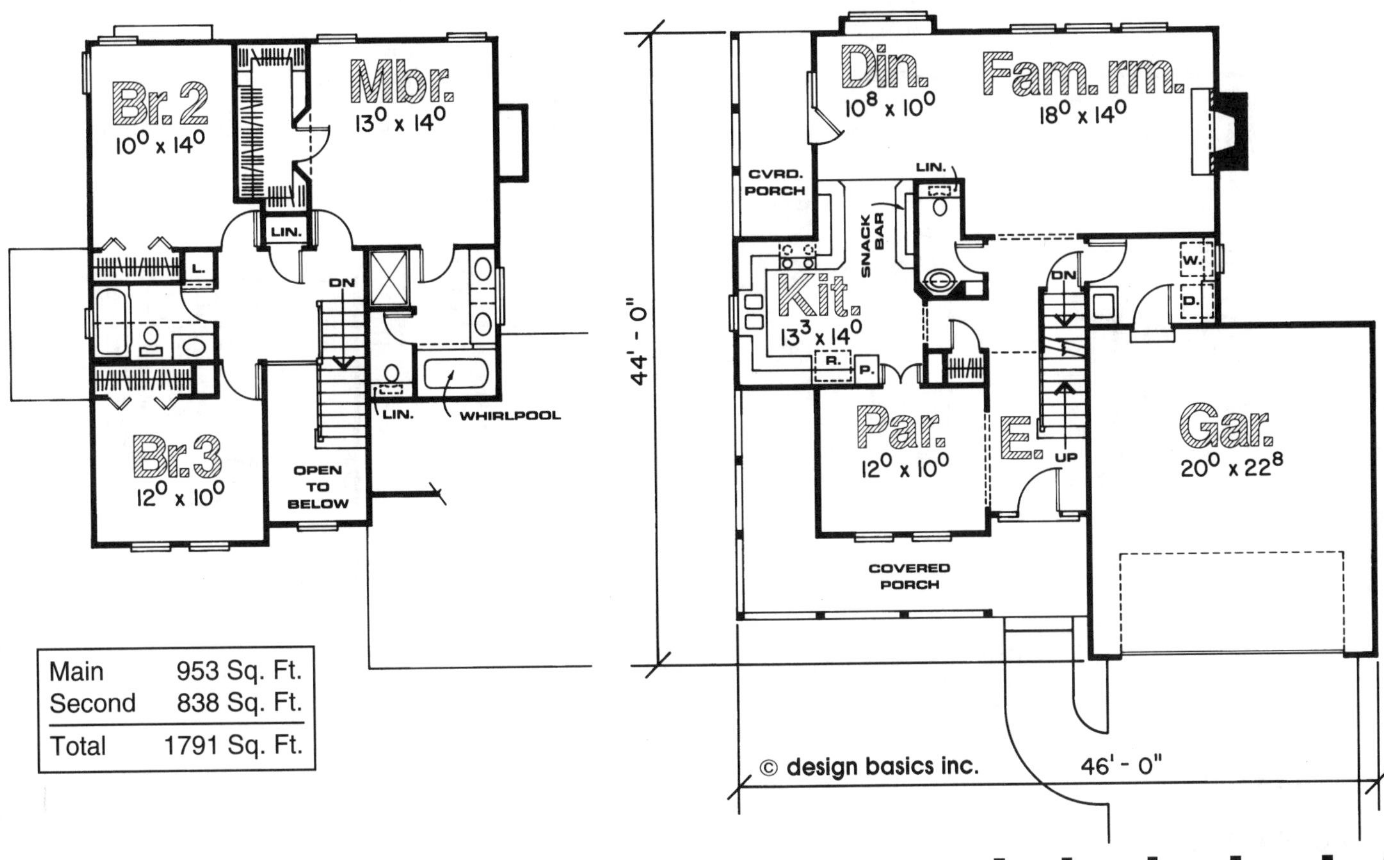

Main	953 Sq. Ft.
Second	838 Sq. Ft.
Total	1791 Sq. Ft.

design basics inc.® HOME PLAN DESIGN SERVICE

9F-1868 Somerset price code: 18

Gold Seal HOME PLANS™

- High quality, erasable, reproducible vellums
- Shipped via 2nd day air within the continental U.S.

- appealing porch graces elevation
- light and airy 2-story entrance with large guest closet and plant shelf above
- formal dining room encourages intimate meals or entertaining options
- row of picture/awning windows show-case great room with striking fireplace
- expansive island kitchen and bayed breakfast area with open view to back yard
- secondary bedrooms afford comfort and privacy
- lovely master suite with tiered ceiling in-cludes compartmented bath, two walk-in closets, dual lavs and whirlpool tub

Rear Elevation

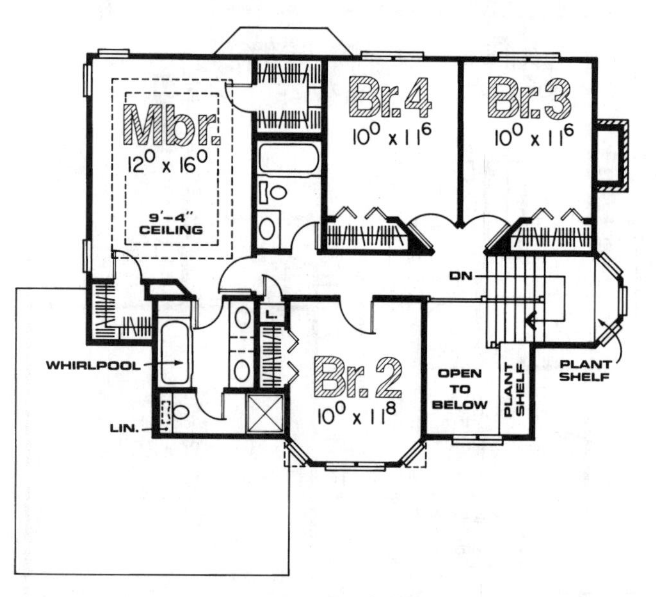

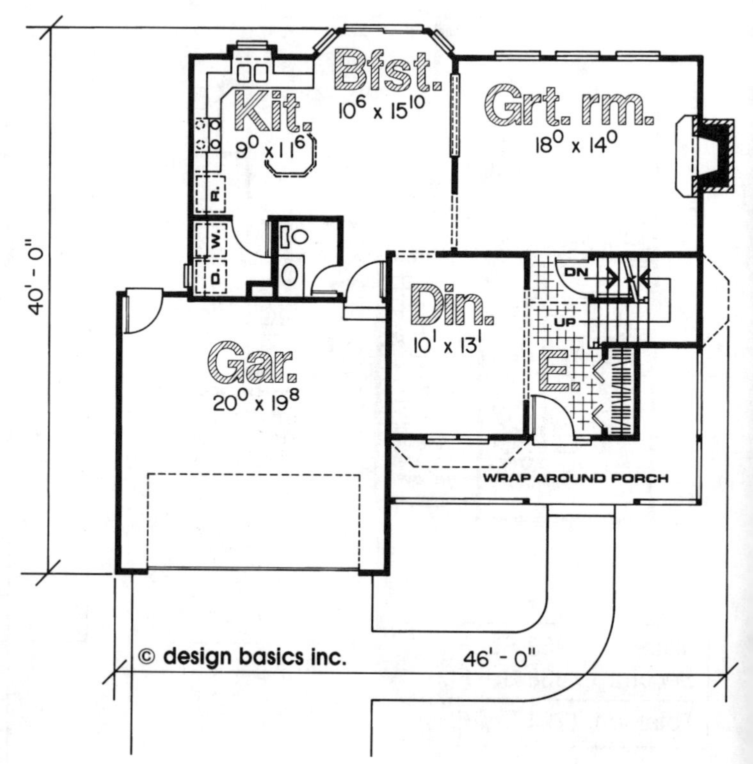

Main	919 Sq. Ft.
Second	923 Sq. Ft.
Total	1842 Sq. Ft.

ORDER DIRECT
7:00-6:00 Mon.-Fri. CST
800-947-7526

9F-2950 Herald price code: 18

Gold Seal HOME PLANS™

- ▸ High quality, erasable, reproducible vellums
- ▸ Shipped via 2nd day air within the continental U.S.

- parlor off entry has dining room option and French doors to family room
- back yard door shared by large family room and bayed breakfast area with pantry
- island kitchen open to breakfast area features a second pantry and 2 lazy Susans
- desirable mud porch allows side yard access to utility area with 1/2 bath and laundry room
- back stairs lead to well-planned second level
- secondary bedrooms share hall bath
- amenities abound in master suite with whirlpool bath, built-in linen cabinet and ample walk-in closet off dressing area

Rear Elevation

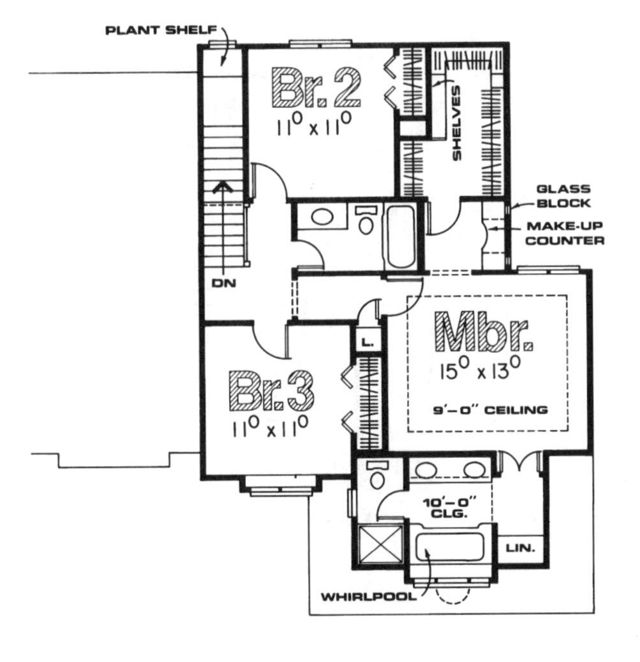

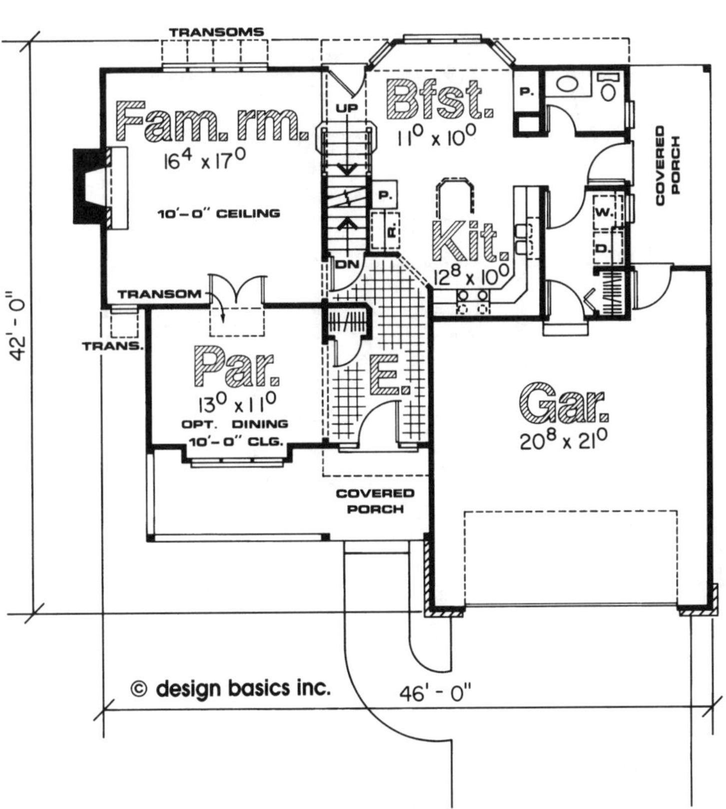

Main	972 Sq. Ft.
Second	877 Sq. Ft.
Total	1849 Sq. Ft.

design basics inc.®
HOME PLAN DESIGN SERVICE

9F-746 Monroe price code: 18

- High quality, erasable, reproducible vellums
- Shipped via 2nd day air within the continental U.S.

- covered front porch
- step-down from entry into volume living room open to formal dining room with vaulted ceiling
- window in compartmented main-floor laundry area
- awning window centers above bookcase in family room with fireplace
- well-planned kitchen with lazy Susan, pantry and many cabinets is open to breakfast area
- cathedral ceiling in master bedroom
- skylit dressing area and compartmented stool in master bath, plus walk-in closet
- volume ceiling in front bedroom with beautiful arched window

Rear Elevation

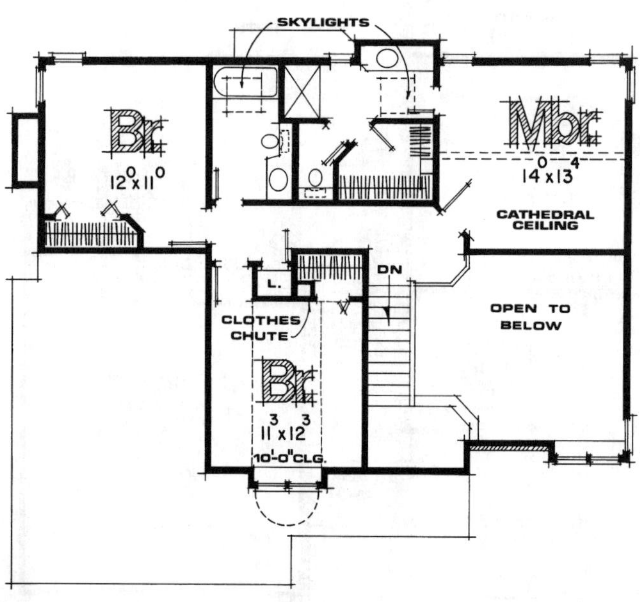

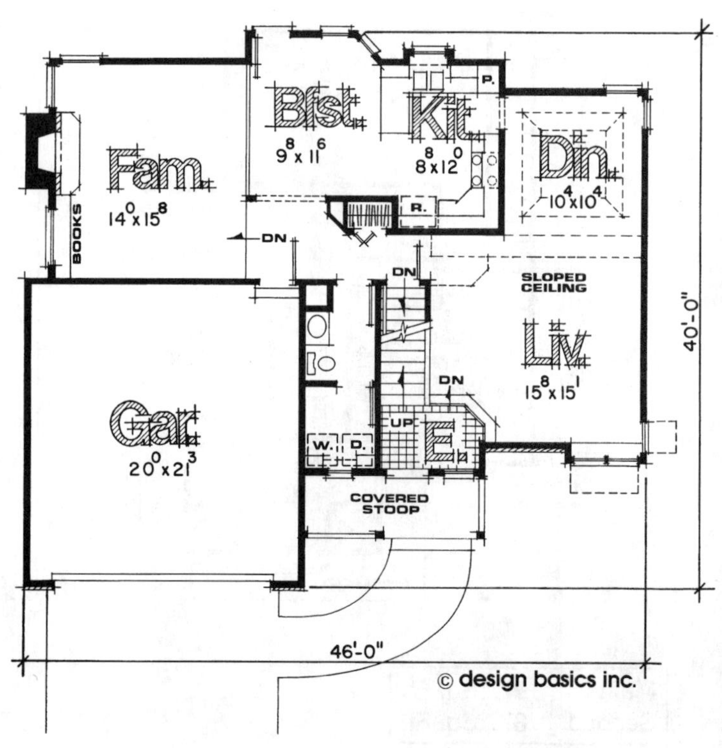

© design basics inc.

ORDER DIRECT
7:00-6:00 Mon.-Fri. CST
800-947-7526

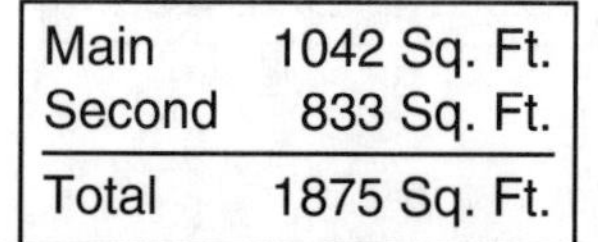

Main	1042 Sq. Ft.
Second	833 Sq. Ft.
Total	1875 Sq. Ft.

9F-2305 Austin price code: 18

Gold Seal™ HOME PLANS

- High quality, erasable, reproducible vellums
- Shipped via 2nd day air within the continental U.S.

- elegant lines of this two-story elevation give additional enticement
- dramatic tiled entry hall leads conveniently to all areas
- adjacent living and dining areas enhance every entertaining pursuit
- kitchen and bayed breakfast area located strategically to serve both the formal dining area and the family room
- bright picture window and lovely raised hearth fireplace highlight family room
- second level arrangement offers unique privacy to secondary bedrooms and gives seclusion to master suite
- sumptuous master suite features two closets and a sunlit whirlpool tub and dressing area

Rear Elevation

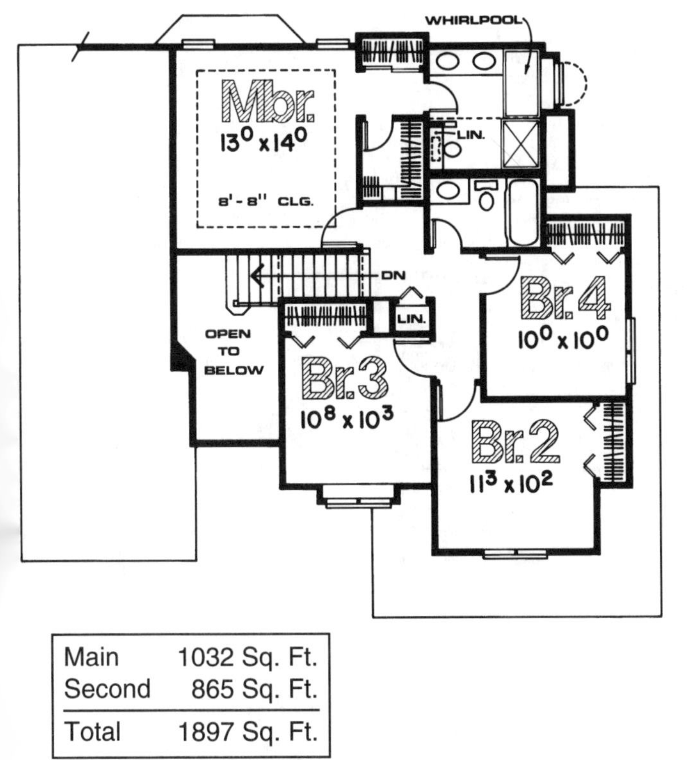

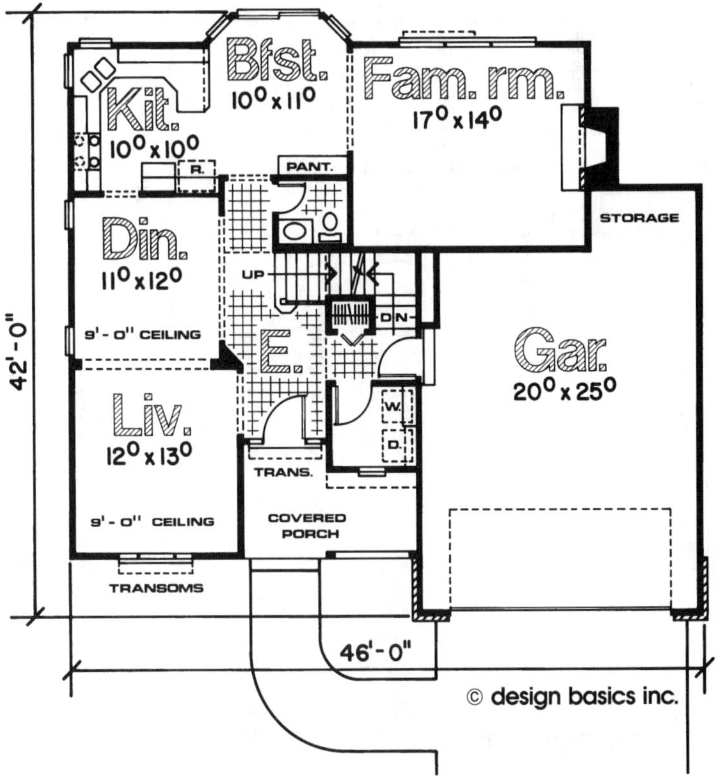

Main	1032 Sq. Ft.
Second	865 Sq. Ft.
Total	1897 Sq. Ft.

9F-1769 Hampton price code: 20

Gold Seal™ HOME PLANS

- High quality, erasable, reproducible vellums
- Shipped via 2nd day air within the continental U.S.

- large hall coat closet and nearby laundry room convenient to garage entrance into home
- volume living room opens to large dining room for entertaining
- efficient kitchen with pantry and planning desk open to bayed dinette
- sunken family room, private from entry, has fireplace and many windows
- central trafficways throughout
- extra storage space in garage
- secondary bedrooms segregated for privacy share skylit hall bath
- large master bedroom with elaborate skylit master bath includes walk-in closet, double vanity and compartmented stool and shower

Rear Elevation

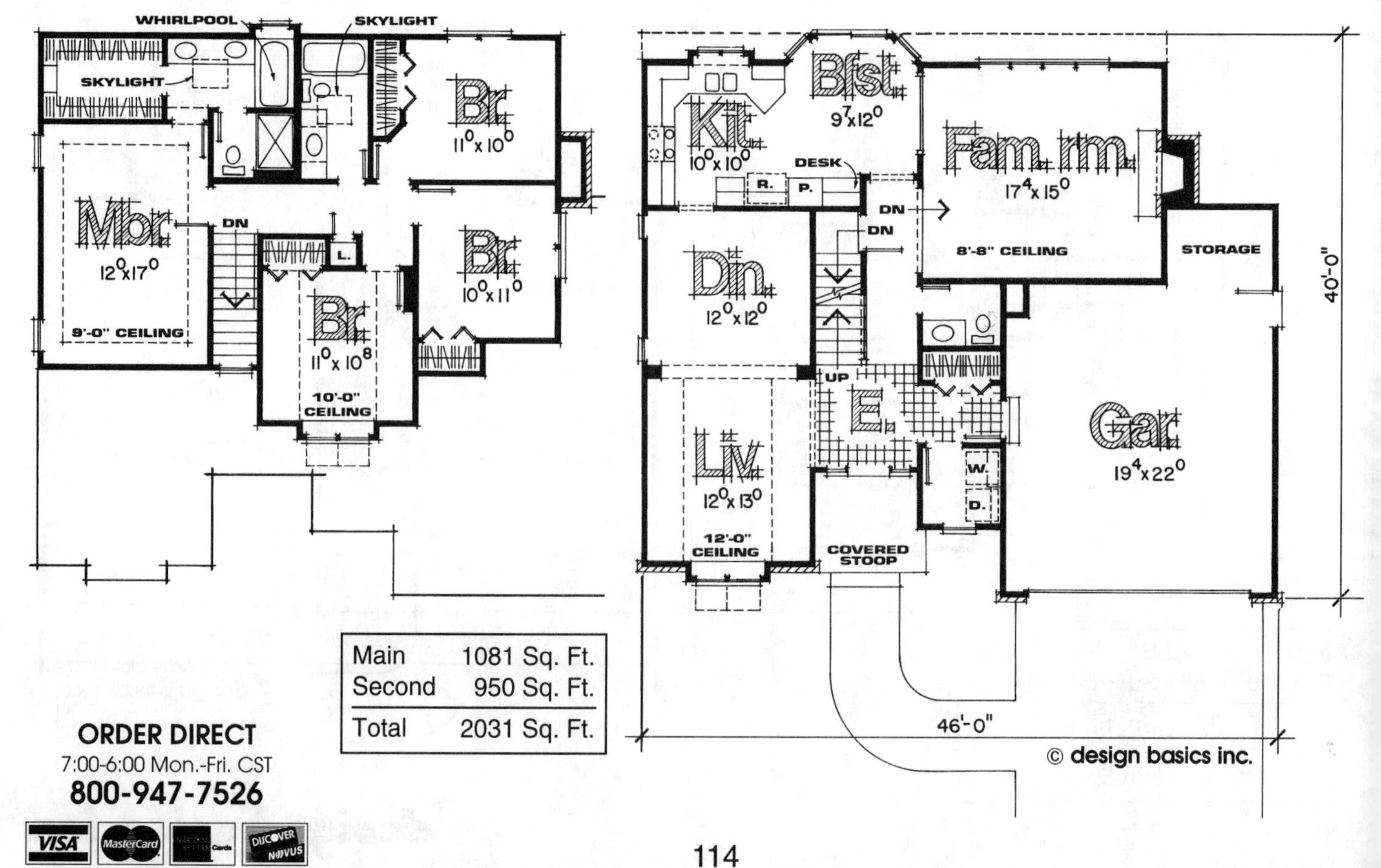

Main	1081 Sq. Ft.
Second	950 Sq. Ft.
Total	2031 Sq. Ft.

ORDER DIRECT
7:00-6:00 Mon.-Fri. CST
800-947-7526

9F-846 Ardmore price code: 20

Gold Seal™ HOME PLANS

- High quality, erasable, reproducible vellums
- Shipped via 2nd day air within the continental U.S.

- entry offers immediate view of living room with open access to formal dining room for entertaining options
- sunken family room offers built-in bookcase and fireplace
- kitchen features lazy Susan, pantry and window over sink
- wood railing separates sunny breakfast area from family room, enhancing the open feeling
- upstairs balcony overlooks living room below
- master suite includes deluxe dressing/ bath area featuring skylight, walk-in closet and private compartmented stool
- secondary bedrooms share skylit hall bath

Rear Elevation

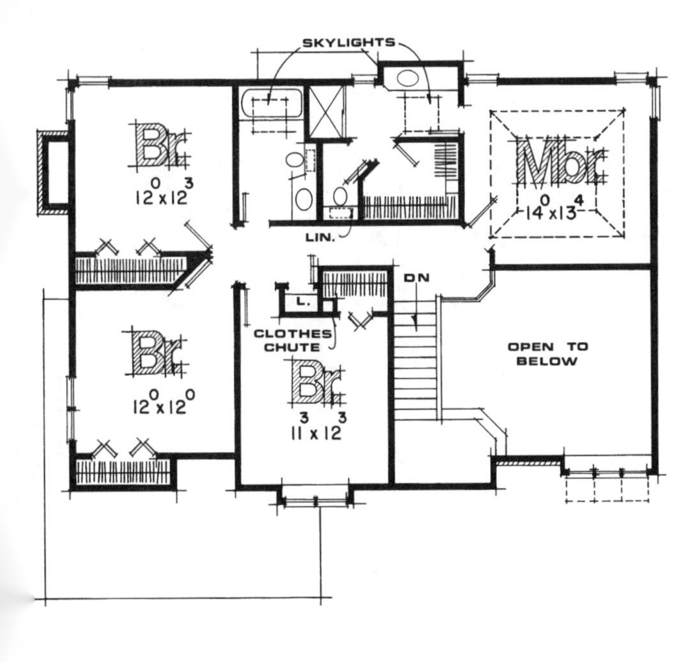

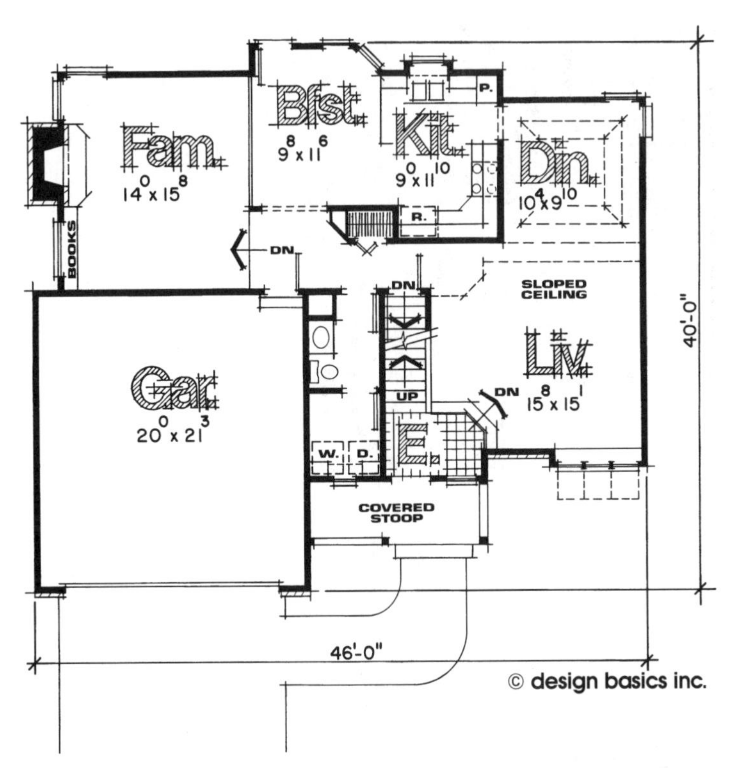

Main	1042 Sq. Ft.
Second	1020 Sq. Ft.
Total	2062 Sq. Ft.

9F-1870 Bristol price code: 20

- High quality, erasable, reproducible vellums
- Shipped via 2nd day air within the continental U.S.

- charming porch and arched windows of elevation allude to elegance within
- parlor with large bayed window and sloped ceiling harks back to simpler life
- formal dining area open to parlor invites entertaining with ease from kitchen
- bright kitchen and bayed breakfast area features wrapping counters, pantry and desk
- step down into expansive gathering room with fireplace and abundant windows
- ample secondary bedrooms share nearby skylit bath
- indulging master bedroom with skylit dressing area, dual lavs, whirlpool tub and large walk-in closet

Rear Elevation

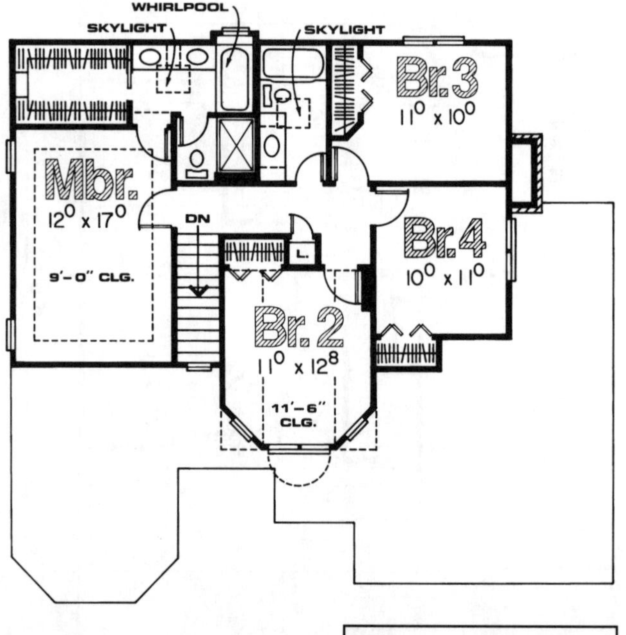

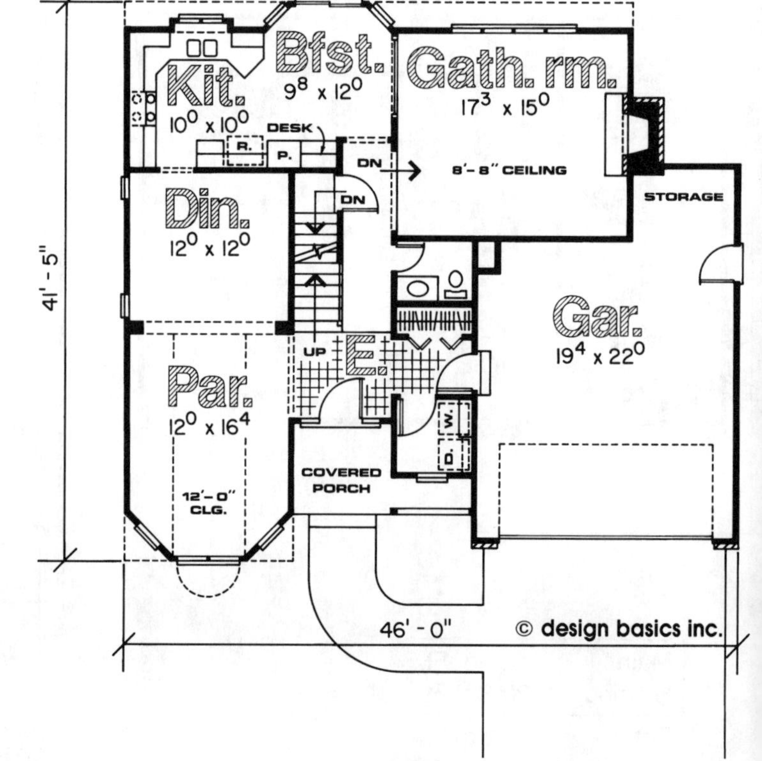

Main	1113 Sq. Ft.
Second	965 Sq. Ft.
Total	2078 Sq. Ft.

9F-1536 Livingston price code: 21

- High quality, erasable, reproducible vellums
- Shipped via 2nd day air within the continental U.S.

- simplified foundation
- volume living room opens to dining room with formal ceiling
- powder bath off entry
- planning desk and pantry in island kitchen
- bayed breakfast area open to family room
- step-down family room with beamed ceiling and raised hearth fireplace
- secondary bedrooms share hall bath
- efficient second level laundry
- large master bedroom with vaulted ceiling and corner windows
- luxurious master bath with window over corner whirlpool, walk-in closet, double vanity and compartmented stool and shower

Rear Elevation

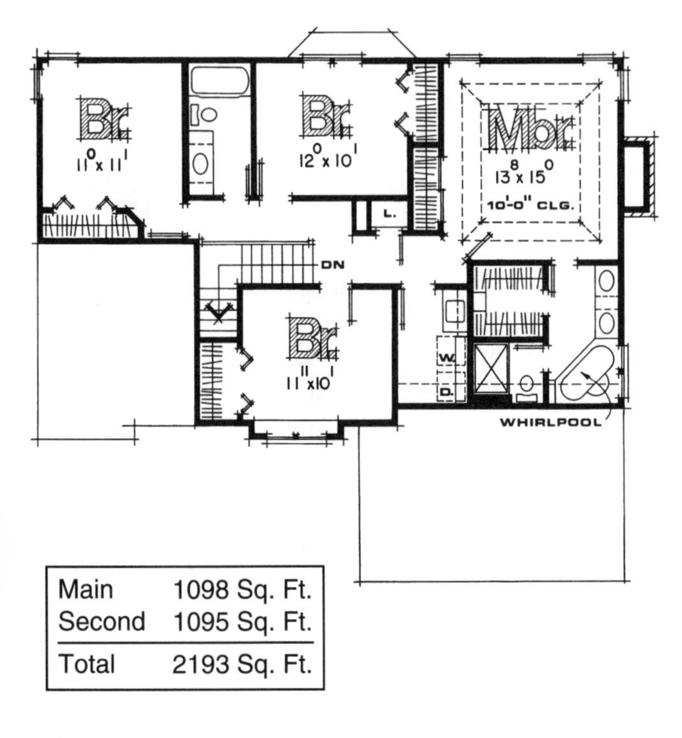

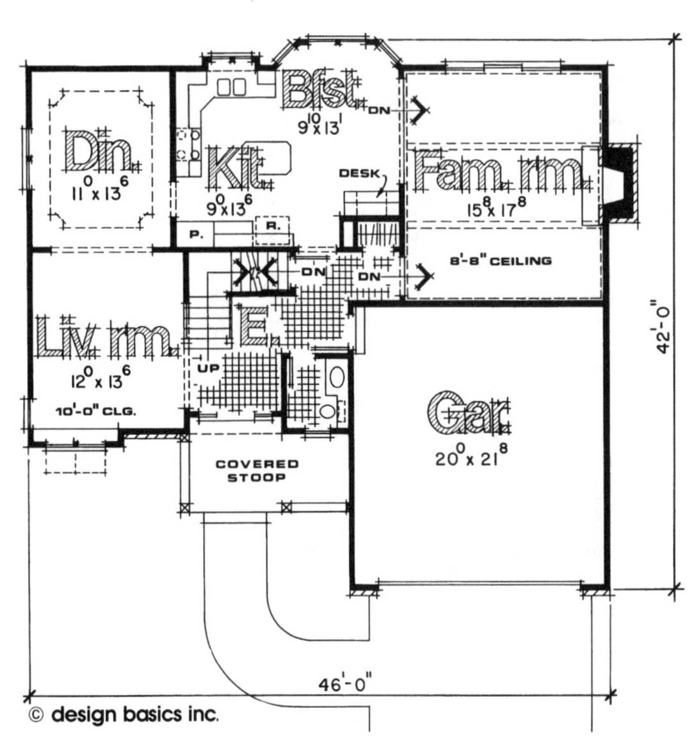

Main	1098 Sq. Ft.
Second	1095 Sq. Ft.
Total	2193 Sq. Ft.

9F-2408 Crawford price code: 22

- High quality, erasable, reproducible vellums
- Shipped via 2nd day air within the continental U.S.

- elevation enhanced by expansive covered porch
- spacious 2-story entry surveys formal dining room with hutch space
- entertainment center and see-thru fireplace highlight great room
- kitchen/breakfast/hearth room areas feature gazebo dining, wrapping counters and numerous amenities
- bedroom #3 features half round transom and volume ceiling
- bedroom #4 includes built-in desk
- convenient compartmented bath and large walk-in linen storage serves secondary bedrooms
- luxurious master suite with vaulted ceiling enjoys his/her vanities, walk-in closet and whirlpool

Rear Elevation

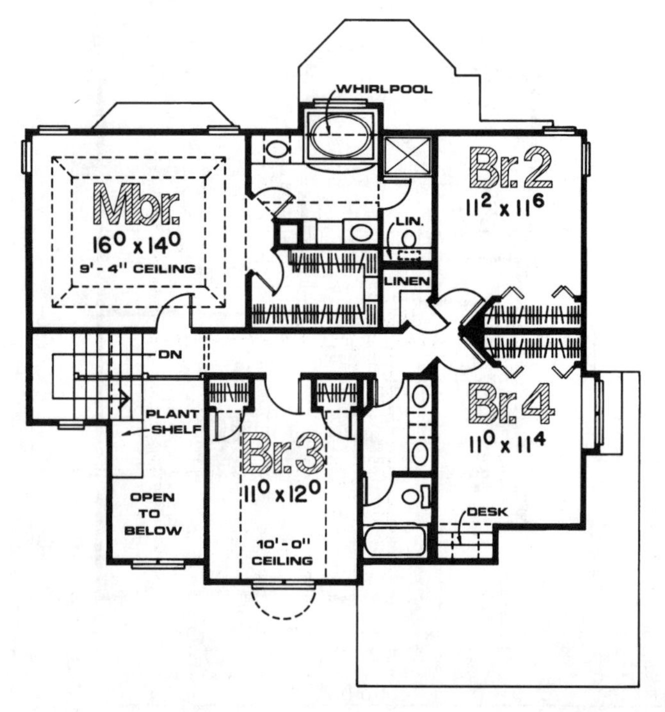

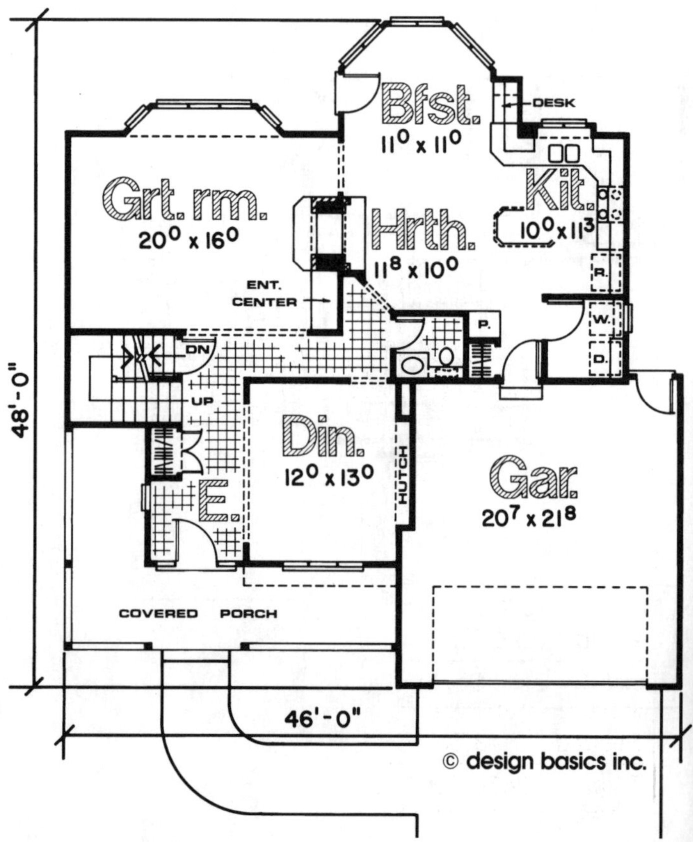

© design basics inc.

ORDER DIRECT
7:00-6:00 Mon.-Fri. CST
800-947-7526

Main	1150 Sq. Ft.
Second	1120 Sq. Ft.
Total	2270 Sq. Ft.

9F-2792 Primrose price code: 24

- ▶ High quality, erasable, reproducible vellums
- ▶ Shipped via 2nd day air within the continental U.S.

- charming wrap-around porch and quaint window treatment create country mood
- formal dining room is distinguished by columned entry and charming bowed window
- two pantries and desk line one side of dinette
- dinette and family room join together creating tremendous openness
- on upper level, enjoy dramatic view of family room
- master suite boasts walk-in closet and luxurious bath highlighted by whirlpool and dual lavs
- round, arched window and window seat along with 10-foot-high ceiling add distinctiveness to 4th bedroom

Rear Elevation

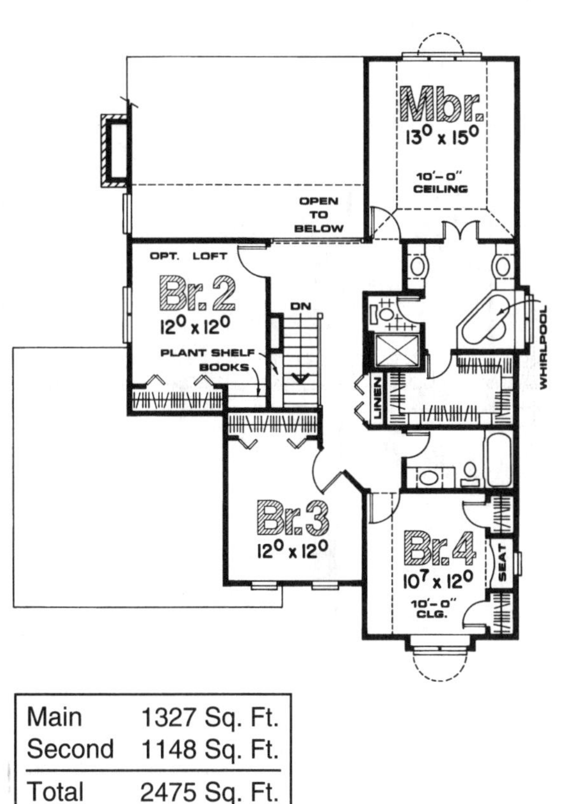

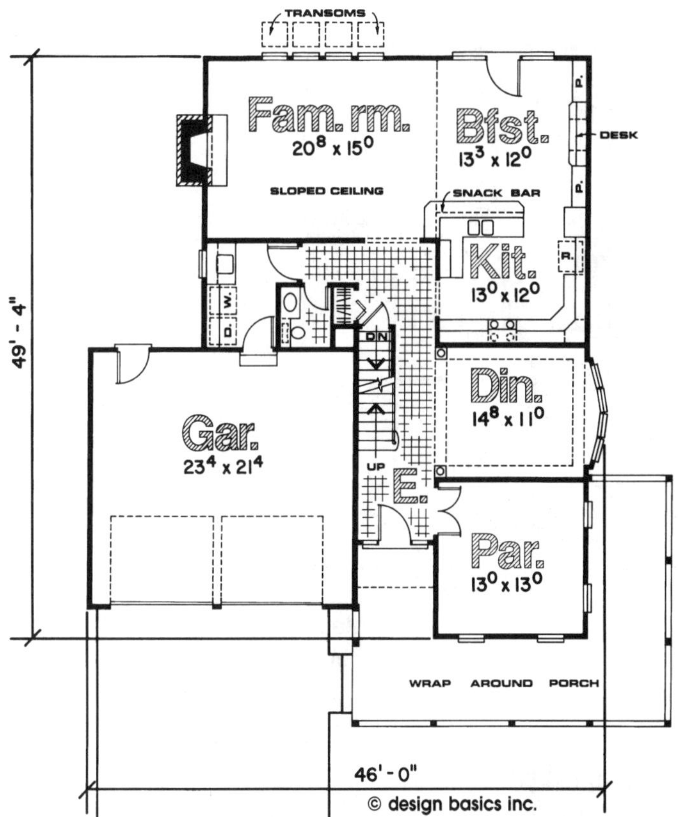

Main	1327 Sq. Ft.
Second	1148 Sq. Ft.
Total	2475 Sq. Ft.

9F-2948 Peyton price code: 18

- ▶ High quality, erasable, reproducible vellums
- ▶ Shipped via 2nd day air within the continental U.S.

- covered porch paired with cedar shakes and stone create a charming elevation
- 2-story entry captures picturesque views of elegant colonnade framing entry to great room and open U-stairs with plant ledge above landing
- formal dining room, open to great room and entry, has direct access from kitchen
- bayed dinette open to great kitchen featuring large pantry, 2 lazy Susans and snack bar
- spacious garage has storage area
- upstairs hallway overlooking entry leads to secondary bedrooms sharing sun-lit bath
- master suite highlighted by vaulted ceiling and whirlpool bath with dramatic angled walls, sloped ceiling and spacious walk-in closet

Rear Elevation

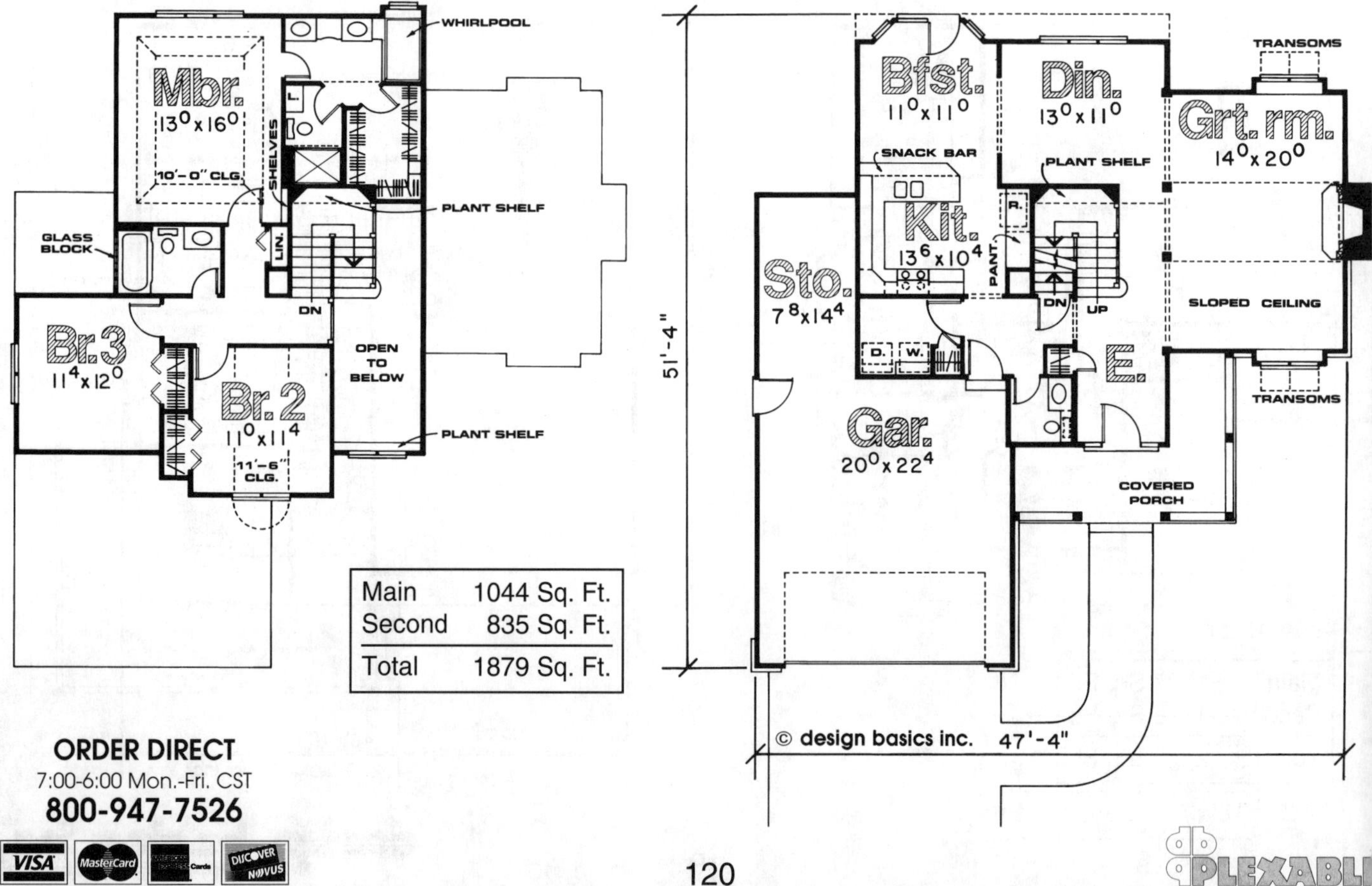

Main	1044 Sq. Ft.
Second	835 Sq. Ft.
Total	1879 Sq. Ft.

9F-3028 Ferguson price code: 20

- High quality, erasable, reproducible vellums
- Shipped via 2nd day air within the continental U.S.

- built-in bookcase with window between 2 coat closets add charm to entry
- view of colonnade and U-stairs enhance sun-filled great room
- formal dining room well located for entertaining
- peninsula kitchen with large pantry and 2 lazy Susans shares snack bar with bayed dinette
- garage features convenient access to kitchen and laundry room and has extra storage area
- 3 secondary bedrooms share large compartmented bath
- bedroom #2 has walk-in closet
- vaulted ceiling and whirlpool bath with spacious walk-in closet complete lavish master suite

Rear Elevation

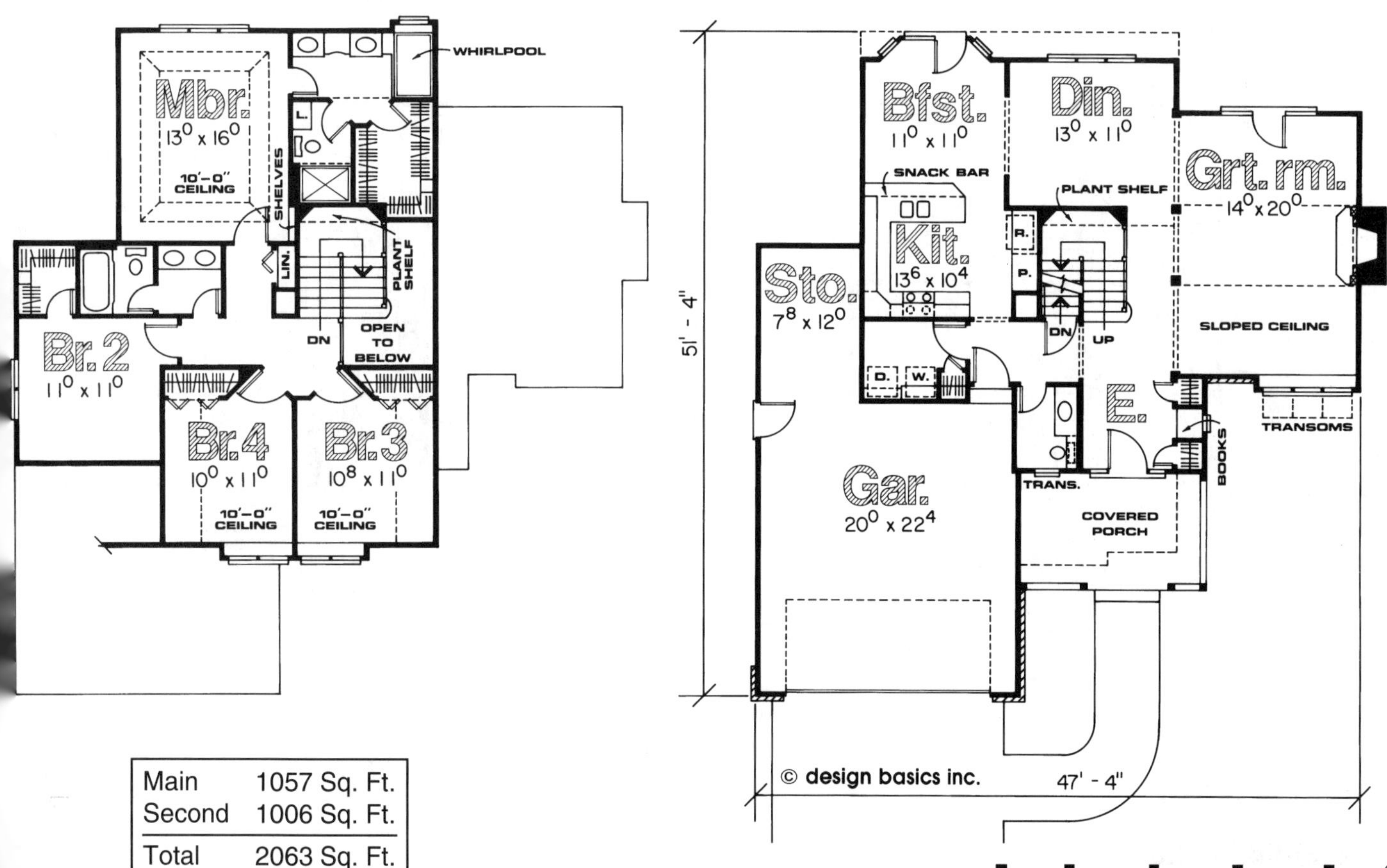

Main	1057 Sq. Ft.
Second	1006 Sq. Ft.
Total	2063 Sq. Ft.

9F-3459 Jamestown price code: 15

- High quality, erasable, reproducible vellums
- Shipped via 2nd day air within the continental U.S.

Gold Seal PLUS

- quaint traditional elevation with economy in mind
- oak floor entry with convenient coat closet
- dining room is enriched with oak flooring
- sunny windows brighten family room with fireplace
- wrapping counters, large pantry and lovely windows accentuate kitchen and breakfast area
- organized utility area designates laundry room and powder room
- quick grocery traffic from garage to kitchen
- second floor unfolds master suite with twin vanities, whirlpool tub and walk-in closet
- secondary bedrooms share full bath

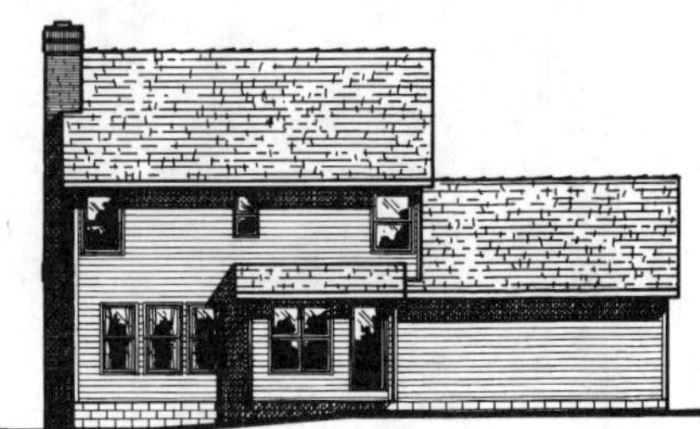

Rear Elevation

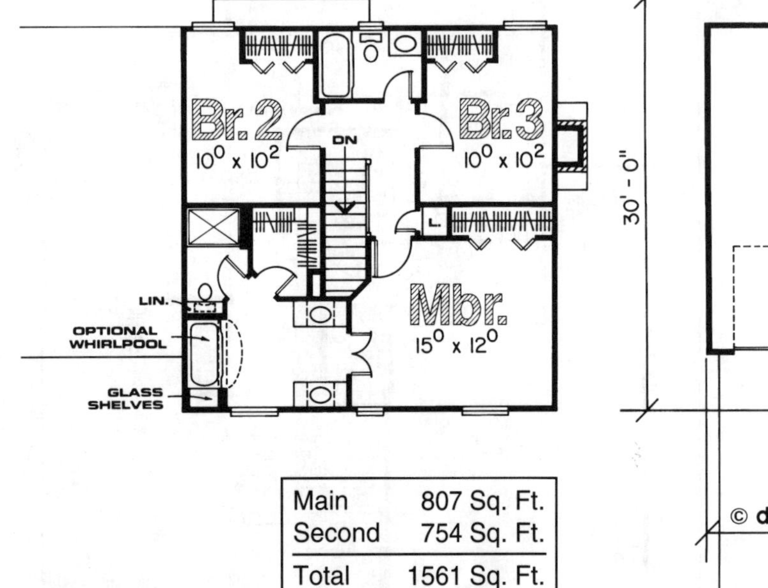

Bfst.
11^0 x 7^6
SNACK BAR
Fam. rm.
13^8 x 17^0
Gar.
19^8 x 23^4
Kit.
10^0 x 10^0
P.
R.
DN
UP
D.
W.
Din.
11^0 x 10^0
E.
STOOP
30' - 0"
48' - 0"

Main	807 Sq. Ft.
Second	754 Sq. Ft.
Total	1561 Sq. Ft.

9F-3554 Cheyenne price code: 17

- High quality, erasable, reproducible vellums
- Shipped via 2nd day air within the continental U.S.

- inviting, traditional elevation
- sophisticated parlor boasts bayed windows and French doors to family room
- raised-hearth fireplace and gorgeous picture awning windows highlight large family room
- staircase has convenient second floor access from kitchen and family room
- spacious breakfast area offers great view and backyard access
- wrapping counters and two lazy Susans accommodate kitchen
- master suite has French door access to bath with sloped ceiling and large walk-in closet
- centralized hall bath serves two secondary bedrooms
- bedroom #2 features 10'-0" ceiling

Rear Elevation

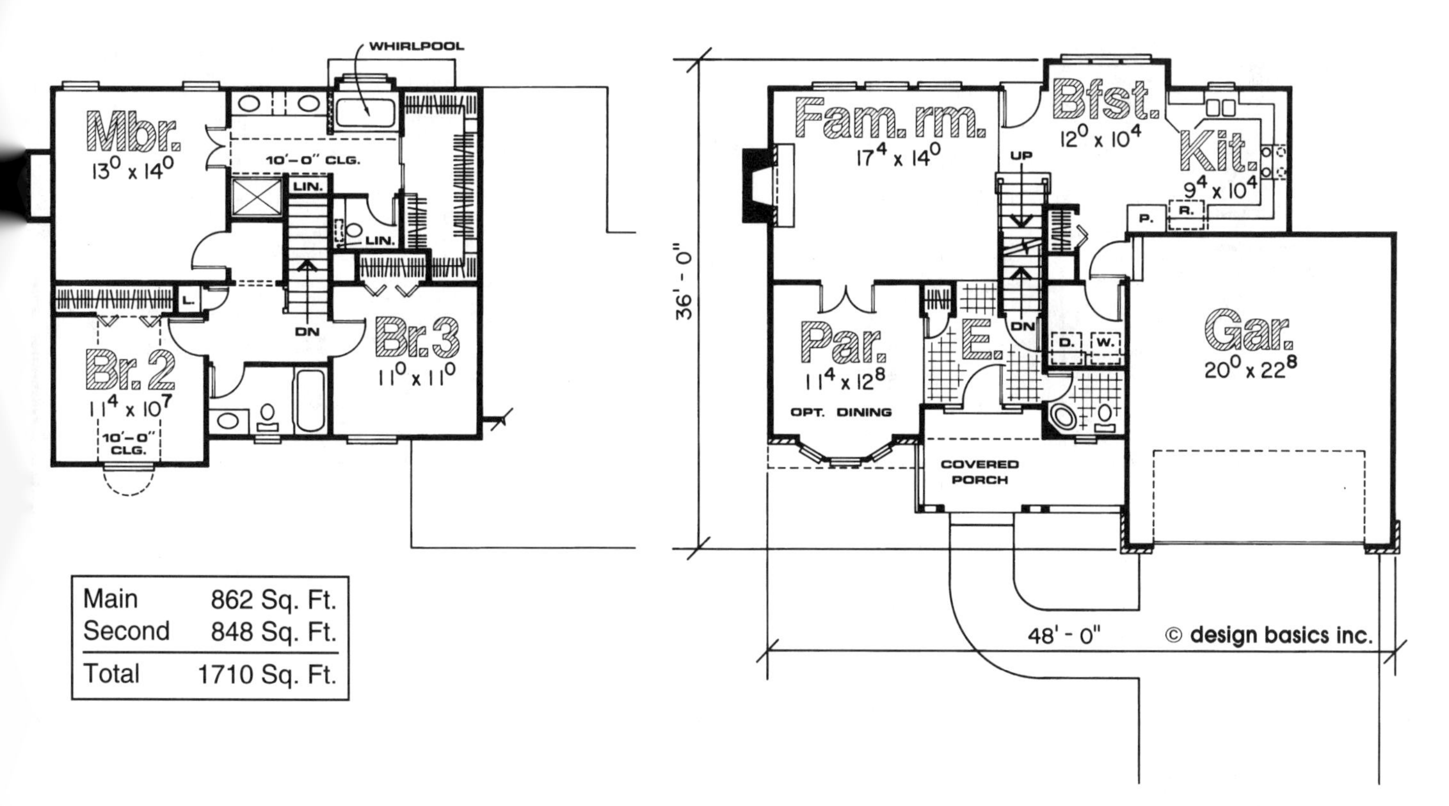

Main	862 Sq. Ft.
Second	848 Sq. Ft.
Total	1710 Sq. Ft.

9F-2100 Fenton price code: 18

Gold Seal HOME PLANS™

- High quality, erasable, reproducible vellums
- Shipped via 2nd day air within the continental U.S.

- quaint front porch
- staircase and formal volume living room seen from entry
- dining room open to living room for entertaining ease
- pantry, lazy Susan and window above sink in kitchen
- bright bayed dinette overlooks family room
- step down into family room with handsome fireplace and wall of windows out the back
- powder bath centrally located
- angles add interest to bedroom #3
- private master bedroom with boxed ceiling features walk-in closet and pampering dressing area with double vanity and whirlpool on angle under window

Rear Elevation

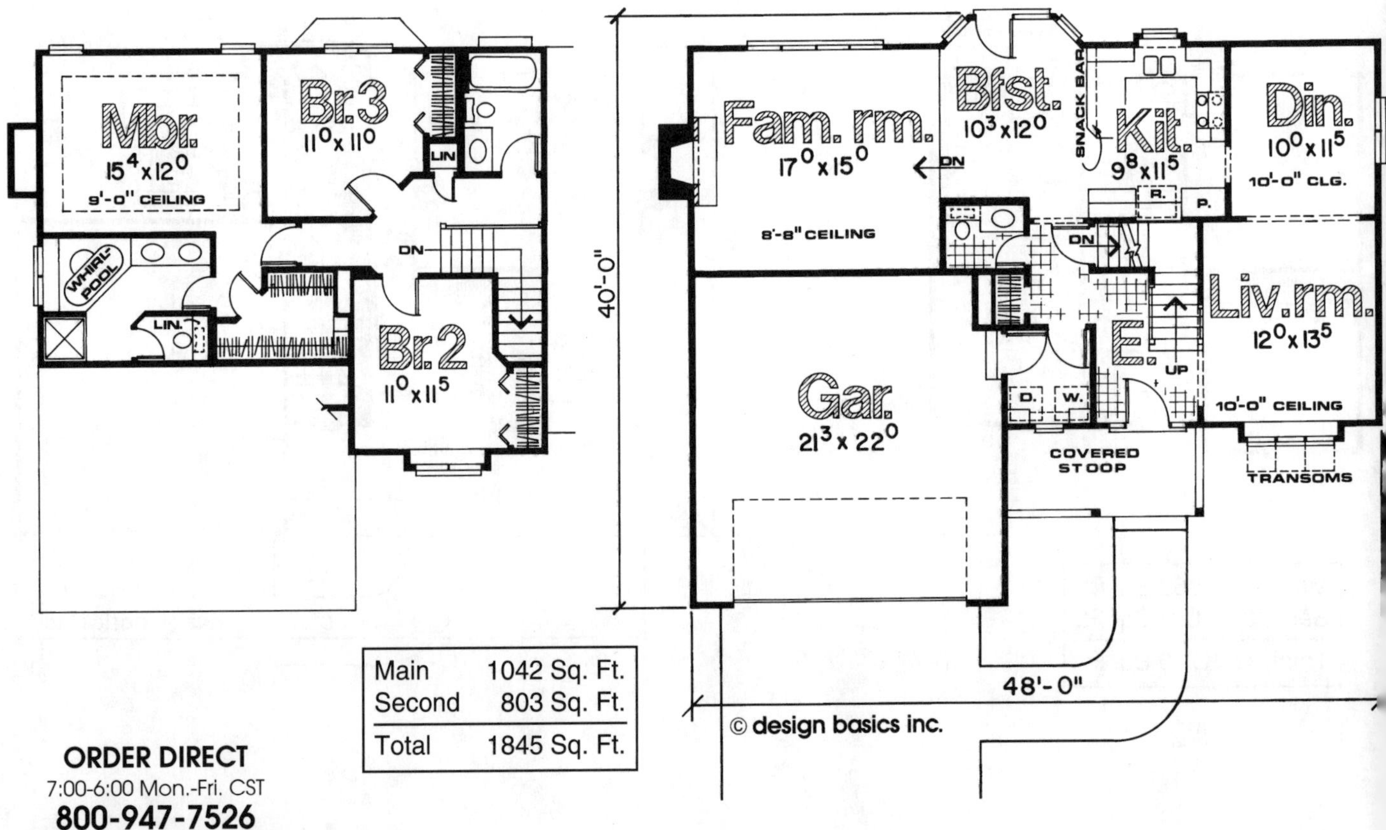

Main	1042 Sq. Ft.
Second	803 Sq. Ft.
Total	1845 Sq. Ft.

ORDER DIRECT
7:00-6:00 Mon.-Fri. CST
800-947-7526

9F -3567 Yorktown price code: 18

- High quality, erasable, reproducible vellums
- Shipped via 2nd day air within the continental U.S.

- front porch brings charming twist to this economical elevation
- oak flooring adds elegance to entry and dining room
- bright windows and fireplace compliment relaxed family room
- breakfast area conveniently accesses both backyard and garage
- kitchen enhanced with peninsula snack bar
- organized laundry and powder room off kitchen
- master suite reveals dual sink vanity and romantic corner whirlpool tub
- bedroom #3 offers walk-in closet
- extra storage space in deep garage

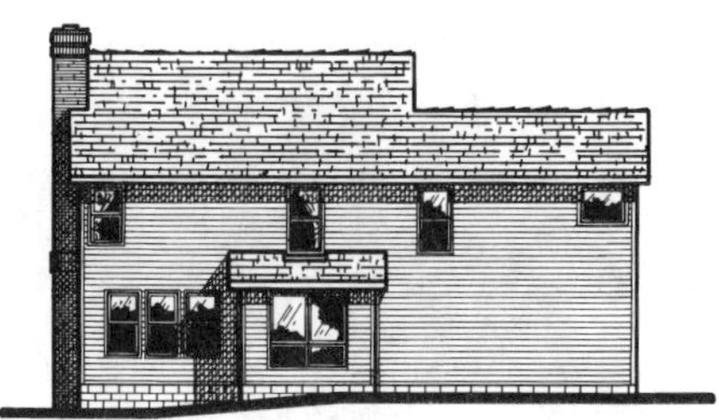

Rear Elevation

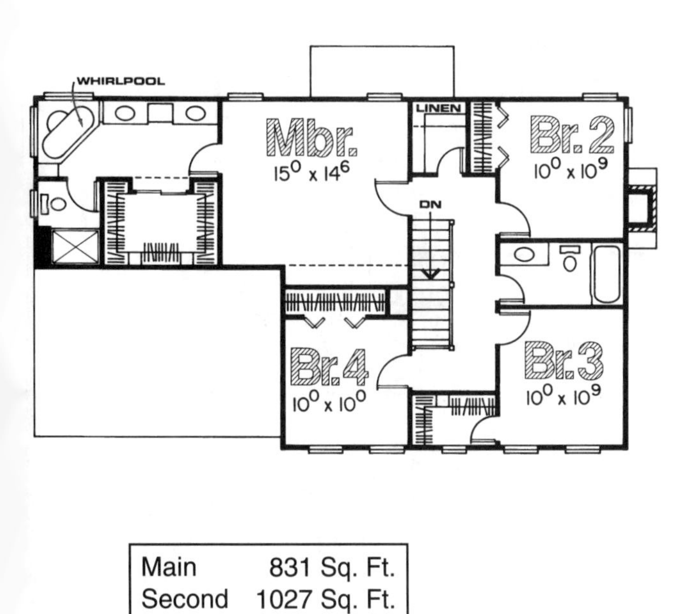

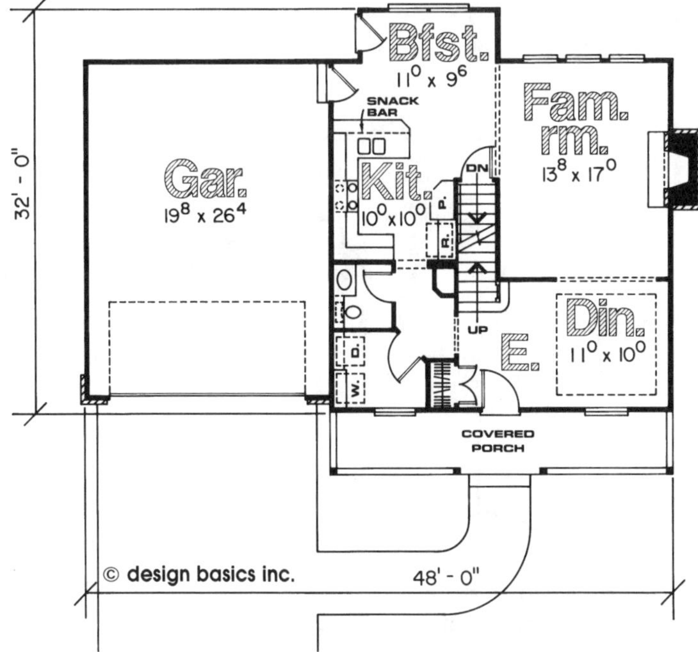

Main	831 Sq. Ft.
Second	1027 Sq. Ft.
Total	1858 Sq. Ft.

9F-3386 Mansell price code: 19

- High quality, erasable, reproducible vellums
- Shipped via 2nd day air within the continental U.S.

- gingerbread comes alive in elevation packed with traditional flair
- large living room with 10-foot ceiling and bayed windows is seen from entry
- both kitchen and living room benefit from nearby dining room with 10-foot ceiling
- snack bar, wrapping counters and two lazy Susans in kitchen
- gigantic sunken family room fosters activity with its fireplace and sunny windows
- bayed breakfast area has access to backyard
- master suite features 9-foot boxed ceiling, bayed windows and walk-in closet
- whirlpool and dual lavs in master bath
- bayed windows and 10-foot ceiling highlight bedroom #2

Rear Elevation

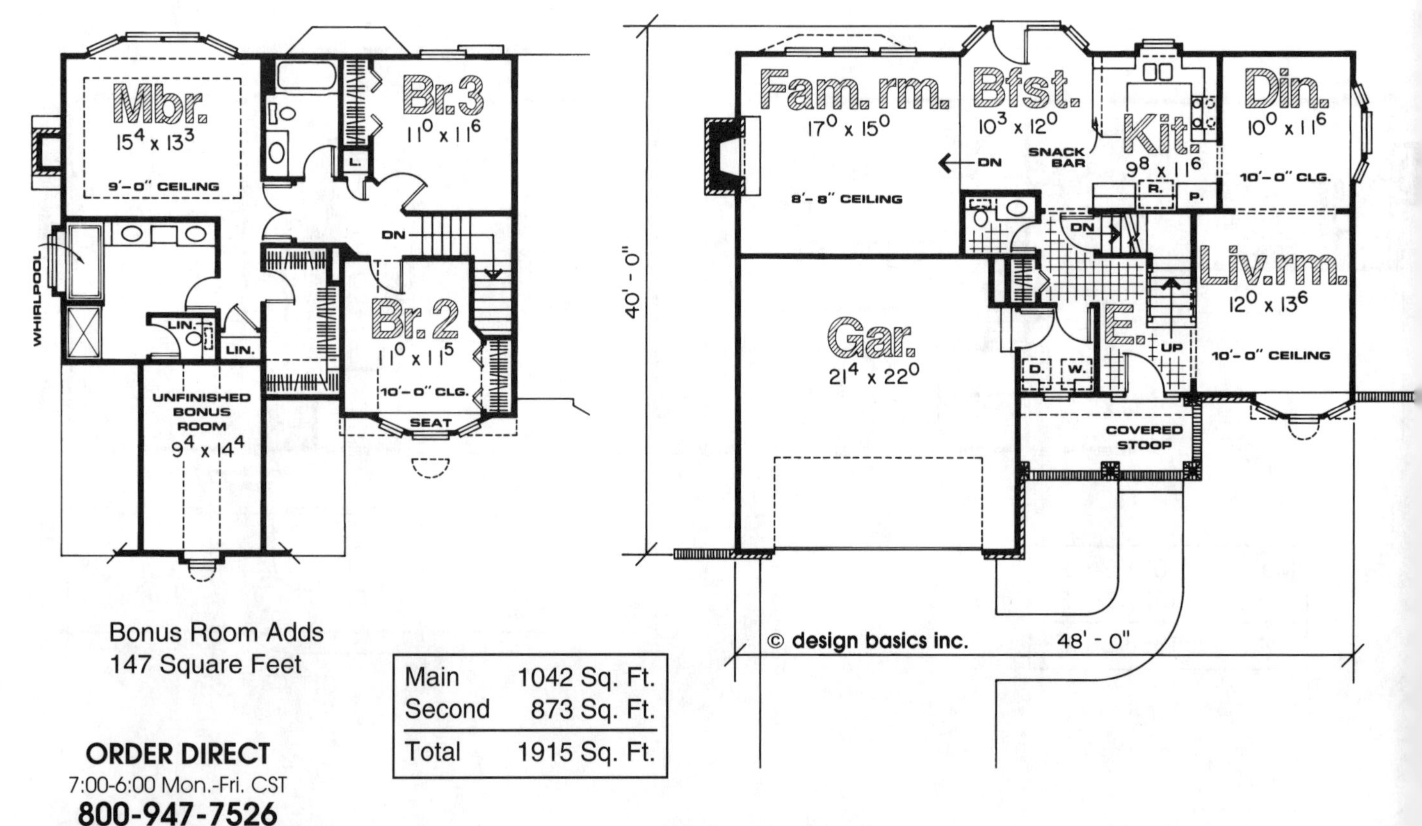

Bonus Room Adds
147 Square Feet

Main	1042 Sq. Ft.
Second	873 Sq. Ft.
Total	1915 Sq. Ft.

9F-2154 Galvin price code: 19

- ▶ High quality, erasable, reproducible vellums
- ▶ Shipped via 2nd day air within the continental U.S.

- volume living room seen from entry with beautiful boxed window
- formal dining room open to living room for versatility
- informal and formal areas well segregated for comfortable living
- step down into large family room with handsome fireplace and wall of windows out to the back
- bayed dinette open to kitchen with snack bar, pantry and 2 lazy Susans
- private master bedroom with formal boxed ceiling
- master dressing area features walk-in closet, double vanity and angled whirlpool under window

Rear Elevation

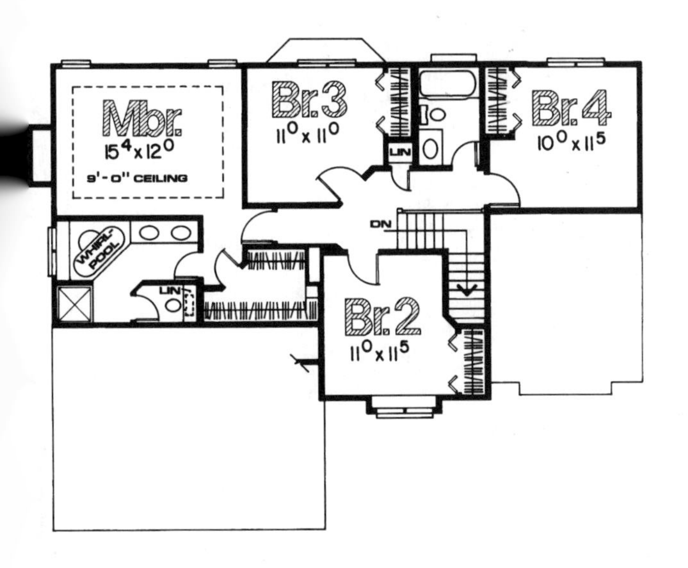

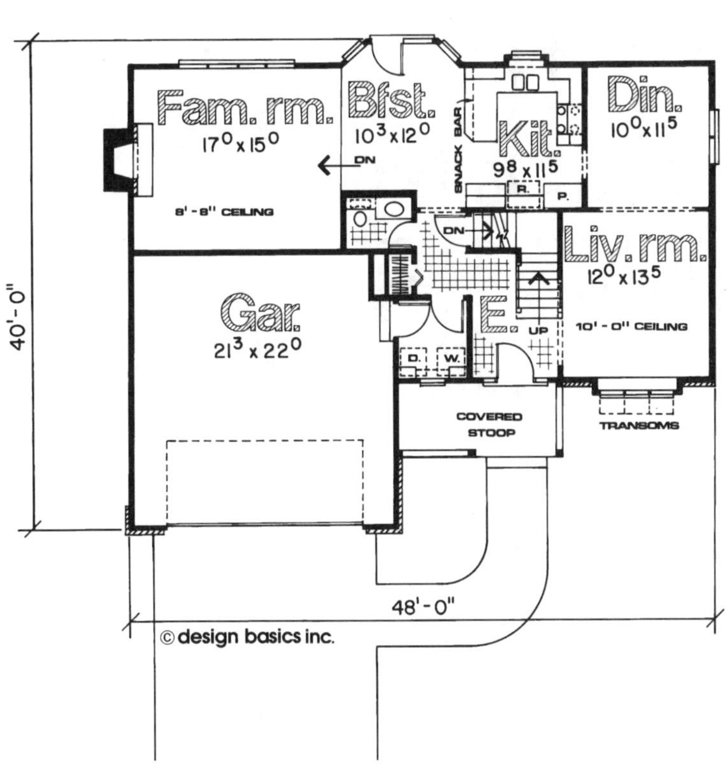

Main	1042 Sq. Ft.
Second	953 Sq. Ft.
Total	1995 Sq. Ft.

9F-1179 Sawyer price code: 20

- High quality, erasable, reproducible vellums
- Shipped via 2nd day air within the continental U.S.

- main level footage optimized and second level footage maximized
- private door onto spacious wrap-around porch from kitchen
- large kitchen includes pantry, island counter, roll-top desk and lazy Susan
- convenient main floor powder bath
- great room opens to staircase at the rear brightened with window on landing
- double doors to large master bedroom
- deluxe master bath area with whirlpool, transom windows and sloped ceiling
- laundry room with soaking sink on same level as bedrooms
- 3 linen closets on second level
- secondary bedrooms share centrally located bath with double vanity

Rear Elevation

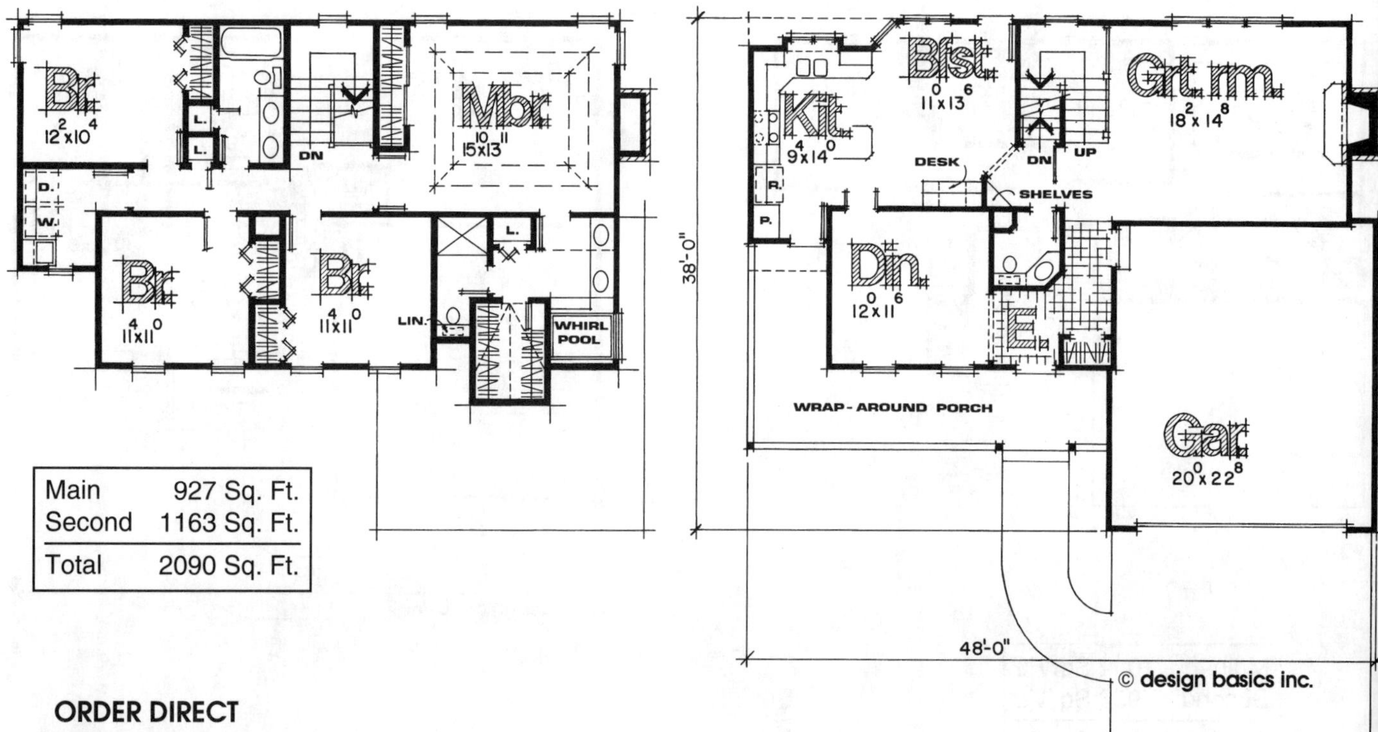

Main	927 Sq. Ft.
Second	1163 Sq. Ft.
Total	2090 Sq. Ft.

9F-1552 Landon price code: 20

Rear Elevation

- ▸ High quality, erasable, reproducible vellums
- ▸ Shipped via 2nd day air within the continental U.S.

Gold Seal™ HOME PLANS

- volume entry expands into unique staircase
- showcase dining room with bayed window and hutch space
- French doors into den or optional guest bedroom
- efficient kitchen with corner windows
- strategically located bath
- naturally lit staircase leading to a loft with plant shelf overlooks entry area
- secondary bedrooms share a skylit bath
- large master bedroom with tiered ceiling
- arched window above whirlpool tub in beautiful master bath
- laundry room with sink conveniently located on second level

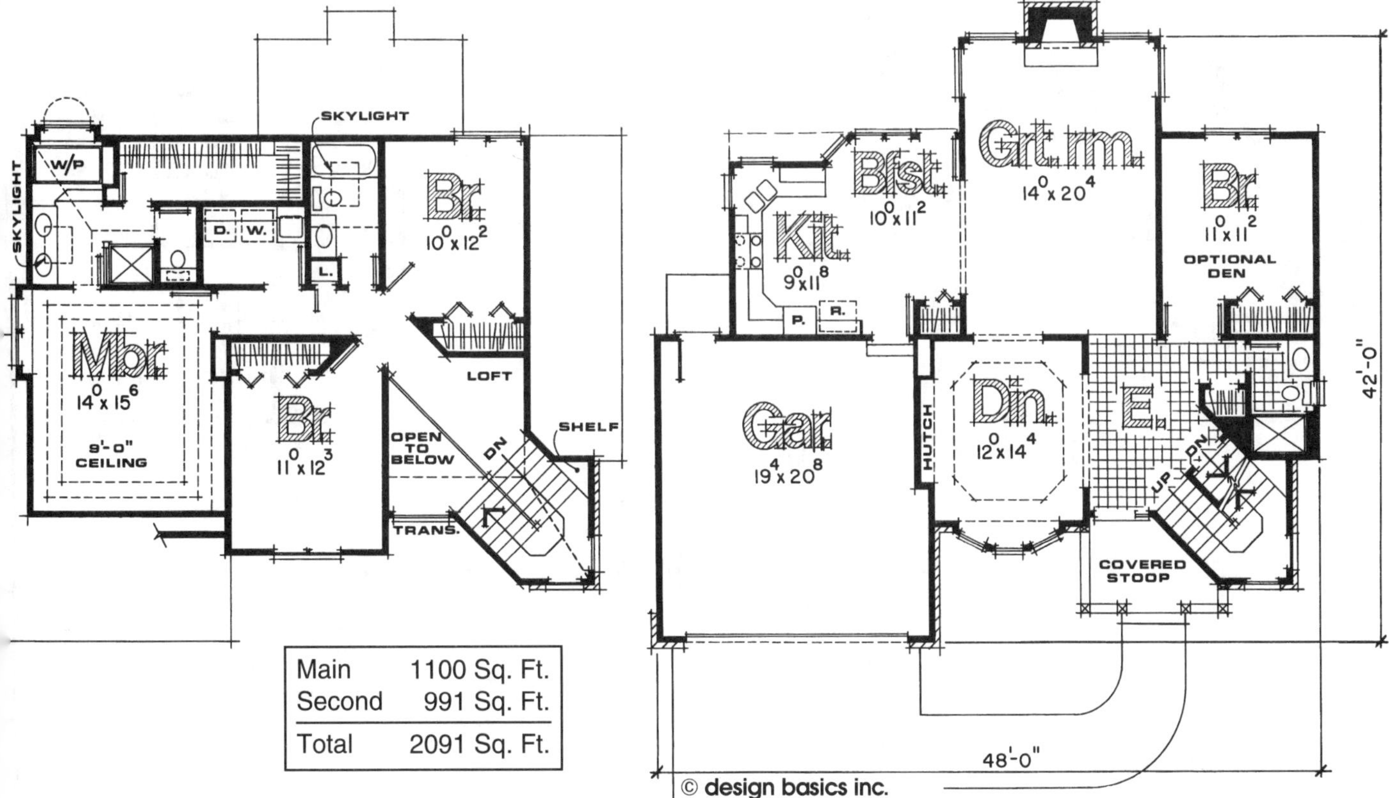

Main	1100 Sq. Ft.
Second	991 Sq. Ft.
Total	2091 Sq. Ft.

9F-2156 Graham price code: 20

- High quality, erasable, reproducible vellums
- Shipped via 2nd day air within the continental U.S.

- quaint front porch
- formal living room with 10-foot ceiling seen from entry
- dining room open to living room for entertaining options
- snack bar, pantry and window above sink in kitchen
- dinette open to informal family room for comfortable gathering
- step down into sunken family room with fireplace and windows out the back
- beautiful arched window and volume ceiling for bedroom #2
- secondary bedrooms share skylit hall bath
- private master suite with tiered ceiling and walk-in closet features angled whirlpool under window

Rear Elevation

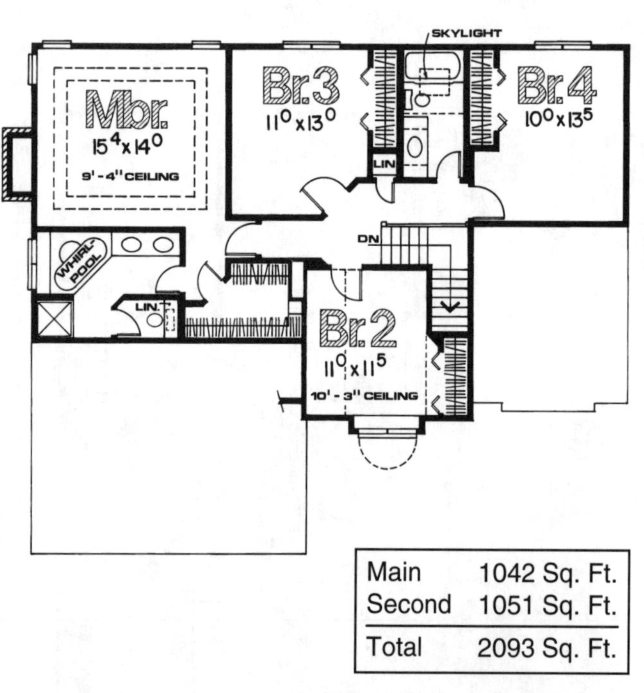

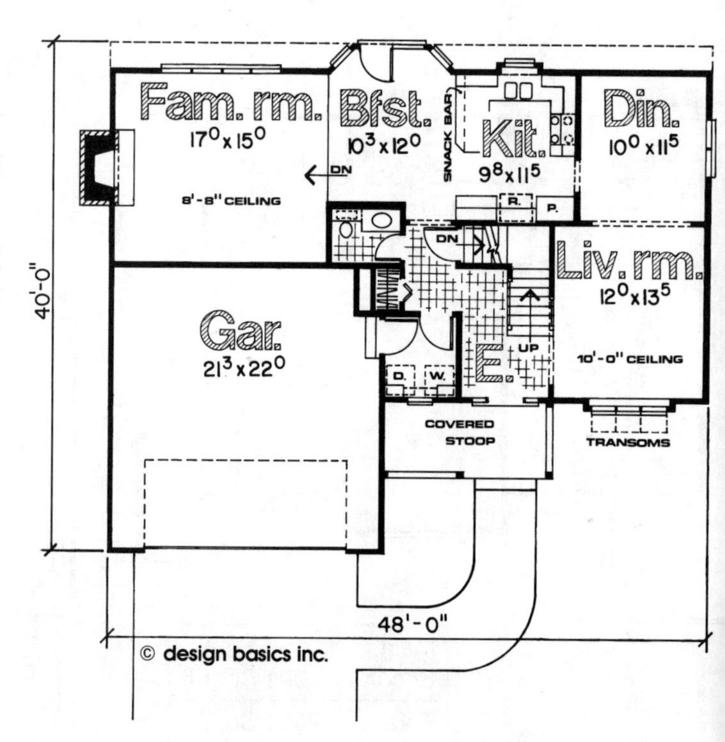

Main	1042 Sq. Ft.
Second	1051 Sq. Ft.
Total	2093 Sq. Ft.

ORDER DIRECT
7:00-6:00 Mon.-Fri. CST
800-947-7526

9F-3209 Foresman price code: 20

- ▶ High quality, erasable, reproducible vellums
- ▶ Shipped via 2nd day air within the continental U.S.

- large covered porch is attractive feature for this 2-story
- great room off entry is warmed by fireplace
- formal dining, with interesting ceiling detail, is located near kitchen
- French doors open to well-organized peninsula kitchen with snack bar
- breakfast area provides pantries, desk area and convenient access to powder and laundry rooms
- built-in work bench in garage is added benefit
- master suite features large walk-in closet, sloped ceiling in dressing area, dual lavs, linen cabinet and whirlpool
- nice-sized bedrooms share hall bath

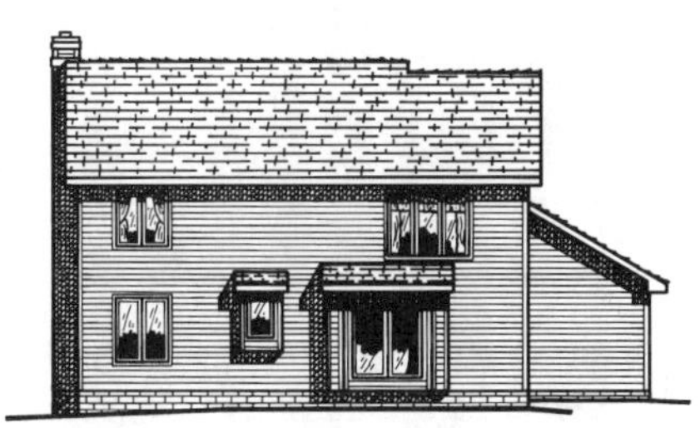

Rear Elevation

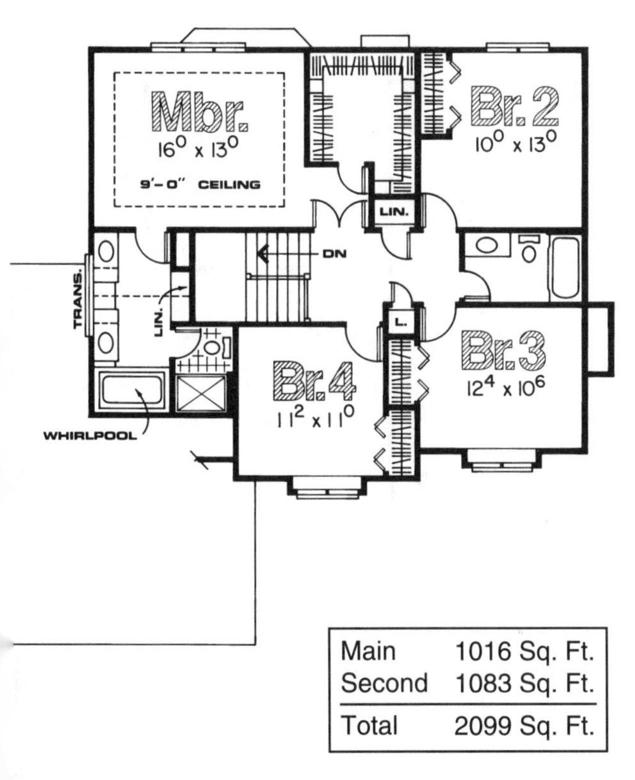

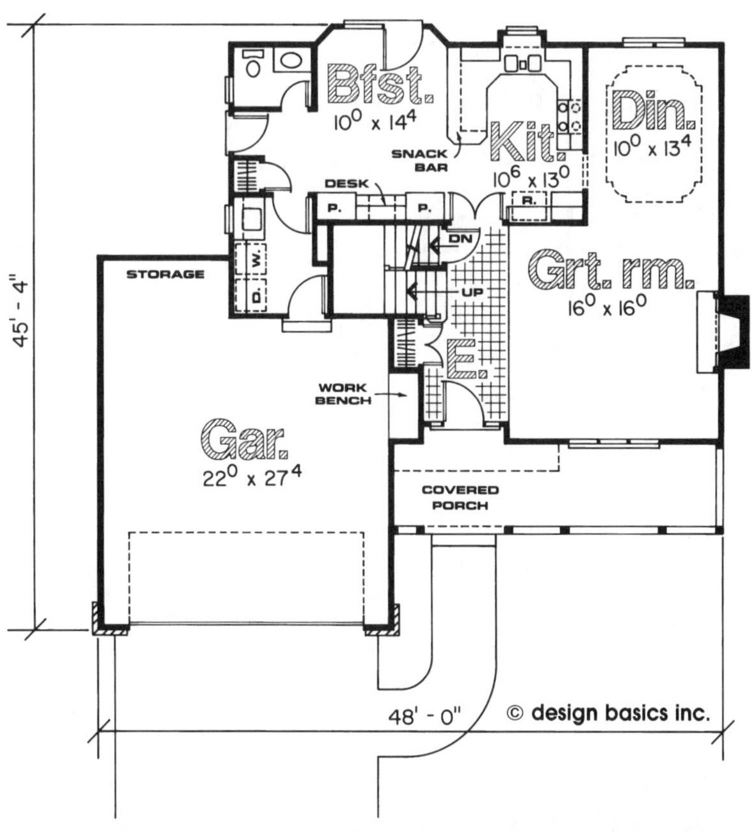

Main	1016 Sq. Ft.
Second	1083 Sq. Ft.
Total	2099 Sq. Ft.

9F-2216 Collier price code: 21

- High quality, erasable, reproducible vellums
- Shipped via 2nd day air within the continental U.S.

- inviting covered porch
- entry open to formal living room with volume ceiling
- abundant windows throughout
- dining room open to living room for versatility
- step down into comfortable family room with fireplace
- den with bookcase can easily open up to family room with French doors if desired
- pantry and desk in kitchen open to bayed dinette
- upstairs, bedroom #2 offers volume ceiling and half-round window
- skylit hall bath
- private master suite features plant shelf, whirlpool, skylight above vanity and walk-in closet

Rear Elevation

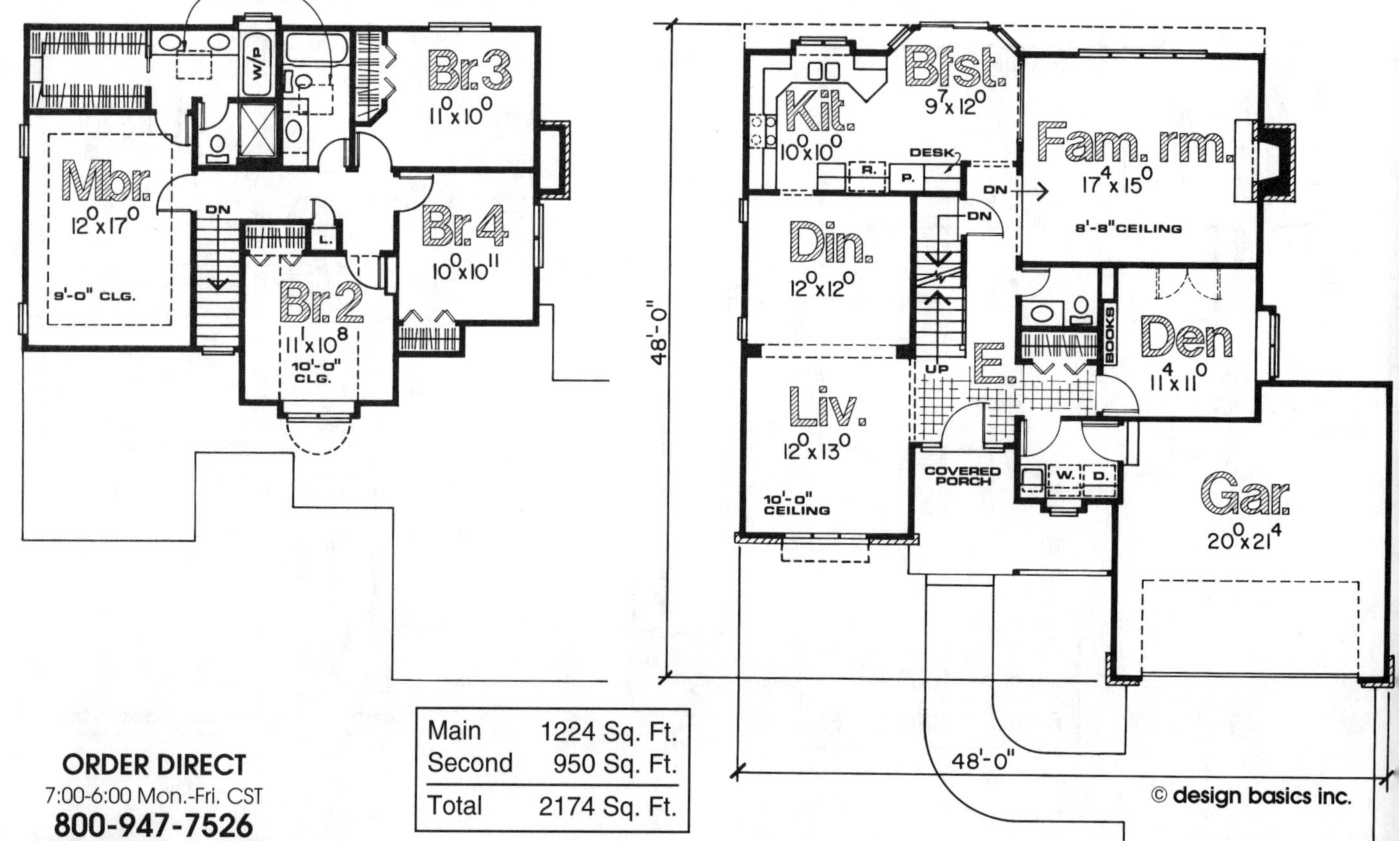

Main	1224 Sq. Ft.
Second	950 Sq. Ft.
Total	2174 Sq. Ft.

9F-669 Kinston price code: 21

- ▶ **High quality, erasable, reproducible vellums**
- ▶ **Shipped via 2nd day air within the continental U.S.**

- large hard-surfaced entry open to dining room
- step down to spacious great room which is visually open to breakfast area and kitchen
- central powder bath location
- airy island kitchen features a planning desk, pantry and corner sink with windows above
- bright breakfast area with many windows and access to outside
- convenient main floor laundry
- master suite ume ceiling in corner whirlpoo light and compa shower completing

Rear Elevation

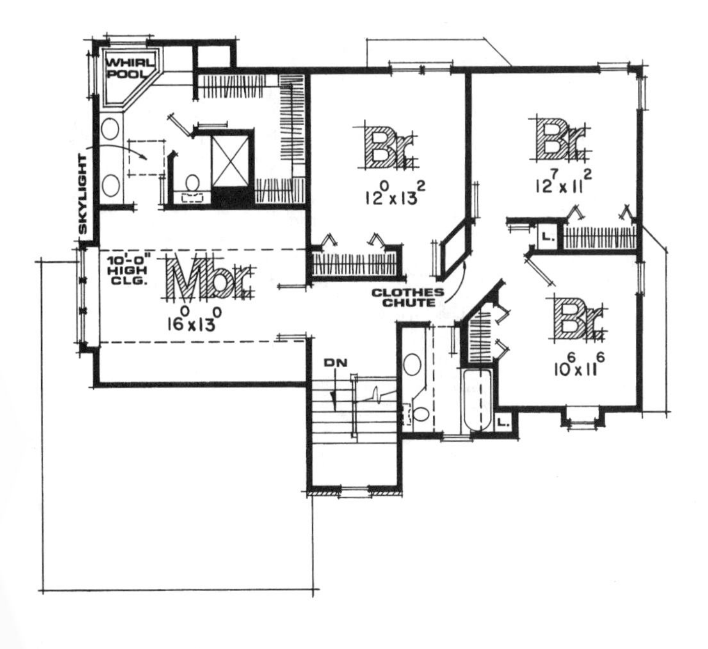

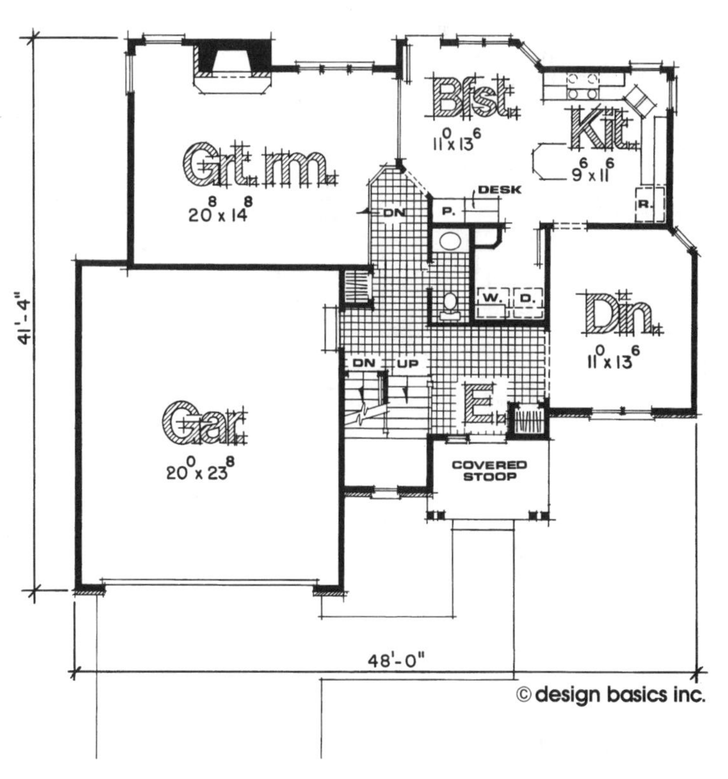

© design basics inc.

Main	1048 Sq. Ft.
Second	1143 Sq. Ft.
Total	2191 Sq. Ft.

price code: 22

- ...into gathering room with cozy ...d inviting view to the back
- ...n and bayed breakfast fea-...rapping counter, pantry
- ...floor laundry with sink
- location of secondary bedrooms affords privacy to all
- luxurious master suite includes vaulted ceiling, his and her closets, dual lavs, corner whirlpool and compartmented bath

Rear Elevation

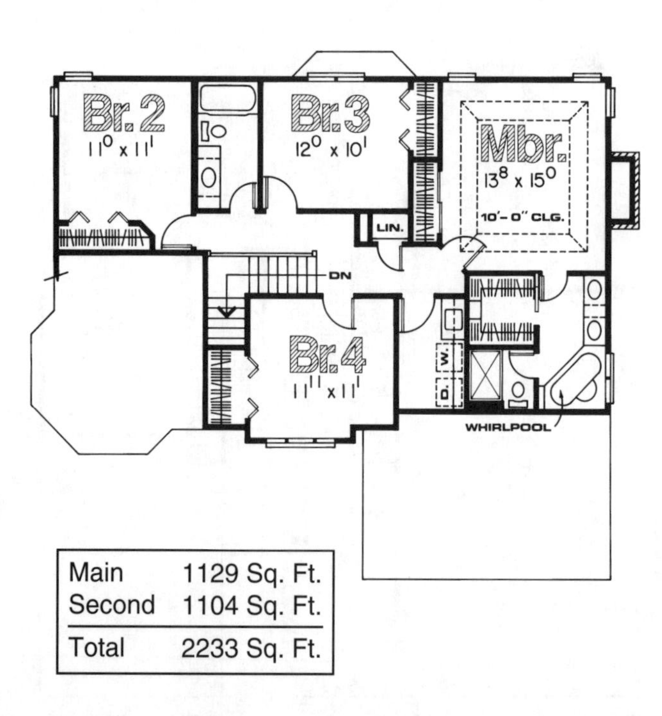

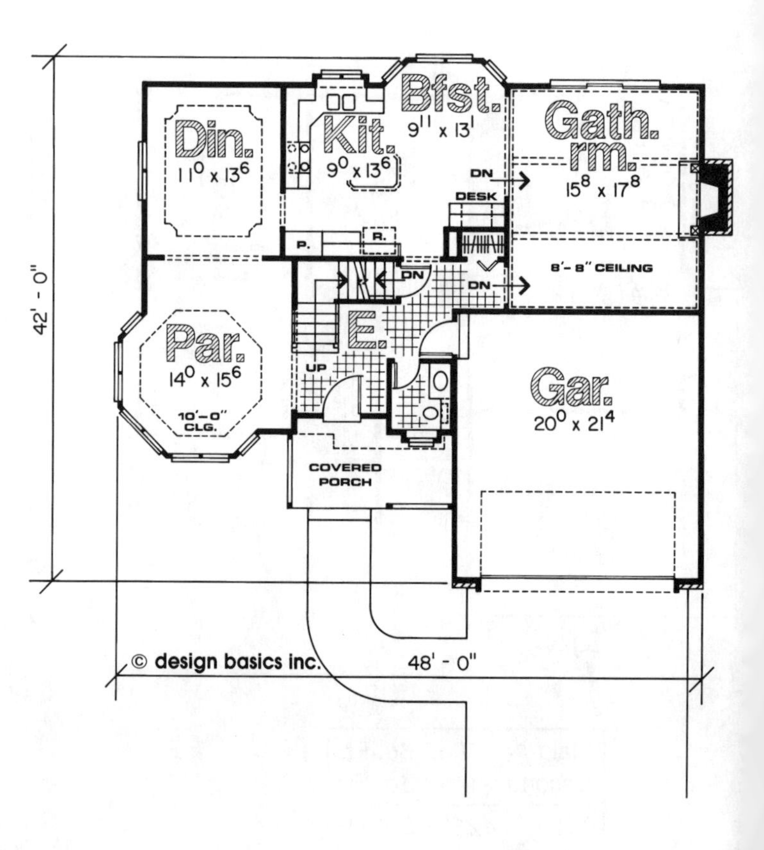

Main	1129 Sq. Ft.
Second	1104 Sq. Ft.
Total	2233 Sq. Ft.

9F-2157 Lauderdale price code: 23

- High quality, erasable, reproducible vellums
- Shipped via 2nd day air within the continental U.S.

- volume living room with transoms atop elegant bayed windows is open to dining room with hutch space
- efficient kitchen includes pantry and snack bar
- central powder bath location
- bayed breakfast area open to sunken family room with raised hearth fireplace
- laundry area doubles as mud entry from garage
- maximized second level footage
- elaborate master suite boasts tiered ceiling, dual entrances to large bath, luxurious vanities with see-thru surrounding glass detail, shower and separate whirlpool, 2 compartmented stools and huge walk-in closet

Rear Elevation

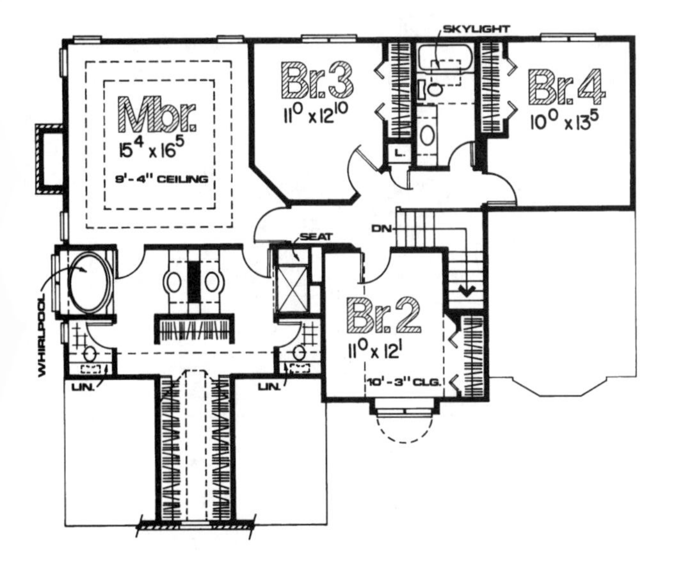

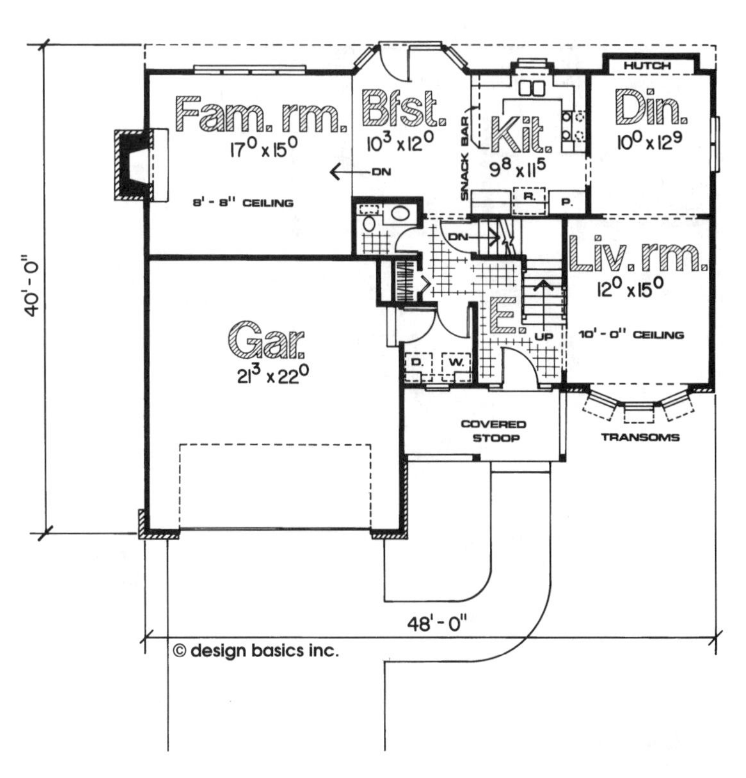

Main	1063 Sq. Ft.
Second	1242 Sq. Ft.
Total	2305 Sq. Ft.

9F-1754 Sydney price code: 23

- High quality, erasable, reproducible vellums
- Shipped via 2nd day air within the continental U.S.

Gold Seal™ HOME PLANS

- volume entry with plant ledge above
- unique angled staircase off entry
- dining room open to living room for expanded entertaining
- sunken family room with see-thru fireplace and beamed ceiling
- island kitchen with pantry adjoins sunny dinette
- convenient laundry off kitchen
- extra depth in garage
- upstairs, landing overlooks entry below
- segregated secondary bedrooms share centralized bath with 2 lavs
- tiered ceiling in master bedroom with his and her walk-in closets
- master bath offers window over 2-person whirlpool plus his and her vanity

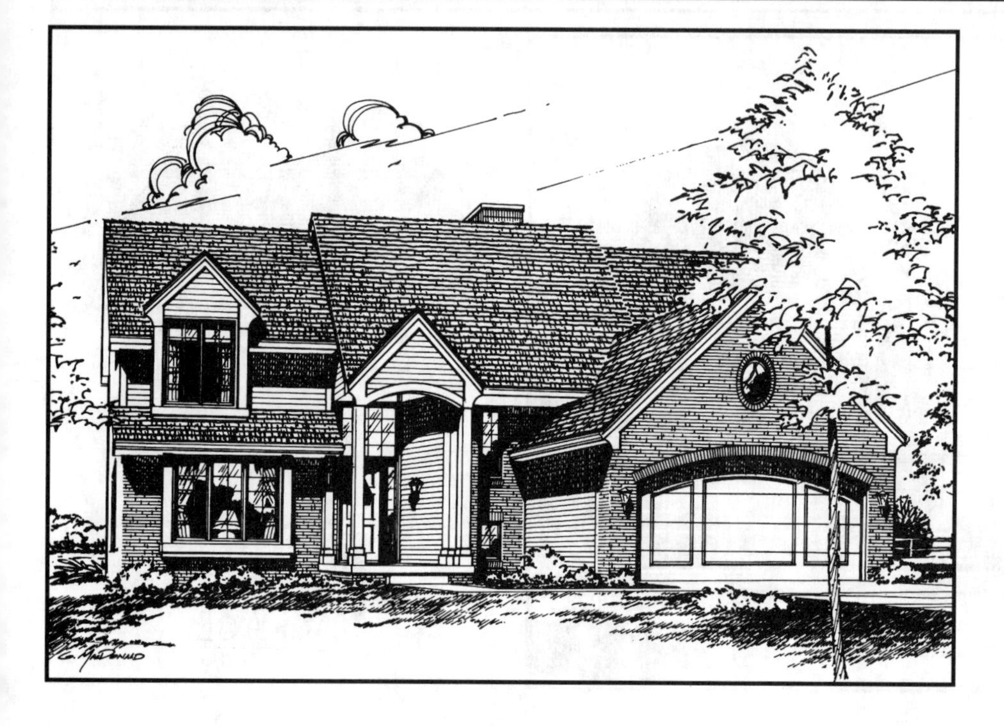

Rear Elevation

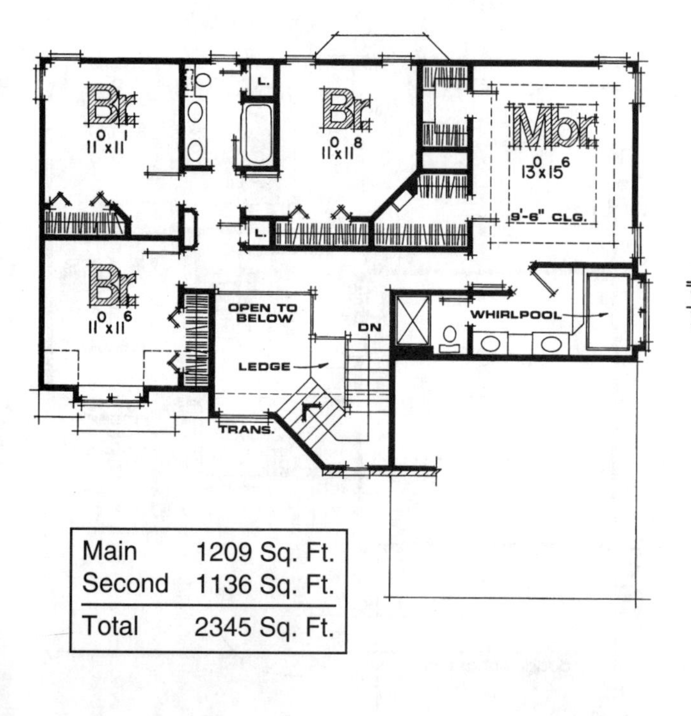

Main	1209 Sq. Ft.
Second	1136 Sq. Ft.
Total	2345 Sq. Ft.

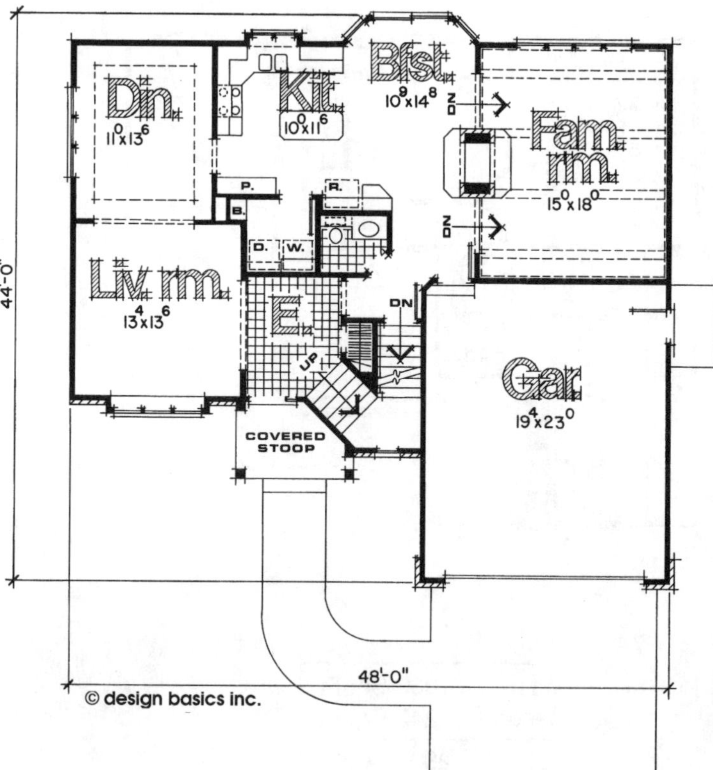

9F-3568 Melrose price code: 19

- ▶ **High quality, erasable, reproducible vellums**
- ▶ **Shipped via 2nd day air within the continental U.S.**

- intricate details bring out tradition of days past
- window seat and volume ceiling upon entry
- parlor creates elegant atmosphere and is flexible as dining room
- kitchen/breakfast area offers island counter, boxed windows and lazy Susan
- view of backyard can be seen from spacious family room through lovely windows
- back staircase location is convenient to living areas of the home
- French doors reveal 9'-0" ceiling, whirlpool tub and plant shelf in master suite
- bedroom #2 has 10'-0" ceiling and shares full bath with bedroom #3
- optional bonus room on second floor

Rear Elevation

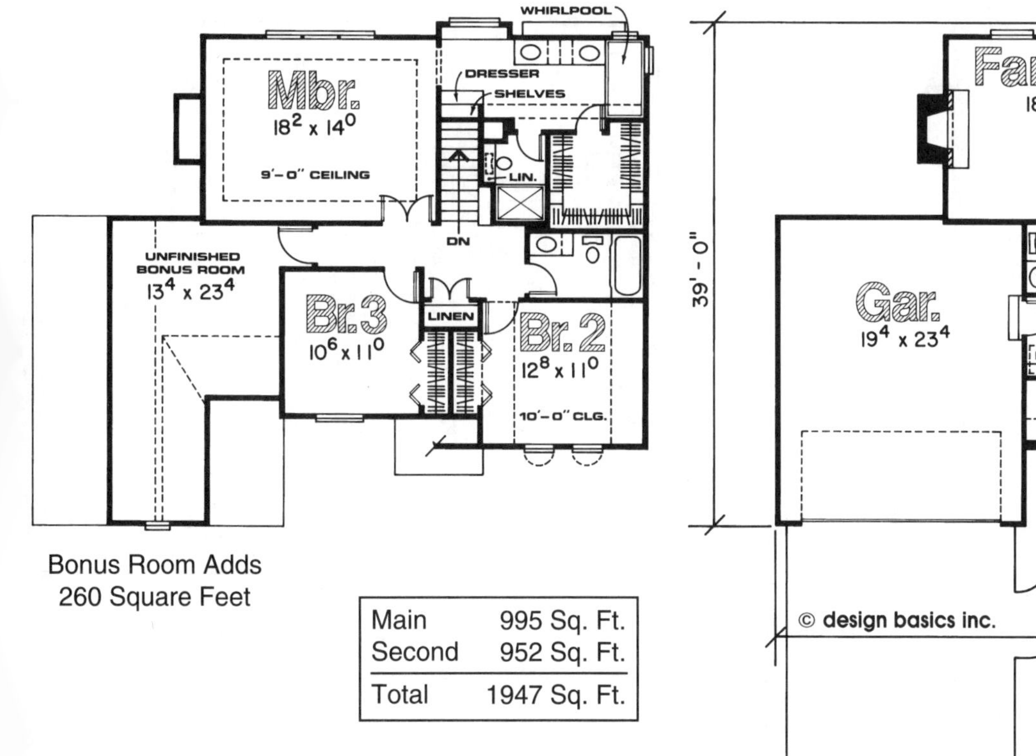

Bonus Room Adds
260 Square Feet

Main	995 Sq. Ft.
Second	952 Sq. Ft.
Total	1947 Sq. Ft.

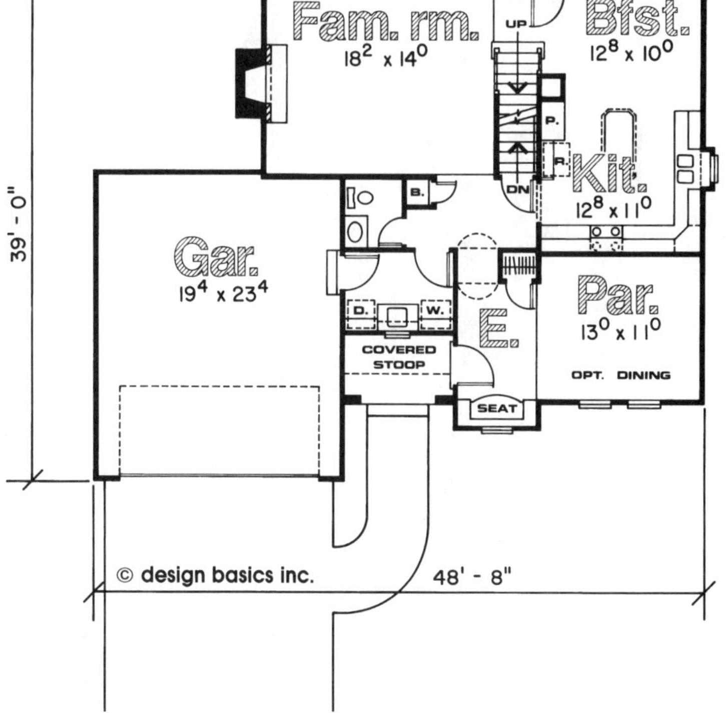

9F-3384 Frederick price code: 19

Gold Seal™ HOME PLANS

- High quality, erasable, reproducible vellums
- Shipped via 2nd day air within the continental U.S.

- exterior details combine to evoke emotion
- living room boasts 10-foot ceiling and boxed window
- dining room openly connected to living room - perfect for formal gatherings
- wrapping counters and corner sink in kitchen open to bayed breakfast area
- laundry room and back hall closet convenient features near garage entry
- master bedroom with boxed ceiling and walk-in offers perfect place to retreat
- pampering master bath presents whirlpool tub under arched window plus separate shower
- bedroom #2 has large walk-in closet

Rear Elevation

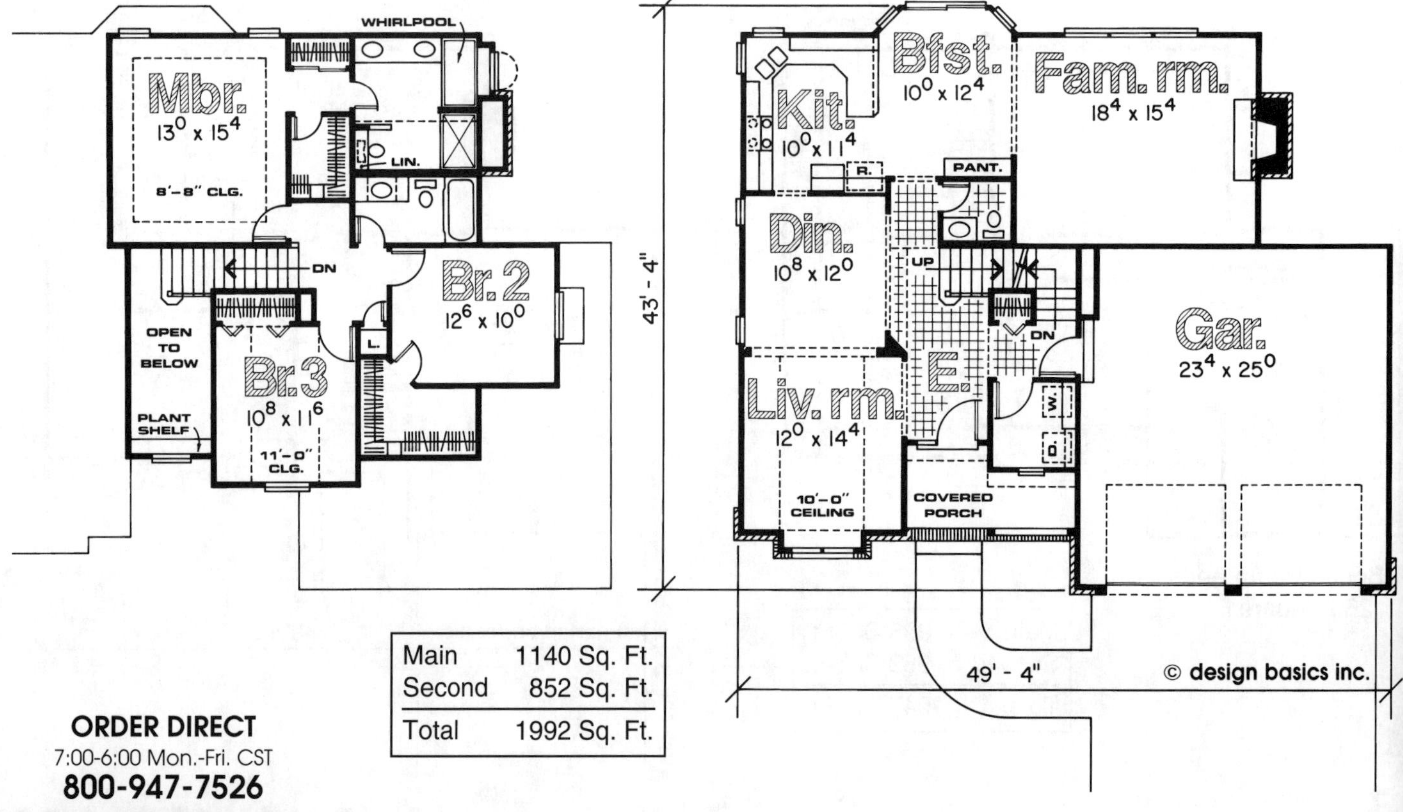

Main	1140 Sq. Ft.
Second	852 Sq. Ft.
Total	1992 Sq. Ft.

9F-2648 Cyprus price code: 19

Gold Seal™ HOME PLANS

- ▶ High quality, erasable, reproducible vellums
- ▶ Shipped via 2nd day air within the continental U.S.

- brilliant design character captures great livability in this striking 2-story home
- whether used as office, library, or as formal living room, parlor with privacy is valuable design
- T-shaped staircase smooths traffic flow
- well-appointed kitchen is just steps away from dinette and dining room
- integrated design of family room, dinette and kitchen capitalize on comfortable family living and easy entertaining
- charming window seat complements comfortable master bedroom
- all desired amenities such as walk-in closet, dual lavs and whirlpool are featured in master bath

Rear Elevation

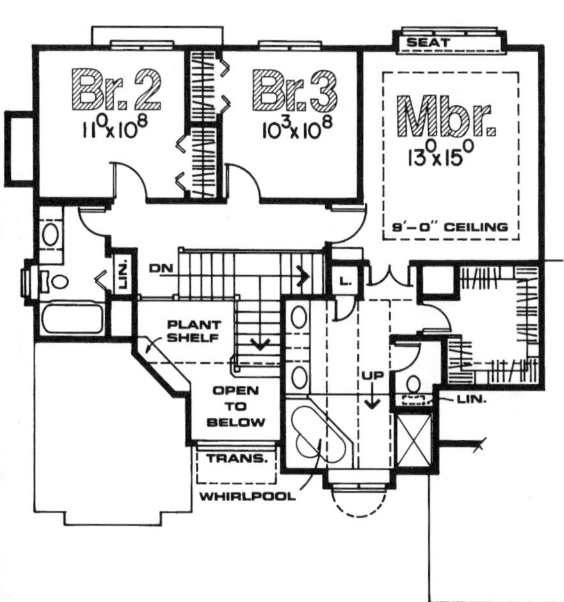

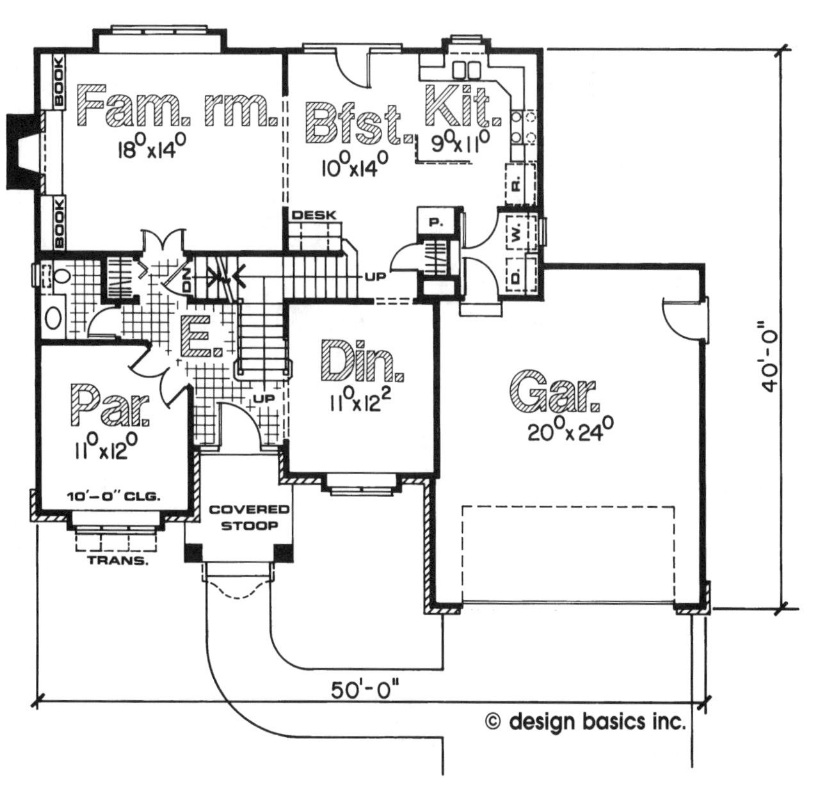

Main	1082 Sq. Ft.
Second	869 Sq. Ft.
Total	1951 Sq. Ft.

9F-3552 Ballobin price code: 20

- High quality, erasable, reproducible vellums
- Shipped via 2nd day air within the continental U.S.

Gold Seal HOME PLANS™

- front elevation captures attention with alluring windows and porch
- dining room opts as formal parlor
- convenient coat closet in oak entry
- front and back covered porches to enjoy outdoors
- abundant counter space serves kitchen
- bayed breakfast area accesses snack bar
- large family room presents cathedral ceiling and windows framing warm fireplace
- French doors reveal 9'-0" boxed ceiling, dual lavs and whirlpool in master suite
- compartmented hall bath with twin lavs serves secondary bedrooms
- bedroom #3 possesses walk-in closet

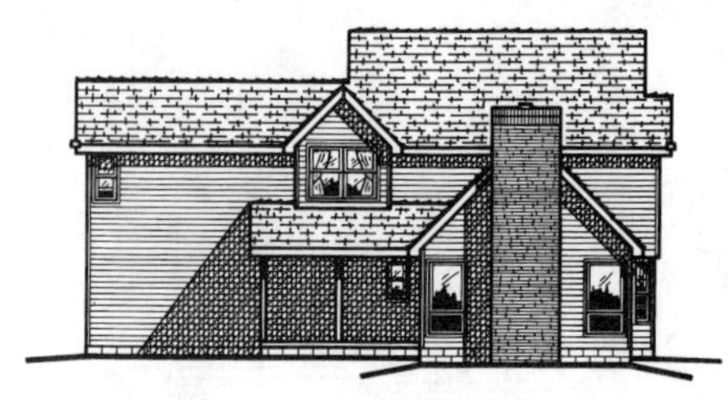

Rear Elevation

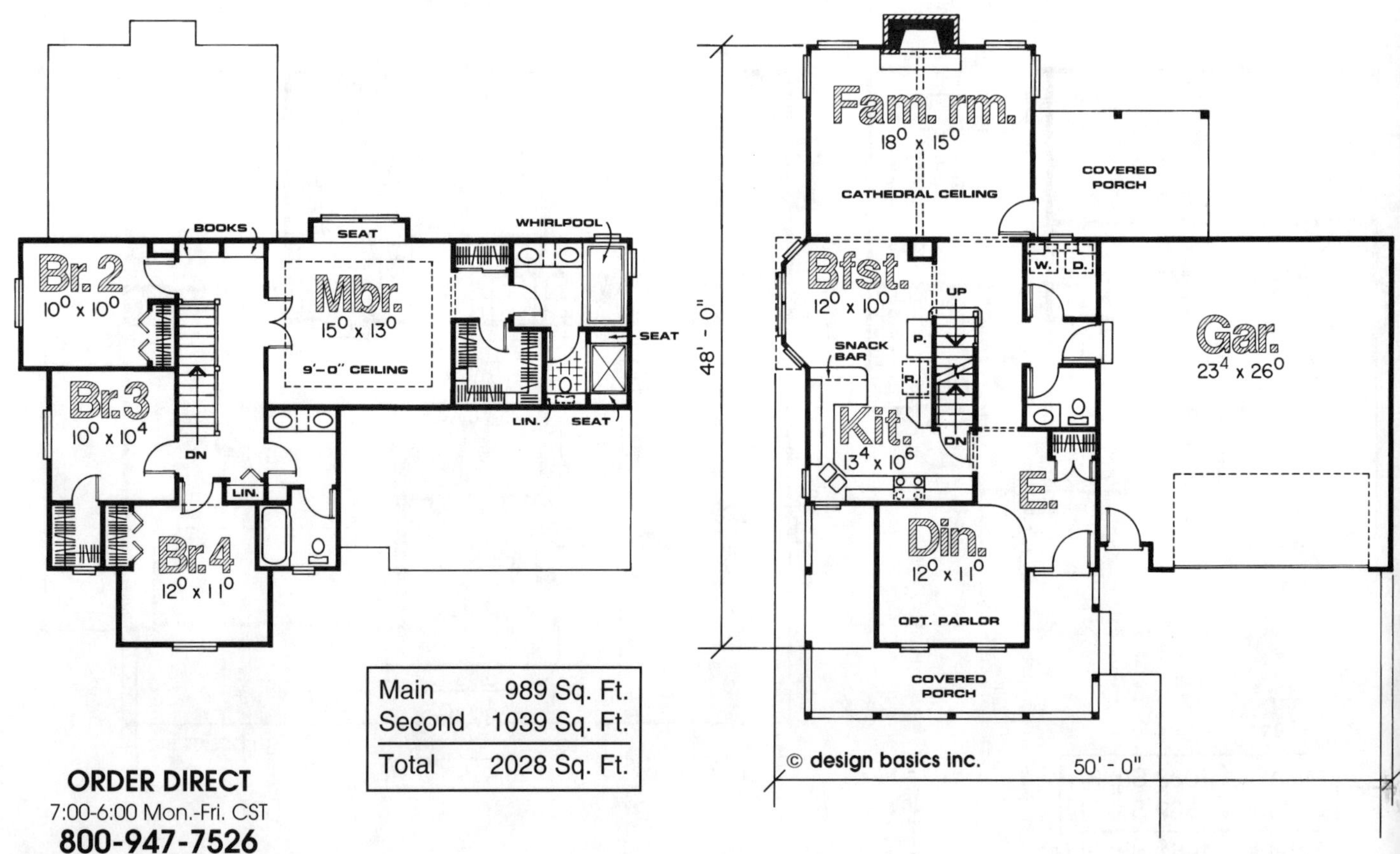

Main	989 Sq. Ft.
Second	1039 Sq. Ft.
Total	2028 Sq. Ft.

9F-2638 Linden price code: 21

- ▶ High quality, erasable, reproducible vellums
- ▶ Shipped via 2nd day air within the continental U.S.

- covered porch invites you into this country style home
- handsome bookcases frame fireplace in spacious family room
- double doors off entry provide family room added privacy
- kitchen features island, lazy Susan a[…] easy access to walk-in laundry
- master bedroom features boxed ce[…] and separate entries into walk-in cl[…] and master bath

Rear Elevation

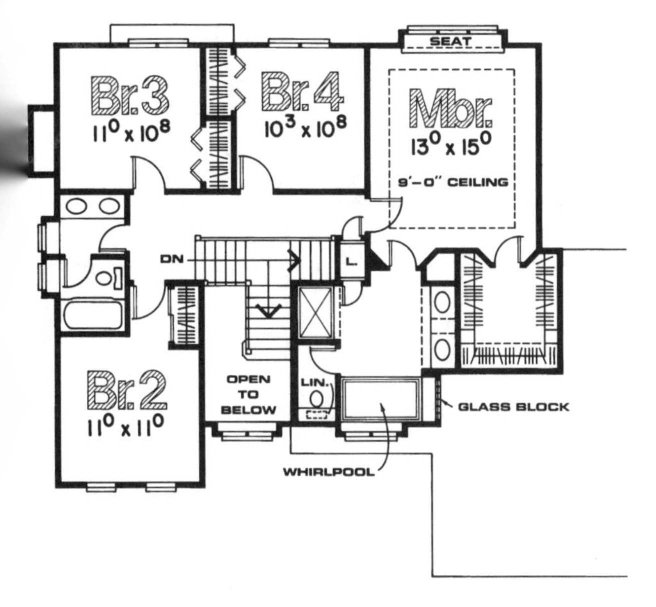

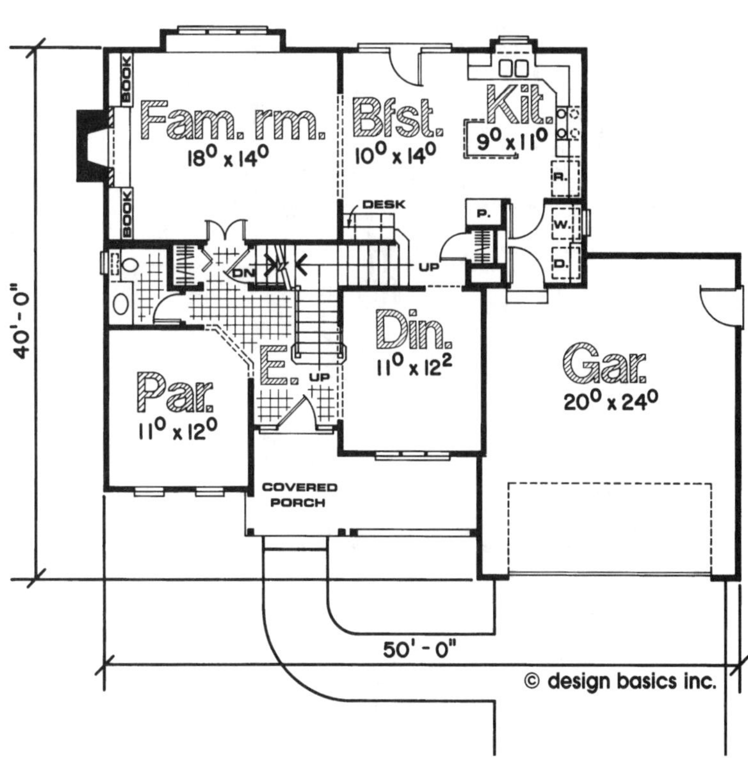

Main	1082 Sq. Ft.
Second	1021 Sq. Ft.
Total	2103 Sq. Ft.

...man price code: 21

...ucible vellums
...hin the continental U.S.

- ...nsight into home
- ...d with arched win-
- ...eiling
- ...s to kitchen through
- wet bar, fireplace and beautiful windows in casual family room
- bayed breakfast area accesses back
- kitchen includes island counter and two lazy Susans
- soaking sink in laundry room
- master suite has 9'-0" ceiling, skylight and whirlpool tub with separate shower
- room for expansion on second floor

Rear Elevation

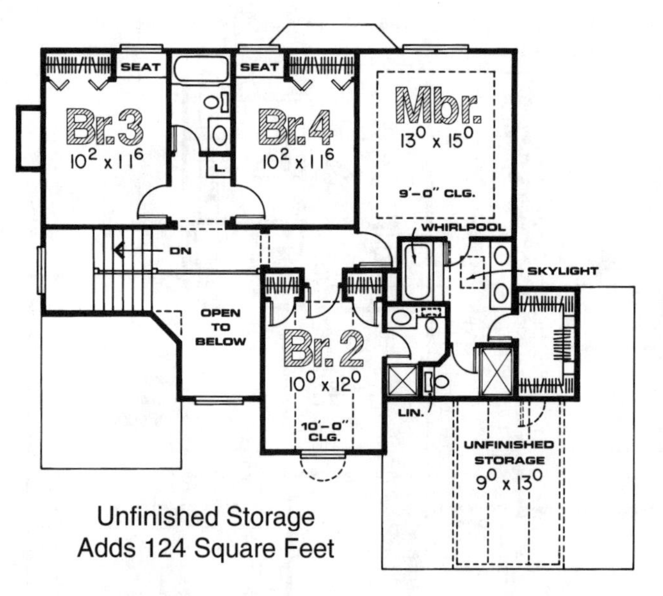

Unfinished Storage
Adds 124 Square Feet

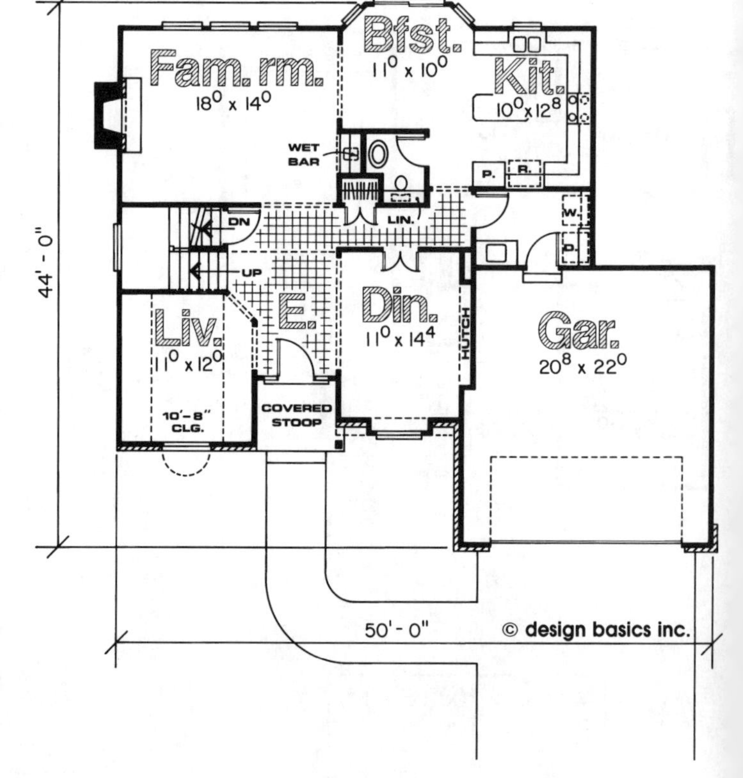

Main	1179 Sq. Ft.
Second	1019 Sq. Ft.
Total	2198 Sq. Ft.

9F-790 Cormorant price code: 22

- High quality, erasable, reproducible vellums
- Shipped via 2nd day air within the continental U.S.

- interesting angled staircase at entry
- volume living room and dining room are open to easily accommodate larger gatherings
- high transom windows in dining room spotlight hutch or buffet
- sunken family room with fireplace
- well planned kitchen boasts 2 lazy Susans, pantry and windows above sink
- planning desk in breakfast area
- centrally located powder bath
- large laundry area with sink and window
- double doors open into master bedroom with vaulted ceiling
- skylit master bath/dressing area has whirlpool, double lavs and large walk-in closet
- second bedroom converts easily to den

Rear Elevation

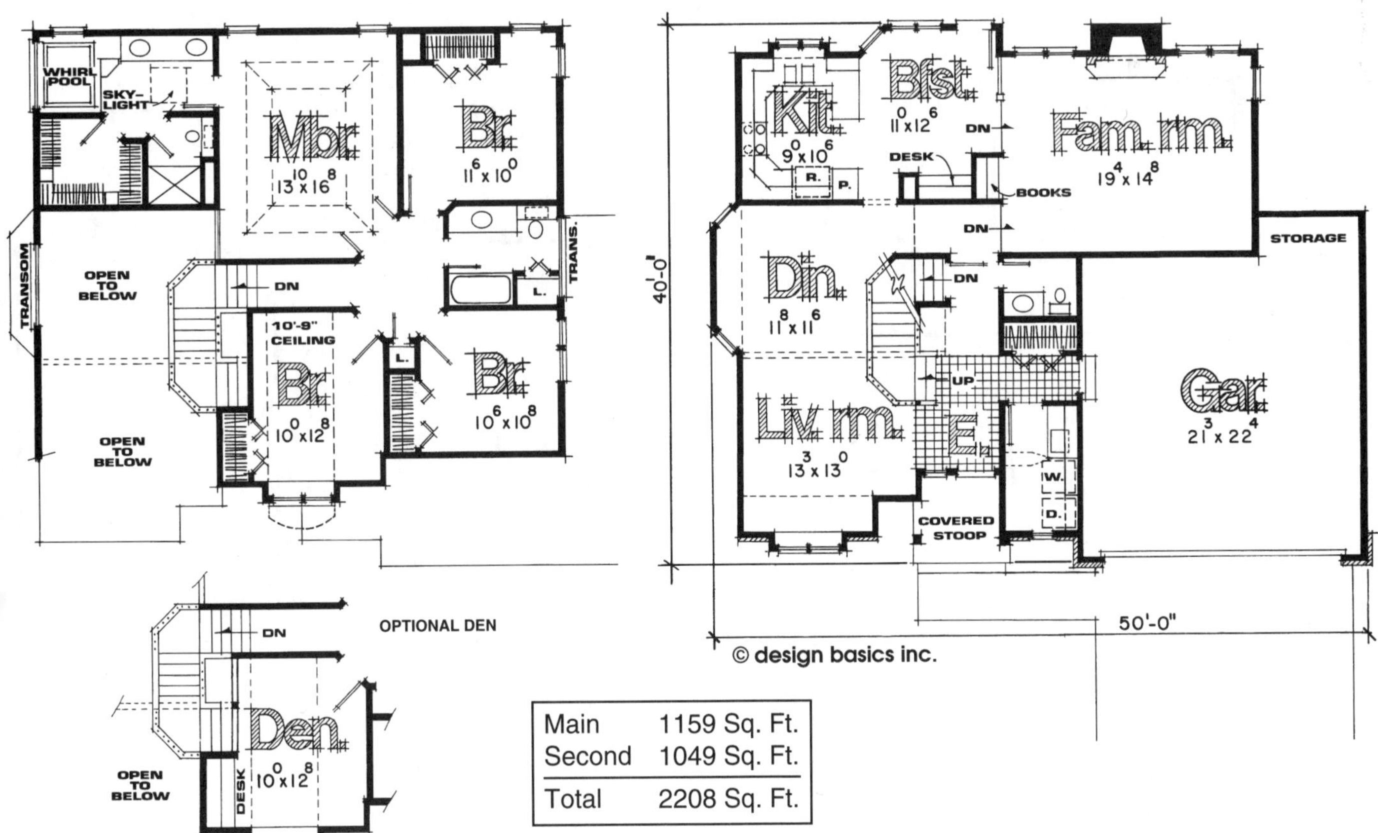

Main	1159 Sq. Ft.
Second	1049 Sq. Ft.
Total	2208 Sq. Ft.

9F-1857 Cambridge price code: 22

Gold Seal HOME PLANS™

- ▶ High quality, erasable, reproducible vellums
- ▶ Shipped via 2nd day air within the continental U.S.

- elevation's picturesque turret-shaped porch has impactful curb appeal
- unique staircase adds intrigue to large entrance hall
- both parlor and adjoining dining room include sunny bayed windows
- bright kitchen and breakfast area features desk, pantry, wrapping counters and access door to outside
- step down into spacious gathering room with bayed window, raised hearth fireplace and built-in bookcase
- skylit hall bath with handy linen closet
- comfortable secondary bedrooms
- French door entry to elegant master suite with vaulted ceiling and pampering skylit master bath with walk-in closet, whirlpool tub and dual lavs

Rear Elevation

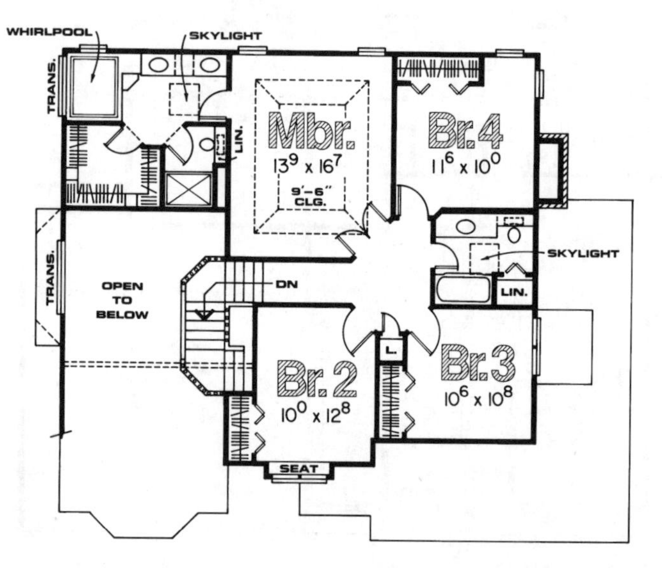

Bfst. 10^{8} x 12^{6}
Kit. 9^{0} x 10^{6}
R. P.
DESK
DN
Gath. rm. 19^{3} x 16^{7}
BOOKS
8'-8" CEILING
DN
STORAGE
Din. 11^{8} x 11^{5}
16'-10" CLG.
DN
UP
E.
Gar. 21^{4} x 22^{4}
Par. 13^{3} x 15^{0}
IRON-A-WAY
W. D.
COVERED PORCH
TRANSOMS
40' - 0"
50' - 0"

Main	1202 Sq. Ft.
Second	1049 Sq. Ft.
Total	2251 Sq. Ft.

9F-1033 Santee price code: 24

- High quality, erasable, reproducible vellums
- Shipped via 2nd day air within the continental U.S.

- entry spotlights angled staircase and formal living room
- dining room with hutch space open to living room for expanded entertaining
- family room offers beamed ceiling, bookcase and fireplace framed by windows
- kitchen is well planned with wrapping counter, pantry, desk and corner sink
- bayed window in breakfast area which provides access to the outside
- laundry room with sink and iron-a-way
- discrete main-floor powder bath
- master suite with his and her closets in bedroom, plus dressing/bath area featuring wrapping vanity, walk-in closet and 2-person whirlpool tub
- third bedroom includes walk-in closet

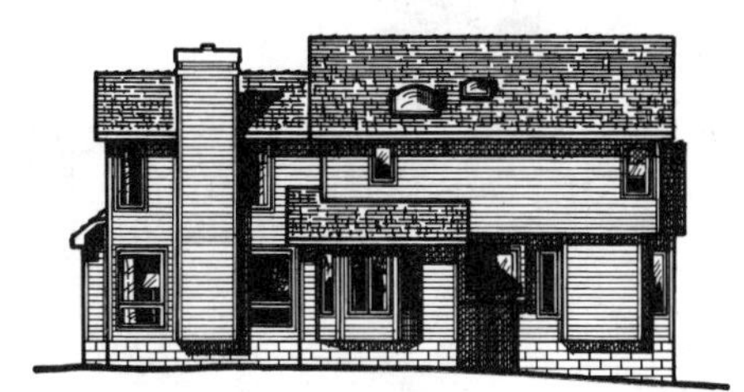

Rear Elevation

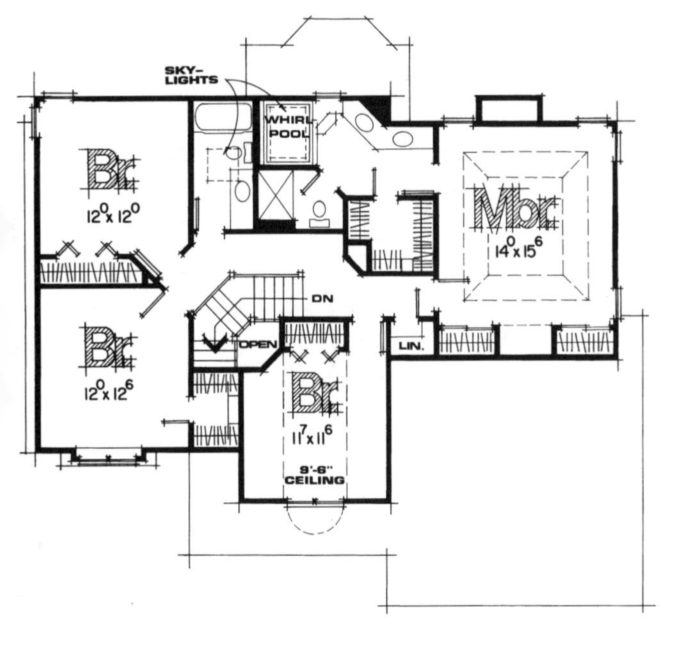

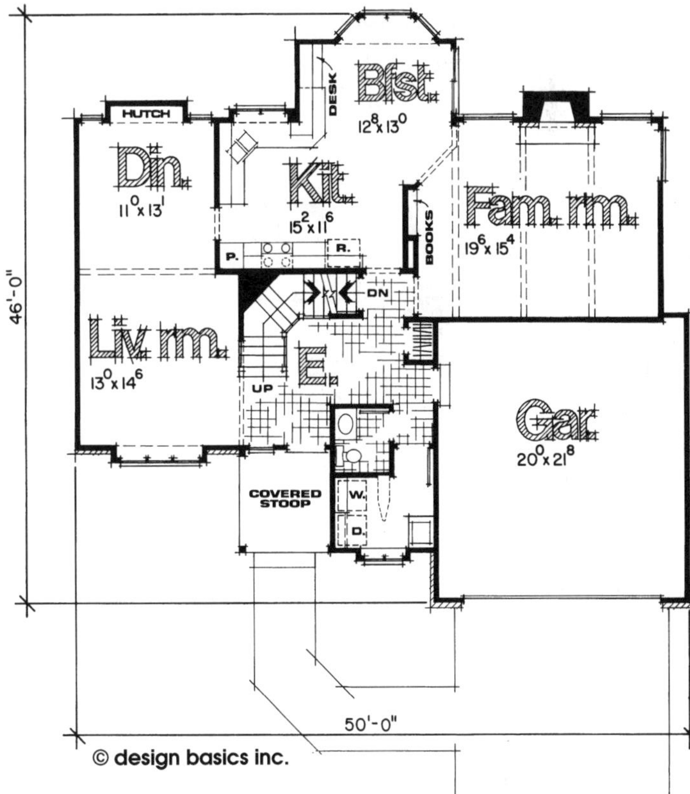

Main	1247 Sq. Ft.
Second	1183 Sq. Ft.
Total	2430 Sq. Ft.

design basics inc.®
HOME PLAN DESIGN SERVICE

9F-3274 Whitmore price code: 25

- intricate trim work and covered porch create sense of family appeal
- 9'-0" main level walls
- formal living and dining rooms are decorated by box ceilings and round columns
- efficient kitchen values snack bar, 2 pantries, desk and lazy Susans
- sunny atrium door in bayed breakfast area opens to outdoors
- family room with box beam ceiling details and brick fireplace is ideal for gatherings
- master suite includes large walk-in, ample dressing area with dual lavs and whirlpool
- secondary bedrooms share compartmented hall bath with 2 lavs
- spacious bonus room available for future expansion

Rear Elevation

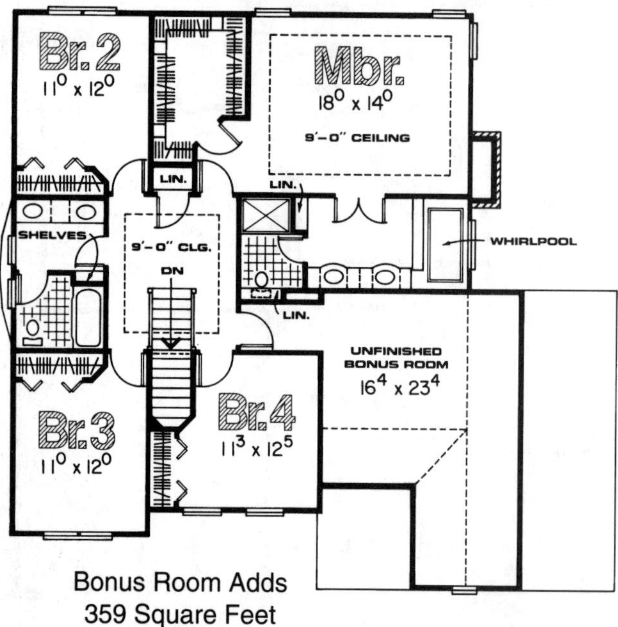

Bonus Room Adds 359 Square Feet

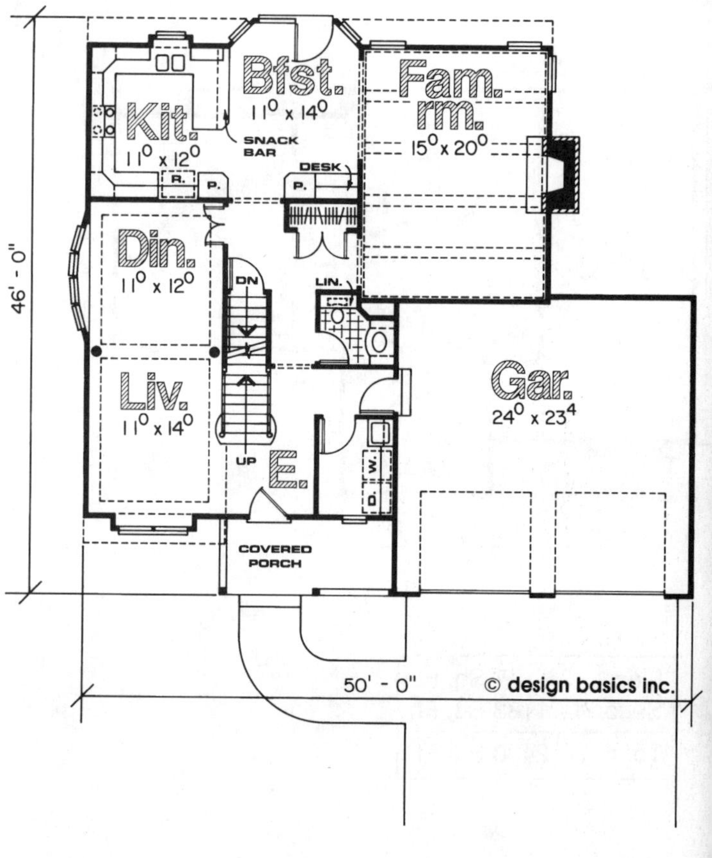

Main	1255 Sq. Ft.
Second	1262 Sq. Ft.
Total	2517 Sq. Ft.

GOLD SEAL™ HOME PLANS

BASE PLAN INFORMATION				
PAGE NO.	WIDTH	PLAN NO.	PLAN NAME	SQ. FT.
149	44'-0"	851	Medford	1201
150	48'-0"	1581	Drake	1458
152	50'-0"	978	Savannah	1556
151	48'-0"	1477	Emerson	1690
148	42'-0"	1041	McNary	1699

MULTI LEVEL HOMES

9F-1041 McNary price code: 16

- High quality, erasable, reproducible vellums
- Shipped via 2nd day air within the continental U.S.

- formal living room featuring boxed window and volume ceiling open to entry with coat closet
- centrally located powder bath
- private lower-level family room with fireplace framed by windows
- lower level laundry room including sink and iron-a-way also serves as mud room with walk-out access to the back
- efficient kitchen with desk and walk-in pantry adjoins sunny bayed breakfast area with special ceiling detail
- master suite with skylit dressing/bath area features double vanity, walk-in closet and whirlpool tub
- secondary bedrooms with boxed windows share convenient hall bath

Rear Elevation

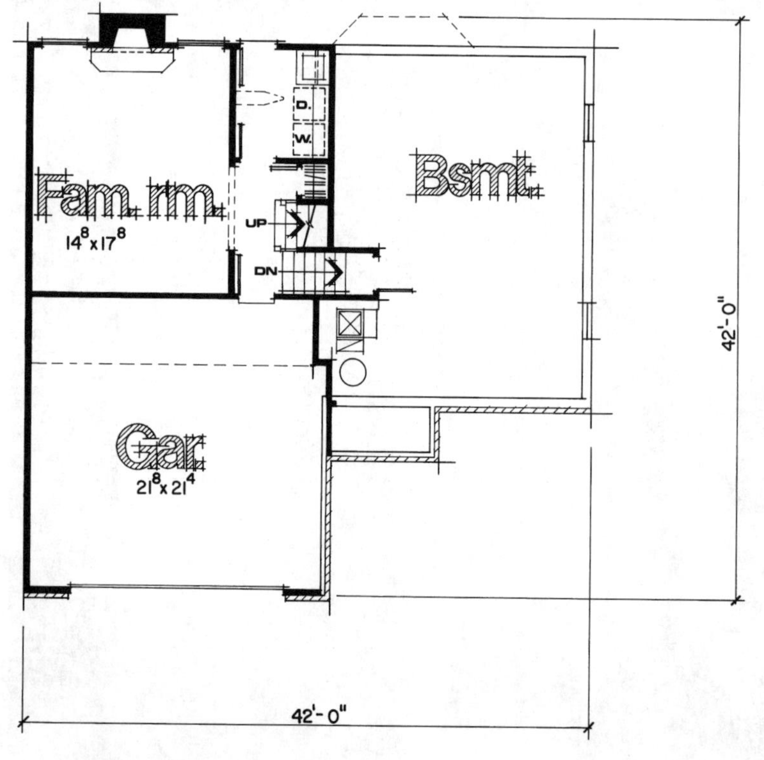

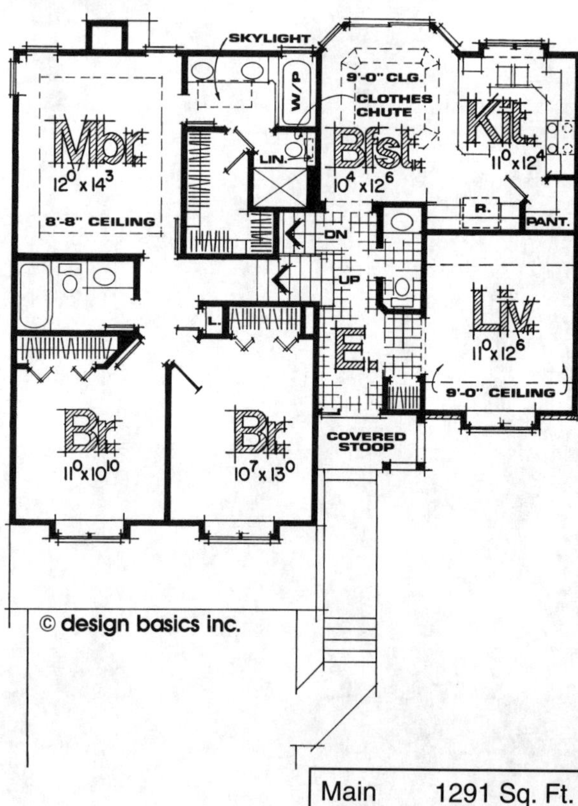

Main	1291 Sq. Ft.
Second	408 Sq. Ft.
Total	1699 Sq. Ft.

9F-851 Medford price code: 12

- ▸ High quality, erasable, reproducible vellums
- ▸ Shipped via 2nd day air within the continental U.S.

- entry opens to volume great room with fireplace and large boxed window
- conveniently located laundry room is only one-half flight down on garage level
- well-planned kitchen features wrapping counter, corner sink with windows, pantry, lazy Susan and snack bar serving sunny breakfast area
- master bedroom with walk-in closet and compartmented stool and shower
- hall bath shared by secondary bedrooms

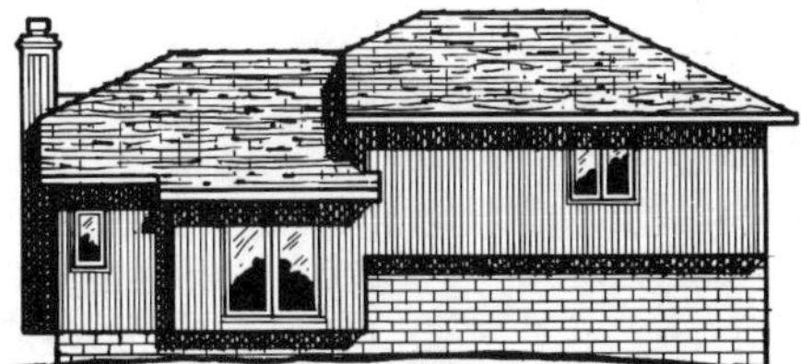

Rear Elevation

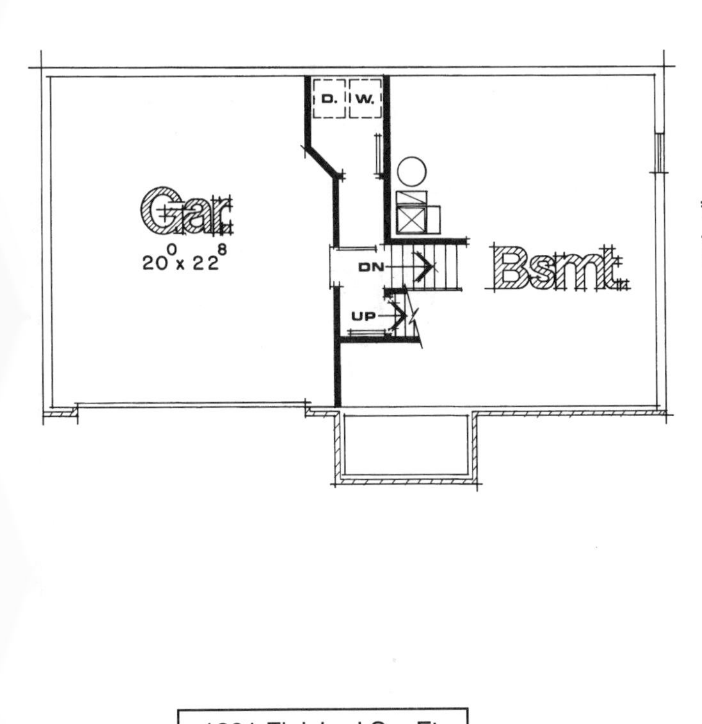

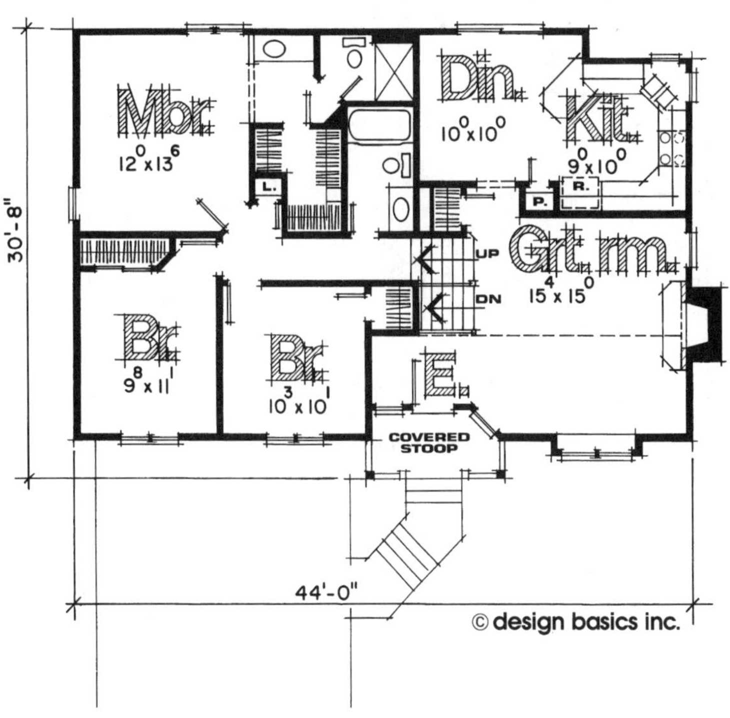

1201 Finished Sq. Ft.

9F-1581 Drake price code: 14

Gold Seal™ HOME PLANS

- High quality, erasable, reproducible vellums
- Shipped via 2nd day air within the continental U.S.

- front door commands expansive, impressive views of high volume entry, great room and dining room, skylit stairwell and plant ledges above
- perceived space from diagonal views through the house
- coat closet at entry
- fireplace centered under great room's valley cathedral ceiling framed by large windows
- efficient kitchen with pantry and planning desk
- separate dining room and dinette
- luxurious master suite features mirrored bi-pass doors for large walk-in closet, dressing area and private bath
- corridor hallway to bedrooms

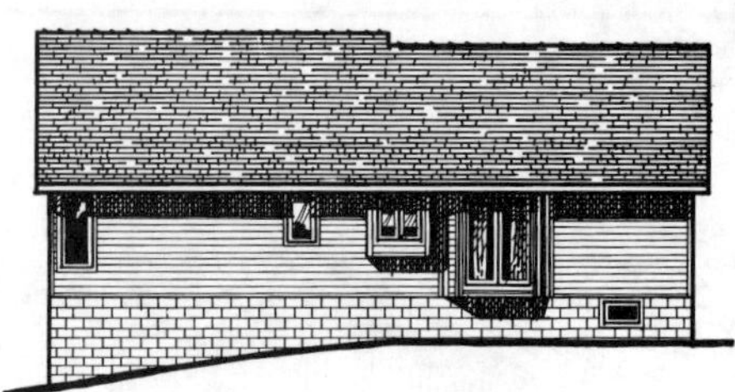

Rear Elevation

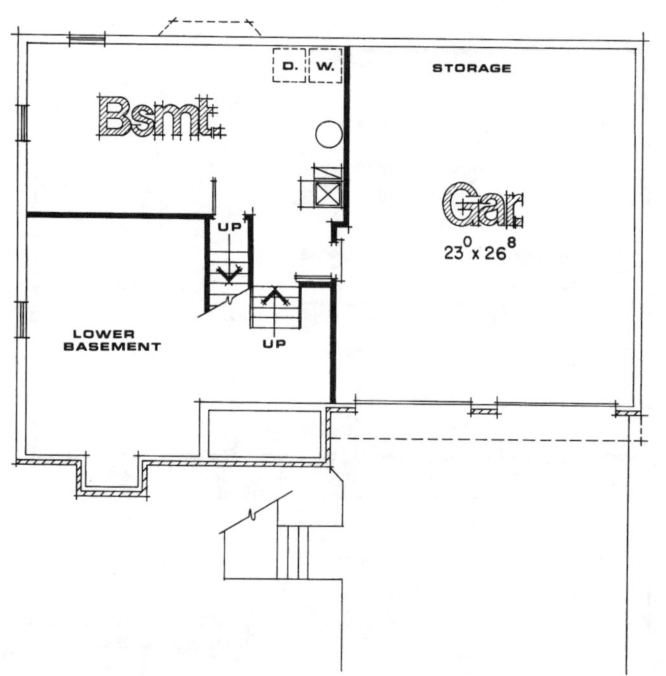

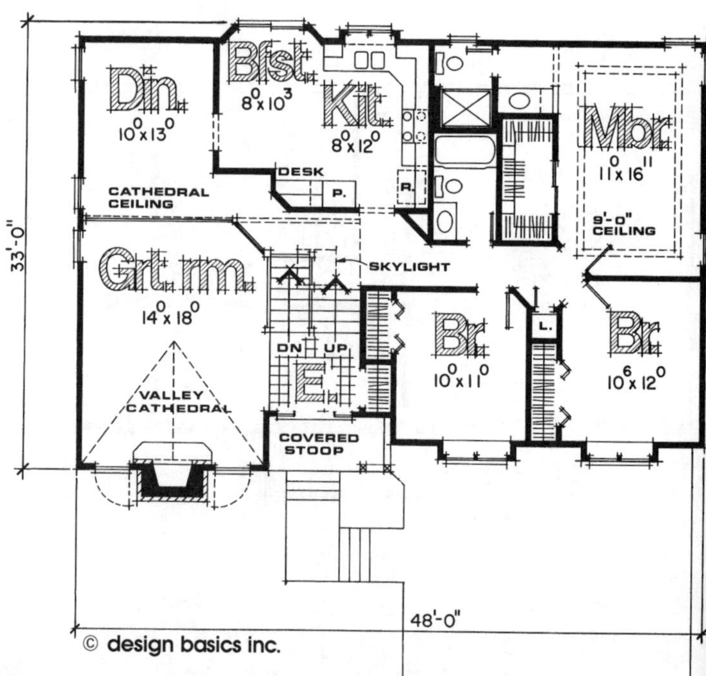

1458 Finished Sq. Ft.

ORDER DIRECT
7:00-6:00 Mon.-Fri. CST
800-947-7526

9F-1477 Emerson price code: 16

Gold Seal HOME PLANS™

- ▶ High quality, erasable, reproducible vellums
- ▶ Shipped via 2nd day air within the continental U.S.

- main level mud/laundry room
- comfortable living room with bayed window and vaulted ceiling open to formal dining room
- efficient kitchen overlooking family room with raised hearth fireplace
- bayed breakfast area with planning desk
- back stairs into kitchen
- storage space in garage
- full basement
- large hall linen closet
- secondary bedrooms share functional hall bath
- vaulted ceiling in large master bedroom with window seat, walk-in closet and private bath

Rear Elevation

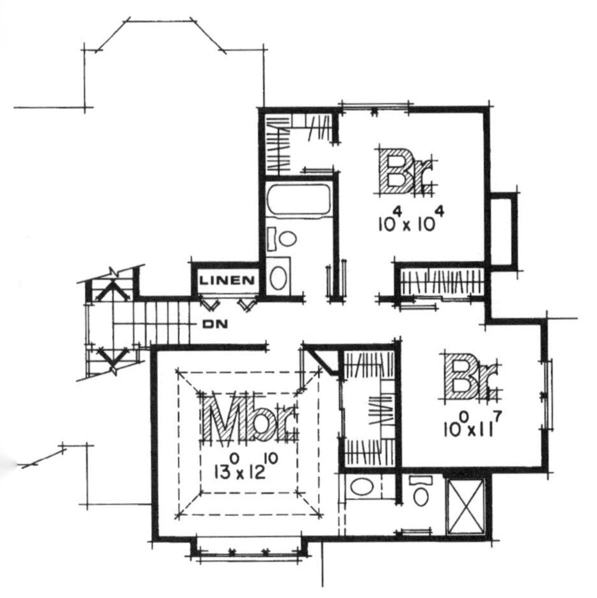

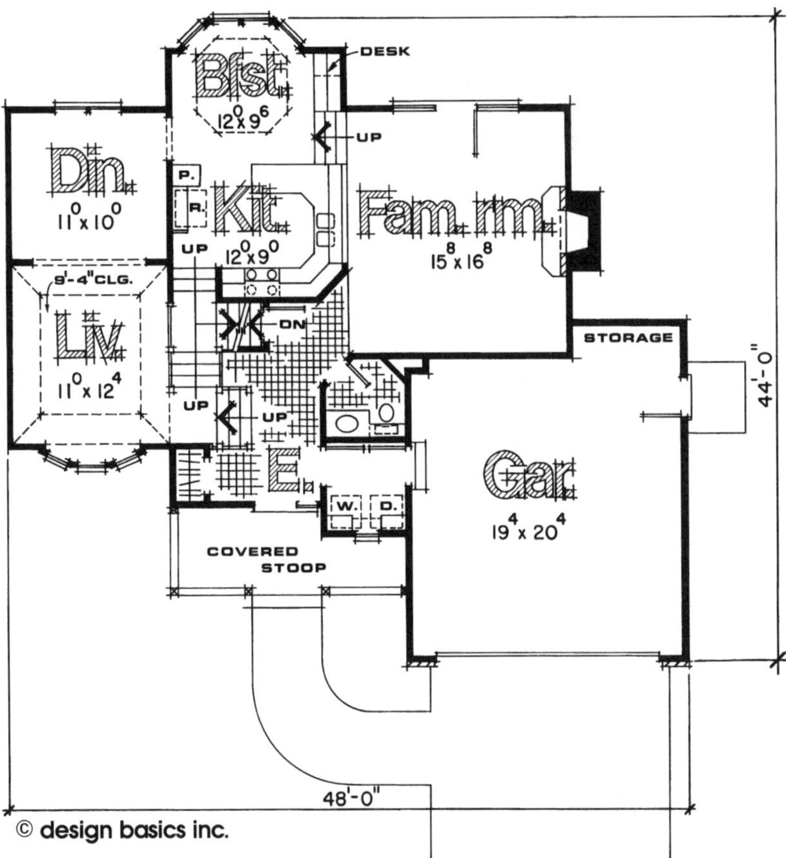

Main	1015 Sq. Ft.
Second	675 Sq. Ft.
Total	1690 Sq. Ft.

design basics inc.®
HOME PLAN DESIGN SERVICE

9F-978 Savannah price code: 15

- high-impact entry
- formal dining room with ceiling detail and boxed window open to entry
- volume great room has handsome brick fireplace and large windows with transoms to the back
- kitchen with wrapping counter, corner sink, lazy Susan and pantry adjoins bayed breakfast area with sloped ceiling and arched transom window
- bathroom and bedrooms situated for privacy in central hallway
- master suite includes skylit dressing/bath area with double vanity, walk-in closet and whirlpool tub
- secondary bedrooms share hall bath
- garage with extra storage space

Rear Elevation

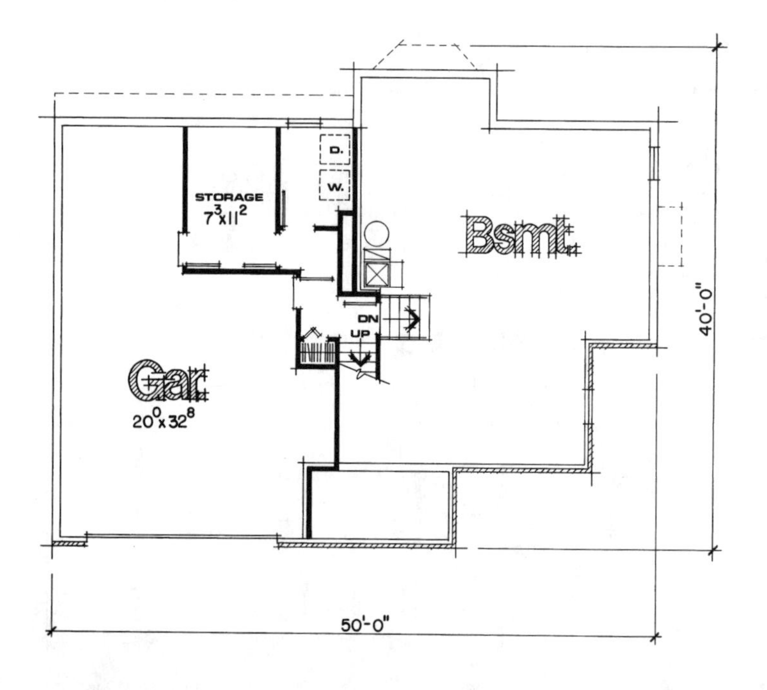

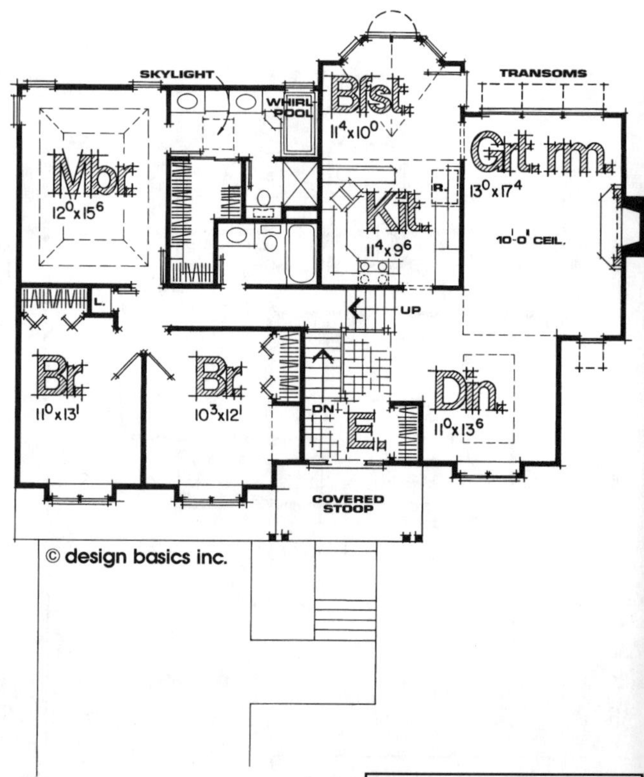

Main	1499 Sq. Ft.
Second	57 Sq. Ft.
Total	1556 Sq. Ft.

Welcome to

Heartland Home Plans™

Designs with a New Appreciation for Traditional American Values

Homes from the Heartland Home Plans™ collection are a part of a philosophy based on designing homes for true practicality and livability. The elevations are unpretentious, warm and immediately welcoming. They are characterized by uncomplicated rooflines, clean, sharp gables and traditional elements such as brick and lap siding. Front porches help create a softer, more inviting look from the street. The design of each floor plan allows for flexibility in the selection of materials and amenities. The floor plans as a whole center on buyers' everyday lifestyles, so one can easily imagine themselves cooking in the kitchen, watching television in the family room and getting ready for the day in the master suite. Regardless of a home's square footage, each floor plan is efficient in its use of space. Together, all of these factors make Heartland homes a value for those who will live in them. The following pages feature 67 Heartland home plan designs – each one appropriate for narrow building sites. Many are "Plexable™", meaning they can be configured into duplex plans, enhancing the entire collection's practicality and adaptability to individual lifestyles. Homes from the Heartland Home Plans™ Collection. It makes sense to live in them – which is what one wants most out of a great design.

HEARTLAND

HOME PLANS™

Plan Index & Guide to Symbols

5 - DAY SELECT PLAN CHANGE GUARANTEE

Plan changes listed in the *Select Plan Change Directory* guaranteed complete in 5 business days for Heartland and Gold Seal Plus™ plans. See page 293 in the back of the book for further details.

RIGHT-READING REVERSE PRINTS

Available for Heartland and Gold Seal Plus™ plans. See page 297 in the back of the book for details.

ROOF CONSTRUCTION PACKAGE

Detailed roof framing plans available for all Design Basics plans. See page 297 in the back of the book for details.

PLEXABLE OPTIONS AVAILABLE

Plexable™ plans can be configured into a variety of duplex designs. See page 294-295 in the back of the book for further details.

HEARTLAND HOME PLANS™

BASE PLAN INFORMATION				
PAGE NO.	WIDTH	PLAN NO.	PLAN NAME	SQ. FT.
156	32'-0"	8161	Morton Grove	1162
159	39'-4"	8163	Trinity Acres	1162
161	40'-0"	8093	Kirby Farm	1212
157	34'-0"	8164	Sabino Canyon	1333
163	42'-0"	8013	Gabriel Bay	1392
158	36'-0"	8165	Sarasota Falls	1398
169	50'-0"	8089	Chandler Hills	1433
162	40'-8"	8160	Bradford Pointe	1449
167	48'-8"	8090	Spring Valley	1453
168	49'-4"	8088	Shadow Pines	1520
164	42'-0"	8159	Skyline Woods	1562
165	42'-0"	8158	Jacobs Bay	1593
170	50'-0"	8080	Maple Grove	1628
166	42'-0"	8079	Belle Harbor	1633
160	39'-4"	8168	Sonora Springs	1705

ONE STORY HOMES

Morton Grove

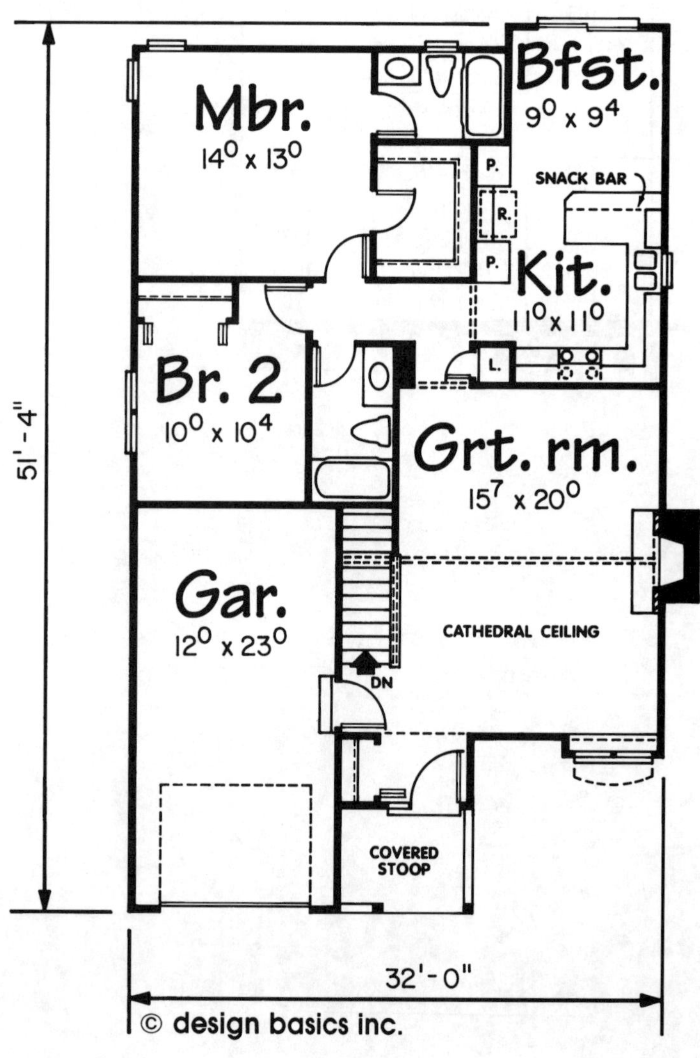

9F-8161

*The dashing **Morton Grove:** In the great room, a cathedral ceiling for a feeling of openness, and a fireplace for a sense of welcome. The snack bar in the kitchen, to serve or eat upon. Two bathrooms, one exclusive to the master suite and the other easily serving the secondary bedroom and all other areas of the home.*

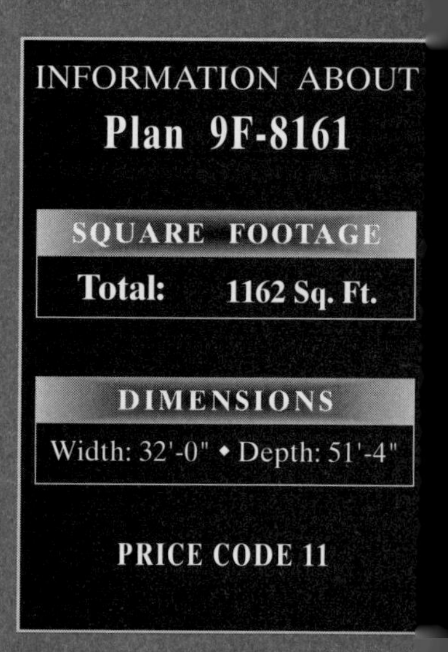

INFORMATION ABOUT
Plan 9F-8161

SQUARE FOOTAGE

Total: 1162 Sq. Ft.

DIMENSIONS

Width: 32'-0" • Depth: 51'-4"

PRICE CODE 11

Order Direct

800-947-7526

(7:00-6:00 Mon.-Fri. CST)

Sabino Canyon

9F-8164

The spunk of Sabino Canyon: *On the elevation, a porch for greeting those walking by. An angled entry, to provide intrigue to those walking in. Counters wrapping around the kitchen, making themselves useful in a variety of ways. And a spacious family room at the rear, providing an area to enjoy a fire and a terrific view.*

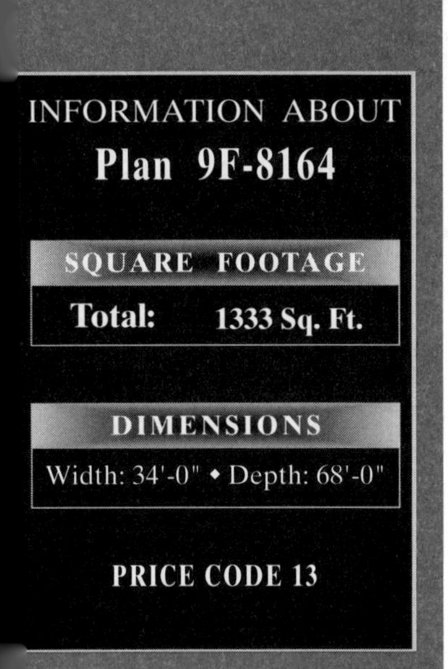

INFORMATION ABOUT
Plan 9F-8164

SQUARE FOOTAGE

Total: **1333 Sq. Ft.**

DIMENSIONS

Width: 34'-0" • Depth: 68'-0"

PRICE CODE 13

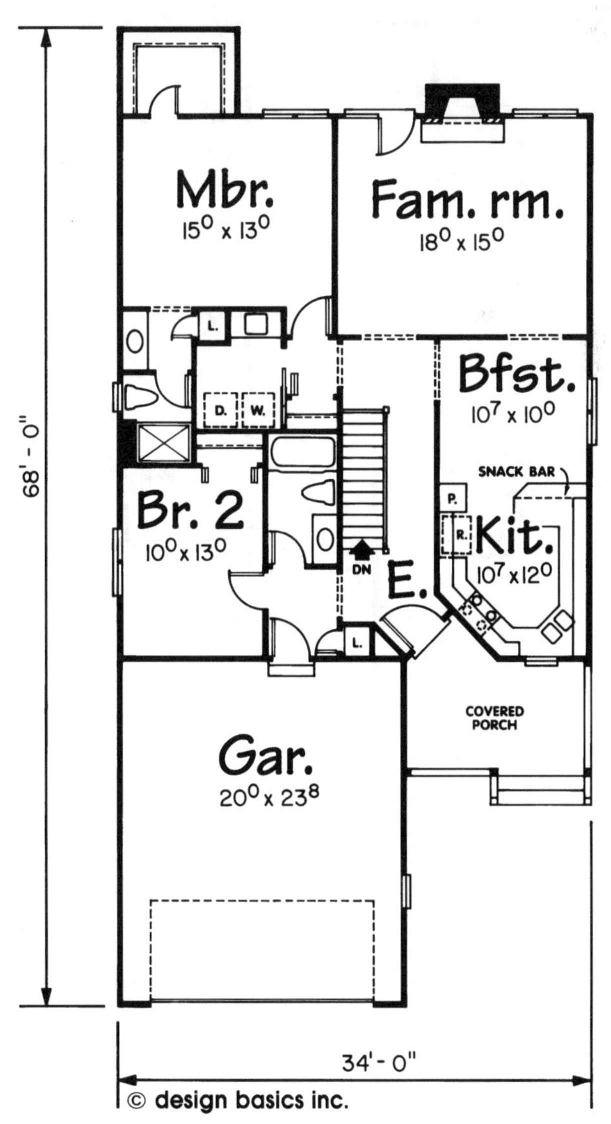

All plans on high quality, erasable, reproducible vellum.

Sarasota Falls

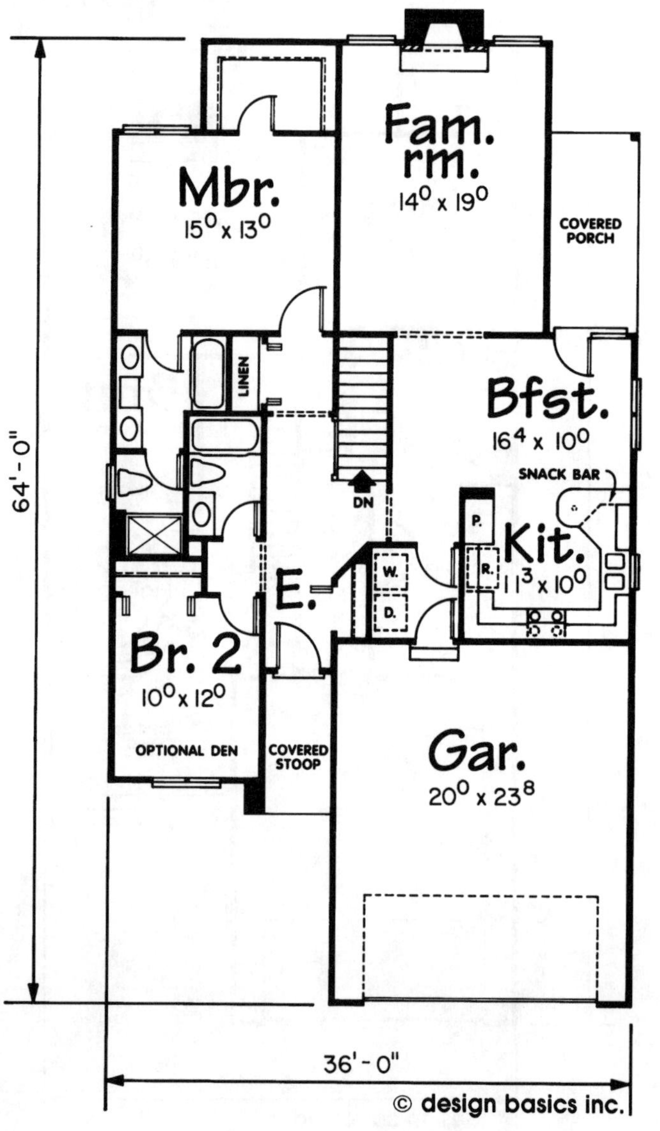

9F-8165

The sleek Sarasota Falls: *An expandable dinette for larger groups. The privately located family room with tall windows, for a clear view of nature. A back porch to watch the children play in the yard. And a snack bar to accommodate a buffet meal.*

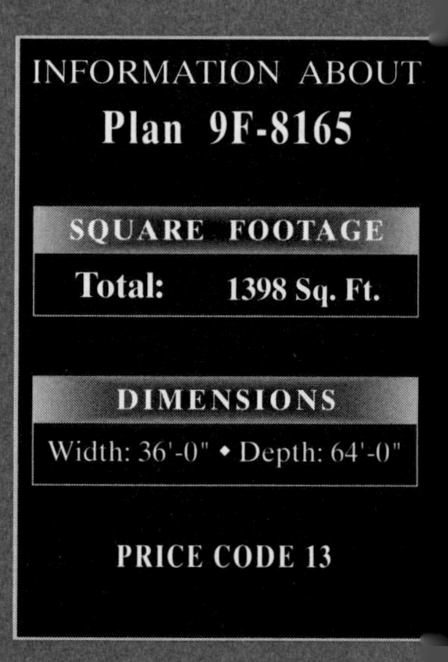

INFORMATION ABOUT

Plan 9F-8165

SQUARE FOOTAGE

Total: 1398 Sq. Ft.

DIMENSIONS

Width: 36'-0" • Depth: 64'-0"

PRICE CODE 13

Order Direct

800-947-7526

(7:00-6:00 Mon.-Fri. CST)

Trinity Acres

9F-8163

The shape of Trinity Acres: The fireplace in the great room, equally at home on formal and informal occasions. Two pantries helping to organize the kitchen. The breakfast area, opened up for natural light. And the master suite placed at the back of the home for an easy get-away spot.

INFORMATION ABOUT
Plan 9F-8163

SQUARE FOOTAGE	
Total:	1162 Sq. Ft.

DIMENSIONS

Width: 39'-4" • Depth: 53'-4"

PRICE CODE 11

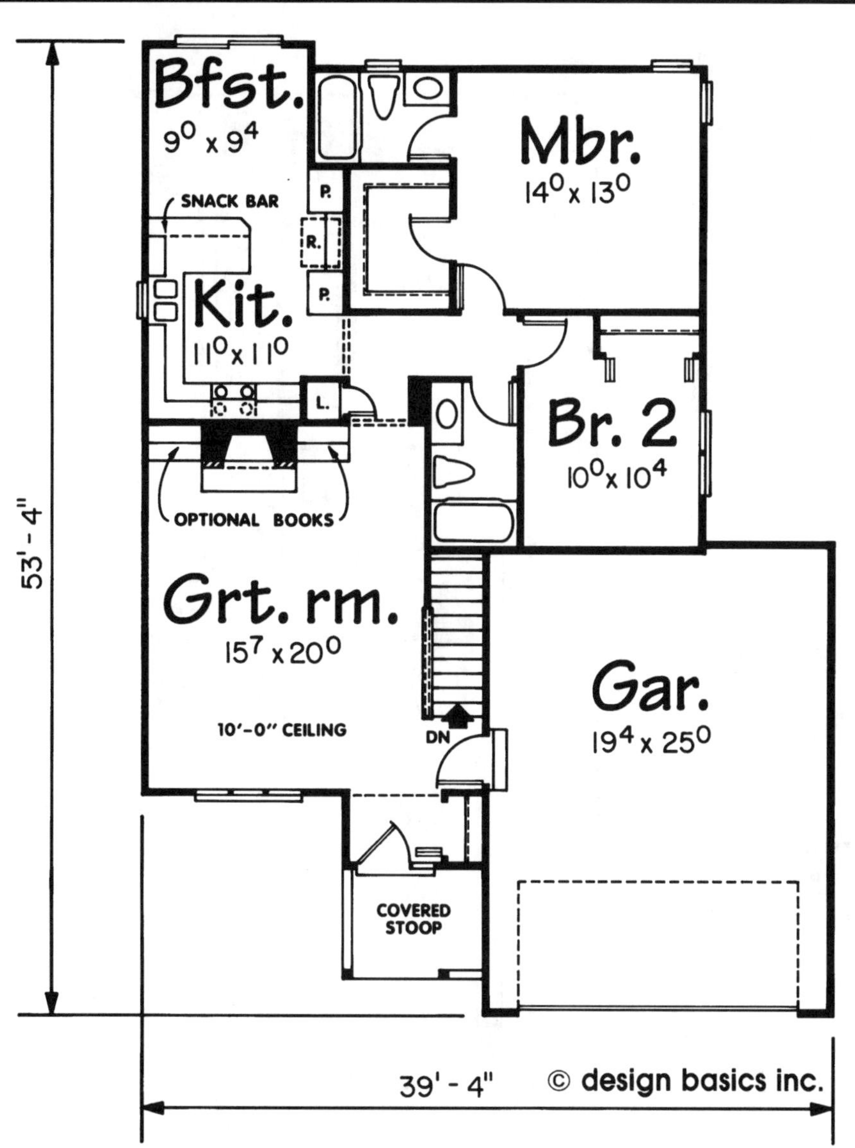

All plans on high quality, erasable, reproducible vellum.

Sonora Springs

9F-8168

The varied Sonora Springs: A den with French doors doubling as a bedroom. A walk-through kitchen to freely access more areas of the main floor. A back porch, adding leisure space to the master bedroom. And an expandable great room and dining room so there's room for everyone.

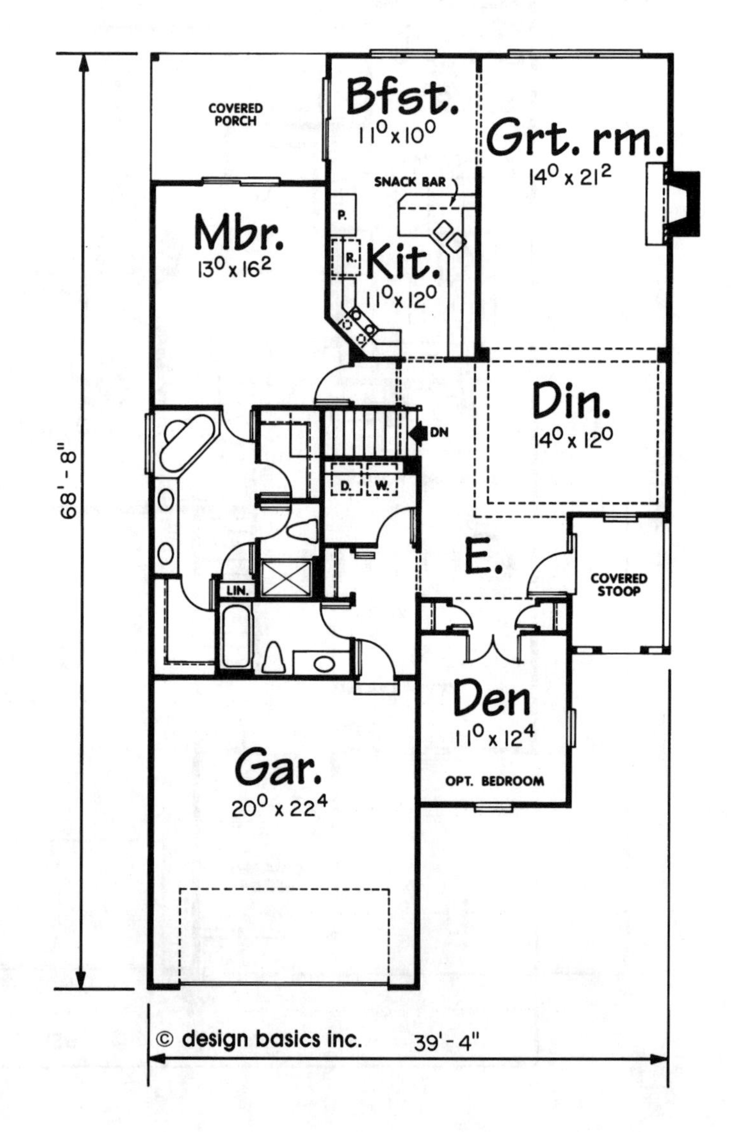

INFORMATION ABOUT
Plan 9F-8168

SQUARE FOOTAGE	
Total:	**1705 Sq. Ft.**

DIMENSIONS
Width: 39'-4" • Depth: 68'-8"

PRICE CODE 17

Order Direct
800-947-7526
(7:00-6:00 Mon.-Fri. CST)

Kirby Farm

9F-8093

The uncomplicated Kirby Farm: Living, eating and cooking areas designated as the center of activity in open, unrestricted space. Other features: a front coat closet for guests; a linen closet for hanging clothes in the laundry room; and a large master suite closet with room for storage and a sizeable wardrobe.

INFORMATION ABOUT
Plan 9F-8093

SQUARE FOOTAGE

Total:	1212 Sq. Ft.

DIMENSIONS

Width: 40"-0" • Depth: 47'-8"

PRICE CODE 12

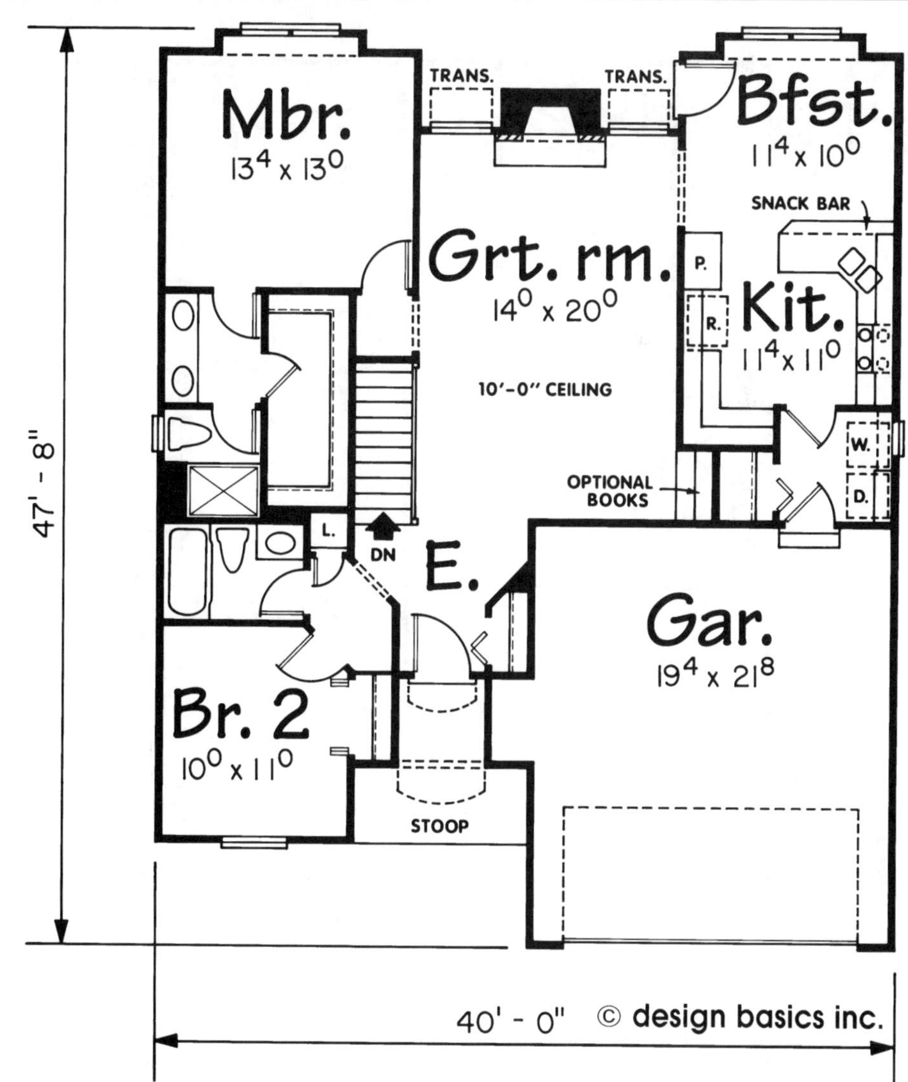

All plans on high quality, erasable, reproducible vellum.

Bradford Pointe

Br. 2
$11^{0} \times 10^{4}$

Mbr.
$14^{0} \times 13^{4}$

COVERED PORCH

Br. 3
$11^{0} \times 10^{0}$

L.

R. P.

Bfst.
$12^{6} \times 11^{0}$

Din.
$12^{8} \times 10^{4}$

Kit.
$10^{6} \times 11^{0}$

P.

DN

Grt. rm.
$16^{8} \times 16^{0}$

Gar.
$19^{4} \times 23^{8}$

E.

COVERED PORCH

56'-8"

40'-8"

9F-8160

*The plentiful **Bradford Pointe:** Two porches for sipping summertime drinks with leisure. A secluded bedroom wing for quiet places to retire to. And easy connection between the living areas, making daily traffic uninhibited.*

INFORMATION ABOUT
Plan 9F-8160

SQUARE FOOTAGE	
Total:	**1449 Sq. Ft.**

DIMENSIONS
Width: 40'-8" • Depth: 56'-8"

PRICE CODE 14

Order Direct
800-947-7526
(7:00-6:00 Mon.-Fri. CST)

Gabriel Bay

9F-8013

Life in the Gabriel Bay:

Office space or hobby room options in two secondary bedrooms. Room for meals and entertaining in the kitchen/ breakfast area coupled with the great room. In the master retreat, a sunny picture window for reading and corner tub for basking in relaxation.

INFORMATION ABOUT
Plan 9F-8013

SQUARE FOOTAGE

Total: 1392 Sq. Ft.

DIMENSIONS

Width: 42'-0" • Depth: 54'-0"

PRICE CODE 13

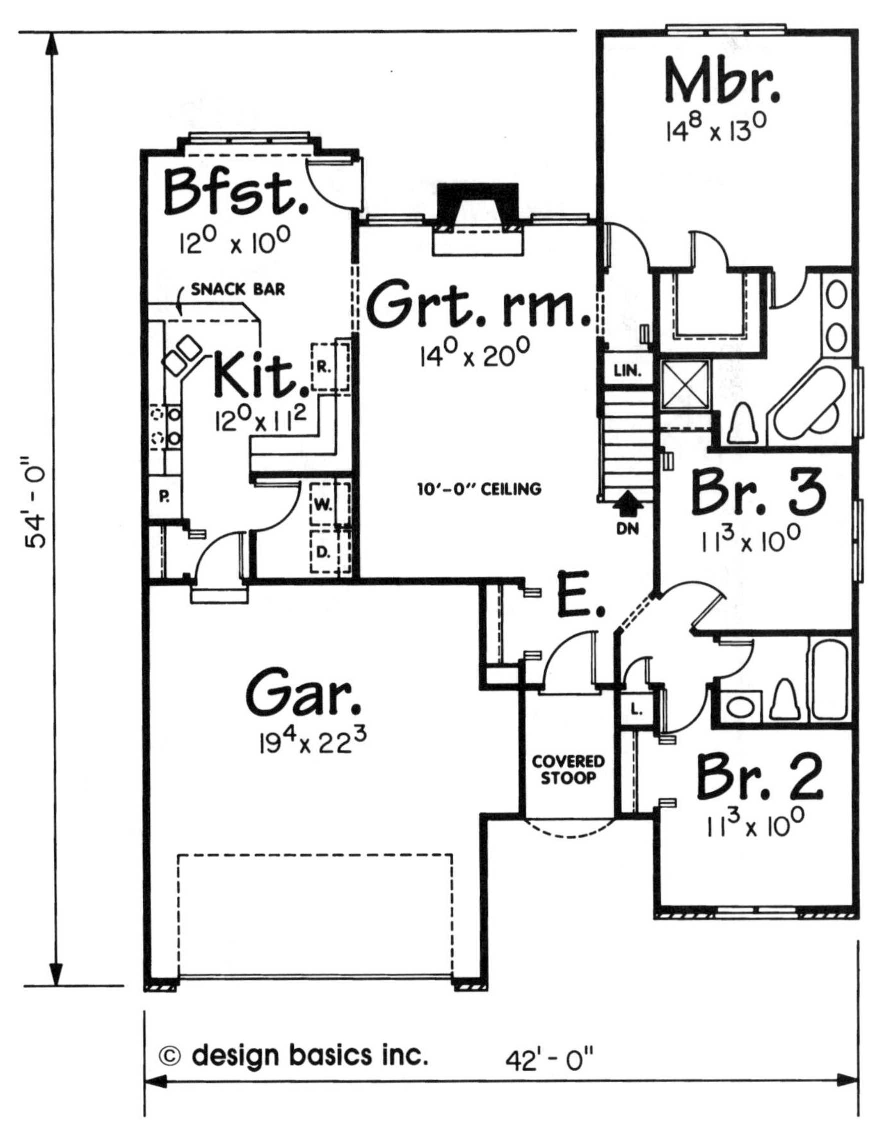

All plans on high quality, erasable, reproducible vellum.

Skyline Woods

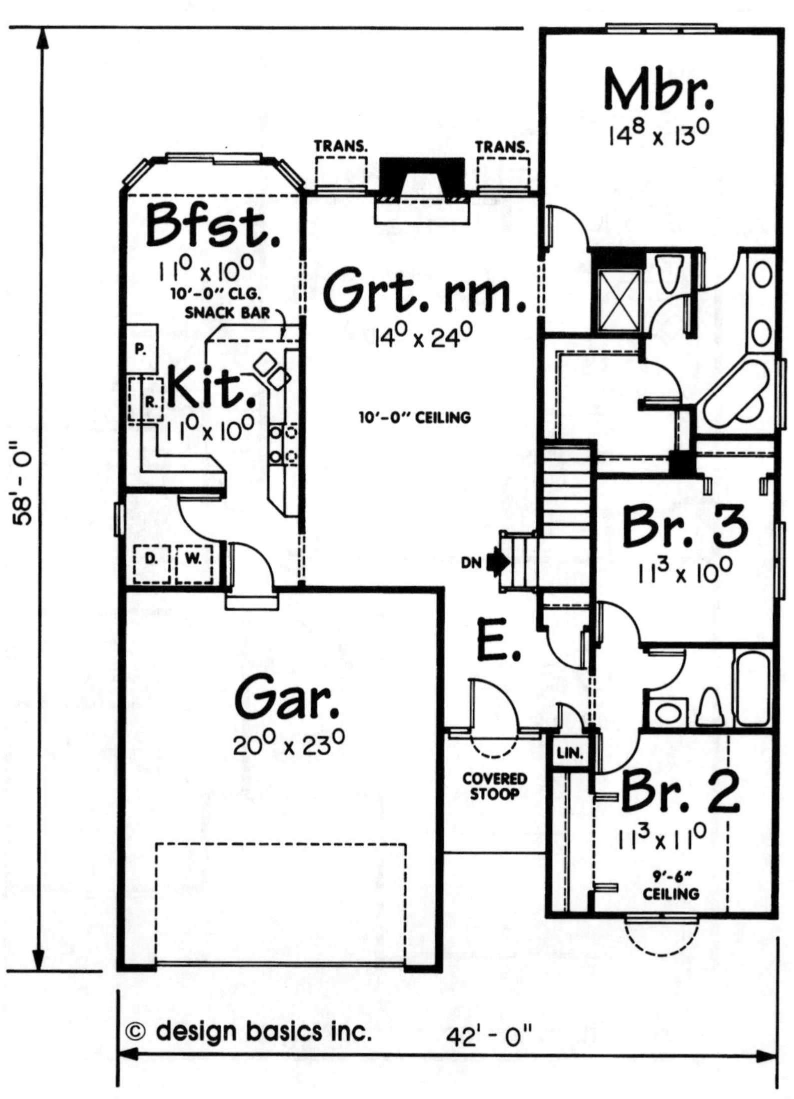

9F-8159

*The attractive **Skyline Woods:** A large great room for when the family comes home. Two secondary bedrooms for sleeping areas or places to explore a hobby. Streamlined traffic from garage to kitchen for unloading the car after grocery shopping. And bayed windows in the breakfast area providing natural light in the morning.*

INFORMATION ABOUT
Plan 9F-8159

SQUARE FOOTAGE	
Total:	**1562 Sq. Ft.**

DIMENSIONS
Width: 42'-0" • Depth: 58'-0"

PRICE CODE 15

Order Direct
800-947-7526
(7:00-6:00 Mon.-Fri. CST)

Jacobs Bay

9F-8158

*The adjustable **Jacobs Bay:** An optional walk-out basement for extra bedrooms, storage and living space. A spacious island kitchen for the one who loves to cook. A den, which could easily accommodate an overnight guest. And an entertaining area that's versatile for holidays and gatherings.*

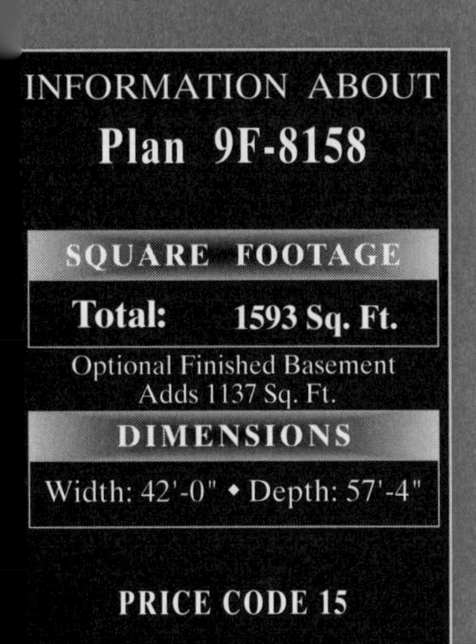

INFORMATION ABOUT
Plan 9F-8158

SQUARE FOOTAGE

Total: 1593 Sq. Ft.

Optional Finished Basement Adds 1137 Sq. Ft.

DIMENSIONS

Width: 42'-0" • Depth: 57'-4"

PRICE CODE 15

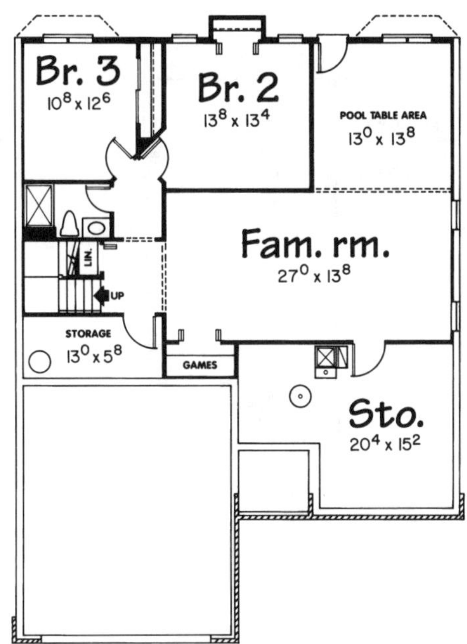

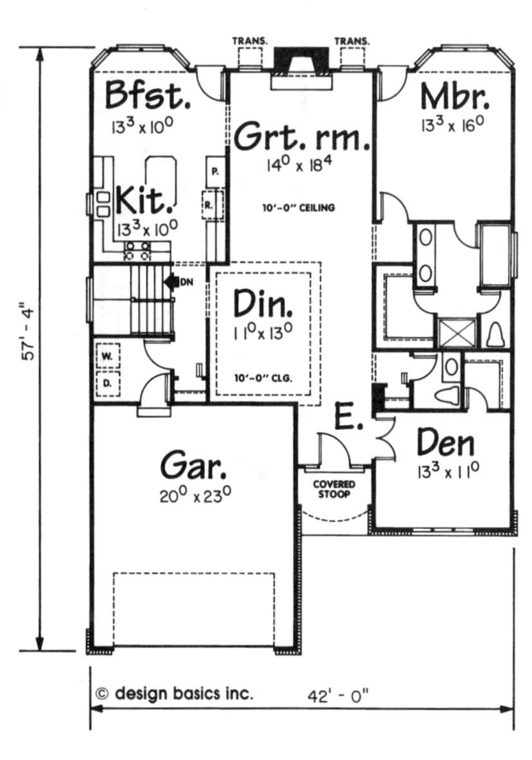

All plans on high quality, erasable, reproducible vellum.

Belle Harbor

Mbr.
14^{8} x 16^{0}

TRANSOMS

COVERED PORCH

Bfst.
12^{0} x 11^{4}

Grt. rm.
14^{0} x 20^{0}
11'-0" CEILING

P.

R.

SNACK BAR

Kit.
12^{0} x 13^{0}

DN

Din.
13^{4} x 10^{0}
11'-0" CEILING

E.

W.

D.

L.

Br. 2
11^{4} x 12^{0}

Gar.
19^{4} x 23^{0}

COVERED STOOP

60' - 0"

42' - 0"

9F-8079

*A flair of its own – the **Belle Harbor.** For a sense of unity, the entry, dining room and great room with 11-foot ceilings. In the master bath, his and her vanities and a corner soaking tub for a feeling of luxury. And a lazy welcome to the outdoors on a long back porch.*

INFORMATION ABOUT
Plan 9F-8079

SQUARE FOOTAGE	
Total:	**1633 Sq. Ft.**

DIMENSIONS

Width: 42'-0" • Depth: 60'-0"

PRICE CODE 16

Order Direct

800-947-7526

(7:00-6:00 Mon.-Fri. CST)

Spring Valley

9F-8090

A longing for Spring Valley. A front covered porch to escape and dream upon. In the kitchen, an island counter for added space to prepare and cook meals. A large dinette open to both formal and informal eating. And a master bedroom with the option of a second closet if needed.

INFORMATION ABOUT
Plan 9F-8090

SQUARE FOOTAGE

Total:	1453 Sq. Ft.

DIMENSIONS

Width: 48'-8" • Depth: 44'-0"

PRICE CODE 14

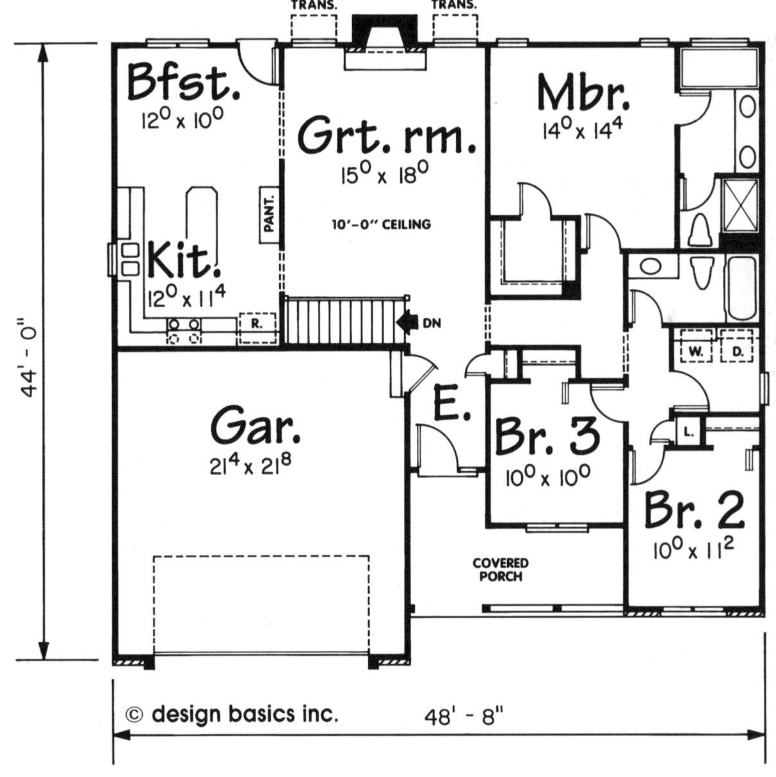

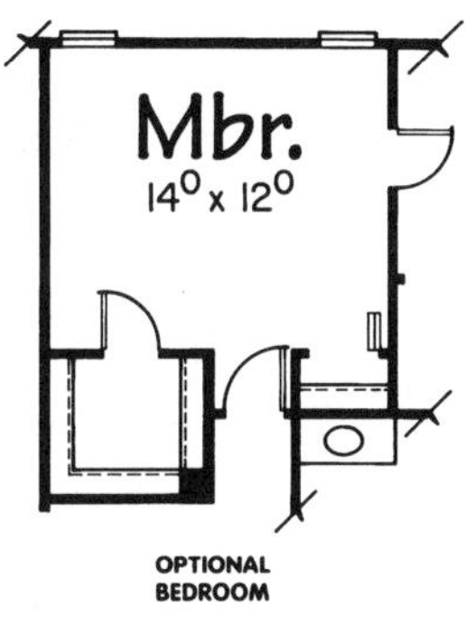

OPTIONAL BEDROOM

All plans on high quality, erasable, reproducible vellum.

Shadow Pines

9F-8088

A view of the Shadow Pines: Sloped ceiling in the great room and warmth by a crackling fireplace. Patio doors in the breakfast area for leading to backyard fun and letting in sunshine. And bayed dining room windows adding definition to memories created there.

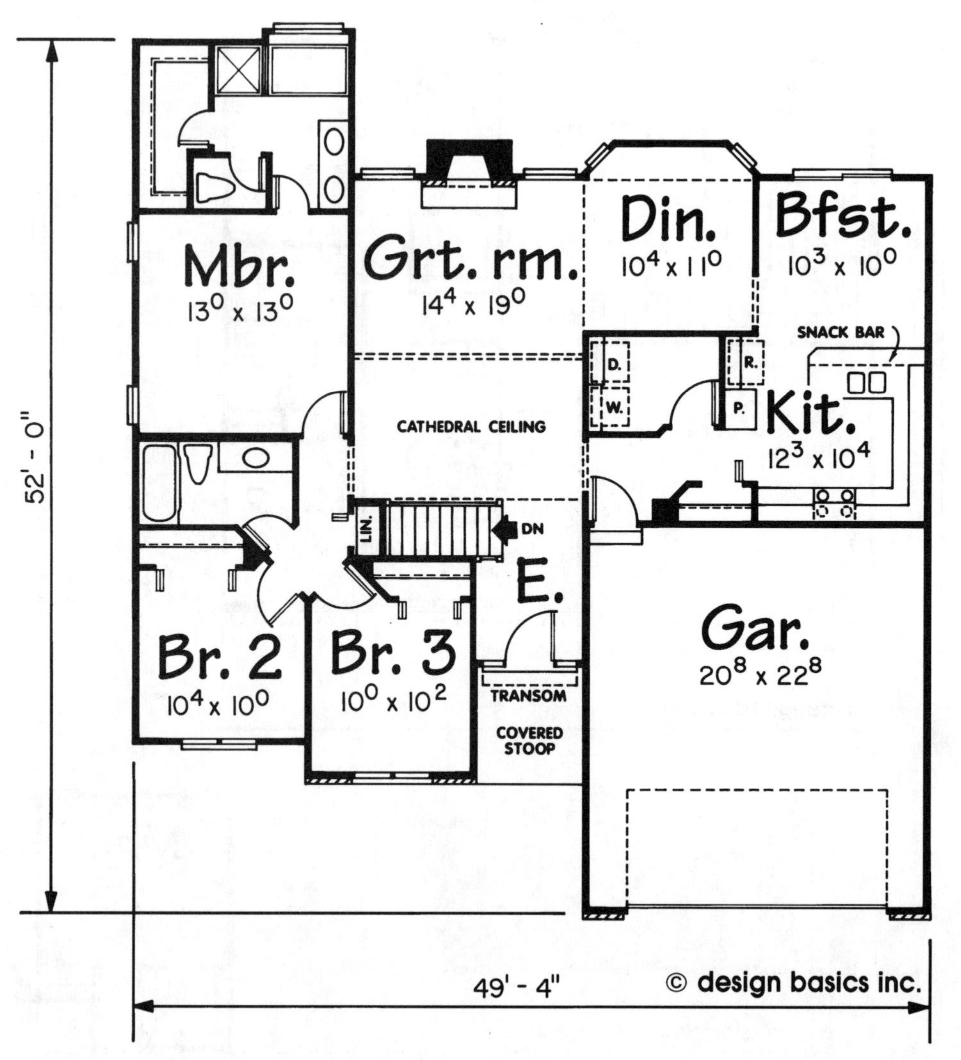

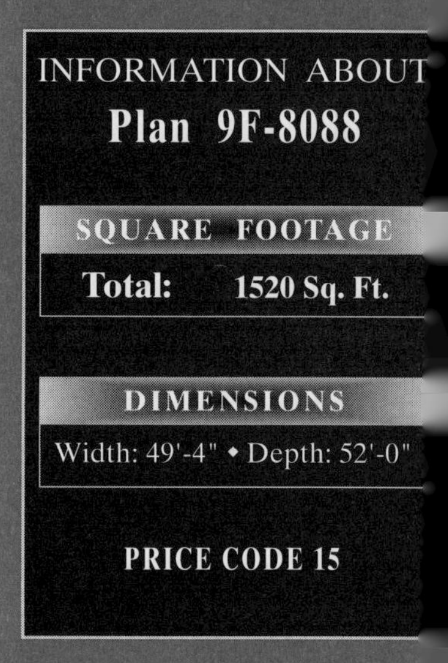

INFORMATION ABOUT
Plan 9F-8088

SQUARE FOOTAGE	
Total:	**1520 Sq. Ft.**

DIMENSIONS

Width: 49'-4" • Depth: 52'-0"

PRICE CODE 15

Order Direct

800-947-7526

(7:00-6:00 Mon.-Fri. CST)

Chandler Hills

9F-8089

*The allure of **Chandler Hills:** Arches and columns on a front porch dedicated to summer. A tall, sloping great room ceiling to naturally prompt warm comments from guests who relax there. And the master suite at the rear of the home for secluded peace and quiet.*

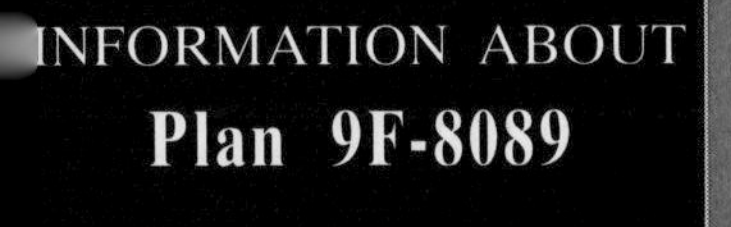

INFORMATION ABOUT

Plan 9F-8089

SQUARE FOOTAGE	
Total:	**1433 Sq. Ft.**

DIMENSIONS

Width: 50'-0" • Depth: 58'-0"

PRICE CODE 14

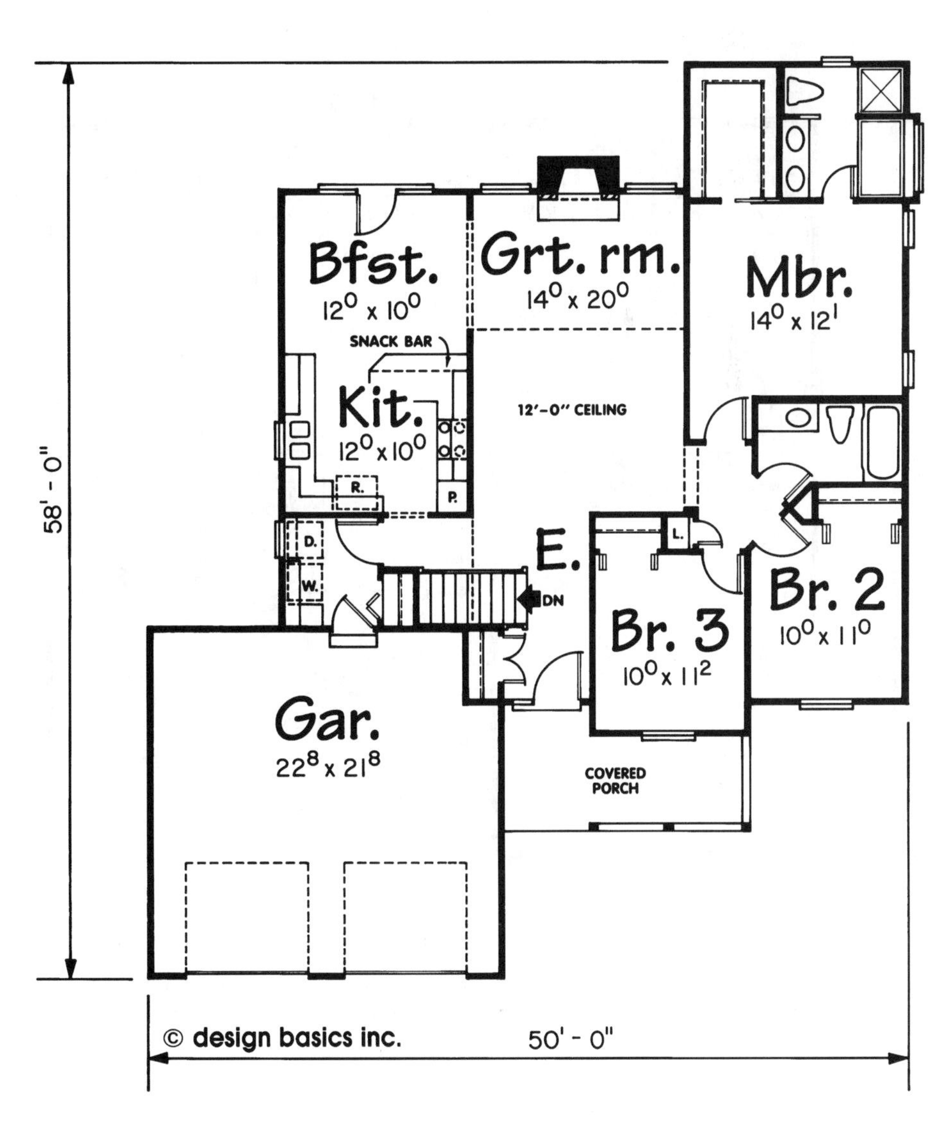

All plans on high quality, erasable, reproducible vellum.

Maple Grove

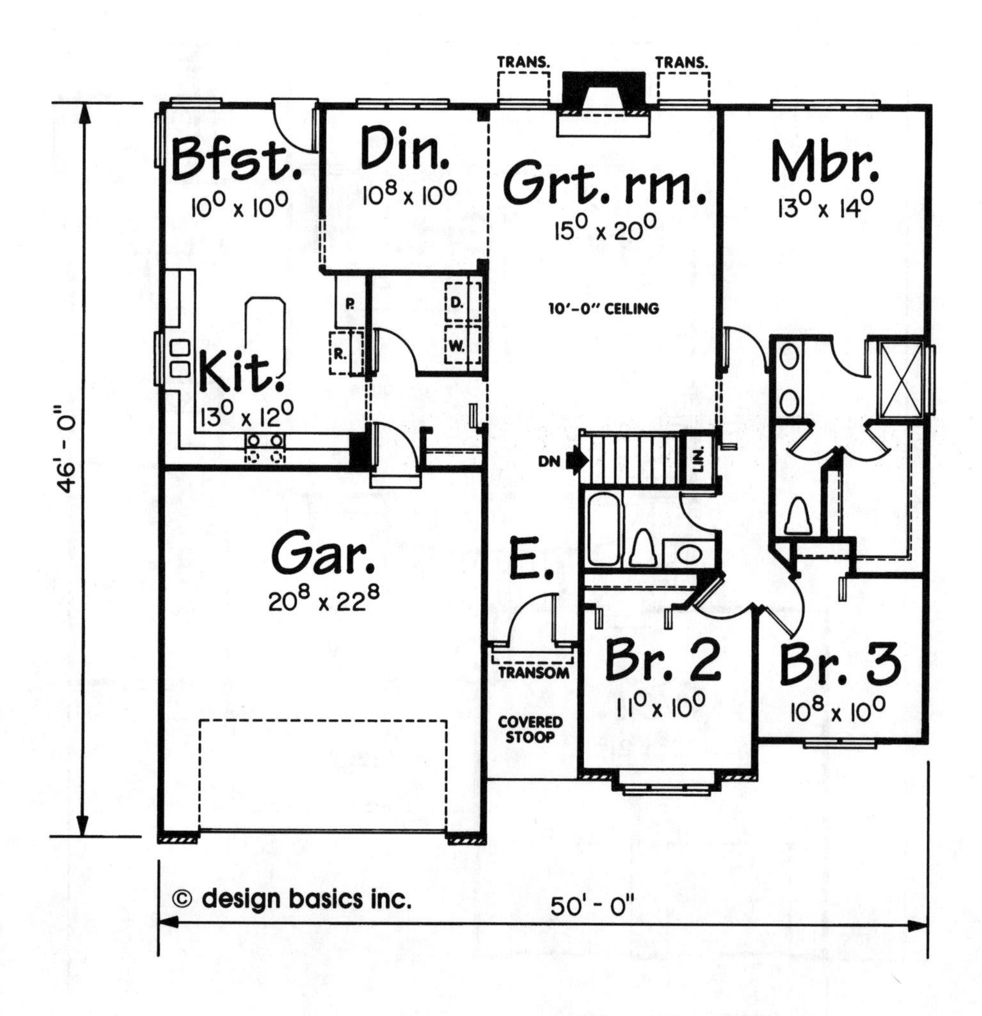

9F-8080

*The sensibility of **Maple Grove:** An island counter in the kitchen to help prepare meals for cooking and serving. Formal and informal eating areas near each other, convenient as extra space when larger groups stay to eat. Three bedrooms for families to dream away the night.*

INFORMATION ABOUT

Plan 9F-8080

SQUARE FOOTAGE

Total: **1628 Sq. Ft.**

DIMENSIONS

Width: 50'-0" • Depth: 46'-0"

PRICE CODE 16

Order Direct

800-947-7526

(7:00-6:00 Mon.-Fri. CST)

HEARTLAND HOME PLANS™

BASE PLAN INFORMATION				
PAGE NO.	WIDTH	PLAN NO.	PLAN NAME	SQ. FT.
188	50'-0"	8027	Ellies Knoll	1615
179	40'-8"	8094	Angel Cove	1715
172	28'-0"	8137	Liberty Creek	1772
186	48'-0"	8037	Carriage Hills	1802
174	34'-0"	8166	Vista Springs	1827
176	38'-0"	8171	Brentwood Falls	1844
189	50'-0"	8126	Orchard Trail	1953
180	40'-8"	8085	Wood Hollow	1967
181	42'-0"	8076	Holly Mills	1973
190	50'-0"	8125	Park Hills	1974
182	42'-0"	8151	Grand Oaks	2001
173	32'-0"	8169	Arapaho Valley	2018
177	38'-0"	8170	Pershing Acres	2097
183	42'-0"	8154	Elm Creek	2152
175	34'-0"	8172	Eldridge Acres	2183
187	48'-0"	8063	Abbott Lane	2208
184	42'-0"	8153	Echo Valley	2231
178	39'-4"	8167	Castle Ridge	2260
185	42'-0"	8155	Stafford Run	2320

1½ STORY HOMES

Liberty Creek

9F-8137

The smooth lines of Liberty Creek: Volume in the entry expanding to the second floor for an impressive balcony view. In the great room, a cathedral ceiling to lend a spacious feel to gatherings. And two private get-aways at the rear – the master suite and a covered porch.

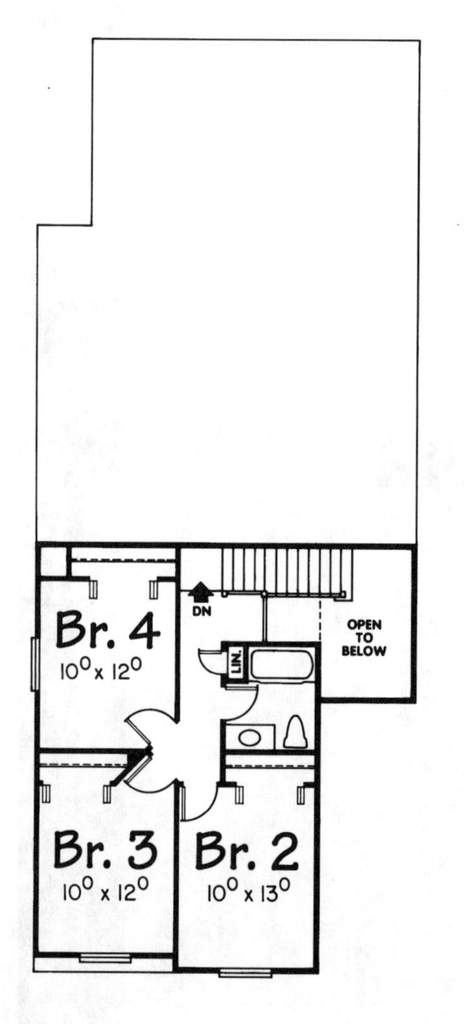

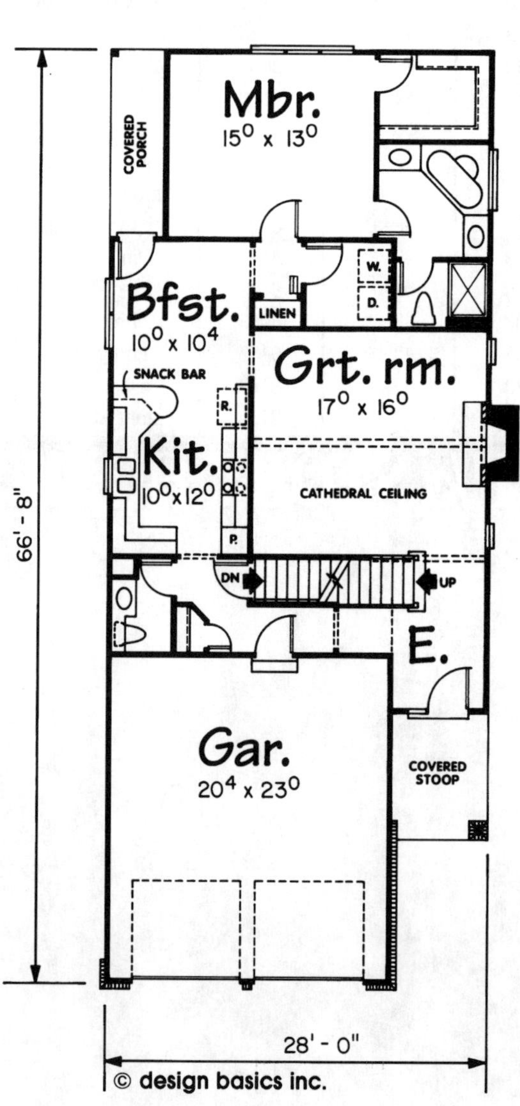

INFORMATION ABOUT
Plan 9F-8137

SQUARE FOOTAGE

Total:	**1772 Sq. Ft.**
Level 1:	1189 Sq. Ft.
Level 2:	583 Sq. Ft.

DIMENSIONS

Width: 28'-0" • Depth: 66'-8"

PRICE CODE 17

Arapaho Valley

9F-8169

An interpretation of the Arapaho Valley: A spacious kitchen to prepare meals with ease. Abundant views in the living room making it feel unrestricted when sitting there. And a master suite with plenty of features to be enjoyed by him and her.

INFORMATION ABOUT
Plan 9F-8169

SQUARE FOOTAGE

Total:	**2018 Sq. Ft.**
Level 1:	1508 Sq. Ft.
Level 2:	510 Sq. Ft.

DIMENSIONS

Width: 32'-0" • Depth: 76'-0"

PRICE CODE 20

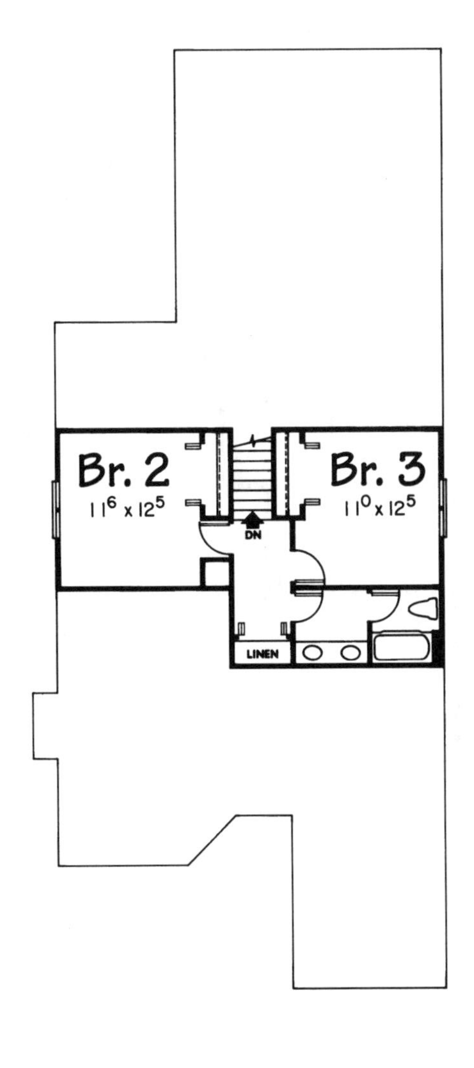

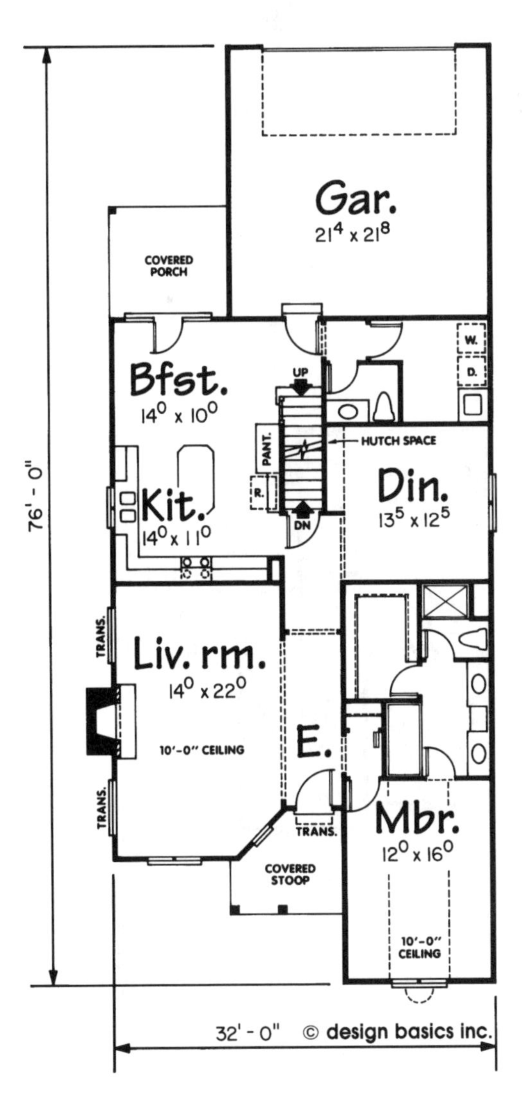

All plans on high quality, erasable, reproducible vellum.

Vista Springs

9F-8166

The capable ***Vista Springs:*** *A balanced elevation with a front porch to relax on in the evening. A tall ceiling in the great room to make it feel bigger than it is. A U-shaped stairway leading the children upstairs at bedtime. And a rear covered stoop to get some air after dinner.*

Br. 4 10⁰ x 12⁸
LINEN
OPEN TO BELOW
DN
Br. 3 10⁰ x 12³
Br. 2 10⁰ x 12⁷

62' - 0"

Mbr. 13⁰ x 15⁰
COVERED STOOP
Bfst. 10⁰ x 10⁰
SNACK BAR
SLOPED CEILING
Grt. rm. 14⁰ x 19⁰
17'-0" CEILING
Kit. 10⁰ x 12⁸
P.
R.
D.
W.
E.
UP
Gar. 20⁴ x 23⁰
COVERED PORCH

34' - 0"

INFORMATION ABOUT
Plan 9F-8166

SQUARE FOOTAGE	
Total:	**1827 Sq. Ft.**
Level 1:	1204 Sq. Ft.
Level 2:	623 Sq. Ft.

DIMENSIONS

Width: 34'-0" • Depth: 62'-0"

PRICE CODE 18

Eldridge Acres

9F-8172

*The durable **Eldridge Acres:** A wide front porch to sit and rest upon. A fireplace to warm those who kick back in the great room. In the kitchen, a long snack bar to serve everyone breakfast. And plenty of windows in the upstairs bedrooms making them feel open and spacious.*

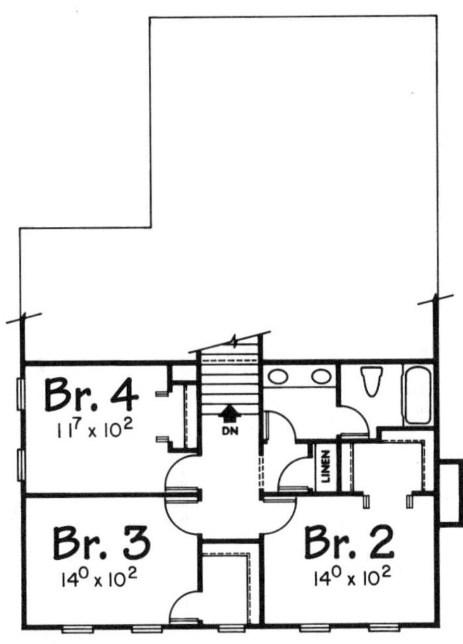

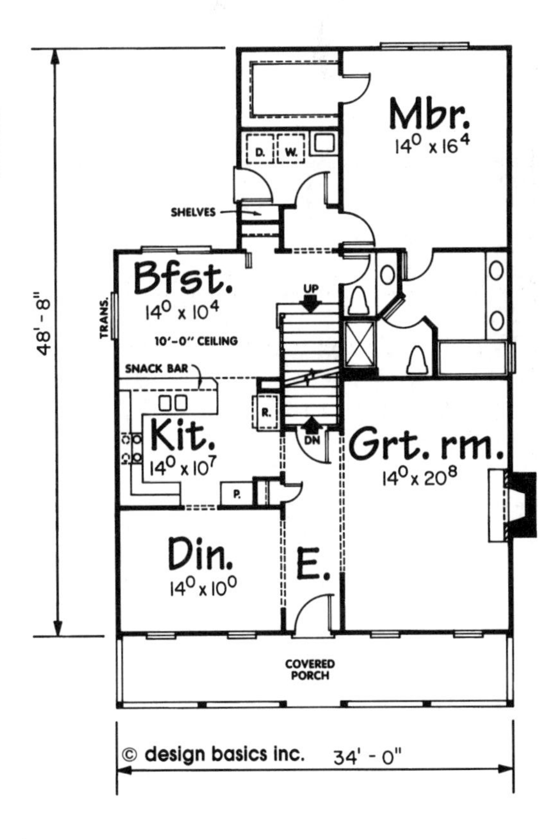

INFORMATION ABOUT
Plan 9F-8172

SQUARE FOOTAGE

Total:	**2183 Sq. Ft.**
Level 1:	1477 Sq. Ft.
Level 2:	706 Sq. Ft.

DIMENSIONS

Width: 34'-0" • Depth: 48'-8"

PRICE CODE 21

All plans on high quality, erasable, reproducible vellum.

Brentwood Falls

9F-8171

A presentation of Brentwood Falls: Upon entry, a view of the dining room - flexible as a living space also. Close connection between the great room and kitchen to quickly grab snacks when watching a movie. Unfinished storage upstairs to be used in any number of ways.

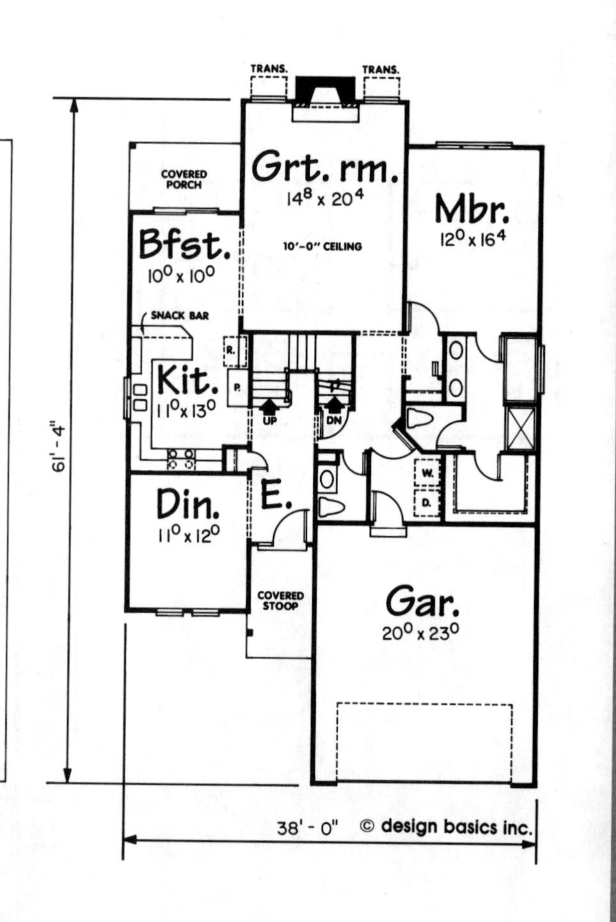

INFORMATION ABOUT
Plan 9F-8171

SQUARE FOOTAGE

Total:	**1844 Sq. Ft.**
Level 1:	1397 Sq. Ft.
Level 2:	447 Sq. Ft.

DIMENSIONS

Width: 38'-0" • Depth: 61'-4"

PRICE CODE 18

Order Direct

800-947-7526

(7:00-6:00 Mon.-Fri. CST)

Pershing Acres

9F-8170

*A classic representation of **Persing Acres:** A spacious great room that expands into a nearby dining room offering great connection between eating and living arrangements. A secluded master bedroom, compartmentalized for storage and getting ready. And three secondary bedrooms upstairs linked to main-floor living by a U-shaped stairway.*

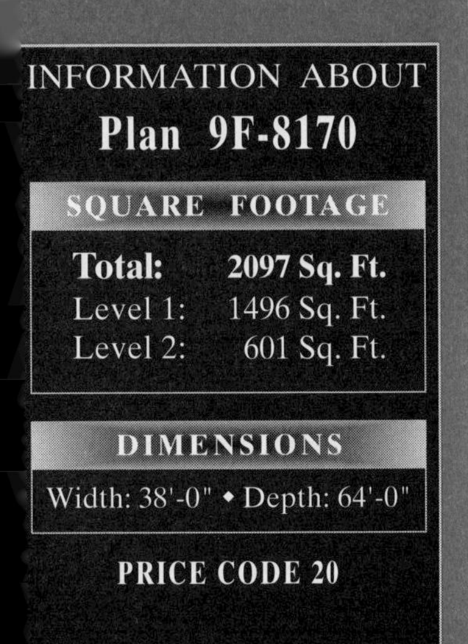

INFORMATION ABOUT
Plan 9F-8170

SQUARE FOOTAGE

Total:	**2097 Sq. Ft.**
Level 1:	1496 Sq. Ft.
Level 2:	601 Sq. Ft.

DIMENSIONS

Width: 38'-0" • Depth: 64'-0"

PRICE CODE 20

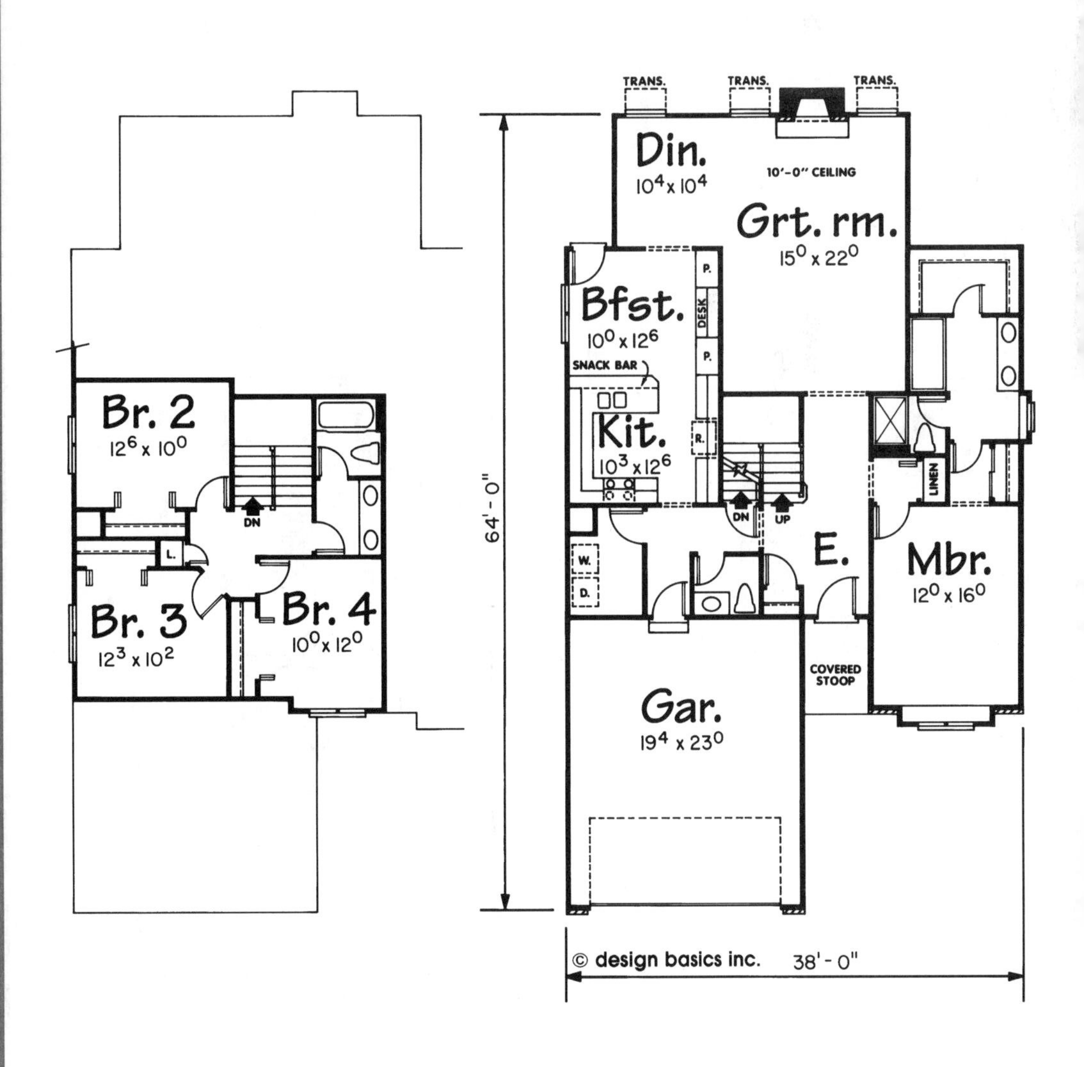

All plans on high quality, erasable, reproducible vellum.

Castle Ridge

9F-8167

The convenience of Castle Ridge: An entry expanding into the warmth of the great room. Two covered porches for plenty of room to contemplate. The master suite, secluded for romance. And on the second floor, a loft for use as a bedroom, study or living space.

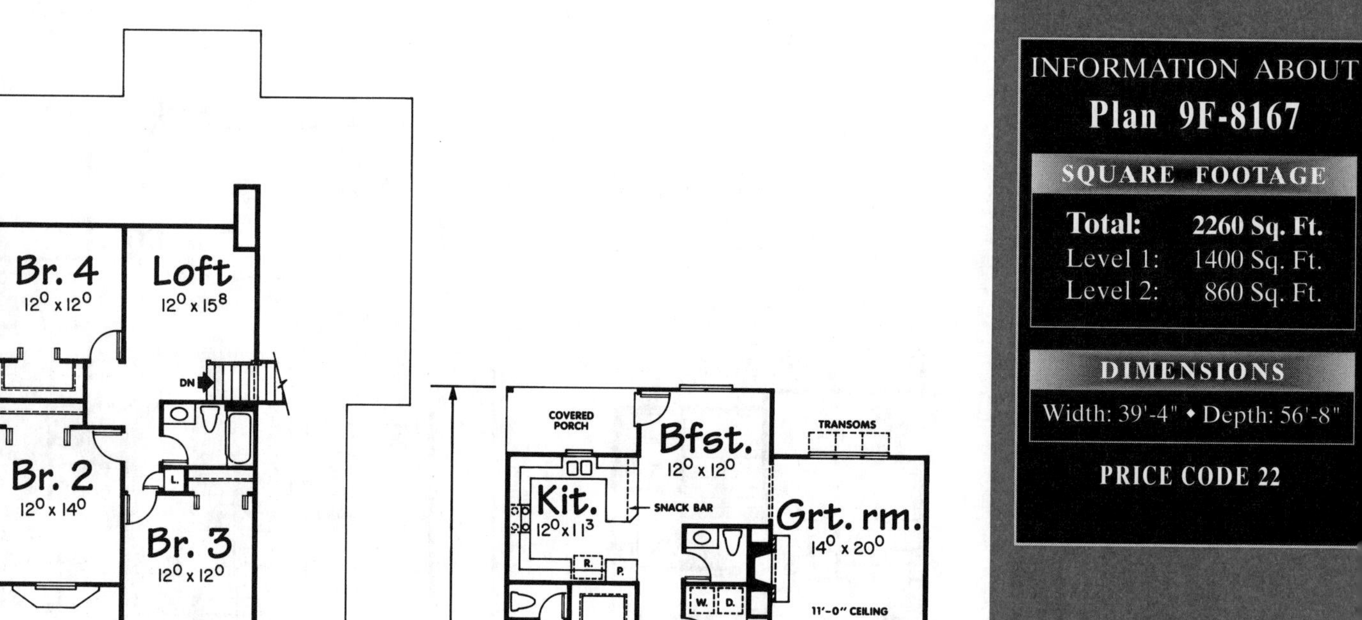

INFORMATION ABOUT
Plan 9F-8167

SQUARE FOOTAGE

Total:	**2260 Sq. Ft.**
Level 1:	1400 Sq. Ft.
Level 2:	860 Sq. Ft.

DIMENSIONS

Width: 39'-4" ◆ Depth: 56'-8"

PRICE CODE 22

Order Direct

800-947-7526

(7:00-6:00 Mon.-Fri. CST)

Angel Cove

9F-8094

A fancy for Angel Cove:

The master bedroom on the main floor for convenient access from the living areas. A snack bar in the kitchen for an easy place to eat breakfast. And a second-floor bonus room to add a fourth bedroom or convert into hobby space.

INFORMATION ABOUT
Plan 9F-8094

SQUARE FOOTAGE

Total:	**1715 Sq. Ft.**
Level 1:	1324 Sq. Ft.
Level 2:	391 Sq. Ft.

Unfinished Bonus Room Adds 212 Sq. Ft.

DIMENSIONS

Width: 40'-8" • Depth: 54'-0"

PRICE CODE 17

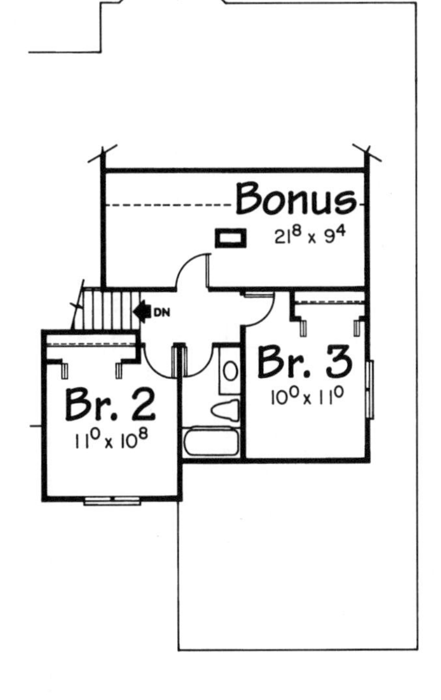

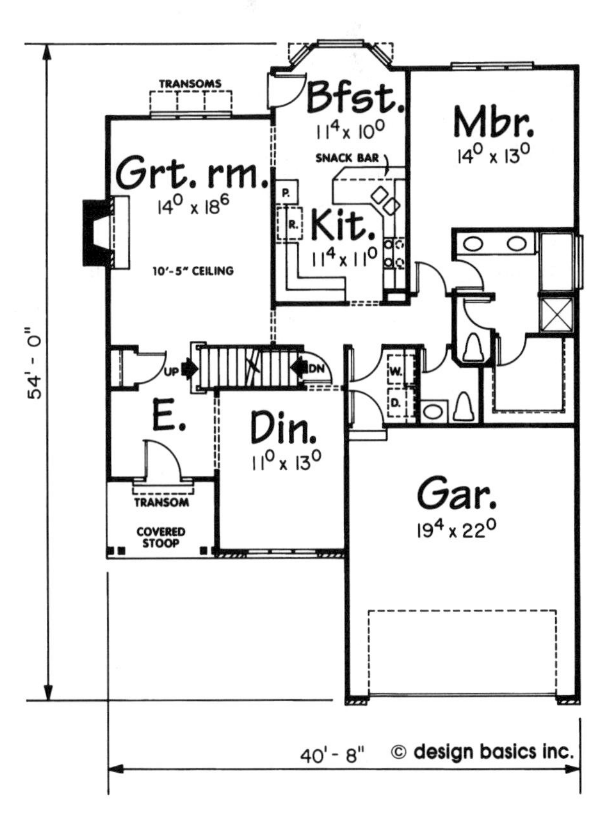

All plans on high quality, erasable, reproducible vellum.

Wood Hollow

9F-8085

The livability of Wood Hollow: A front porch, L-shaped and entirely suitable to summer sitting around. The dining room, open for admiration and elegant for entertaining. A 10-foot vaulted ceiling in the master bedroom to heighten its appeal. And three bedrooms on the second floor for separation from noise and activity below.

INFORMATION ABOUT
Plan 9F-8085

SQUARE FOOTAGE

Total:	**1967 Sq. Ft.**
Level 1:	1391 Sq. Ft.
Level 2:	576 Sq. Ft.

DIMENSIONS

Width: 40'-8" • Depth: 56'-0"

PRICE CODE 19

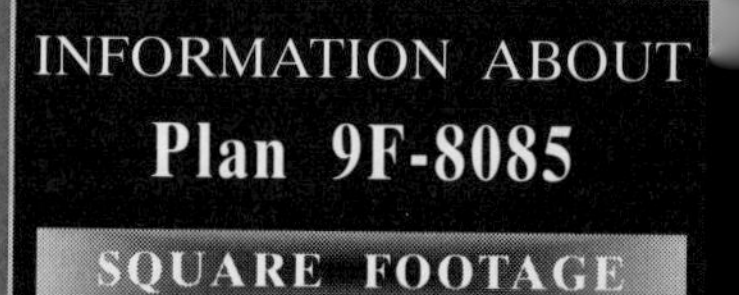

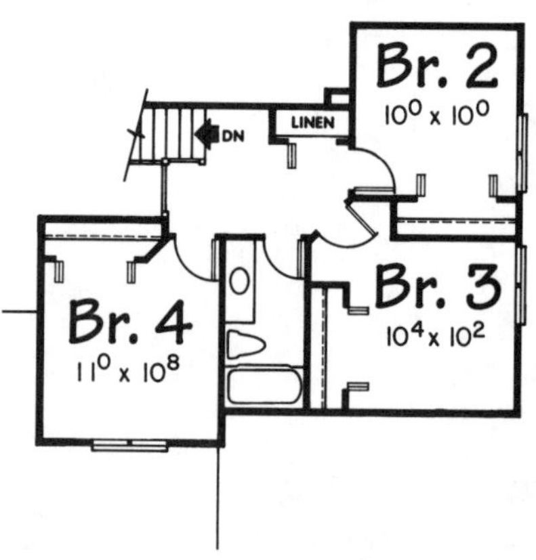

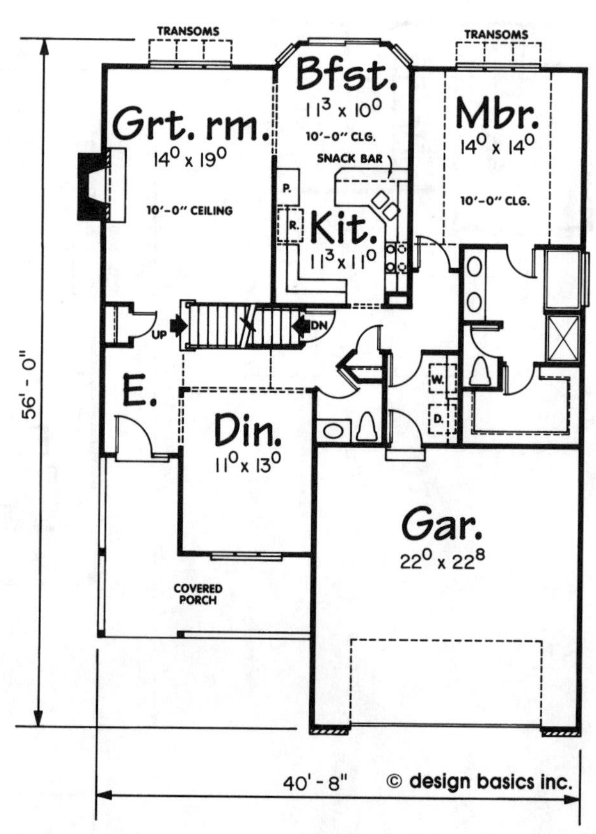

Order Direct

800-947-7526

(7:00-6:00 Mon.-Fri. CST)

Holly Mills

9F-8076

The ease of ***Holly Mills:***

An open dining room to view from or expand into the entry. Additional wrapping counter space in the kitchen, designated to prepare, cook and serve food. Two bedrooms on the main floor and two upstairs providing options for varied, changing lifestyles. And a bonus room fulfilling the need for more space.

INFORMATION ABOUT
Plan 9F-8076

SQUARE FOOTAGE

Total:	**1973 Sq. Ft.**
Level 1:	1534 Sq. Ft.
Level 2:	439 Sq. Ft.

Unfinished Bonus Room Adds 313 Sq. Ft.

DIMENSIONS

Width: 42'-0" • Depth: 54'-0"

PRICE CODE 19

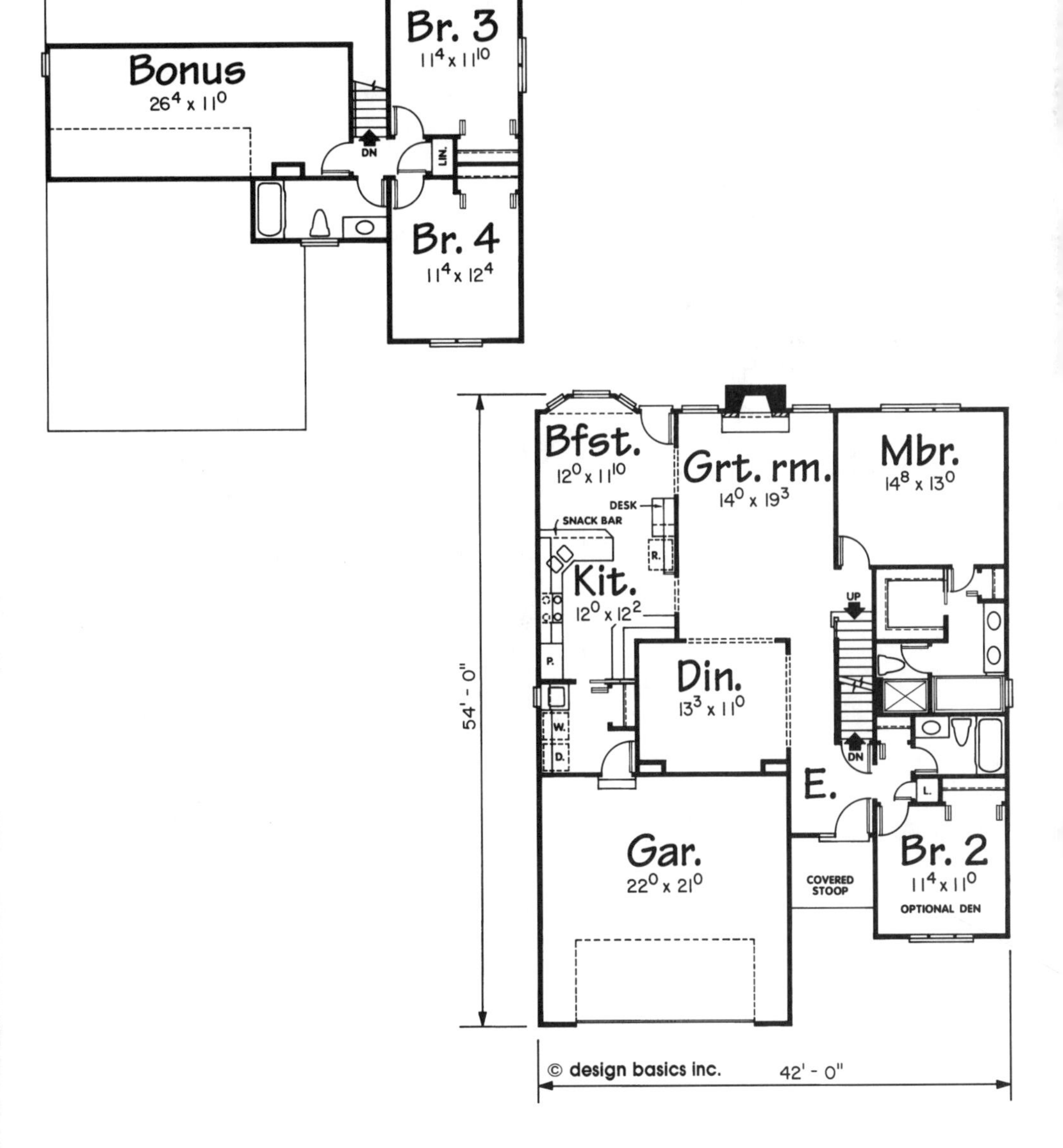

All plans on high quality, erasable, reproducible vellum.

Grand Oaks

9F-8151

The satisfaction of ***Grand Oaks:*** *The formal dining room to view upon entry. The great room, reveling in enough space and height so one will feel comfortable there. Extra counter space in the dinette for use as a work space or computer center. A walk-in linen closet upstairs to meet the needs of two bedrooms and a full, compartmentalized bath.*

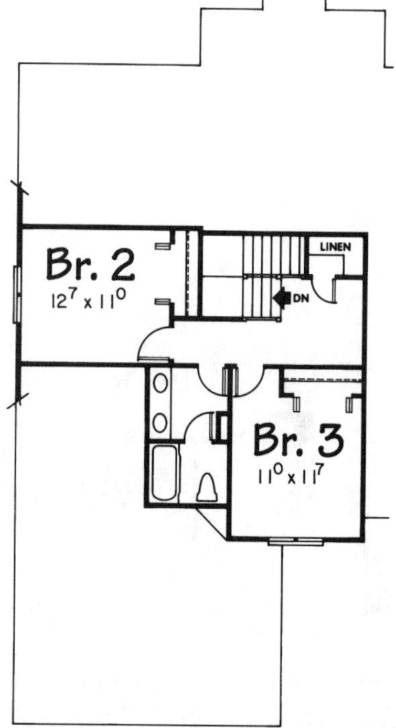

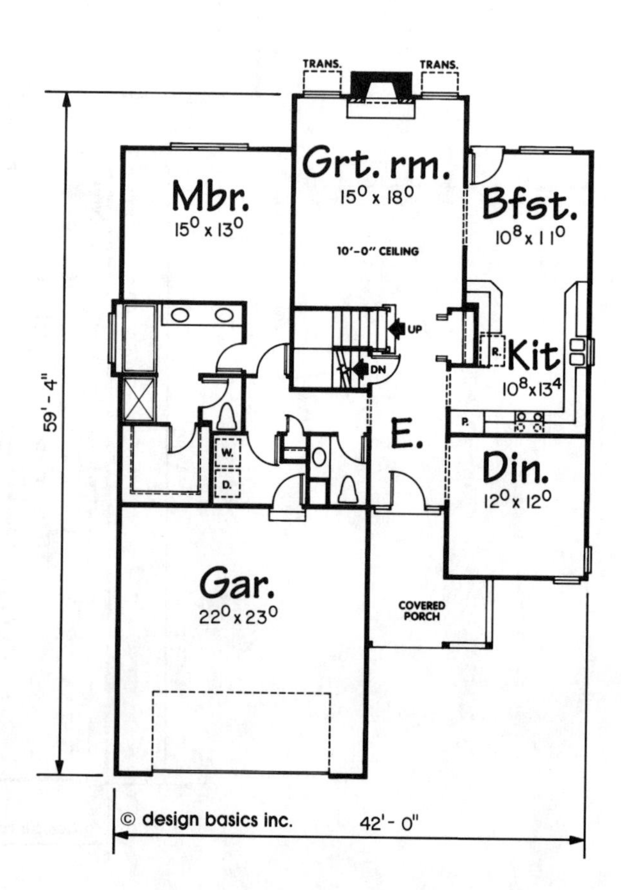

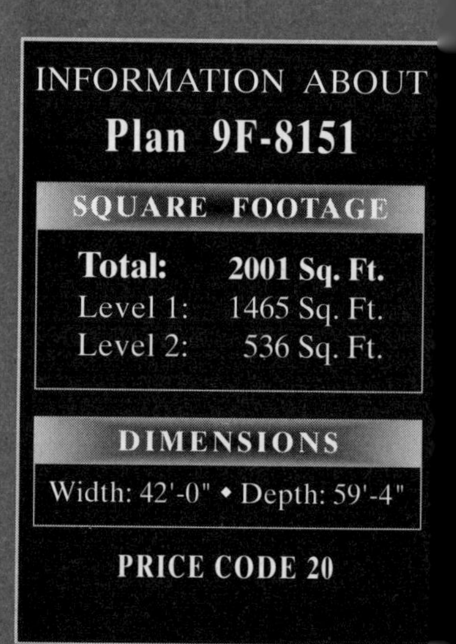

INFORMATION ABOUT
Plan 9F-8151

SQUARE FOOTAGE

Total:	**2001 Sq. Ft.**
Level 1:	1465 Sq. Ft.
Level 2:	536 Sq. Ft.

DIMENSIONS

Width: 42'-0" • Depth: 59'-4"

PRICE CODE 20

Order Direct

800-947-7526

(7:00-6:00 Mon.-Fri. CST)

Elm Creek

9F-8154

The specially finished Elm Creek: The dining room, close enough to the kitchen for easy serving and enclosed enough to be versatile as another living space. A secluded master suite, to enjoy the soaking tub and dual-sink vanity. And a U-shaped stairway connecting the main floor to the three upstairs bedrooms.

INFORMATION ABOUT

Plan 9F-8154

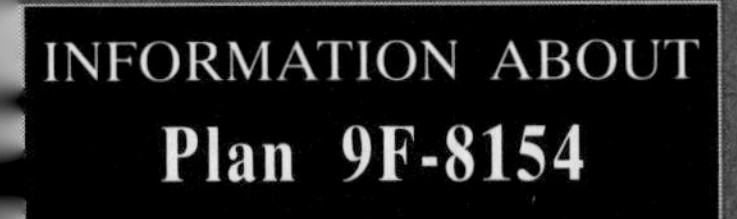

SQUARE FOOTAGE	
Total:	**2152 Sq. Ft.**
Level 1:	1465 Sq. Ft.
Level 2:	687 Sq. Ft.

DIMENSIONS

Width: 42'-0" • Depth: 59'-4"

PRICE CODE 21

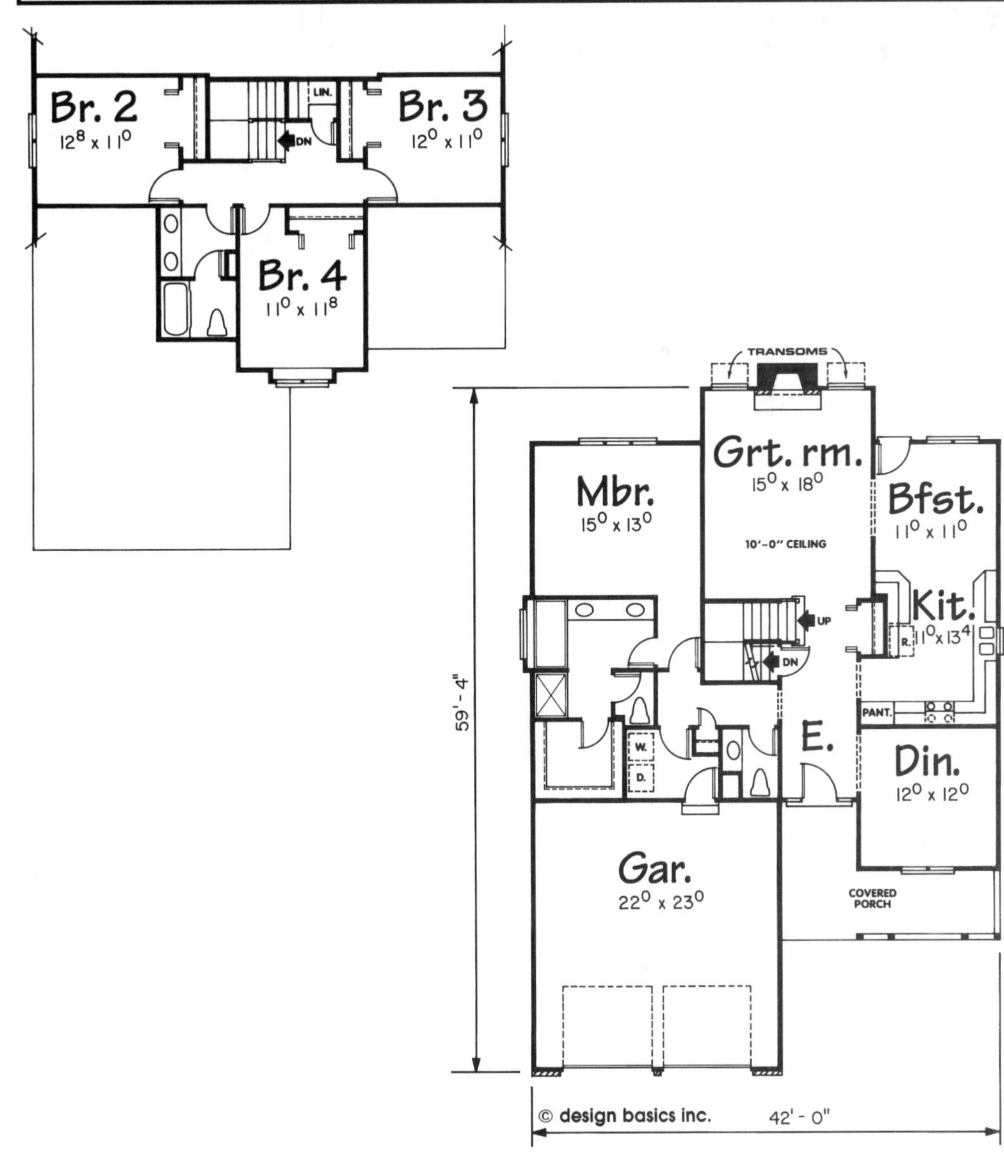

All plans on high quality, erasable, reproducible vellum.

Echo Valley

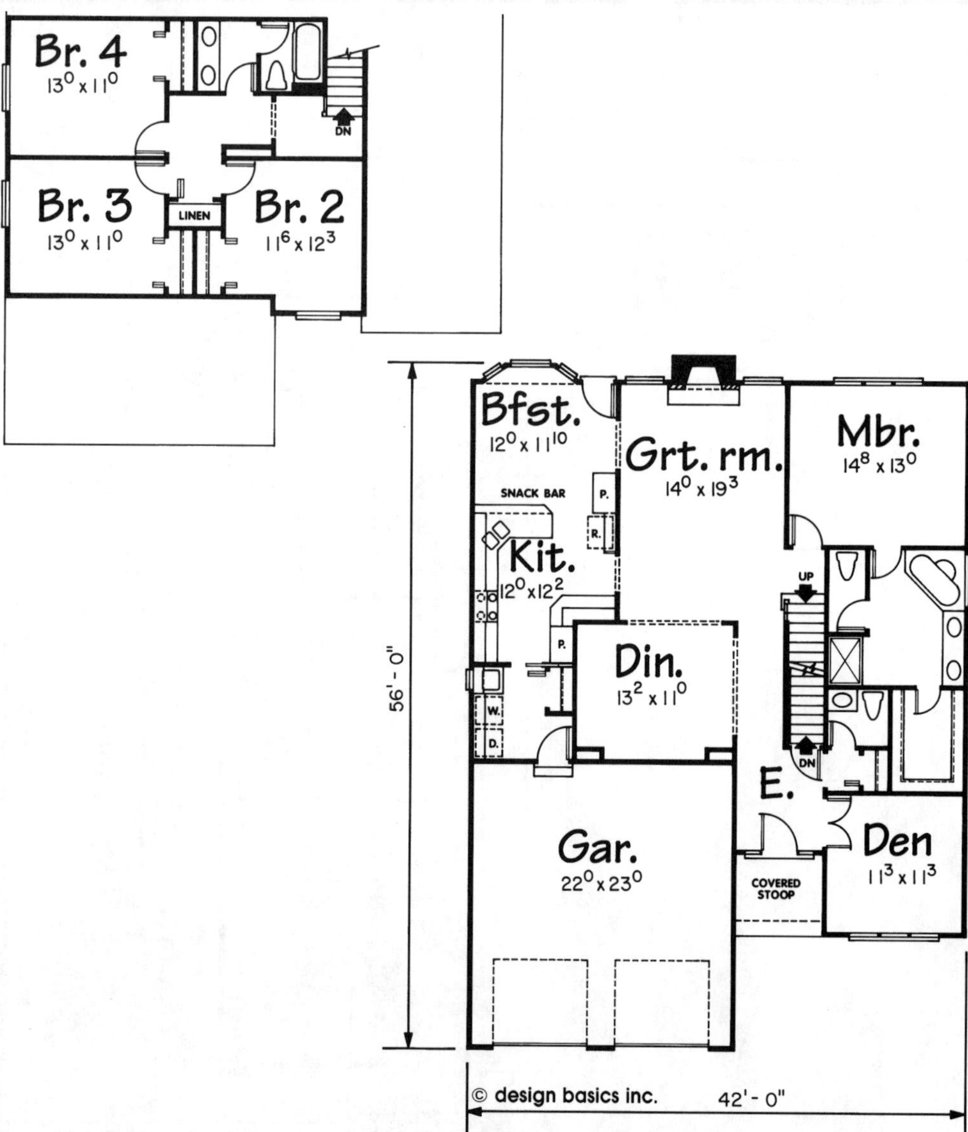

9F-8153

The significance of Echo Valley: A back stairway to seclude the traffic to the second floor. A den enclosed behind French doors for privacy. Special counter space in the kitchen to help serve the dining room. And the master suite on the main floor, for those who prefer to comfortably access the living area from it.

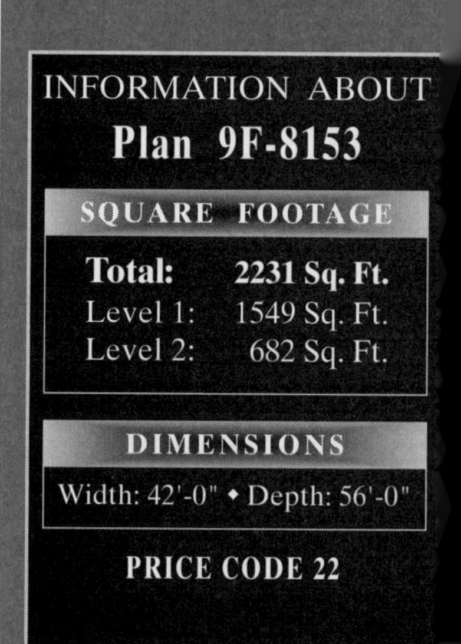

INFORMATION ABOUT
Plan 9F-8153

SQUARE FOOTAGE

Total:	**2231 Sq. Ft.**
Level 1:	1549 Sq. Ft.
Level 2:	682 Sq. Ft.

DIMENSIONS

Width: 42'-0" • Depth: 56'-0"

PRICE CODE 22

Stafford Run

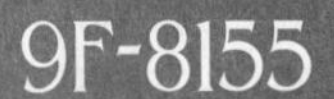

The infinitely subtle Stafford Run: Openness in the great room and dining room, for a unique connection between living and eating. A den at the rear, to work in peace. A sloped ceiling in the great room adding interest to entertainment and relaxation. And a large walk-in closet and dressing area in the master bath to make getting ready easier.

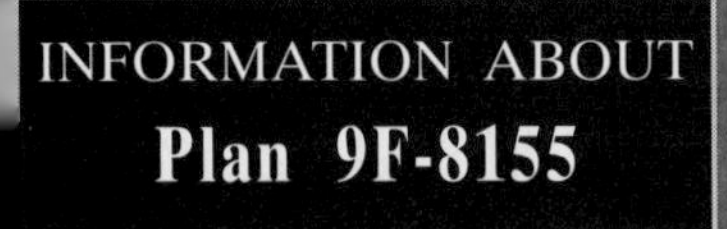

SQUARE FOOTAGE

Total:	**2320 Sq. Ft.**
Level 1:	1653 Sq. Ft.
Level 2:	667 Sq. Ft.

DIMENSIONS

Width: 42'-0" • Depth: 60'-0"

PRICE CODE 23

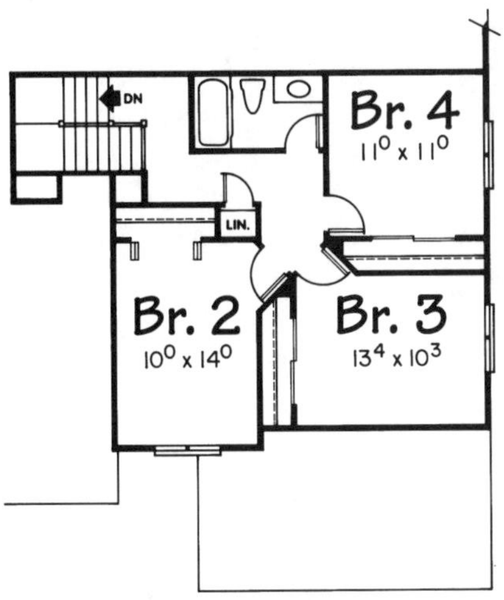

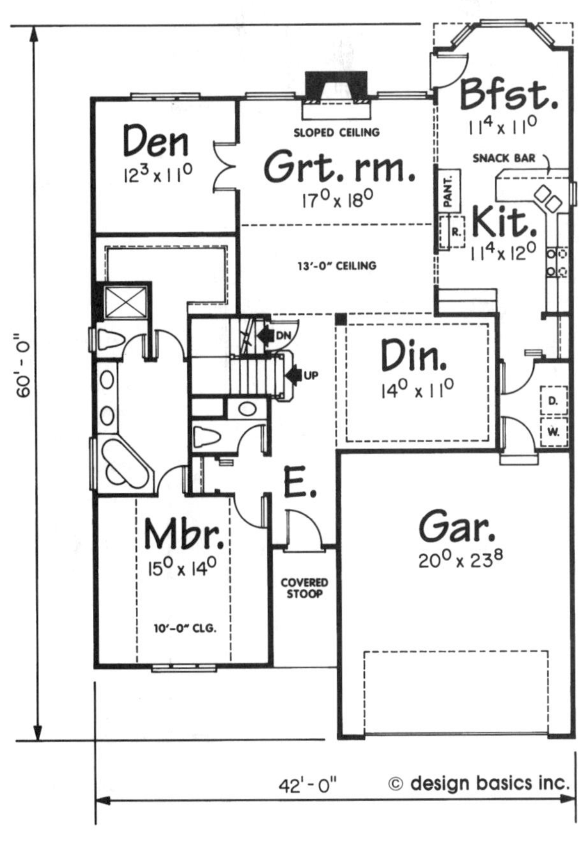

All plans on high quality, erasable, reproducible vellum.

Carriage Hills

9F-8037

Aspects of the Carriage Hills: A covered stoop that feels like a porch. A great room with both width and height to encourage feelings of freedom when in it. A sunny perspective of meals in the bayed breakfast area. And a formal dining room for those special times when its needed.

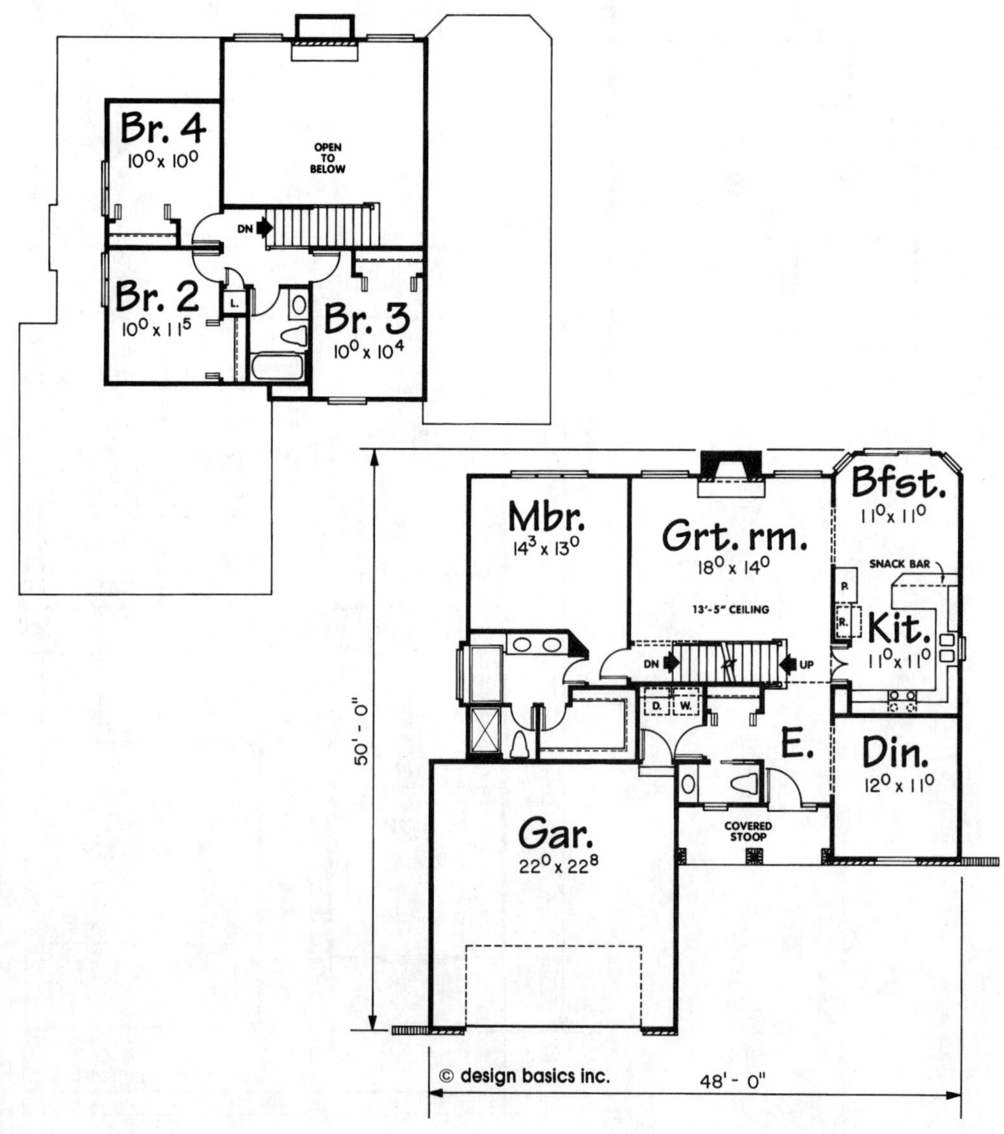

INFORMATION ABOUT
Plan 9F-8037

SQUARE FOOTAGE

Total:	**1802 Sq. Ft.**
Level 1:	1284 Sq. Ft.
Level 2:	518 Sq. Ft.

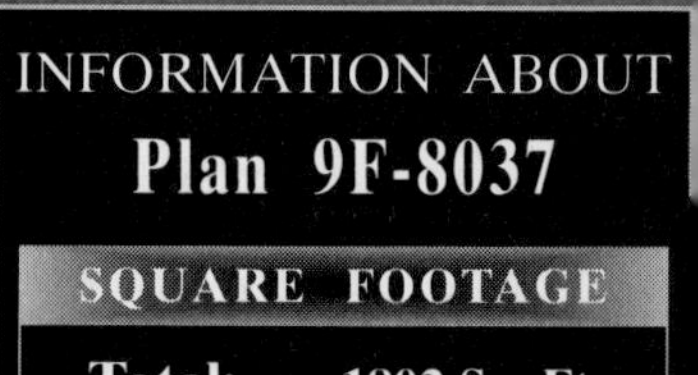

DIMENSIONS

Width: 48'-0" • Depth: 50'-0"

PRICE CODE 18

Abbott Lane

9F-8063

The hominess of **Abbott Lane:** *A wrapping porch to forget the anxiety of the day. A fireplace and windows to beckon sitting and talking in the great room. A sunlit U-shaped stairway to lead to three upstairs bedrooms and an optional storage area, large enough for a studio.*

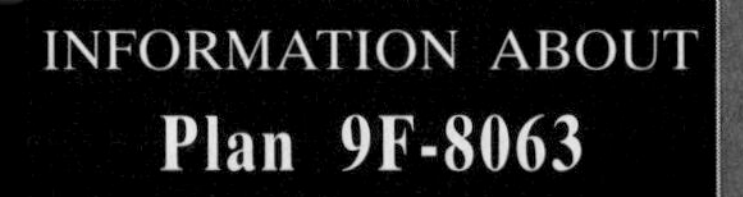

SQUARE FOOTAGE

Total:	**2208 Sq. Ft.**
Level 1:	1496 Sq. Ft.
Level 2:	712 Sq. Ft.

Unfinished Storage Adds 317 Sq. Ft.

DIMENSIONS

Width: 48'-0" • Depth: 54'-4"

PRICE CODE 22

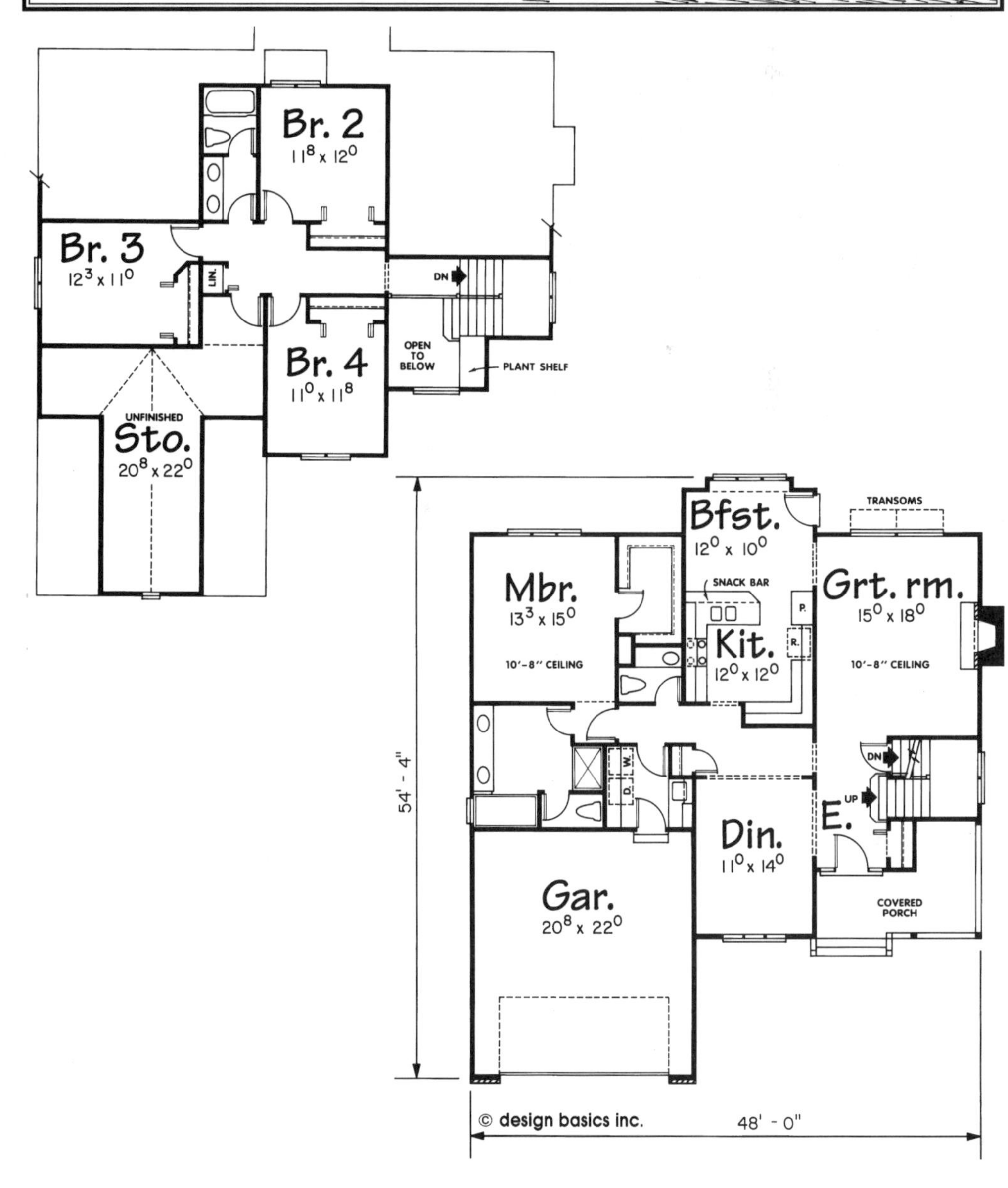

All plans on high quality, erasable, reproducible vellum.

PLEXABLE™

Ellies Knoll

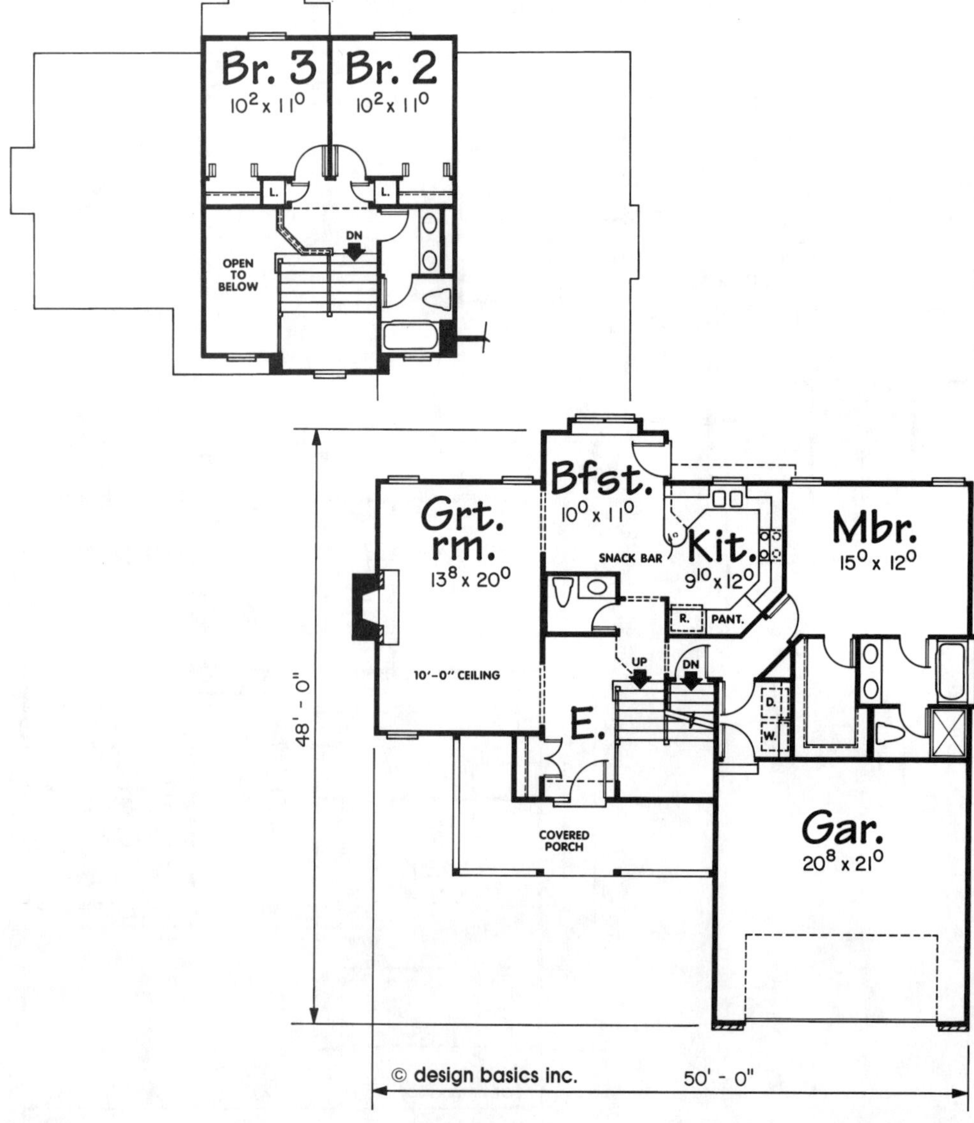

9F-8027

*A blend of the basics – the **Ellies Knoll**. A front porch and rooflines with admirable style. A spacious great room with three sources of outside light for sun-filled reading and relaxation. A corner snack bar and large pantry in the kitchen to organize the cooked and uncooked. And a U-shaped stairway with a second-floor overlook of life below.*

INFORMATION ABOUT
Plan 9F-8027

SQUARE FOOTAGE

Total:	**1615 Sq. Ft.**
Level 1:	1210 Sq. Ft.
Level 2:	405 Sq. Ft.

DIMENSIONS

Width: 50'-0" • Depth: 48'-0"

PRICE CODE 16

Orchard Trail

9F-8126

*The radiance of **Orchard Trail:** A charming covered porch for watching the sunrise. An island counter in the kitchen for convenience when cooking. A combined great room and dining room to easily host parties and holiday gatherings. And a back patio to escape to after dinner.*

INFORMATION ABOUT

Plan 9F-8126

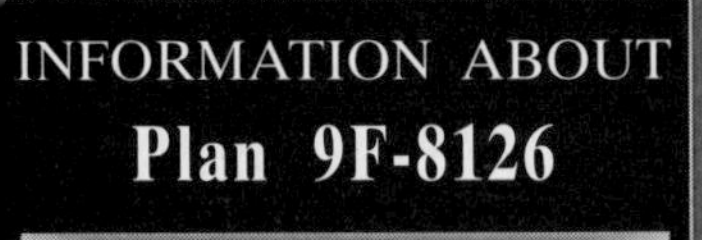

SQUARE FOOTAGE	
Total:	**1953 Sq. Ft.**
Level 1:	1491 Sq. Ft.
Level 2:	462 Sq. Ft.

DIMENSIONS

Width: 50'-0" • Depth: 58'-0"

PRICE CODE 19

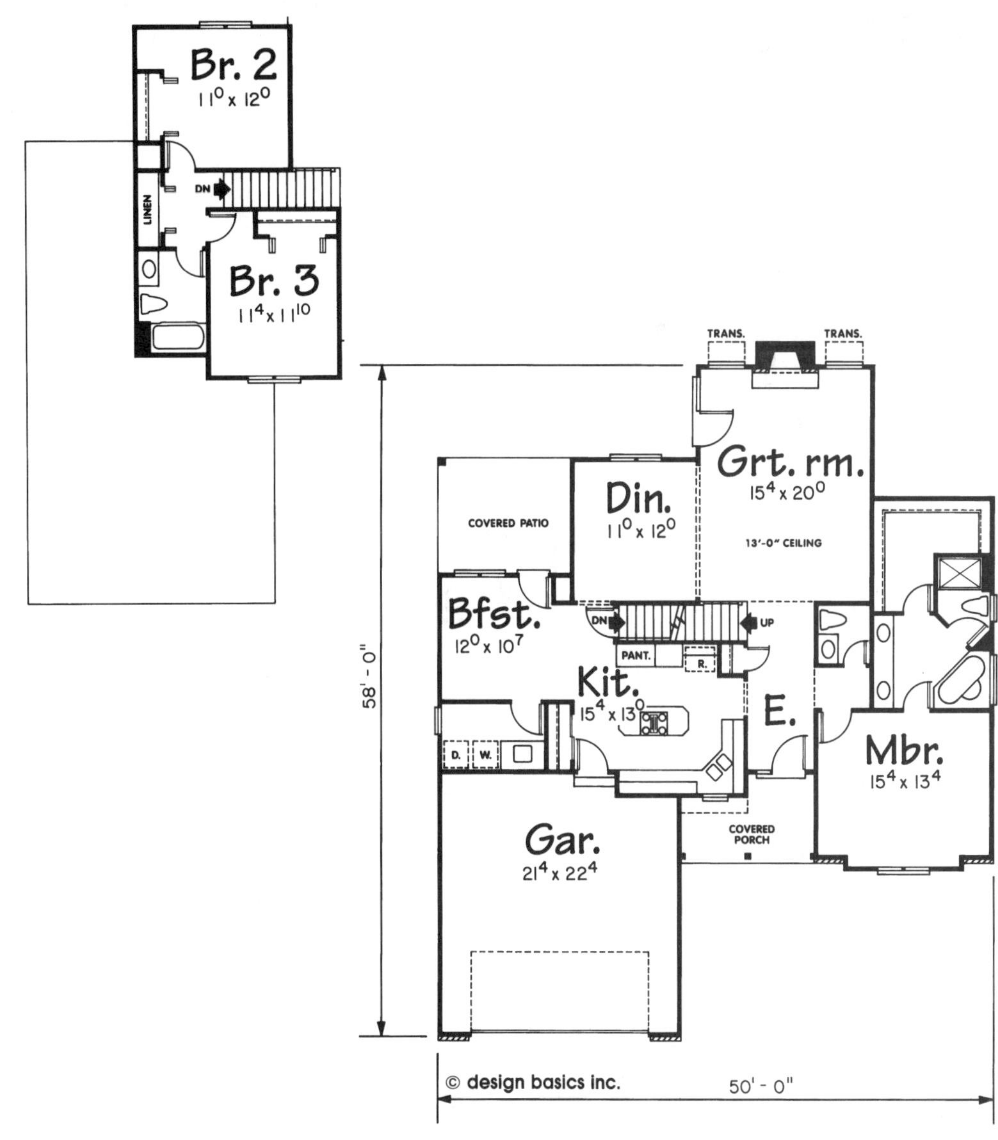

All plans on high quality, erasable, reproducible vellum.

Park Hills

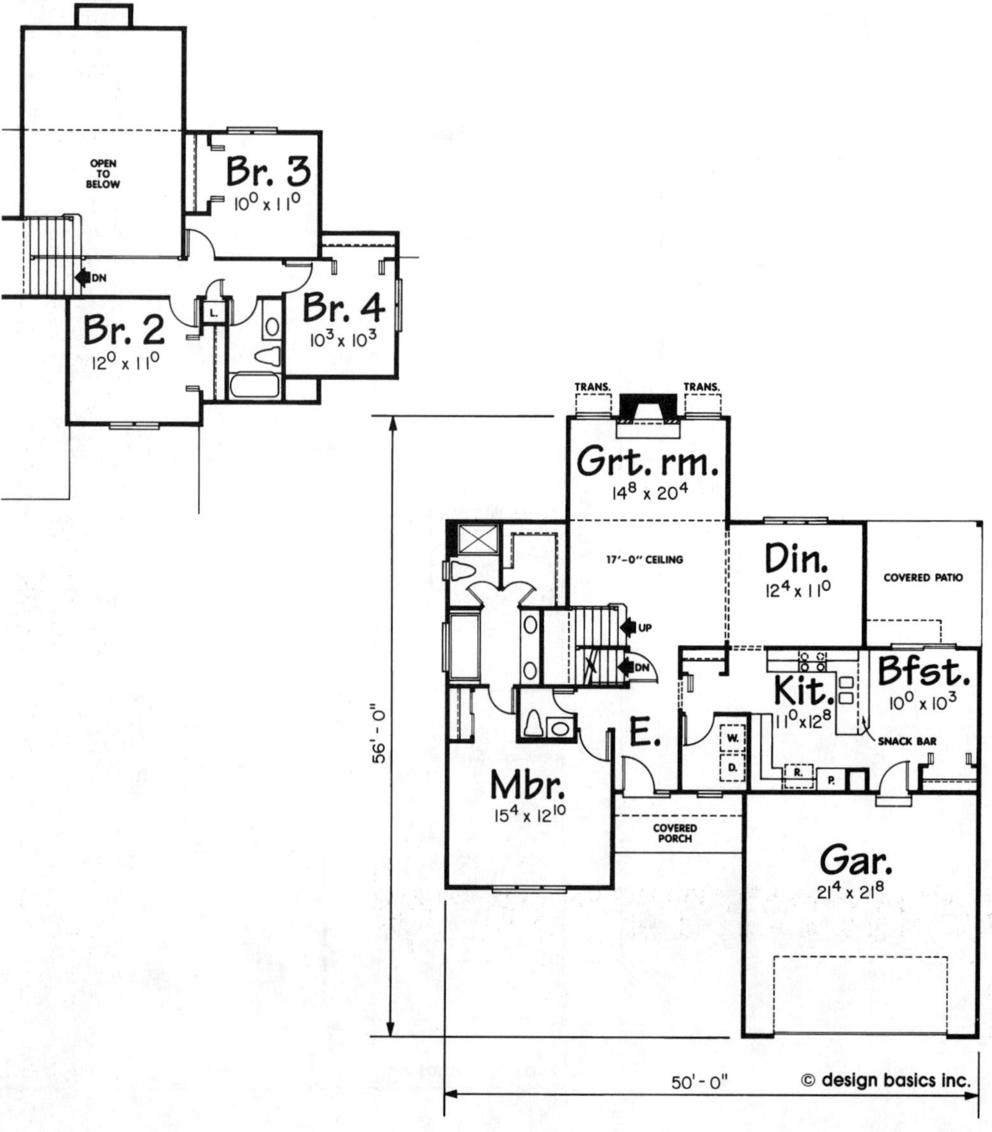

9F-8125

The friendly ***Park Hills:***

A two-story great room lending a sense of spaciousness to the main floor. A rear covered patio and front porch – both meant to be relaxed upon. And in the kitchen, a snack bar peninsula for an easy place to enjoy breakfast.

INFORMATION ABOUT Plan 9F-8125

SQUARE FOOTAGE

Total:	**1974 Sq. Ft.**
Level 1:	1394 Sq. Ft.
Level 2:	580 Sq. Ft.

DIMENSIONS

Width: 50'-0" • Depth: 56'-0"

PRICE CODE 19

Order Direct

800-947-7526

(7:00-6:00 Mon.-Fri. CST)

HEARTLAND HOME PLANS™

BASE PLAN INFORMATION

PAGE NO.	WIDTH	PLAN NO.	PLAN NAME	SQ. FT.
222	50'-0"	8109	Apple Woods	1608
199	40'-0"	8028	Tilmers Run	1642
198	39'-4"	8139	Harbor Lane	1654
204	41'-4"	8162	Majesty Oaks	1672
206	42'-0"	8105	Adams Creek	1685
209	44'-0"	8108	Rose Hollow	1705
195	38'-0"	8142	Royal Ridge	1737
196	38'-0"	8148	Topeka Canyon	1745
214	48'-0"	8107	Ashland Park	1752
212	44'-8"	8029	Linden Acres	1753
200	40'-0"	8141	Knights Bridge	1806
220	48'-8"	8102	Henley Mills	1817
192	28'-0"	8136	Camden Place	1818
208	42'-8"	8106	Chimney Ridge	1830
210	44'-0"	8100	Pebble Creek	1844
205	41'-4"	8104	Ridge Crest	1852
193	29'-4"	8138	Chrystal Bay	1852
215	48'-0"	8099	Duncan Valley	1877
216	48'-0"	8098	Sherman Oaks	1881
211	44'-0"	8030	Burton Place	1885
197	38'-0"	8140	Amber Cove	1899
207	42'-0"	8101	Bailey Falls	1919
217	48'-0"	8081	Oak Hollow	1926
218	48'-0"	8031	Robins Lane	2029
194	30'-0"	8173	Wichita Falls	2074
221	48'-8"	8073	Wilson Creek	2084
223	50'-0"	8072	Hamilton Farm	2095
219	48'-0"	8060	Chapel Hills	2211
213	46'-0"	8011	Jones Farms	2292
201	40'-0"	8145	Turtle Creek	2346
202	40'-0"	8143	Wilkins Woods	2380
224	50'-0"	8014	Rogers Point	2469
203	40'-0"	8147	Kellys Walk	2526

TWO STORY HOMES

Camden Place

9F-8136

The easy feel of ***Camden Place:*** *A casual great room centered on a fireplace for warmth and windows for natural light. Wrapping counters and two pantries in the kitchen to help organize the cook. And on the second floor, three bedrooms with a large laundry room to serve them.*

SQUARE FOOTAGE

Total:	**1818 Sq. Ft.**
Level 1:	829 Sq. Ft.
Level 2:	989 Sq. Ft.

DIMENSIONS

Width: 28'-0" • Depth: 54'-0"

PRICE CODE 18

Mbr. $14^0 \times 14^0$

LIN.

DN

OPEN TO BELOW

PLANT SHELF

D.

W.

Br. 2 $10^0 \times 13^0$

Br. 3 $10^0 \times 13^0$

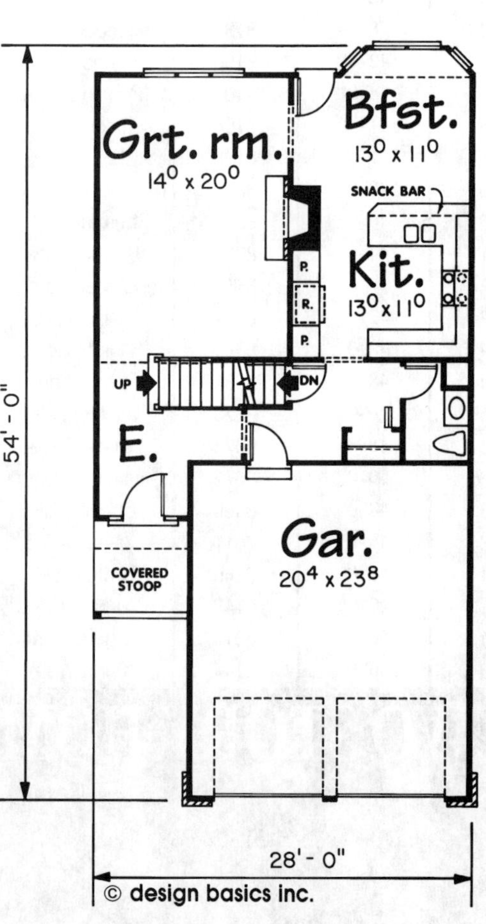

Order Direct

800-947-7526

(7:00-6:00 Mon.-Fri. CST)

Chrystal Bay

9F-8138

The polished **Chrystal Bay:** *A wide entry drawn into the great room for a feeling of welcome. A snack bar, island counter and sizable pantry helping the kitchen serve the dinette. And the laundry room on the second floor to accommodate all the bedrooms.*

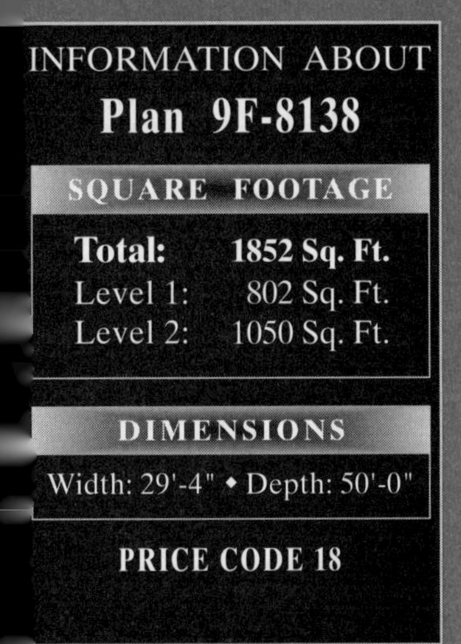

INFORMATION ABOUT
Plan 9F-8138

SQUARE FOOTAGE

Total:	**1852 Sq. Ft.**
Level 1:	802 Sq. Ft.
Level 2:	1050 Sq. Ft.

DIMENSIONS

Width: 29'-4" • Depth: 50'-0"

PRICE CODE 18

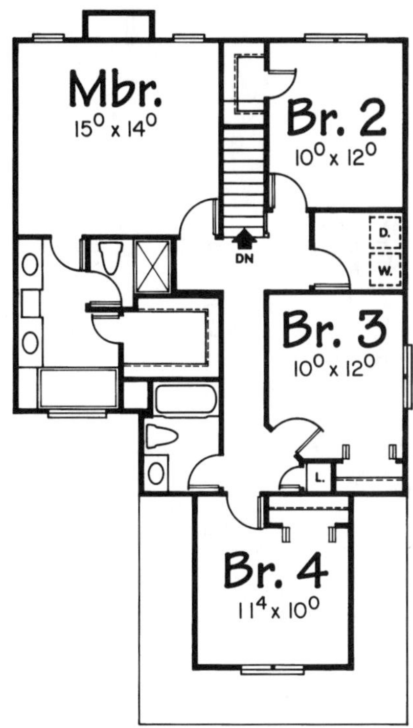

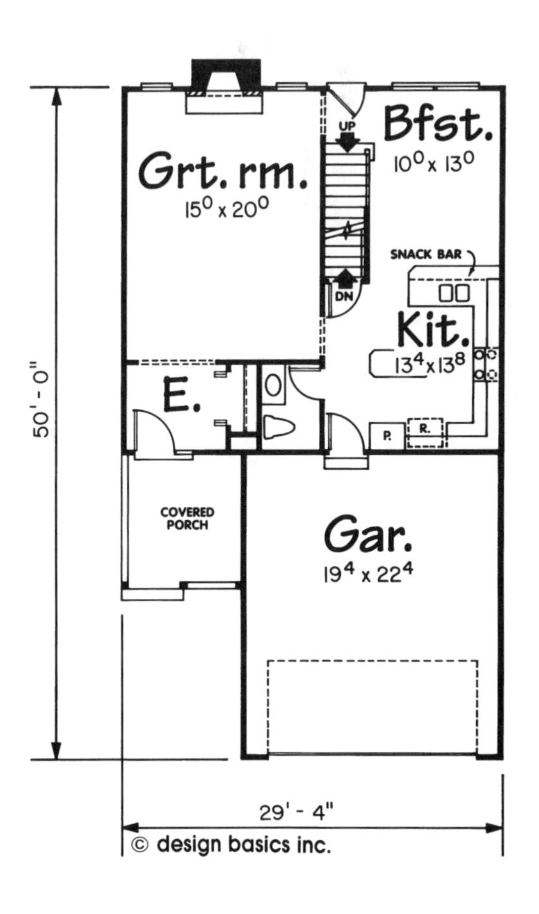

All plans on
high quality, erasable,
reproducible vellum.

PLEXABLE™

Wichita Falls

9F-8173

*The functional **Wichita Falls:*** *Bayed windows in the breakfast area illuminating cooking as well as eating. Angled stairs adding interest to the distance upstairs. A loft viewing the great room, for use as a reading area.*

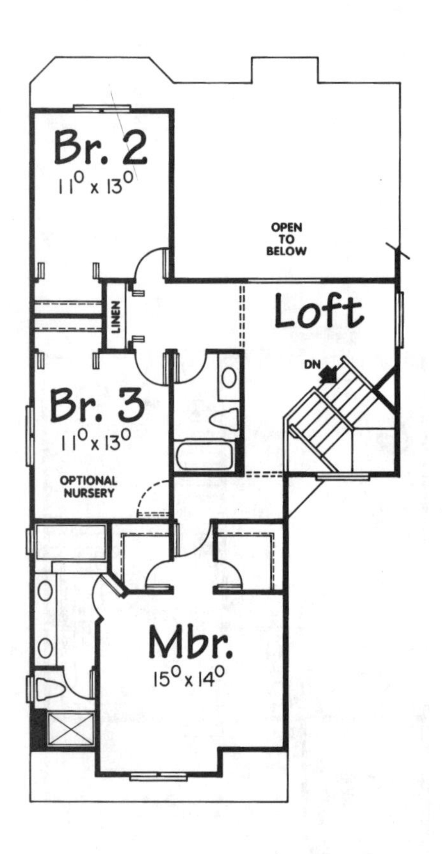

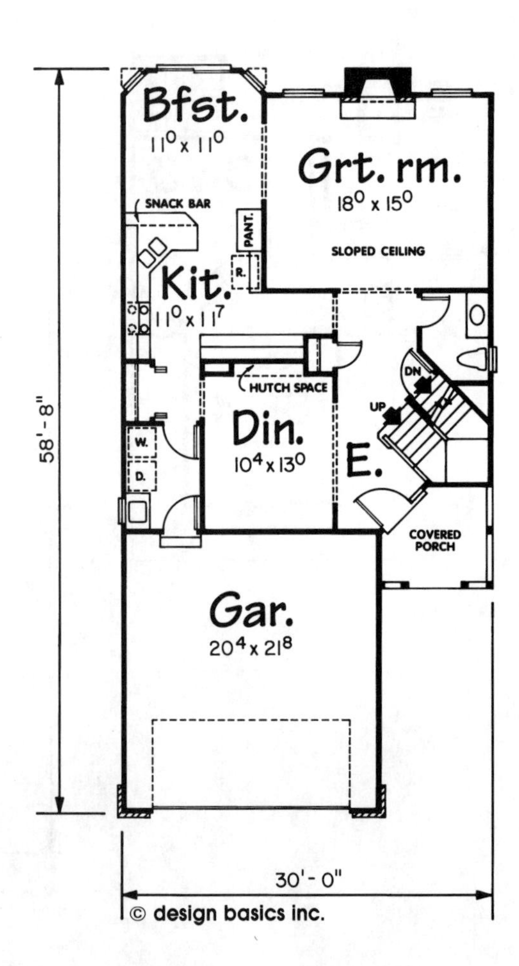

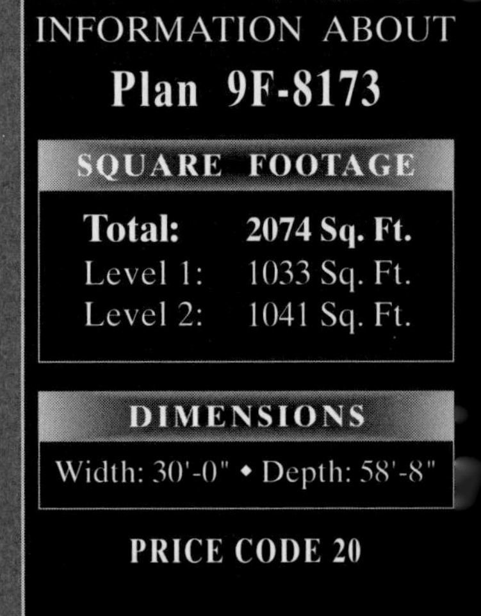

INFORMATION ABOUT
Plan 9F-8173

SQUARE FOOTAGE

Total:	**2074 Sq. Ft.**
Level 1:	1033 Sq. Ft.
Level 2:	1041 Sq. Ft.

DIMENSIONS

Width: 30'-0" • Depth: 58'-8"

PRICE CODE 20

Royal Ridge

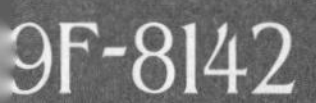

The comfort of ***Royal Ridge:*** *A front porch for waving at the neighbors. A well-placed kitchen for pouring drinks and serving snacks to the eating areas. A fireplace in the great room to improve the view. And three upstairs bedrooms with relaxation in mind for all.*

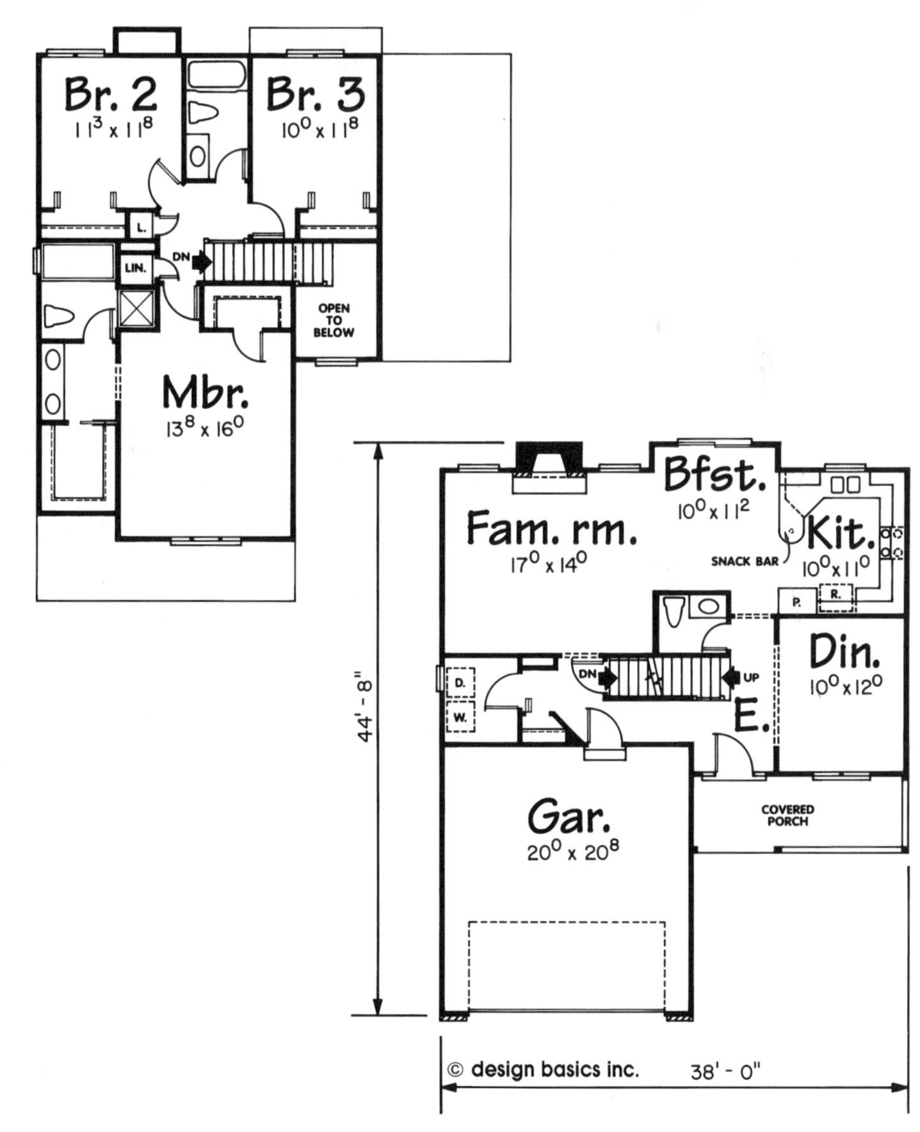

INFORMATION ABOUT
Plan 9F-8142

SQUARE FOOTAGE

Total:	**1737 Sq. Ft.**
Level 1:	886 Sq. Ft.
Level 2:	851 Sq. Ft.

DIMENSIONS

Width: 38'-0" • Depth: 44'-8"

PRICE CODE 17

All plans on high quality, erasable, reproducible vellum.

Topeka Canyon

9F-8148

The refined **Topeka Canyon:** *The great room with the option of expanding into the dining room if necessary. At the rear, a private office for a place to work at home. A laundry room that also serves as a mud room in bad weather. And a sitting area in the master suite for reading the newspaper or checking out the sunrise.*

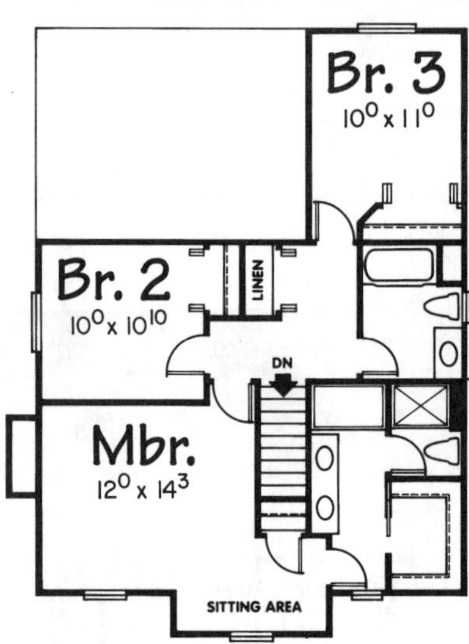

INFORMATION ABOUT Plan 9F-8148

SQUARE FOOTAGE

Total:	**1745 Sq. Ft.**
Level 1:	934 Sq. Ft.
Level 2:	811 Sq. Ft.

DIMENSIONS

Width: 38'-0" • Depth: 45'-4"

PRICE CODE 17

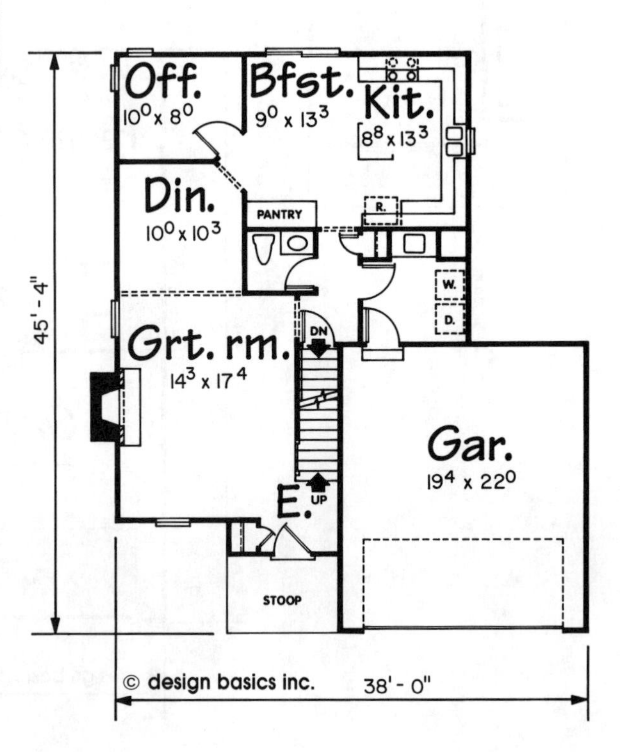

Amber Cove

9F-8140

The flair of Amber Cove:

A cathedral ceiling in the great room enhancing the time spent here. An office at the back for use as a den or when working out of the home. An island kitchen that blends with the dinette for a spacious feel. And four bedrooms upstairs to retreat to.

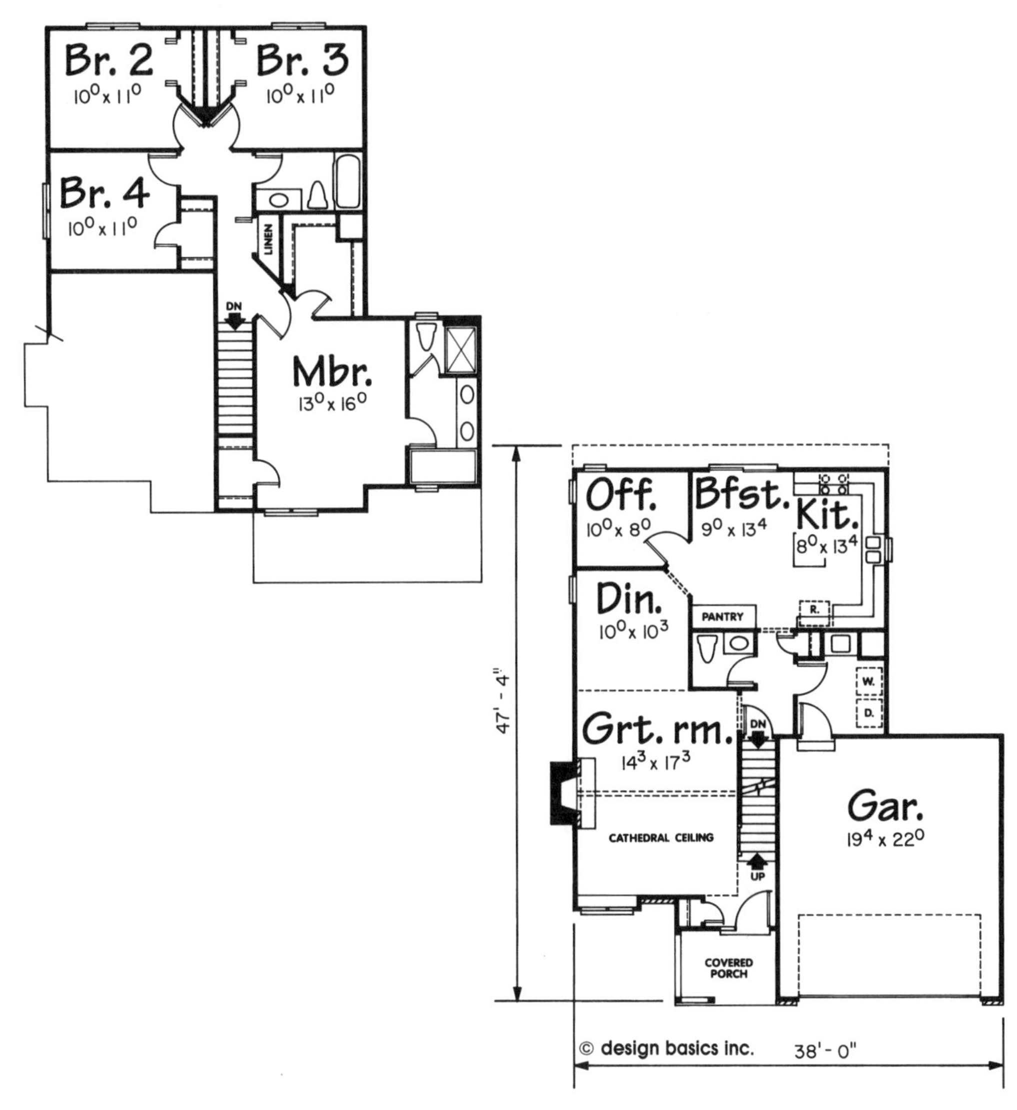

INFORMATION ABOUT

Plan 9F-8140

SQUARE FOOTAGE

Total:	**1899 Sq. Ft.**
Level 1:	919 Sq. Ft.
Level 2:	980 Sq. Ft.

DIMENSIONS

Width: 38'-0" • Depth: 47'-4"

PRICE CODE 18

All plans on high quality, erasable, reproducible vellum.

Harbor Lane

9F-8139

*The classic **Harbor Lane**.*

An L-shaped porch providing an essential place to unwind. The sunny family area with elements like a snack bar and fireplace for day-to-day living. A master suite with a lovely window and a soaking tub to retreat to. And a nice place for a workbench in the garage.

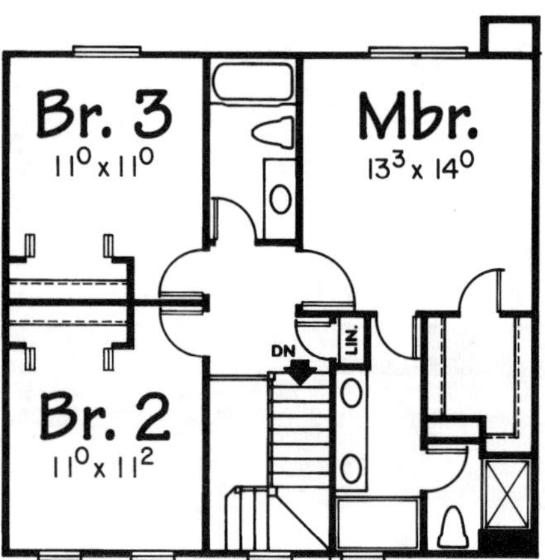

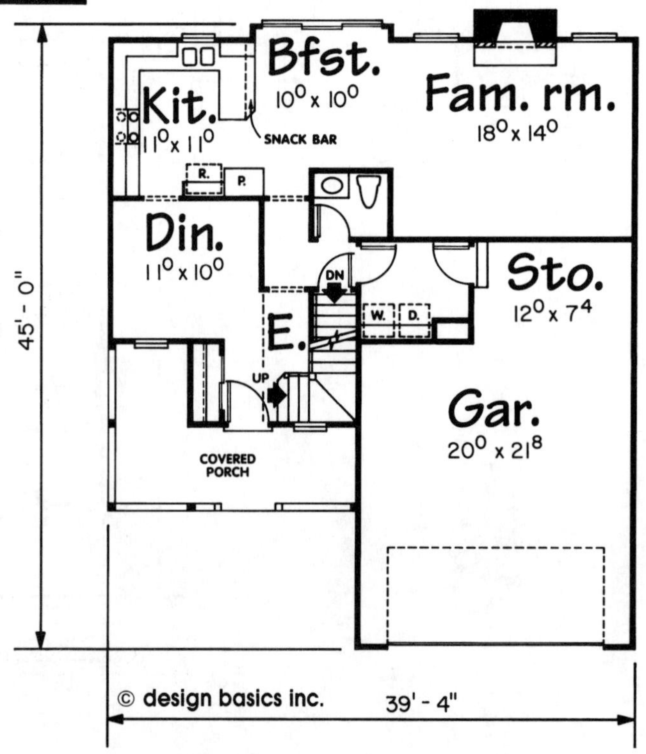

INFORMATION ABOUT Plan 9F-8139

SQUARE FOOTAGE

Total:	**1654 Sq. Ft.**
Level 1:	866 Sq. Ft.
Level 2:	788 Sq. Ft.

DIMENSIONS

Width: 39'-4" • Depth: 45'-0"

PRICE CODE 16

Tilmers Run

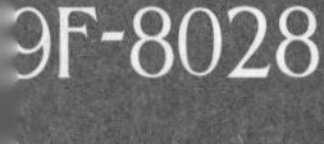

9F-8028

The identity of Tilmers Run: A wide, gabled porch to charm the outdoors. A dining room that expands into the great room for ready relaxation after meals. Two informal eating options in the kitchen – at the snack bar or by a bayed window. On the second floor, an unfinished bonus room leaves options for more closet or storage space in the master suite.

INFORMATION ABOUT
Plan 9F-8028

SQUARE FOOTAGE

Total:	**1642 Sq. Ft.**
Level 1:	862 Sq. Ft.
Level 2:	780 Sq. Ft.

Unfinished Storage Adds 132 Sq. Ft.

DIMENSIONS

Width: 40'-0" • Depth: 44'-0"

PRICE CODE 16

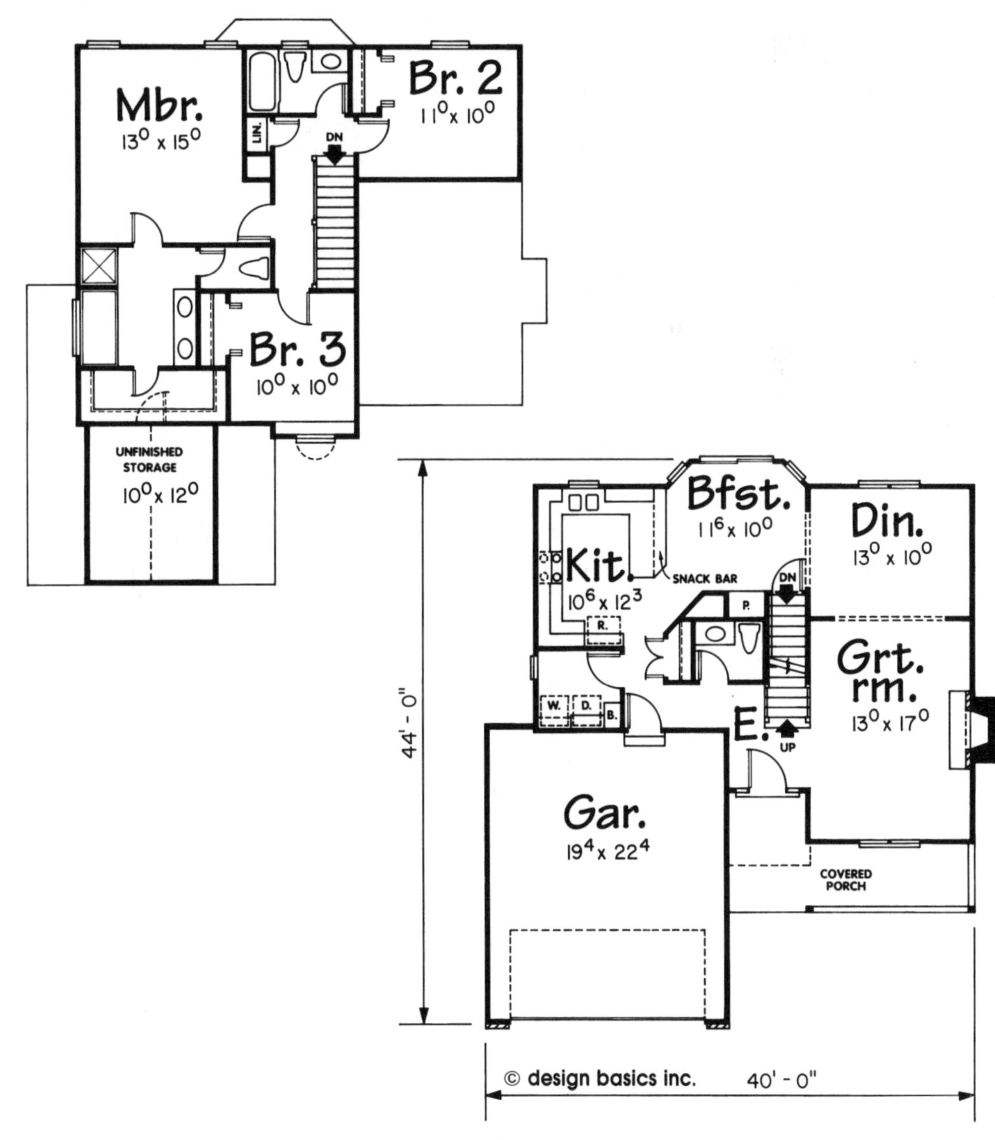

All plans on high quality, erasable, reproducible vellum.

Knights Bridge

9F-8141

The charm of ***Knights Bridge:*** *A volume entry that coaxes one to cozy up to the fireplace in the great room. Formal and informal eating areas – each for the right occasion. And an organized trafficway to easily get to the powder bath, laundry room, garage and kitchen.*

INFORMATION ABOUT
Plan 9F-8141

SQUARE FOOTAGE

Total:	**1806 Sq. Ft.**
Level 1:	946 Sq. Ft.
Level 2:	860 Sq. Ft.

DIMENSIONS

Width: 40'-0" • Depth: 46'-0"

PRICE CODE 18

Mbr. 15^0 x 14^0
LIN.
Br. 2 11^0 x 11^0
DN
OPEN TO BELOW
Br. 3 11^0 x 11^0

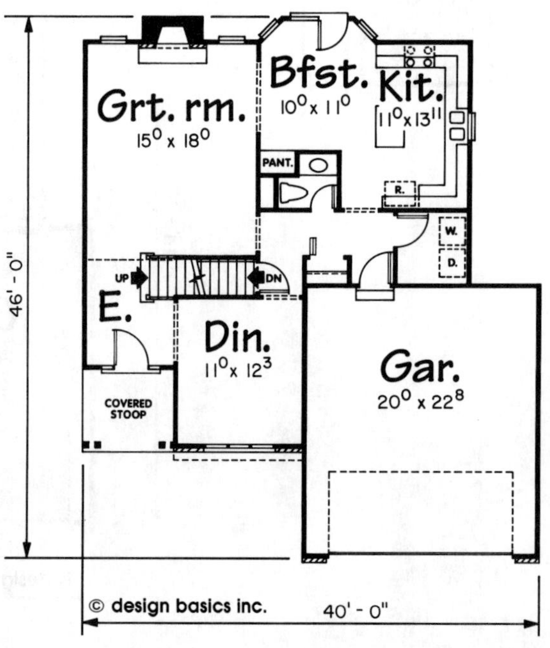

Order Direct

800-947-7526

(7:00-6:00 Mon.-Fri. CST)

Turtle Creek

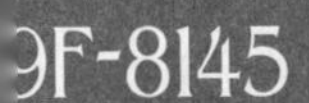

9F-8145

The approachable **Turtle Creek:** *Open living and dining rooms to expand parties and holiday gatherings. The secluded family area at the rear for everyday activity. An office with possible use as a bedroom. And a laundry room large enough to handle the whole family.*

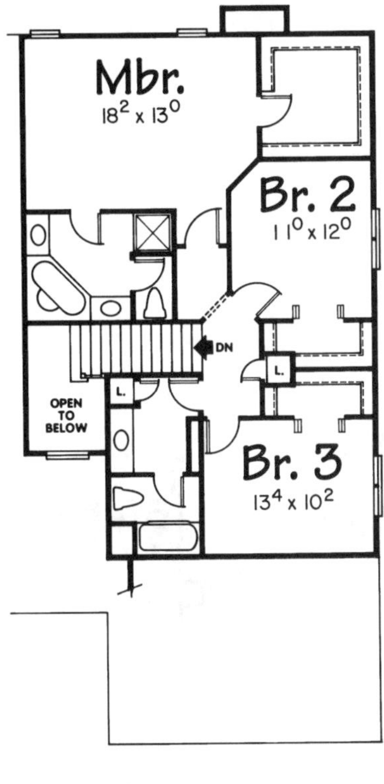

INFORMATION ABOUT Plan 9F-8145

SQUARE FOOTAGE

Total:	**2346 Sq. Ft.**
Level 1:	1381 Sq. Ft.
Level 2:	965 Sq. Ft.

DIMENSIONS

Width: 40'-0" • Depth: 54'-0"

PRICE CODE 23

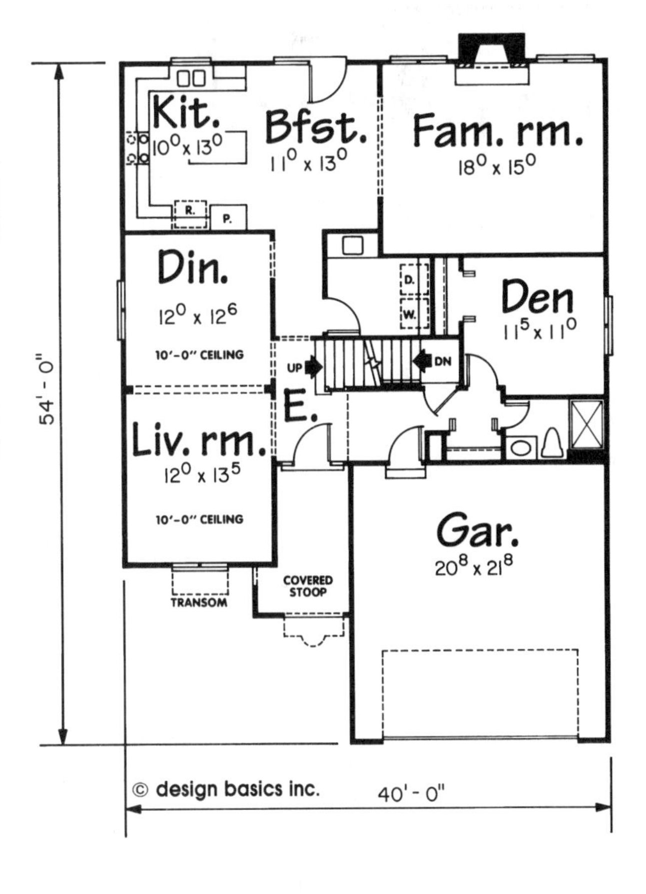

All plans on high quality, erasable, reproducible vellum.

Wilkins Woods

9F-8143

*The stately **Wilkins Woods:** Angled French doors to a den positioned for retreat and privacy. Bayed windows in the dining room so that meals are open to natural light. A U-shaped stairway for access to four second-floor bedrooms and the two baths that serve them.*

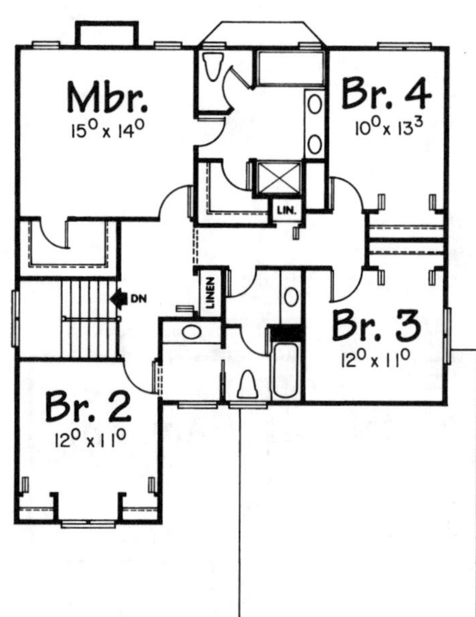

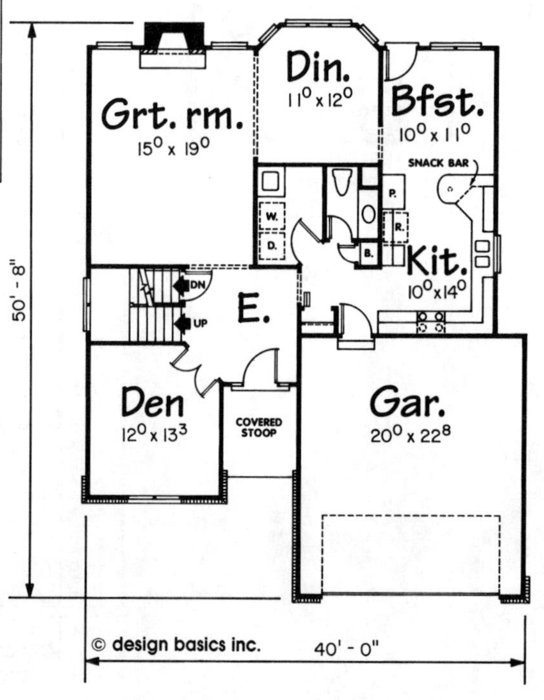

INFORMATION ABOUT
Plan 9F-8143

SQUARE FOOTAGE

Total:	**2380 Sq. Ft.**
Level 1:	1189 Sq. Ft.
Level 2:	1191 Sq. Ft.

DIMENSIONS

Width: 40'-0" • Depth: 50'-8"

PRICE CODE 23

Kellys Walk

The lustre of ***Kellys Walk:***

Natural light sources to expand the entry into the living, dining and family rooms. A see-through fireplace bonding the living areas. A wide-open kitchen to easily access all areas of the main floor. And the second-floor master suite with two walk-in closets meeting his and her needs.

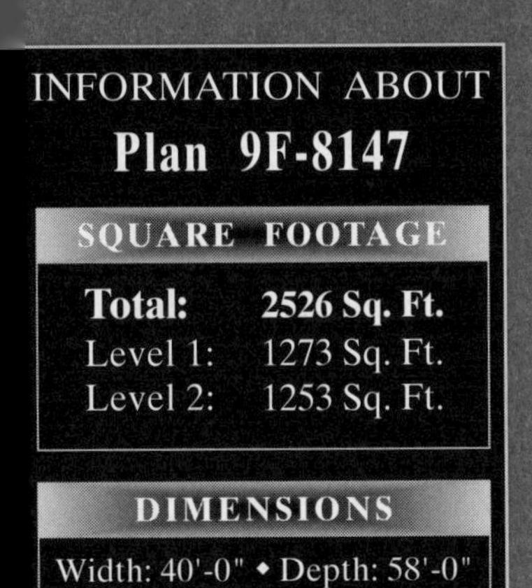

INFORMATION ABOUT
Plan 9F-8147

SQUARE FOOTAGE

Total:	**2526 Sq. Ft.**
Level 1:	1273 Sq. Ft.
Level 2:	1253 Sq. Ft.

DIMENSIONS

Width: 40'-0" • Depth: 58'-0"

PRICE CODE 25

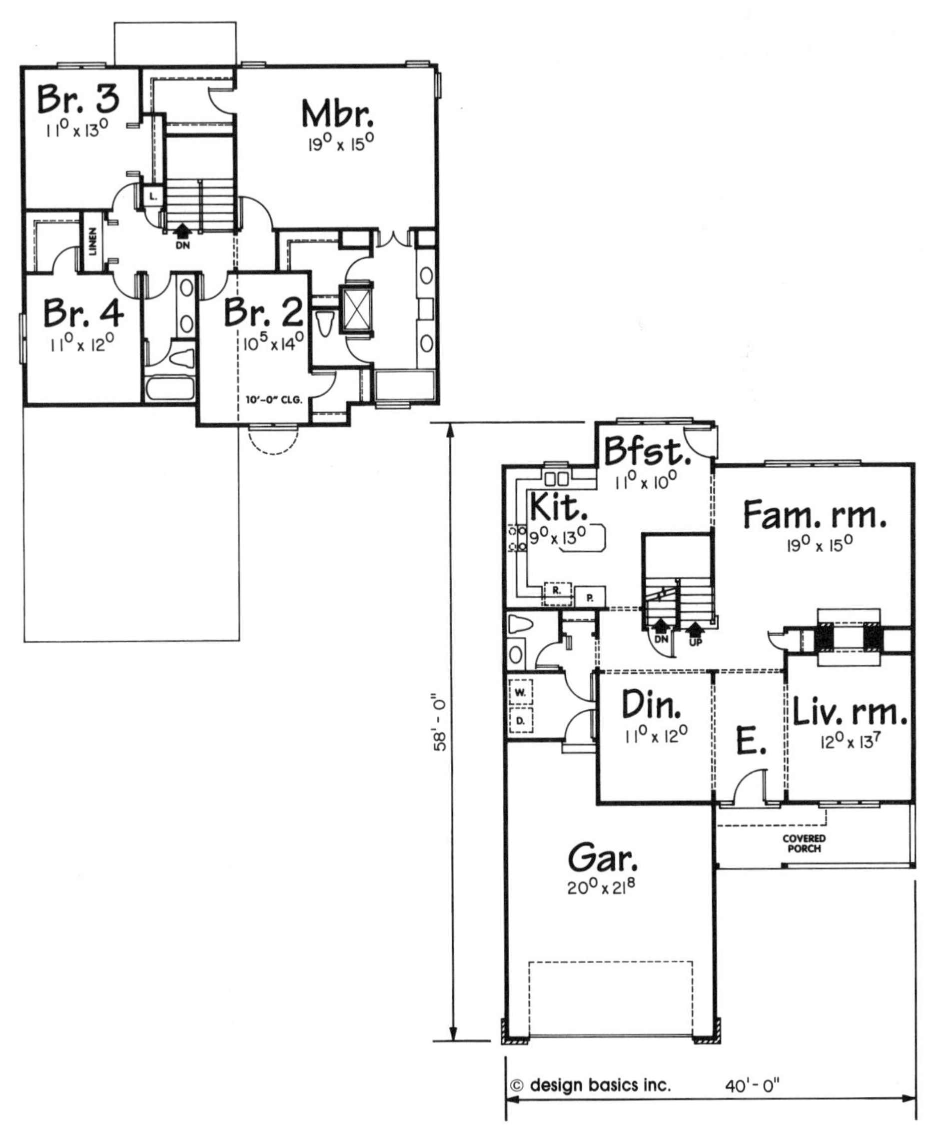

All plans on
high quality, erasable,
reproducible vellum.

Majesty Oaks

9F-8162

*The grand **Majesty Oaks:** A great room that expands into the dining room and vice versa, if necessary. The kitchen positioned to serve the breakfast area informally and the dining room formally. A second-floor laundry room to serve three bedrooms. And a spacious master bath for relaxing.*

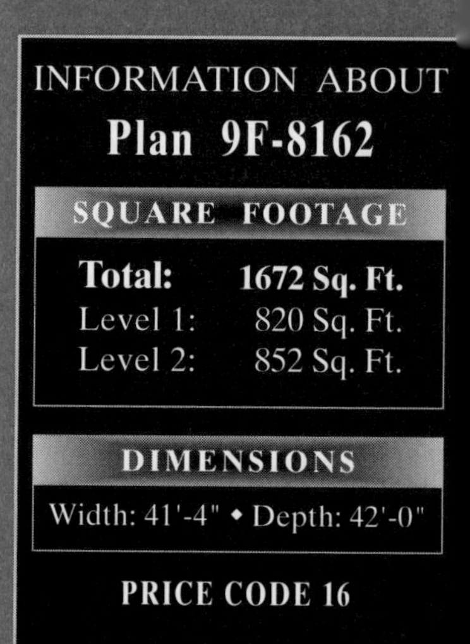

INFORMATION ABOUT
Plan 9F-8162

SQUARE FOOTAGE

Total:	**1672 Sq. Ft.**
Level 1:	820 Sq. Ft.
Level 2:	852 Sq. Ft.

DIMENSIONS

Width: 41'-4" • Depth: 42'-0"

PRICE CODE 16

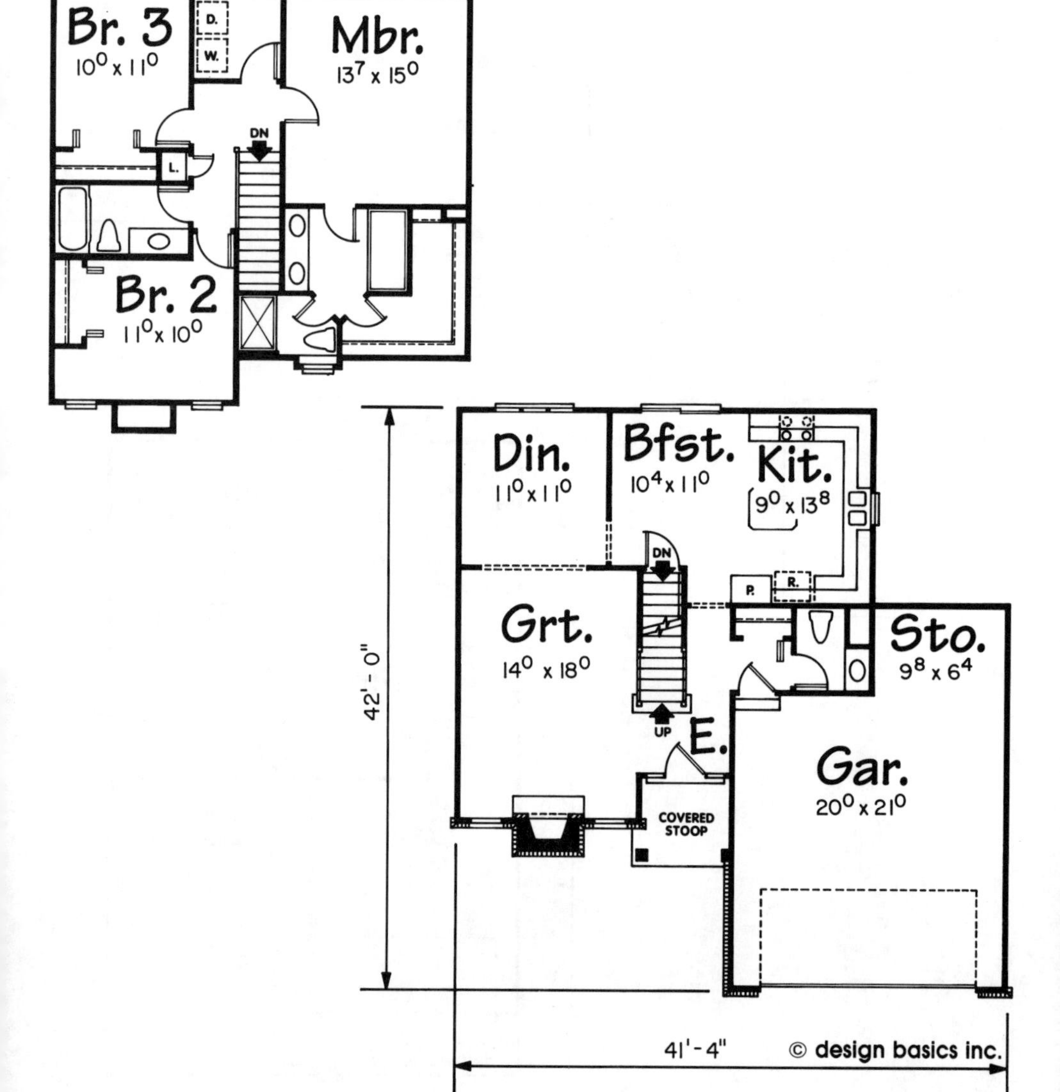

Order Direct

800-947-7526

(7:00-6:00 Mon.-Fri. CST)

Ridge Crest

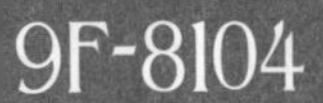

The design of the ***Ridge Crest:*** *A quaint porch enlightening the elevation and offering a place to relax. Bayed windows in the family room for sunlit living. A long snack bar in the kitchen, doubling as counter space for the cook. And a T-shaped stairway for quick access upstairs.*

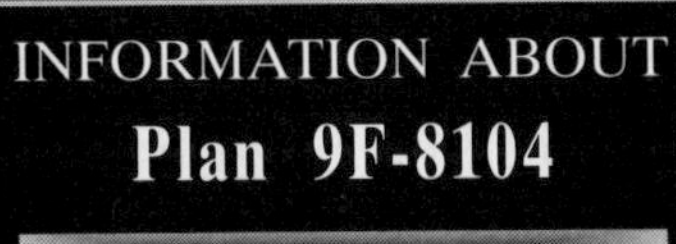

SQUARE FOOTAGE

Total:	**1852 Sq. Ft.**
Level 1:	802 Sq. Ft.
Level 2:	1050 Sq. Ft.

DIMENSIONS

Width: 29'-4" ◆ Depth: 50'-0"

PRICE CODE 18

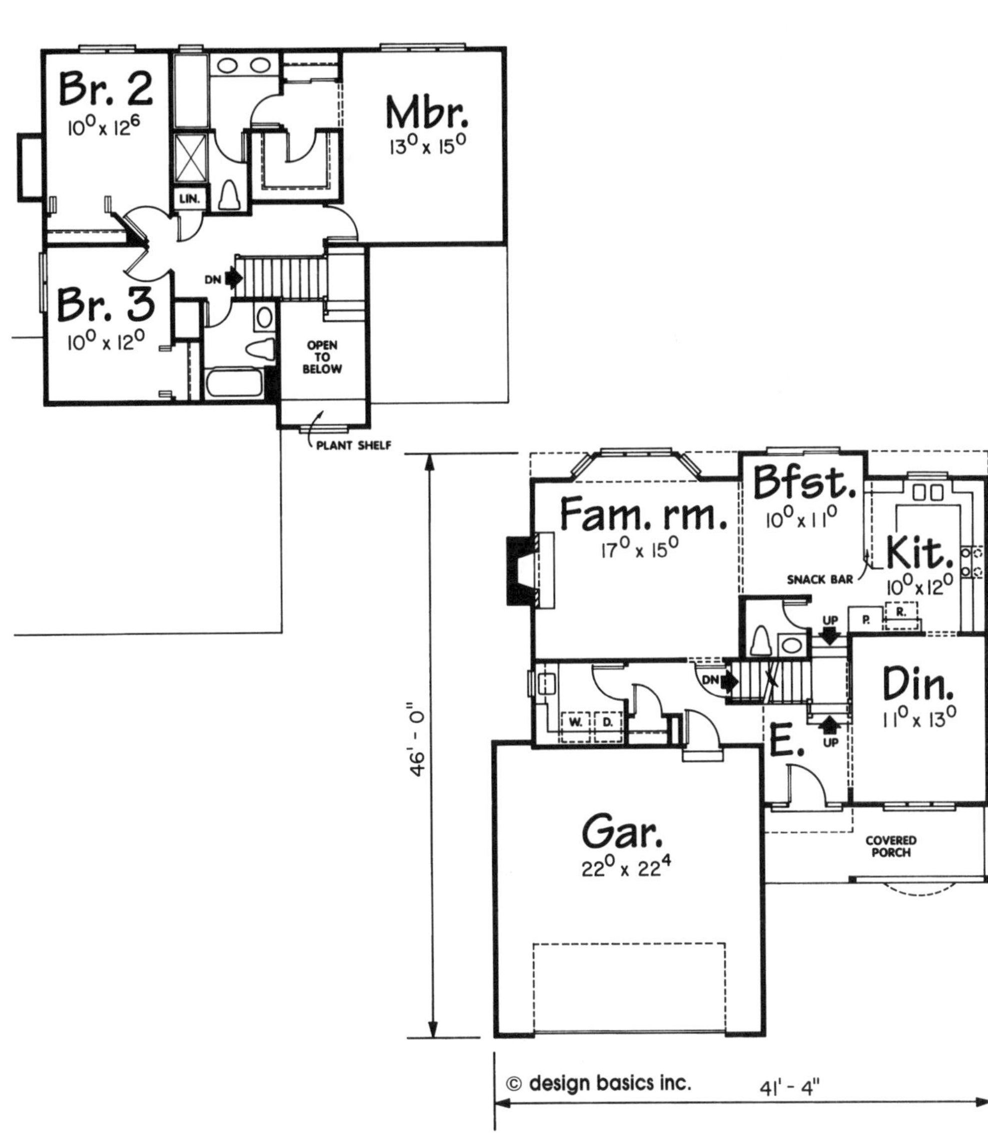

All plans on
high quality, erasable,
reproducible vellum.

Adams Creek

9F-8105

The adaptable ***Adams Creek:*** *A great room that can expand into the dining room for more space. A kitchen with the option of serving meals at the snack bar, breakfast area or dining room. A U-shaped stairway leads to a balcony for a view of the entry. And a bonus room with sloped ceilings to build into a studio or hobby room.*

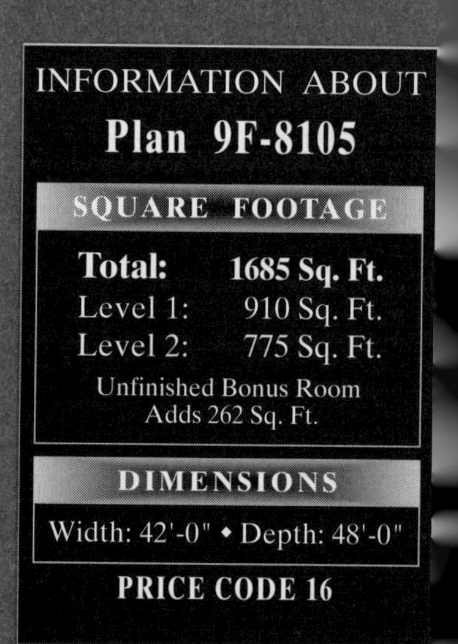

INFORMATION ABOUT
Plan 9F-8105

SQUARE FOOTAGE

Total:	**1685 Sq. Ft.**
Level 1:	910 Sq. Ft.
Level 2:	775 Sq. Ft.

Unfinished Bonus Room Adds 262 Sq. Ft.

DIMENSIONS

Width: 42'-0" • Depth: 48'-0"

PRICE CODE 16

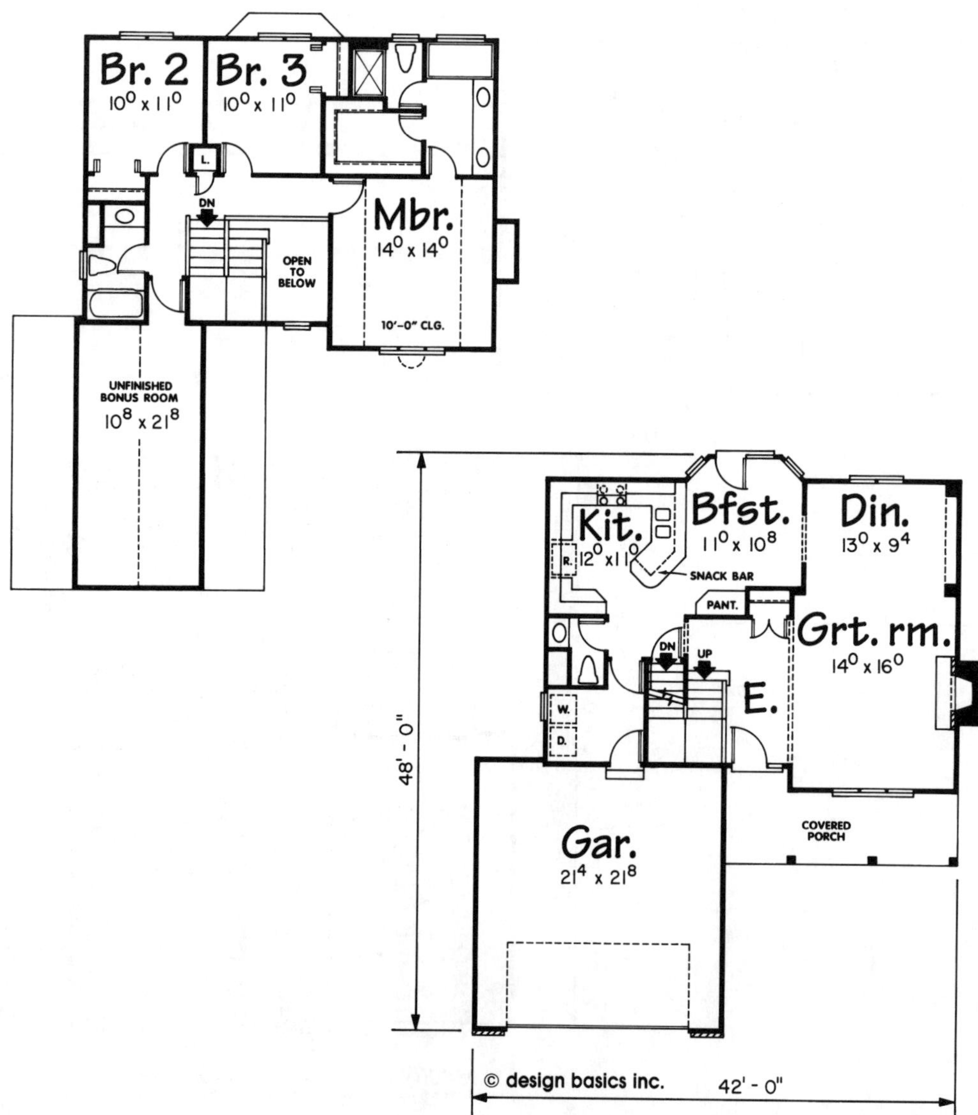

Bailey Falls

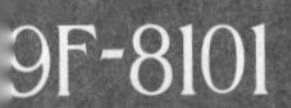

9F-8101

The carefree Bailey Falls:

An 11-foot ceiling in the spacious living room to enhance a glass of tea with neighbors who've dropped by. A prominent fireplace in the family room warms activity throughout the breakfast area and kitchen. And four bedrooms separated on the second floor for the solitude it provides.

INFORMATION ABOUT
Plan 9F-8101

SQUARE FOOTAGE

Total:	**1919 Sq. Ft.**
Level 1:	1007 Sq. Ft.
Level 2:	912 Sq. Ft.

DIMENSIONS

Width: 42'-0" • Depth: 46'-0"

PRICE CODE 19

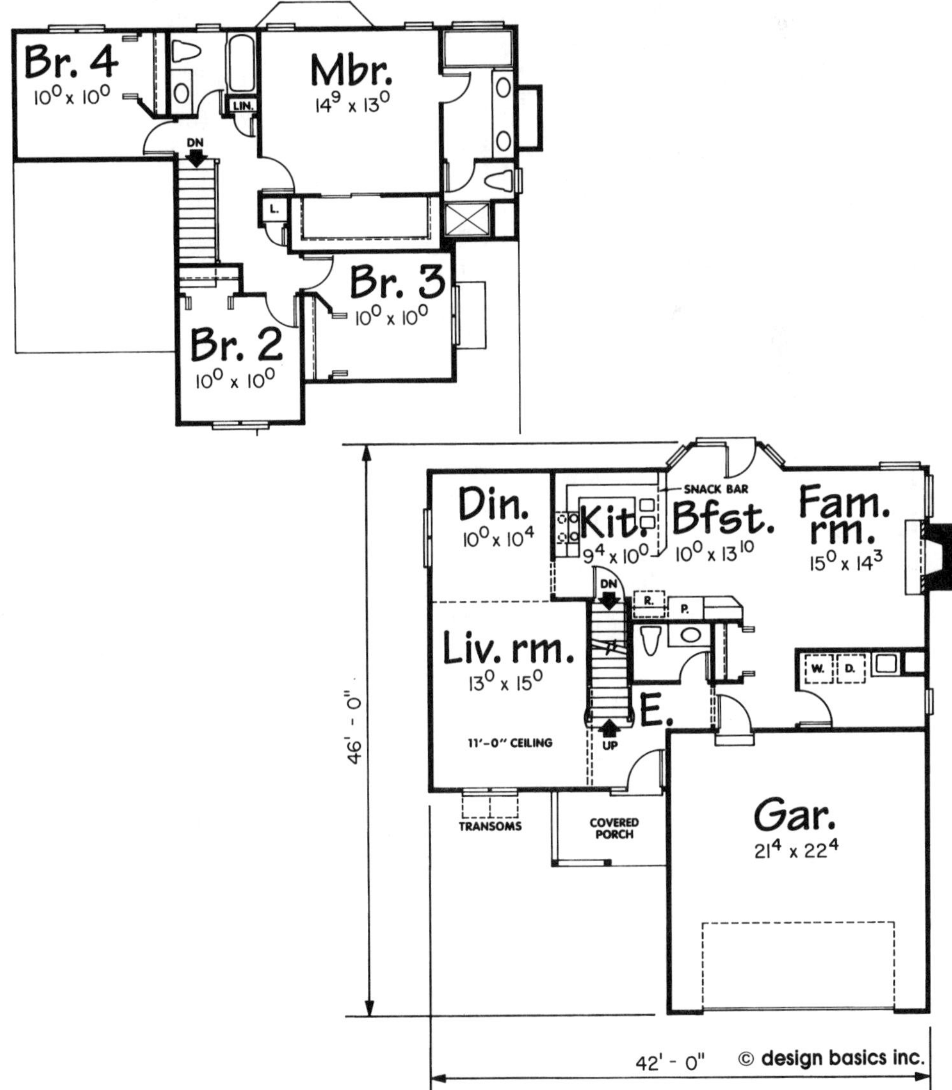

All plans on high quality, erasable, reproducible vellum.

Chimney Ridge

9F-8106

*The tone of **Chimney Ridge:** A boxed window and fireplace in the great room to provide light and warmth to family fun. For occasions that call for formal cuisine, a dining room at the rear. On the second floor, four bedrooms and a bonus room to enhance, expand or revamp the master bath.*

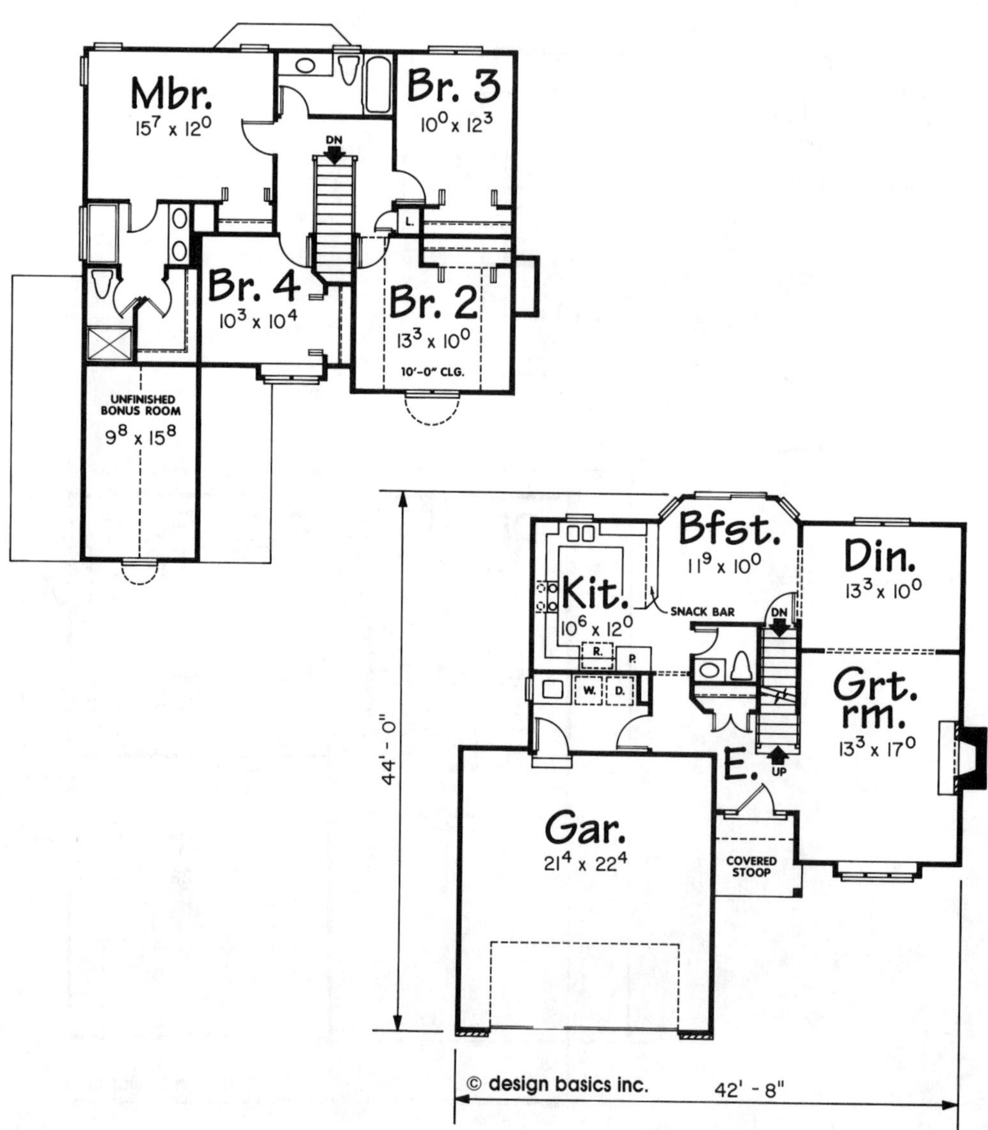

INFORMATION ABOUT
Plan 9F-8106

SQUARE FOOTAGE

Total:	**1830 Sq. Ft.**
Level 1:	879 Sq. Ft.
Level 2:	951 Sq. Ft.

Unfinished Bonus Room Adds 160 Sq. Ft.

DIMENSIONS

Width: 42'-8" • Depth: 44'-0"

PRICE CODE 18

Rose Hollow

9F-8108

Shades of Rose Hollow:

In the volume entry, a plant shelf and second-floor balcony adding charm. An expansive great room that welcomes group gatherings. A bright window in the kitchen allowing sunlight and a view of backyard activity while cooking. All bedrooms on the second floor for those who prefer seclusion from the main floor.

INFORMATION ABOUT

Plan 9F-8108

SQUARE FOOTAGE

Total:	**1705 Sq. Ft.**
Level 1:	924 Sq. Ft.
Level 2:	781 Sq. Ft.

Unfinished Bonus Room Adds 193 Sq. Ft.

DIMENSIONS

Width: 44'-0" • Depth: 40'-0"

PRICE CODE 17

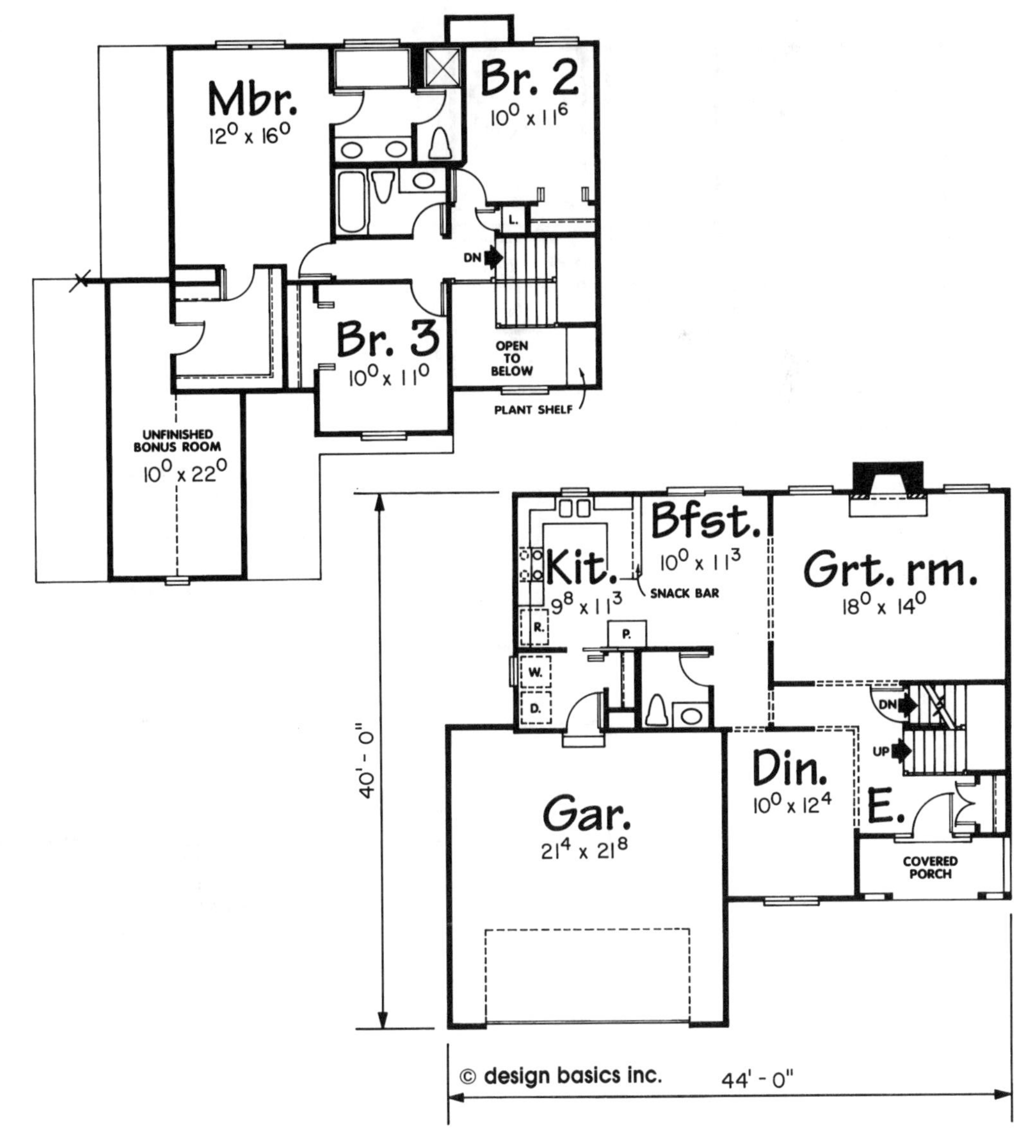

All plans on high quality, erasable, reproducible vellum.

Pebble Creek

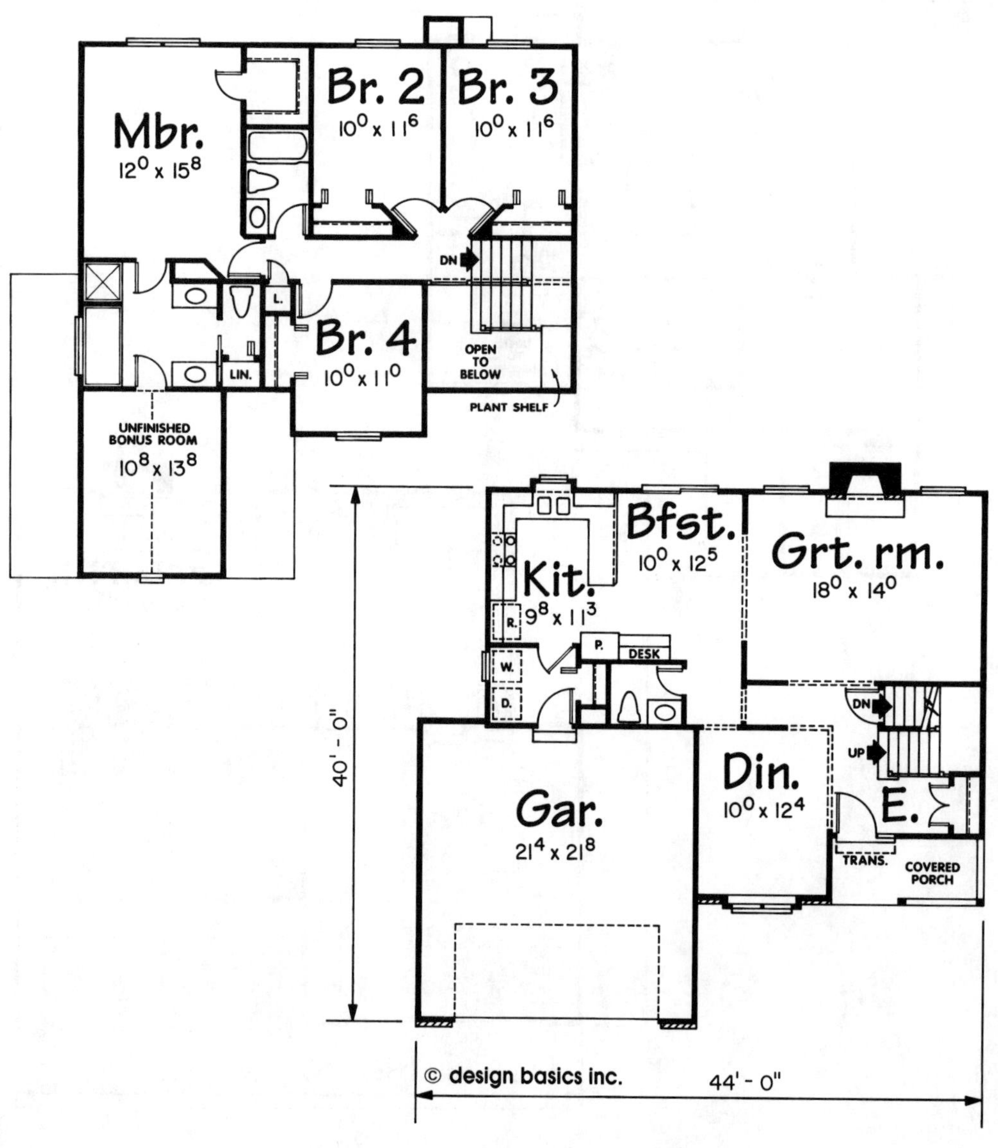

9F-8100

The fun inside ***Pebble Creek:*** *A U-shaped stairway and plant shelf adding a relaxed, quaint atmosphere to entering the home. The great room, breakfast area and kitchen live together, anticipating family games, and cooking and eating favorite meals. On the second floor, a bonus room for the option of an additional 159 square feet of space to play around.*

INFORMATION ABOUT
Plan 9F-8100

SQUARE FOOTAGE

Total:	**1844 Sq. Ft.**
Level 1:	924 Sq. Ft.
Level 2:	920 Sq. Ft.

Unfinished Bonus Room Adds 159 Sq. Ft.

DIMENSIONS

Width: 44'-0" • Depth: 40'-0"

PRICE CODE 18

Burton Place

The presence of the Burton Place: *Easy traffic flow on the main floor, making room to room transition smooth and uncalculated. A family room with fireplace and large picture window to inspire conversation or quiet thinking. A U-shaped stairway, plant shelf and second-floor balcony – giving those in the entry something pleasant to view.*

INFORMATION ABOUT

Plan 9F -8030

SQUARE FOOTAGE

Total:	**1885 Sq. Ft.**
Level 1:	925 Sq. Ft.
Level 2:	960 Sq. Ft.

DIMENSIONS

Width: 44'-0" • Depth: 42'-0"

PRICE CODE 18

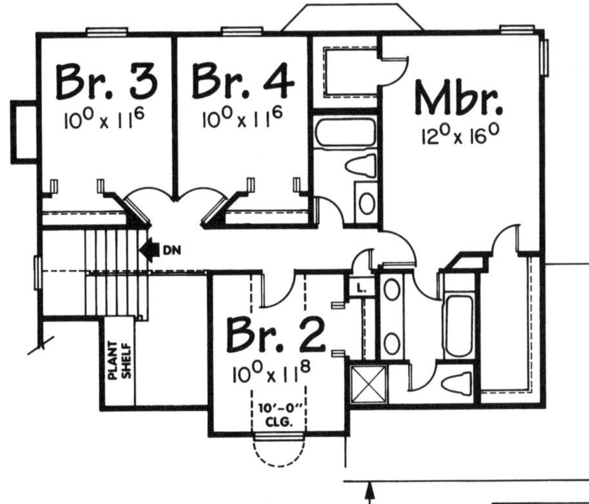

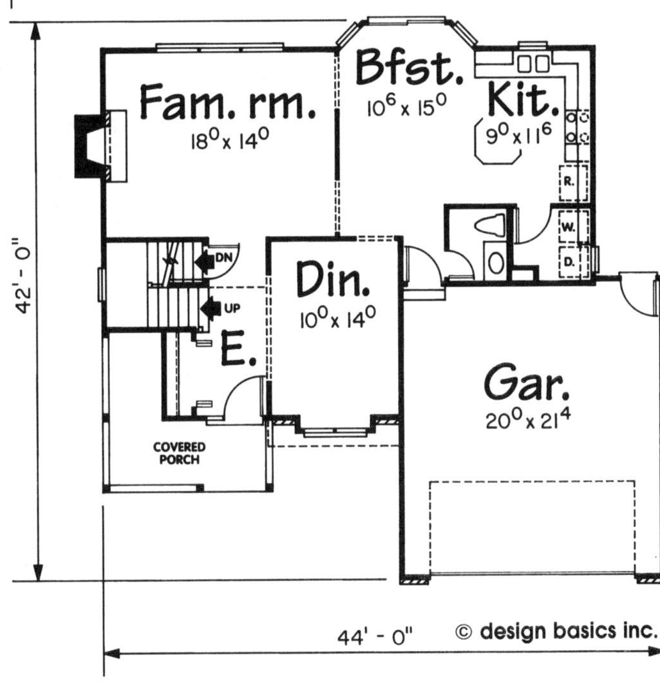

All plans on high quality, erasable, reproducible vellum.

Linden Acres

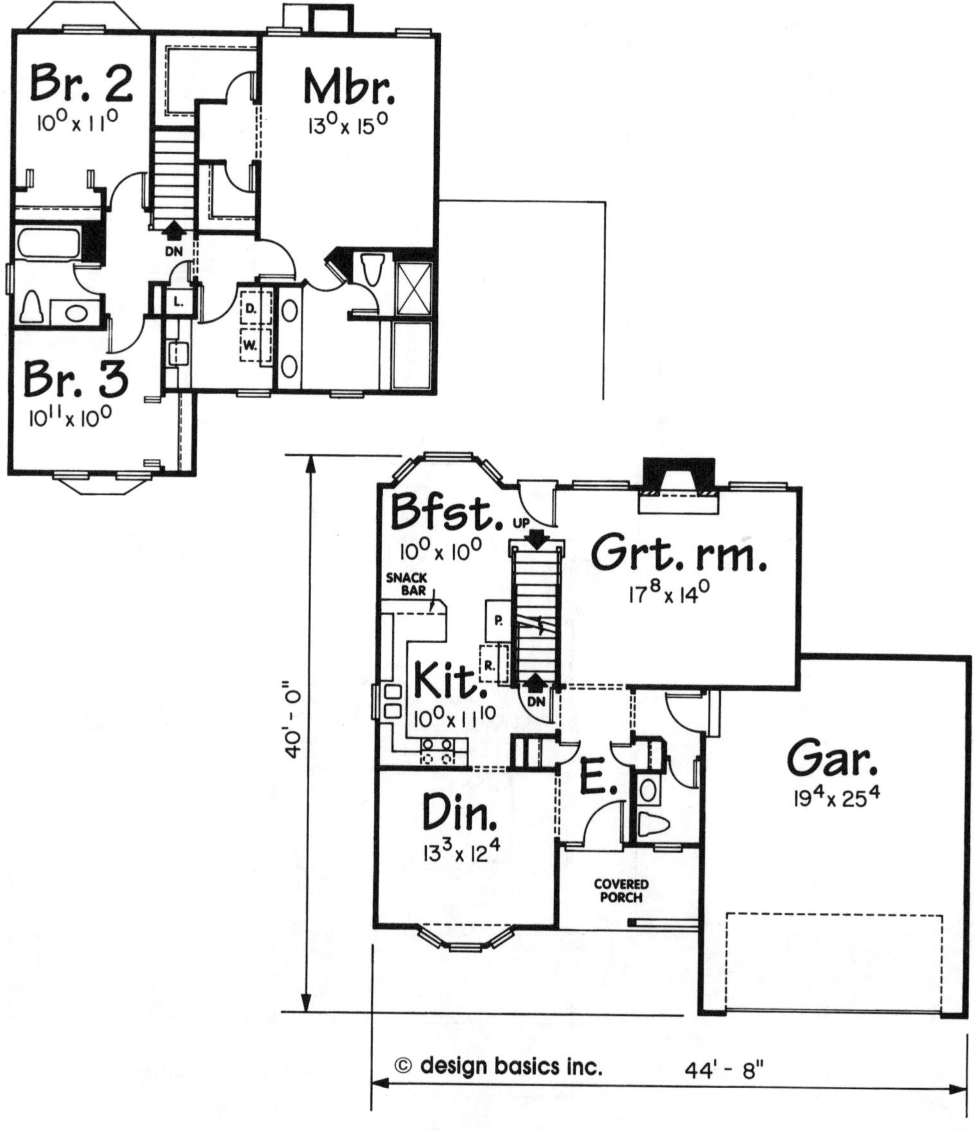

9F-8029

Tradition in the ***Linden Acres:*** *Dining room elegance with quick service from the kitchen and a bayed view of the front. Semi-seclusion in the great room to entertain guests or inspire family fun. A rear staircase for more privacy and accessibility upstairs. And two master suite closets for his and her preference.*

INFORMATION ABOUT
Plan 9F-8029

SQUARE FOOTAGE

Total:	**1753 Sq. Ft.**
Level 1:	860 Sq. Ft.
Level 2:	893 Sq. Ft.

DIMENSIONS

Width: 44'-8" • Depth: 40'-0"

PRICE CODE 17

Order Direct

800-947-7526

(7:00-6:00 Mon.-Fri. CST)

Jones Farm

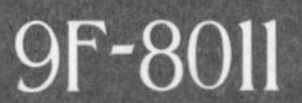

9F-8011

*The **Jones Farm** appeal:*

A wrapping, covered porch for rocking away afternoons. A quick path from the garage to the kitchen for unloading groceries. Eating and working options in the breakfast area. And designated space for stories and warmth around the see-through fireplace of the hearth room.

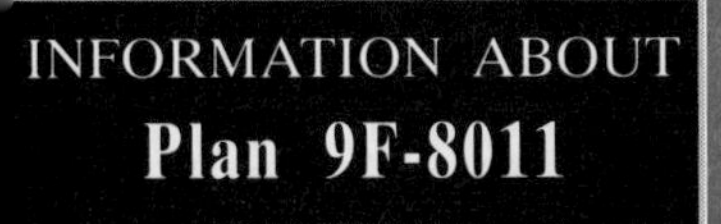

INFORMATION ABOUT
Plan 9F-8011

SQUARE FOOTAGE

Total:	**2292 Sq. Ft.**
Level 1:	1158 Sq. Ft.
Level 2:	1134 Sq. Ft.

Unfinished Bonus Room Adds 84 Sq. Ft.

DIMENSIONS

Width: 46'-0" • Depth: 47'-10"

PRICE CODE 22

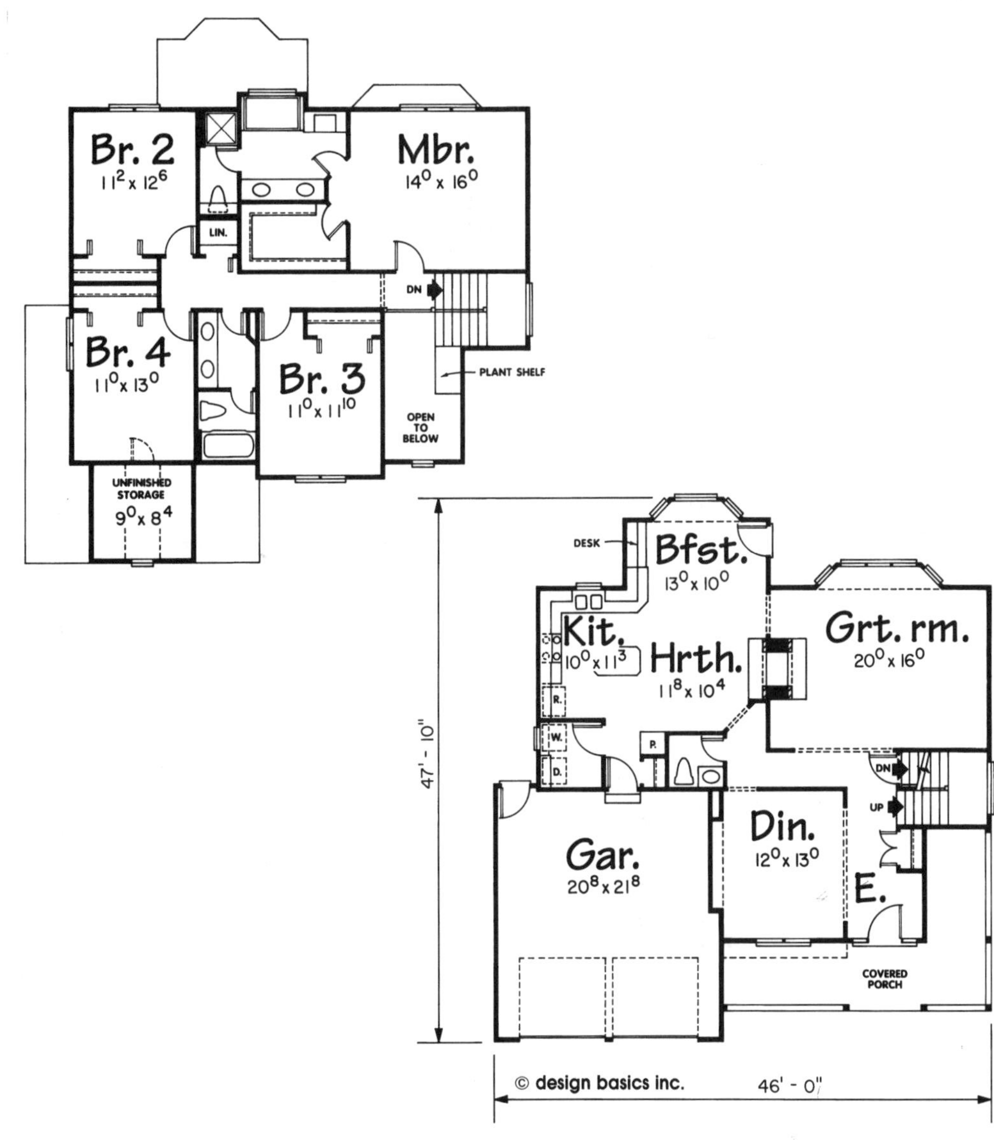

All plans on high quality, erasable, reproducible vellum.

Ashland Park

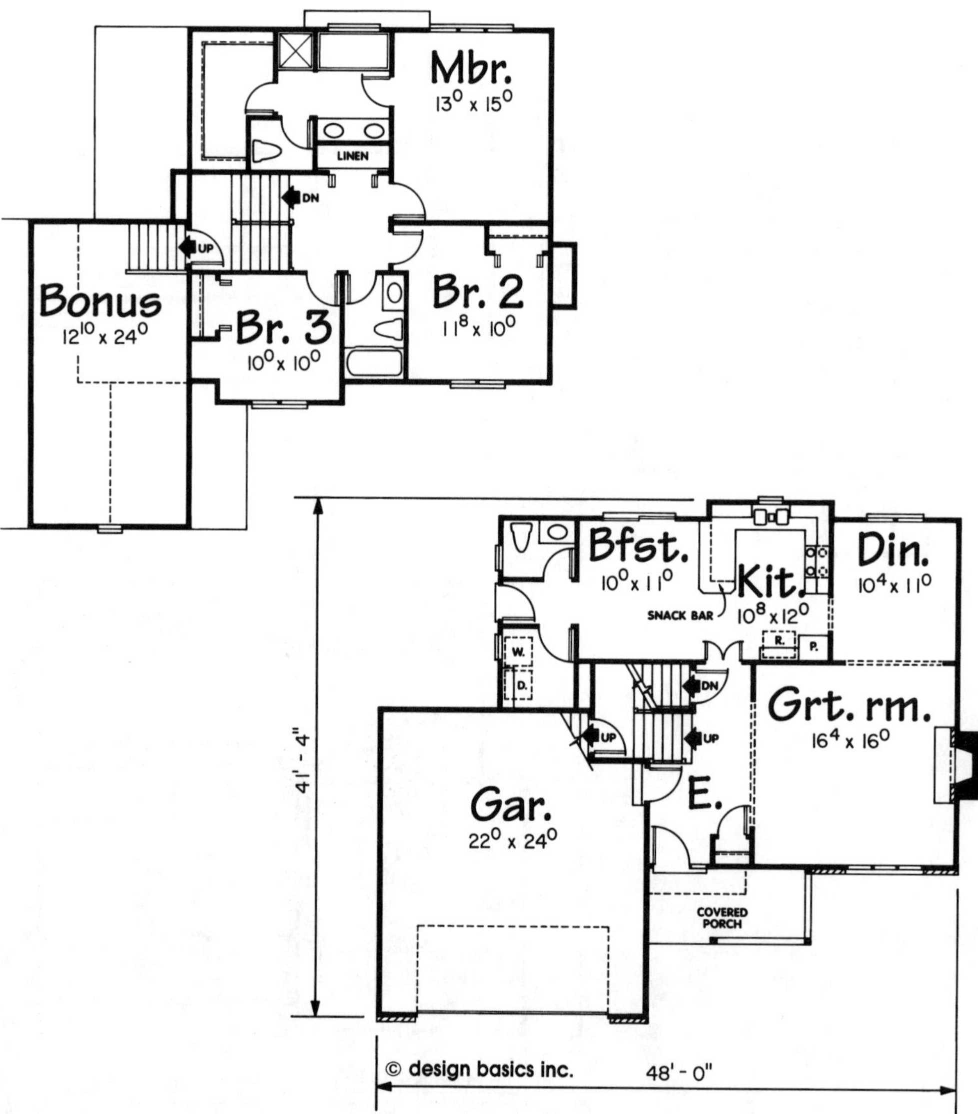

9F-8107

*The favorable **Ashland Park:** Welcoming guests to relaxation, a large great room off the entry. A U-shaped stairway that leads to an optional mid-level bonus room – perfect as an office or study. And a spacious walk-in closet in the master bath for easy access from the dressing area.*

INFORMATION ABOUT
Plan 9F-8107

SQUARE FOOTAGE

Total:	**1752 Sq. Ft.**
Level 1:	944 Sq. Ft.
Level 2:	808 Sq. Ft.

Unfinished Bonus Room Adds 324 Sq. Ft.

DIMENSIONS

Width: 48'-0" • Depth: 41'-4"

PRICE CODE 17

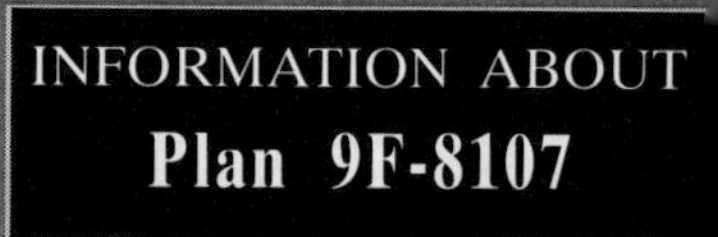

800-947-7526

(7:00-6:00 Mon.-Fri. CST)

Duncan Valley

The assurance of Duncan Valley: *Two living spaces, both strategically open to eating areas of the home for after-meal relaxation. A covered porch at the front, offering shelter from the elements. And a master bathroom featuring a large dressing area and walk-in closet with the ability to expand into a bonus room.*

INFORMATION ABOUT
Plan 9F-8099

SQUARE FOOTAGE

Total:	**1877 Sq. Ft.**
Level 1:	1040 Sq. Ft.
Level 2:	837 Sq. Ft.

Unfinished Bonus Room Adds 174 Sq. Ft.

DIMENSIONS

Width: 48'-0" • Depth: 40'-0"

PRICE CODE 18

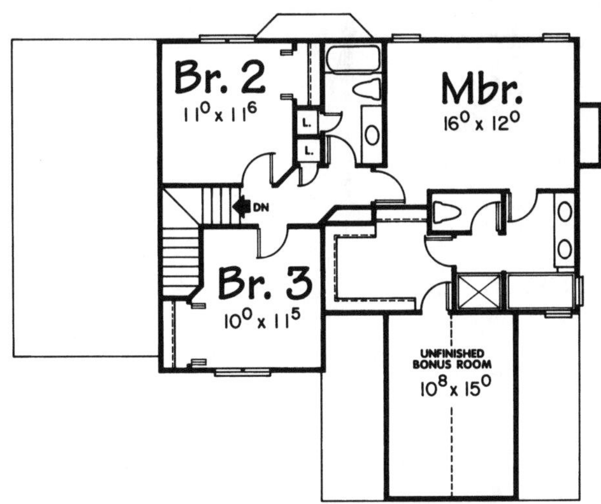

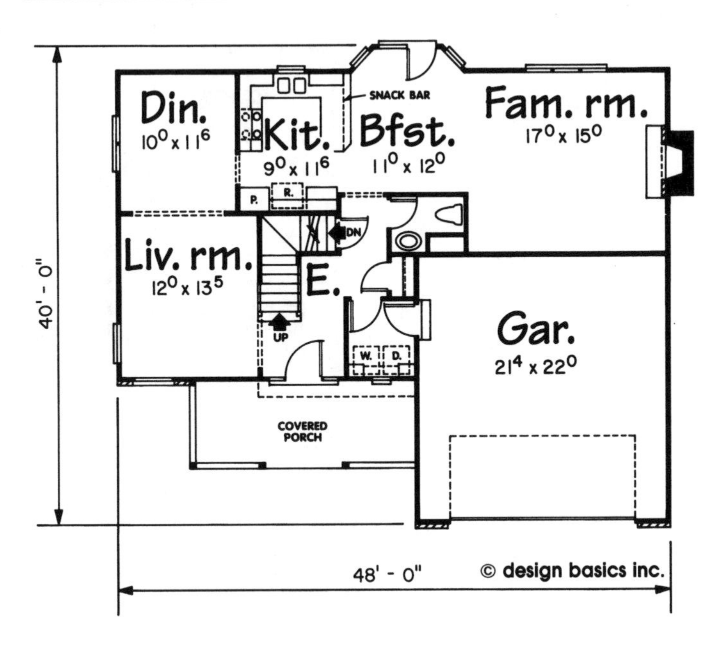

All plans on high quality, erasable, reproducible vellum.

Sherman Oaks

9F-8098

The Sherman Oaks effect: A front porch promoting timeless liesure. A bright window enhancing dining room meals and conversation. A roomy breakfast area with a way to the backyard. And a large master bedroom to indulge its occupants in a spacious retreat.

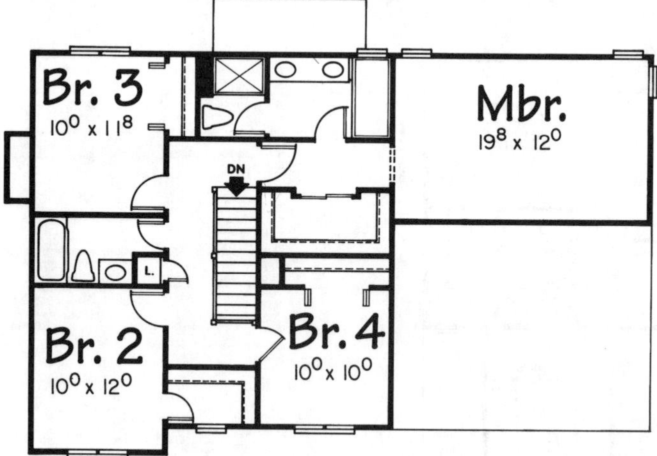

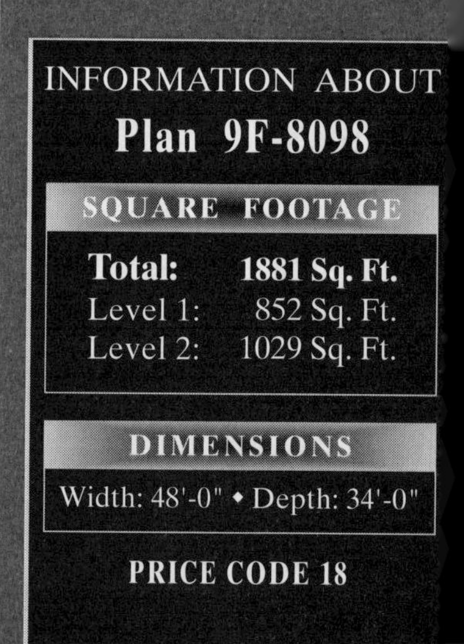
INFORMATION ABOUT
Plan 9F-8098

SQUARE FOOTAGE

Total:	**1881 Sq. Ft.**
Level 1:	852 Sq. Ft.
Level 2:	1029 Sq. Ft.

DIMENSIONS

Width: 48'-0" • Depth: 34'-0"

PRICE CODE 18

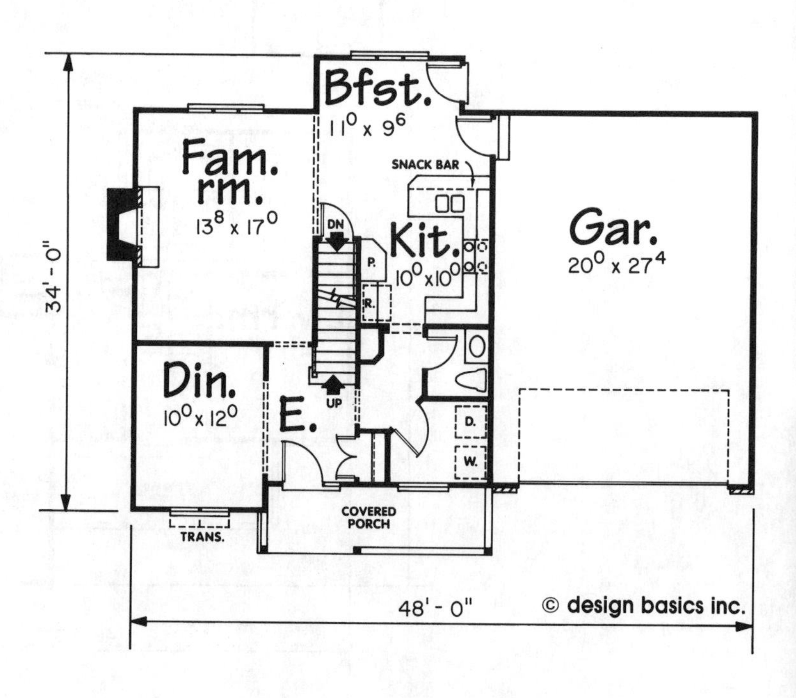

Oak Hollow

9F-8081

*The exceptional **Oak Hollow:** Two living areas for activity both formal and casual. Bayed windows to define the breakfast area. Another large window in the family room to emphasize the outdoors. And an extra closet in the master suite for added wardrobe space.*

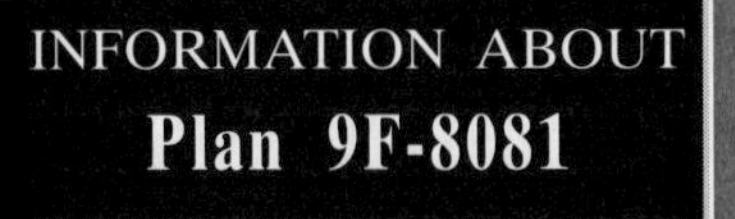

INFORMATION ABOUT
Plan 9F-8081

SQUARE FOOTAGE

Total:	**1926 Sq. Ft.**
Level 1:	1057 Sq. Ft.
Level 2:	869 Sq. Ft.

DIMENSIONS

Width: 48'-0" • Depth: 42'-0"

PRICE CODE 19

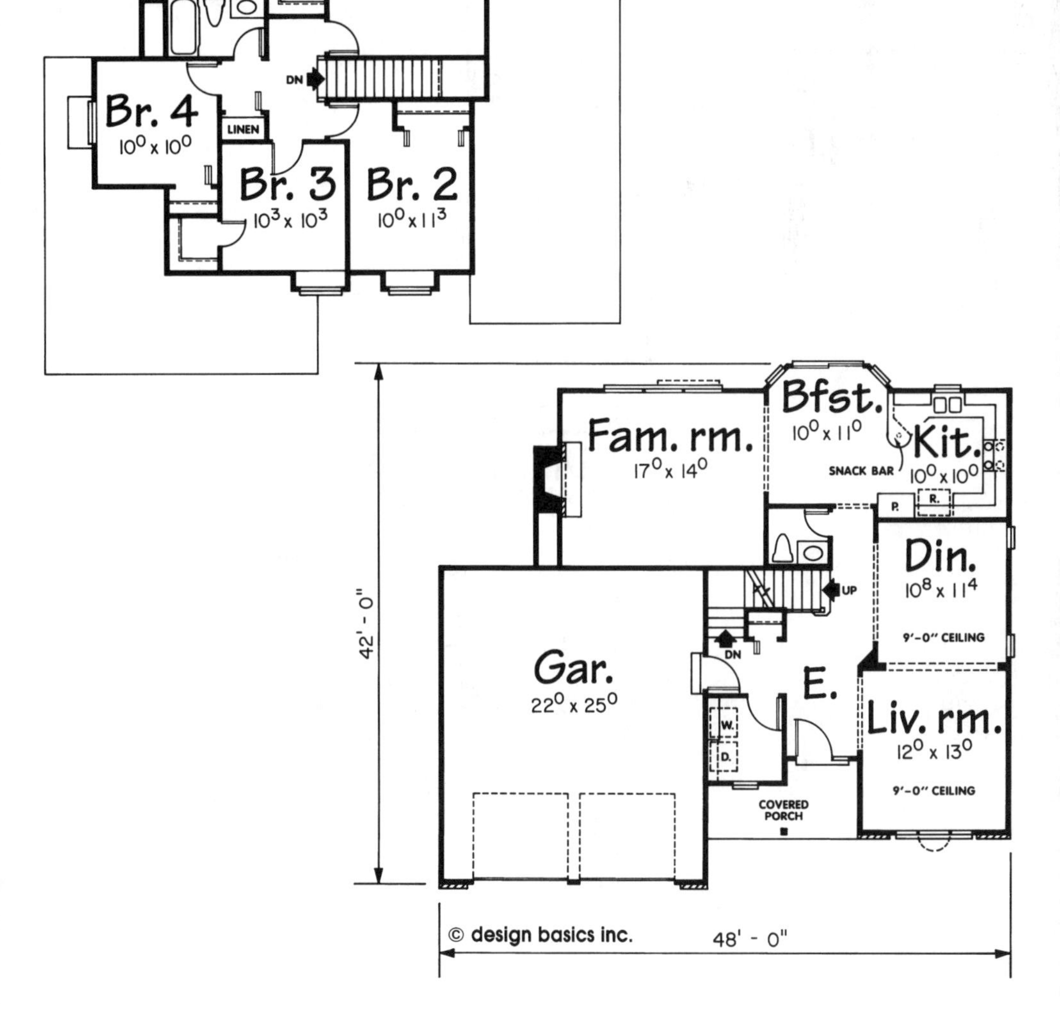

All plans on
high quality, erasable,
reproducible vellum.

Robins Lane

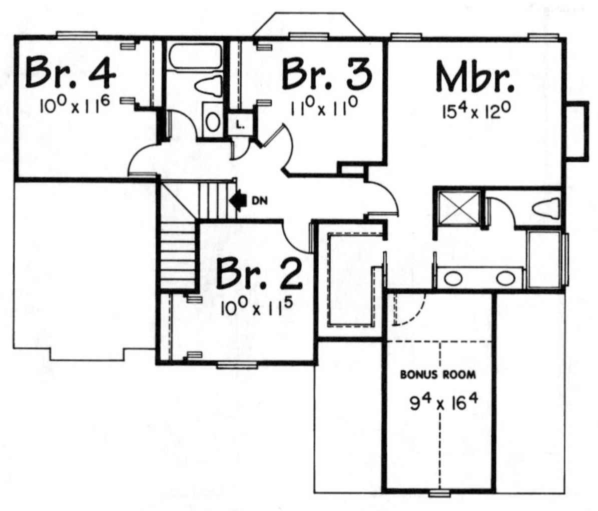

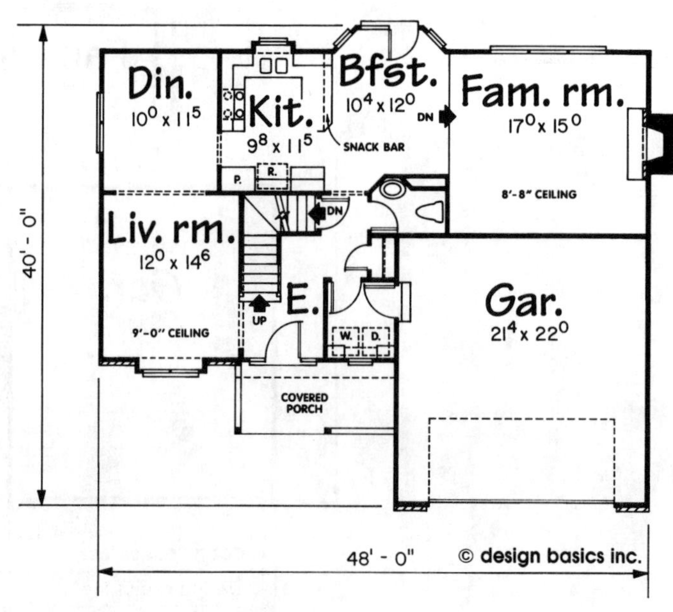

9F-8031

The pleasure of ***Robins Lane:*** *Two living spaces for those with the need to entertain and the need for entertainment. The kitchen in the center, well-positioned to serve the formal rooms and bring a sense of hominess to the family area. A second-floor bonus room opts to expand the master suite.*

INFORMATION ABOUT

Plan 9F-8031

SQUARE FOOTAGE

Total:	**2029 Sq. Ft.**
Level 1:	1046 Sq. Ft.
Level 2:	983 Sq. Ft.

Unfinished Bonus Room Adds 165 Sq. Ft.

DIMENSIONS

Width: 48'-0" • Depth: 40'-0"

PRICE CODE 20

Order Direct

800-947-7526

(7:00-6:00 Mon.-Fri. CST)

Chapel Hills

9F-8060

The appearance of Chapel Hills: The formal rooms – defined enough to be separate and open enough to combine for entertaining. A bayed breakfast area to facilitate traffic from the kitchen to the family room. A second-floor laundry room to serve four bedrooms. And an optional storage area to perhaps enlarge the master suite's walk-in closet.

INFORMATION ABOUT
Plan 9F-8060

SQUARE FOOTAGE

Total:	**2211 Sq. Ft.**
Level 1:	1108 Sq. Ft.
Level 2:	1103 Sq. Ft.

Unfinished Storage
Adds 149 Sq. Ft.

DIMENSIONS

Width: 48'-0" • Depth: 44'-0"

PRICE CODE 22

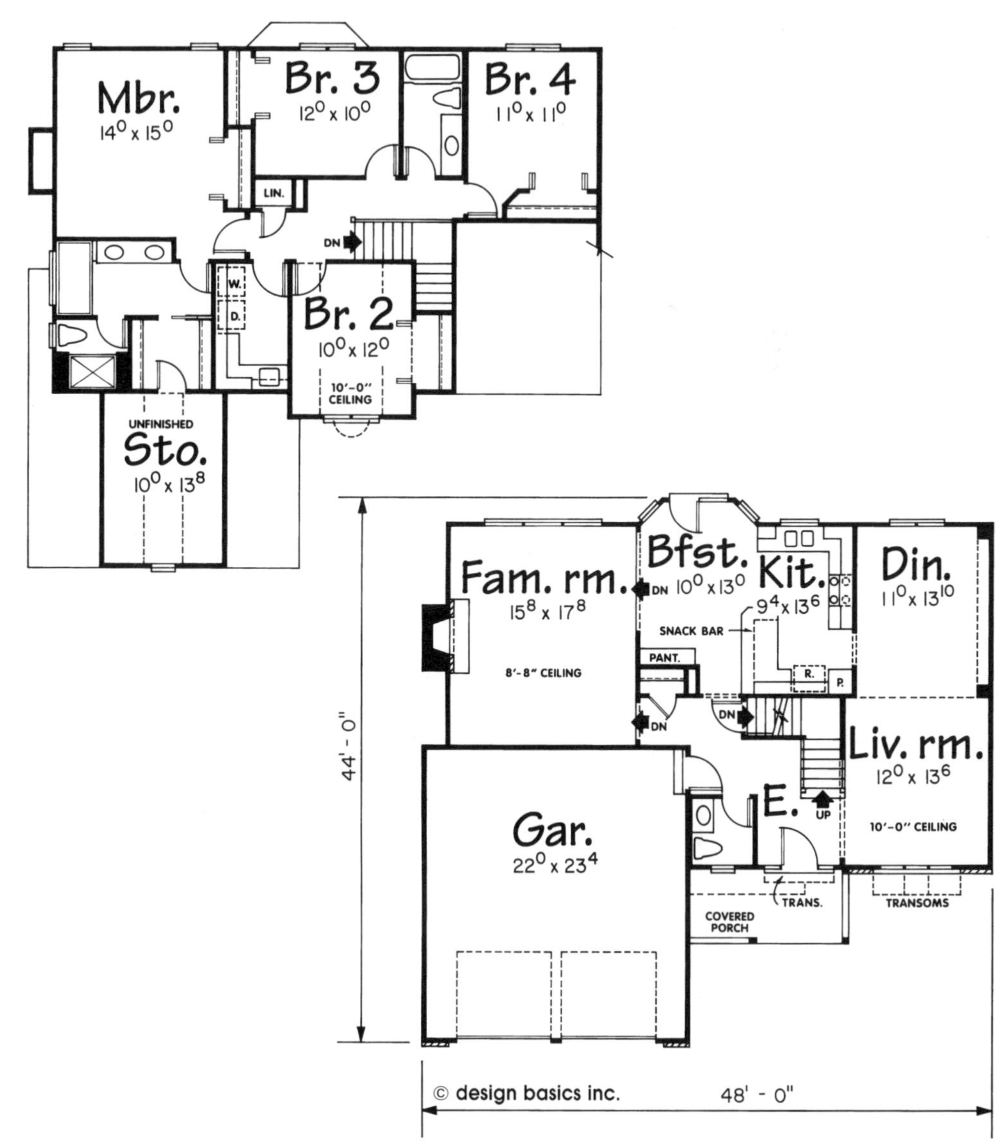

All plans on
high quality, erasable,
reproducible vellum.

Henley Mills

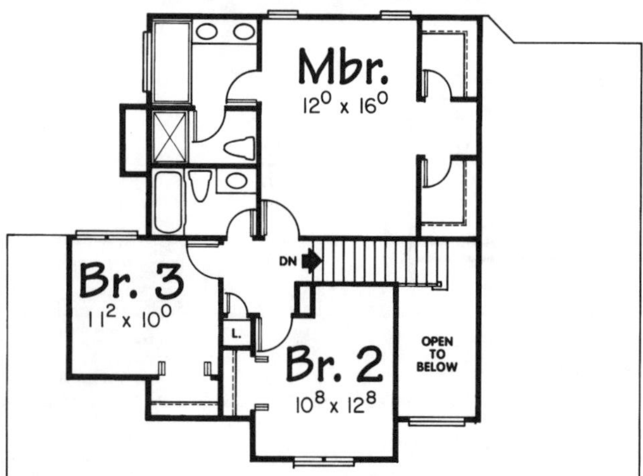

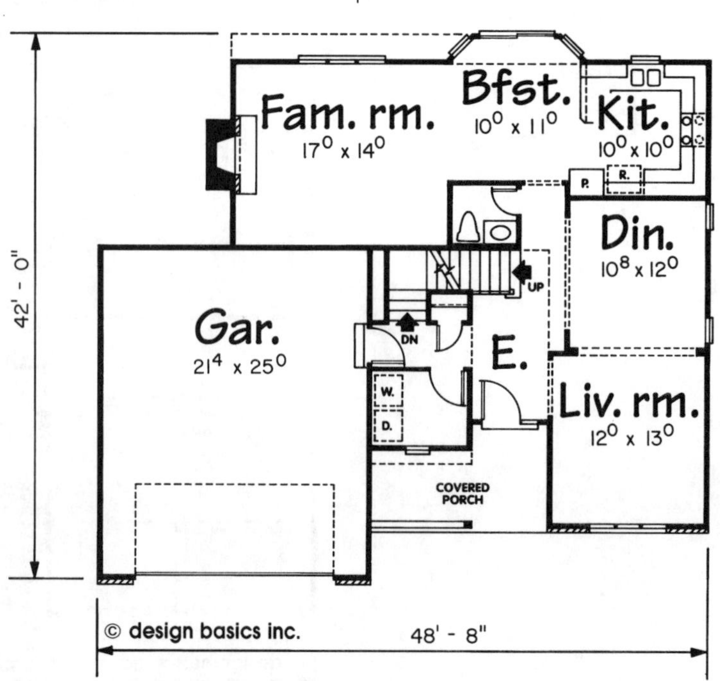

9F-8102

The togetherness of ***Henley Mills:*** *Open living and dining rooms for formal gatherings. A bayed dinette providing sunlight for breakfast and linking the kitchen and family room for casual day-to-day activity. His and her walk-in closets in the master suite for the preference of separated wardrobes or additional storage space.*

INFORMATION ABOUT Plan 9F-8102

SQUARE FOOTAGE

Total:	**1817 Sq. Ft.**
Level 1:	1053 Sq. Ft.
Level 2:	764 Sq. Ft.

DIMENSIONS

Width: 48'-8" • Depth: 42'-0"

PRICE CODE 18

Wilson Creek

The lofty lines of ***Wilson Creek:*** *Shutters, a front porch and planter box on the elevation, beckoning a sense of country days and summer's ays. The family room at the ear – a secluded area for play nd laughing loudly. And a large onus room in the second-floor naster suite to complete as nother room or closet.*

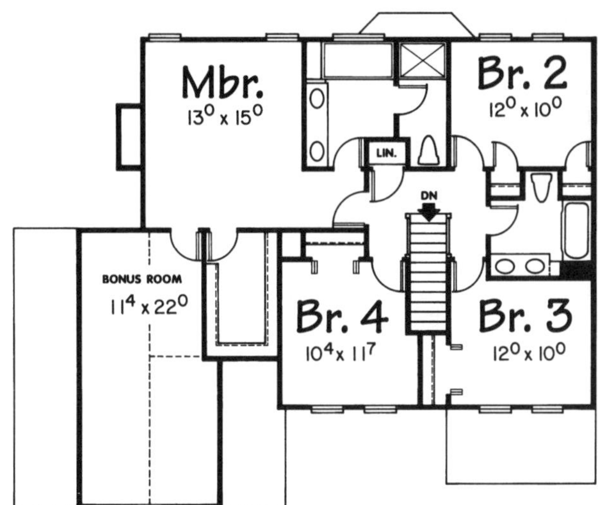

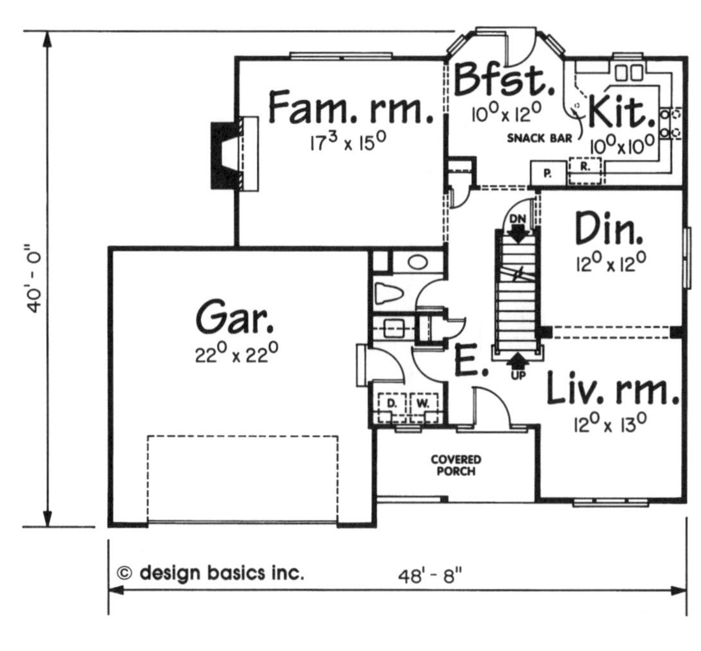

NFORMATION ABOUT Plan 9F-8073

SQUARE FOOTAGE

Total:	**2084 Sq. Ft.**
Level 1:	1070 Sq. Ft.
Level 2:	1014 Sq. Ft.

Unfinished Bonus Room Adds 253 Sq. Ft.

DIMENSIONS

Width: 48'-8" • Depth: 40'-0"

PRICE CODE 20

All plans on high quality, erasable, reproducible vellum.

Apple Woods

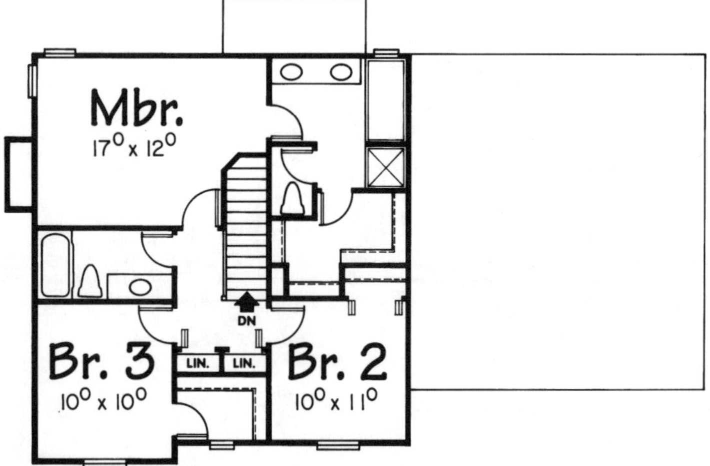

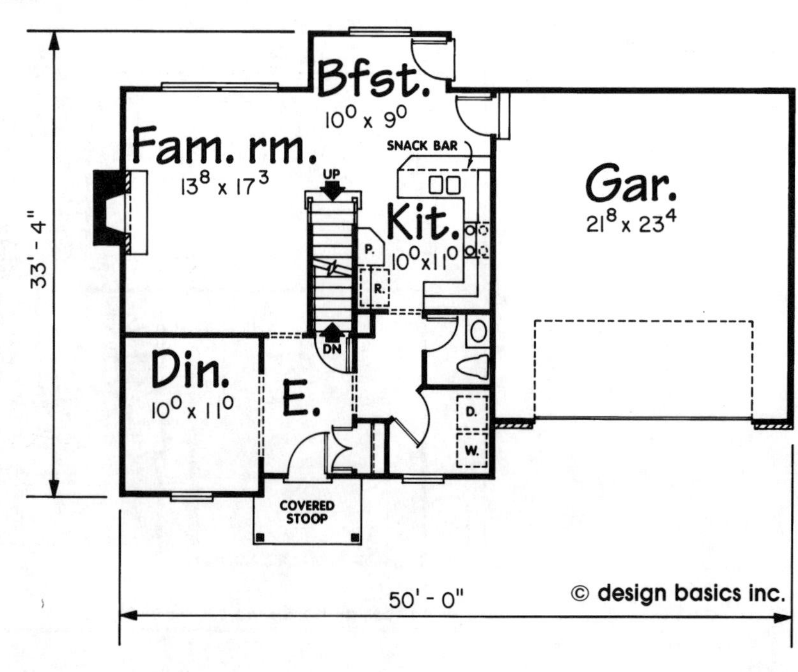

9F-8109

The simple appeal of Apple Woods: *The dining room off the entry, adding character and elegance to guests' first impressions. A snack bar in the kitchen to serve light meals informally. And an expansive family room for lounging about with friends and family.*

INFORMATION ABOUT
Plan 9F-8109

SQUARE FOOTAGE

Total:	**1608 Sq. Ft.**
Level 1:	840 Sq. Ft.
Level 2:	768 Sq. Ft.

DIMENSIONS

Width: 50'-0" • Depth: 33'-4"

PRICE CODE 16

Order Direct

800-947-7526

(7:00-6:00 Mon.-Fri. CST)

Hamilton Farm

9F-8072

*The country confidence of **Hamilton Farm:** A wrapping front porch with two ways in and out for twice the enjoyment. A spacious kitchen and breakfast area so that a number of people can gather together there. A second-floor laundry to cut down on stairway traffic from the four bedrooms.*

INFORMATION ABOUT
Plan 9F-8072

SQUARE FOOTAGE

Total:	**2095 Sq. Ft.**
Level 1:	948 Sq. Ft.
Level 2:	1147 Sq. Ft.

DIMENSIONS

Width: 50'-0" • Depth: 38'-0"

PRICE CODE 20

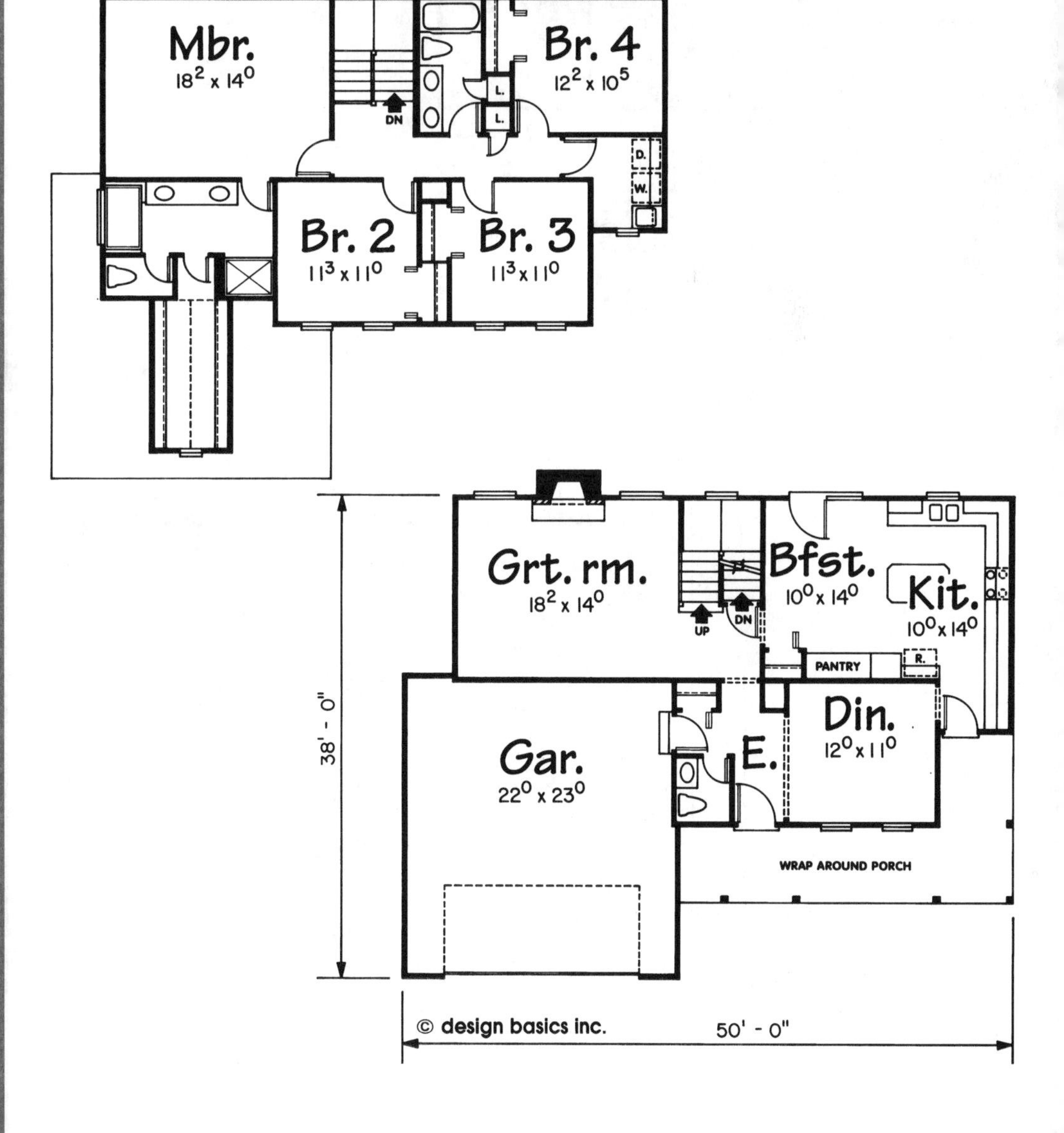

All plans on high quality, erasable, reproducible vellum.

Rogers Point

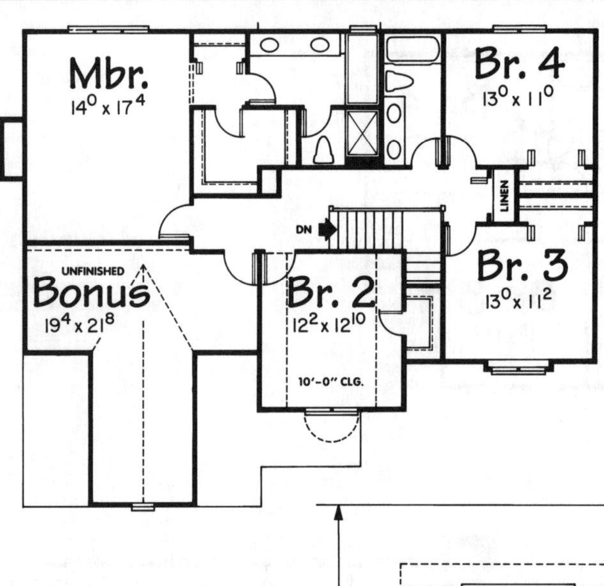

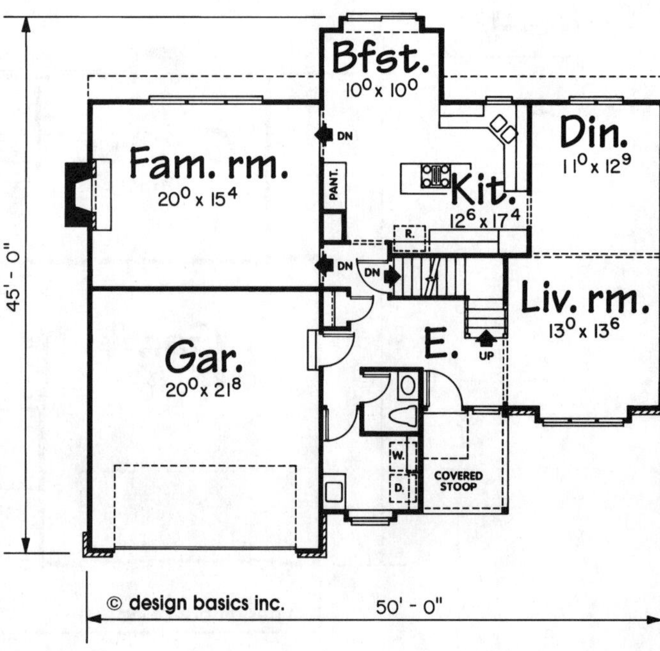

9F-8014

All the comforts of Rogers Point: Two living spaces for large or intimate, formal or informal get-togethers. The convenience of an island cooktop that frees up counter space in the kitchen. And upstairs, four bedrooms, two baths and an optional bonus room for storage.

INFORMATION ABOUT
Plan 9F-8014

SQUARE FOOTAGE

Total:	**2469 Sq. Ft.**
Level 1:	1254 Sq. Ft.
Level 2:	1215 Sq. Ft.

Unfinished Bonus Room Adds 310 Sq. Ft.

DIMENSIONS

Width: 50'-0" • Depth: 45'-0"

PRICE CODE 24

Nostalgia Home Plans™

Designs that are rooted in the traditions of the past, while still maintaining the popular floor plan features of today.

Why is it that we find ourselves drawn to the homes of the past? Is it because they remind us of where we came from? Is it because we long for a time when life seemed to move at a more peaceful pace? Is it because we miss their craftsmanship – seemingly abandoned in favor of the so-called "faster, cheaper, better" production of homes in recent years? For perhaps all these reasons and many more, the following designs from the Nostalgia Home Plans Collection™ were created. Each design is rooted in the traditions of the past with elegant mouldings and trim, while still maintaining the popular floor plan features of today, such as bonus rooms and home office space. These plans can help you rediscover the warmth and beauty of homes you can be proud of. And of course, at no more than 50 feet wide, each design included here was designed to conform to a narrower lot.

INDEX OF PLANS

SEPARATE LAUNDRY ROOMS

If there's one comment we've heard over and over through the years, it's that the laundry room placement is very important in the home. In these designs, we've taken special care to provide separate laundry room facilities. And in the few exceptions where this wasn't possible, we tried to design the laundry room large enough to accommodate the traffic and also serve as a mud room.

SIMPLER FOUNDATIONS

While buyers will appreciate the old-world feel of these homes, we think they will also appreciate the lengths we went to, throughout the design process, to save them money on the construction of the home. For example, any protrusion or 'jog' in the foundation costs money. The simpler the foundation, the less costly it becomes. As much as we could, we tried to limit any protrusions in the foundation to the front of the home, to focus the most dramatic effects there. Conversely, we often squared off the foundations in the back for cost effectiveness.

One-story Homes

Plan Index

Page #	Width	Plan #	Plan Name	Sq. Ft.
228	42'-0"	5180	Holbrook	1339
232	49'-8"	5034	Payson	1472
230	48'-8"	5001	Anson	1653
234	50'-0"	5177	Cedric	1679

Holbrook

❶ This home provides the efficiency of today's lifestyle needs with the detailing and charisma of homes typically larger.

❷ An angled counter in the kitchen helps define the space and organize the working areas.

❸ The large great room draws guests inside with its fireplace and access to a nearby bookshelf.

❹ A full bath serves the main floor as well as the second bedroom.

❺ A large walk-in closet is located off the master bath creating a private dressing area to avoid disturbing a sleeping spouse.

❻ The garage offers an alcove to build a work bench or shelves.

For More Information
on our Copyrights see page 298.

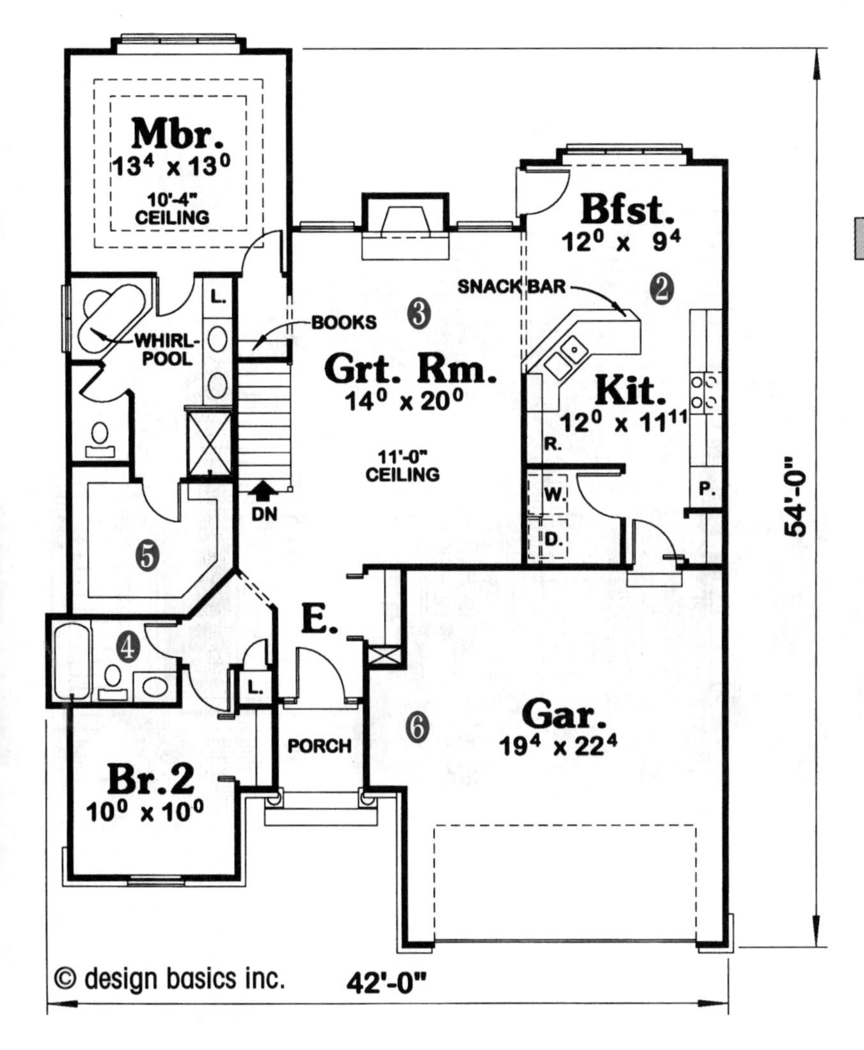

1339 Finished Sq. Ft.

NOTE: 9 ft. main level walls

EXTERIOR HIGHLIGHT

Since a deep covered stoop, such as the one on this home, has the potential to "hide" the front door, this home's entry was elevated to give it stature. Columns and a circle-top window draw further eye-catching appeal.

Anson

❶ A front porch reminiscent of the 1920s sets the tone on this charming one-story home.

❷ Walking into this home reveals twin coat closets in the entry and an inviting great room with fireplace.

❸ Plenty of extra space in the master bath leaves room to fully utilize the corner make-up counter and his and her vanities.

❹ With the option of converting to a bedroom, the den offers a bayed window overlooking the charming front porch.

❺ A built-in workbench in the garage provides a place for tools.

❻ The spacious kitchen and dinette facilitate good circulation for daily use.

AVAILABLE FOR ALL PLANS

For More Information
on Parade Home Packages see page 29

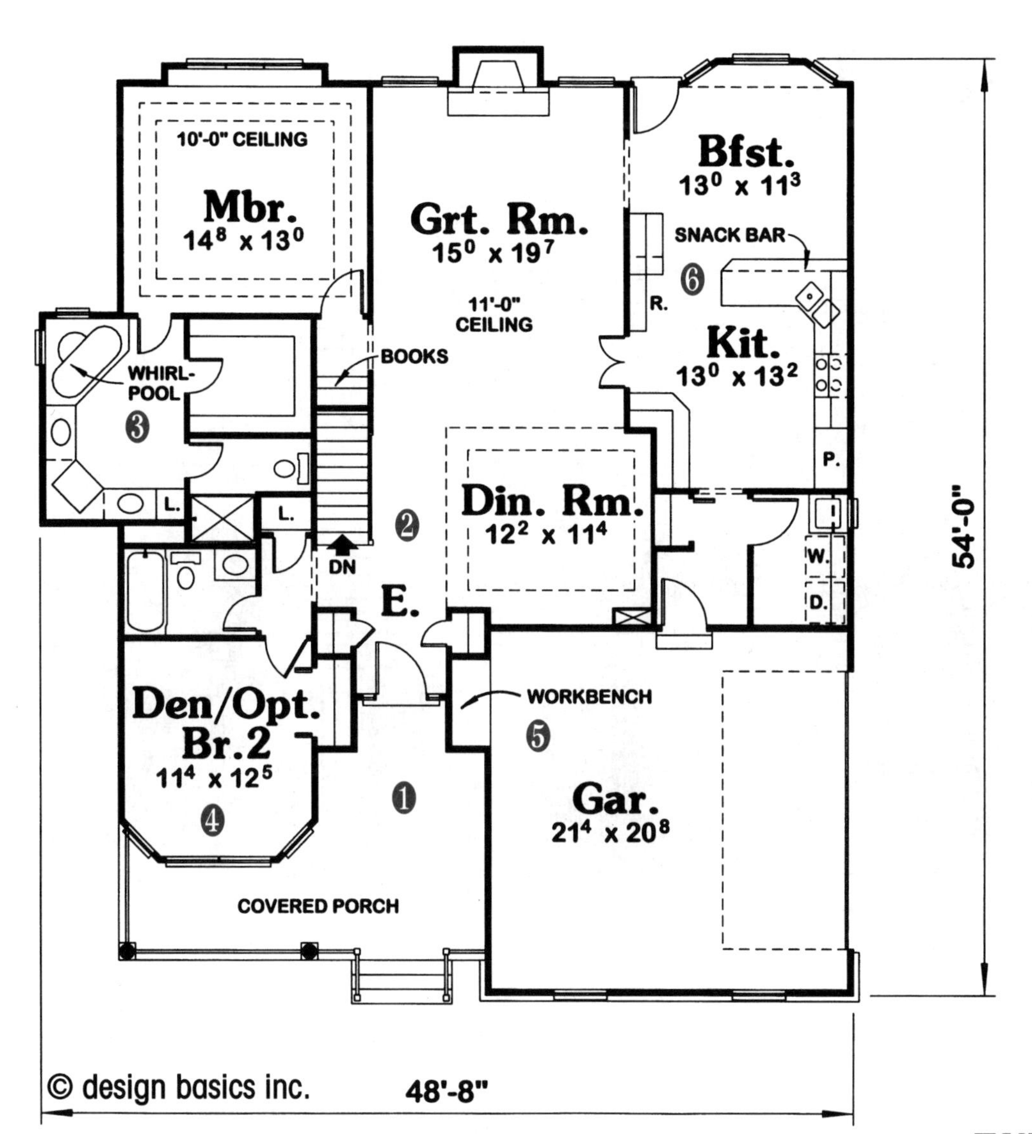

1653 Finished Sq. Ft.

NOTE: 9 ft. main level walls

EXTERIOR HIGHLIGHT

A multi-paned front door is a beautiful addition to this home's entry. A deep front porch was designed to amply accommodate the protruding bay window.

TO ORDER THIS PLAN CALL
1-800-947-7526

Nostalgia

Payson

❶ This country cottage is updated with a hip roof and eyebrow arches.

❷ Traffic flows neatly through the den just inside the entry.

❸ With no wasted space, the kitchen and breakfast area function as a large living area organized with a island counter.

❹ His and her walk-in closets offer plenty of practical storage options in the master suite.

❺ An optional finished basement provides the possibility of creating an apartment for a live-in relative.

❻ Extra bedrooms in the basement are perfect for occasional visits from friends and relatives.

AVAILABLE FOR ALL PLANS

For More Information
on our Roof Construction Package
see page 297.

MAIN FLOOR

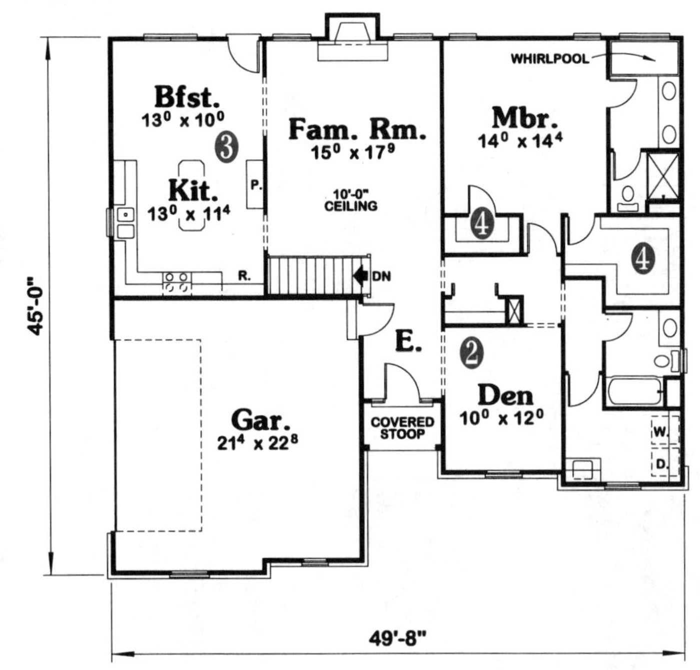

1472 Finished Sq. Ft.

NOTE: 9 ft. main level walls

LOWER FLOOR

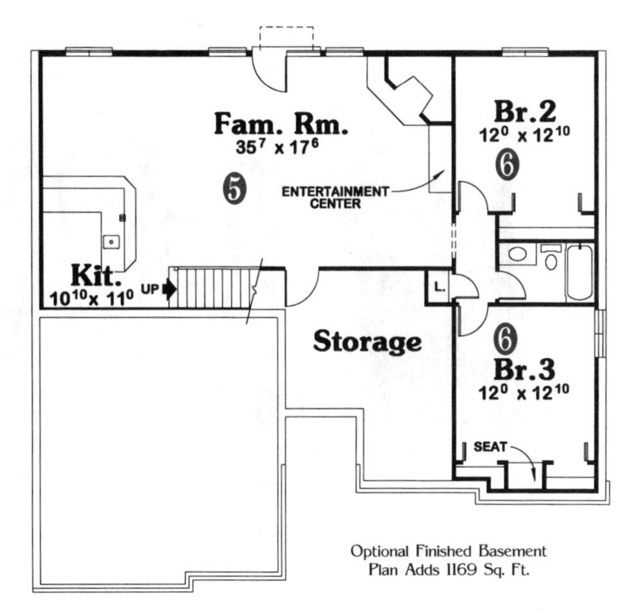

Optional Finished Basement Plan Adds 1169 Sq. Ft.

EXTERIOR HIGHLIGHT

Designing stone to stucco helps comfortably move the eye to the central focus of this design - the front door. Other detailing, such as batten board shutters and decorative lintels add a French country flair.

Cedric

❶ Brick pedestals anchoring tapered columns and a detailed entablature provide the framework of this nostalgic front porch.

❷ Bedroom 3 could easily become a den with double doors opening to the entry.

❸ Both the dining room and breakfast area are near the kitchen and readily expand into one another.

❹ A boxed ceiling offers beauty in the master bedroom which also features a large walk-in closet and whirlpool tub.

❺ Extra counter area in the laundry room extends its available working space.

❻ A bench near the garage entry provides a place to take off one's muddy shoes.

AVAILABLE FOR ALL PLANS

For More Information
on our Custom Changes see page 29

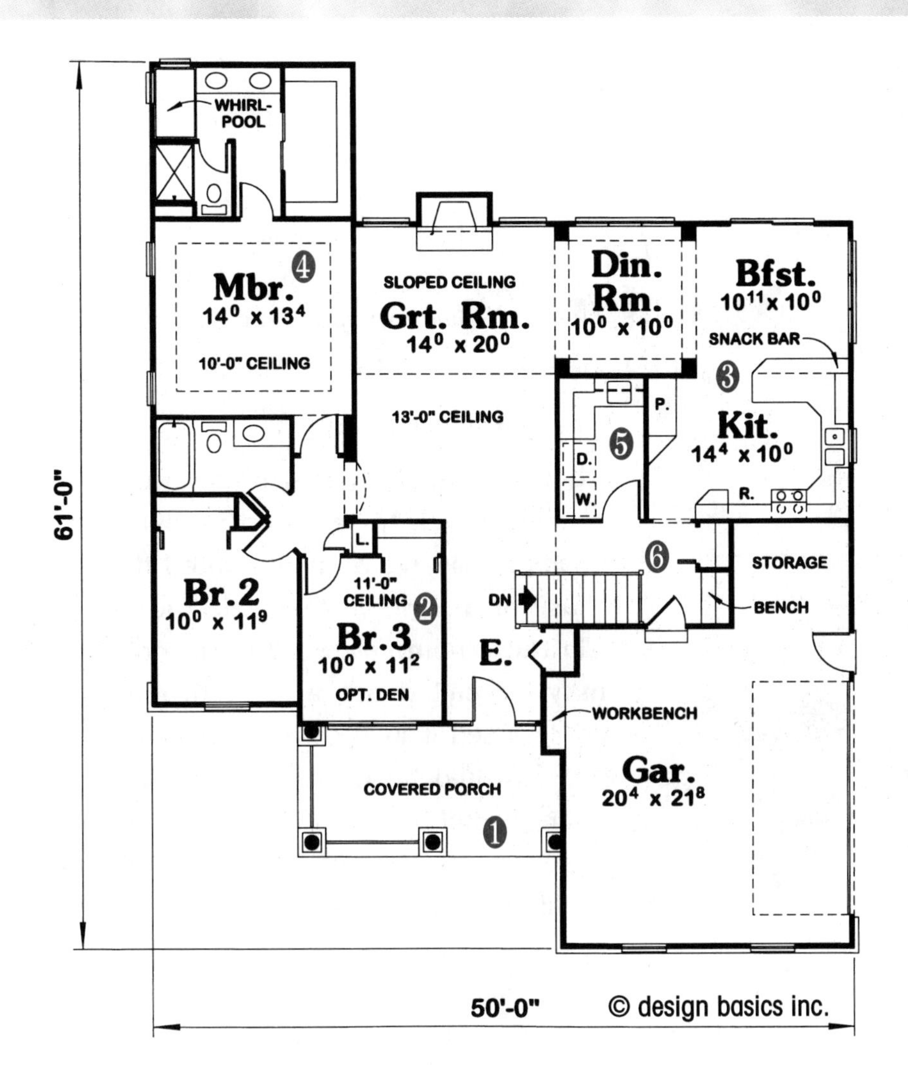

1679 Finished Sq. Ft.

NOTE: 9 ft. main level walls

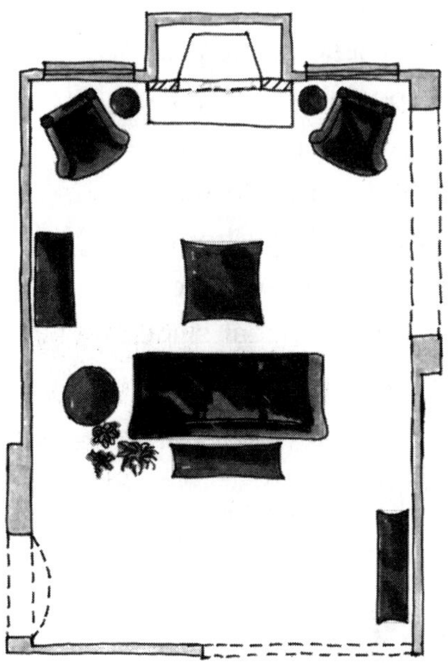

DECORATOR DESIGN TIPS

GREAT ROOM - Traffic flow is driven behind the main focal area and sets up a space conducive for TV watching or fireplace enjoyment. If a room like this were arranged with furniture along the walls, proximity to each other between the TV area and fireplace becomes a problem.

TO ORDER THIS PLAN CALL
1-800-947-7526

design basics inc.
HOME PLAN DESIGN SERVICE

In the **Nostalgia** *Collection you will find...*

FLEXIBLE ROOMS

Because the same design may work equally well for an empty-nester *and* family, we've incorporated the use of a variety of flexible rooms in these home plans. While a room may be called out as a bedroom, we've designed it in such a way to suggest that it could be used as an office, exercise room or hobby room. These spaces can really serve a variety of functions and greatly benefit the home's resale value.

ECONOMIC USE OF SPACE

Home buyers are continually looking for larger and larger storage areas. They're also looking for the most economical home for their dollar. So, in every inch of these homes, we tried to use the space that's available, especially the space directly under the roof. You'll find plenty of bonus rooms, attics, lofts and second-floor bedrooms with dormers to make the rooms more useable. And all but a few of these homes offer nine-foot main level walls. Buyers can use these spaces as they see fit and will also enjoy the aesthetic appeal since many of these areas create charming nooks with quaintly sloped ceilings.

$1\frac{1}{2}$-story Homes

Plan Index

Chambers

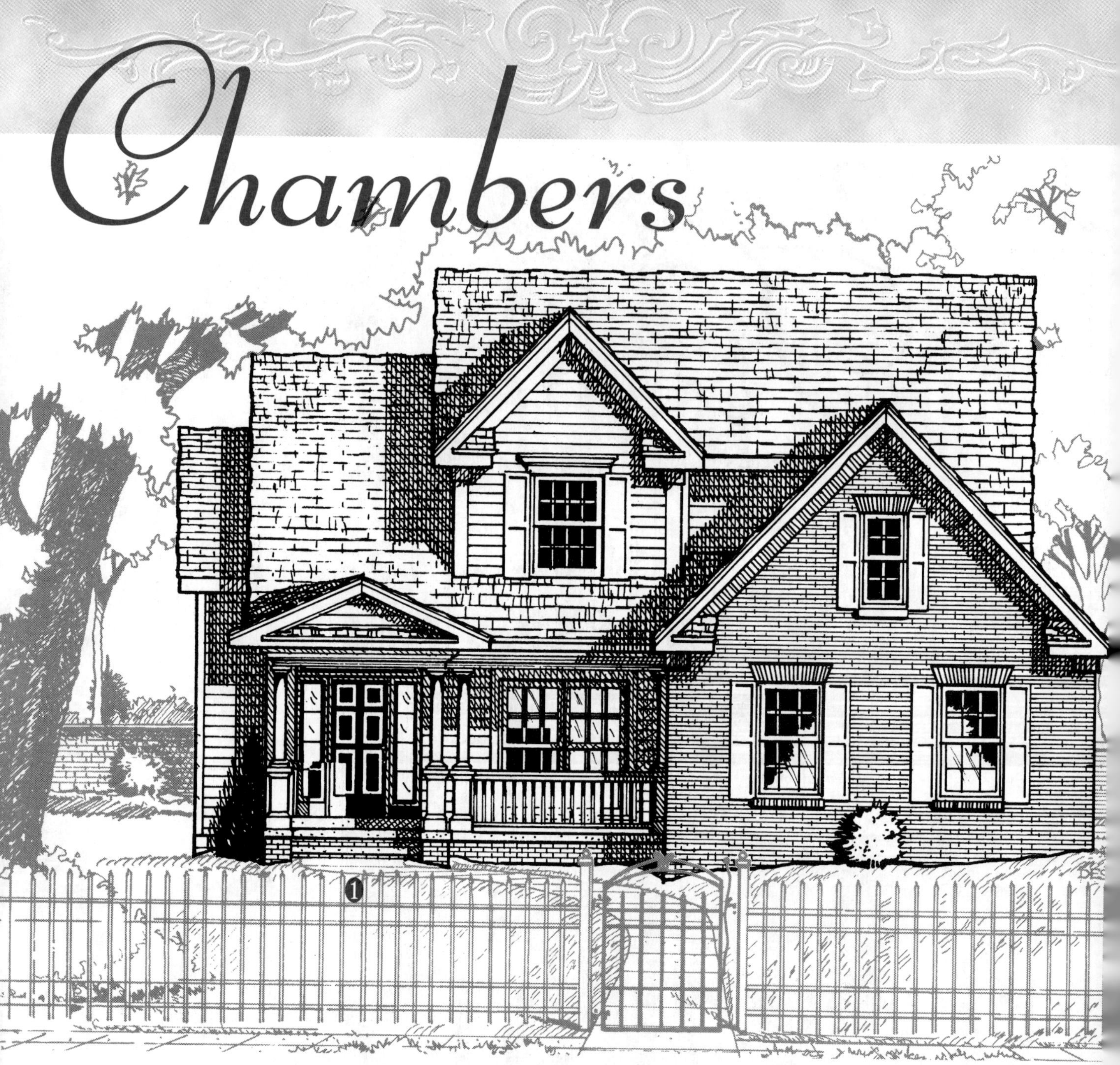

❶ A classical pediment frames the entry and porch on this home and anchors the front elevation.

❷ A singular, free-standing column brings a hint of timelessness to the dining room.

❸ A corner fireplace encased with two sides of windows illuminates the great room.

❹ The kitchen is brightened with plenty of light from the breakfast area and great room.

❺ A second-floor loft overlooks the dinette and creates the perfect family computer center.

❻ An unfinished bonus room offers flexibility as a fourth bedroom, exercise room or storage for seasonal items.

AVAILABLE FOR ALL PLANS

For More Information on Reverse Plans see page 297.

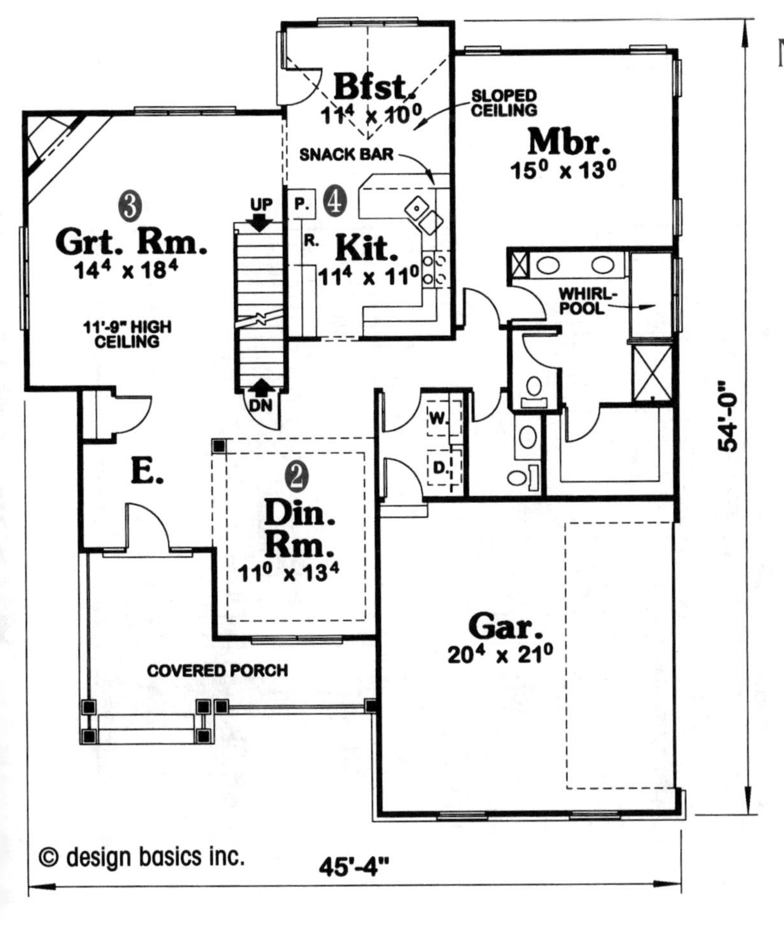

Main	1457 Sq. Ft.
Second	686 Sq. Ft.
Total	2143 Sq. Ft.

NOTE: 9 ft. main level walls

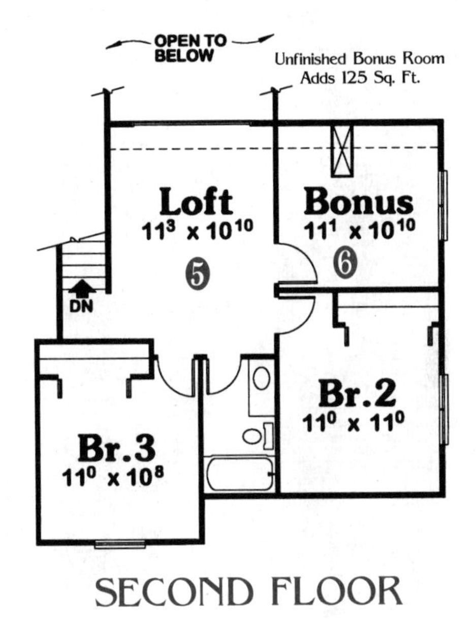

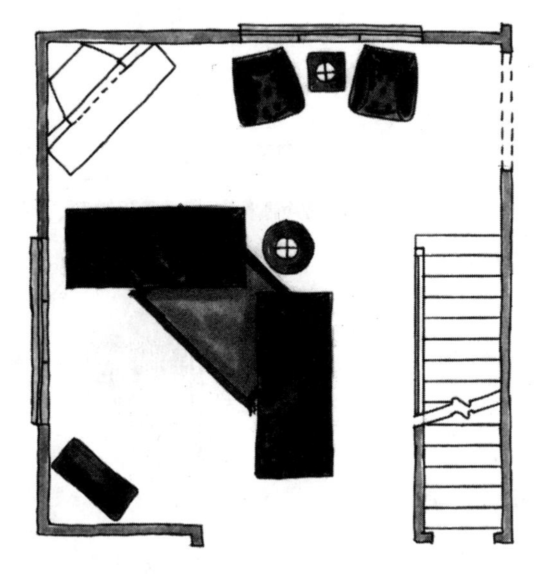

DECORATOR DESIGN TIPS

GREAT ROOM - If including an entertainment unit in this room, the sofas are pulled to the lower half of the room and placed in an "L" shape around the TV unit. A secondary seating area is placed behind the sofas, next to the fireplace, for those who want a more private area. If this room does not require a TV unit, the sofas could flip the opposite way to face the fireplace, while staying in an "L" shape. If the upholstery gets spread too far apart, an ineffective combination is created and isn't conducive for entertaining and conversation.

Magrath

❶ A classic Greek-style entry brings structure to this asymmetrical design.

❷ A study located on the second floor is perfect as a homework area.

❸ Angled walls and a 10-foot ceiling define the dining room and establish its pleasant ambiance.

❹ A hall leads to a private master suite with a large sitting room, great for relaxing or catching up on office work.

❺ Quaint window seats charm bedrooms 2 and 3.

❻ A large bonus room above the garage is beneficial for seasonal storage.

AVAILABLE FOR ALL PLANS

For More Information
on Parade Home Packages see page 29

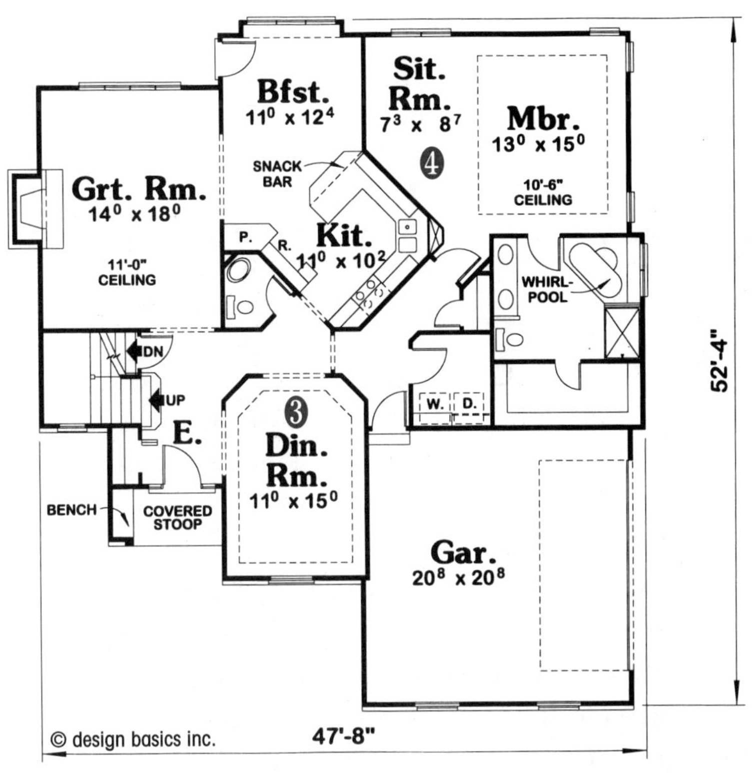

MAIN FLOOR

Main	1554 Sq. Ft.
Second	867 Sq. Ft.
Total	2421 Sq. Ft.

NOTE: 9 ft. main level walls

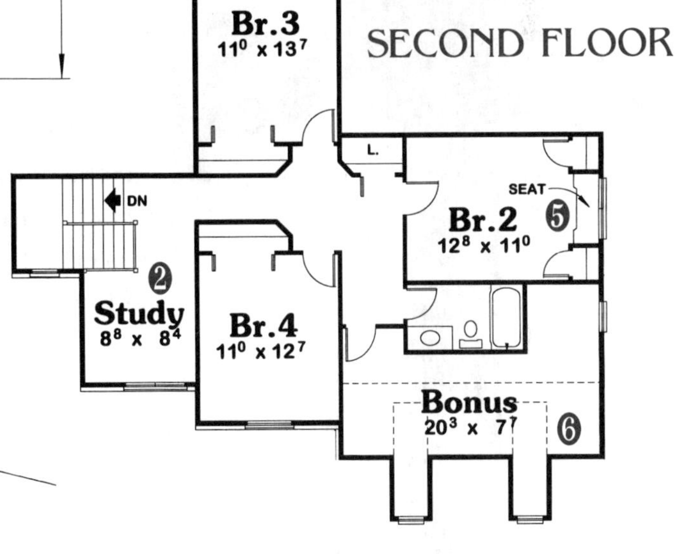

SECOND FLOOR

Unfinished Bonus Room
Adds 240 Sq. Ft.

INTERIOR VIEW

KITCHEN - An open kitchen and breakfast area arrangement offers fluidity between working and family activity. A snack bar offers a place for family and guests to interact with those in the kitchen.

In the **Nostalgia** *Collection you will find...*

SIDE-LOAD GARAGES

Probably one of the most difficult things to work around in home design is the garage. Since it is large to begin with, and getting larger all of the time, designers like ourselves do everything we can to 'de-emphasize' its presence. The majority of the homes in this collection feature side-load garages, in part, to help replicate the architectural styles of homes before there were garages. But doing so also creates an easier option to change the garage to a front-load entry than vice versa.

WORK SPACE

With the popularity of 'do-it-yourself' home improvement, we as designers have to ask ourselves where the buyer will put a work bench or lawn equipment, when designing the garage. We tried as much as we possibly could to design alcoves and obvious storage areas into the garages in this collection. This will, in many cases, allow buyers and builders to include a garden center or work bench in the construction of the home.

Two-story Homes

Plan Index

Page #	Width	Plan #	Plan Name	Sq. Ft.
256	49'-4"	4999	Sanders	1628
260	50'-0"	4642	Ackerly	1712
258	50'-0"	4997	Rocklund	1778
244	41'-4"	5084	Cohasset	1893
248	46'-0"	5085	Branford	1928
252	49'-0"	4949	Darius	1938
254	49'-4"	4996	Amesbury	2069
246	43'-8"	4952	Caldera	2144
262	50'-0"	4135	Gerard	2349
250	48'-0"	4950	Neville	2808

Cohasset

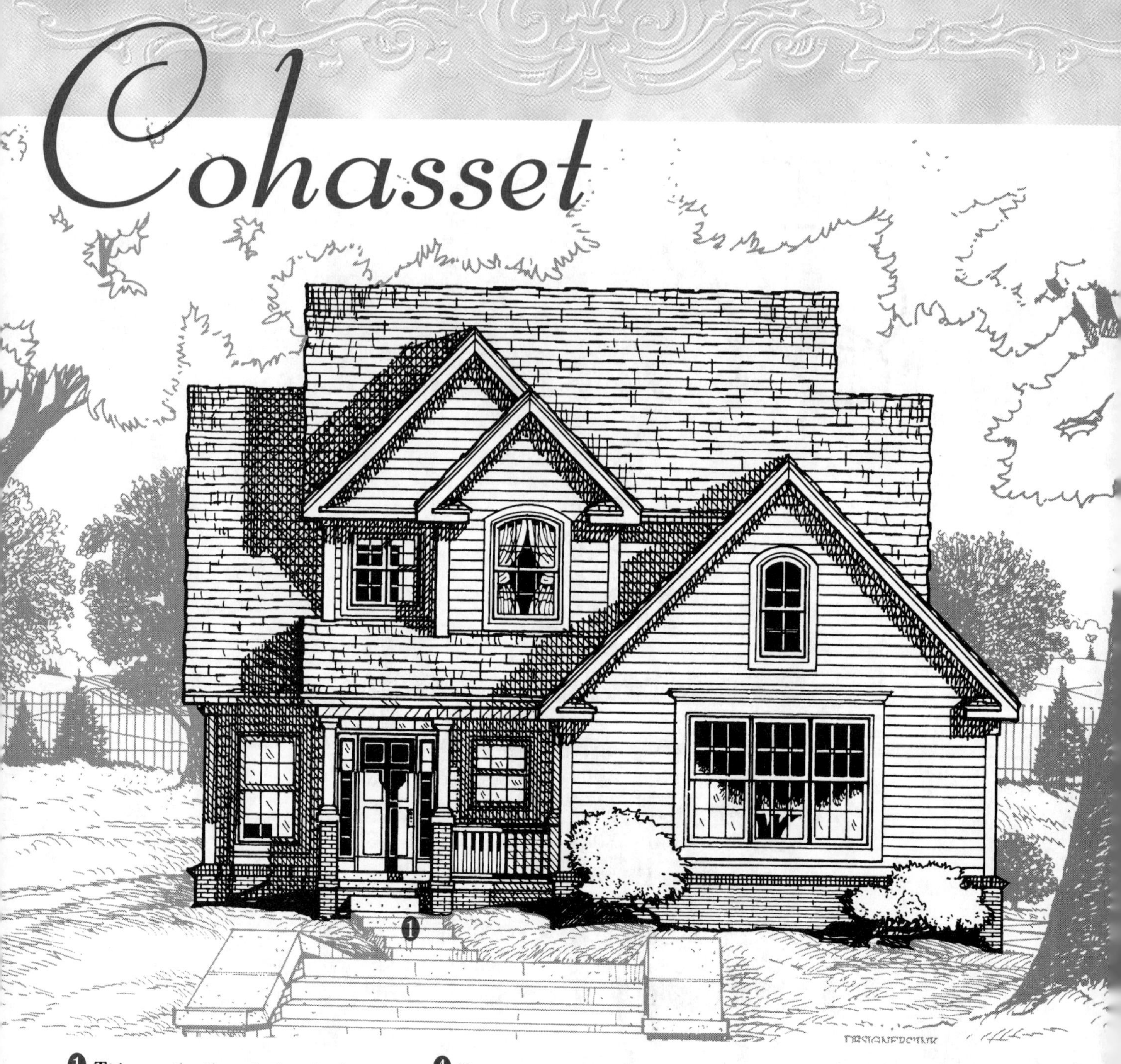

❶ This captivating design features beautiful windows set off with traditional, simplified trim.

❷ Upon walking in, the front room has a variety of options including a parlor or, with its close vicinity to the kitchen, a dining room.

❸ Bookshelves and a fireplace add a comfortable atmosphere to the family room.

❹ Extra storage space in the garage welcomes shelves or a work bench.

❺ Ample space is offered in the secondary bedrooms, both of which have a walk-in closet.

❻ Unfinished storage above the garage would make a great addition to the master suite's closet, especially for seasonal storage.

AVAILABLE FOR ALL PLANS

For More Information on our Roof Construction Package see page 297.

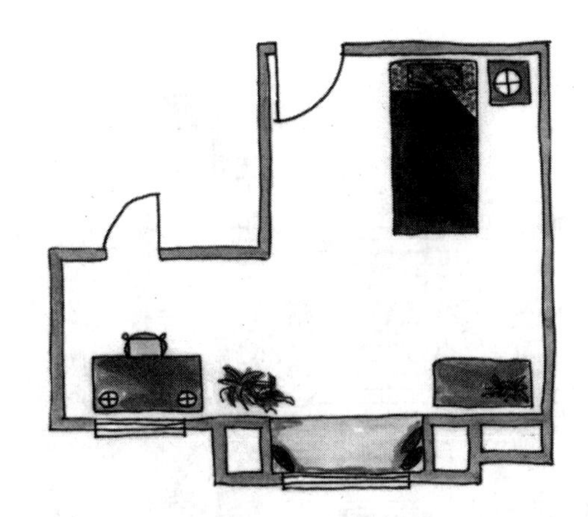

SECOND FLOOR

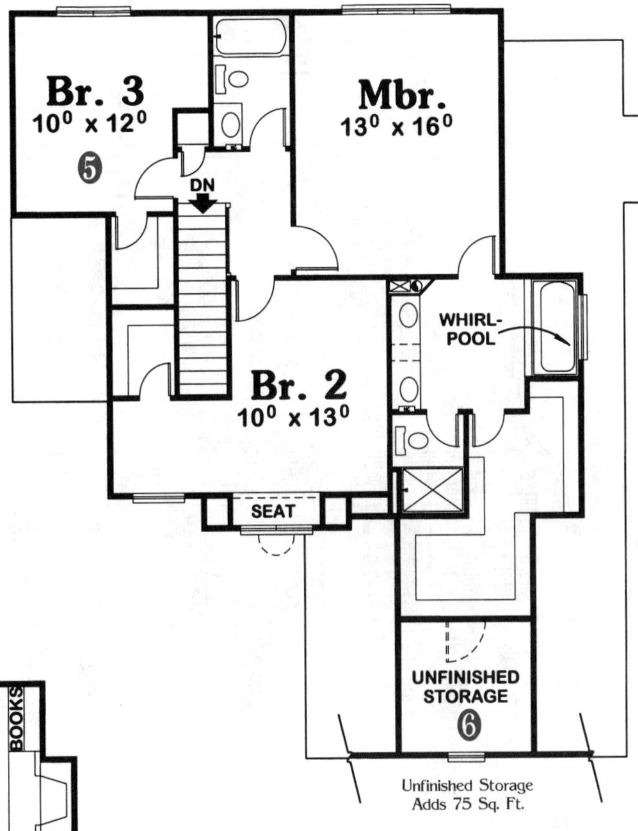

DECORATOR DESIGN TIPS

BEDROOM 2 - This bedroom has the perfect shape to arrange special areas. By tucking a desk in front of the window, a private study area is created. The window seat allows for a comfortable space to read in the sun.

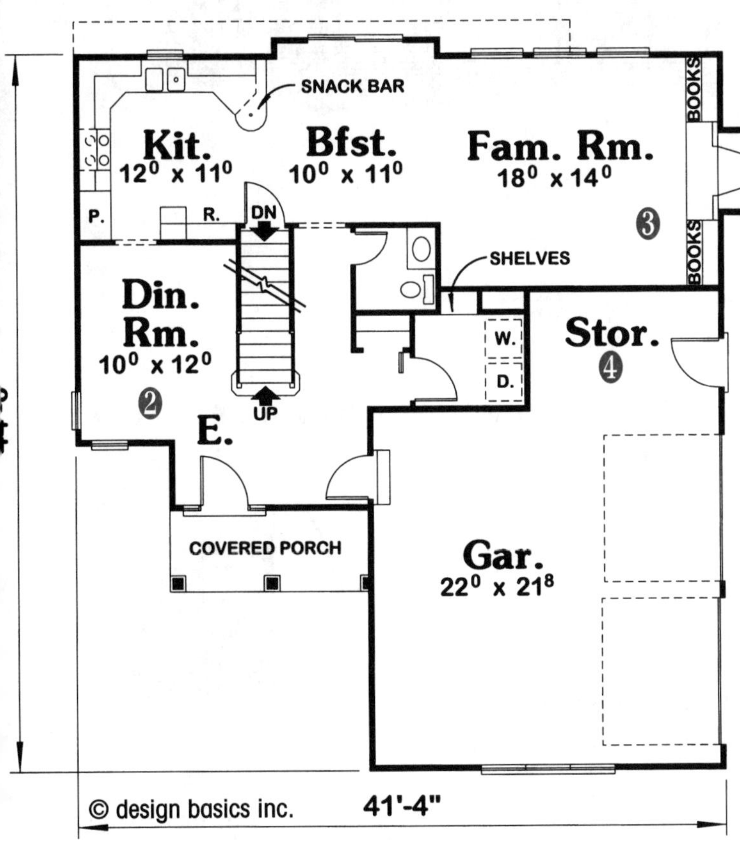

Main	920 Sq. Ft.
Second	973 Sq. Ft.
Total	1893 Sq. Ft.

NOTE: 9 ft. main level walls

MAIN FLOOR

Caldera

❶ Through the front covered porch is a lovely entry that views the staircase, and offers a large coat closet with old-fashioned double doors.

❷ The great room is warmed by a fireplace and opens to the dining room for ease when entertaining.

❸ The kitchen has ample counter space and a snack bar that serves the breakfast area.

❹ The master suite is spacious, with its giant walk-in closet that further opens to more storage space.

❺ Three secondary bedrooms, one with a handy built-in desk, share a full hall bath.

❻ A pocket door leads to the laundry room providing a soaking sink.

AVAILABLE FOR ALL PLANS

For More Information on Reverse Plans see page 297.

EXTERIOR HIGHLIGHT

The recessed, arched entry on this home helps keep the frontage to a minimum. For that reason this home would work well on a narrower lot.

SECOND FLOOR

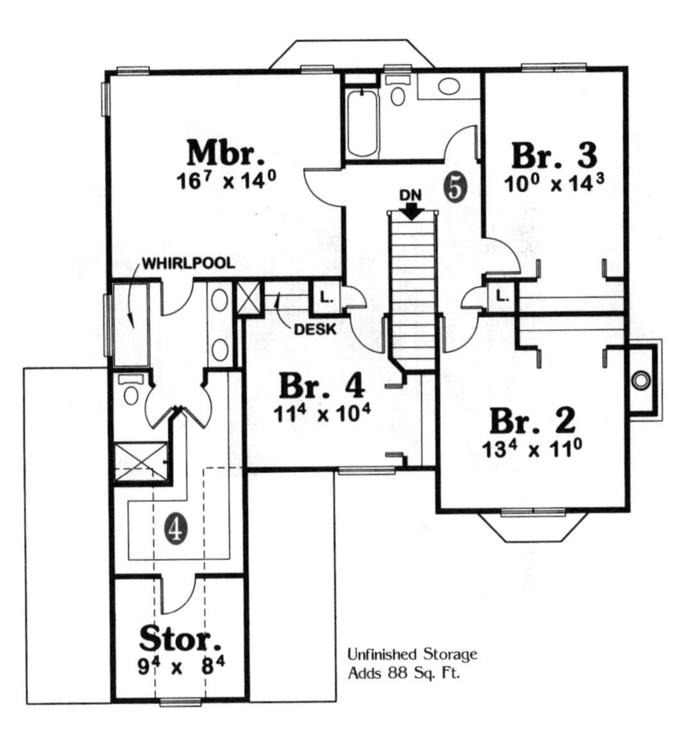

MAIN FLOOR

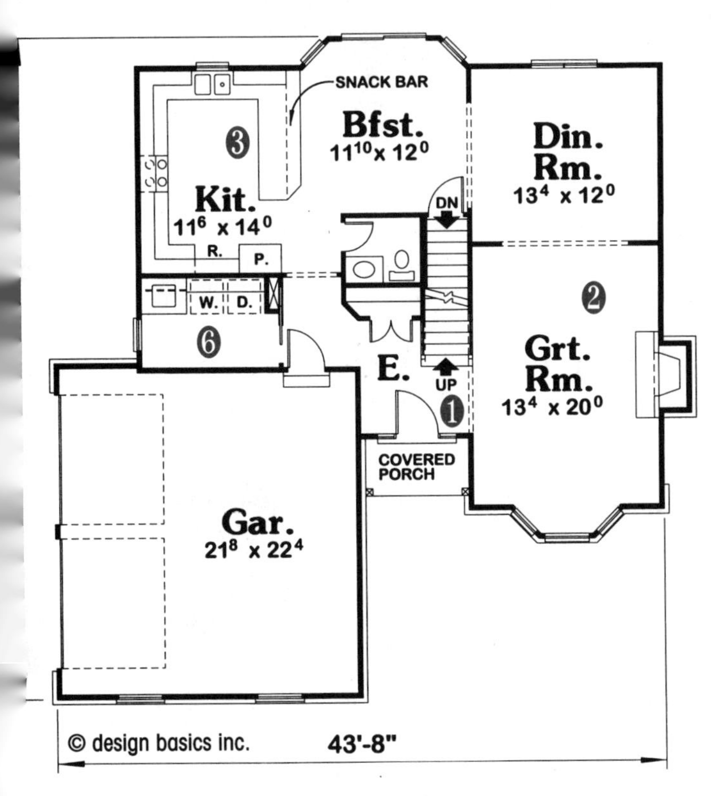

Main	1008 Sq. Ft.
Second	1136 Sq. Ft.
Total	2144 Sq. Ft.

NOTE: 9 ft. main level walls

Branford

❶ Soldier coursing charms the windows of this home, which will make a good candidate for a narrower lot situation.

❷ In its traditional role, the living room in this home welcomes guests as they walk in the door.

❸ The hearth room offers a bookcase and shares a see-thru fireplace with the living room.

❹ A computer area at the top of the stairway is perfect for homework or finishing up office work.

❺ The unfinished bonus room on the second-floor, is a great place to expand into a studio.

❻ 9-foot main level walls bring a sense of spaciousness to all rooms on the first floor.

AVAILABLE FOR ALL PLANS

For More Information
on Parade Home Packages see page 29

MAIN FLOOR

Main	1002 Sq. Ft.
Second	926 Sq. Ft.
Total	1928 Sq. Ft.

NOTE: 9 ft. main level walls

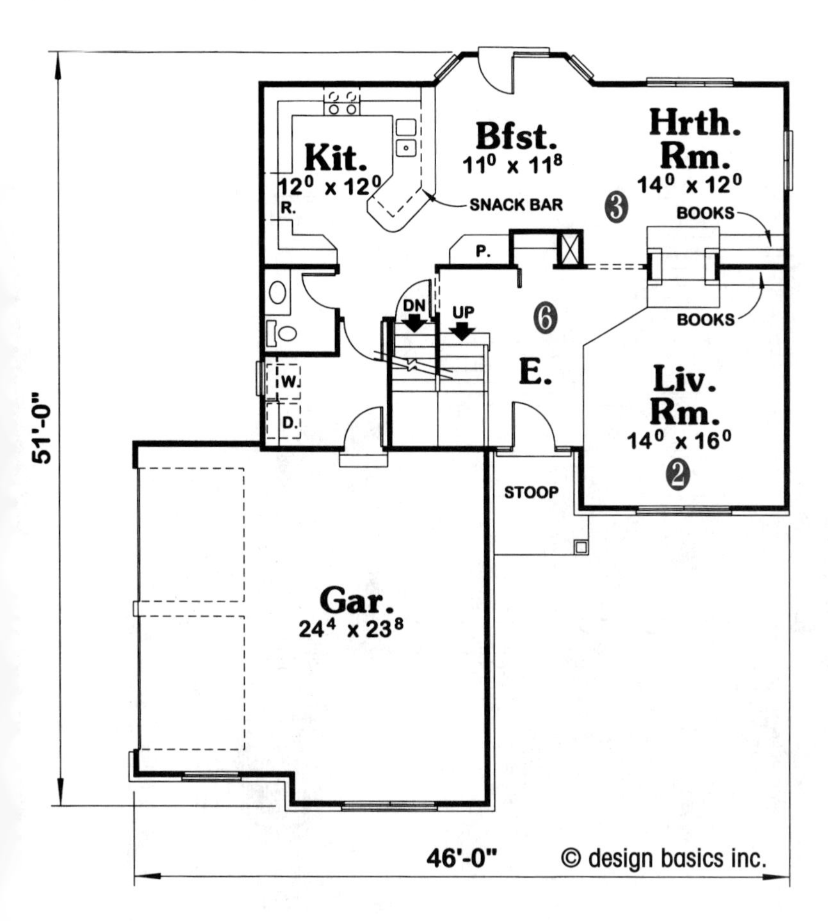

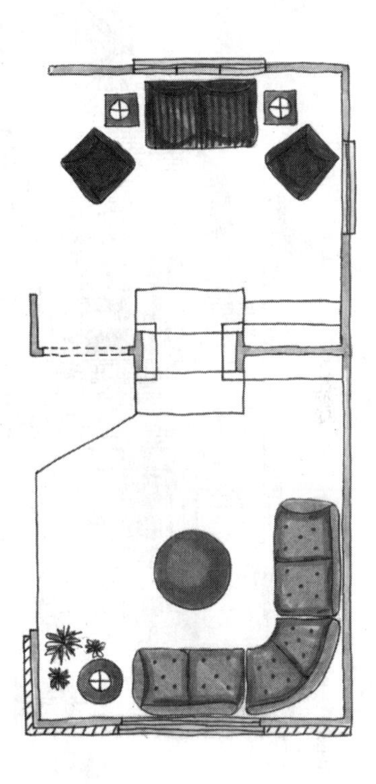

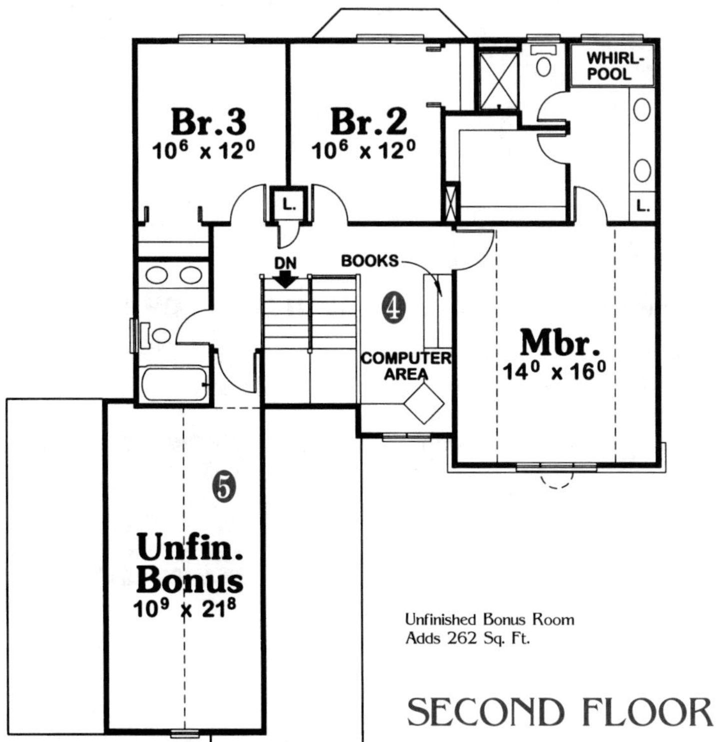

Unfinished Bonus Room
Adds 262 Sq. Ft.

SECOND FLOOR

DECORATOR DESIGN TIPS

LIVING/HEARTH ROOM - These fairly open living spaces require an easy transition from one room to another. By using a large sectional piece in the living room, and smaller pieces in the hearth room, a nice composition of scale and shape is created. Too many pieces of the same size and proportion makes a space feel overdone and "busy."

TO ORDER THIS PLAN CALL
1-800-947-7526

design basics inc. HOME PLAN DESIGN SERVICE

Neville

❶ A covered porch with columns is an inviting way to lure guests inside this home, while remaining a perfect place to observe the neighborhood from a porch swing.

❷ The double doors that open to the dining room allow for quiet dining and are a signature trait of this home.

❸ The master suite offers a walk-in closet with his-and-her aisles.

❹ Window benches in the upstairs landing and bedroom 4 add to the home's subtle charm.

❺ Optional storage space off of bedroom 4 allows for expansion of its walk-in closet.

❻ An unfinished attic offers abundant yet careful storage of a family's memories.

AVAILABLE FOR ALL PLANS

For More Information
on Reverse Plans see page 297.

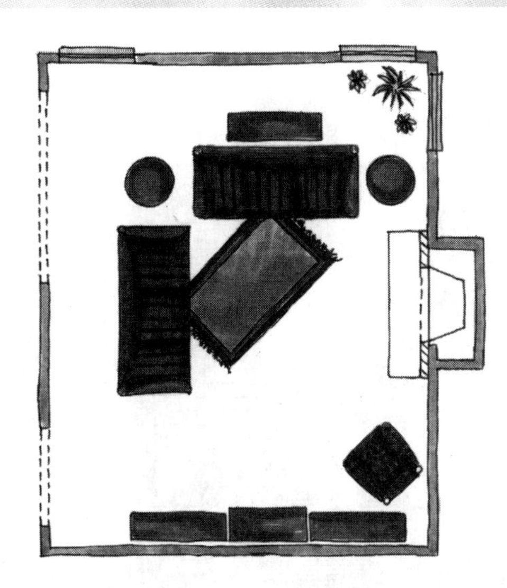

DECORATOR DESIGN TIPS

FAMILY ROOM - This room is large enough for two sofas. By placing them in an "L" shape, an intimate, cozy area is created by the fireplace. Traffic is kept behind the conversation area. The only wall without an opening or window works well to place an entertainment unit surrounded by bookcases. Tucking a chair by the fireplace makes a great place to read.

SECOND FLOOR

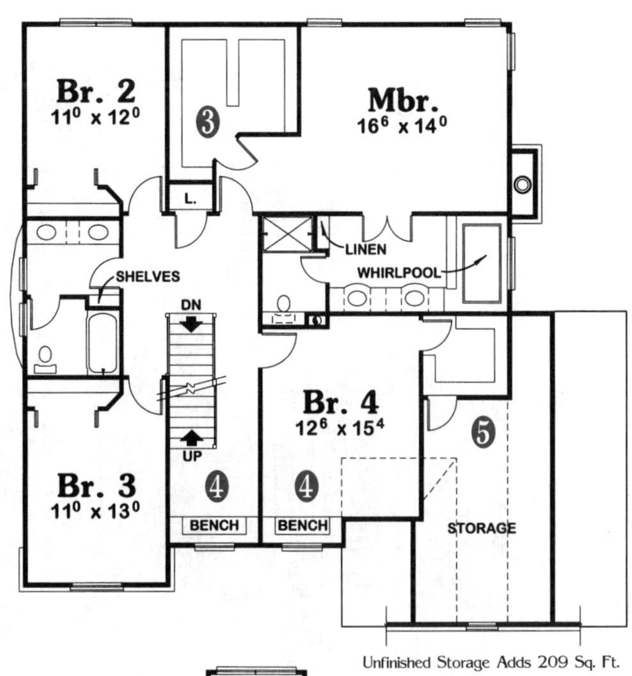

Unfinished Storage Adds 209 Sq. Ft.

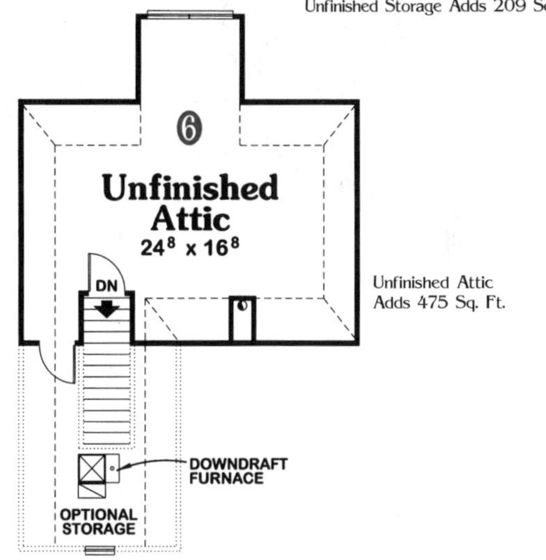

Unfinished Attic Adds 475 Sq. Ft.

MAIN FLOOR

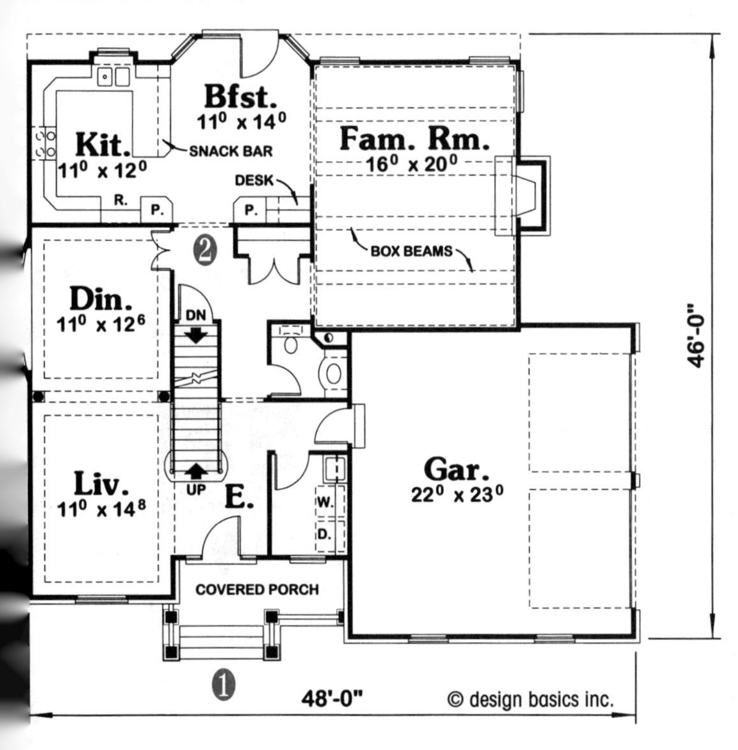

Main	1304 Sq. Ft.
Second	1504 Sq. Ft.
Total	2808 Sq. Ft.

NOTE: 9 ft. main level walls

Darius

❶ With its wistful gazebo porch and subtle outside window details, viewing this home brings to life memories of homes of the past.

❷ A view of the living room, with elegant columns, sets the mood for the rest of the home.

❸ The dining room, when paired with the living room, shares space for formal occasions.

❹ The kitchen and breakfast area open spaciously to the family room, and are ideal for family celebrations.

❺ Upstairs, the master bedroom offers many options with its unfinished bonus space, great for storage or especially a private office.

❻ The master bath is lavish with its corner whirlpool tub and novel sloped ceiling.

AVAILABLE FOR ALL PLANS

For More Information
on our Custom Changes see page 29

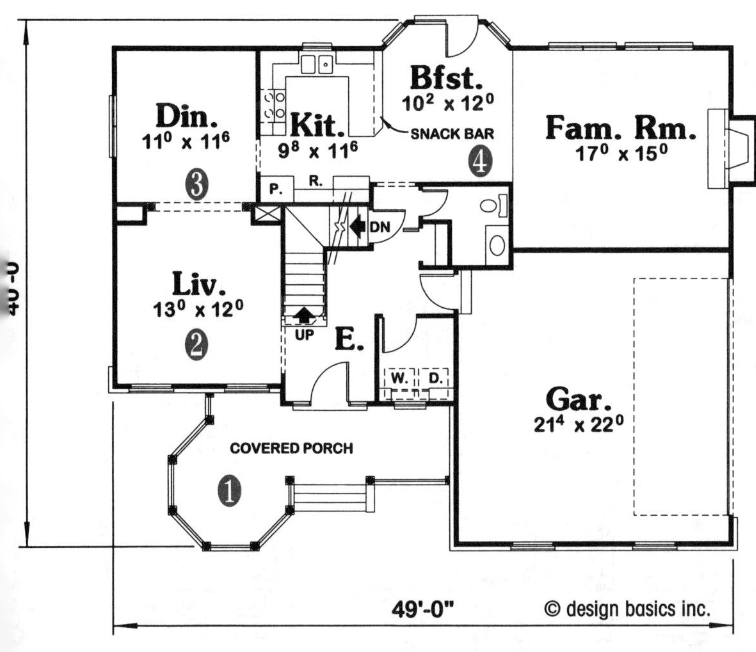

MAIN FLOOR

Main	1091 Sq. Ft.
Second	847 Sq. Ft.
Total	1938 Sq. Ft.

NOTE: 9 ft. main level walls

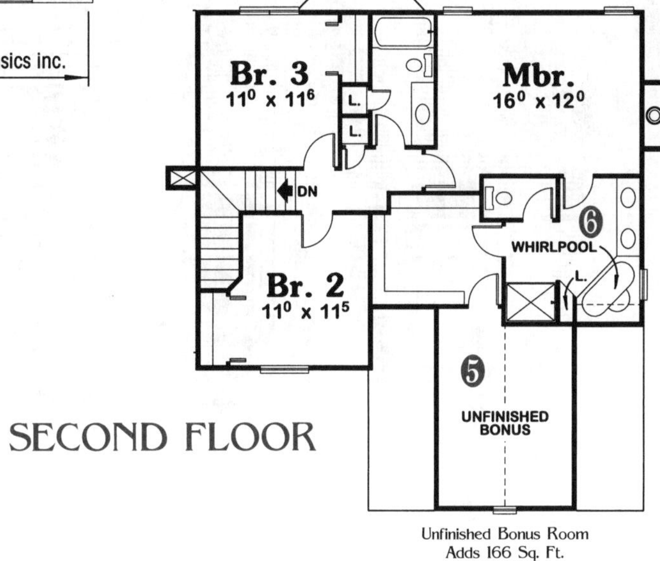

SECOND FLOOR

Unfinished Bonus Room
Adds 166 Sq. Ft.

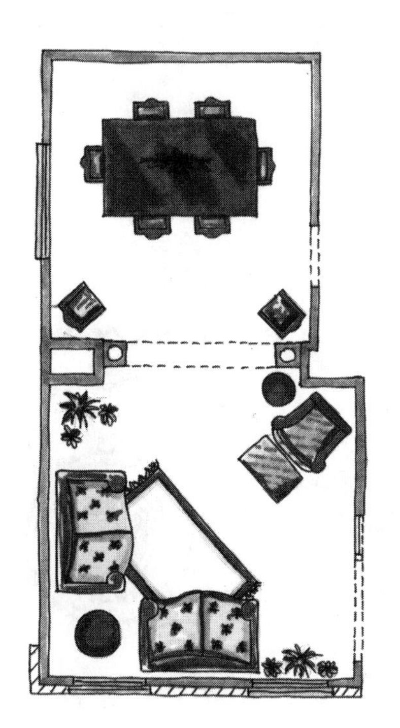

DECORATOR DESIGN TIPS

LIVING/DINING ROOM - The decorating choices in the living and dining rooms need to coincide since they are open to each other. In the living room, an angled rug ties two loveseats together to form a nice conversation area. Since this is a smaller room, loveseats work better together than larger furniture pieces. Also, choosing a more delicate style of furniture won't over-fill the space.

Amesbury

❶ Upon walking in, a formal room easily adaptable as a dining room or living room is enhanced with a bayed window.

❷ Prominent columns and a ceiling sloped on two sides add an airy comfort to the great room.

❸ A butcher's block, pantry and oven form an efficient working triangle in the kitchen.

❹ Storage space in the garage is a welcome amenity for a work bench or equipment storage.

❺ The second-floor corridor overlooks the entry and leads to two secondary bedrooms that share a full bath.

❻ The master bedroom is enhanced with a vaulted ceiling and shelves for displaying books.

For More Information
on our Copyrights see page 298.

EXTERIOR HIGHLIGHT

To recess a porch such as this, on a home that already has a deep-set entry, could potentially "de-emphasize" the entry. The treatment works on this home because the Doric column detailing and the large sidelights and transom around the front door serve to capture attention.

SECOND FLOOR

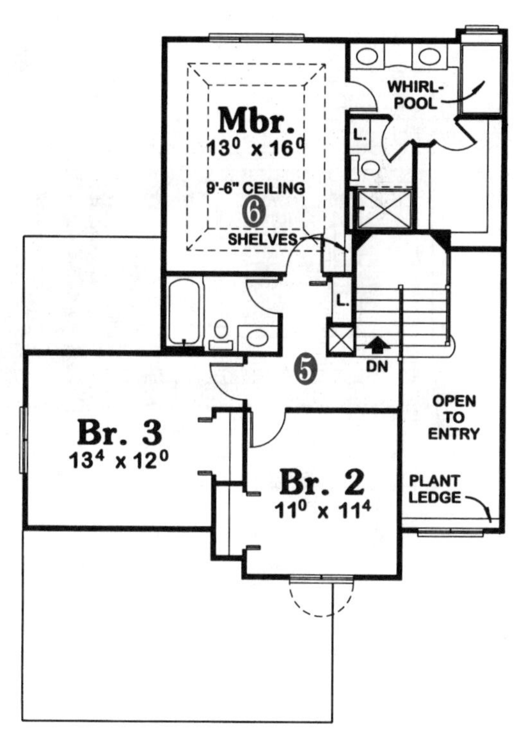

MAIN FLOOR

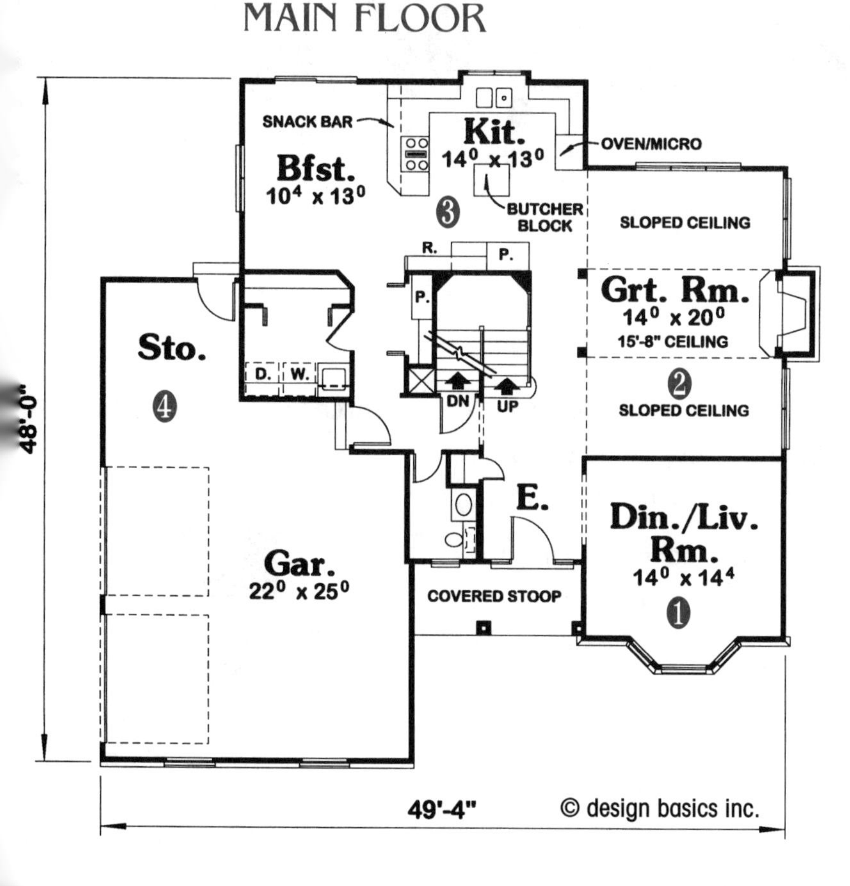

Main	1209 Sq. Ft.
Second	860 Sq. Ft.
Total	2069 Sq. Ft.

NOTE: 9 ft. main level walls

Sanders

❶ The covered porch of this home, together with a lovely transom window above the front door, create a desirable front elevation.

❷ Adding to the entry's impressive view of the French doors leading to a secluded den, is the beautiful staircase.

❸ Indented double doors add interest to the den.

❹ Three large windows and a raised-hearth fireplace add character to the already-inviting family room.

❺ Wrapping counters in the kitchen are convenient for the chef of the house, as are a snack bar, lazy Susan and pantry.

❻ The breakfast area resembles a cozy nook with access to the outside.

AVAILABLE FOR ALL PLANS

For More Information on our Custom Changes see page 29

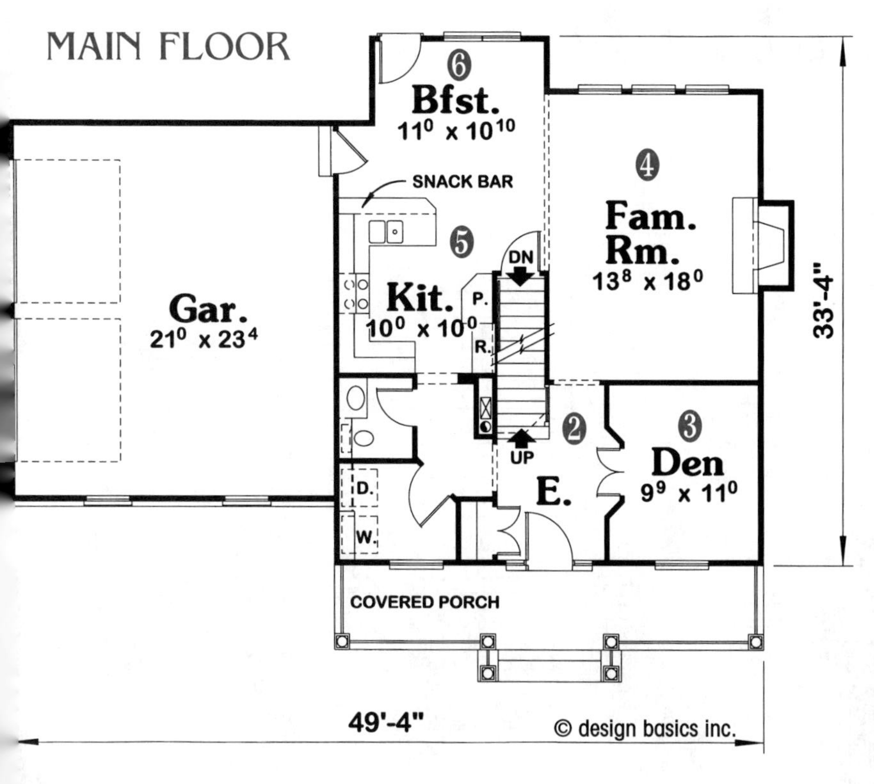

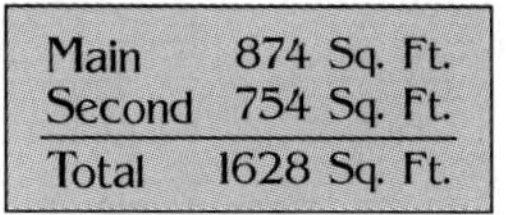

Main	874 Sq. Ft.
Second	754 Sq. Ft.
Total	1628 Sq. Ft.

NOTE: 8 ft. main level walls

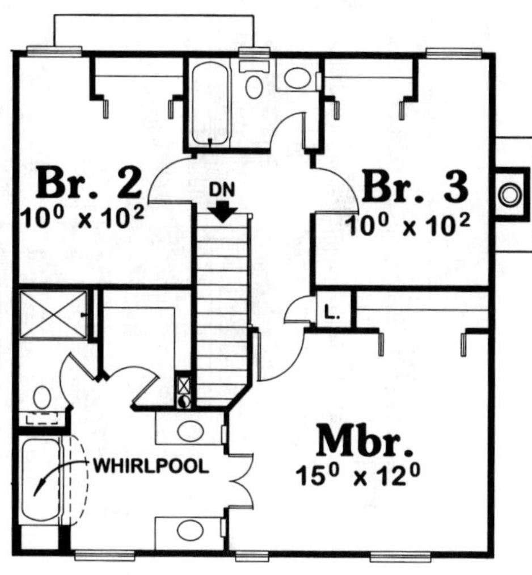

INTERIOR VIEW

MASTER BATH - His and her vanities are exceptional conveniences in this luxurious master bath. A relaxing whirlpool tub draws you inside where a large walk-in closet and compartmental shower offer further benefits.

TO ORDER THIS PLAN CALL
1-800-947-7526

Rocklund

❶ Double doors seclude the parlor from the family room but also provide the possibility of expansion for larger groups.

❷ A built-in curio cabinet in the family room is a great place to decorate with books or family photos.

❸ A walk-in pantry offers storage to both the kitchen and breakfast area.

❹ Plenty of storage space in the garage is perfect for a work bench or lawn equipment.

❺ Expansion space above the garage provides the option to expand the master suite closet or create a storage area.

❻ Two linen closets provide extra storage on the second floor.

AVAILABLE FOR ALL PLANS

For More Information
on Reverse Plans see page 297.

SECOND FLOOR

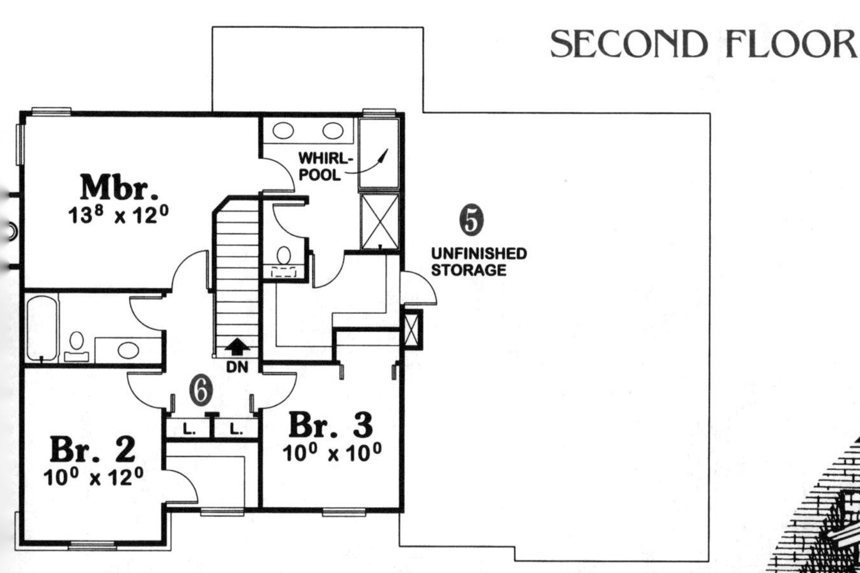

Main	1003 Sq. Ft.
Second	775 Sq. Ft.
Total	1778 Sq. Ft.

NOTE: 9 ft. main level walls

EXTERIOR HIGHLIGHT

Wide brick steps and pilasters help bring back the feel of homes from the Arts and Crafts era. An extension of this brick is carried on throughout the exterior of this facade.

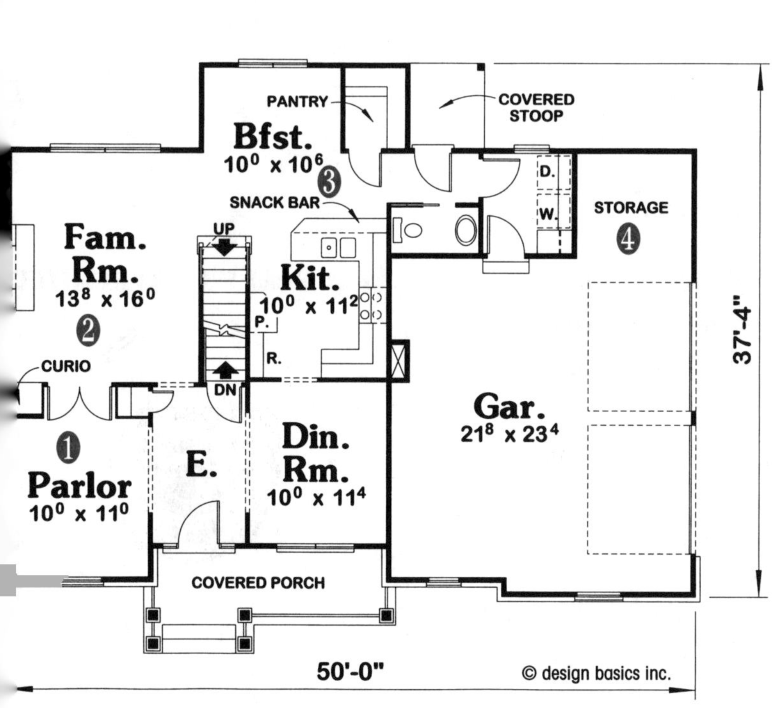

MAIN FLOOR

TO ORDER THIS PLAN CALL
1-800-947-7526

Ackerly

❶ This charming design features lap siding and shutters to set off its All-American appeal.

❷ A large covered stoop opens to an informal floor plan with the kitchen located to the front.

❸ A snack bar serves the dinette, which could function both formally and informally.

❹ A media room – perfect for a family work area with home computer – could also become a dining room or hobby area.

❺ A cathedral ceiling centers on the fireplace in the dramatic family room.

❻ A nook in the master bedroom can be used as an entertainment center or bookshelf.

For More Information
on our Copyrights see page 29

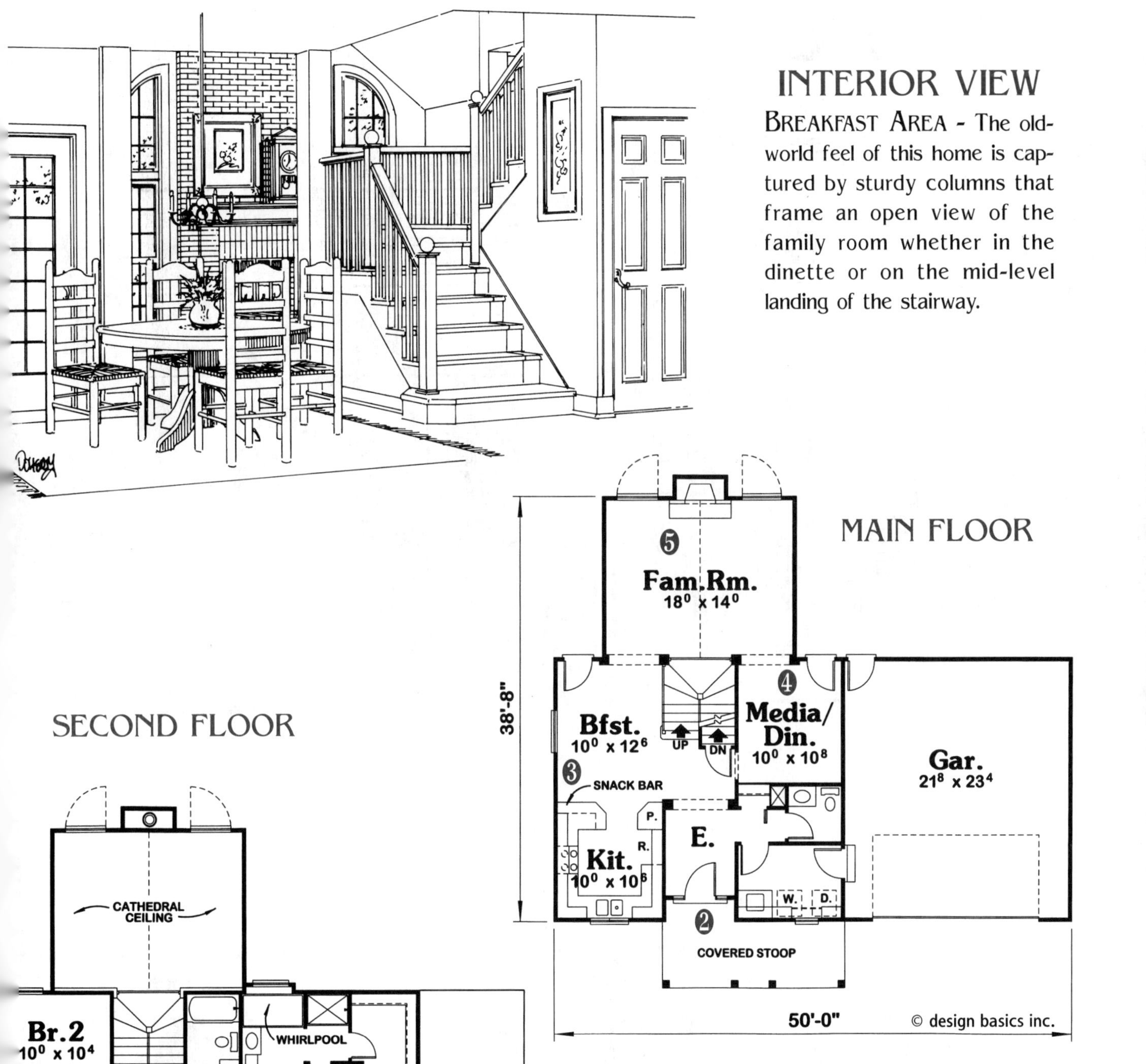

INTERIOR VIEW

BREAKFAST AREA - The old-world feel of this home is captured by sturdy columns that frame an open view of the family room whether in the dinette or on the mid-level landing of the stairway.

Main	932 Sq. Ft.
Second	780 Sq. Ft.
Total	1712 Sq. Ft.

NOTE: 9 ft. main level walls

TO ORDER THIS PLAN CALL
1-800-947-7526

Gerard

❶ The elevation's understated styling is enhanced by the use of a variety of timeless architectural elements, such as its double-hung windows and shutters.

❷ A wet bar in the family room is convenient when entertaining formally or informally.

❸ The living and dining rooms will comfortably entertain guests and make beautiful places to show off antiques.

❹ Bedroom 2 with its own private bath, makes the perfect guest bedroom or in-law suite.

❺ Unfinished storage offers the potential for expansion.

❻ At 50 feet in width, the Gerard helps solve a narrow lot situation.

AVAILABLE FOR ALL PLANS

For More Information
on our Roof Construction Packag
see page 297.

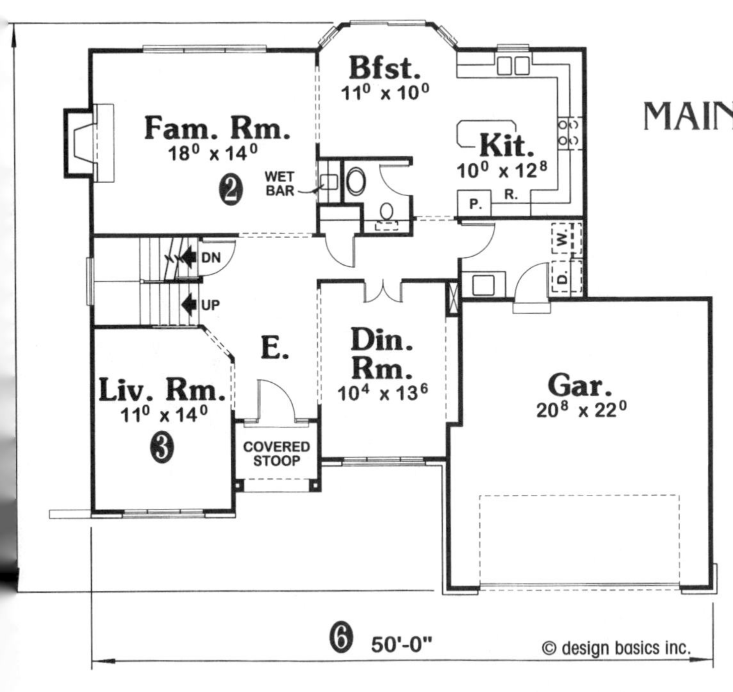

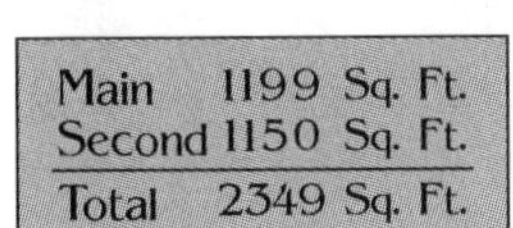

Main	1199 Sq. Ft.
Second	1150 Sq. Ft.
Total	2349 Sq. Ft.

NOTE: 9 ft. main level walls

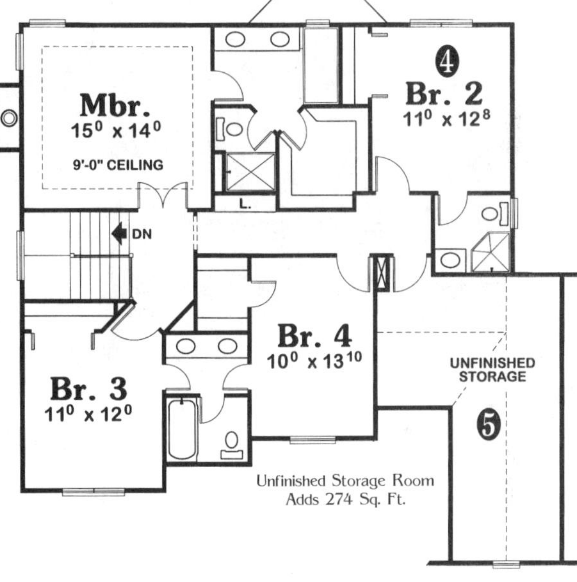

EXTERIOR HIGHLIGHT

Keystones showcased on decorative trim board and soldier coursing are repeated throughout the windows on this home. This detailing, mixed with a stucco and brick combination, makes a perfect design presentation.

Welcome to

Duplex Home Plans™

Multi-family designs including our most popular design concepts.

Those who are interested in multi-family designs are sure to enjoy the following designs in this special duplex plan feature in The Narrow Home™ Collection. All the favorite amenities and logistical room design that builders and home buyers have come to expect in our Gold Seal™ and Heartland collections, are now available in the form of 22 duplex plans, 2 triplex designs and one fourplex concept, showcased on the following pages. These designs, featuring thought-thru traffic patterns, and attractive elevations, will make a beautiful streetscape in any development. But whether you are building in a planned neighborhood or not, each of these multi-family designs includes our most popular design concepts to further enhance their saleability. Additionally, many of the designs that you've seen throughout the book can be formulated into duplex designs. See our Plexable ad on page 294-295 for more information or call one of our Customer Support Specialists with an inquiry.

DUPLEX • TRIPLEX • 4-PLEX
HOME PLANS™

Plan Index & Guide to Symbols

CUSTOM CHANGES AVAILABLE

Changes can be made to any Design Basics plan. See page 293 in the back of the book for details.

PLEXABLE OPTIONS AVAILABLE

Plexable™ plans can be configured into a variety of duplex designs. See page 294-295 in the back of the book for further details.

PARADE HOME PACKAGE

Available for any Gold Seal™ plan. Includes *Materials and Estimator's Workbook, Color Rendering, Customized Promotional Handout Artwork* and acrylic literature holder. Only $149. See page 297 in the back of the book for details on each product.

PRICE CODE

9F 4630 2x

- High quality, erasable, reproducible vellums
- Shipped via 2nd day air within the continental U.S.

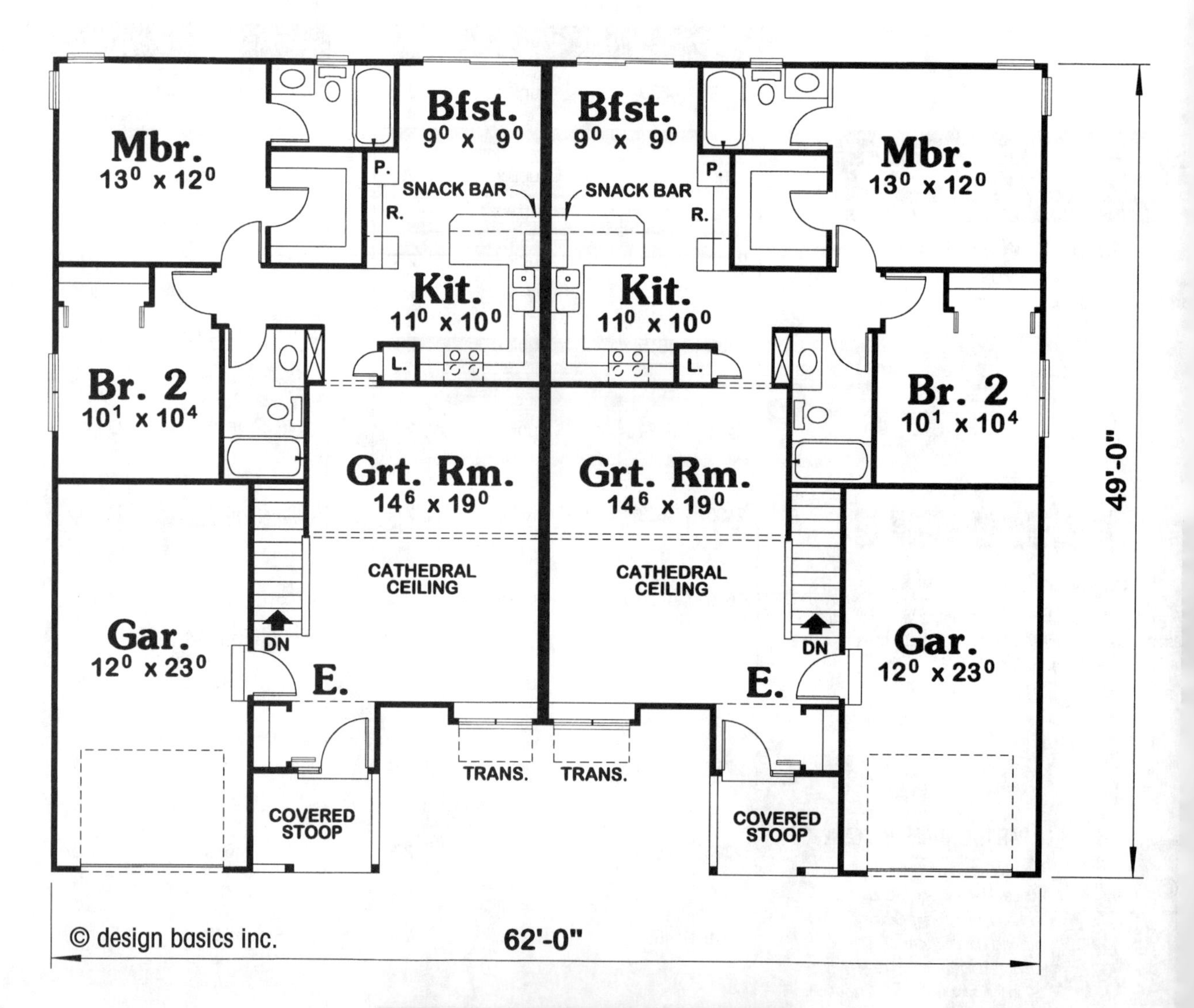

LEFT SIDE	RIGHT SIDE
Main 1079 sq. ft.	Main 1079 sq. ft.

PRICE CODE

F 4626 2x

▸ High quality, erasable, reproducible vellums
▸ Shipped via 2nd day air within the continental U.S.

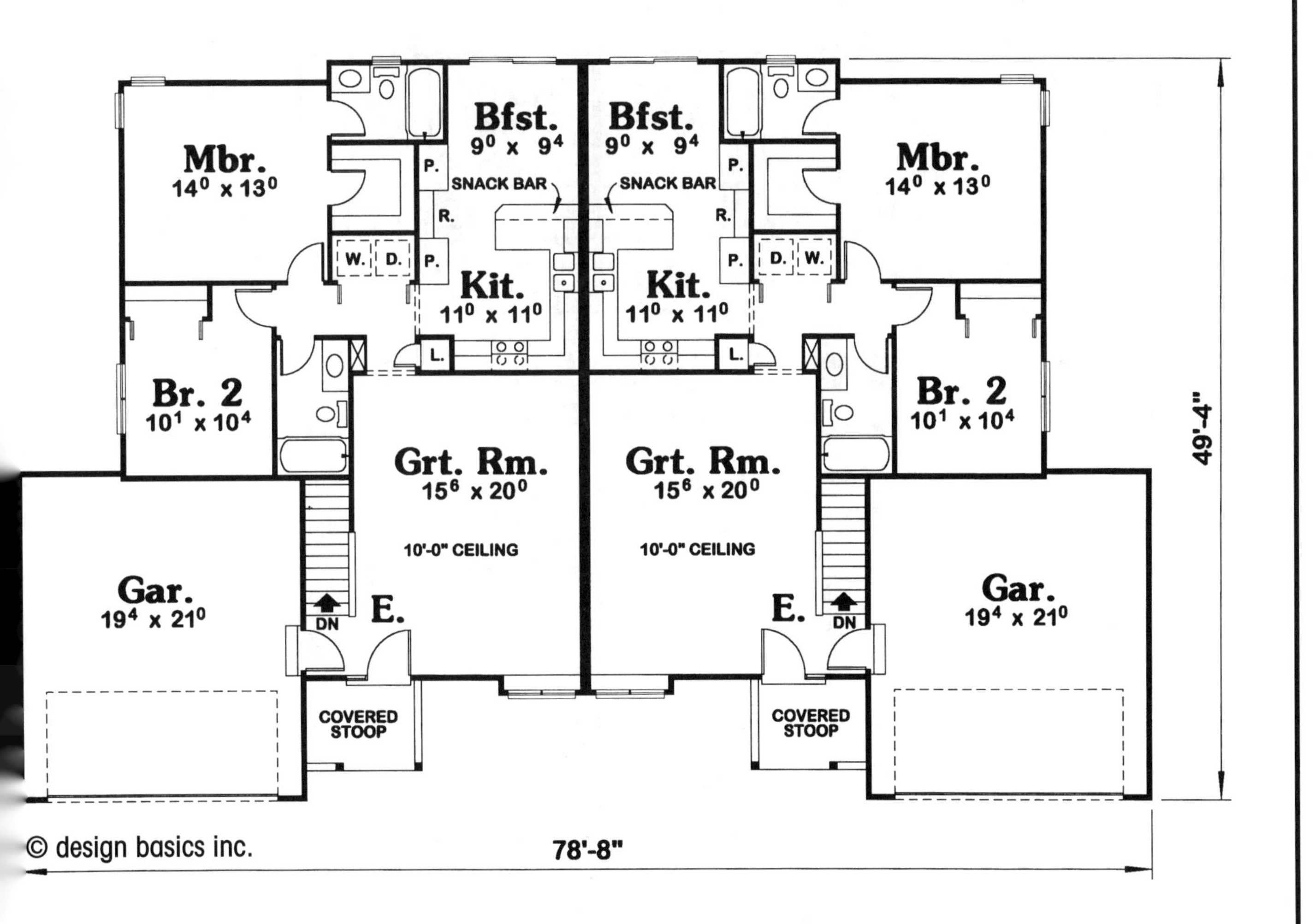

LEFT SIDE	RIGHT SIDE
Main 1140 sq. ft.	Main 1140 sq. ft.

PRICE CODE

9F 4614 2x

- High quality, erasable, reproducible vellums
- Shipped via 2nd day air within the continental U.S.

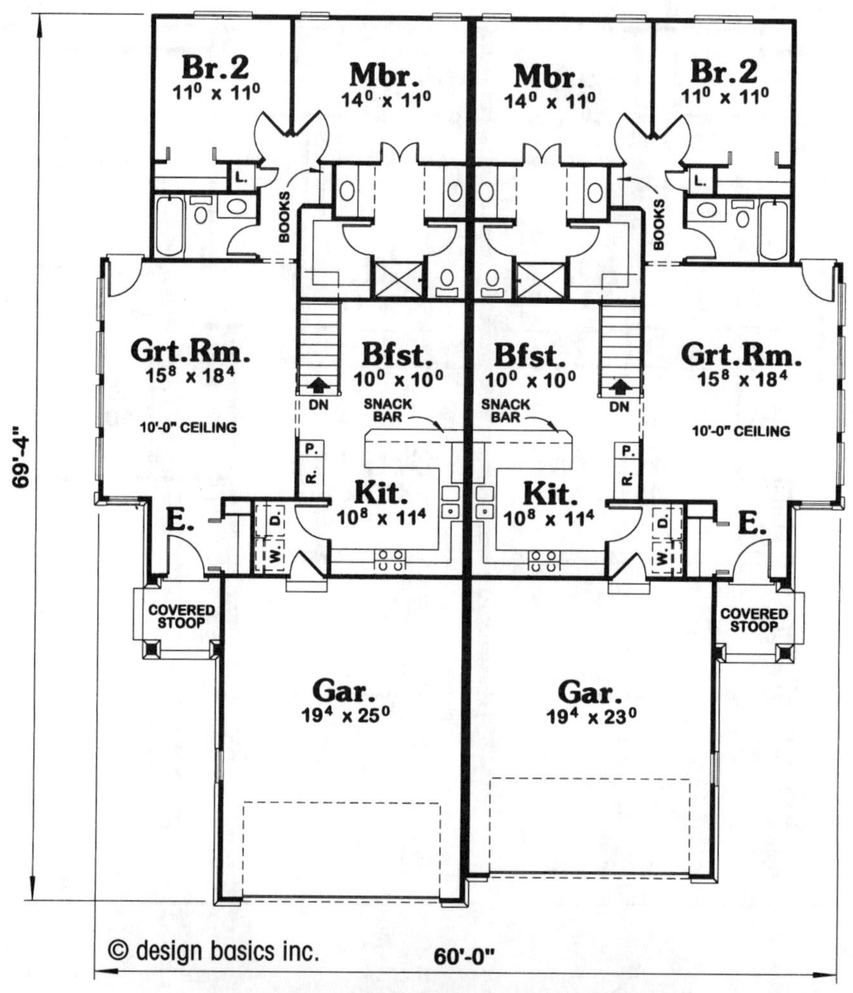

LEFT SIDE	RIGHT SIDE
Main 1218 sq. ft.	Main 1218 sq. ft.

- High quality, erasable, reproducible vellums
- Shipped via 2nd day air within the continental U.S.

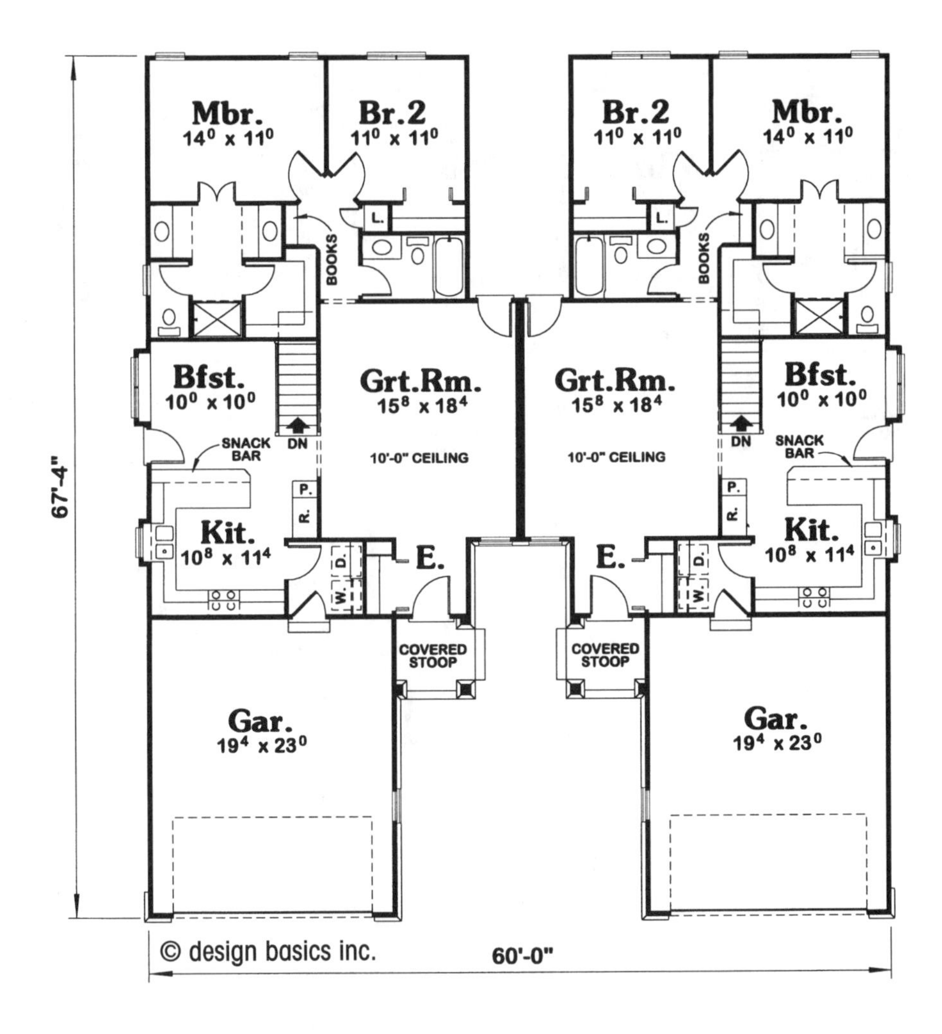

LEFT SIDE	RIGHT SIDE
Main 1218 sq. ft.	Main 1218 sq. ft.

ORDER DIRECT
:00-6:00 Mon.-Fri. CST
300-947-PLAN

PRICE CODE

9F 8174 2X

- High quality, erasable, reproducible vellums
- Shipped via 2nd day air within the continental U.S.

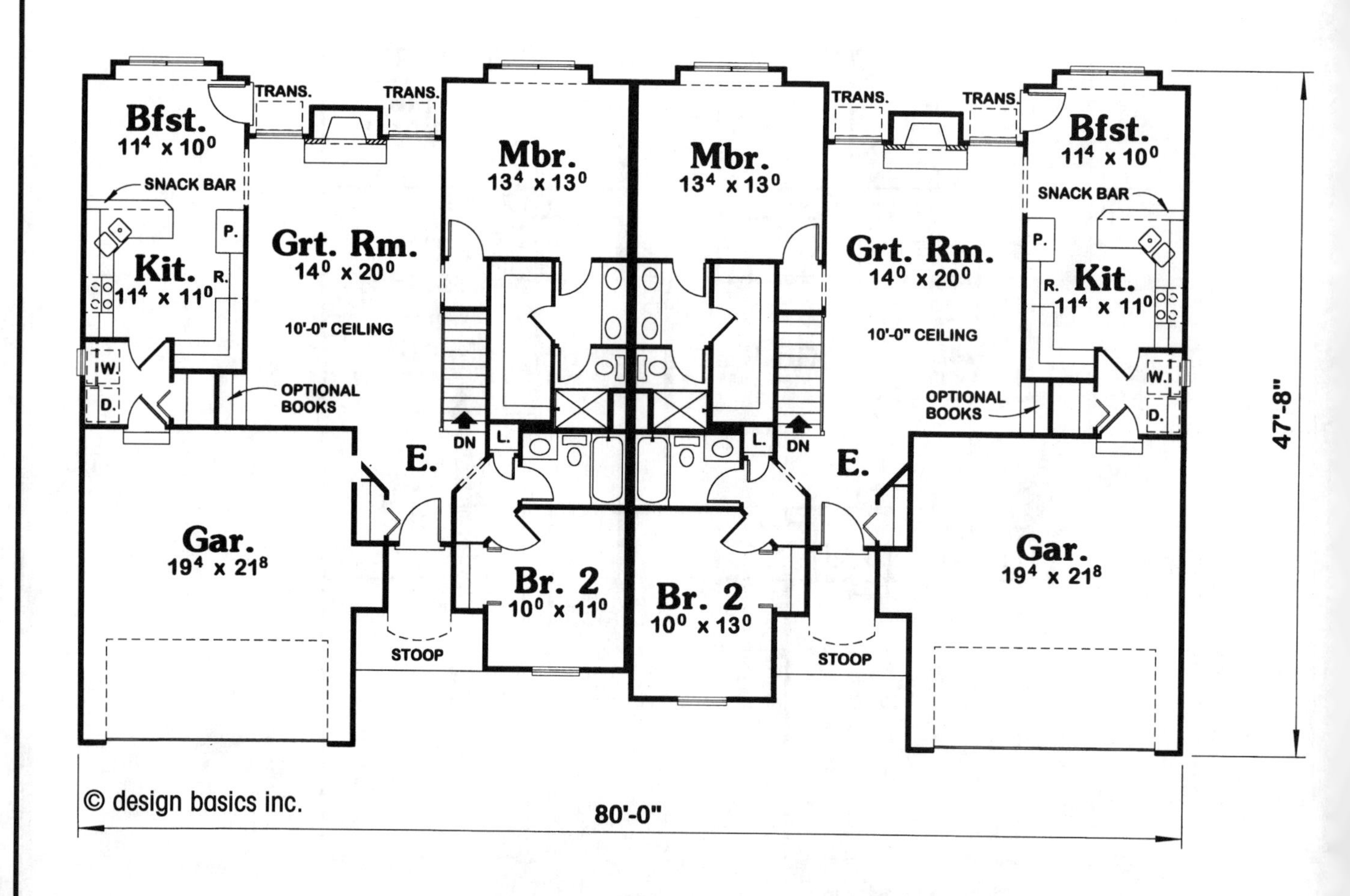

PRICE CODE

F 4623 2x

- High quality, erasable, reproducible vellums
- Shipped via 2nd day air within the continental U.S.

Gold Seal HOME PLANS™

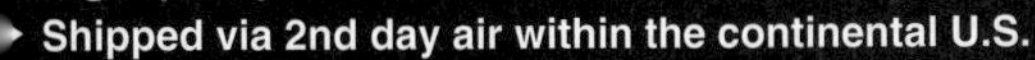

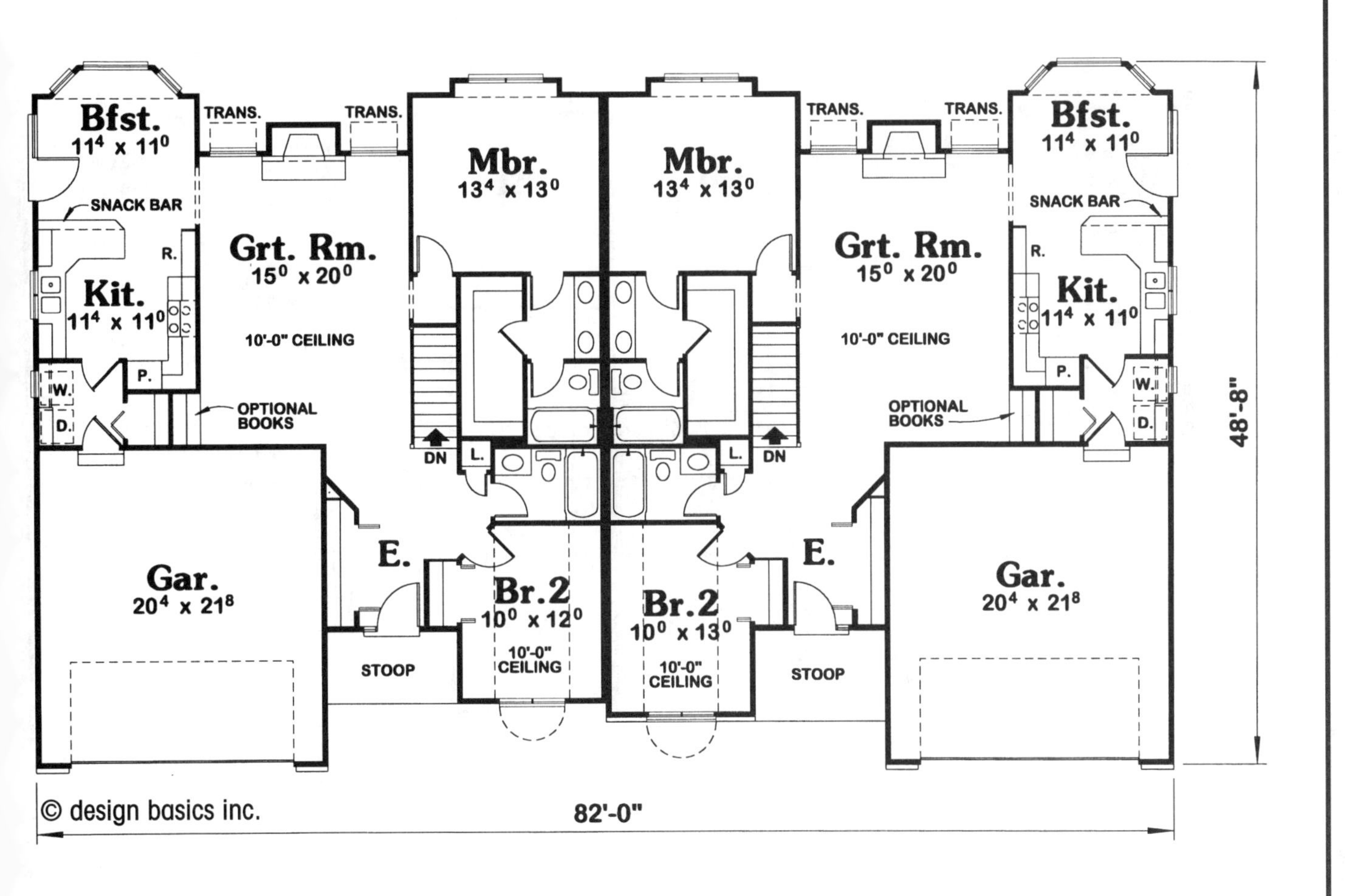

LEFT SIDE	RIGHT SIDE
Main 1242 sq. ft.	Main 1253 sq. ft.

PRICE CODE

9F 4620 2x

- High quality, erasable, reproducible vellums
- Shipped via 2nd day air within the continental U.S.

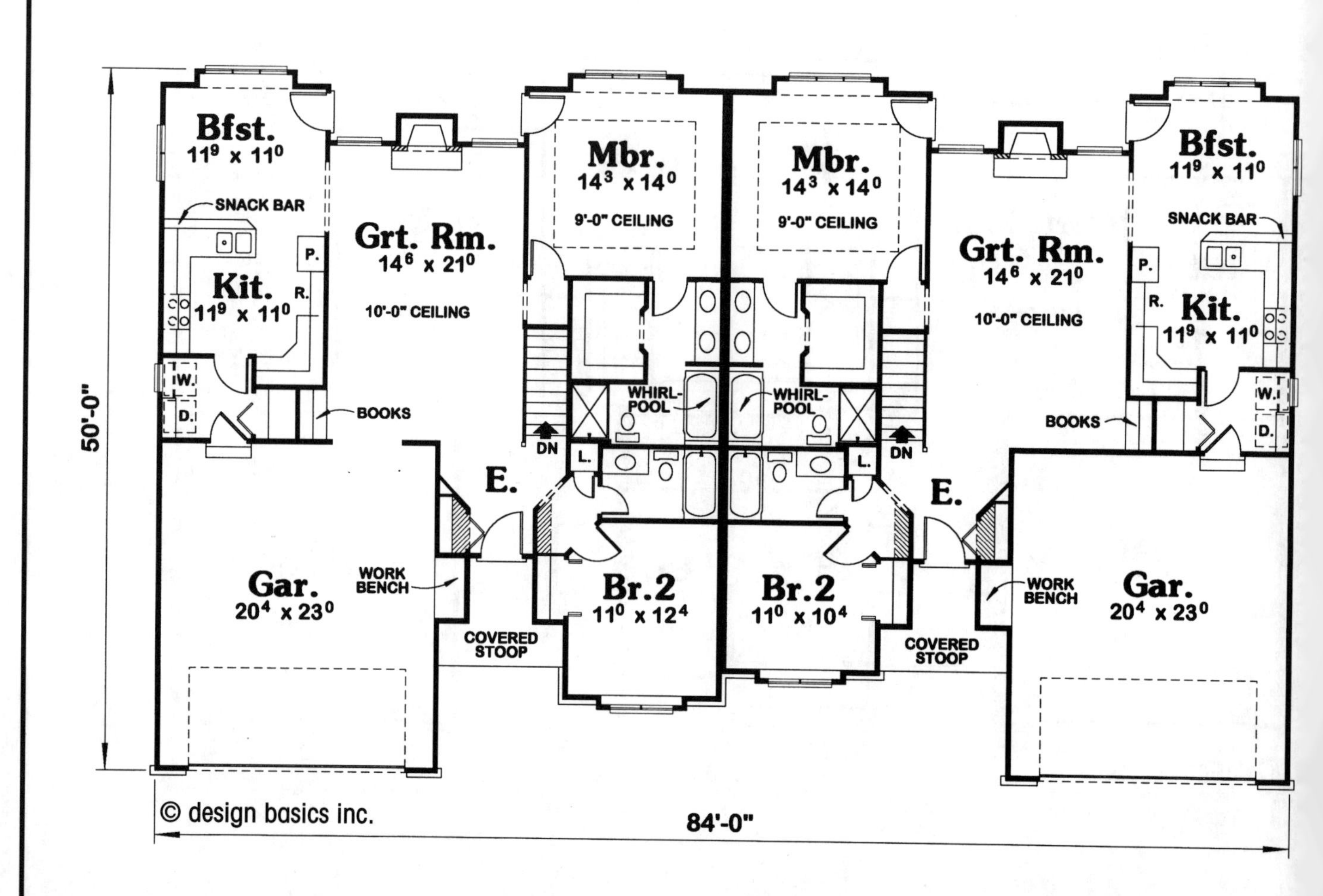

LEFT SIDE	RIGHT SIDE
Main 1331 sq. ft.	Main 1308 sq. ft.

PRICE CODE

F 4625 2x

- High quality, erasable, reproducible vellums
- Shipped via 2nd day air within the continental U.S.

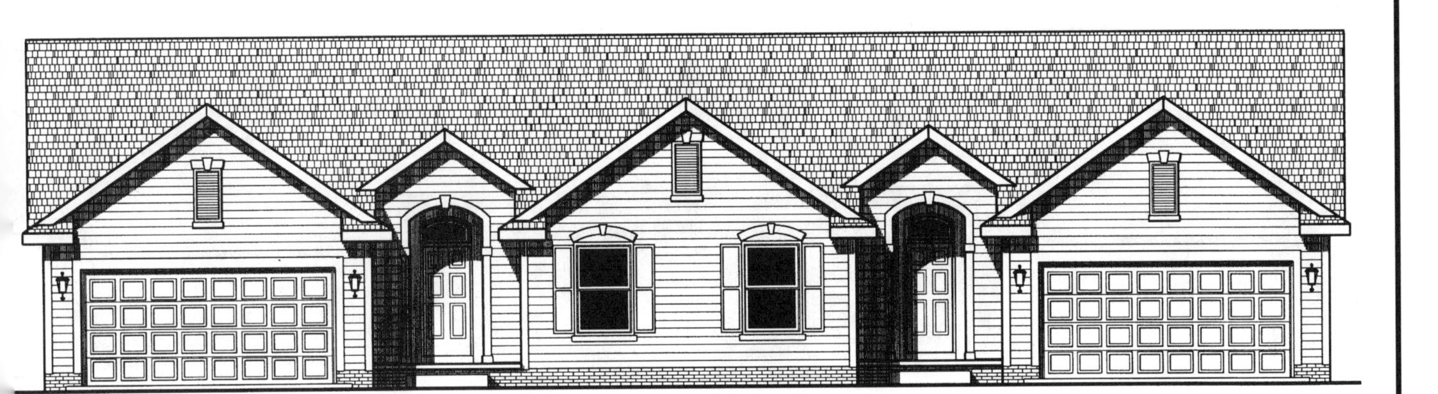

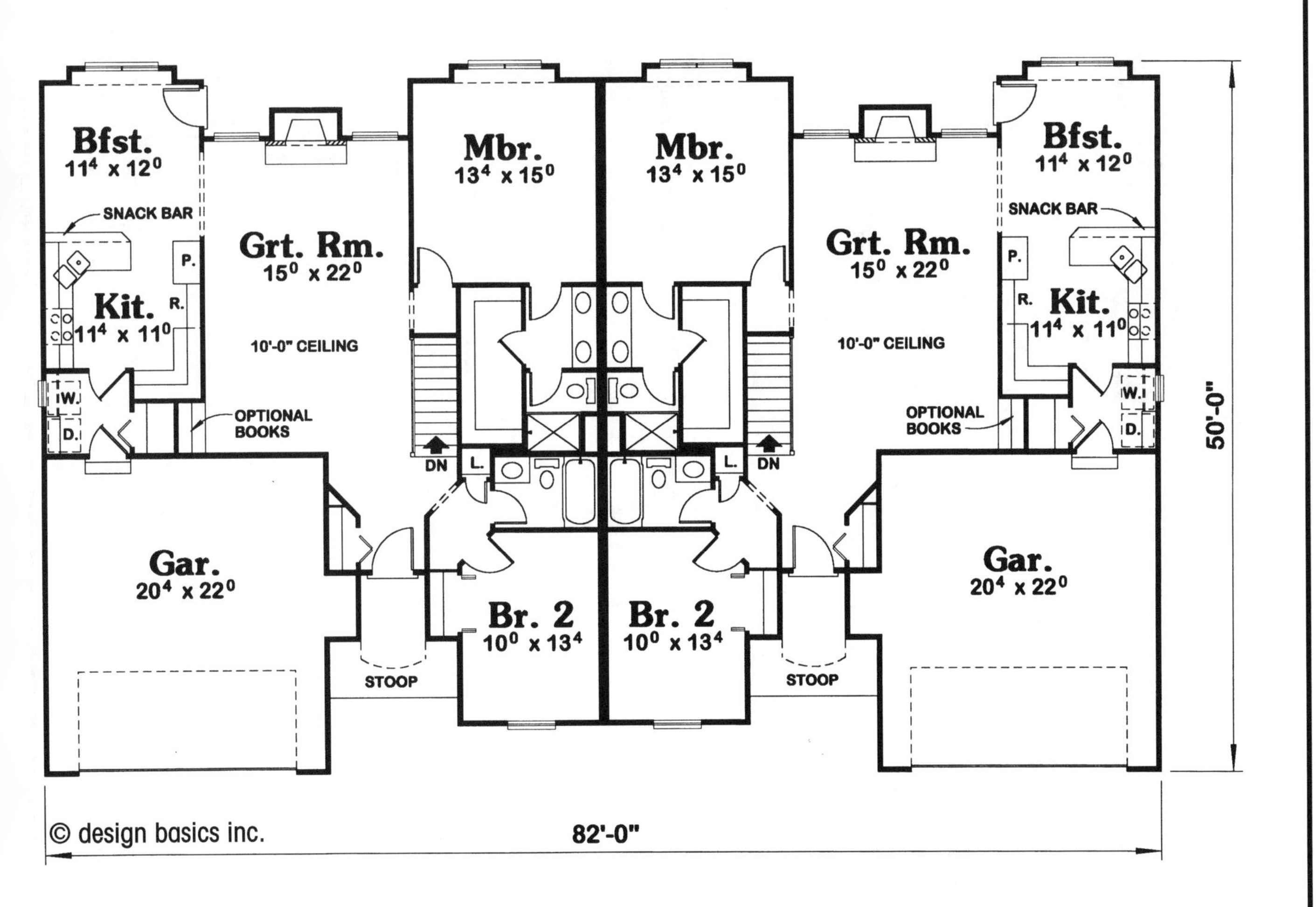

LEFT SIDE	RIGHT SIDE
Main 1344 sq. ft.	Main 1344 sq. ft.

PRICE CODE

9F 4629 2x

- High quality, erasable, reproducible vellums
- Shipped via 2nd day air within the continental U.S.

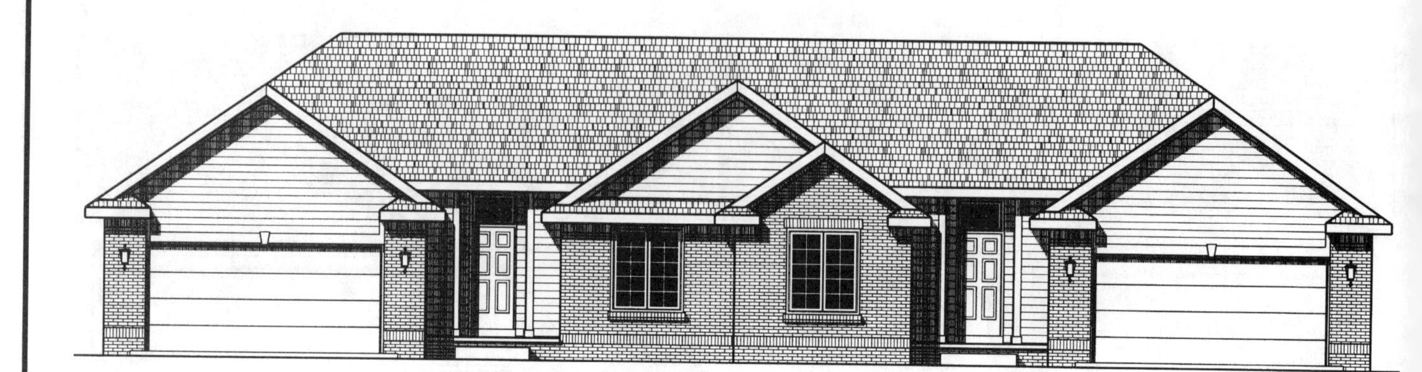

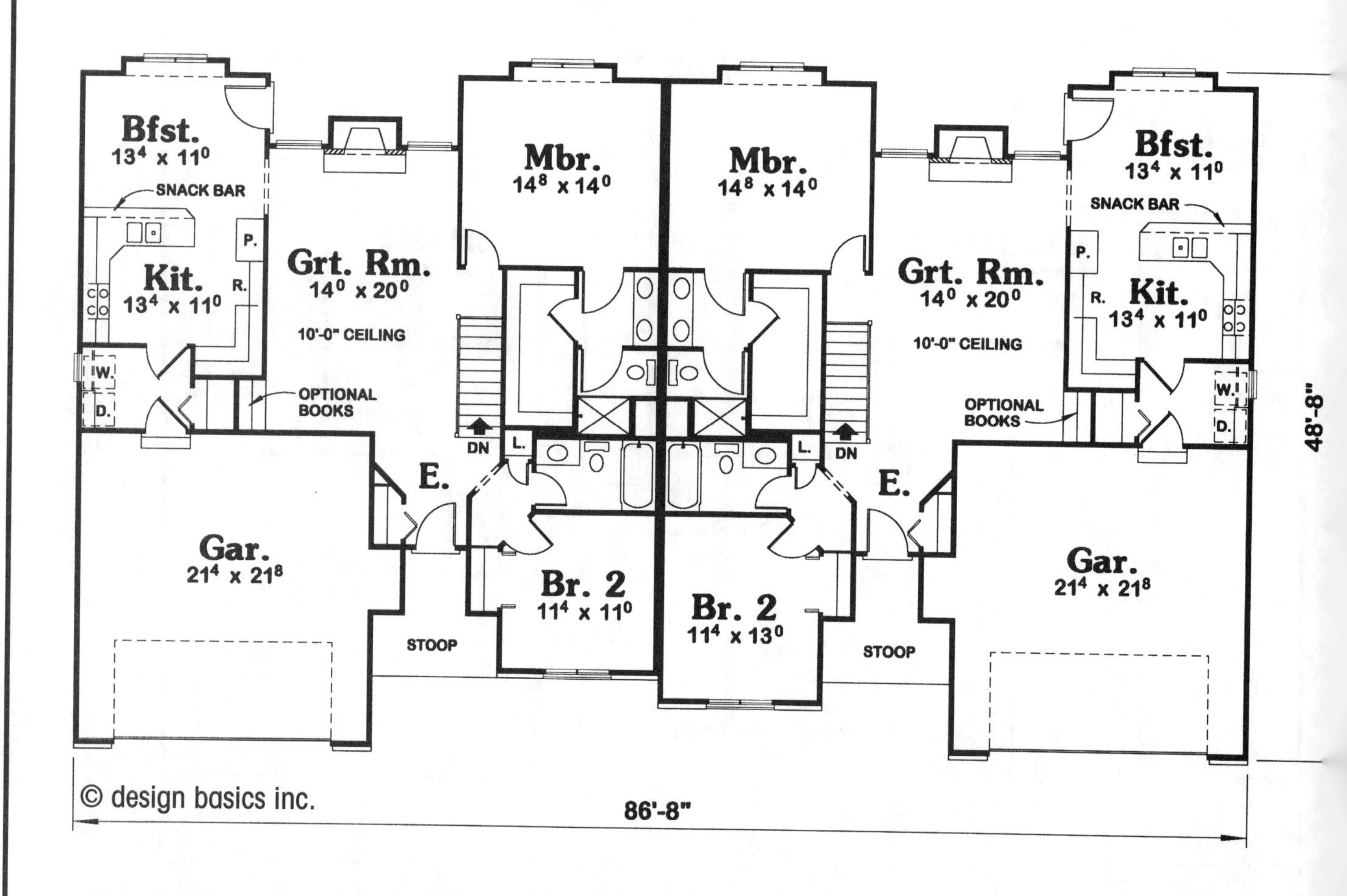

LEFT SIDE		RIGHT SIDE	
Main	1346 sq. ft.	Main	1370 sq. ft.

PRICE CODE

F 4618 2x

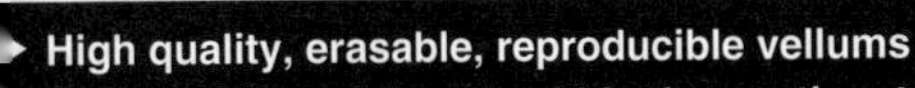

- High quality, erasable, reproducible vellums
- Shipped via 2nd day air within the continental U.S.

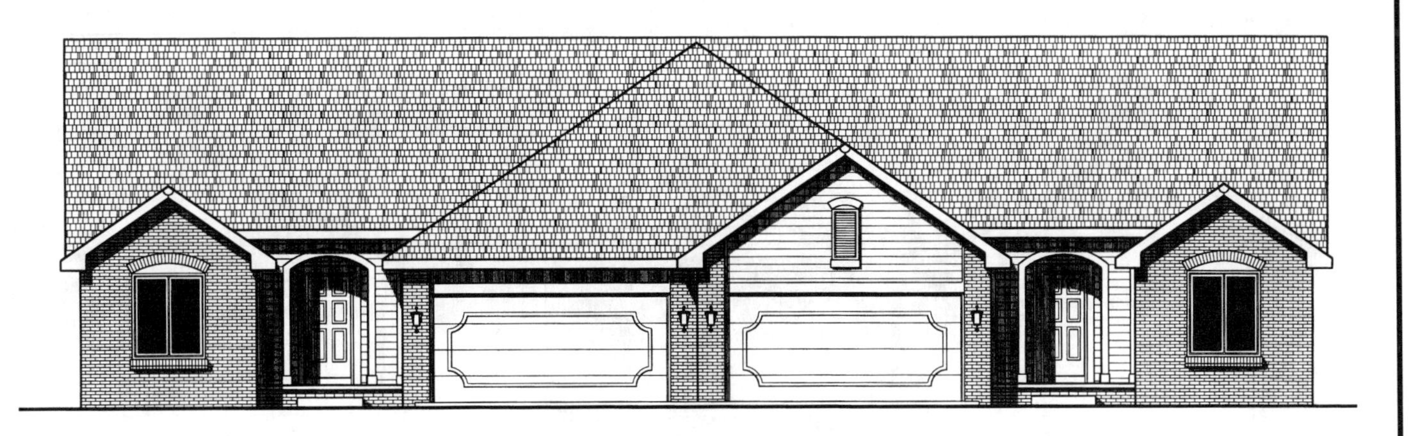

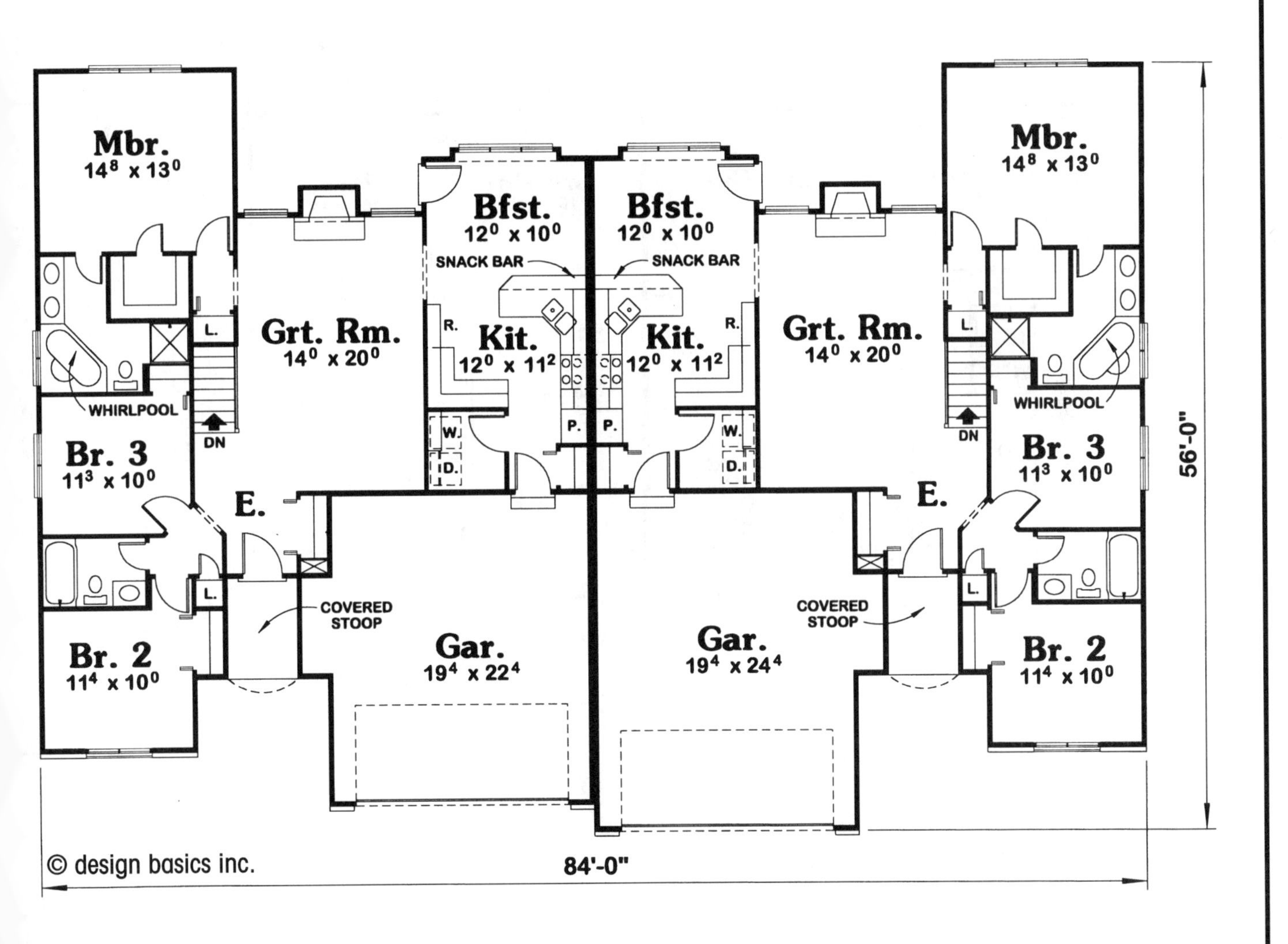

LEFT SIDE	RIGHT SIDE
Main 1392 sq. ft.	Main 1392 sq. ft.

PRICE CODE

9F 4631 2x

- High quality, erasable, reproducible vellums
- Shipped via 2nd day air within the continental U.S.

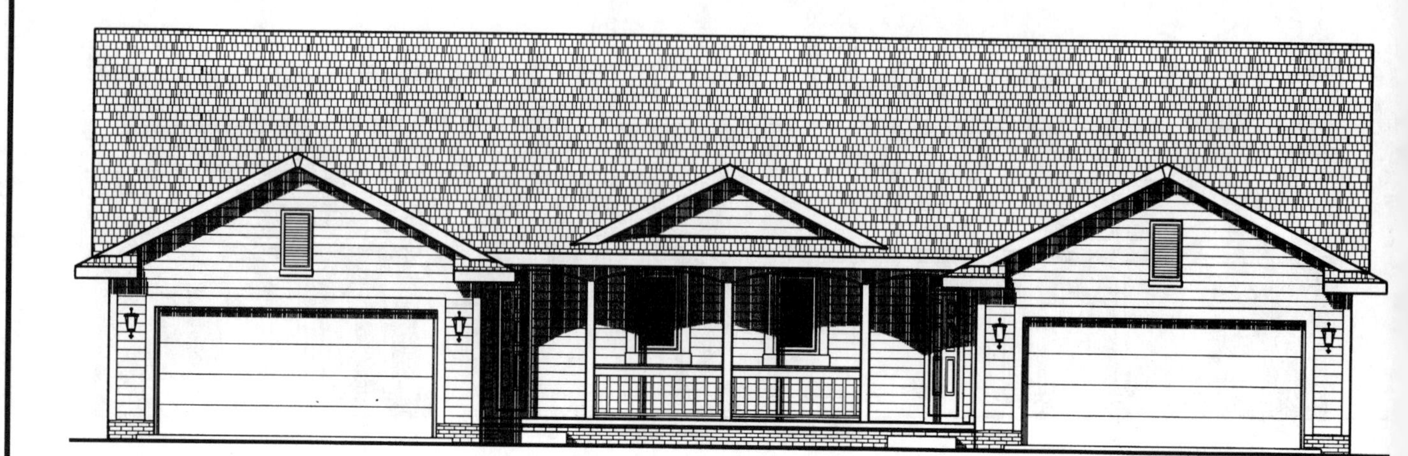

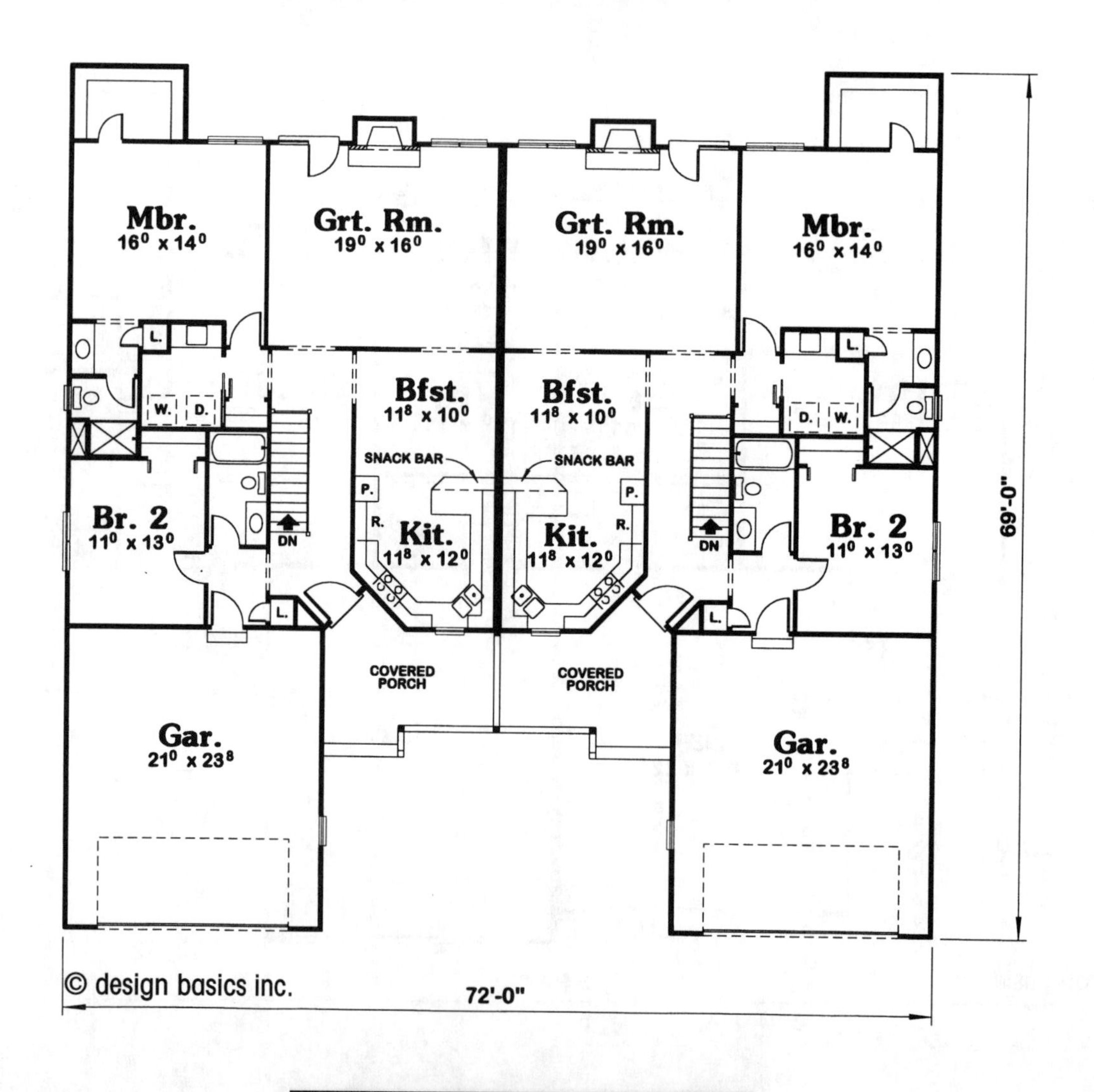

LEFT SIDE	RIGHT SIDE
Main 1455 sq. ft.	Main 1455 sq. ft.

PRICE CODE

F 4632 2x

- High quality, erasable, reproducible vellums
- Shipped via 2nd day air within the continental U.S.

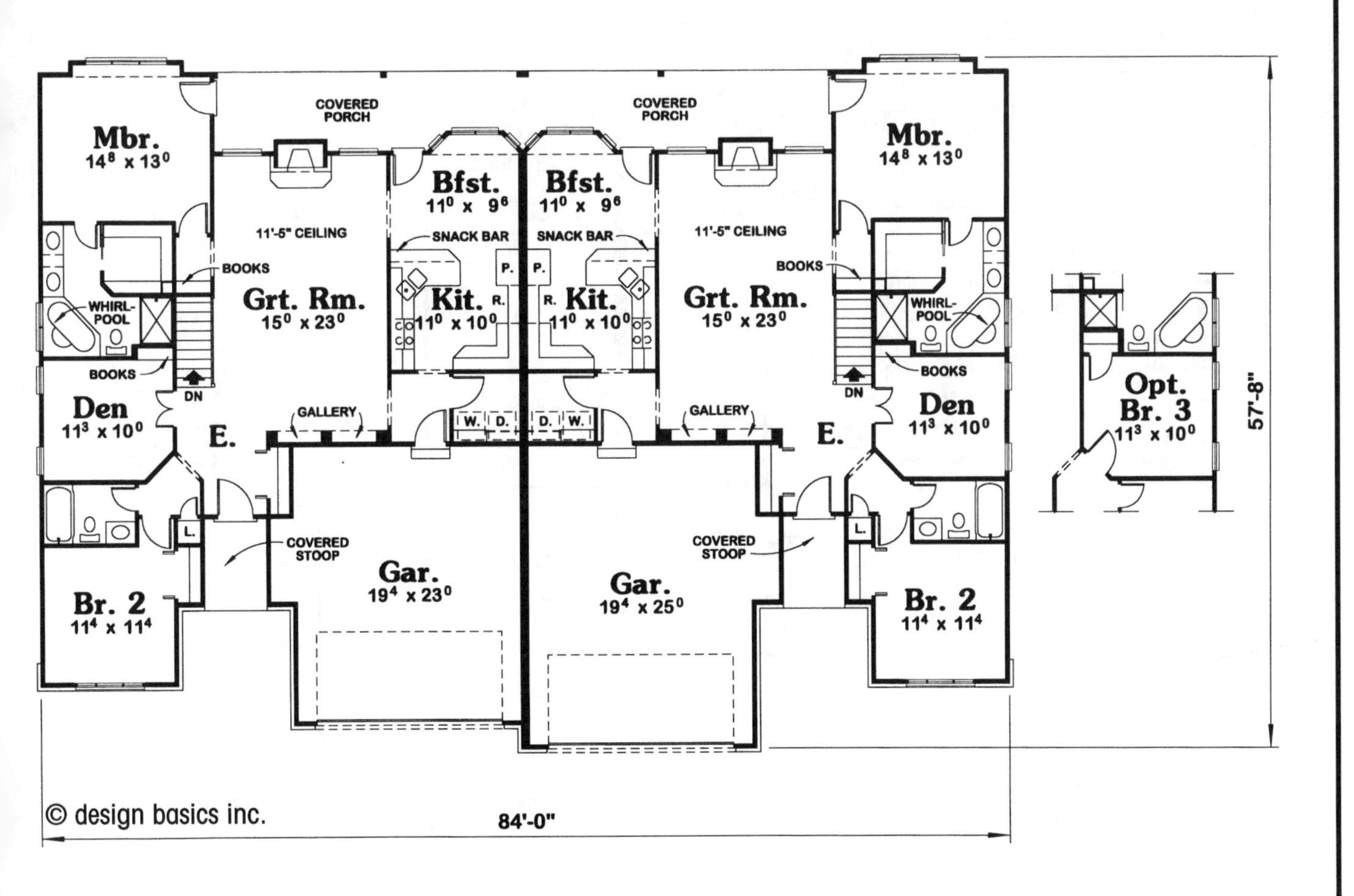

LEFT SIDE	RIGHT SIDE
Main 1478 sq. ft.	Main 1478 sq. ft.

9F 4619

PRICE CODE **2x**

- High quality, erasable, reproducible vellums
- Shipped via 2nd day air within the continental U.S.

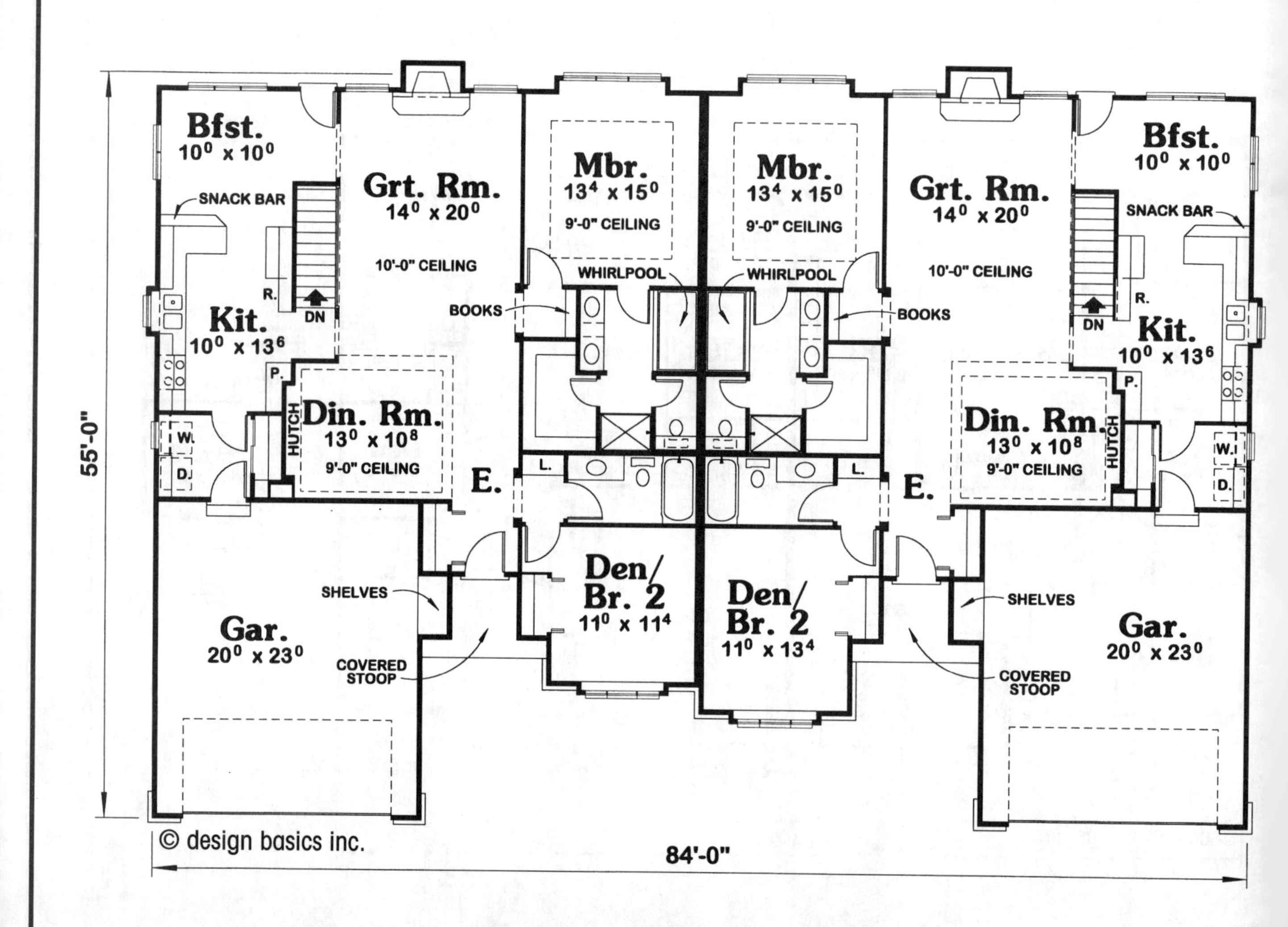

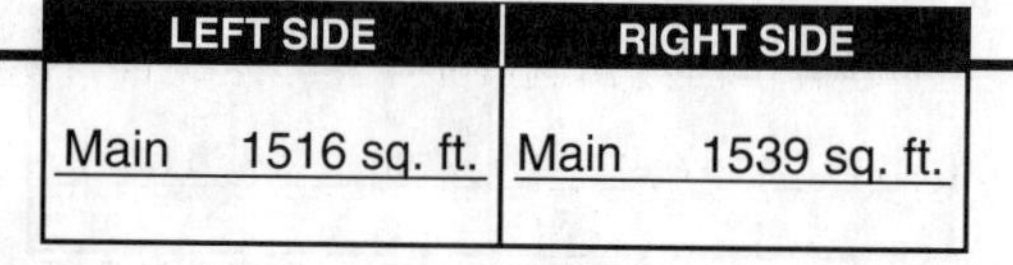

LEFT SIDE	RIGHT SIDE
Main 1516 sq. ft.	Main 1539 sq. ft.

F 4616 PRICE CODE 2x

- High quality, erasable, reproducible vellums
- Shipped via 2nd day air within the continental U.S.

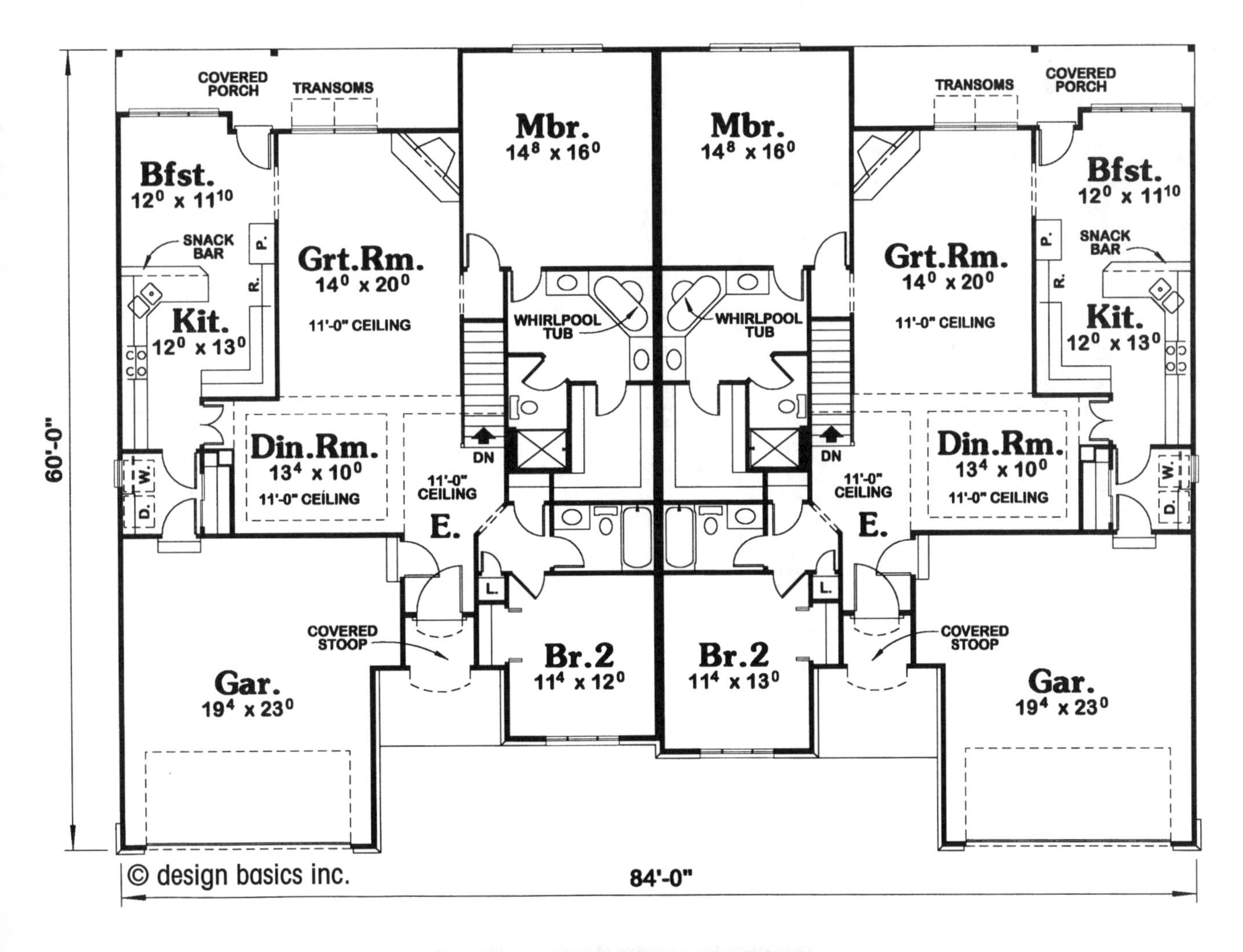

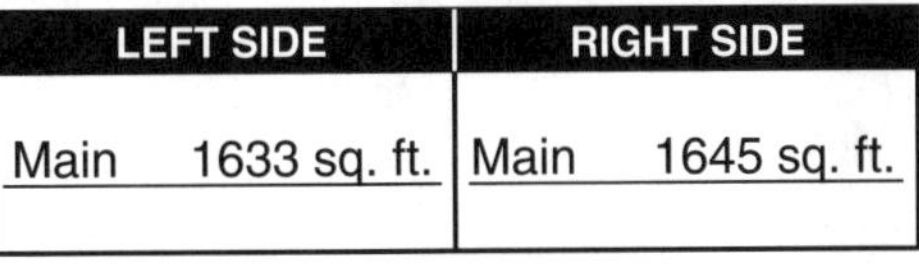

LEFT SIDE	RIGHT SIDE
Main 1633 sq. ft.	Main 1645 sq. ft.

9F 8175

PRICE CODE **2x**

- High quality, erasable, reproducible vellums
- Shipped via 2nd day air within the continental U.S.

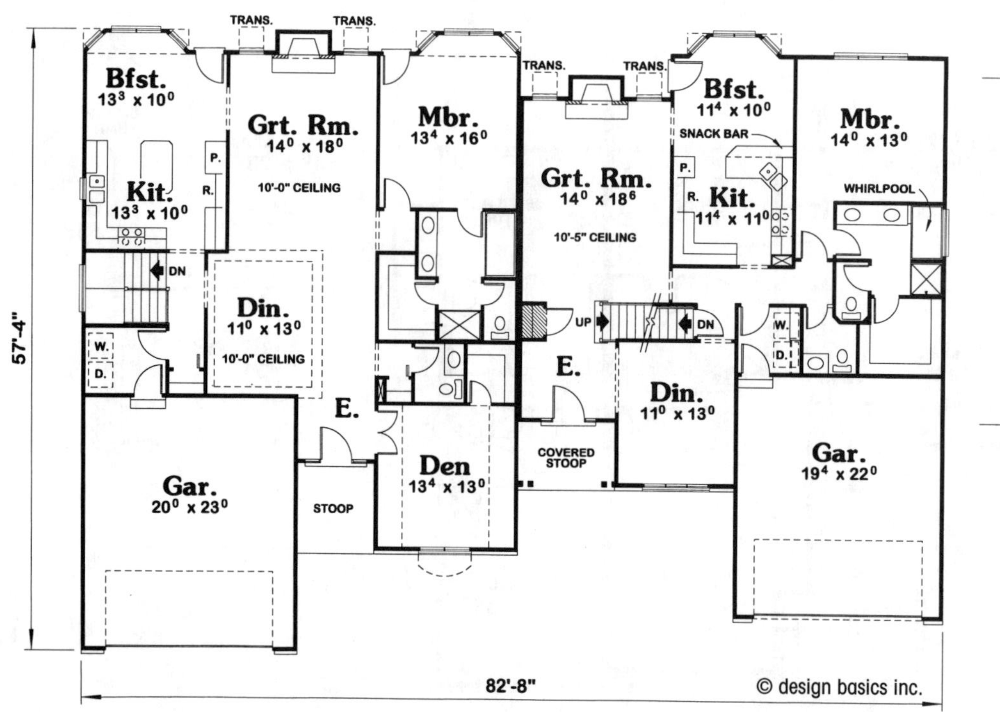

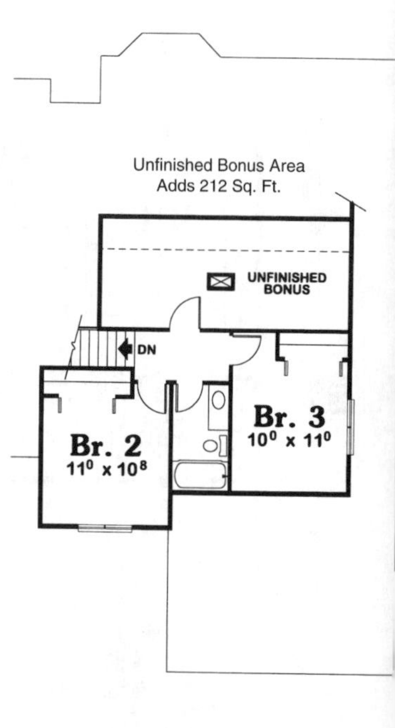

LEFT SIDE	RIGHT SIDE
Main 1621 sq. ft.	Main 1324 sq. ft. Second 391 sq. ft. Total 1715 sq. ft.

PRICE CODE

F 4633 2x

▶ High quality, erasable, reproducible vellums
▶ Shipped via 2nd day air within the continental U.S.

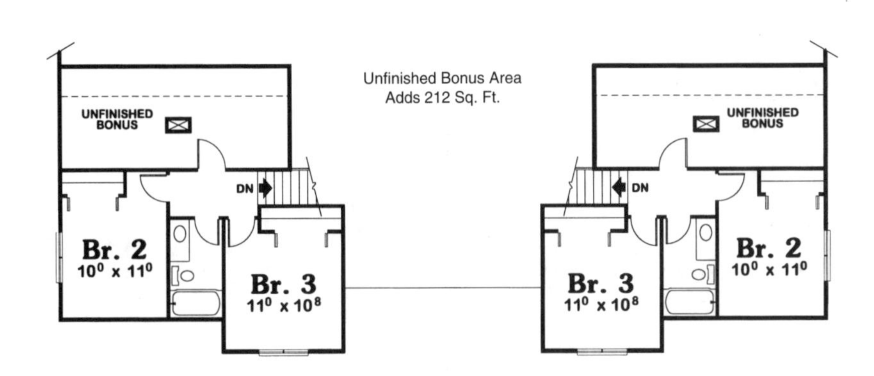

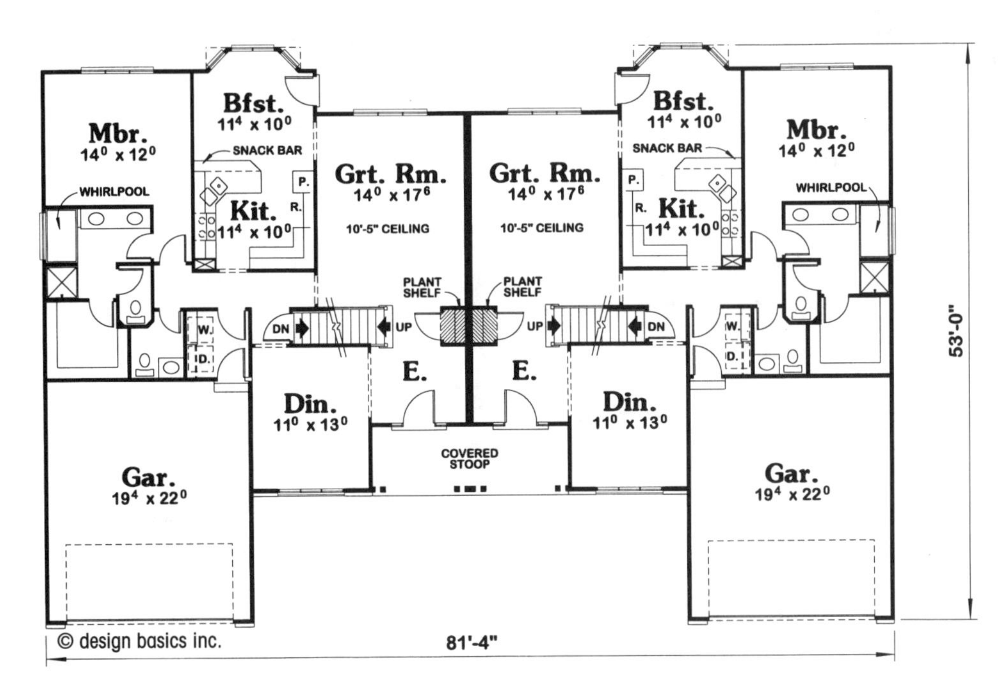

LEFT SIDE		RIGHT SIDE	
Main	1284 sq. ft.	Main	1284 sq. ft.
Second	391 sq. ft.	Second	391 sq. ft.
Total	1675 sq. ft.	Total	1675 sq. ft.

PRICE CODE

9F 4627 2x

- High quality, erasable, reproducible vellums
- Shipped via 2nd day air within the continental U.S.

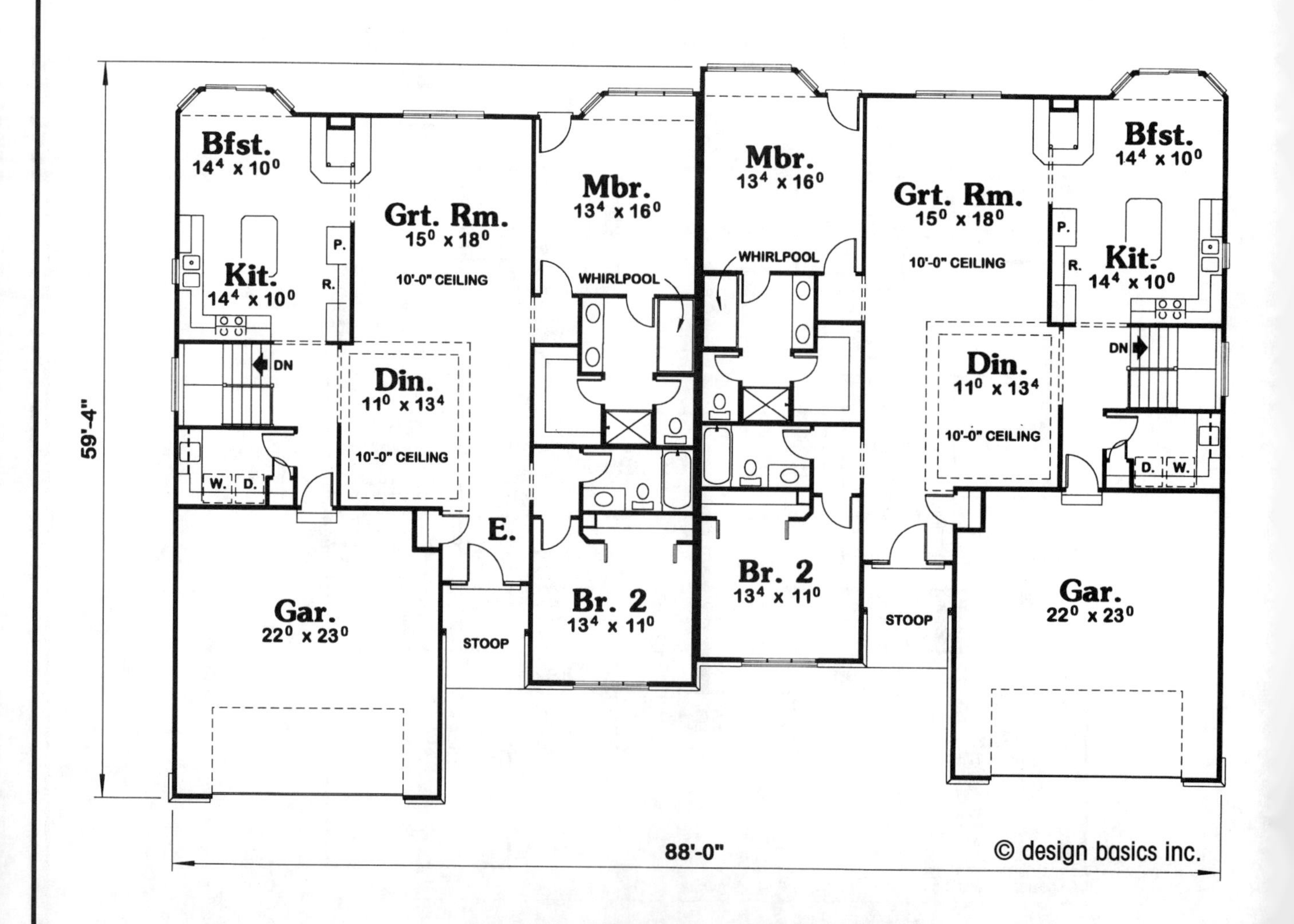

LEFT SIDE	RIGHT SIDE
Main 1685 sq. ft.	Main 1685 sq. ft.

PRICE CODE

4622 2x

High quality, erasable, reproducible vellums
Shipped via 2nd day air within the continental U.S.

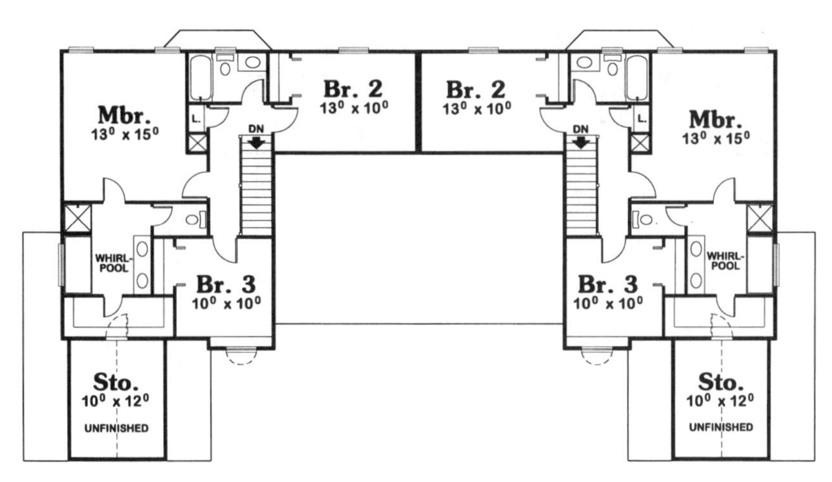

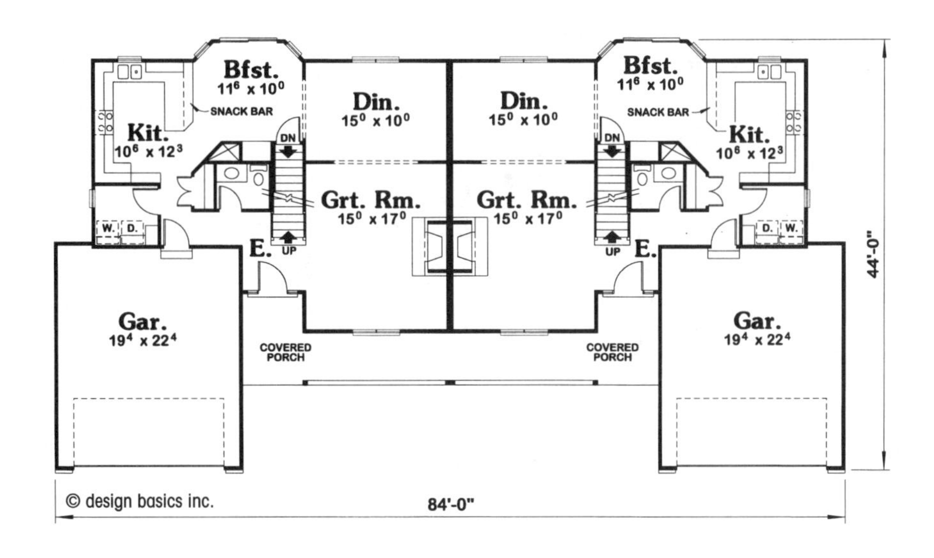

LEFT SIDE		RIGHT SIDE	
Main	918 sq. ft.	Main	918 sq. ft.
Second	802 sq. ft.	Second	802 sq. ft.
Total	1720 sq. ft.	Total	1720 sq. ft.

PRICE CODE

9F 4617 2x

- High quality, erasable, reproducible vellums
- Shipped via 2nd day air within the continental U.S.

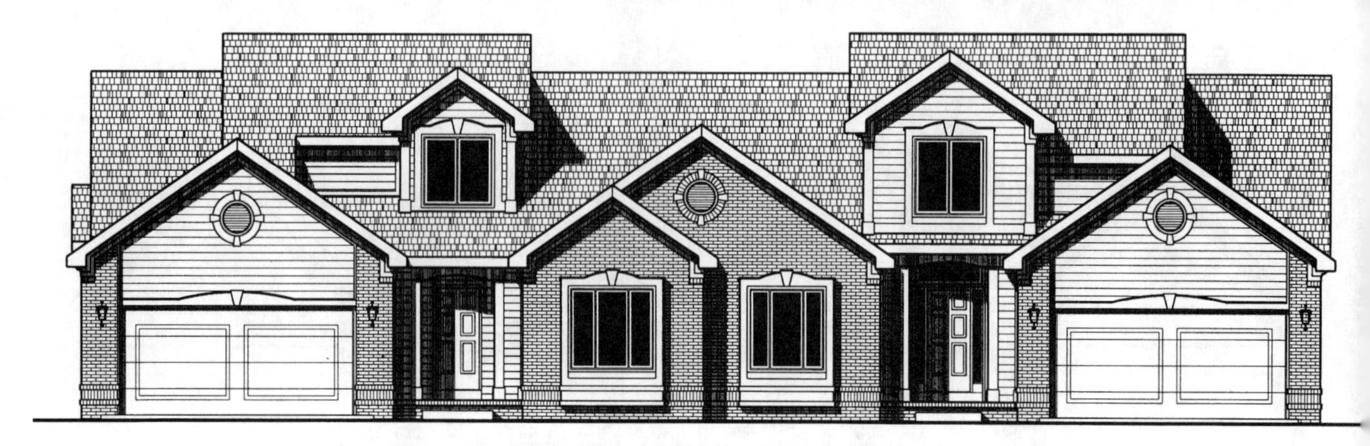

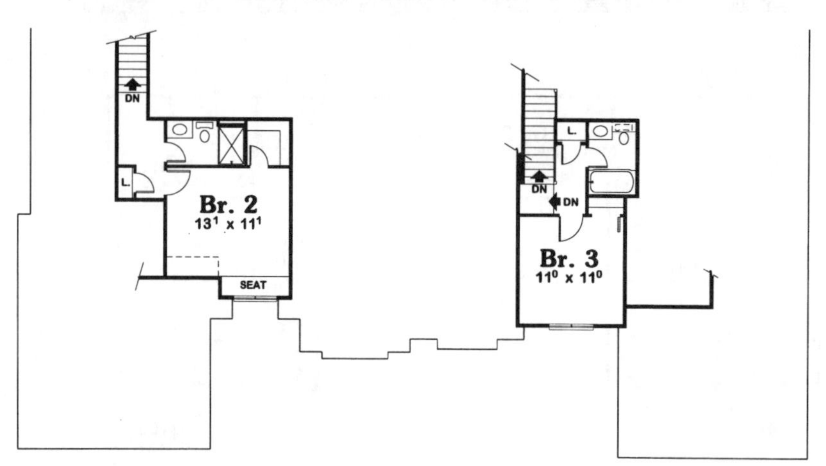

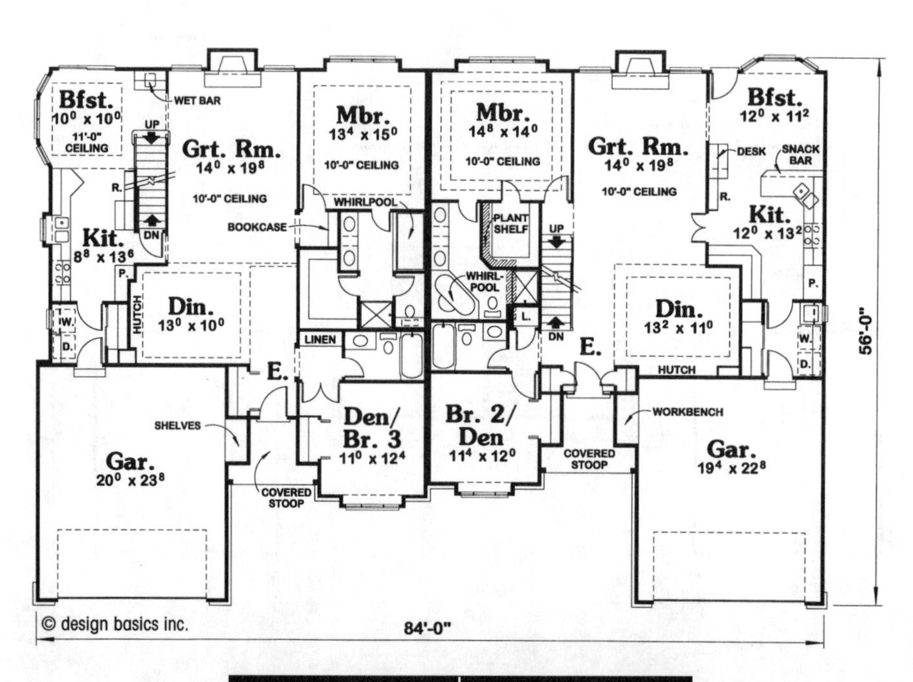

LEFT SIDE		RIGHT SIDE	
Main	1486 sq. ft.	Main	1517 sq. ft.
Second	286 sq. ft.	Second	234 sq. ft.
Total	1772 sq. ft.	Total	1751 sq. ft.

PRICE CODE

F 4624 3x

High quality, erasable, reproducible vellums
Shipped via 2nd day air within the continental U.S.

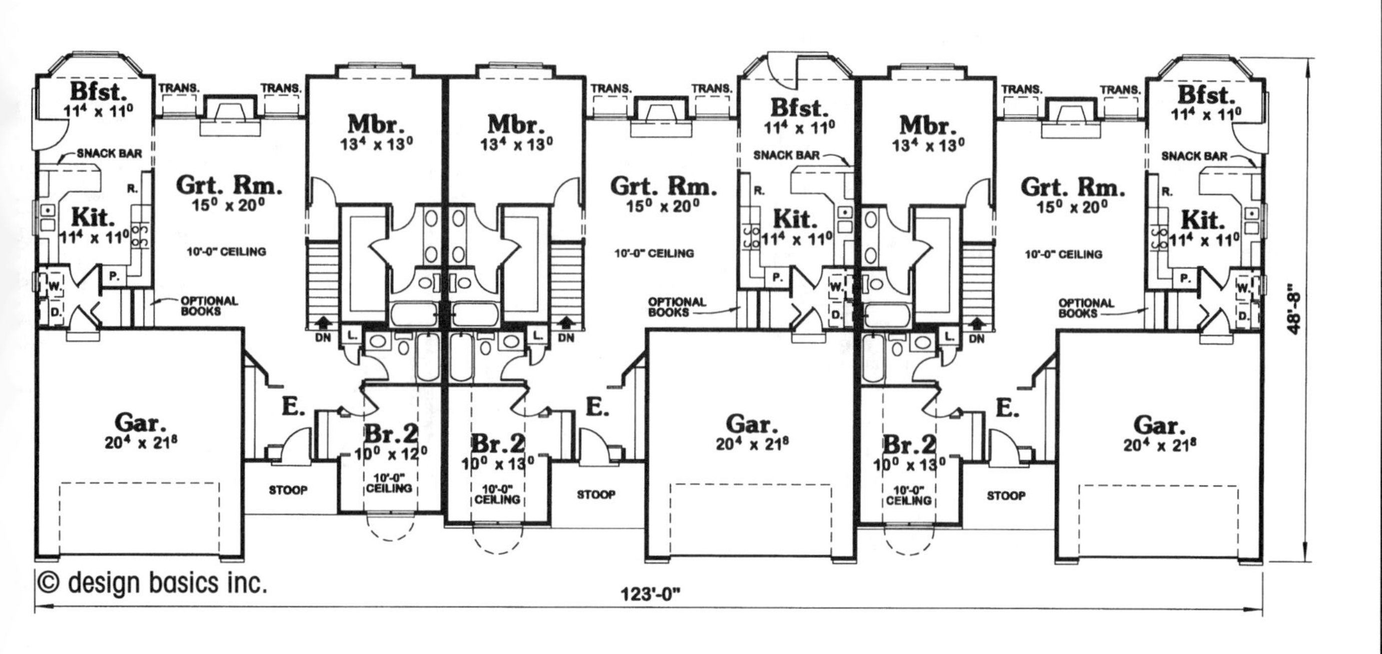

LEFT SIDE	MIDDLE	RIGHT SIDE
Main 1242 sq. ft.	Main 1253 sq. ft.	Main 1253 sq. ft.

ORDER DIRECT
-6:00 Mon.-Fri. CST
0-947-PLAN

PRICE CODE

9F 5283 3x

- High quality, erasable, reproducible vellums
- Shipped via 2nd day air within the continental U.S.

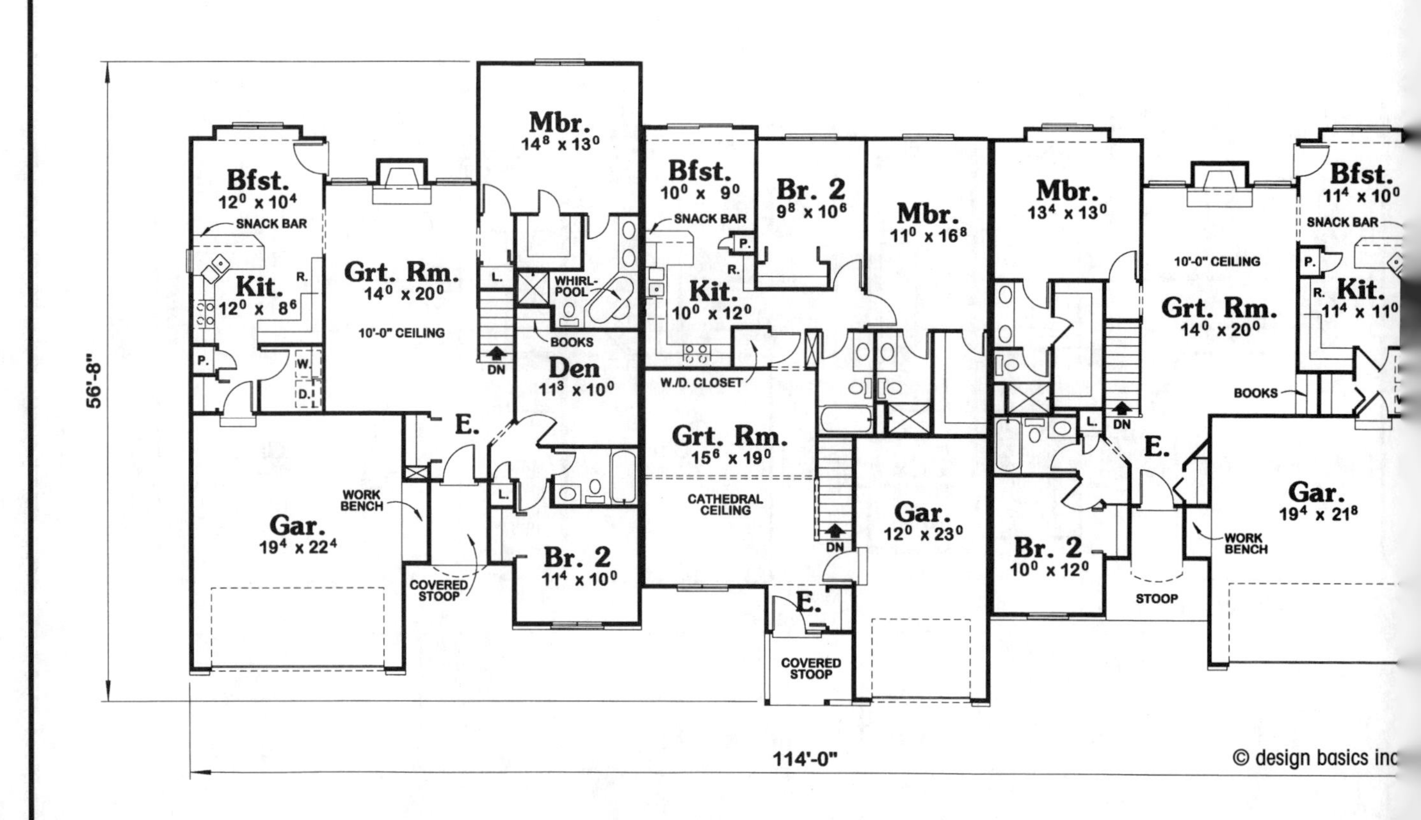

LEFT SIDE	MIDDLE	RIGHT SIDE
Main 1393 sq. ft.	Main 1160 sq. ft.	Main 1223 sq. ft.

PRICE CODE

- High quality, erasable, reproducible vellums
- Shipped via 2nd day air within the continental U.S.

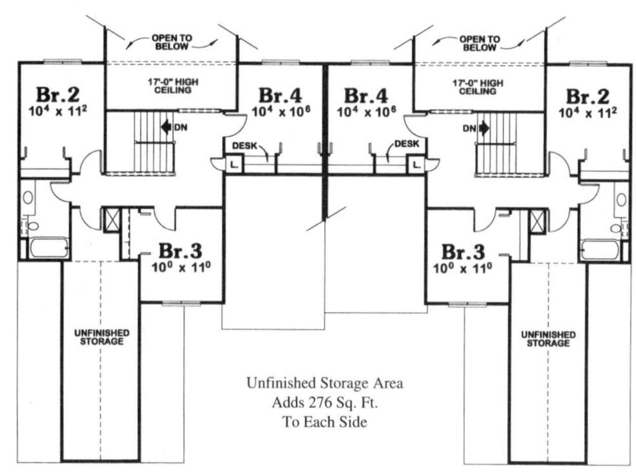

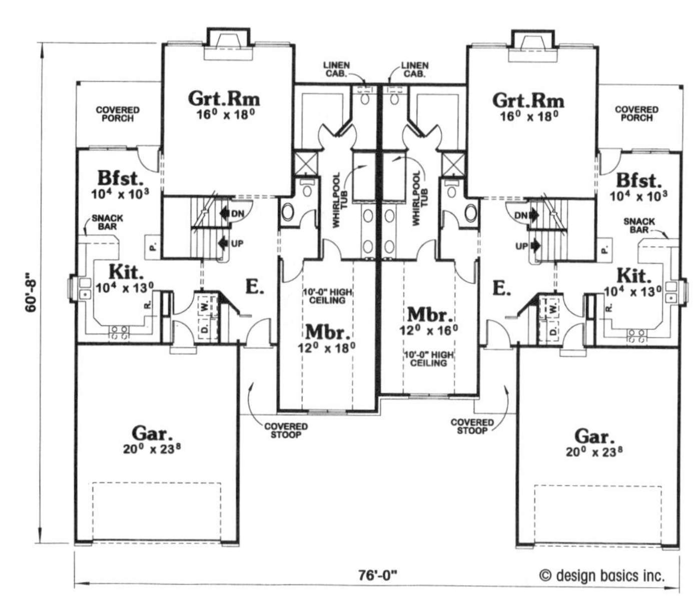

LEFT SIDE		RIGHT SIDE	
Main	1308 sq. ft.	Main	1284 sq. ft.
Second	645 sq. ft.	Second	645 sq. ft.
Total	1953 sq. ft.	Total	1929 sq. ft.

PRICE CODE

9F 4628 2x

- High quality, erasable, reproducible vellums
- Shipped via 2nd day air within the continental U.S.

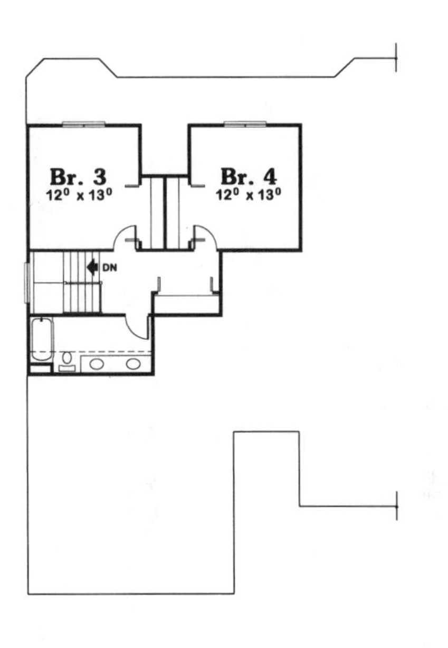

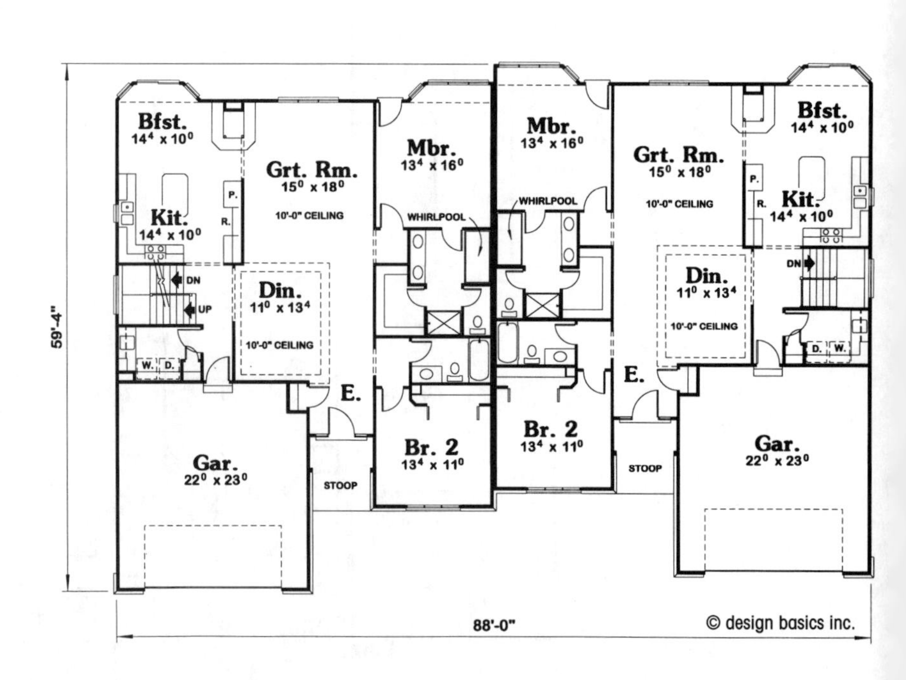

LEFT SIDE	RIGHT SIDE
Main 1685 sq. ft. Second 576 sq. ft. Total 2261 sq. ft.	Main 1685 sq. ft.

ORDER DIRECT
7:00-6:00 Mon.-Fri. CST
800-947-PLAN

PRICE CODE

F 4012 2x

- High quality, erasable, reproducible vellums
- Shipped via 2nd day air within the continental U.S.

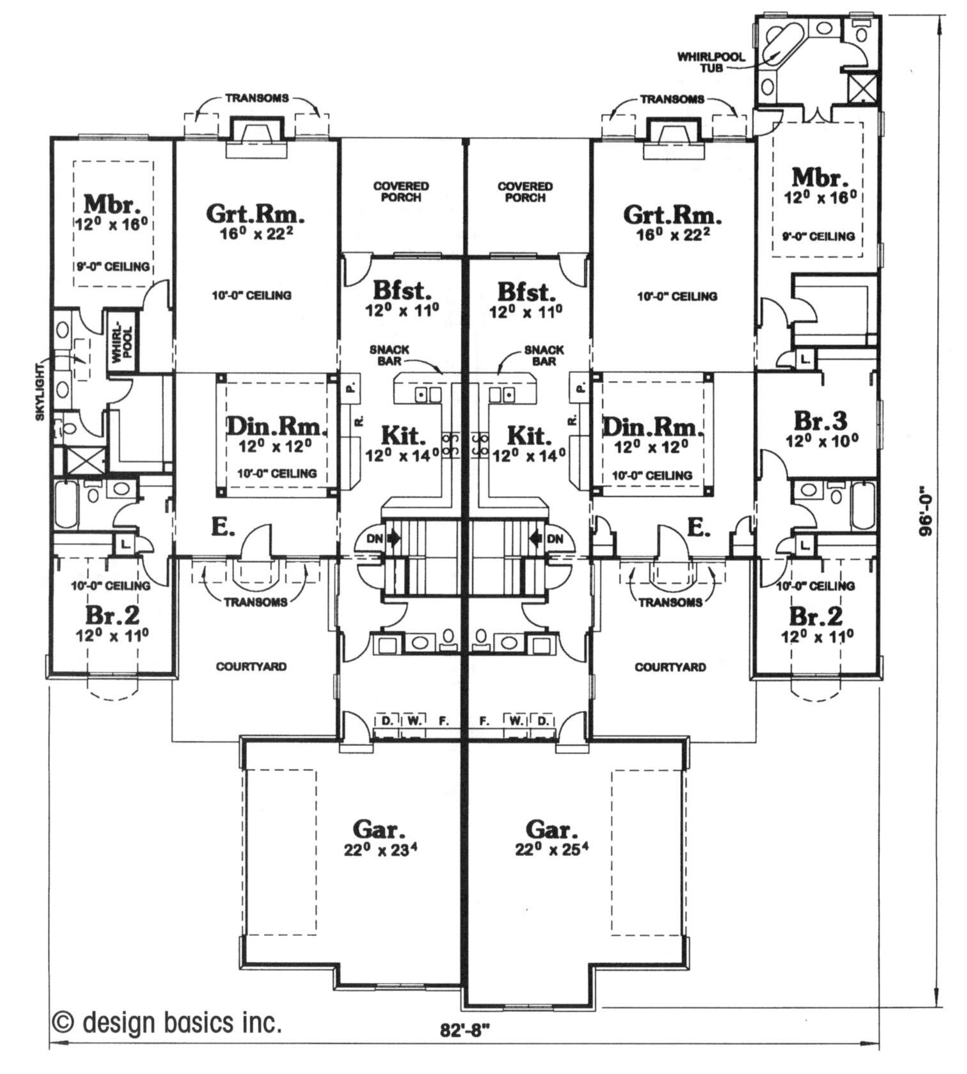

LEFT SIDE	RIGHT SIDE
Main 1908 sq. ft.	Main 2060 sq. ft.

PRICE CODE

9F 4621 4x

- High quality, erasable, reproducible vellums
- Shipped via 2nd day air within the continental U.S.

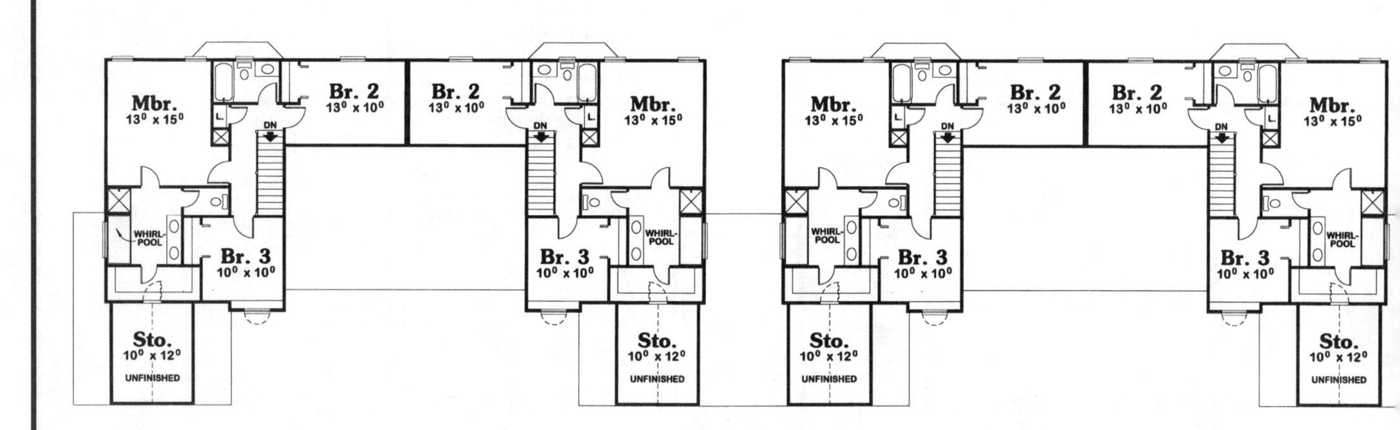

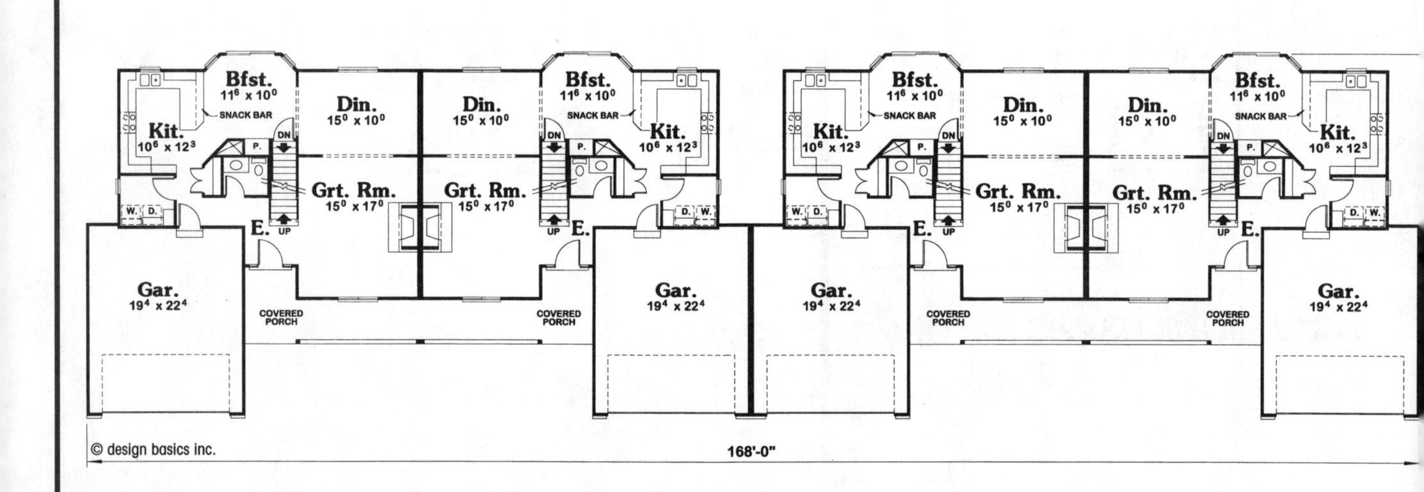

LEFT		LEFT CENTER		RIGHT CENTER		RIGHT	
Main	918 sq. ft.	Main	918 sq. ft.	Main	918 sq. ft.	Main	918 sq. ft.
Second	802 sq. ft.	Second	802 sq. ft.	Second	802 sq. ft.	Second	802 sq. ft.
Total	1720 sq. ft.	Total	1720 sq. ft.	Total	1720 sq. ft.	Total	1720 sq. ft.

Quality Plans ~ Dependable Designs

Design Basics home plans come to you on high-quality, erasable, reproducible vellums and include the following

1. COVER PAGE. Each Design Basics home plan features the rendered elevation and informative reference sections including: general notes and desig criteria*; abbreviations; and symbols for your Design Basics plan. 2. ELEVATIONS. Fully detailed showing materials used, and drafted at 1/4" scale fo the front and 1/8" scale for the rear and sides. An aerial view of the roof is provided showing all hips, valleys and ridges. For a more thorough understanding a Roof Construction Package (see pg. 158) is available showing roof framing and dimensional layouts. Additionally, fascia and railing sections are provide when necessary. 3. FOUNDATIONS. Drafted at 1/4" scale. Block foundations and basements are standard. We also show the suggested HVAC layou structural information*, steel beam and pole locations and the direction and spacing of the floor system above. 4. MAIN LEVEL FLOOR PLAN. 1/4 scale. Fully dimensioned from stud to stud for ease of framing. 2"x4" walls are standard. The detailed drawings include such things as ceiling treatment structural header locations*, flooring materials, framing layout, supply air locations and kitchen layout.

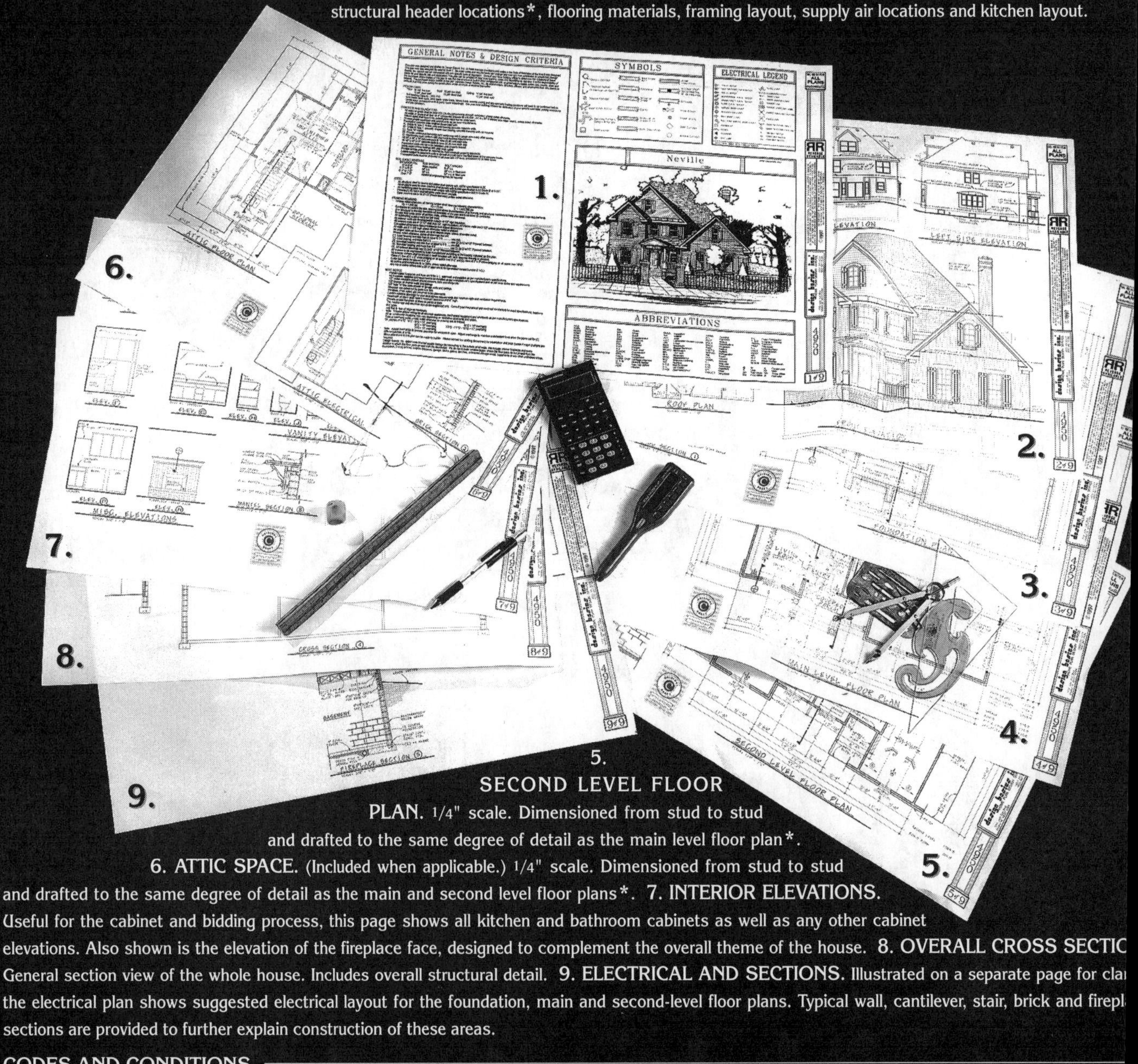

5. SECOND LEVEL FLOOR PLAN. 1/4" scale. Dimensioned from stud to stud and drafted to the same degree of detail as the main level floor plan*. 6. ATTIC SPACE. (Included when applicable.) 1/4" scale. Dimensioned from stud to stud and drafted to the same degree of detail as the main and second level floor plans*. 7. INTERIOR ELEVATIONS. Useful for the cabinet and bidding process, this page shows all kitchen and bathroom cabinets as well as any other cabinet elevations. Also shown is the elevation of the fireplace face, designed to complement the overall theme of the house. 8. OVERALL CROSS SECTIC General section view of the whole house. Includes overall structural detail. 9. ELECTRICAL AND SECTIONS. Illustrated on a separate page for clai the electrical plan shows suggested electrical layout for the foundation, main and second-level floor plans. Typical wall, cantilever, stair, brick and firepl sections are provided to further explain construction of these areas.

CODES AND CONDITIONS

** Our plans are drafted to meet average codes and conditions in the state of Nebraska, at the time they are designed. Because codes and requirements can change may vary from jurisdiction to jurisdiction, Design Basics Inc. cannot warrant compliance with any specific code or regulation. All Design Basics plans can be adapte your local building codes and requirements. It is the responsibility of the purchaser and/or builder of each plan to see that the structure is built in strict compliance wit governing municipal codes (city, county, state and federal).*

ERASABLE VELLUMS. *Before making changes to your plan, PLEASE NOTE the following: ➻ To erase, you must use an electric eraser with a white #73 refill (we recommend a Eberhard Faber refill #75214.) ➻ Use a 2H graphite lead to re-draft. If you have any further questions, contact our Customer Support Specialists at (800) 947-7526.*

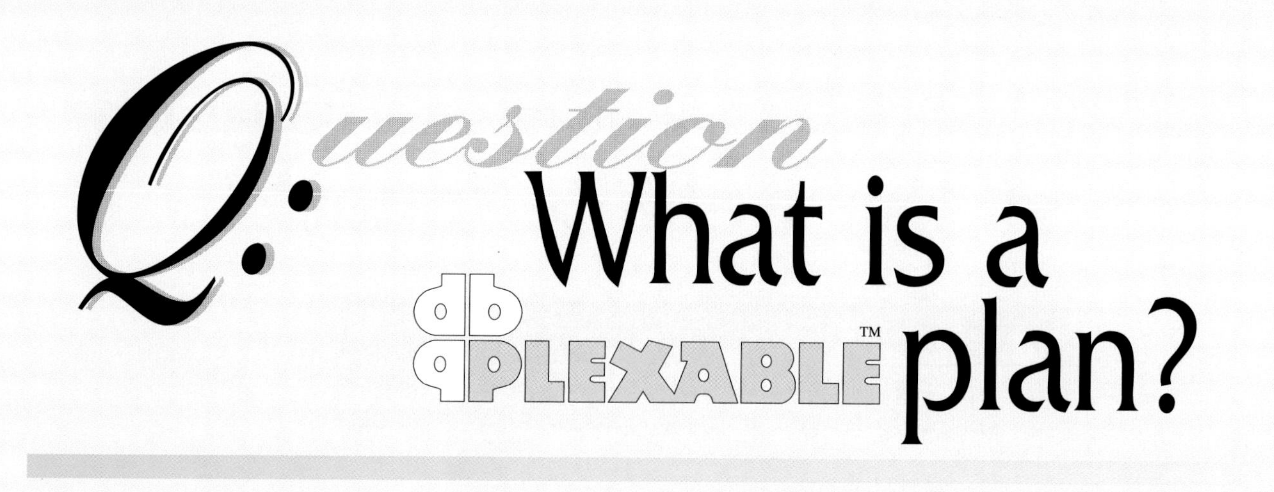

Tier One 9F-8174

Tier One lets you take a plan and join it with a duplicate version of the same plan. There are four different ways to join duplicate plans: Standard Side by Side; Side by Side Reverse; Mirror Left, and Mirror Right.

Left Side	Right Side
1212 Sq. Ft.	1233 Sq. Ft.

Price – $695

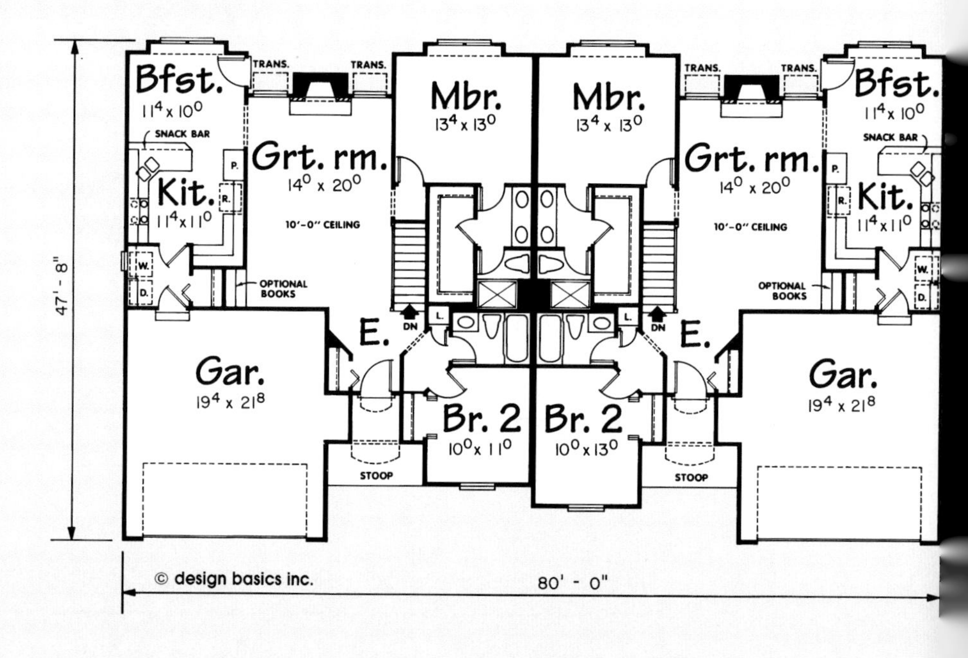

Call • 800-947-7526 • FOR PRICING INFORMATION

Answer:

Throughout The Narrow Home™ Collection, you'll find our PLEXABLE™ logo at the bottom right corner on many of the pages. Each of these plexable plans can be configured into duplex homes – according to your specifications – by Design Basics custom change designers.

Whether you want us to duplicate the same design side-by-side (our Tier One option), or merge two different plans together (Tier Two), we can help turn your multi-family dreams into reality.

Plexable plan possibilities are practically endless, but an example of Tier One and Tier Two options are shown below.

Tier Two 9F-8175

Tier Two lets you join two completely different plans. Since the possible combinations are nearly endless, you can create your own unique Plexable design. Our Customer Support Specialists can help you select plans and determine the feasability of your design.

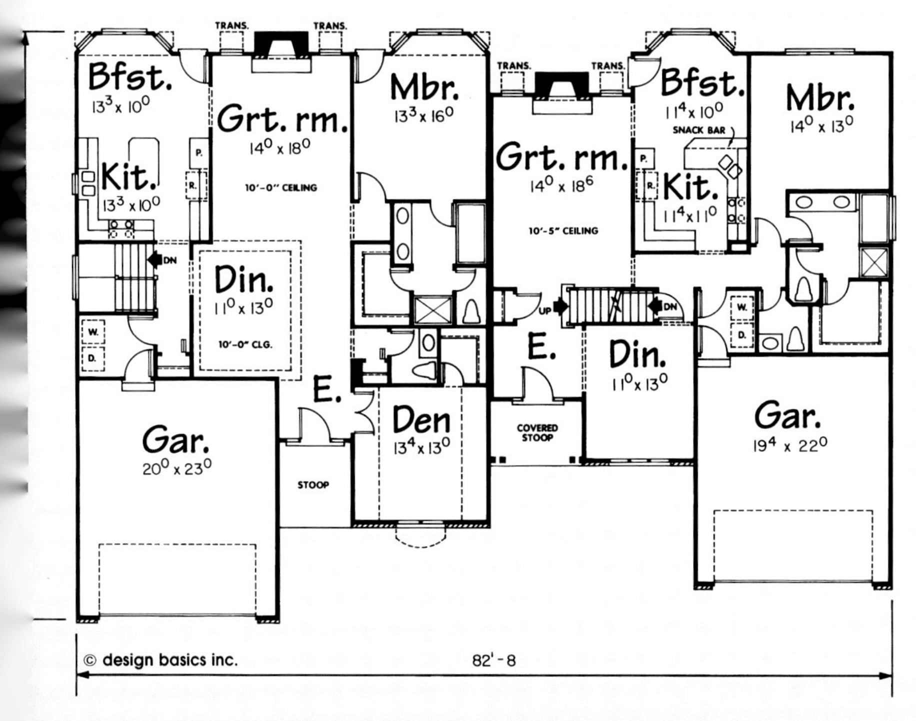

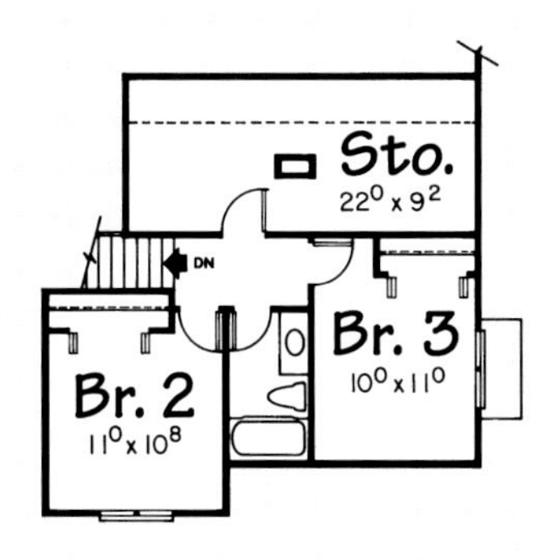

Left Side	Right Side
1621 Sq. Ft.	1715 Sq. Ft.

Price – $695

CUSTOMIZED PLAN CHANGES

PRICE SCHEDULE

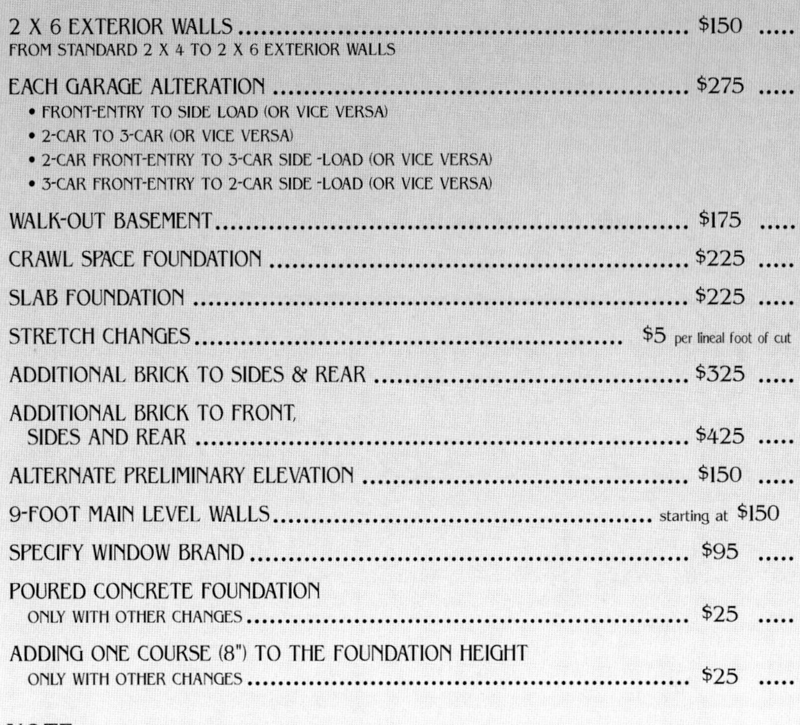

Change	Price
2 X 6 EXTERIOR WALLS FROM STANDARD 2 X 4 TO 2 X 6 EXTERIOR WALLS	$150
EACH GARAGE ALTERATION • FRONT-ENTRY TO SIDE LOAD (OR VICE VERSA) • 2-CAR TO 3-CAR (OR VICE VERSA) • 2-CAR FRONT-ENTRY TO 3-CAR SIDE -LOAD (OR VICE VERSA) • 3-CAR FRONT-ENTRY TO 2-CAR SIDE -LOAD (OR VICE VERSA)	$275
WALK-OUT BASEMENT	$175
CRAWL SPACE FOUNDATION	$225
SLAB FOUNDATION	$225
STRETCH CHANGES	$5 per lineal foot of cut
ADDITIONAL BRICK TO SIDES & REAR	$325
ADDITIONAL BRICK TO FRONT, SIDES AND REAR	$425
ALTERNATE PRELIMINARY ELEVATION	$150
9-FOOT MAIN LEVEL WALLS	starting at $150
SPECIFY WINDOW BRAND	$95
POURED CONCRETE FOUNDATION ONLY WITH OTHER CHANGES	$25
ADDING ONE COURSE (8") TO THE FOUNDATION HEIGHT ONLY WITH OTHER CHANGES	$25

NOTE

- All plan changes come to you on erasable, reproducible vellums.
- An unchanged set of original vellums is available for only $50 along with your plan changes.
- Design Basics changes are not made to the artist's renderings, electrical, sections or cabinets.
- Prices are subject to change.

As a part of our commitment to help you achieve the "perfect" home, we offer an extensive variety of plan changes for any Design Basics plan. For those whose decision to purchase a home plan is contingent upon the feasibility of a plan change, our Customer Support Specialists will, in most cases, be able to provide a FREE price quote for the changes.

call us toll-free at

(800) 947-7526

to order plan changes listed here, or if you have questions regarding plan changes not listed

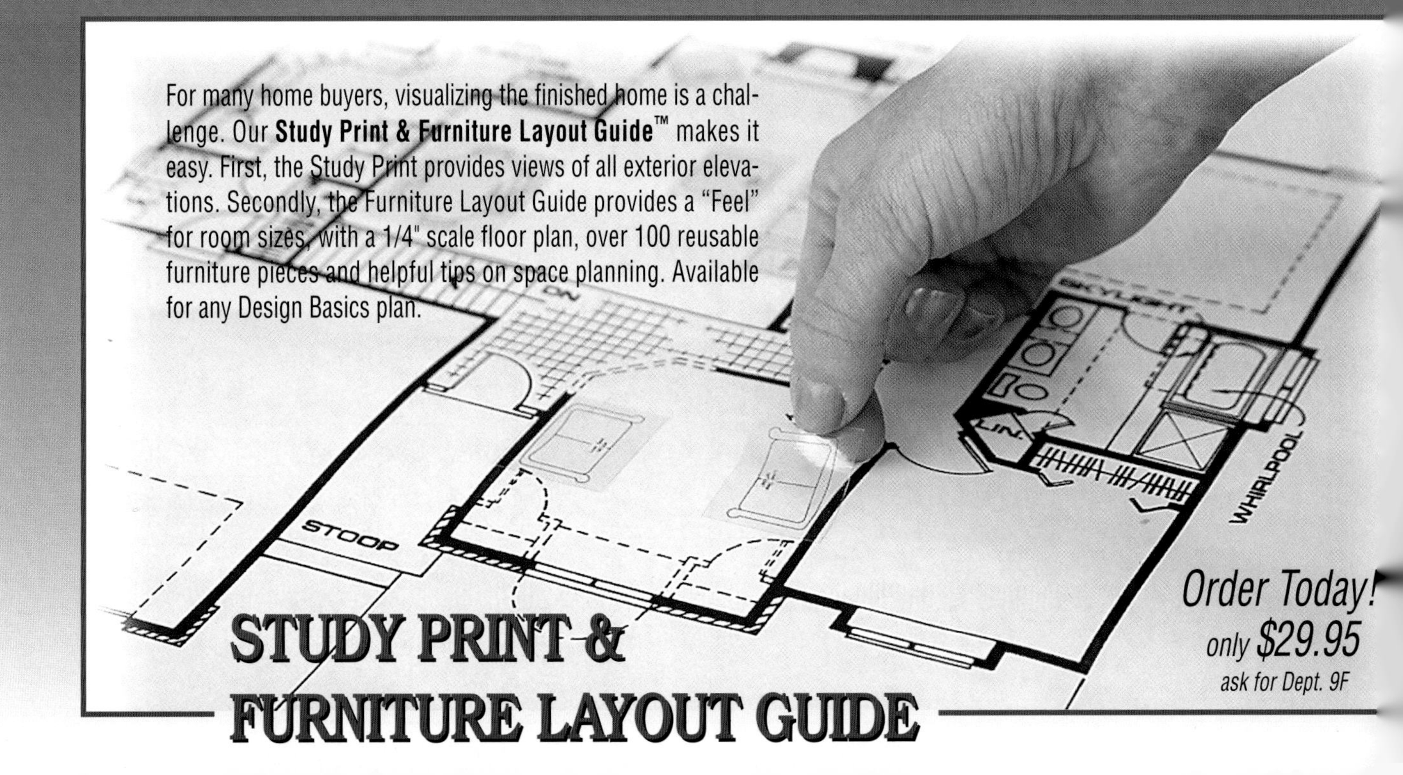

Don't Underestimate our Roofs!

Roof Construction Package

FOR · ALL · PLANS

- *Prepare accurate bids.*
- *Eliminate costly mistakes and waste.*
- *Save time and money during construction.*

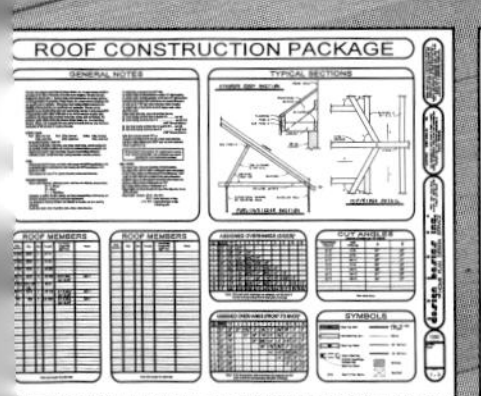

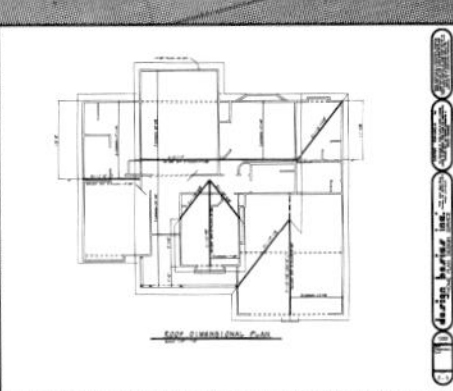

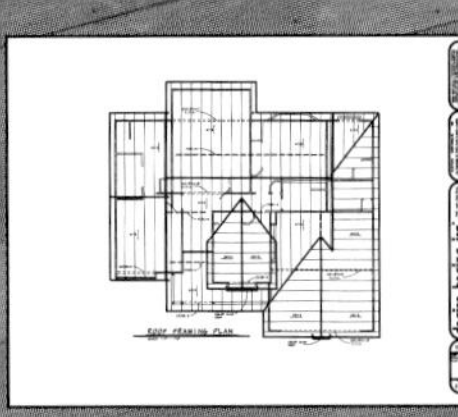

Available for each Design Basics plan, our Roof Construction Package is a complete roof framing and dimensional layout, including:

1) Aerial views of the roof showing hips, valleys, ridges, rafters and roof supports.

2) A dimensional plan showing lengths, runs, ridge heights and wall plate heights.

$100 within seven days of plan purchase. *$150 after seven days.
*Please have Construction License Number Available

Right-Reading Reverse Plans

Get the convenience and flexibility of **Right-Reading Reverse Plans** on any Gold Seal Plus™, Heartland and Nostalgia home design. Our CAD-generated reverse versions are available at the same price as originally drafted plans.

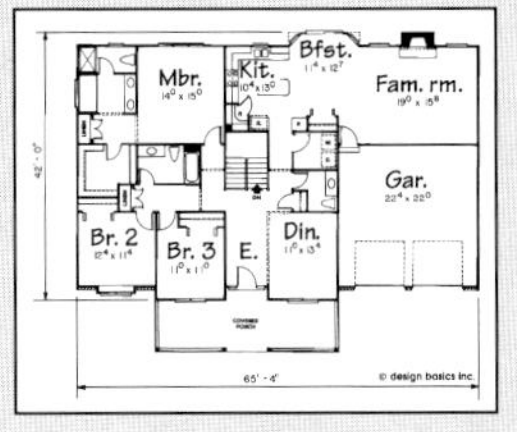

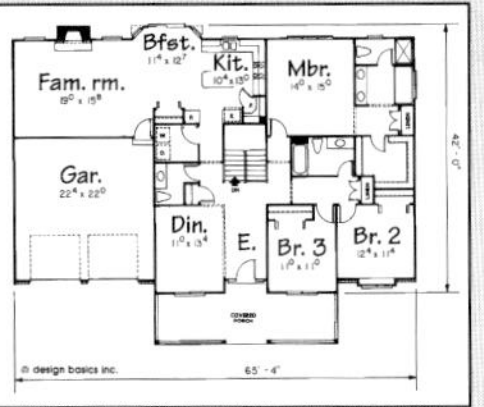

Order the reverse version within seven days of the original plan purchase for only $200. After seven days for $300.

Triple Your Sales Efforts! with the Design Basics

Parade Home Package *available for all plans*

PARADE HOME PACKAGE

Materials and Estimators Workbook
Help ensure accurate bids through a detailed cost breakdown.
Regularly $50

Promotional Handout Artwork
Customized with your name and logo, this 8 1/2" x 11" reproducible master is perfect for on-site handouts or newspaper advertising. ***Regularly $69***

Color Renderings
Choose an artist's original for **$130.00** or a beautiful color replica for only **$60.00**. It's mounted in a 13" x 16" black metal frame, with your choice of a gray marble or black matte.

Get all three products for only $149

($224.00 if you choose the original rendering.)

COPYRIGHT
Cans & Cannots

These days, it seems almost everybody has a question about what can or cannot be done with copyrighted home plans. At Design Basics, we know US copyright law can sometimes get complex and confusing, but here are a few of the basic points of the law you'll want to remember.

Once you've purchased a plan from us and have received a Design Basics construction license,

You Can . . .

- Construct the plan as originally designed, or change it to meet your specific needs.
- Build it as many times as you wish *without* additional reuse fees.
- Make duplicate blueprint copies as needed for construction.

You Cannot . . .

- Build our plans without a Design Basics construction license.
- Copy *any* part of our original designs to create another design of your own.
- Claim copyright on changes you make to our plans.
- Give a plan to someone else for construction purposes.
- Sell the plan.

PROTECT YOUR RIGHTS
to build, modify and reproduce our home plans with a Design Basics construction license.

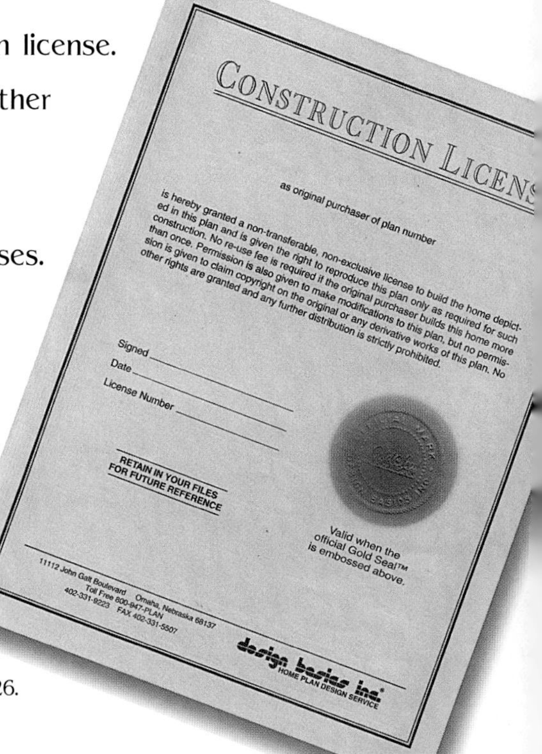
CONSTRUCTION LICENS

as original purchaser of plan number

is hereby granted a non-transferable, non-exclusive license to build the home depicted in this plan and is given the right to reproduce this plan only as required for such construction. No re-use fee is required if the original purchaser builds this home more than once. Permission is also given to make modifications to this plan, but no permission is given to claim copyright on the original or any derivative works of this plan. No other rights are granted and any further distribution is strictly prohibited.

Signed

Date

License Number

RETAIN IN YOUR FILES FOR FUTURE REFERENCE

Valid when the official Gold Seal™ is embossed above.

11112 John Galt Boulevard Omaha, Nebraska 68137
Toll Free 800-947-PLAN
402-331-9223 FAX 402-331-5507

design basics inc.
HOME PLAN DESIGN SERVICE

The above points are provided as general guidelines only. Additional information is provided with each home plan purchase, or is available upon request at (800) 947-7526.

DESIGN BASICS' HOME PLAN LIBRARY

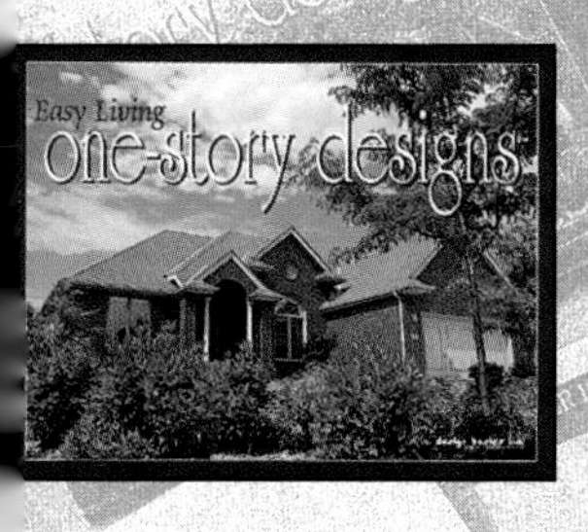

2.

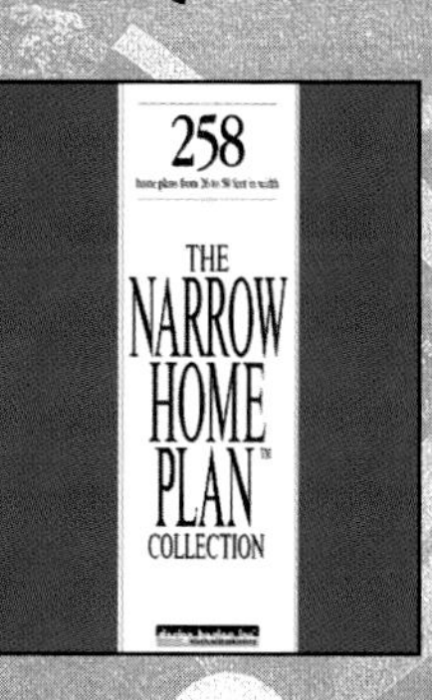

3.

4.

5.

6.

7.

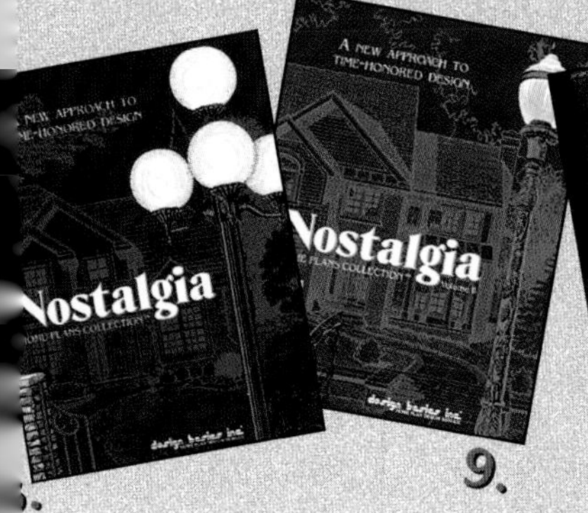

9.

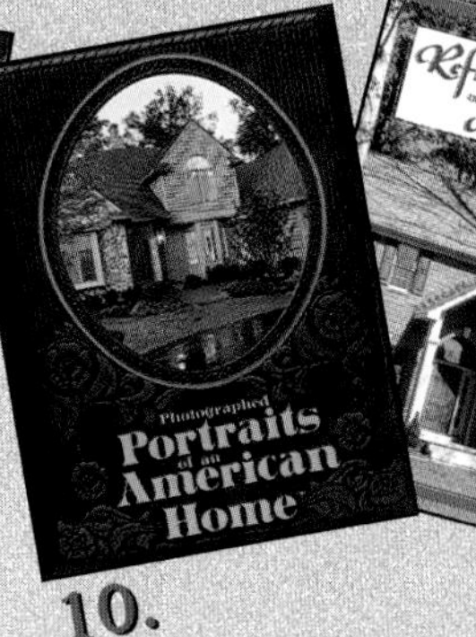

10.

11.

12.

13.

14.

Easy Living One-Story Designs™ – *155 one-story home ...gns from the Gold Seal™, Heartland Home Plans™ and ...eless Legacy™ collections, together in one plan book.* $7.95

Timeless Legacy™, A Collection of Fine Home ...igns by Carmichael & Dame – *52 breathtaking luxury ...e designs from 3300' to 4500'. Includes artful rear views of ... home.* $25.00

...he Narrow Home Plan™ Collection – *258 one-story, 1 1/2 ... and 2-story home plans that are from 26 to 50 feet wide. Many ... be joined together to create customized duplex plans.* $14.95

...Heartland Home Plans™ – *120 plan ideas designed for ...yday practicality. Warm, unpretentious elevations easily ...pt to individual lifestyles. From 1212' to 2631'.* $8.95

...n the Porch™ – A Designer's Journal of Notes and ...tches – *64 designs from Gold Seal™, Heartland Home ...s™ and Timeless Legacy™ – each one with a porch. Includes ...s on the porch and it's role in traditional design.* $2.95

6) Gold Seal™ Home Plan Book Set – *442 of today's most sought-after one-story, 1 1/2 story and 2-story home plan ideas.* All 5 books for $84.95 or $19.95 each

- Homes of Distinction – 86 plans under 1800'
- Homes of Sophistication – 106 plans, 1800'-2199'
- Homes of Elegance – 107 plans, 2200'-2599'
- Homes of Prominence – 75 plans, 2600'-2999'
- Homes of Grandeur – 68 plans, 3000'-4000'

7) Gold Seal Favorites™ – *100 best selling plans from the famous Gold Seal™ Collection, including 25 duplex designs.* $6.95

8) Nostalgia Home Plans Collection™ – A New Approach to Time-Honored Design – *70 designs showcasing enchanting details and unique "special places." From 1339' to 3480'.* $9.95

9) Nostalgia Home Plans Collection™ Vol. II – A New Approach to Time-Honored Design – *70 designs bringing back the essence of homes of the past.* $9.95

10) Photographed Portraits of an American Home™ – *100 of our finest designs, beautifully photographed and tastefully presented among charming photo album memories of "home". A must for any sales center's coffee table.* $14.95

11) Reflections of an American Home™ Vol. III – *50 photographed home plans with warm remembrances of home and beautiful interior presentations. From 1341' to 3775'.* $4.95

12) Seasons of Life™ – Designs for Reaping the Rewards of Autumn – *100 home plans specially tailored to today's empty-nester. From 1212' to 3904'.* $4.95

13) Seasons of Life™ – Designs for Living Summer's Journey – *100 designs from, 1605' to 3775' for the move-up buyer.* $4.95

14) Seasons of Life™ – Designs for Spring's New Beginnings – *100 home plans for first-time buyers. Presentations unique to this lifestyle. From 1125' to 2537'.* $4.95

Order the complete Seasons of Life™ set (all three books) for only $9.00

ORDERING INFORMATION – ATTENTION DEPT. 9F

Name ______________________ Company ______________________

Address ______________________ Title ______________________

(For UPS Delivery – Packages cannot be shipped to a P.O. Box.)

Above Address ☐ business address ☐ residence address

City ____________ State ________ Zip ________

Phone ( ) ____________ FAX ( ) ____________

☐ Visa ☐ AMEX

☐ MasterCard ☐ Discover

Credit Card: ☐☐☐☐☐☐☐☐☐☐☐☐☐☐☐☐ ☐☐ / ☐☐ Expiration Date

☐ Check enclosed (All orders payable in U.S. funds only)

All COD's must be paid by Certified Check, Cashier's Check or Money Order.
(Additional $10.00 charge on COD orders)

Signature ______________________

Follow this example for ordering PLANS:

PLAN NUMBER	PLAN NAME	AMOUNT
9F - 8174	*Tier One Duplex*	$695
Additional set of prints w/plan purchase	ea. $10.00	
	SUBTOTAL	

Follow this example for ordering PRODUCTS and BOOKS:

PLAN NUMBER	DESCRIPTION	QTY.	AMOUNT
9F - 8174	*Materials and Estimator's Workbook*	1	$50

BOOK NAME / DESCRIPTION	QTY.	AMOUNT

SHIPPING & HANDLING
(CONTINENTAL US)

Home plans
- 2nd Business Day .... N/C
- Next Business Day $15.00

Books & Products
- UPS Ground (4-5 business days) .... $ 4.95
- 2nd Business Day $10.00
- Next Business Day $20.00
- Any Single Plan Books .... $ 4.95
- Any Combination of Plan Books .... $ 4.95

SAME DAY SHIPPING IF ORDERED BY 2:00 P.M. CT.

SUBTOTAL OF PLANS, PRODUCTS AND BOOKS	
NE Res. Add 6% Sales Tax	
Shipping & Handling (see chart at left)	
No refunds or exchanges, please. **TOTAL**	

All Design Basics home plans come with a basement foundation. Alternate foundations available for additional charges. Home plans do not carry an architect's/engineer's stamp. You may need to obtain an architect's/engineer's stamp to comply with your local building codes.

design basics inc.®
HOME PLAN DESIGN SERVICE

PLAN PRICE SCHEDULE

Plan Price Code	*Total Square Feet*	*1 Set Master Vellums*
9	900' - 999'	$425
10	1000' - 1099'	$435
11	1100' - 1199'	$445
12	1200' - 1299'	$455
13	1300' - 1399'	$465
14	1400' - 1499'	$475
15	1500' - 1599'	$485
16	1600' - 1699'	$495
17	1700' - 1799'	$505
18	1800' - 1899'	$515
19	1900' - 1999'	$525
20	2000' - 2099'	$535
21	2100' - 2199'	$545
22	2200' - 2299'	$555
23	2300' - 2399'	$565
24	2400' - 2499'	$575
4X	4-Plex	$895

PLEASE CALL US FOR CURRENT PRICES 800-947-7526

Prices subject to change.

Free 2nd Business Day Delivery

All plan orders received prior to 2:00 p.m. C... be processed, inspected and shipped out th... afternoon via 2nd business day delivery wit... continental U.S. All other product orders ... sent via UPS ground service or US Postal Serv...

FOR FASTEST SERVICE CALL (800) 947-7526 OR FAX (402) 331-5507

Monday - Friday, 7:00 a.m. to 6:00 p.m. C.T.

Design Basics Inc. • 11112 John Galt Boulevard • Omaha, Nebraska 68137-2384

STANDARDS OF EXCELLENCE – *Each complete Design Basics Home Plan comes to you on high quality, erasable, reproducible vellum.*